Elementary Classroom Teachers as Movement Educators

THIRD EDITION

Susan K. Kovar
Wichita State University

Cindy A. Combs
Harvey County Special Education Cooperative,
Newton Public Schools, Newton, Kansas

Kathy Campbell
Arizona State University

Gloria Napper-Owen
University of New Mexico

Vicki J. Worrell
Emporia State University

 **Higher Education**

Boston   Burr Ridge, IL   Dubuque, IA   New York   San Francisco   St. Louis
Bangkok   Bogotá   Caracas   Kuala Lumpur   Lisbon   London   Madrid   Mexico City
Milan   Montreal   New Delhi   Santiago   Seoul   Singapore   Sydney   Taipei   Toronto

Higher Education

Published by McGraw-Hill, an imprint of The McGraw-Hill Companies, Inc., 1221 Avenue of the Americas, New York, NY 10020. Copyright © 2009, 2007, 2004. All rights reserved. No part of this publication may be reproduced or distributed in any form or by any means, or stored in a database or retrieval system, without the prior written consent of The McGraw-Hill Companies, Inc., including, but not limited to, in any network or other electronic storage or transmission, or broadcast for distance learning.

 This book is printed on recycled, acid-free paper containing a minimum of 50% total recycled fiber with 10% postconsumer de-inked fiber.

1 2 3 4 5 6 7 8 9 0 QPD/QPD 0 9 8

ISBN 978-0-07-337646-2
MHID 0-07-337646-9

Editor in Chief: *Michael Ryan*
Editorial Director: *William R. Glass*
Executive Editor: *Christopher Johnson*
Marketing Manager: *William Minick*
Director of Development: *Kathleen Engelberg*
Developmental Editor: *Julia Akpan*
Production Editor: *Holly Paulsen*
Manuscript Editor: *Patricia Ohlenroth*
Design Manager: *Ashley Bedell*
Text Designer: *Linda Robertson*
Cover Designer: *Mary-Presley Adams*
Photo Research: *Nora Agbayani*
Production Supervisor: *Tandra Jorgensen*
Composition: *10.5/12.5 Garamond Light by Laserwords*
Printing: *PMS 362, 45# New Era Matte Plus Recycled, Quebecor World*
Cover: Masterfile Royalty-Free

Library of Congress Cataloging-in-Publication Data has been applied for.

The Internet addresses listed in the text were accurate at the time of publication. The inclusion of a website does not indicate an endorsement by the authors or McGraw-Hill, and McGraw-Hill does not guarantee the accuracy of the information presented at these sites.

www.mhhe.com

Brief Contents

Contents

· ·

3 Movement Components and Skill Development   53

4 Exercise Concepts and Fitness Education   91

6 Physical Education Curriculum   167

7 Managing and Teaching the Physical Education Lesson   199

8 Curriculum Integration in the Classroom   231

9 Motivating Children to Be Physically Active   265

Preface

Vision and Goals

Preservice elementary classroom teachers across the country take a course designed to educate them about the teaching of physical education. Our book, *Elementary Classroom Teachers as Movement Educators,* is a textbook for that course. We believe the most important objective of the course is to convince elementary classroom teachers that their students need (1) quality, daily physical education, (2) movement experiences in the classroom throughout the school day, and (3) quality recess time. In addition, the course should focus on teaching elementary classroom teachers how to include movement in their classrooms, how to turn students on to participating in physical activities, and how to become comfortable teaching physical activities.

Our goal in writing this book is to create a text written directly to the elementary classroom teacher who has no formal training in physical education. Most elementary physical education textbooks talk to physical educators, not to elementary classroom teachers. Thus the books assume the reader has formal education in physical education. (And, indeed, that formal education is necessary to fully understand the concepts discussed.) Our book is designed to inform elementary classroom teachers about the discipline of physical education and the key role they play in producing physically active children who are also skilled movers. We hope that preservice elementary classroom teachers will be more willing to study the material and put it into practice if it is addressed directly to them. Our book has information and tools that reflect the variety of situations in which elementary classroom teachers may find themselves with respect to the physical education time of their students, from supporting a physical education specialist with classroom activities to managing physical education lessons independently for their students. It provides a strong introduction to fundamental physical education concepts as well as hundreds of sample activities and lessons.

Content

Elementary Classroom Teachers as Movement Educators covers the traditional knowledge bases of physical education curriculum and assessment, motor development, motor learning, exercise physiology and fitness, movement concepts and skill development, legal issues, and managing and teaching physical education lessons. In addition, our book includes unique coverage designed especially for elementary classroom teachers:

- We address the need for elementary classroom teachers to include more movement in their regular classroom activities and lessons. Many of the books currently available for elementary physical education courses talk about and give examples for integrating math, science, reading, and so on, from the classroom into the physical education lesson— and we do that also. But in addition, we integrate movement and exercise knowledge and practice into the regular classroom (Chapter 8).
- We also address the need for physical educators and elementary classroom teachers to consider recess time as important movement time. The guidelines of the National Association for Sport and Physical Education (NASPE) recommend that elementary school children accumulate between 60 and 120 minutes of physical activity every day. We believe school recess time can be profitably used to help children meet those guidelines, and we discuss how to make that happen (Chapter 12).
- Because we believe classroom teachers play such an important role in motivating and socializing children to be physically active, we include chapters on how to create an environment that stimulates children to be active (Chapter 9) and how to manage the current sociological issues involved in children moving (Chapter 10).
- This book contains a special emphasis on children with special needs. An in-depth chapter is provided on planning for children with diverse and special needs (Chapter 5). In addition, activities and issues related to special populations are integrated throughout the text, and specific suggestions for including all students are provided in lessons and activities.

Organization

The overall organization of the book reflects the courses we teach, but we have designed it to be flexible. Each chapter stands by itself, so users may cover chapters in whatever order best suits their course and way of teaching. The following descriptions of the chapter contents will be helpful in planning the order in which to cover various topics.

Chapter 1, "What Is Physical Education?" introduces the movement needs of elementary school children, the importance of physical education in meeting those movement needs, the NASPE content standards, the role of the classroom teacher as a movement educator, and the role of recess in the school curriculum.

Chapter 2, "Motor Development and Motor Learning for Children," introduces the process of motor development through which children progress as well as principles of motor learning from which developmentally appropriate teaching practices are based. Instructional strategies to facilitate learning are covered, and commonly seen inappropriate practices are discussed. Students are encouraged to reflect on the role physical activity plays in the development of children.

Chapter 3, "Movement Components and Skill Development," introduces the movement map to identify the underlying components of movement. Movement components are concepts that can be applied to any movement form. Movement components include ways the body moves (body movements), what the body can do (body awareness), where the body moves (space awareness), how the body moves (qualities of movement), and how the body relates (relationships). Descriptions of basic locomotor skills, nonlocomotor movements, and manipulative skills are included and accompanied with activities that can be used to develop these skills.

Chapter 4, "Exercise Concepts and Fitness Education," describes the role of the classroom teacher as a fitness educator and how to implement fitness education in the classroom. Health risk factors are identified, and the physiology of movement and exercise is covered (cardiorespiratory system, musculoskeletal system, and body composition). NASPE guidelines on intermittent activity bursts are also addressed. This chapter includes many Quick Lessons for use in the classroom.

Chapter 5, "Planning for Children with Diverse and Special Needs," describes children who have special needs (Reality Tours), in order to deepen the teacher's understanding of various disabilities, and details the role classroom teachers play in educating children with special needs. The book presents disability as one aspect of diversity and suggests ways teachers may reach all children. Specific physical, mental, and emotional disabilities are identified, and the impact of those disabilities on the physical skills of children

is discussed. Movement modifications and safety recommendations are identified that allow children with special needs to participate fully in movement lessons.

Chapter 6, "Physical Education Curriculum," identifies the characteristics of a quality elementary physical education program and discusses who is responsible for producing such a program. Physical education curriculum content (scope and sequence) is included as well as a framework for and examples of writing objectives for the physical education lesson. Assessment theory and practice is covered in depth.

Chapter 7, "Managing and Teaching the Physical Education Lesson," presents the mechanics of teaching physical education lessons—teaching methods, organizing the lesson and the students, class management techniques and discipline strategies that help children choose responsible behavior, and guidelines for providing effective feedback to students.

Chapter 8, "Curriculum Integration in the Classroom," discusses how integrating movement with other curricular subject areas may benefit elementary school students. The role movement plays in learning is substantiated by citing brain-based research, and its implications for teachers are discussed. Examples of ready-to-use movement activities and games that can be integrated into various subject areas are listed and described.

Chapter 9, "Motivating Children to Be Physically Active," presents ideas and information useful to motivate children to be physically active now and throughout their lifetime. Ideas include instilling feelings of motor skill competency, building intrinsic motivation to be active, involving students in the teaching-learning process, and teachers being role models.

Chapter 10, "Sociological Aspects of Children Moving," describes the socialization process as it applies to children in their role of being physically active and examines movement as a socializing agent. Teaching and assessing the social skills of sportsmanship, fair play, responsibility, and respect are covered. Inclusion is discussed as a socialization issue, and diversity issues (cultural, ethnic, gender, and disability) are identified relative to the movement setting.

Chapter 11, "Creating a Physically Safe Movement Environment," identifies the unique safety concerns and legal issues relevant in situations where children are involved in physical activities. Current "best practices" in selecting curriculum content and implementing instruction are discussed with specific recommendations for conducting physical activity in a safe manner. How to maintain safe indoor and outdoor movement environments is covered.

Chapter 12, "Recess as Quality Movement Time," discusses the role and benefits of recess in the educational process. The primary emphasis of the chapter is how to help children construct their own quality recess time and still allow recess to be free play.

The book concludes with four units of lesson plans and six appendixes, which are described in detail in the section "Pedagogical Features and Learning Aids."

New to the Third Edition

Key changes to the third edition include the following:

- *Updated government regulations:* Coverage has been added throughout the text regarding the Child Nutrition and WIC Reauthorization Act of 2004, established by Congress, which requires school districts with federally funded, school-meals programs to implement wellness policies that address nutrition and physical activity for children in the school.
- *Thoroughly revised chapters:* Chapter 1 makes the case for having physical activity in the schools and adds new information on state physical activity standards that impact the classroom teacher. Chapter 2 includes expanded coverage of modifications that can be made to games that have traditionally been considered inappropriate due to elements of elimination or minimal physical activity. Chapter 3 contains revised rubrics which more thoroughly describe the performance levels of students. Chapter 5 introduces a great fitness activity (snowshoeing) that allows *all* students to participate actively (no snow required), and outlines a series of questions movement educators can ask themselves to identify ways to modify or change activities to help students be successful. Chapter 9 is now organized to emphasize the two major functions of the classroom teacher in terms of motivating students to be physically active (i.e., using motivational pedagogical techniques and promoting physical activity). Chapter 10 is more tightly focused on classroom teachers as they operate in the classroom and as they direct physical activity. Appendix A, "Progressive Activities for Motor Skill Development," contains additional activities (within each motor skill list) that reinforce rhythmic development.
- *Updated coverage of key topics:* Updated topics include the OMNI picture scale of perceived exertion for children; the MyPyramid especially

designed for "kids"; new research showing positive links between movement and academics; new cultural integration resources in the Passport to Play curriculum; more clearly defined movement forms; and new and expanded information on the theory and term MVPA (moderate to vigorous physical activity), safety issues (medicine use, air quality and humidity, dangerous activities, and first aid kit contents), gender equity, Hellison's responsibility model, parental influence on a child's activity, and handling bullying in the classroom and during recess.

- *Design changes:* The third edition features a new chapter opening design. We have also addressed the reviewers' concerns about the difficulty in distinguishing the various pedagogical features by giving them each a more distinctive look. In addition, a video icon has been added to highlight areas in the text where video clips of sample activities are available.

The instructor and student supplements, described in detail later in the preface, have also been expanded and updated.

Pedagogical Features and Learning Aids

The book provides many helpful pedagogical features and learning aids.

Video clips of sample activities from the text, taught by a master teacher, are available on the Instructor's Resource DVD-ROM for presentation during lecture and in a lower-resolution format on the Online Learning Center (www.mhhe.com/kovar3e) for individual viewing by students. A video guide, complete with discussion questions and instructor notes, is included in the Instructor's Manual.

COMPLETE LESSON PLANS

At the end of the book, four units of physical education lesson plans with progressive lessons for specific grade levels are included. These lesson plans are complete and include NASPE standards, objectives, activity descriptions (introductory activities, lesson focus activities, physical fitness activities, closing activities), and assessments. Each lesson also has a classroom movement activity that corresponds to the objectives and content of the physical education lesson. This combination demonstrates how classroom and physical education activities can work together to achieve movement objectives. Experienced physical education specialists, in conjunction with the authors, created these lesson plan units.

INSTANT ACTIVITY BOXES

Each chapter includes one or more Instant Activities that classroom teachers can use immediately with their students in the classroom. They are flexible and include enough activities to fill 10–30 minutes of activity time (depending on the time available to the teacher). These appear in boxes throughout the chapters and are designed so the classroom teacher can simply read the activity description and teach the activity immediately, without much additional planning and preparation time. In some cases, the activity may require that you obtain equipment from the physical educator or reorganize the desks in the classroom to create an activity space.

QUICK LESSONS, CLASSROOM LEARNING STATIONS, AND SPECIAL EVENTS

Each chapter ends with the following three types of lessons and activities:

 Quick Lessons: One or more Quick Lessons appear at the end of each chapter, with lesson content that relates to chapter topics. Quick Lessons are designed primarily for use in the classroom and contain student objectives, activities, and assessments that guide classroom teachers in their lesson preparation and implementation. They provide future classroom teachers with ready-to-use movement lessons. Quick Lessons are more in-depth than Instant Activities but less so than the fully developed physical education lessons presented at the end of the text. Quick Lessons indicate the NASPE standard the activity is designed to meet, as well as include hints on how to adapt the activities so that all students can be successful and on how to integrate the activities into subject areas such as math, science, and reading.

Classroom Learning Stations: At least one Classroom Learning Station plan appears at the end of each chapter. Each Learning Station is tied to the specific content of the chapter and describes a learning area relating to physical education that can be set up in a corner of the classroom. These Learning Station plans provide ready-to-use physical education content materials and

physical activities that can be integrated into the classroom. The station may remain set up and usable for several weeks until each student or groups of students have the free time to complete the specified activities.

 Special Events: A plan for a Special Event—an event that can be hosted by the elementary classroom teacher (for just one classroom or for several classrooms) that celebrates something related to physical education—appears at the end of each chapter.

ADDITIONAL LEARNING AIDS

Each chapter opens with a purpose statement, a list of objectives, and a scenario featuring a classroom teacher in a movement education setting. Each chapter concludes with a summary and a list of suggested chapter activities. These activities include projects that can help preservice elementary classroom teachers put key concepts from the chapter into action. We firmly believe that just presenting information to pre-service teachers is not sufficient; they must become involved in using that information in order to actually provide appropriate movement for their students.

HELPFUL APPENDIXES

The six appendixes provide important resource materials:

- Appendix A, "Progressive Activities for Motor Skill Development," includes dozens of activities designed to reinforce key components of the movement map.
- Appendix B, "Rubrics for Locomotor and Manipulative Skills," provides 19 ready-to-use rubrics for assessing basic skills performance.
- Appendix C, "Recess Games and Activities," includes a variety of quality recess games and activities for elementary school children that can help build basic motor skills.
- Appendix D, "Lesson Plan Resource Materials," provides materials for selected lessons that appear in the text—including such items as animal movement cards, physical education bingo pieces, and carpet square activity cards.
- Appendix E, "Content Included in Each Movement Form," contains a more in-depth listing than that provided in Chapter 6 of physical activities included in each movement form.
- Appendix F, "Activity Listings by Grade Level, Movement Form, and Integration Area," contains an

overall index of all the activities and lessons in the book, organized by grade level, movement form, and integration area, for easy future reference. This appendix is also available from the book's Online Learning Center as a downloadable Excel file; the activity listings can be sorted electronically by any category, including grade level, movement form, NASPE standard, activity location (classroom, playground, gymnasium), knowledge content, and integration area.

Supplements

A comprehensive package of supplementary materials designed to enhance teaching and learning is available with *Elementary Classroom Teachers as Movement Educators.*

INSTRUCTOR'S RESOURCE DVD-ROM

The Instructor's Resource DVD-ROM presents key teaching resources in an easy-to-use format. It is organized by chapter and works in both Windows and Macintosh environments. It includes the following teaching tools:

- *Instructor's Manual* with a sample syllabus, student objectives, key terms, chapter summaries, chapter outlines, suggested classroom learning activities and student assessment activities, and recommended readings.
- *PowerPoint slides* with key lecture points.
- *Image bank* with photos and illustrations from the text in digital format.
- *Test bank* with true/false, multiple-choice, and short-answer questions; for the third edition, the test bank was prepared by Glenn Hushman, University of New Mexico.
- *Video clips* of sample activities from the text, taught by a master teacher; the videos are accompanied by instructor notes and discussion questions.

The test bank is also available on the Instructor's Resource DVD-ROM with the *EZ Test computerized testing software.* EZ Test provides a powerful, easy-to-use test maker to create printed quizzes and exams. For secure online testing, exams created in EZ Test can be exported to WebCT, Blackboard, PageOut, and EZ Test Online. EZ Test comes with a Quick Start Guide, and once the program is installed, users have access to a User's Manual and Flash tutorials. Additional help is available at www.mhhe.com/eztest.

ONLINE LEARNING CENTER
www.mhhe.com/kovar3e

The Online Learning Center provides additional resources for both instructors and students. Instructor tools include downloadable versions of the Instructor's Manual, PowerPoint slides, image bank, and video guides. There are also links to professional resources.

For students, the Online Learning Center includes resources to help them succeed in the course and in their teaching experiences:

- *Learning objectives, self-quizzes, and glossary flashcards* for review of key concepts and exam preparation.
- *Suggested portfolio activities and extensive links* to help students expand their personal collection of teaching resources and experiences.
- *Video clips of sample activities* from the text, taught by a master teacher, which provide models of excellence and many teaching tips to help students become better movement educators.

PRIMIS ONLINE
www.mhhe.com/primis

Primis Online is a database-driven publishing system that allows instructors to create customized textbooks, lab manuals, or readers for their courses directly from the Primis website. The custom text can be delivered in print or electronic (eBook) form. A Primis eBook is a digital version of the customized text sold directly to students as a file downloadable to their computer or accessed online by password. *Elementary Classroom Teachers as Movement Educators* can be customized using Primis Online.

MOVING INTO THE FUTURE: NATIONAL STANDARDS FOR PHYSICAL EDUCATION
(ISBN 0-8831-4909-5)

A copy of *Moving into the Future,* the physical education content standards developed by NASPE, is packaged free with each new copy of the textbook. These standards clearly identify what elementary school students should know and be able to do as a result of a quality physical education program. *Moving into the Future* also includes performance benchmarks and a variety of assessment techniques appropriate for assessing student achievement.

Additional supplements and packaging options are available; check with your local sales representative for more information.

Acknowledgments

We have many special people (including children) to whom we owe much gratitude for the completion of this book. Without them this book would be ordinary, but with them, it has become extraordinary. First, a heartfelt thank you to the students in USD 373 (Newton, Kansas), who allowed us to take their photographs. These students spent three full Saturdays with us as we managed to take 400 photos of them moving. And to their parents, how can we adequately thank you for your willingness to bring your children to and from the photo shoots and entrust us with their care for three days? Parents, you are truly very special people! Second, to the photographer, a special thanks, as you and your equipment survived the three all-day photo shoots. Steve Stephens provided us with quality digital photos as well as a cooperative spirit and congenial atmosphere during the photo sessions. Third, to the authors of the lesson plans—Cindy Chrisman, Virginia Hammersmith, Rebecca Nicholas, and Susan Oldfather—thanks for working with us to produce tried-and-true units of instruction in physical education. These units will come in handy when classroom teachers begin their careers and teach movement activities for the first time to their own students.

Finally, to the many people who reviewed the text in its many stages of development, we can only imagine the number of hours you must have spent in providing us with such in-depth and useful information and questions. Although we sometimes hated to read those comments and suggestions—as they entailed much work on our part to implement—we know the book is much better because of your input. Thanks so much for sharing your knowledge with us!

Reviewers of the Second Edition

Roberta E. Faust, *Eastern Michigan University*
Deborah A. Garrahy, *Illinois State University*
Bill R. Gordon, **Jr.**, *Oral Roberts University*
Christine P. Heusser, *California State University, Fullerton*
Beatrice W. Katz, *Cleveland State University*
Clay P. Sherman, *California State University, Fullerton*
Donald F. Staffo, *Stillman College*
Nannette Wolford, *Missouri Western State College*
Bill Yongue, *Florida International University*

Reviewers of the Third Edition

Judy Chandler, *Central Michigan University*
Carol Conley, *University of Oklahoma—Norman*
Lena-Marie Cool, *Kalamazoo Valley Community College*
Lorri Engstrom, *Kutztown University of Pennsylvania*
Heather Erwin, *University of Kentucky*
Dana Espinosa, *East Carolina University*
Nadene Davidson, *University of Northern Iowa*
Carol Girdler, *University of Iowa—Iowa City*
Monica Magner, *Morehead State University*
Lori Peterson, *University of Wisconsin—La Crosse*
Virginia Trummer, *University of Texas San Antonio*
Mark Urtel, *Indiana University-Purdue University Indianapolis*

About the Authors

Susan K. Kovar

Susan K. Kovar is a professor of physical education and dean of the graduate school at Wichita State University. Susan has spent her 25-year career in higher education preparing elementary physical educators and classroom teachers to meet the movement needs of elementary-aged children. Much of her scholarship (research, publication, and presentations) over that period focused on issues in physical education and methods of teaching elementary physical education. She received a BS from the University of Nebraska, an MS from the University of Illinois, and a PhD from the University of Minnesota. She is an active member of AAHPERD and NASPE, having served on a number of NASPE committees. For seven years, she was a reader for the NASPE/NCATE process for accreditation of undergraduate physical education preparation programs in institutions of higher education. For an additional five years, she served as one of seven NASPE/NCATE adjudicators who made final recommendations to NCATE regarding these programs. She is a reviewer for *JOPERD* and *Strategies.* In 1987 she was named CAPEHE Young Scholar by the Central Association for Physical Education in Higher Education, and in 1998 she was named Central District AAHPERD Scholar. She has been recognized by NAKPEHE as a distinguished administrator (in 2002) and as the Amy Morris Homans lecturer in 2004.

Cindy A. Combs

Cindy A. Combs has taught Adapted Physical Education (APE) for 21 years and implemented the first APE program in the Harvey County Special Education Cooperative in Newton, Kansas, in 1984. She received her BS in health and physical education and in special education from Bethel College, in Kansas, and her MS in curriculum and instruction from Wichita State University. Cindy is a past president of the Kansas AHPERD. She currently serves as a field editor for *Palaestra.* She was the 2006 AAPAR National Adapted Physical Education Teacher of the year. In 1999 she was awarded the National Shaklee Teacher Award "to recognize ten of the country's most outstanding teachers of children with disabilities." Cindy has served as

adjunct faculty teaching adapted physical education and courses in qualitative research.

Kathy Campbell

Kathy Campbell, EdD, FACSM, is currently a lecturer at Arizona State University's Polytechnic campus in Mesa, Arizona. Recently Kathy worked in the private sector as an exercise physiologist and manager of cardiac rehabilitation at Advanced Cardiac Specialists in Apache Junction, Arizona. Her background includes teaching, coaching, and curriculum development in public schools and at four universities. She has worked in the field of exercise science, wellness, and physical education for over 20 years, is a Fellow of the American College of Sports Medicine, and possesses certification in Advanced Cardiac Life Support, ACSM Exercise Specialist, and ACSM Exercise Test Technologist. Kathy earned her EdD and MS in health, physical education and leisure from Oklahoma State University and her BS in biology with a minor in physical education from New Mexico State University. Kathy's interest in daily physical activity in the schools is evidenced by former work with elementary school teachers in workshops and short courses for fitness education in the public schools. She has several publications and presentations in the area of exercise and fitness, is a former chair of the Applied Exercise Science Council (NASPE), and a past president of the central states chapter of ACSM.

Gloria E. Napper-Owen

Gloria Napper-Owen is an associate professor in physical education–teacher education and chair of the Department of Health, Exercise, and Sports Sciences at the University of New Mexico. She also serves as program coordinator for the undergraduate physical education teacher education program and the graduate curriculum and instruction program. Gloria's teaching expertise is in elementary physical education and the alignment of curriculum, instruction, and assessment. In 2007 Gloria was a key member of the College of Education's NCATE Task Force and helped prepare the institution and program reports for a successful accreditation review. In 2001 Gloria received the Southwest District AAHPERD Honor Award, the highest award given at the district level, and in 2005 she received the Professional Honor Award from New Mexico AHPERD. She has held leadership roles within AAHPERD, SWDAAHPERD, and NMAHPERD. Gloria has authored articles on beginning teacher induction, teacher development, and issues in elementary physical education. She has made numerous presentations at national, district, and state conventions on the topics of her research focus.

Vicki J. Worrell

Vicki J. Worrell is an associate professor at Emporia State University in Kansas. Vicki has been in higher education for 10 years and taught elementary physical education in public schools for 19 years. She received a BS from Wichita State University, an MEd from the University of Kansas, and an EdD from Oklahoma State University. Vicki has served as chair of the Council of Physical Education for Children (COPEC) and chair of the NASPE Public Relations Committee, and has served a three-year term as a member of the NASPE Cabinet. She currently serves on the AAHPERD Strategic Planning Committee. Vicki has recently completed a three-year leadership term as president-elect, president and past president of the Central District AHPERD. Vicki continues to serve as the executive director for the Kansas Association for Health, Physical Education, Recreation and Dance. Recently she was a coauthor for two books that were published by NASPE: *Never Play Leapfrog with a Unicorn* and *Roadblocks to Quality Physical Education*. Vicki was the 2006 NASPE Joy of Effort recipient and the 1993 National Elementary Teacher of the Year.

CHAPTER 1

What Is Physical Education?

The purpose of this chapter is to describe the need for physical activity and physical education in the school curricula. The chapter focuses on the benefits of physical education (instruction time in movement) and physical activity to the growing child, the content of physical education in the schools today, the role recess (unstructured play) fulfills in meeting the movement needs of children, and how the elementary classroom teacher serves as a movement educator.

Objectives

After studying this chapter, you will be able to do the following:

- Cite requirements of Public Law 108–265, Section 204.
- Define and describe physical education as it is practiced in elementary schools today.
- Cite five qualities of a physically educated person.
- Articulate the benefits of daily physical education for elementary school children.
- Cite the National Association for Sport and Physical Education (NASPE) content standards.
- Articulate the benefits of physical activity to the growing child.
- Articulate the role of the elementary classroom teacher in providing quality physical activity for students.
- Express the educational value of a recess period for elementary school children.
- Articulate the role of the elementary classroom teacher in providing quality recess time.
- Express the differing goals and purposes of physical education versus recess.

It is Friday afternoon, and the children in the second-grade classroom are becoming restless and inattentive. Normally at this time the students have physical education class (taught by a certified physical education teacher); however, today they did not. The classroom teacher decides to provide a short physical education lesson for the children focused on controlling the body while moving and understanding movement concepts. The teacher is able to take the children outdoors because the weather is favorable and a play space is available. Each child finds a space within the area designed by the teacher. On the teacher's cue, the children perform various movements:

- Walk forward; walk backward; walk in a circle. (The movement concept is direction.)
- Walk slowly; walk quickly; walk with smooth, gliding steps; walk with jerky steps. (The movement concept is speed.)
- Walk with big steps; walk with small steps. (The movement concept is size.)
- Walk with knees lifted high; walk and clap hands under thighs on each step. (The movement concept is body shape.)
- Walk and lower the body; walk and raise the body. (The movement concept is level.)

The children perform similar movements while practicing other locomotor skills, such as running, hopping, jumping, leaping, skipping, galloping, and sliding. The teacher emphasizes that students must be in control of their bodies (and have no contact with other students) while performing and moving within the designated play area. The teacher observes the students and corrects those who are not performing the locomotor skills correctly. The teacher ends the lesson by calling the students together in a group. Various students, selected by the teacher, demonstrate the different locomotor skills. Students must then correctly name the skill just demonstrated. In addition, the teacher mentions the movement concepts that were explored in the lesson and asks the students to define them (direction, speed, size, body shape, and level).

The Case for Physical Activity in the School

A revolution is occurring in America today concerning the value, benefit, and place of physical activity and physical education within the schools. Parents, education administrators, school board members, and national health agencies and experts have become increasingly convinced that physical education and daily physical activity play a critical role in both overcoming childhood obesity and physical inactivity and in preparing children to achieve academically. Several recent national polls indicate parental support for physical education in schools and daily physical activity. Eighty-five percent of parents polled believe that students should have daily physical education at every grade level with a program emphasis on healthy lifestyle choices, including one that leads to a lifetime of being physically active (RWJF 2003). Ninety-one percent believe that schools should provide more physical education for children than they currently offer, particularly to help combat childhood obesity (HSPH 2003), and 95 percent of parents polled believe that daily physical activity leads to higher academic achievement in children (NASPE 2003).

There is also strong support within the federal government. In the early months of 2007, Health and Human Services Secretary Mike Leavitt indicated the agency would announce in late 2008 the availability of comprehensive physical activity guidelines, including specific recommendations for subgroups such as children. In 2004, with the passage of the Child Nutrition Reauthorization Act (**Public Law 108–265, Section 204**), Congress required that school districts with federally funded school-meals programs develop and implement wellness policies for the 2006–07 school year (USDA 2007). The policies are to address both the nutritional and physical activity needs of students. This act has greatly increased efforts to include physical activity into the daily lives of schoolchildren. As a result of this act, schools across the nation have begun to implement some of the same principles and programs espoused in this textbook since its first edition, namely:

1. Provide quality, daily physical education classes for all students in elementary schools
2. Provide additional daily opportunities for students to be physically active through:
   a. Free-play recess time (before, during, and after school hours)
   b. Physical activity in the classroom that uses movement to teach subject content during a subject lesson and to simply provide a break between subject lessons
   c. Community sport clubs and programs

Strong support is also coming from various national organizations. The National Association for Sport and Physical Education (NASPE) (NASPE 2004a) recommends that children accumulate at least 60 minutes of moderate and vigorous physical activity on a daily basis and discourages extended periods of inactivity during daytime hours. The National Alliance for Nutrition and Activity (NANA) developed a set of wellness policies to help local school districts respond to the congressional act (NANA 2005). Both NASPE and NANA recommend instructional physical education time totaling 150 minutes a week. The NANA model also recommends students receive at least 60 minutes of daily physical activity (physical education, recess, classroom activity, etc.), and specifically states that physical activity opportunities beyond the physical education class are needed to encourage students to adopt regular physical activity as a lifetime personal choice. The scenario at the beginning of this chapter illustrates this recommendation, showing how a classroom teacher takes a break from lessons with a short period of physical activity, during which students are physically active while they learn about movement (e.g., define the concept of direction). Today, educators may find many opportunities to develop partnerships among school personnel to provide daily physical activity and physical education for students, and to collaborate with community groups on ways to provide students with physical activities outside of school.

Increasing public support may be the result of the overwhelming empirical evidence of the benefits of a quality, daily physical education program. Programs stimulate student growth and development in three domains: cognitive, psychomotor, and affective (Kretchmar 2006; Le Masurier and Corbin 2006). *Cognitively,* students learn how to move effectively, how to recognize the importance of lifelong participation in physical activity, and how to develop health-related self-management skills, which lead to increased physical activity levels. Students also develop their own individuality as moving human beings, coming to know themselves in terms of what activities they like to participate in and what activities they are skilled in performing. *Physically* (psychomotor domain), students maintain proper body weight, improve muscular strength and endurance, strengthen the heart muscle, build bone and muscle mass, improve motor skills, maintain flexibility, and lower blood pressure. *Emotionally* (affective domain), students lower their anxiety and stress levels, improve their self-esteem and sense of well-being, express their creativity, discover a part of themselves and what they can do, and experience the fun of moving. *Socially* (affective domain), students learn to interact with others in a positive manner and to develop the skills of teamwork, cooperation, and leadership.

The evidence of and support for the benefits of a quality, daily physical education program for children has never been stronger. Unfortunately, many school districts still lag behind in efforts to improve physical education opportunities for students. In fact, most children in grades K–12 do not participate in physical education with the frequency recommended by the agencies previously mentioned. Part of the problem may stem from the lack of federal mandates for physical education programming, so each state is free to decide what kind of program and/or time requirements are implemented. The *Shape of the Nation Report* (NASPE 2006a) indicated the following data on physical education requirements across the country:

- Thirty-six states have mandates for elementary physical education. Eleven of those states have time requirements, but only two states (Louisiana and New Jersey) meet the national recommendation of 150 minutes or more per week.
- Illinois and Massachusetts are the only states that require daily physical education for all K–12 students, while New Jersey and Rhode Island require daily physical education for students in grades 1–12.
- Of all the states, fifteen require that students be assessed in physical education.

In addition, the report indicates that 28 states require certified physical education teachers to teach physical education classes, and in the other states either certified physical education or classroom teachers may teach the elementary physical education classes. A certified physical education teacher is someone who has completed an undergraduate degree in physical education pedagogy and is certified by the state to teach physical education in K–12 schools within the state. A certified **physical education teacher** is also called a physical educator. Although many classroom teachers will teach physical education to their students, we refer to these teachers as **movement educators** since they do not technically have the same professional preparation as physical educators.

The Shape of the Nation data clearly indicate that physical educators, classroom teachers, parents, school administrators and school boards have much work to do to achieve the recommendations coming from the public, government agencies, and national associations. Given this environment, you may be asking, what is the role of the classroom teacher in this arena?

The Role of the Classroom Teacher as a Movement Educator

As an elementary classroom teacher and movement educator, you may find yourself in one of three different situations in relation to physical education programming. In one situation, you may be totally responsible for the physical education of the students in your classroom (just as you are responsible for teaching reading, mathematics, etc.). In another situation, you may still be responsible for teaching physical education to the students in your classroom; however, the school district has available a certified physical education teacher who serves a number of schools in the district. Generally, this teacher's role is to assist you in preparing the physical education curriculum, selecting appropriate activities, and evaluating students. In this situation, the physical education teacher is a valuable resource to the classroom teacher. The physical education teacher can provide in-service training, help plan the physical education curriculum, shift equipment among schools as needed, help outline daily lesson plans, assist in discipline efforts, and provide teaching cues for the various motor skills.

In the third situation, you may not have any official responsibility for the physical education program, as your school has a physical education teacher hired to teach physical education to your students. In this last circumstance, we recommend that you work closely with the physical educator to integrate each other's content matter into your teaching. For example, the physical educator might integrate reading into the gymnasium, and the classroom teacher might integrate movement into the classroom. Regardless of your situation, as a classroom teacher you play a role as a movement educator. You can help achieve the physical education program objectives and the school's wellness objectives. You should do so to further the physical, social, and mental development of your students. Your role includes the following:

■ Advocating and providing daily physical activity for your students
■ Forming partnerships with the physical education teacher
■ Knowing and using national and state standards
■ Enhancing your physical education teaching skill
■ Supporting the value of lifelong physical activity
■ Joining schoolwide initiatives to achieve wellness

ADVOCATING AND PROVIDING DAILY PHYSICAL ACTIVITY FOR ELEMENTARY SCHOOL CHILDREN

Advocating for daily physical activity for children in elementary school means supporting and providing three types of physical activity times during the school day:

■ physical education class,
■ short bouts of physical activity interspersed throughout the day in the classroom setting, and
■ quality recess time.

By providing these three types of daily physical activity periods, you give students an opportunity to become physically educated. Research has shown that the amount of time spent in physical education class is not sufficient, in and of itself, to achieve the NASPE standards (Castelli 2005). Additional daily, high-quality physical activity in the classroom and during recess may provide the necessary time to produce desired results.

Elementary classroom teachers, as a group, can be strong advocates for daily physical education within their own schools. Recognizing the value of physical education, they can work with the physical educator and the school principal to produce a class schedule that allows daily physical education for their students. The Council on Physical Education for Children recommends at least 30–60 minutes of daily instruction in physical education for elementary students (COPEC 2001). This instruction time is exclusive of time allotted for recess, free and/or supervised play periods, and noon-hour activities.

In addition to daily physical education, classroom teachers might consider adding short bouts of supervised movement times (10–15 minutes in length) throughout the school day in the classroom (or outdoors) for their children. Even 10–15 minutes of physical activity can

benefit the students (NASPE 2004a; Maeda and Murata 2004). During the short bouts, the physical activities could provide a break from the academic subject being studied and/or support the learning of the academic subject by integrating movement into the subject being taught (see Instant Activity 1.1).

Additional physical activity time can be structured before and/or after school, during recesses, and on special occasions (such as monthly Friday afternoon game days). How to structure recess periods that are high-quality activity times is addressed later in this chapter. The Special Event (Celebrating National Physical Education and Sport Week) at the end of the chapter provides one example of a special occasion filled with movement activities.

FORMING PARTNERSHIPS WITH PHYSICAL EDUCATION TEACHERS

Classroom teachers can support quality physical education by forming partnerships with physical educators. The classroom teacher and physical education teacher become partners working to meet the movement needs of elementary school children. Together, these professionals can address issues such as these:

■ What movement skills and concepts should students practice and be able to master for their grade level?
■ Are the students improving their movement skills?
■ How long should recess periods be?
■ What equipment should be available during recess?
■ How can physical education concepts and movement experiences be integrated into the classroom?
■ How can subject area content be integrated into physical education?
■ How can the students' social skills be improved?

KNOWING AND USING NATIONAL AND STATE STANDARDS

Whatever the specific situation of classroom teachers in providing physical education, they will find it helpful to know the NASPE content standards and the corresponding student expectations for the children in the grade level they teach. In addition, since 47 states and the District of Columbia (Shape of the Nation Report 2006) have their own physical education curricula and requirements, knowing your state's standards is also imperative. Physical education standards for all the states are available online. Information may be found at www.education-world.com/standards/state/toc/index.shtml or by searching keywords "physical education state standards."

INSTANT ACTIVITY 1.1 Dice Math

Grades K–6

Equipment Needed

Play dice

Activity

In the classroom, students form a circle. Using two or three large play dice, do the following math and movement tasks. Children take turns throwing the dice. Always throw the dice into the center of the circle so all the students can view the numbers rolled.

For Young Children

Add the dice totals and do that many elbow swings with a partner.
Add the dice totals and do that many sit-ups.
Add the dice totals and make that number using your body.
Add the dice totals and hop or jump that many times in place.

Add the dice totals and skip or gallop around the circle that many times.
Add the dice totals and do that many push-ups.
Add the dice totals and do that many crab-walk steps (forward or backward).
Add the dice totals and do that many jumping jacks in place.

For Older Students

Perform the same movement skills, but alter the math skills to match the students' abilities. For example,

Add the blue and yellow dice, but subtract the red.
Using two dice, multiply the two numbers.
Add the blue and yellow dice, and then multiply by the red.

With young children, the teacher can determine the movements. With older students, the student who rolls the dice can select the movement to be performed.

In today's schools, either alone or in concert with the physical education teachers, classroom teachers are responsible for using standards to provide experiences that allow their students to achieve the physical education program goals for their grade level as well as to develop a physically active lifestyle. For example, North Carolina state standards mandate a minimum of 30 minutes of moderate to vigorous physical activity (MVPA) daily for all K–8 students. If a child does not have physical education on a particular day, classroom teachers are expected to provide 30 minutes of MVPA during recess or classroom time. Many other states recommend that classroom teachers integrate physical activity in the classroom to meet school wellness policies (e.g., Montana has a Mind and Body program and South Dakota uses the Minds in Motion program).

ENHANCING PHYSICAL EDUCATION TEACHING SKILLS

We recommend classroom teachers enhance their physical activity teaching skills on a continuing basis, by completing in-service training, by communicating with physical education teachers, and by attending physical education conferences. These activities allow teachers to discover new teaching methods, obtain new program activities, and discuss issues and problems with other practicing professionals. North Carolina provides in-service training so classroom teachers can effectively provide MVPA in 10-minute bouts called classroom energizers. (Information on energizers that connect physical activity with academic concepts is on the web at www.ncpe4me.com).

SUPPORTING THE VALUE OF LIFELONG PHYSICAL ACTIVITY

The classroom teacher can support the value of being physically active throughout life. As the literature today indicates, perhaps the most important element to helping children remain active throughout their lives is for them to develop a positive attitude toward physical activity. The words and actions of the classroom teacher can significantly affect those attitudes, so aim to portray the fun, excitement, and benefits of participating in physical activity. Just as classroom teachers help students develop appropriate skills in and attitudes about math, science, and reading, they help students develop skills in and attitudes about the value of being physically active throughout life.

JOINING SCHOOLWIDE INITIATIVES TO ACHIEVE WELLNESS

Passage of the Child Nutrition Reauthorization Act has forever changed the landscape for school personnel. They are now mandated to include parents, students, school board members, and community leaders in establishing and implementing a local wellness policy for the school. The policy, at a minimum, must (1) have nutrition education and physical activity goals, (2) meet nutrition guidelines for food served in schools, and (3) have a plan for measuring the success of the policy. Obviously, classroom teachers will be deeply involved in providing nutrition education and physical activity experiences for students in ways determined by the wellness policy. In addition, they may be involved in assessing progress toward nutrition and physical activity goals. Classroom teachers may have the opportunity to collaborate with other professionals to establish "whole-school" approaches to activity promotion (Lee and Solmon 2007), wellness information, and healthy eating (Jefferies and Mathias 2007). Opportunities may also exist to establish before- and after-school physical activities for the students (Hastie 2007).

Physical Education and Movement Defined

A number of movement terms have been used in the text already. It might prove useful to define those terms that have subtle distinctions in meaning. As major players in developing their students' motor skills and advocating an active lifestyle, classroom teachers will use movement terms quite often. **Physical education is a movement program sponsored by K–12 schools and institutions of higher education.** Physical education classes in the K–12 school curriculum provide a planned sequence of developmentally appropriate movement activities, games, and sports designed by the teacher or the school district for the purpose of educating all students about and through movement. Similar to other subject areas taught in the K–12 curriculum (e.g., math and science), physical education establishes goals and objectives for the program and the learner. Assessment of the learner occurs to determine progress toward the program goals. The aim is for students to become skilled movers who are physically active and who appreciate the value of movement, activity, and fitness in their lives. Currently, emphasis is on students developing a lifestyle of wellness within the framework of becoming a physically educated person (see Box 1.1).

BOX 1.1
Characteristics of a Physically Educated Person

A physically educated person

- *has* learned skills necessary to perform a variety of physical activities
- *is* physically fit
- *does* participate regularly in physical activity
- *knows* the implications of and benefits from involvement in physical education
- *values* physical activity and its contribution to a healthful lifestyle

Reprinted from *Moving into the Future: National Standards for Physical Education* (2004), with permission from the National Association for Sport and Physical Education (NASPE), 1900 Association Drive, Reston, VA 20191-1599.

LEARNING ABOUT AND THROUGH MOVEMENT

As a discipline, the term physical education is used to describe all learning (education) that occurs *about* human movement and *through* human movement. **Learning about movement** emphasizes the development of physical fitness and skilled motor performance. Physical fitness involves using movement to strengthen the body systems (the heart, lungs, and major muscles and tendons of the body) in order to lead a healthier life. Skilled motor performance involves perfecting the basic movement skills (e.g., throwing, running) and applying them effectively in specific situations (e.g., playing baseball or softball). Thus learning about movement occurs whenever children are practicing their motor skills or developing their physical fitness. Learning about movement also occurs when the knowledge content associated with physical fitness or motor skill development is taught. For example, learning about movement occurs when students learn the benefits of exercising on a regular basis or study movement principles based on the laws of physics (e.g., where to keep their center of gravity when performing a handstand and how to produce force when throwing a ball).

Learning through movement emphasizes that participating in movement experiences can contribute to the development of the whole person (socially, emotionally, and intellectually, as well as physically). Learning through movement entails coming to know

Successful elementary physical education programs can help children develop positive attitudes about movement and promote a lifetime of physical activity.

ourselves as moving human beings—what are we capable of doing, what do we like to do, what are the feelings we experience? Learning through movement can also occur as we learn to get along with each other—for example, when students learn to cooperate with others by playing cooperative games or when they learn to respect others while playing sports. Learning through movement also refers to the knowledge necessary to dance, to play a game, or to strategize a new soccer play. Even a baby at the moment of birth begins to participate in physical education, because he or she learns intellectually through movement (i.e., through physically moving in the environment and manipulating objects in the environment). In the remainder of this textbook, we use the term physical education to mean a course of study offered within the K–12 school system.

MOVEMENT TERMINOLOGY

Watch preschool children for a while. What do they do all day? They constantly move. In fact, they never stop moving unless forced to do so by caregivers who want them to sit and eat or lie down to sleep. We call this constant **movement** "playing," and it entails walking, running, manipulating objects, climbing, opening cupboards, pulling objects out of the toy box, putting objects into containers, riding a bicycle, and so on.

We could just as well call this playing "physical education." Instead, our culture uses different names for movement experiences that occur in particular settings for a particular purpose. Thus we use terms such as *play, games, sport, athletics, exercise,* and *physical*

activity to denote movement experiences that occur under certain conditions.

Play The term *play* generally refers to activity done by children. **Play** refers to movement activities that children do during their free time, such as the ones mentioned previously. Usually play activities are only minimally supervised by adults. During play, children select and engage in activities that hold their interest. During a play period, a child usually tries many different play activities, not just one. Children play because it is fun, and they move because that is how they learn about the world in which they live.

Games Once several children begin to play together (not just in the presence of others), they develop relationships with each other as well as with the movement. Physical educators tend to call these creative or regularized movement activities **games.** Movement games include activities such as playing shadow tag or tetherball; pretending "Barbie," "Superman," or "cops and robbers"; and playing jacks or hopscotch. As children grow older, play activities take on a subtle organization. These games have arbitrary rules (established by the participants on any given day), and the game participants enforce the rules. Children play movement games for the same reasons they play—because playing is fun.

Organized Sport Activities and Athletics Organized sport activities occur in the school setting with school-age children after or before school as part of the extracurricular program. **Sports** are organized games that have established, accepted, published rules of play. At the elementary school level, ideally, children engaged in sport activities should have fun; learn fundamental skills, teamwork, and fair play; practice skills in game situations without pressure from adults; and be able to socialize with their friends. Under these conditions, sport participation is a very valuable experience for the child.

Sport activities develop into organized **athletics** at an early age. Although more common in middle and high school, athletics are also available for young children, generally as a component of a community effort to have young children involved in sports. Eventually, the primary goal of athletic programs is to produce a few highly skilled players who can compete successfully against individuals or teams from other schools. In athletics, students may self-select to try out for a team based on their interests and talent, but only those chosen by the coaches will be members of the team. In addition, in athletics, participants do not self-regulate the breaking of the rules. Officials are employed to monitor players and enforce the rules.

In recent times, children have begun playing sports, beginning at very early ages (first and second grades) and continuing throughout their years in elementary school. Community recreation agencies and private businesses offer many of these competitive sports (such as soccer, gymnastics, dance, and T-ball). These highly structured sport activities are replacing the unstructured, free-play activities that children in the past engaged in after school and on the weekends. Although children may learn specific movement skills more quickly in a structured setting, they miss the development of social and creative skills that occurs when children play together without direct adult supervision. It is important to children's development that they have opportunities for free play during their years in elementary school.

Instant Activity 1.2 is designed to help children improve their sport skills, and Classroom Learning Station 1.1 (at the end of the chapter) is designed to help children become knowledgeable about sports. The text preface contains an explanation of Instant Activities and Classroom Learning Stations, as well as other pedagogical features, including why these elements appear in each chapter and how the classroom teacher might use them.

Exercise   Defined as movement engaged in by adults for the improvement or maintenance of physical fitness, **exercise** is planned, structured, repetitive, and purposeful. Usually children do not exercise or work out; they play or engage in physical activity.

Physical Activity   A relatively new term in the field, **physical activity** is a broad term that includes all large

INSTANT ACTIVITY 1.2
Striking Practice

Grades K–6
Equipment Needed
A balloon or ball for each student

Activity
Have the children stand by their desks or have them scattered throughout the room. Using balloons for less-skilled children and Nerf volleyballs for skilled children, practice the following striking skills:

Grades K–2

Hit (with hands) and catch (work for control).
Hit to self with other body parts (head, elbow, etc.).
Hit underhand.
Hit overhand.
Hit sidearm.

Grades 3–4

Hit forward and walk around the room (do not
  interfere with others).
Serve overhand to a partner.
Serve underhand to a partner.
Serve sidearm to a partner.
Volley consecutively to self (count number of hits).
Volley with a partner.

Grades 5–6

Volley with a partner and count the number of
  consecutive hits.
Volley, jump, and catch.
Volley, in groups of three, with two balls.

muscle movement performance (that increases energy expenditure) engaged in at any age (by children, adolescents, and adults). Thus a small child learning to walk, children playing a game during recess, adolescents playing basketball at the neighborhood court, and adults playing golf or walking on the treadmill are all engaged in physical activity.

Elementary Physical Education Today

Physical education is essential for the developing child. Its unique role in the elementary school curriculum is to provide children with movement learning opportunities that improve their motor skills, develop fitness, increase their knowledge of movement, and stimulate their desire to remain physically active. Given these learning opportunities, children come to possess the characteristics of a **physically educated person.** The benefits, to society and to the individual, of possessing these characteristics are many. Individually, regular physical activity helps maintain a proper weight; improves muscular strength and endurance; strengthens the heart muscle and bone mass; lowers blood pressure, anxiety, and stress; and improves self-esteem. Children must possess these characteristics in order for society to begin to reverse the devastating effects of childhood obesity and inactivity. A U.S. Federal Interagency Forum (2004) indicated that the proportion of children 6–18 years old who were overweight has steadily increased (6 percent were overweight in 1976–1980, 11 percent in 1988–1994, and 16 percent in 1999–2002). Data for 2003–04 indicated that 17.1% of children and adolescents (2–19 years of age) were overweight (NCHS 2006). Most alarming is the fact that this percentage indicates the prevalence of overweight children and adolescents has almost tripled since 1976–1980.

A quality program leads to children who are not only physically educated but also academically ready to learn. Physical activity stimulates not only physical development but also cognitive development. The body-mind connection is receiving renewed emphasis as research and empirical evidence continue to show a positive relationship between academic achievement and physical activity. Based on the premise that movement causes actual changes in the brain (growth of nerve cells), researchers are using brain scans and electrodes to discover exactly what happens in the brain during physical activity and exercise. Preliminary evidence supports providing physical activity and physical education in the schools to improve brain functioning, mental alertness, and attitude (Blakemore 2003).

The quality physical education program consists of the following elements:

■ Developing, expanding, and refining the child's motor skills through participation in a wide range of basic movement forms. Children improve their performance of fundamental movement patterns through participation in movement exploration, games, dance, tumbling, and sport activities.
■ Improving heart-lung functioning as well as muscular strength and endurance through participation in fitness activities that are challenging and fun.
■ Enhancing the child's current (and future) interest in pursuing physical activity as a lifestyle choice by creating an environment that fosters not only

the physical development of the child, but also the cognitive and social development of the child.
■ Promoting social, cooperative, and problem-solving skill development through group participation.
■ Increasing the child's knowledge of the basic movement forms, movement principles for quality performance, health and fitness concepts, and injury prevention by integrating such knowledge into movement experiences.

To achieve this quality program, NASPE (2004b) guidelines indicate that the program include the following components: the opportunity to learn, meaningful content, and appropriate instruction. These components emphasize the need for adequate instructional time, equipment, and facilities to teach a variety of motor skills using well-designed lessons that facilitate student learning. In addition to these components, the quality program contains a curriculum that adheres to national standards and practices, emphasizes the goal of promoting lifetime physical activity, and connects with classroom content in educating the whole student (mind and body).

ADHERES TO PRINCIPLES AND STANDARDS

Today the physical education profession recognizes the unique physical, social, and cognitive needs of elementary school children and has established specific curriculum standards and appropriate teaching practices to guide classroom teachers and physical education teachers.

NASPE Content Standards Physical education professionals from across the country developed the national physical education standards. These standards, published by the National Association for Sport and Physical Education (**NASPE**) in *Moving into the Future: National Standards for Physical Education* (2004b), specify what a student should know, value, and be able to do in order to become a "physically educated person." The six content standards in physical education are listed below.

The content standards reflect the current trend in education of establishing national standards for the various subject areas taught within the schools. However, content standards in a particular subject area (developed within the educational reform movement) do *not* establish a national curriculum. In physical education, the **NASPE content standards** indicate *what a student should know, value, and be able to do.*

In addition to the six broad content standards, *Moving into the Future* identifies student expectations by grade levels (K–2, 3–5, 6–8, and 9–12). The student expectations for the grade levels build upon the previous grade level; so each year the students make further progress toward the attainment of being a physically educated person. The sample grade-level performance outcomes provide a guide for what knowledge, values, and abilities students should have acquired by the completion of that grade level.

The six national content standards are as follows:

Standard 1: Students demonstrate competency in motor skills and movement patterns needed to perform a variety of physical activities. To meet this standard at the K–6 level, students practice (to a mastery level) the basic motor and manipulative skills identified in Chapter 3. See Quick Lesson 1.1 (Match the Diagram) for a sample lesson designed to help students meet Standard 1.

Standard 2: Students demonstrate understanding of movement concepts, principles, strategies, and tactics as they apply to the learning and performance of physical activities. Students must not only practice their physical skills but also acquire the knowledge of how to move correctly. Using their movement knowledge, students can improve their performance and assess their own performance and that of others. The movement concepts and principles the students study are detailed in Chapter 3. See Quick Lesson 1.2 (Challenge Long Jump) for a sample lesson designed to help students meet Standard 2.

Standard 3: Students participate regularly in physical activity. Students learn to participate in physical activity during physical education class, in their elementary classroom, during school recesses, and during nonschool hours. Students are encouraged to seek opportunities to be physically active and to learn activities they can do in various movement settings. The knowledge base for this standard is presented in Chapters 8, 9, 10, and 12. See Quick Lesson 1.3 (Chase the Leader) for a sample lesson designed to help students meet Standard 3.

Standard 4: Students achieve and maintain a health-enhancing level of physical fitness. Students participate in physical activity following the time, intensity, and duration principles for achieving fitness. In addition, they learn to plan activity sessions that meet the guidelines for achieving fitness. This knowledge base is presented in Chapter 4. See Quick Lesson 1.4 (Jump for Fitness) for a sample lesson designed to help students meet Standard 4.

Standard 5: Students exhibit responsible personal and social behavior that respects self and others in physical activity settings. Students develop the social skills needed to participate in physical activities with others. Emphasis is on being able to control one's behavior in a physical setting (alone, with a partner, and in small and large groups) so that learning may occur. This knowledge base is presented in Chapter 10. See Quick Lesson 1.5 (Create Your Own Sport) for a sample lesson designed to help students meet Standard 5. Students also develop attitudes, beliefs, and behavioral practices that contribute to inclusive behavior when in a physical activity setting (inclusive regardless of gender, ethnic background, and disability). This knowledge base is presented in Chapters 5 and 10. See Quick Lesson 1.6 (Opposite Hand) for an additional sample lesson designed to help students meet Standard 5.

Standard 6: Students value physical activity for health, enjoyment, challenge, self-expression, and/or social interaction. Students become aware of participation in physical activity as a source of personal meaning and enhancement. This knowledge base is presented in Chapter 9. See Quick Lesson 1.7 (My Physical Activity Journal) for a sample lesson designed to help students meet Standard 6.

The content standards are connected to curriculum planning in Chapter 6. The standards are used to design physical education programs that produce physically educated children. To demonstrate this connection between the standards and the program activities selected for specific lessons, the lessons included in this book clearly identify the standard being met.

Appropriate Teaching Practices The Council on Physical Education for Children (**COPEC**) developed for NASPE a number of appropriate practices for elementary physical education. The document specifies appropriate instructional and curriculum practices to help the educator implement programs that produce physically educated children and to counteract the use of inappropriate practice. For example, one inappropriate practice is to use lesson activities that require many children to wait before participating (e.g., relays, taking turns on equipment, playing Duck, Duck, Goose). The appropriate practice is to use lesson activities that allow full participation by all students all of the time.

These practices recognize that educators must teach the whole child—physically, intellectually, and socially (NASPE 2000).

■ Physically, the programs have the unique opportunity to teach students movement skills (e.g., throwing, running, backstroke, two-step) from a wide array of movement forms (e.g., game skills, creative and rhythmic skills, gymnastics, swimming). After exploring many movement forms during their school years, students become proficient in a few select activities enabling them to be active throughout their lifetime.

- Intellectually, the programs teach about the following:
  1. How to perform movement activities (e.g., game rules and strategies)
  2. How to perform specific movement skills (e.g., throwing and catching a football, doing a forward roll, doing an elbow swing in square dance)
  3. The benefits of regular physical activity and exercise in sustaining health and well-being
  4. How to achieve and maintain physical fitness
- Socially, the programs facilitate interaction between and among diverse student populations in order to prepare students for the cooperative and competitive experiences they will face in the future. The programs also encourage participants to value being physically active.

The appropriate practices, as identified by NASPE, are discussed throughout this book whenever they are relevant to the topics being addressed. The entire NASPE document (*Appropriate Practices for Elementary School Physical Education*) is available online (under pull-down menu "publications" at www .aahperd.org/naspe/).

Elementary physical education has come a long way in the last 20 years. The profession has focused content standards for the program and has identified teaching and curriculum practices to ensure that students become physically educated.

EMPHASIZES LIFETIME PHYSICAL ACTIVITY

Educators play an important part in the profession's efforts to promote lifetime physical activity by supporting the NASPE guidelines (2004a) for the amount of time elementary school children should be physically active each day. Each child should accumulate at least 60 minutes of physical activity each day, and 50 percent of the minutes should be in bouts of 15 minutes or more. These activity bouts might occur during recess, classroom activity times, physical education, and sports practices. Each child should have daily physical education for a minimum of 30 minutes (weekly minimum of 150 minutes) and additional free-play time each day. The **surgeon general** (USDHHS 2007) supports this guideline by recommending that schools provide quality daily physical education classes in all school grades

and build physical activity into children's regular routines and playtime. Educators should strive to follow these recommendations when planning physical activity time for elementary school children because there is a direct link between inactivity during childhood and sedentary lifestyles in adults. Inactive children are likely to become inactive adults.

The Benefits of Lifetime Physical Activity In addition to supporting the NASPE guidelines for the amount of physical education time in the schools, the surgeon general documents the **benefits of regular physical activity** for people of all ages. These benefits include reduced risk of coronary heart disease, diabetes, hypertension, obesity, and certain cancers. Although these benefits are most salient later in life (during adulthood), other benefits are more immediate, such as improved movement skills, improved physical fitness levels, reduction of stress, healthier mental states, feelings of success, improved cooperation skills, and weight management. By balancing calories consumed and calories expended, this weight management aspect is critical to reducing the incidence of obesity and diabetes in children. Weight gain appears to be associated with increased caloric intake and decreased caloric expenditure (inactivity). Increasing activity levels to balance caloric intake and output is of great concern, as evidence suggests that overweight adolescents are at increased risk to become overweight adults (NCHS 2006).

The Important Role of Elementary Physical Education Programs Because children are inherently active, many people believe children do not need to engage in organized physical education programs to promote physical activity. Yes, it is true that children are inherently active, and they can obtain a certain amount of physical activity time during recess and before and after school. However, several factors support the contention that children need to participate in physical education throughout their elementary school years.

First, as we will examine in more detail later in the chapter, the focus and goals of recess and physical education are quite different. One cannot substitute for the other. Second, although elementary students are the most physically active group within America's population, regular participation in physical activity declines sharply with increasing age. Recent data indicate that only 35.8 percent of high school students had been physically active enough to raise their heart rate and breathe hard for at least 60 minutes on at least five of the seven days preceding the survey (CDC

2006a). In addition, activity levels were higher among boys (43.8 percent) than girls (27.8 percent). Only 24 percent of adults in the United States engage in vigorous physical activity (lasting 10 minutes or more) three or more times a week (CDC 2006b). Third, it does not appear that children compensate for the loss of physical education time in the curriculum by increasing their activity levels outside of school time (Dale, Corbin, and Dale 2000). In fact, children were more active outside of school time on days when their physical education time was increased.

Thus it is important to have elementary physical education programs in the school curriculum as a primary means of intervention before inactivity becomes a part of the student's lifestyle. Since values are established at an early age, the idea of valuing physical activity as part of a healthy lifestyle should be introduced early (in elementary school) and reiterated throughout the child's school years. Physical education programs have the potential to make significant contributions to the lives of children across the country. With today's emphasis on school-based wellness, the physical education program should be the cornerstone of the school physical activity initiatives (Lynn 2007). Quick Lesson 1.7, at the end of the chapter, is designed to improve understanding of the benefits of an active lifestyle, and Instant Activity 1.3 contains activities students can perform in the classroom to be active for 10 to 15 minutes.

CONNECTS TO THE CLASSROOM

Physical education today, in addition to adhering to national standards and emphasizing lifetime physical activity, also connects more fully to the content being learned by the students in the classroom.

Integrating Content in the Classroom and Gymnasium   It is not unusual for the physical educator and classroom teacher to collaborate so that subject content matches occur in the classroom and gymnasium. For example, the mathematical concepts of addition and subtraction might be taught concurrently in the classroom (using flash cards) and in the gymnasium (using objects and bodily movement). The health concepts of weight management might be taught in the gymnasium (using fun activities to burn off calories) and in the classroom (keeping a log of foods eaten each day for a month). The movement concept of visual focus point might be taught in the gymnasium (performing balance activities) and in the classroom (discussing how to use mind-focusing techniques to

stay on task within the classroom). The examples just provided are simple, one-time integration experiences. Teachers may more fully integrate subject content by jointly developing and teaching a series of lessons that allow students to experience the subject content in multiple ways over time. We encourage classroom teachers and physical educators to plan for integration throughout the school year, where student learning of subject content is supported in both classroom and gymnasium, thus providing students with more meaningful learning opportunities.

Evidence (Blakemore 2003) continues to mount that movement is essential to learning and that increased time in physical education does not have negative effects on students' academic achievement. Classroom teachers should have students move for the same reason physical educators have students count, calculate, read, write, and name the colors (Jensen 2000). Integrated learning intertwines the many "core curriculums" (e.g., art, music, physical education, drama, math, science, reading, writing) to enhance student learning. The Classroom Learning Station at the end of the chapter outlines an integrated learning experience.

Educating the Whole Child   The strong connection between the classroom and gymnasium, where the integration of subject content occurs on a regular basis, also provides the opportunity to **educate the whole child.** A number of recent educational theories, such as the multiple intelligences theory and brain-based education, emphasize that the learner is a whole human being who interprets educational experiences holistically (i.e., physically, socially, emotionally, and intellectually all at the same time). These theories are moving educational practices in the classroom and gymnasium to a new level—from the traditional emphasis on memorization of facts in lecture settings that are teacher-dominated to reflective learning in experiential settings that are student-led. Although physical education has always occurred in experiential settings, teachers still dominated the learning process and demanded rote repetition of teacher-selected activities. Today physical educators are revamping teaching techniques—choices, goal setting, problem solving, challenge, feedback, rehearsal time, arousal, and music—to activate the brain and increase learning (Blakemore 2004). These techniques are described at length in Chapter 9.

Howard Gardner's **multiple intelligences theory** espouses the viewpoint that individuals have a number of intelligences—not just one intellect measured by standardized IQ tests (logical-mathematical intelligence) (Gardner 2006). Gardner has proposed eight independent, but interacting, intelligences:

INSTANT ACTIVITY 1.3 Marching

Grades K–6

Equipment Needed

Tape player and audiotape with appropriate music

Activity

Play music that has a strong, basic beat. It should be fast enough to raise the children's heart rates while performing. Have the children stand by their desks in the classroom and do the following:

Grades K–3

March in place to the beat.
March with knees high.
March with knees low.
March on tiptoes.
March loudly (stomping).
March softly.
March with arms overhead.
March with hands on hips.
March with hands clapping.

Grades 3–4

March forward for eight counts.
March backward for eight counts.
March while beating a drum.
March while beating rhythm sticks.
March and snap fingers.
March mirroring a partner.

Grades 5–6

March a pattern:
    Forward for eight counts
    Backward for eight counts
    Turning in place for four counts
    Repeat
March double time.
March double time while clapping the beat.
March beat while clapping double time.
March in patterns created by the students.

Note: Select music the students enjoy, or better yet ask the students to bring in their favorite music, and then use a selection they bring in.

---

linguistic, logical-mathematical, spatial, musical, bodily-kinesthetic, interpersonal, intrapersonal, and naturalist. A unique combination of these intelligences forms an individual's cognitive structure. According to Gardner and others, students possess a "profile of intelligences" with relative strengths and weaknesses in the various intelligences (Moran, Kornhaber, and Gardner 2006). The theory implies that educators should offer students learning experiences that engage many of their intelligences, not just one. This allows the intelligences to interact *within* the student. In addition, these learning experiences tend to be collaborative in nature so that students learn from each other in group or partner activities. This allows the intelligences to interact *across* students. For example, the learning experience in Classroom Learning Station 1.1 allows the intelligences to interact both within and across students by asking students to:

- Touch and manipulate equipment (using bodily-kinesthetic intelligence)
- Read stories (linguistic intelligence)
- Examine spatial relationships among game players (spatial intelligence)
- Play with others (interpersonal intelligence)

Brain-based education involves using new knowledge about the neurological workings of the mind and the implications of this knowledge for the teaching and learning process. The theory purports that the brain changes physiologically as the result of challenging, nurturing experiences. In addition, it asserts that emotions and cognition cannot be separated, as the emotional impact of a lesson may determine present and future learning (King-Friedrichs 2001). Students learn best when experiences are positive (not threatening) and viewed (by the student) as useful (Phillips 2005). Brain research supports learning experiences in which students interact with each other, solve problems, complete projects, use music and rhyme, and construct (art objects, drawings, movement sequences, etc.) to represent events, timelines, and ideas (Wolfe 2006).

Many educators are using teaching strategies based on the theory of multiple intelligences and brain-based education. As these strategies are developed, implemented, and evaluated for effectiveness, educators are making significant changes in their classrooms and gymnasiums. We believe that as these theories continue to develop, the importance of movement in the educational processes will be recognized and classroom teaching methods will allow for children to learn through movement experiences, not just through reading textbooks and viewing videotapes. We also believe that physical educators will use these new findings to develop learning experiences that promote student reflection, student interaction, and student diversity.

Recess as Quality Movement Time

During the school day, students have two primary opportunities to be physically active: physical education class and recess. Most elementary students are provided with a recess each morning and afternoon. Generally, "to take a recess" means to withdraw temporarily from the business one is currently engaged in; thus students recess from the formal process of studying in the classroom. **Recess** is play time provided to allow students a break from the rigors of academic learning.

THE BENEFITS OF RECESS

During recess, students tend to play games or sports, play on the playground equipment, or stand around and talk to friends. Any of these activities serves the purpose of refreshing their minds for further academic learning, but most professionals encourage students to be physically active because the body was not made to sit for long periods of time (as students sit at desks in the classroom). This physical activity is encouraged by taking the students outdoors to wide-open spaces with playground equipment so they can run, jump, swing, climb, skip, kick balls, and so on. Given certain spaces and equipment, students self-select activities they want to participate in and then self-direct the activities with only minor intervention from the teachers who supervise the recess.

Many educators provide recess periods for their children because they recognize that the benefits of this type of play go way beyond just refreshing the children's minds. Self-selection of activities allows students to participate in an activity of their choice with the individuals of their choice, thus building their decision-making skills, developing relationships with others, and creating self-confidence. Engaging in self-directed (versus teacher-directed) physical activities allows students to practice (and learn) valuable social interaction skills, such as the following:

- Taking responsibility for one's actions
- Setting rules and regulations for the group's behavior
- Setting consequences for breaking the rules
- Taking turns

Access to playground equipment during recess encourages physical activity; by self-selecting and self-directing their activities, these students can improve fitness and social interaction skills and boost self-confidence.

- Caring for others
- Leading and following in the group's activities
- Allowing others to participate

Children who participate vigorously in physical activities during recess improve their heart and lung (cardiorespiratory) fitness. Students playing on the jungle gym improve their upper-arm strength, and students playing games or sports improve their movement skills. In addition, children benefit cognitively from the peer interaction they experience while playing with other children. A study from NASPE (2006b) indicates that physical activity during recess "may improve attention, focus, behavior, and learning in the classroom."

We know that the physical education class is the primary mechanism for teaching movement concepts and activities within the school; however, we also know that physical education alone cannot solve the inactivity patterns of youth today. Even if children participate in daily physical education for 30 minutes, that alone does not meet the NASPE (2004a) recommendation of 60 minutes of daily physical activity. Thus we need to look for additional activity time within the school day. Within a typical day, recess periods provide anywhere from 30 to 90 minutes of additional activity time. It behooves us to view and establish recess as quality education time designed to stimulate free play and the love of being physically active.

THE ROLE OF THE CLASSROOM TEACHER

Of course, the extent to which social skills, movement skills, and physical fitness are improved depends on the spaces and equipment provided and the activities

Classroom teachers can promote physical activity during recess by offering students equipment.

students are encouraged to participate in. Although students self-select activities, professionals limit or provide access to certain activities by providing particular spaces and equipment and by giving certain kinds of encouragement to the students. For example, students cannot play hopscotch unless the lines are permanently painted on a paved area, or students are allowed to draw their own on the sidewalk (with chalk), or a dirt area is provided where they can draw the hopscotch boxes. Students cannot play basketball without basketballs and hoops. Thus classroom teachers have an important role in providing appropriate movement spaces, equipment, and activities for their students during recess. Classroom teachers should encourage students to participate in active recess play and never withhold recess time from students (as punishment for misbehavior or as time for the students to complete missed homework). Students may gain many of the already-mentioned benefits when classroom teachers do the following:

- Provide appropriate equipment and play spaces.
- Provide sufficient equipment and spaces for many groups to play simultaneously.
- Challenge students to find a new game appropriate for use at recess time (using varied sources—the library, the Internet, and other people).
- Ask students who are just standing around if they would like to do one of the following activities:
  - Play a new game (and then teach them a new game).
  - Select and use a piece of equipment from the traditional and innovative equipment available on a cart.
  - Walk with you around the perimeter of the play area.
  - Join a game already in progress (help the student ask whether he or she can join the activity).
- Help groups establish and enforce fair game and sport rules.
- Identify and reinforce expected recess behaviors, so students know that teasing, fighting, name-calling, and the like are inappropriate behaviors that will not be allowed to occur.
- Encourage play groups to include students who ask to join the group.
- Recognize whether certain students are loners (never playing with anyone), and then take steps to help them overcome whatever obstacles prevent them from playing with others.
- Observe what's happening on the playground (who plays what games with whom, who the activity leaders are, who's left out, who always fights, who plays fairly), and use that information to improve the activity levels of the children.
- Observe what games (activities) are being played, thus providing insight into what the students like to do so that additional activities of a similar nature (e.g., different tag games) can be taught.

Considerable debate has occurred over the role of play in the child's development and the need for schools to schedule play periods for children. Theorists continue to suggest that during play children learn and practice various physical, cognitive, and social skills. Chapter 12 provides an in-depth discussion of recess within the schools, including a description of recess activities that classroom teachers might use to encourage their students to participate actively during recess and tips on how classroom teachers can make recess a profitable movement time for their students.

Summary

As a discipline, physical education describes all learning that occurs *about movement* and *through movement*. Learning about movement emphasizes the development of physical fitness and sport skill performance. Learning through movement emphasizes that participating in movement experiences can contribute to the development of the whole person (socially, emotionally, and intellectually, as well as physically). A number of recent educational theories emphasize that the learner is a whole human being who interprets educational experiences holistically (i.e., physically, socially, emotionally, and intellectually all at the same time). As these theories become more accepted and practiced, the importance of movement to the learning process will be better recognized.

The immediate benefits of a quality physical education program for children include improved movement skills and fitness levels, reduction in stress, healthier mental states, experiences of success, and improved cooperation skills. If children continue to be physically active throughout their lives, the benefits include reduced risk of coronary heart disease, diabetes, obesity, hypertension, and certain cancers.

Elementary physical education today offers children a movement program that is specifically designed for the physical, social, and mental abilities they possess. Using established curriculum standards and appropriate teaching practices, classroom teachers and physical education teachers strive to help their students become physically educated. Children should spend 150 minutes a week in physical education class, and they should spend additional time in free-play activities during recess and before and after school. In addition, the classroom teacher can provide movement experiences in the classroom that supplement the physical education program and encourage children to be active throughout the day.

Classroom teachers can help meet the physical education program objectives by doing the following:

- Supporting the benefits of a quality daily physical education program when interacting with children
- Being strong advocates for daily physical education within their school community
- Being partners with the physical education teacher to meet the movement needs of their students

- Enhancing their own skills relative to teaching physical education
- Supporting the value of being physically active throughout life
- Providing quality physical activities and recess experiences for their students
- Joining schoolwide initiatives to achieve wellness

Chapter Activities

1. In your own words, write a paragraph describing what physical education entails in schools today. Include how play, athletics, organized sport activities, and recess are different from physical education.
2. List the things you liked and disliked about the physical education classes you participated in while in elementary school. For the disliked items, indicate how you might change the situations so that they would be positive instead of negative. Also name and describe your favorite physical education activity in elementary school and indicate why you liked it best.
3. Write a paragraph explaining your view on how important recess is as an educational experience.
4. Read an article about elementary physical education from one of these publications: *Strategies; Journal of Physical Education, Recreation, and Dance; Teaching Elementary Physical Education;* or SPEAK, the advocacy kit produced by the American Alliance for Health, Physical Education, Recreation and Dance (AAHPERD).
5. Write a two-page paper that presents an argument you could use to convince your school board that quality daily physical education should be a priority for your school. Use the resources mentioned in this chapter to support your argument.
6. Obtain a copy of the NASPE content standards and grade-level performance outcomes as well as the state physical education standards for the state in which you plan to teach.
7. Visit the NASPE website (go to www.aahperd.org and click on NASPE to get to the NASPE homepage). Locate the NASPE resources listed in the bibliography below.

Internet Resources

American Alliance for Health, Physical Education, Recreation and Dance; National Association for Sport and Physical Education. Contains numerous position papers related to physical education for children. **www.aahperd.org/naspe**

BrainGym International. Official BrainGym website of the Educational Kinesiology Foundation.
www.braingym.org

Centers for Disease Control and Prevention: Healthy Schools, Healthy Youth! Health and safety topics, recent research, and health statistics specifically pertaining to children.
www.cdc.gov/HealthyYouth

Centers for Disease Control and Prevention: National Center for Health Statistics. The nation's principal health statistics agency.
www.cdc.gov/nchs

Dietary Guidelines for Americans. Guidelines published jointly every five years by the Department of Health and Human Services and the Department of Agriculture.
www.healthierus.gov/dietaryguidelines

Dr. Thomas Armstrong website. Contains Dr. Armstrong's work in the field of multiple intelligences.
www.thomasarmstrong.com

Education World. Contains educational resources for teaching using the theory of multiple intelligences.
www.education-world.com/a_curr/curr054.shtm

Federal Interagency Forum on Child and Family Statistics. Provides access to statistics and reports on children and families, including population and family characteristics, economic security, health, behavior and social environment, and education.
www.childstats.gov

Healthy People 2010. National initiative establishing health objectives for the nation to achieve by 2010.
www.healthypeople.gov

National Center for Chronic Disease Prevention and Health Promotion, Division of Nutrition and Physical Activity. Division of the Centers for Disease Control that addresses the role of nutrition and physical activity in improving the public's health and preventing and controlling chronic diseases.
www.cdc.gov/nccdphp/dnpa

New Horizons for Learning. An international network of people, programs, and products dedicated to successful, innovative learning; contains information on multiple intelligences theory.
www.newhorizons.org/strategies/mi/front_mi.htm

PE4life. Many links to information on physical education, sports, and fitness.
www.PE4life.com

Robert Wood Johnson Foundation. Contains information on childhood obesity; foundation seeks to improve the health and health care of all Americans.
www.rwjf.org

Bibliography

Blakemore, C. L. 2003. Movement is essential to learning. *Journal of Physical Education, Recreation and Dance* 74(9): 22–25, 41.

———. 2004. Brain research strategies for physical educators. *Journal of Physical Education, Recreation and Dance* 75(1): 31–36, 41.

Castelli, D. 2005. *Are the national physical education standards achievable?* Presented at National Association for Kinesiology and Physical Education in Higher Education, Tucson, AZ.

Centers for Disease Control and Prevention (CDC). 2006a. Youth risk behavior surveillance—United States, 2005. *Morbidity and Mortality Weekly Report* 55 (SS–5): 1–108.

———. 2006b. Summary health statistics for U.S. adults: National health interview survey, 2005. *Vital and Health Statistics* 10(232): 1–153.

Council of Physical Education for Children (COPEC). 2001. *Physical education is critical to a complete education.* Reston, VA: National Association for Sport and Physical Education, an association of the American Alliance for Health, Physical Education, Recreation and Dance. Position paper at www.aahperd.org/naspe/.

Dale, D., C. B. Corbin, and K. S. Dale. 2000. Restricting opportunities to be active during school time: Do children compensate by increasing physical activity levels after school? *Research Quarterly for Exercise and Sport* 71: 240–248.

Gardner, H. 2006. *Multiple intelligences: New horizons.* New York: Basic Books.

Harvard School of Public Health. 2003. *Obesity as a public health issue: A look at solutions.* Boston: Harvard School of Public Health.

Hastie, P. A. 2007. Physical activity opportunities: Before and after school. *Journal of Physical Education, Recreation and Dance* 78(6): 20–23.

Jefferies, S., and K. Mathias. 2007. The physical educator's role in enacting the mandated school wellness policy: School nutrition. *Journal of Physical Education, Recreation and Dance* 78(6): 24–28.

Jensen, E. 2000. *Brain-based learning.* San Diego: The Brain Store.

King-Friedrichs, J. 2001. Brain-friendly techniques for improving memory. *Educational Leadership* 59(3): 76–79.

Kretchmar, R. S. 2006. Ten reasons for quality physical education. *Journal of Physical Education, Recreation and Dance* 77(9): 6–9.

Lee, A., and M. Solmon. 2007. School programs to increase physical activity. *Journal of Physical Education, Recreation and Dance* 78(5): 22–24, 28.

Le Masurier, G., and C. B. Corbin. 2006. Top 10 reasons for quality physical education. *Journal of Physical Education, Recreation and Dance* 77(6): 44–53.

Lynn, S. 2007. The case for daily physical education. *Journal of Physical Education, Recreation and Dance* 78(5): 18–21.

Maeda, J. K., and N. M. Murata. 2004. Collaborating with classroom teachers to increase daily physical activity: The GEAR Program. *Journal of Physical Education, Recreation and Dance* 75(5): 42–46.

Moran, S., M. Kornhaber, and H. Gardner. 2006. Orchestrating multiple intelligences. *Educational Leadership* 64(1): 22–27.

National Alliance for Nutrition and Activity. 2005. *Model school wellness policies*. www.schoolwellnesspolicies.org/.

National Association for Sport and Physical Education (NASPE). 2000. *Appropriate practices for elementary physical education*. Reston, VA: National Association for Sport and Physical Education, an association of the American Alliance for Health, Physical Education, Recreation and Dance. www.aahperd.org/naspe/.

———. 2003. *Parents' views of children's health and fitness: A summary of results*. Reston, VA: National Association for Sport and Physical Education, an association of the American Alliance for Health, Physical Education, Recreation and Dance.

———. 2004a. *Physical activity for children: A statement of guidelines for children ages 5–12*. Reston, VA: National Association for Sport and Physical Education, an association of the American Alliance for Health, Physical Education, Recreation and Dance.

———. 2004b. *Moving into the future: National standards for physical education*. St. Louis, MO: Mosby.

———. 2006a. *Shape of the nation report: Status of physical education in the USA*. Reston, VA: National Association for Sport and Physical Education, an association of the American Alliance for Health, Physical Education, Recreation and Dance.

———. 2006b. *Recess for elementary school students*. Reston, VA: National Association for Sport and Physical Education, an association of the American Alliance for Health, Physical Education, Recreation and Dance. www.aahperd.org/naspe/.

National Center for Health Statistics (NCHS). 2006. *Prevalence of overweight among children and adolescents: United States, 2003–2004*. www.cdc.gov/nchs/products/pubs/pubd/hestats/overwght_child_03.htm.

Phillips, J. M. 2005. From neurons to brainpower: Cognitive neuroscience and brain-based learning. ERIC, 490–546.

Robert Wood Johnson Foundation (RWJF). 2003. *Healthy schools for healthy kids*. Seattle, WA: Pyramid Communications. www.rwjf.org/publications/other.jsp.

U.S. Department of Agriculture (USDA). 2007. Local Wellness Policy Requirements. http://www.fns.usda.gov/tn/Healthy/Wellness_Policyrequirements.html.

U.S. Department of Health and Human Services (USDHHS). 2007. Overweight and obesity: A vision for the future. www.surgeongeneral.gov/topics/obesity/.

U.S. Federal Interagency Forum on Child and Family Statistics. 2004. America's children: Key national indicators of well-being 2004. http://childstats.gov.

Wolfe, P. 2006. Brain-compatible learning: Fad or foundation? Neuroscience points to better strategies for educators, but sorting out claims on brain-based programs is essential. *School Administrator* 63(11): 10–15.

GRADES K–6

NASPE STANDARD 1 Students demonstrate competency in motor skills and movement patterns needed to perform a variety of physical activities.

LESSON OBJECTIVES

- Students identify and perform the eight basic locomotor movements.
- Students identify and perform various pathways.
- Students use different speeds and levels.

EQUIPMENT NEEDED A sheet of paper and a pencil for each child

PREPARATION TIME None

KNOWLEDGE CONTENT Asking children to draw a pathway and then execute it may involve the following:

- Basic locomotor skills: movements that take children from one space to another
  - *Walking:* transferring of weight from one foot to the other with one foot always in contact with the ground
  - *Running:* transferring of weight from one foot to the other with momentary loss of contact with the ground by both feet while moving
  - *Jumping:* springing evenly into the air from both feet and landing on both feet while moving
  - *Hopping:* going up into the air and back to the ground on the same foot
  - *Skipping:* performing a step-hop on one foot, followed by a step-hop on the other foot
  - *Leaping:* taking off on one foot and landing on the other foot (using an elongated running step with flight)
  - *Sliding:* moving sideways with the same foot leading
  - *Galloping:* moving forward with the same foot leading
- Pathways: direction traveled
  - Direct
  - Zigzag
- Speed: rate at which the student travels
  - Fast
  - Intermediate
  - Slow

- Levels: position of height of the body
  - High: on tiptoes
  - Regular: normal walking position
  - Medium: half squat position
  - Low: full squat position

CLASSROOM ACTIVITY

- Give each child a pencil and a sheet of paper.
- Tell children to draw a pathway (curved, zigzag, straight, etc.) and include several locomotor skills, levels, and speeds while they travel their pathway.
- Scatter children around the room and ask them to perform their drawing. Remind them to be careful of obstacles and not to bump into each other.
- Pathways should be more intricate and motor patterns more difficult for students in grades 3 through 6.

ASSESSMENT Observe the match between the drawing and the performance. Ask students to discuss how they executed their drawing. Give feedback pertaining to drawing and performance. Review the terms listed in the lesson content section.

SUCCESS FOR ALL If an individual student will not be successful because of motor deficits, have a student helper or paraprofessional assist that student. A classmate might serve as helper if he or she is mature enough to handle the assignment.

INTEGRATION WITH OTHER SUBJECT AREAS
You might integrate this activity into Social Studies lessons in the following ways:

- Examine a pathway Christopher Columbus took to find the Americas.
- Examine a pathway that the space shuttle *Endeavour* has taken in space.
- Examine the pathways traveled by European settlers (e.g., the Oregon Trail) as they crossed North America to settle in the western part of the continent.
- Examine the pathways traveled by Native American tribes as they made their seasonal migrations.

QUICK LESSON 1.2
Challenge Long Jump

GRADES K–6

NASPE STANDARD 2 Students demonstrate understanding of movement concepts, principles, strategies, and tactics as they apply to the learning and performance of physical activities.

LESSON OBJECTIVES

- Students demonstrate competency in body management through standing long jump and running long jump (grades 3–6).
- Students demonstrate competency in body management through standing long jump (grades K–2).
- Students apply principles of speed and force.

EQUIPMENT NEEDED Mat to land on if performing running long jump

PREPARATION TIME Five minutes

KNOWLEDGE CONTENT Participating in a running long jump will teach and reinforce the following skills and concepts (grades 3–6):

- Speed: the ability of the body to perform movement in a short period of time. The running long jump reinforces the use of body parts to generate speed. The student runs to a designated place (a line taped on the floor), plants the dominant or stronger foot, thrusts both arms forward and upward to accelerate through the air, and then lands on both feet.
- Force: the effort expended in movement. Force is applied throughout the run and in the explosive movement of the jump.

Participating in a standing long jump will teach and reinforce the following skills and concepts (grades K–2):

- Coordinating the arms and legs to produce force
- Landing softly (knees bent to absorb the force)
- Landing with body weight forward (so as not to fall backward) on landing
- Use of arm action to produce force

CLASSROOM ACTIVITY

- Divide the class into three or four teams.
- A member of each team jumps (standing long jump) alternately with a member of the opposing team.
- The distance of each jumper is added to that of his or her teammates.
- When everyone has jumped, the team having the longest total distance jumped is the winner.
- For grades 3–6, repeat this activity performing the running long jump (for safety reasons, run only for several steps and have a gymnastics mat placed where the students will land).

ASSESSMENT Peer assessment: after the first group competition, ask the teams to discuss how they might improve their jumping distances. Repeat the activity.

SUCCESS FOR ALL Students in a wheelchair may "jump" by throwing an object, and students with severe motor deficits may jump with helpers on both sides of their body holding onto a belt that is secured around the jumper's waist.

QUICK LESSON 1.3
Chase the Leader

GRADES 3–6

NASPE STANDARD 3 Students participate regularly in physical activity.

LESSON OBJECTIVES

- Students demonstrate cardiovascular fitness.
- Students experience moderate to vigorous activity through jogging and sprinting.
- Students cooperate in a group effort to complete the task.

EQUIPMENT NEEDED None

PREPARATION TIME None

KNOWLEDGE CONTENT Having the students engage in moderate to vigorous activity promotes the following:

- Use of the overload principle. Overload is necessary to improve physical fitness in that it stresses the body physiologically and causes it to adapt or adjust, thus improving physical conditioning. There are three ways to overload the body through exercise. One or more of the following components of overload must be increased:
  1. *Frequency:* increasing how often you exercise
  2. *Intensity:* increasing the effort of the exercise (i.e., the speed of a run, the amount of weight lifted, the length a muscle is stretched)
  3. *Time* (or duration): increasing the length of time you exercise
- Cardiovascular fitness. Although cardiovascular fitness is a vital area of physical fitness, total fitness should not be ignored. Here are four other areas of health-related physical fitness:
  1. *Muscular strength:* the amount of force that can be exerted by a single contraction of the muscle
  2. *Muscular endurance:* the ability of a muscle group to continue muscle movement over a length of time
  3. *Flexibility:* the ability of a joint and muscle group to move through a maximum range of motion
  4. *Body composition:* the percentage of body weight that is fat compared with tissue, which is bone and muscle
- A feeling that a cardiovascular workout can be fun.

CLASSROOM TO PLAYGROUND ACTIVITY

- Arrange class in lines of six players each (there is an unlimited number of lines).
- The first person is the leader, who begins leading the line by jogging slowly.
- When the leader speeds up slightly, the last person in line sprints to the beginning of the line and becomes the new leader, who then slows down and jogs slowly again.
- This continues until everyone completes the circuit. The circuit can be done more than once.

ASSESSMENT The teacher discusses with students how they felt about the different running speeds, about being the leader, and about improving their ability to sustain the activity.

SUCCESS FOR ALL This activity is very strenuous, so when introducing the activity have the leaders jog rather than run. Then leaders can increase their speed as their cardiovascular endurance improves. If you know the fitness levels of your students, you could form homogeneous groups according to fitness levels. That would provide a more appropriate workout for each student.

INTEGRATION WITH OTHER SUBJECT AREAS

The knowledge content specified in this lesson could be integrated into health lessons.

QUICK LESSON 1.4
Jump for Fitness

GRADES K–6

NASPE STANDARD 4 Students achieve and maintain a health-enhancing level of physical fitness.

LESSON OBJECTIVES

- Students identify that the heart beats faster when exercising.
- Students understand and discuss how physical activity makes them healthier.

EQUIPMENT NEEDED None

PREPARATION TIME None

KNOWLEDGE CONTENT Having students recognize their heartbeat before and after vigorous physical activity helps them understand the following:

- That exercise increases heart rate (increases the number of times the heart beats per minute).
- That the pulse can be taken at the wrist (just below the thumb) or on the neck below the earlobe, where the carotid arteries are located.
- That arteries pump oxygenated blood from the heart to the rest of the body.

- That the pulse is taken by counting the number of beats per minute.

CLASSROOM ACTIVITY

1. Ask students to feel their pulse while at rest.
2. Ask students to jump up and down 25 times.
3. Ask students to feel their pulse again after jumping.

ASSESSMENT Ask students to draw a picture of their heart resting and a picture of their heart exercising. Have them share their drawings with the class and discuss their feelings about vigorous activity.

SUCCESS FOR ALL If students cannot jump up and down to raise their heart rate, have them do one of the following activities: do sit-ups, roll their wheelchair around the room, or lift hand weights (up and down from shoulder level to above head).

INTEGRATION WITH OTHER SUBJECT AREAS
This lesson could be integrated into science lessons teaching how the heart functions and how the blood flows through the body.

QUICK LESSON 1.5
Create Your Own Sport

GRADES 3–6

NASPE STANDARD 5 Students exhibit responsible personal and social behavior that respects self and others in physical activity settings.

LESSON OBJECTIVES

- Students identify necessity for rules and boundaries in physical activity.
- Students display positive attitude toward following rules.

EQUIPMENT NEEDED Mixture of physical education equipment (balls, cones, jump ropes, scoops, sticks, etc.)

PREPARATION TIME Ten minutes to collect the equipment.

KNOWLEDGE CONTENT The students creating a game learn to understand and value the following:

1. That a game or sport must have the following:
   —Rules governing the activity
   —Boundaries, or the area within which the activity must occur
   —A specified time period to play
   —A specific number of players, whether one-on-one (as in singles tennis) or a team (as in basketball)
   —Specific equipment to be used in specific ways
   —Specific movement skills
   —An ultimate goal to be accomplished

2. That adherence to the rules is necessary for the individual or team to accomplish the goal. This is where sport acts like a mini-society and instills the concept of being a good citizen.
3. The efforts of self, teammates, and opponents in playing by the rules to accomplish the goal.

CLASSROOM OR PLAYGROUND ACTIVITY

- Place a mixture of physical education equipment (balls, cones, jump ropes, scoops, sticks, etc.) in the center of the classroom or play field.
- Divide the class into groups of four or five.
- Ask each group to choose some equipment and create a game.
- The game must have rules and boundaries.
- Allow each group to present its game to the class and have everyone play the game.

ASSESSMENT Have the students discuss why they created the rules and boundaries of their game and the importance of everyone playing by the rules.

SUCCESS FOR ALL Groups must develop games that allow everyone in their group to participate. You may have to help the group in this effort.

INTEGRATION WITH OTHER SUBJECT AREAS You could integrate this activity into a social studies lesson that is studying the rules of different societies, why the rules come into being, and how the rules serve the members of the society.

GRADES 3–6

NASPE STANDARD 5 Students exhibit responsible personal and social behavior that respects self and others in physical activity settings.

LESSON OBJECTIVES

- Students identify the difficulties experienced in throwing with the nondominant hand.
- Students understand and describe the cooperation necessary to participate in physical activity with people of different abilities.

EQUIPMENT NEEDED A foam ball for every two students.

PREPARATION TIME None

KNOWLEDGE CONTENT Asking students to throw with their nondominant hand helps them experience the physical challenges of children with lesser abilities or disabilities in the following ways:

- If the student is right-handed, throwing with the left hand will feel awkward because the neuromuscular development of the left arm is not the same as that of the right arm.
- People are of value in and of themselves and should be included in physical activity with possible adaptations for them to participate.
- Everyone has a role in physical education class and in life in general, and all people are to be valued (regardless of ability or disability).

CLASSROOM ACTIVITY

- Group students in pairs, spaced far enough apart to throw back and forth to each other.
- Using foam balls, ask students to toss back and forth to each other, throwing first with their dominant hand and then with their nondominant hand.
- Allow time for students to throw 15 to 20 times each way.

ASSESSMENT Ask the students to write one or two paragraphs describing how they felt about throwing with their nondominant hand. Were they accurate in their throwing? Did it feel awkward? Ask them to relate these feelings to the feelings of students with disabilities. Have them share their written work with the class.

SUCCESS FOR ALL Students unable to throw may be assisted by the teacher or other classroom helper. Stand behind the student, grasp his or her hand (the one with the ball in it), and perform the throwing motion with the student.

QUICK LESSON 1.7
My Physical Activity Journal

GRADES K–6

NASPE STANDARD 6 Students value physical activity for health, enjoyment, challenge, self-expression, and/or social instruction.

LESSON OBJECTIVES (K–2 students will need assistance from their parents or other caregivers.)

- Students identify the amount of time per day spent on physical activity.
- Students describe their feelings and attitudes toward physical activity each day.
- Students increase their daily physical activity by the end of a week.

EQUIPMENT NEEDED Copies of the Activity Journal page (see next page).

PREPARATION TIME For K–2 students, 30 minutes to draft a letter to parents asking for their assistance in this lesson.

KNOWLEDGE CONTENT Asking students to keep a week-long physical activity journal helps them do the following:

- Become aware of the time they spend being sedentary versus being active.

- Design a plan to incorporate more physical activity into their day.
- Discover feelings associated with physical activity.

CLASSROOM ACTIVITY

- Either copy the Activity Journal or ask students to create their own activity journal.
- Ask students to log an entry every day for one week. K–2 students will need assistance from their parents.
- Challenge students to increase their daily physical activity by the end of the week.

ASSESSMENT Ask students to share their physical activity journals and their feelings about engaging in physical activity.

SUCCESS FOR ALL Parental assistance can be given to any child who needs it.

ACTIVITY JOURNAL

I got up today at
_____ A.M.

I was in class _____ hours today.
Today in physical education class we_____
_____.

After school I _____
_____.

I spent _____ hours watching television, playing
video games, or using the computer today.

The physically active things I did today were _____
_____
_____.

I went to bed at _____ P.M.
How I feel about my physical activity:_____
_____
_____.

CLASSROOM LEARNING STATION 1.1
Today's Popular Sports

GRADES K–6

NASPE STANDARD 6 Students value physical activity for health, enjoyment, challenge, self-expression, and/or social interaction.

LESSON OBJECTIVES

- Students improve their reading skills.
- Students play lead-up games (games leading up to various sports).
- Students interact with peers while teaching and playing lead-up games.
- Students enjoy playing the lead-up games.
- Students become motivated to be interested in physical activity and sport.
- Students examine the spatial relationships among game players as they play the lead-up games.

EQUIPMENT NEEDED Teachers can determine equipment needs based on what they have available.

PREPARATION TIME Limit the amount of planning time by collaborating with the school librarian and physical educator. Ask the librarian to select several sport-topic books (representing the different reading levels of students in your class*), or go online to barnesandnoble.com, select an age group (4–8 or 9–12), and browse by subject "Sports & Adventure" to find appropriate books. Ask the physical educator to develop the activity sheet and choose a lead-up game based on the books selected.

KNOWLEDGE CONTENT The knowledge content of this learning station depends on the particular reading materials that can be used in your classroom and the reading level of your students. Books, magazines, and newspaper articles could teach the following:

- About sport teams or personalities
- About social issues related to sport
- About sport activities for girls versus boys
- How to collect sport cards
- How to adapt sport for persons with disabilities
- The fun of participation
- The challenge of adventure activities
- The self-expression in dance activities
- The social interaction of team sports

CLASSROOM ACTIVITY

The learning station asks pairs or groups of students to do the following:

1. Read a grouping of materials placed at the station (based on students' reading ability and interest).
2. Complete a corresponding brief activity sheet. The activity sheet, developed by the teacher to correspond with the reading experience, should focus on what the teacher wants students to learn as they read.
3. Read a written explanation of how to play a lead-up game related to the sport being studied. The lead-up game should contain movement skills similar to those needed for the actual sport.
4. Attempt (with the teacher's help) to play the lead-up game at recess time.

ASSESSMENT The teacher inspects the thoroughness of answers provided by the student on the activity sheet (knowledge evaluation) and visually observes the students while they play the lead-up game at recess time (socialization and enjoyment evaluation).

SUCCESS FOR ALL A variety of reading materials and activity sheets should be at the station to represent the various reading abilities of the students in your class and the sport interests of the boys, girls, ethnic groups, and students with disabilities. If visually impaired students are members of the class, be sure the reading materials are available on audiotapes.

INTEGRATION WITH OTHER SUBJECT AREAS

Several ways exist to integrate this learning station with regular classroom subjects:

1. Select spelling words from the reading materials in this station.
2. Select some of the reading materials placed in the station and read them aloud to the class.
3. Reinforce library skills by having students find books in the school library on the same topic as the one highlighted in the station.

*Sample books for:
  Ages 4–8 *Play Ball, Amelia Bedelia* (baseball/softball)
        The Kid Who Only Hit Homers (baseball)
        Arthur Makes the Team (baseball)
  Ages 9–12 *Mia Hamm* (sport personalities)
        On the Field with . . . Alex Rodriguez
        Wilma Unlimited: How Wilma Rudolph Became the World's Fastest Woman
        Satch & Me

GRADES K–6

NASPE STANDARDS 1, 3, 5

- Students demonstrate competency in motor skills and movement patterns needed to perform a variety of physical activities.
- Students participate regularly in physical activity.
- Students exhibit responsible personal and social behavior that respects self and others in physical activity settings.

LESSON OBJECTIVES

- Students celebrate National Physical Education and Sport Week.
- Students are physically active during the school day.
- Students have fun participating in physical activity.
- Students practice movement skills.
- Students recognize the importance of being active.
- Students treat their peers with respect.
- Students follow the rules established for each station.

EQUIPMENT NEEDED Depends on activities selected. Have sufficient equipment at each station so each child is active all the time (without waiting in line for a turn).

PREPARATION TIME Planning and setup: five hours.

KNOWLEDGE CONTENT The teacher includes explanations of why we celebrate National Physical Education and Sport Week, why being physically active is so important to our health and well-being, and what behaviors constitute respect for peers and teachers. National Physical Education and Sport Week occurs the first week in May of each year.

PLAYGROUND ACTIVITY: PLAY DAY Set up physical activity stations on the playground. The number of stations needed depends on the number of students participating. Form groups of students, but keep the number of children in each group to three or four so they can all be active most of the time. For a class of 24 students with groups of four, you would need six stations.

The groups of students will rotate through all the stations, so it doesn't matter where students begin. Just place them at the various stations to begin the play day. The groups will rotate on signal (probably a whistle or the teacher's voice over a megaphone); therefore, it's important that the activities at each station take

approximately the same time to complete. If you are unsure about the time needed to perform certain activities, do a trial run.

You will need adults (high school or intermediate-grade students, paraprofessional staff, parents, etc.) to staff each station. Adults should organize and supervise the station as well as help children who are having trouble performing the skills.

The purpose of the day's activities is to have fun and celebrate. We suggest that scores not be kept, so that the emphasis remains on the fun of doing the activities.

In general, station activities are activities familiar to the students because then little time needs to be spent explaining skills. Station activities (and equipment needed) could include the following:

- Running sprints
- Jumping rope
- Dribbling soccer balls
- Throwing balls for distance (football, fox tail, Frisbee)
- Kicking balls for distance (soccer)
- Kicking balls for accuracy (at a target)
- Throwing balls for accuracy (at a target)
- Juggling balls (or scarves for young children)
- Performing agility drills (running certain patterns through hula hoops placed on the ground)
- Practicing the grapevine step running
- Using a hula hoop (twirling around the waist)
- Running over hurdles
- Running or crawling through a maze
- Tossing water balloons

Be sure to adapt the station activities to the abilities of your students. Have enough equipment so each child is active all the time at each station. (Do not take turns with the equipment.) Do not place stations that work the same muscle groups side by side. For instance, separate the sprint running and jump rope stations.

You might begin the play day by raising the U.S. flag (with proper respect and behavior) and having a celebrity say a few words about the purpose of the play day. Ideally the celebrity would stay to help with the play day. You might end the day by calling everyone together to congratulate them (and to distribute participation ribbons if you wish).

Organizing the play day for just your class is quite easy and not very time consuming. Plan just for your class the first time; then expand as you become more sure of the organization needed to include more students.

Note: A packet containing information about and ideas for celebrating National Physical Education and

Sport Week is available from AAHPERD Publications (at www.aahperd.org).

ASSESSMENT *Have each adult* who is supervising a station complete the supervisor assessment sheet (see next page) at the end of the play day. Adults should know before the play day begins exactly what behaviors they should be noting during the play day so they can complete the assessment afterward.

Have each student who participates complete the student assessment sheet (see next page) at the end of the play day (for older children only). For younger children, the teacher could hold a class discussion using the questions on the assessment sheet.

SUCCESS FOR ALL Be sure all students can perform the station activities, or make alterations as needed.

INTEGRATION WITH OTHER SUBJECT AREAS
During the week following the play day, have students make journal entries in which they answer (with complete sentences to practice writing skills) the following questions:

1. Why did you like (or not like) participating in the play day?
2. What activities did you perform the best?
3. What new activities would you include in next year's play day?

Assessment Sheet (for Supervisors)

<u>Directions:</u> Circle an appropriate number using the following response key to indicate how strongly you agree or disagree with the statement based on behavior the children displayed at your station throughout the play day.

    1 = strongly agree
    2 = agree
    3 = disagree
    4 = strongly disagree

At my station (Station # _____), throughout the day, in general, the students

were physically active most of the time.	1	2	3	4
were able to correctly perform the movements required.	1	2	3	4
treated each other with respect.	1	2	3	4
treated teachers and supervisors with respect.	1	2	3	4
followed the rules at each station.	1	2	3	4
appeared to enjoy the activity.	1	2	3	4

Assessment Sheet (for Students)

<u>Directions:</u> Circle "yes" or "no" after each question below. Answer "yes" or "no" based on how you behaved today during the play day.

I was physically active most of the time at each station.	Yes	No
At each station I mostly watched others perform.	Yes	No
I was able to perform the activities at most of the stations.	Yes	No
I treated other students with respect most of the time.	Yes	No
I listened to teachers and supervisors as they gave instructions.	Yes	No
I followed the rules for the activities at each station.	Yes	No
I had fun today doing the play day activities.	Yes	No

CHAPTER 2

Motor Development and Motor Learning for Children

The purpose of this chapter is to identify and discuss the process of motor development through which children progress. Principles of motor learning and developmentally appropriate teaching practices for elementary school children are presented. You are encouraged to reflect on the role physical activity plays in the development of children.

Objectives

After studying this chapter, you will be able to do the following:

- Describe the normal process of motor development of children ages 3 through 12.
- Discuss the concepts of motor learning that influence children's motor skill acquisition.
- Identify developmentally appropriate teaching progressions for motor skill attainment.
- Comprehend how regular physical activity benefits children's growth and development.

Ms. Jones was observing her second-grade students out on the playground; they were successfully engaged in throwing to targets. She had discussed this lesson with Ms. Key, the physical educator, and the objective was for children to demonstrate overhand throwing to targets. She saw Sally standing about ten feet away from a wall throwing a tennis ball to a big *X* target on the wall. She saw Karen throwing a foam ball through a hula hoop suspended from the basketball rim. Randy was throwing a small football over John's head to his partner, Susan. Ms. Jones could see that students were experiencing success because of the equipment they were able to choose from.

The children chose their equipment based on their comfort level and the challenge of the activity. As Ms. Jones walked around and talked to the children, she was pleased about how they enjoyed the activity and what they could tell her about the overhand throw. It was apparent to Ms. Jones that they were becoming more competent with the overhand throw, and the equipment they had to choose from was helping to create a successful activity.

Introduction to Motor Development and Motor Learning

Motor development is defined as the changes that occur in human movement across the life span. Motor development does not occur in isolation as a child matures from infancy to adolescence. Rather, motor development will be influenced by biological characteristics that a child possesses (such as heredity and maturation) and by the environment in which the child lives. Opportunities for movement that are found within the environment (such as toys, swing sets in the backyard, stairs to climb in the home) influence motor development.

Motor learning refers to a relatively permanent change in performance as a result of practice or experience. Although learning cannot be directly observed, it can be inferred during a motor performance. Through repeated observations of a child's performance, you will be able to infer whether or not a skill has been learned or refined. When assessing performance and making instructional decisions, three elements will be considered: the learner, the task, and the environment.

For example, you might ask yourself the following questions:

- Has the learner acquired easier components of a skill before being asked to combine the parts into one movement?
- Does the task require that an object be manipulated while the child moves within the classroom space?
- Are objects within the classroom stationary or moving?

Understanding motor development and motor learning is important if you are to help children improve their motor performance. Such an understanding also requires knowledge of development in the physical, cognitive, and affective domains because these domains all interact with the motor domain. For example, improved movement performance may impact feelings of self-worth or status in a peer group. Since these domains are in constant interaction, we need to look at the interrelationships of the domains before we create learning experiences for elementary school children.

PHYSICAL GROWTH AND MOTOR DEVELOPMENT IN CHILDREN

What is the typical height and weight of an eight-year-old child? Why do third-grade children have so many different abilities when it comes to throwing a ball? How do boys and girls differ in their physical development? Should boys and girls participate together in elementary school physical education activities? As you plan physical activities for elementary school children, it is important that you understand the characteristics of children and how to plan your learning activities to meet their needs. As you look at a group of children in a classroom, you will notice that no two children look the same. Their physical characteristics differ, and their motor skills do as well.

Growth Patterns   Although growth patterns of children are genetically determined, there is a predictable pattern that children experience. However, the timing for that pattern will vary from child to child. During childhood, height, weight, and muscle mass steadily increase, although the increases are not as rapid as during infancy. Growth gradually slows throughout childhood until the adolescent growth spurt. The annual height gain from early childhood to puberty decelerates from 2.75 inches per year (at ages three

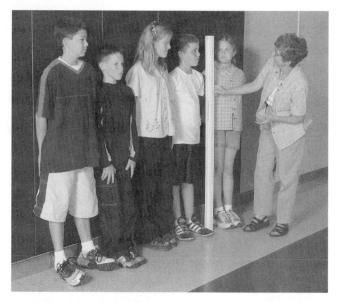

Children of the same age can display variations in growth.

through five) to 2.25 inches per year (from age six through adolescence). The average weight gain is about 4.5 pounds per year during early childhood, with an average increase to 6.5 pounds per year from age six to adolescence. These years of slow but steady growth enable children to explore how their bodies function and to move when called upon to do so.

Gender Similarities   If you were to see a boy and girl from the same kindergarten class out on the playground from a posterior perspective, you would find these two children to be similar in appearance. Boys and girls have similar amounts of muscle and bone mass during preschool and early primary grades, and they show a similar gradual decrease in fatty tissue through age eight. As children continue to advance to age 12, both boys and girls have greater limb growth than trunk growth. Slight differences are apparent in that boys tend to have longer legs and arms, and girls tend to have greater hip and thigh width.

Physical differences between boys and girls are minimal until the onset of preadolescence (see Instant Activity 2.1). The similarities in growth patterns for boys and girls during the elementary school years allow them to participate together during physical activity periods. We encourage you to take an active role in letting boys and girls interact during physical activity so that they learn to understand and respect the similarities and differences among children in the movement setting.

INSTANT ACTIVITY 2.1 Tracking Height

Grades K–6

Equipment Needed

Ruler

Activity

Place a ruler on the wall of your classroom and let students periodically check how much they have grown. Ask them to write their height in their own personal notebook, and discuss the following questions with them.

Grades K–2

How can you tell that you have grown taller?
When we started school, were you taller than most students, shorter, or somewhere in between?
Are you taller, shorter, or somewhere in between now?
Is everyone in the class the same height? Why not?

Grades 3–4

How much have you grown since the beginning of the school year?

By what other ways besides measuring yourself can you tell you have grown?
When you stand next to adult members of your family, how can you tell that you have grown?

Grades 5–6

How has your height changed since the beginning of the school year?
How does your height compare with that of others in your family?
Are you taller, shorter, or somewhere in between when you compare yourself with your classmates?
Why is it okay for you to be different from everyone else in the classroom?
If one of your friends complained about his or her body height, what might you say to help your friend feel good about his or her height?
What can we do to accept ourselves and our friends just the way we are?

COGNITIVE IMPLICATIONS FOR MOTOR DEVELOPMENT

Once children learn to walk upright unassisted, verbal communication rapidly improves. Walking allows children to explore the environment and expand their conceptual knowledge of the world in which they live. As children learn concepts—for example, dogs and cats have four legs or dogs bark and cats meow—their ability to communicate verbally becomes more efficient.

Between the ages of two and four, children learn to role-play as they pretend play. It is not unusual to see children dress up as their mother or father and walk around the house talking as they have heard their parent talk. During their pretend play, props, such as clothing, makeup, and jewelry, may be used to symbolize objects to make play more enjoyable as the child imitates a favorite activity of the parent. Such activity benefits motor development as well as enhances the child's cognitive development to communicate.

A noticeable characteristic of children between the ages of two and four is their egocentrism. They view the world only from their own perspective and have a

difficult time sharing or cooperating with others. It is all about "Me!" The movement educator must be careful to plan activities that avoid large group participation, as children of these ages will not work together toward a group goal. Participation in individual exploratory movement with progression to cooperative partner and small group movement opportunities will increase social interaction among children and encourage them to learn to be more sensitive to the feelings of others.

Between the ages of four and seven, children have a difficult time thinking about more than one aspect of a motor problem at a time. If you have seen young children play soccer on a Saturday morning, you may have noticed that most of the children are trying to kick the ball. Their attention is focused so much on kicking the ball that they do not even consider the possibility of passing the ball to a teammate who might be away from the crowd. Children are more successful participating in movement activities that are low in complexity and require focus on one movement at a time. For example, a game of Four-Square that requires children to hit a ball with an underhand striking motion is easier than a game of modified volleyball in which children must decide to strike with the forearms, or overhead set, or one-handed hit.

Upper elementary school children, ages 7 to 11, develop the ability to problem-solve on more than one task at a time. However, tasks that demand their focus must be within their real-world or personal experiences rather than a hypothetical situation. Children who have attained the cognitive ability to focus on more than one task can begin to develop strategies in movement activities that include offensive and defensive tactics. On any given Saturday morning in the fall, you can see children of these ages successfully countering an opponent's dribbling tactics on soccer fields across the country. Because of the ability to focus attention on multiple tasks, the child can anticipate what an opponent will do, formulate a strategy to counterattack, and execute the movement.

AFFECTIVE IMPLICATIONS FOR MOTOR DEVELOPMENT

Play is an important factor in children's socialization and motor development. Through play children interact and develop an awareness of each other and begin to form social groups. Play typically is based on movement; consequently there is an impact on motor development as well as the affective, social development.

During the early childhood years of 3½ to 4½ years of age, children emerge from playing in solitary and begin interacting with other children as play occurs. They begin to share toys and equipment, but there is little evidence of working within a group, as they are egocentric in their cognitive perspective. When children enter kindergarten, the school becomes a socializing factor that reinforces group interaction in purposeful play activities. Throughout the elementary years, children learn to cooperate, compete, and develop leadership skills. For example, it is very common to hear a classroom teacher say, "Who is the line leader today?"

When children play, it is not unusual to see them running, jumping, laughing, and even screaming in delight. They have a wonderful time moving and interacting with another, whether that is a caregiver or a neighborhood friend. As play evolves into more structured group activity or physical education class during mid-childhood, children become more aware of their competence and social acceptance. They begin to verbalize their feelings of self-worth and self-esteem based on how they see themselves compared with other children. If children view themselves as being

as competent as others in their social group, increased participation in physical activity will enhance both their social and their motor development. However, if they view themselves as a "loser" or a "klutz," they are apt to link physical activity with negative self-worth and low self-esteem. Both their social and motor development may then be hindered because of their self-consciousness of being viewed by others as incompetent.

Movement educators need to be aware of the social behaviors of children as they plan activities. It will be unrealistic to expect children in early childhood to participate in activities with a group goal. These children will be more successful exploring movement individually and learning to enjoy movement as a form of play. Older elementary school children find group activities fun, but such activities need to promote social success and the development of leadership skills of all students. Otherwise, children may perceive a negative relationship between social and motor development. The feeling of success in movement and the simple act of participation within a group can positively affect a child's self-worth and self-esteem.

Motor Development Concepts

General motor development of all humans is quite similar. Although all humans are unique in the characteristics they display during movement, the sequence and predictability of development are similar across the population. Growth and development occur in two directions: from head to toe and from the center of the torso outward to the limbs. Voluntary movement, or movement that is controlled in higher areas of the brain, is evident by the end of the child's first year. While these movements may not always contain all of the elements of the more mature movement of an elementary school aged child, they are recognizable. Voluntary movements may be classified into categories called nonlocomotor, locomotion, and manipulation. These same categories will delineate the basic fundamental motor skills discussed in Chapter 3.

HEAD TO TOE DEVELOPMENT

Because motor development occurs from head to toe, the ability to do voluntary movement begins at the head. Infants at one month may display minimal control of the head and neck while in a supine position.

However, by five months of age, infants in the same position will be able to raise their head and look over their environment. Once control of the head is evident, control of the upper body is important, as the ability to elevate the chest becomes a precursor to rolling to a sitting position. By eight months of age, most children can sit alone, and by ten months of age, most children will control upper and lower areas of the body and pull themselves into a supported standing position.

The ability to stabilize and control the body also continues the progression to upright walking. By raising the chest after rolling to a prone position, children are encouraged to use their arms to crawl across the floor. Use of the legs in this head to toe development will occur later. Initial crawling may be evident by seven or eight months of age. As the upper body is controlled to raise the chest off the floor and the legs are involved, children will begin to creep by the end of the first year.

Upright walking begins with support from a parent at about eight months and progresses to support by a piece of furniture at about ten months. Less support is needed to maintain balance at 11 months, and some children are able to walk unassisted at 12 months of age. If you envision a child learning to walk upright, the child will have stiff knees and ankles. As development continues, the child will eventually gain greater control of the knee joint and then the ankle joint, which allows a more normal walking pattern. A gross, voluntary movement eventually becomes refined to the more controlled movement of walking.

As children walk to explore their surroundings, their strength and balance improve, and soon they begin to propel themselves into the air in a form of running. Other voluntary movements follow and include jumping and hopping. The fundamental skills of galloping, sliding, and skipping take longer to acquire, as children need to combine and coordinate motor skills (for example, a step and a leap combine in a gallop) in order to successfully accomplish the skill. The skip is the last fundamental skill to be learned and may not be evident until age six or seven. The critical period from ages three to eight is when children should master control and coordination of large muscle groups to perform the fundamental motor skills. Children who fail to develop mature fundamental skills during this critical period may experience difficulties coordinating more complex skills required for participation in sport skills and recreational physical activities. (Fundamental motor skills are discussed in Chapter 3. You may refer to the movement map in Chapter 3 for a graphic display of these skills.)

TORSO TO LIMB DEVELOPMENT

Another direction of control for voluntary movement is from the center of the body outward to the limbs. Because children gain control of their body first at the center, **gross motor skills** like those we have been discussing—running, jumping, throwing, body rolling—will be evident before skills requiring fine motor control. Small muscle skills, called **fine motor skills,** require more precise movements, typically of the hand and fingers, and involve eye-hand coordination. Writing, buttoning a shirt, and playing a musical instrument require fine motor skills. Figure 2.1 demonstrates progression in fine motor control as children learn to manipulate a crayon to draw. As children attain greater use of muscles in the hand and fingers, drawings display more precision and detail.

The ability of children to gain control of motor skills is associated with two processes: differentiation and integration. **Differentiation** is the progression of skill development from gross movements of infants to the more refined and useful movements of children. **Integration** is the coordination of muscle and sensory systems as found when movements of the hands and fingers are integrated with the use of the eyes to perform more refined skills. For example, a child will initially trap a ball against the chest in an attempt to catch the ball. Eventually, as the child integrates the visual information with better control of limb movement from the shoulders to the hands, the ball will be caught with the hands and fingers.

Physical activity typically emphasizes the development of large muscle skills, while the classroom environment provides opportunities to practice fine motor skills. Development of both categories of motor skills is critical to the enjoyment of many lifetime pursuits, such as recreational sport activities, musical activities, and occupational skills. We recommend that children receive numerous opportunities to practice and succeed with movements from both categories so that they are confident in their abilities. Smooth coordination of large muscles and precise control of small muscles are essential to successful completion of many tasks that children are called to do during the typical school day.

FACTORS AFFECTING MOTOR DEVELOPMENT

Unfortunately, some children will not experience normal motor development. Recreational drug use, such as alcohol, cocaine, and tobacco, can affect both the mother and the developing fetus. Use of alcohol may

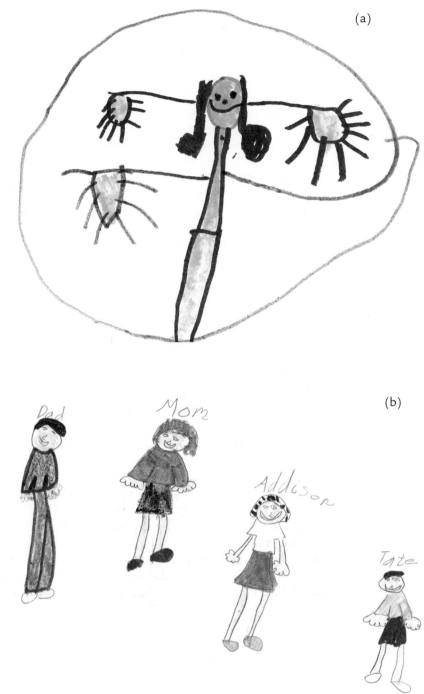

FIGURE 2.1   As children develop greater use of the muscles of the hand and fingers, fine motor control improves. The drawing of a four-year-old child (a) displays little precision, while the drawing of a seven-year-old child (b) displays much more detail and precision due to increasing fine motor control.

result in birth defects known as **fetal alcohol syndrome.** Abnormalities to the fetus may include mental retardation, attention deficit disorder with hyperactivity, and retarded physical growth. Cocaine use during pregnancy may cause brain damage to the fetus as the result of decreased oxygen. During development the fetus and mother may also experience extreme fluctuations in heart rate and blood pressure, which may result in ruptured vessels in the fetus. Blood vessels to the placenta may also constrict and impede the nutrients going to the fetus, resulting in low birth weight and possibly poor blood supply to the fetus. Adverse effects of tobacco use during pregnancy include lack of oxygen to the fetal tissues, due to the interference of carbon monoxide with the capabilities of hemoglobin to carry and release oxygen, and low birth weight.

Use of prescription and nonprescription drugs during pregnancy should be done only in consultation with a physician. Possible effects on the fetus include central nervous system defects, eye defects, congenital heart defects, mental retardation, and hearing loss.

It is important for pregnant women to receive adequate nutrition. Since the mother is the source of nutrients for the fetus, a balanced diet is critical to the development of the fetus. If a mother's diet is deficient in nutrients, the fetus may develop a parasitic effect on the mother and drain the needed nutrients. Deficiencies in nutrients may lead to low birth weight, premature delivery, incomplete brain development, below normal motor development, poor mental functioning, and skeletal growth retardation. For the pregnant woman wishing to exercise, a balanced diet and additional water consumption are needed to maintain appropriate weight and hydration for herself and the fetus.

READINESS TO LEARN

Why is it that one seven-year-old child is able to smoothly skip around the playground while another seven-year-old child looks awkward and clumsy when attempting to do the same thing? When we observe children as they acquire new skills and become competent with those skills, we are reminded of the uniqueness of each child. Each child has her or his own biological timetable for determining the rate and extent of skill development. While the rate of change in motor development varies for all children, the general sequence of development is relatively similar. Therefore, one seven-year-old child may have acquired a skipping movement pattern while another child may yet be gaining coordination and control of the skip.

One of the challenges of providing appropriate movement activities is matching the task to the movement abilities of the children. If a task is too difficult, children become frustrated and lose interest. If a task is too easy, children become bored. Compound this situation by 20 or more students in a class and it is easy to understand the importance and the challenge of providing motor activities that are developmentally appropriate for all students. Developmentally appropriate activity accommodates a "variety of individual characteristics such as developmental status, fitness and skill levels, body size, and age" (NASPE 2000). Thus an appropriate activity for most second graders would be hitting a ball off a tee, whereas an inappropriate activity would be playing a regulation game of softball.

As you consider which activities are developmentally appropriate, you must consider the **developmental readiness** of the children who will experience the activities. Because children demonstrate variability in

their development, you will want to learn whether the children are ready to learn the activities. You may talk with the children to determine whether they have had previous experiences with similar, but easier tasks. You may watch students to see whether they appear awkward and unable to repeat a movement, or whether they are able to perform repetitions of the correct movement. For children to succeed, it is important that you recognize the variability among and within your children and be prepared to modify activities to meet your children at their level of readiness. Movement educators cannot plan activities based on grade level or age and expect all children to be successful. You must take into account children's developmental variability and individual readiness for activity (see Instant Activity 2.2).

STAGES OF PERFORMANCE

The movement educator is responsible for understanding the **stages of performance** of the children in the class and meeting their needs at their particular stage of performance. Progression through these stages is independent of age, yet all learners progress through the distinct sequence of stages of beginning, intermediate, and advanced learner for skills unique to their level of readiness if quality instruction is provided.

Beginning Level The first stage of performing a motor skill may be thought of as the beginning stage. The learner is generally attempting to get an idea of what the movement looks like and how to coordinate the body to perform the skill. However, more likely than not, the movements of the learner are clumsy and awkward. Because the learner is attempting to understand the movement, the learner also becomes overwhelmed by the numerous visual stimuli that the environment presents. Consequently, the learner tires easily because of the mental fatigue that occurs. Beginning students may find it necessary to talk to themselves as they do the movement, thereby possibly creating frustration and mental fatigue if success is not experienced.

Kindergarten children are typically at the early stages of the beginning level. Let's look at a specific example of how children at this level look. If the activity of the day incorporates the locomotor movement of jumping, children at this level generally achieve little flight off the floor when they jump for height or distance. Arm movement is not coordinated to achieve lift off the floor, and the jump is often off two feet in order to maintain balance during the jump. As children progress through the beginning level, they perform basic

INSTANT ACTIVITY 2.2   Wadding Paper into a Ball

Grades K–6

Equipment Needed

Balloons or recycled paper

Activity

In the classroom general area that is away from desks, tables, or chairs, have children sit on the floor. Provide an inflated balloon for younger children. Ask older students to wad a piece of recycled paper into a ball.

Grades K–2

Have children toss and catch the balloon as many times as possible without letting it touch the floor.

Have children repeat the above, but invite them to volley the balloon with the dominant hand, if they choose.

Have children keep the balloon up in the air with the nondominant hand.

- Which way was easiest? Which way was most difficult?
- Which way did you have the most success? Which was most fun? Does everyone have to agree, or is it okay for everyone to have their own favorite way?

Grades 3–6

Have older children volley the paper ball back and forth from one hand to the other. See how many times they can rebound the paper ball without dropping it.

Find a different way to volley the paper ball back and forth using the hands.

From a standing position, volley the paper ball upward from the hand to the thigh that is parallel to the floor. While volleying in a safe manner, find a new way to strike the ball upward.

Provide additional time for students to practice.

- How did you feel while you were volleying the ball?
- Which way was the most challenging? The most frustrating? The easiest? The most fun?
- Did you get better as you practiced?
- Did everyone practice the same way and have the same amount of success?
- Why didn't everyone perform the same? Is it okay that everyone was different? Why isn't everyone the same? Why didn't you find everything to be fun or easy?
- What have you learned about differences among all the students in the class?

---

jumping patterns with more vigorous takeoffs and balanced landings. The arms and legs are used to assist the trajectory of the jump and provide more flight. Landings are aided when children learn to absorb the shock with the hips, knees, and ankles.

When providing instruction to learners in this stage of performance, you should plan activities in which the environment and the object of manipulation remain stable. Keep instructions short and simple. Children develop a better mental picture of the motor skill if they observe a demonstration and if you link the new skill to a motor skill previously learned. As children practice the skills, keep corrections and feedback positive, brief, and immediate so that children continue to develop an understanding of how to perform the motor skill without being overly fatigued mentally (see Box 2.1 for additional teaching hints).

Intermediate Level   The second stage of performance, the intermediate stage, is characterized by refinement of the movement so that it is more consistent and has fewer errors. At this stage children find

movement to be less mentally taxing because they focus less on doing the skill and more on the outcome of their efforts. Not only do children have the mental idea of the movement developed, but they also continue to refine how it feels to perform the skill. Therefore they pay less attention to the numerous distracters that are typically in the environment.

Compared with those at the beginning stage, children performing the jump at this stage exhibit a mature pattern. When jumping for distance, the arms are swung behind as the child crouches to prepare for takeoff. The arms swing forward to shoulder height throughout the flight. The arms continue to reach in front as the body weight moves forward on landing. Children are encouraged to explore jumping in combination with other movements, such as catching a ball, so that they begin to apply these skills in more gamelike situations.

Children in this stage of performance may choose not to progress beyond this stage if they perceive that they have failed in their attempts to learn the new skill. Provide maximum opportunities to practice

BOX 2.1

Hints for Teaching Students at the Beginning Level

Do the following to assist children at the beginning level to learn new movement skills:

- When appropriate, break the skill into parts and introduce one part at a time.
- Provide a demonstration to give children a visual image.
- Provide maximum opportunities for each student to practice with equipment.
- Focus immediate feedback on one critical element at a time.
- Focus on the quality of the movement rather than the product of the movement.

BOX 2.2

Hints for Teaching Students at the Intermediate Level

Do the following to assist children at the intermediate level to learn new movement skills:

- Maintain a positive, safe learning environment.
- Provide practice opportunities that become progressively more challenging.
- Vary practice activities often to maintain motivation.
- Give informative, immediate, and brief feedback.
- Provide authentic challenges that focus on small-group applications to the movement task.
- Meet individual needs by modifying the task to meet the abilities of each learner, because the gap in the skill levels of children widens as they grow older.
- Encourage children to analyze the critical elements of movement tasks and begin to detect errors and identify corrections.

progressively more challenging activities. Give feedback that is positive, immediate, and brief so that children construct the knowledge to detect and identify some of their own errors and begin to make their own corrections (see Box 2.2 for additional teaching hints).

Advanced Level In the final stage of performance, the skill has become almost automatic for the performer, and little conscious thought occurs during execution of the skill. The performer is consistent from one practice attempt to the next and is able to detect and correct errors in his or her movement. To consider our previous example, children performing the jump at the advanced stage are able to carry out complex maneuvers. The skills may be part of a sporting event, such as the high jump, or they may be used for expressive purposes such as creative dance.

The transition across the stages of performance occurs when the performer has many opportunities to practice. Children in elementary school typically do not reach the advanced level of learning because of limited practice opportunities in the two- or three-day-a-week physical education program. You as the elementary classroom teacher can facilitate refinement of the skills by providing practice opportunities that offer authentic, dynamic situations similar to a game environment. Children embarking on the advanced level should be encouraged to think critically about game tactics and strategies for successful participation in game play (see Box 2.3 for additional teaching hints).

Your responsibility in the movement setting, whether in the classroom, on the playground, or in the gymnasium, is to provide children the opportunity to practice, acquire, and refine their motor skills. Children's stages of performance will influence the way you teach. It will be helpful for you to develop a repertoire of teaching styles that you can use to meet the needs and developmental levels of the diverse learners in your class, as well as the objectives of your lessons. In Chapter 7, you will have the opportunity to learn about various teaching styles.

Motor Learning Concepts

As you learned in the concepts of motor development, general motor development is similar for all people. We are born with motor skills that allow us, through maturation and experience, to demonstrate adequate form when reproducing the skills. In order to achieve proficiency in motor skills, however, much instruction and practice is necessary. To provide effective instruction, you need to understand the motor learning concepts that will help children successfully produce movements that achieve desired movement goals. These concepts will form the foundation for all

BOX 2.3
Hints for Teaching Students at the Advanced Level

Do the following to assist children at the advanced level to learn new movement skills:

- Provide opportunities to practice in gamelike situations.
- Encourage students to practice offensive and defensive tactics during game play.
- Provide specific, immediate feedback on critical elements of the movement skill.
- Help the performer practice consistent movement from one practice trial to the next.
- Encourage execution of movement skills with little conscious thought.

of the instructional decisions that you make as you plan activities that are developmentally appropriate for all children in your classroom.

CONCEPT OF ATTENTION LIMITS

There is a limit to how many things children can pay attention to at any given time. When the limit is reached, children will have difficulty paying attention to everything going on in their environment. Consequently, they may demonstrate a slower response to initiate a skill, poorer quality of performance of one or more activities, or a total disregard for an activity that is presented. For example, if a child has not yet mastered kicking a stationary ball against the wall and you ask that child to play one-on-one soccer against a classmate, the child's attention limits may be exceeded, as the child must think about kicking a moving ball and moving in relation to the opponent. The child may have little success completing this task, because the unpredictability of the environment and the difficulty of the task have exceeded the limits of the child's attention. To reduce the likelihood that the limits would be exceeded for this child, you might ask the child first to practice dribbling the soccer ball without a defender. Then, be sure to provide sufficient practice just dribbling the ball before teaching the child to play one-on-one soccer.

Levels of excitement may also affect how much attention a child will give to the task at hand. There is an optimal level of excitement, not too much and not

too little, that will vary across children. When a child fails to be excited about participation, performance often decreases because the child fails to pay attention to what is happening in the movement environment. Conversely, if the child is too excited, performance decreases as the child pays attention to too much in the environment and the attention limit is exceeded. The movement educator needs to understand that each child will have a different optimal level of excitement and to help each child maintain the optimal level of excitement.

CONCEPT OF TRANSFER

As you get to know your students' movement capabilities, determining what previous movement experiences they have had will be helpful. Previous learning may influence new movement experiences, and movement educators desire to make a positive transfer of learning from previous learning to new learning. **Positive transfer** occurs when previous learning experiences facilitate learning to use a skill in a different context or assist with learning a new skill. For example, children's previous experiences punting a round ball should assist in learning to punt a football. The critical elements of the motor skill are similar, but the ball has a different shape. Also, learning to volley a ball off the forearms may positively transfer to volleying a footbag, as both require a flat surface for successful completion.

As you design movement experiences for children, consider the following guidelines outlined by Coker (2004) to promote positive transfer.

- Determine whether components of the skill are similar to previously learned skills. Make comparisons throughout the instruction and practice time to draw attention to similarities of the new skill.
- Use previous learning experiences to create a mental image of the movement. For example, movement educators often suggest that children "reach your hand to the cookie jar on the top shelf" to create an image of how the follow-through on a one-handed basketball shot should look.

CONCEPT OF SKILL DEMONSTRATIONS

When teaching a new skill to children, it will not take long to realize the truth of the old adage "a picture is worth a thousand words." Lengthy, detailed descriptions of how to do a new skill will challenge attention limits as well as decrease children's excitement for attempting the new task. Skill demonstrations create a meaningful visual picture of the movement requirements and how all the components of the skill connect together. It is helpful to perform skill demonstrations at a normal speed rather than slow motion so that children get a sense of the timing of the motor skill. At any time that a slow-motion demonstration is used, a demonstration at normal speed should follow so children again see the correct speed of performance.

Movement educators often worry that they cannot provide a correct demonstration of a new skill because they are not able to do the skill. While a correct demonstration will provide a better visual picture for children, there is much to be said for a demonstration that is performed by a classmate who is also learning the skill. The benefit of having an unskilled child do the demonstration is that other children will not only hear the feedback given by the educator to the performer, but also observe how the performer tries to correct the identified errors. In addition, children become more motivated to try new skills when they see that their classmates may not be any more skilled at performing the movement than they.

All children must be able to see the demonstration and hear the instructions that accompany the demonstration. So, consider what will be the most effective formation of students that enables them to see a complete picture of the movement. Circle formations with the performer in the middle of the circle often confuse children who will observe a mirror image of the way they will do the skill. Circle formations also have some students positioned behind the demonstrator so that it is difficult to hear instructions. Line or half-moon formations with the performer in front may allow more children to see the demonstration. To be effective, the performer should present a mirror image by facing the children, but perform the skill in the same direction that the children are moving. It is also helpful to present demonstrations from multiple angles so that children form a more complete picture of the skill.

CONCEPT OF TASK PROGRESSION

Designing appropriate task progressions is crucial to all skill development. It is not uncommon to walk into a movement setting and find children volleying a ball back to a partner who is tossing the ball during the first half of the class and then playing a six-on-six volleyball game for the remaining minutes of the class. Unfortunately, this practice often ends up with most children in the class not having their needs met. Some students will be frustrated because they are not able to hit the ball back, if it comes their direction during the game. Other students with more experience will find the initial activity too easy, and they will not stay excited about the tasks to be practiced. As a teaching practice, the transition from volleying to a partner to playing the volleyball game is inappropriate. These tasks are at the opposite extreme from each other and therefore should not be included in the same lesson or, realistically, sequence of lessons. Design of appropriate task progressions involves the identification of appropriate changes in the environment to address the level of performance of children in the class.

The **environment** can be described as the context in which children do a skill or in which an object is manipulated by the children. If the environment or the object does not change while a child performs a skill, the skill is classified as a **closed motor skill.** The object waits for the child to do something to it, such as hit the ball off a tee, or kick a ball that is sitting stationary against the wall. Walking through a classroom where tables and chairs do not move describes an unchanging, predictable environment.

The other end of the progression is an **open motor skill** that is performed in an unpredictable environment where the object is in motion or the context is changing. Advancing a ball down the court while playing basketball describes an open skill, as the environment may change due to movement of other players or a change in the speed or direction of the dribble.

Environmental conditions may be adjusted to be more or less predictable by altering space requirements, placing or restricting obstacles or defenders in the path, changing the equipment, or adding or deleting team members to game play. Instant Activity 2.3 shows a task progression designed by children for a recess activity with shooting to a soccer goal as the focus. Palmer and Hildebrand (2005) make the following recommendations for designing task progressions:

- Determine whether larger, open space or smaller, restricted space increases the task difficulty, and adjust the space accordingly. Smaller space does not always equate to less difficulty.
- Obstacle and defender predictability are effective means to adjust the level of task difficulty. Stationary obstacles are appropriate for beginning performers; restricting the movement of defenders to keeping a foot inside a hoop enables intermediate performers to have a more predictable environment; and free-moving defenders create an unpredictable environment for advanced performers.

INSTANT ACTIVITY 2.3 *Child-Designed Physical Activity*

Grades 3–6

Equipment Needed

None

Activity

Ask children to design a recess activity that can be taught to students in all of the classes. In small groups, have older students invent soccer activities for shooting to a goal that begin with the closed skill of shooting a stationary ball to an open goal (appropriate for younger children) and end with the older student dribbling a ball against a defender to a closely guarded goal.

Activity 1. Design a shooting activity in which the ball handler stands still and shoots a ball that is still into an open goal.

Activity 2. Design a shooting activity in which the ball handler is allowed to move but the ball stays still.

Activity 3. Design a shooting activity in which the ball handler stands still but the ball is moving.

Activity 4. Design a shooting activity in which the ball handler and the ball are moving.

Activity 5. Design a shooting activity in which the ball handler can move with the ball to shoot at a goal but a defender must stand still.

Activity 6. Design a shooting activity in which the ball handler can move with the ball to shoot at a goal, the defender must stay behind the ball handler, and the goalie must stay still.

Activity 7. Design a shooting activity in which the ball handler can move with the ball to shoot at a goal, the defender must stay behind the ball handler, and the goalie may move.

Activity 8. Design a shooting activity in which the ball handler can move with the ball to shoot at a goal, the defender may defend the ball, and the goalie may move.

- Large, lightweight, slow-moving equipment is easier to manipulate than regulation-sized equipment. The longer the handle of an implement, the more difficult the task becomes. Beginning performers will be more successful using larger, lightweight balls, "big-head" bats, and shorter-handled implements. Advanced performers may do well with the opportunity to practice with regulation equipment, while intermediate performers may do best by having the choice to select from either the beginning-level equipment or the advanced-level equipment.

- Equipment such as goals and targets may be adjusted similarly to the obstacles and defenders by being stationary or mobile. How predictable the goal or target is will contribute to the degree of difficulty. Beginning performers will have higher success when the goal or target is stationary. Intermediate performers may do well with targets that move slowly in a predictable manner. Unpredictable targets will challenge advanced performers.

- More team members involved in the task equates to a higher level of difficulty. Beginning performers are more successful working individually so they can control all aspects of the task. The gradual addition of team members enables children at the intermediate and advanced levels of performance to learn how to react, cooperate, engage in offense and defense strategies, and participate with changes in the space and opportunities to directly manipulate equipment.

More detailed information and examples to assist in designing and using task progressions may be found in Chapters 7, 9, and 11. Appropriate task progressions will keep students safe and motivated during movement activities.

CONCEPT OF FEEDBACK

Feedback is information learners receive about their performance and comes from sources internal to the learner or external to the learner. **Intrinsic feedback** is information that children will receive as they see the results of their practice attempt. For example, if children roll a ball to knock down bowling pins, they will see how many pins they knocked down and how many were left for their second attempt. As children become more proficient with a motor skill, they receive kinesthetic information regarding how a movement felt as it was performed. The intrinsic feedback that comes visually and kinesthetically helps advanced learners detect and correct their movement errors. **Congruent feedback** gives children information from an external source, such as the movement educator, on their performance directly related to what they were asked to

Large, lightweight balls and closed motor skills are appropriate for beginning-level performers.

do. For example, when children are asked to strike a balloon upward with a paddle, congruent feedback would sound like "keep the paddle flat when hitting the balloon upward."

When movement educators offer congruent feedback to children, children focus their efforts better when they have few cues to think about. Giving too much information can exceed the attention limits of children. Therefore it is wise to focus on one cue at a time. When the movement educator observes the performance of children in the class, it is helpful to look at performance in relation to the focus of the task that children are to accomplish. Appropriate congruent feedback should be given before moving on to feedback over other parts of a child's movement performance.

The sooner feedback is given to children after their performance, the more potential children have to use the information. However, if there is a delay in time between the performance and the feedback, children should be encouraged to reflect on their internal

feedback to give them information about their performance. Movement educators can help children begin to develop their own feedback capabilities by prompting them with questions that will guide children to the answer. For example, in the previous example of hitting a balloon with a paddle, a movement educator might ask a child, "Why did the balloon go backward rather than upward?" The movement educator will guide the child to discover that the paddle face was pointing backward rather than flat and upward.

One way movement educators can maximize the information given to children without exceeding their attention limits is to develop a list of words that characterize what learners should do in relation to the tasks being practiced. Movement educators can provide feedback statements that are brief and focused on the task at hand, so that children can make the necessary corrections to their movement. In Chapter 7 you will learn techniques for application of the motor learning concept of feedback.

Strategies to Facilitate Learning

What can the movement educator do to facilitate development of motor skills? As the movement educator looks to facilitate learning, the motor development and motor learning concepts discussed in this chapter should form the foundation for decisions to be made about the instructional plan. Children should be provided with information about the skills and concepts they are to learn, and they should be taught *how* to do motor skills. Quality instruction is critical if children are to progress through the stages of performance. Instruction should be goal directed, and a positive learning environment should be established so that all children are encouraged to learn. Key strategies for facilitating positive learning experiences include adapting to students' individual learning styles, choosing appropriate practice progressions, and creating appropriate movement opportunities that are developmentally appropriate. With a well thought out program, the movement educator can ensure that children will receive the quality instruction necessary to acquire motor skills.

ADAPTING TO CHILDREN'S LEARNING STYLES

Just as you want to meet the needs of children by selecting appropriate task progressions, you will also facilitate learning by recognizing individual learning styles.

Learning styles are the unique preferences all learners have for receiving and processing new information. Learners take in and process new information through different perceptual modes. Although all learners use all modes to some extent, four types of learners have been identified by their preferred mode of learning: (1) the listener, (2) the thinker, (3) the kinesthetic learner, and (4) the visual learner. Box 2.4 gives examples of teaching for all four learning styles. Careful observation will help you to identify a child's preferred mode. Your challenge is to create a learning environment in which the numerous learning styles may be accommodated. Although you may not address each preferred perceptual mode in each lesson, your ability to frequently match learning strategies to individual learning preferences will enhance learning gains.

Instructional strategies may be outlined to accommodate the four learning modalities. The following suggestions may help you begin to develop your strategies.

1. The listener prefers verbal descriptions, so provide clear, concise discussions about the skills or activities to be performed.
2. The thinker likes to analyze movement challenges, so it is helpful to construct activities that include problem-solving or critical thinking skills.
3. The kinesthetic learner likes to feel what the body should do, so it is helpful to provide teaching aids to guide exploratory movement.
4. The visual learner does best when a visual model is given, so that an idea of the movement pattern may be perceived.

BOX 2.4
Learning Styles in Action

Let's look at all four learning styles in action. The movement activity is balancing on different body parts using wide or narrow shapes. Notice how the activity provides information to the learner according to a preferred perceptual mode.

1. *Demonstration for the visual learner:* Remember when we explored balancing on different body parts? Who can show me a balance on three of your favorite bases of support? [Ask the next question after a student demonstrates.] Is this balance using a wide or narrow shape?
2. *Rhythm for the listener:* I'm going to turn on some music to provide a steady beat to hold your balance for three seconds. [Choose a rhythm to aid the listener.] Create three new balances with a wide shape using a different number of body parts for each balance.
3. *Problem solving for the thinker:* Now I'd like you to create three narrow shape balances using a different number of body parts for each balance. I'd like you to investigate which body shape is easier to balance for three seconds and how many body parts it takes to make balancing easier.
4. *Feeling the movement for the kinesthetic learner:* Create a wide shape using your favorite body parts and then slowly move to a narrow shape. Which shape made you feel stronger and able to hold it for longer than three seconds? What did you have to do to your muscles to hold that balance?

CHOOSING APPROPRIATE PRACTICE PROGRESSIONS

Effective teaching in the movement setting is not too different from effective teaching in the classroom. In order for children *to* learn, the movement educator must teach so children *can* learn. During lesson preparation, the movement educator must reflect upon and choose the most appropriate strategies that will keep students on task and focused on skill acquisition. Movement educators should be familiar with practice progressions that facilitate the learning of motor skills.

Individualized Exploration   When children begin to learn new skills, they need maximum opportunities to practice. For example, for children at the beginning stage of performance who are learning to jump rope, individual work with their own rope is best. Children have more opportunities to learn to control the rope when they have individual ropes. The movement educator can also provide more individualized, congruent feedback when each student works independently.

A question that movement educators often ask themselves when planning for individual exploration is whether children should learn the whole skill, or should they break the skill into smaller segments that can later be combined like putting a puzzle together. One argument for whole practice is that children get a better idea of the flow and coordination of the components of the movement. An argument for part practice is that breaking the movement into smaller parts reduces the movement's difficulty.

Two factors may be considered as you decide to teach a skill as a whole or in parts: the task itself and

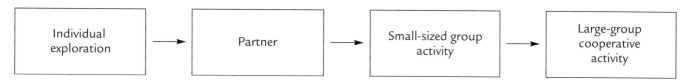

FIGURE 2.2 Recommended Teaching Progressions for Successful Practice Opportunities.

the learner. If the task has parts that cannot easily be separated, such as swinging a bat to strike a ball, teach the skill as a whole. A skill with parts that are difficult for children to learn as a whole may be taught best in parts. In the above example of learning to jump rope, a beginning learner might do best to break the jump rope skill into three progressive parts: (1) learning to self-turn the rope, (2) learning to jump over the rope that has been self-turned and stopped in front of the feet, and (3) learning to combine the jump over the self-turned rope. When you think about the children in your class, consider the limits of their attention span. If learners are unable to concentrate for long periods or remember longer sequences, teach part of the skill and then add the parts together. When children are older, have mature skills, have a longer attention span, and remember longer sequences of movement, the movement may be taught as a whole.

Partner Work with Children Partner work may be introduced to challenge children with the addition of a new dimension to the environment. For example, after children have practiced kicking a stationary ball against the wall and have extended that task to include a running approach to a stationary ball, the addition of a partner to move a few steps in any direction will add a new challenge to the learning situation. A critical mistake that many teachers make is to progress too quickly from individual practice to large-group games without establishing the basic skills that come through partner and small-group practice. Children need to experience learning progressions in a stable environment and then move on to challenges with a single partner before moving to small-group challenges.

We recommend that elementary school children continue to play in small-group activities rather than playing regulation games because of the increased opportunities to practice and be truly active in the game objective. Regulation games tend to exclude the less-skilled children and significantly reduce their chances to acquire motor skills. We believe that all children should experience success in the movement environment and that success comes only through

numerous opportunities to practice and refine skills in individual, partner, and small-group activity (see Figure 2.2). We encourage you to revisit the earlier section "Concept of Task Progression" to assist you in appropriately challenging your children with additional team members.

KEEPING YOUR OPPORTUNITIES DEVELOPMENTALLY APPROPRIATE

The Council on Physical Education for Children (COPEC) has published a position statement on appropriate practices that should be evident in the elementary school movement setting (NASPE 2000). An important factor to consider about practices within the learning environment is that children are not miniature adults. Therefore activities played and equipment used by adults are not appropriate for children. Children must be given opportunities to acquire and refine basic movement skills at an early age in order to gain access to a wide variety of physical activities as they grow older. If children begin to specialize in adult sports at an early age or if they are not given opportunities to master basic skills, they will be limited in their pursuits as they mature.

By now we hope you recognize that at the center of the successful movement experience is a wide variety of motor activity that achieves the physical, emotional, cognitive, and affective development of the child. Although the developmentally appropriate physical education curriculum will be discussed in more detail in Chapter 6, we would like to call your attention to some common activities and games that are contrary to the goals of developmentally appropriate movement activity.

Two journal articles entitled "The Physical Education Hall of Shame" outline games and activities that possess inappropriate features (Williams 1992, 1994). Games and activities included in the Hall of Shame have one or more of the following elements:

- Absence of an educational objective
- Potential to embarrass children
- Elimination of participants

- Overemphasis on fun rather than goal-directed learning
- Lack of emphasis on skill acquisition or fitness development
- Low participation time
- Likelihood of danger or high risk of injury

At the forefront of discussion are the games dodgeball; Duck, Duck, Goose; Red Rover; and Simon Says, which are commonly played in elementary schools. As you consider these games and the Hall of Shame criteria, you will notice the many negative aspects of each game. NASPE (2000) states that these activities "provide limited opportunities for everyone in the class, especially the slower, less agile students who need the activity the most." Many people will argue that modifications to the games within the Hall of Shame will make them worthy of inclusion in the physical education program. Often the most heated arguments surround the game of dodgeball as many believe the game allows a means of practicing the skills of running, dodging, throwing, and catching. In a 2006 position statement on dodgeball, NASPE states, "The students who are eliminated first in dodgeball are typically the ones who most need to be active and practice their skills. Many times these students are also the ones with the least amount of confidence in their physical abilities. Being targeted because they are the 'weaker' players, and being hit by a hard-thrown ball, does not help kids to develop confidence." The selection of activities that are not in the best interests of all children should be eliminated from your repertoire.

Some activities, such as tag games, relays, and kickball, may belong on the Hall of Shame list if played in a traditional manner. Tag games that include elimination, an overemphasis on fun rather than a learning goal, and little emphasis on safety should be in the Hall of Shame. However, tag games may be modified so that elimination is not present, safety is monitored closely, and a focus is on the health-related benefits of a beginning of class instant warm-up activity. Relays may be modified so that there is maximum participation time in small groups and little emphasis on winning and losing. The standard kickball game has little participation time for most students and may be potentially embarrassing to low-skilled children. By modifying the game rules to require all members of the kicking team to run back and forth from home to first as many times as possible, the level of participation increases dramatically. The fielding team could be required to position themselves close together for all to throw and catch one or more balls before running the ball to an "out"

hula hoop. Such modifications will promote greater participation, may include an aerobic benefit, and may promote cooperation rather than competition.

When considering whether to modify games and activities that have inappropriate features, we encourage you to ask yourself whether you want your children exposed to these activities. Will the game or activity promote positive experiences so that children want to be physically active outside of school and throughout their lifetime? Or will participation in the activity create an emotional scar that hinders the development of positive attitudes toward physical activity?

All children should have equal access to meaningful participation in movement activities. Boys and girls and low-skilled and high-skilled children should have their needs met for active participation in all learning experiences. Appropriate equipment for children will accommodate their size and level of motor development and will increase the likelihood of success. We encourage you to provide equipment of various sizes, textures, and weights so that children may choose equipment they can control rather than equipment that will control them.

Most children love to move and play when they are in elementary school. In order to keep their love for fun and enjoyment alive in the movement setting, it is critical that you plan activities that emphasize self-improvement, participation, and cooperation. All too often the movement setting is plagued with inappropriate practices that make children feel fearful, excluded, or frustrated. Situations such as the following decrease the desire to be involved in movement activity:

- Being picked last by a captain for a team
- Struggling to do a pull-up while the entire class watches
- Doing push-ups for punishment
- Being eliminated from a game and sitting out for a long period of time
- Practicing the same activities in all grade levels
- Standing in line to wait for a turn to hit the ball

One inappropriate practice found in the elementary school setting merits discussion. All too often children are disciplined for misbehavior or poor work habits by withholding participation in movement activity or recess opportunities. We strongly discourage this practice because of the message it sends to children about physical activity as unimportant and unnecessary. Children need daily physical activities that aid in the development of healthy minds and bodies. We encourage you to develop other strategies to discipline children that are proportional to the severity of the incident.

Appropriate teaching practices that allow children to integrate the cognitive, affective, and psychomotor aspects of learning will help them understand the contributions of physical activity to good health. We encourage you to recognize the benefits of physical activity for all children and use teaching practices that enable all children to participate regularly in physical activity. Physical activity should be taught through positive learning experiences that provide children of all abilities and interests the foundation of movement skills that lead to lifelong participation.

Summary

As you select, plan, and implement movement experiences, you will want to consider the developmental variability and individual readiness for activity of the children in your class. Because children are not miniature adults, movement experiences should reflect the physical, motor, affective, and cognitive levels of children. The selection of styles, teaching practices, and practice progressions should be made with the interests and abilities of each and every child in mind. Your knowledge of motor development characteristics of children and motor learning concepts will provide you with helpful strategies for selecting movement experiences that will lead to lifelong active and healthy lifestyles.

Chapter Activities

1. Based on what you have learned about variability among children in this chapter, describe what you would recommend the movement educator do in the following situations.

   ▪ Jason and Sally have difficulty skipping through the maze you placed on the floor. The other first-grade students in the class are doing well with the task.

   ▪ Ernie, a small third grader, has difficulty catching a tennis ball that he has tossed against the wall from a distance of eight feet.

   ▪ Within a class of fifth-grade children, it is apparent that four children are at the beginning stage of learning for the task of striking with a short paddle whereas the rest of the class is at the intermediate level of learning.

   ▪ Gayle is a highly skilled soccer player on her recreation league team. She becomes very frustrated during movement activities involving dribbling a ball with her hand. She often asks to sit out during those activities.

2. Construct a list of pros and cons for the inclusion of dodgeball in the movement curriculum. Write a position paper to clarify your views on the merits of this activity in the elementary school curriculum.

3. Based on what you learned in this chapter, construct a series of movement tasks that encourage children to explore the difference between gross movements and fine movements while moving to a rhythmical beat.

4. Your principal questions your request to order balls of various sizes, weights, and textures for use in class. The principal prefers that you order balls of the same size from the district storehouse to save money. How would you justify your request?

5. You are teaching first-grade children to dribble a ball with one hand. Describe how you would accommodate as many learning styles as possible in your instructions to students about dribbling the ball under control.

Internet Resources

American Academy of Pediatrics. Provides information on the development of children and adolescents as well as guidelines for promoting healthy activity.
www.aap.org

Centers for Disease Control and Prevention. Growth charts for height and weight predictions.
www.cdc.gov/growthcharts

Healthy People 2010, Nutrition and Overweight. Objectives for promotion of health and reduction of chronic diseases associated with height and weight.
www.healthypeople.gov

National Association for Sport and Physical Education. Position papers and resources to assist in providing developmentally appropriate instruction.
www.aahperd.org/naspe

PELinks4U. Electronic newsletter for the promotion of active and healthy lifestyles.
www.pelinks4U.org

Bibliography

Coker, C. A. 1996. Accommodating students' learning styles in physical education. *Journal of Physical Education, Recreation, and Dance* 67(9): 66–68.

Gallahue, D., and F. Cleland Donnelly. 2003. *Developmental physical education for all children.* 4th ed. Champaign, IL: Human Kinetics.

Gallahue, D., and J. C. Ozmun. 2006. *Understanding motor development: Infants, children, adolescents, adults.* 6th ed. Boston: McGraw-Hill.

Magill, R. A. 2004. *Motor learning and control: Concepts and applications.* 7th ed. Boston: McGraw-Hill.

National Association for Sport and Physical Education (NASPE). 2000. *Appropriate practices for elementary school physical education.* Reston, VA: AAHPERD.

———. 2006. *Position on dodgeball in physical education.* Reston, VA: AAHPERD. http://www.aahperd.org/naspe/pdf_files/pos_papers/dodgeball.pdf

Palmer, S. E., and K. Hildebrand. 2005. Designing appropriate learning tasks. *Journal of Physical Education, Recreation, and Dance* 76(2): 48–55.

Payne, V. G., and L. D. Isaacs. 2005. *Human motor development: A lifespan approach.* 6th ed. Boston: McGraw-Hill.

Rink, J. E. 2002. *Teaching physical education for learning.* 4th ed. Boston: McGraw-Hill.

Schmidt, R. A., and C. A. Wrisberg. 2004. *Motor learning and performance.* 3rd ed. Champaign, IL: Human Kinetics.

Williams, K. 2004. What's motor development got to do with physical education? *Journal of Physical Education, Recreation, and Dance* 75(6): 35–39.

Williams, N. F. 1992. The physical education hall of shame. *Journal of Physical Education, Recreation, and Dance* 63(6): 57–60.

———. 1994. The physical education hall of shame. *Journal of Physical Education, Recreation, and Dance* 65(2): 17–20.

QUICK LESSON 2.1
Individual Exploration with Balloons

GRADES K–2

NASPE STANDARD 1 Students demonstrate competency in motor skills and movement patterns needed to perform a variety of physical activities.

LESSON OBJECTIVES

- Students explore various body surfaces to manipulate a balloon.
- Students explore striking balloons to different levels.
- Students explore the concept of effort as they strike a balloon.

EQUIPMENT NEEDED A balloon for each child.

PREPARATION TIME Fifteen minutes to blow up balloons.

KNOWLEDGE CONTENT Balloons provide interesting opportunities for exploration. Balloons are inexpensive and float easily, so children may experience success. As children explore striking the balloon, they will become more confident tracking the balloon with their eyes.

Movement concepts of space and effort provide children knowledge of how the body can move by enabling them to learn how motor skills may be modified. Within the concept of space, children may vary movements through the levels of high, medium, and low. Effort of movement may be modified by strong or light force applied to the balloon. Children should be encouraged to explore how their body can move before concentrating on the skill theme of striking.

As children explore effort and space with their balloons, consider the following safety tips:

- Children will need sufficient space to move without interfering with other students.
- To avoid breakage, the balloons should not be overinflated.

CLASSROOM ACTIVITY With each child in his or her own personal space (a child's personal space consists of the space surrounding the child that the child can move in when remaining in basically the same spot on the floor), ask students the following:

- Show me how to keep the balloon in the air above your head.
- Show me how to keep the balloon in the air as high as possible.

- As low as possible.
- Show me how hard you can hit the balloon.
- How soft you can hit the balloon.
- How many different body parts can you use to hit the balloon into the air?
- Can you alternate body parts and hit the balloon above your head?
- Can you alternate body parts and hit the balloon between your knees and shoulders?
- Which body part can you use to hit the balloon low?
- Can you jump and make high contact with the balloon?
- Can you lie on the floor and make contact?
- Can you sit on the floor and make contact?
- Can you explore the same tasks with a partner?
- With a partner, can you explore keeping two balloons in the air at a time while accomplishing the task?

ASSESSMENT Exploratory teaching encourages children to create movement in response to a movement task. Because you want children to feel free to explore and create, there are no right or wrong movements. The teacher observes the children during the exploration and keeps them on target with the movement task. If children begin to stray from the movement task, the teacher should redirect the questions to focus children again.

The teacher should encourage children through motivational feedback. However, the teacher should be cautioned against providing specific feedback about a child's performance. Typically, specific, congruent feedback will cause children to imitate each other rather than create movement themselves.

SUCCESS FOR ALL Exploratory movement should enable all children to enjoy creating movement and to discover what their bodies can do. Children enjoy watching balloons of different colors float through the air, so they will be excited about the activity. With praise and words of encouragement, the teacher can help all children experience the success of exploration of effort and space with balloons.

INTEGRATION WITH OTHER SUBJECT AREAS
Children may be encouraged to count or recite the alphabet as they strike the balloon. A pair of dice might be rolled to integrate math addition, subtraction, or multiplication with the striking activity.

CLASSROOM LEARNING STATION 2.1
Are We All the Same?

GRADES K–6

NASPE STANDARD 5 Students exhibit responsible personal and social behavior that respects self and others in physical activity settings.

LESSON OBJECTIVES

- Students recognize and respect the differences in sizes among their classmates.
- Students recognize and respect the variability of abilities among their classmates.
- Students interact with their classmates as they learn about physical growth.
- Students describe how their bodies change as they grow and how their ability to perform motor tasks also changes.

EQUIPMENT NEEDED A long jump rope or clothesline, clothespins, socks of different sizes.

PREPARATION TIME A few hours should be allotted to gather socks of different sizes, from infant size through adult. The rope should be attached to a wall or another object from low to high, with low being approximately head high for children in class, and high being approximately seven to eight feet. Arrange the socks on the rope by size, with the smallest socks on the low end of the rope. Attach to each sock a tag that identifies the approximate age of the person who wears the sock.

KNOWLEDGE CONTENT The knowledge content of this learning station involves helping children understand how their bodies change as they grow. They should also be able to summarize that at a certain age the body stops growing taller and other body parts also stop growing. As bodies change, so may each child's ability to perform a motor task. Just as we respect our physical differences, we should also respect our differing abilities to do movement activities.

Follow these safety tips for the learning station activity:

- Provide ample space next to the wall free from objects.
- Children should not be allowed to grab onto the rope as they jump.
- Children should be encouraged to bend their knees upon takeoff and landing to avoid leg injuries.
- Children should be encouraged to stretch their ankles and legs in preparation for activity.

CLASSROOM ACTIVITY The learning station asks children to do the following:

- Observe the different socks and describe what is different about each sock.
- Notice that the socks increase in size as one grows older, but also observe that at a certain age the socks no longer increase in size.
- Describe how the body changes physically as a person grows. Identify other body parts that grow and change as we get older.
- Brainstorm on other ways growth occurs as we get older.
- Attempt to determine how individual children of the same height have differing abilities to jump and touch the rope. Ask children to jump from a stationary position next to the wall and touch the rope as high as possible.
- Summarize how bodies change over the years and how abilities change as we grow older and have different experiences.

ASSESSMENT The teacher guides the discussion on physical growth and visually observes the students while they jump as high as they can to touch the rope. The teacher will then lead the discussion on differences in body height and physical ability.

SUCCESS FOR ALL If students with disabilities are present, the activity may be modified so that children may touch the different socks to compare sizes. They may also sit and touch or stand and touch the rope rather than jump to the rope.

INTEGRATION WITH OTHER SUBJECT AREAS
Children may be encouraged to write a short story or draw a picture about things they could do when they were smaller that they can't do now. They may also write or draw about things they look forward to doing as they continue to grow.

Nutrition may be integrated into this activity by having children discuss how a healthy, well-balanced diet will help a body grow.

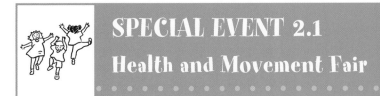

GRADES 3–6

NASPE STANDARD 5 Students exhibit responsible personal and social behavior that respects self and others in physical activity settings.

LESSON OBJECTIVES

- Students comprehend changes in physical and motor development across a school year.
- Students self-assess physical activities and the ability to perform the activities.
- Students respect the differences among peers in the class regarding changes in physical and motor development during the school year.

EQUIPMENT NEEDED Task sheets for each student, as well as the equipment listed in each station description.

Health and Movement Fair
Task Sheet

Student's Name: _____

Station 1:   Height _____   Weight _____

Station 2:

    Shoe length _____

    Arm length _____

    Leg length _____

Station 3:

    Left eye _____   Right eye _____

Station 4:

    Best vertical jump _____

Station 5:

    Best jump rope attempt _____

Station 6:

    Best juggling attempt _____

Station 7:

    Best hula hoop attempt _____

Station 8:

    Best throw/catch attempt _____

Station 9:

    Left foot _____   Right foot _____

Station 10:

    Best keep-it-up attempt _____

PREPARATION TIME Two hours to collect equipment and set up the stations.

KNOWLEDGE CONTENT The students should understand that their bodies grow and change and that their abilities to perform physical activities also change. This activity may be set up in the classroom with learning stations or it may be expanded into the lunchroom or hallways, depending on the number of students involved. To demonstrate changes within individual children, this activity would best be scheduled early in the school year and then again at the end of the school year. The objectives for this activity would be best met if children are able to perform as many of the self-tests with the assistance of another student rather than an adult.

FAIR ACTIVITIES Stations should be set up so children may measure their physical and motor ability tasks (see the following suggested station activities). Allow approximately five minutes at each station. Children should have a task sheet and a pencil with them as they travel throughout the stations.

The teacher should mingle with students and provide assistance as requested by the children. The teacher should provide positive feedback to children who cooperate with each other to complete the tasks.

ASSESSMENT The task sheets completed by the students may be included in a portfolio. Children should be encouraged to draw a picture or write a story about what physical activities they like to do. Their picture or story at the end of the year may be compared with the one from the beginning of the year to demonstrate change. Children should be encouraged to write or talk about how they have changed in their likes and dislikes as well as in their physical and motor development.

SUCCESS FOR ALL Modify tasks and provide ample space between stations so children with disabilities will be able to participate with their classmates.

INTEGRATION WITH OTHER SUBJECT AREAS As noted in the assessment section, integration with language arts and art education is recommended. Math skills and critical thinking activities are included as children compare and contrast their physical dimensions.

STATION 1: HEIGHT AND WEIGHT STATION
Equipment: A scale and a measuring tape secured to the wall

- Have students record their weight and their height on their task sheet.

STATION 2: PHYSICAL MEASUREMENTS
Equipment: Sewing tape measures

- Have students measure the size of their shoe from heel to toe.
- Have students measure the length of their arm from shoulder to tip of the middle finger.
- Have students measure the length of their leg from knee to ankle.

STATION 3: EYE STATION *Equipment:* An eye chart, masking tape, an eye patch

- Have students stand at a piece of tape ten feet from the eye chart, cover one eye, and read the eye chart. Repeat with the other eye.
- Have students record which line they were able to read without mistakes.

STATION 4: VERTICAL JUMP STATION
Equipment: A tape measure, paper hung on a wall, a marker

- Have students stand with their dominant side next to the wall. From a stationary position, students should jump as high as they can, extend the hand with the marker above their head, and make a mark on the piece of paper. After three attempts, measure and have students record the best attempt.

STATION 5: JUMP ROPE STATION *Equipment:*
Five to ten individual ropes of varying lengths for students of various heights

- Students may jump rope in any preferred way and record the number of consecutive jumps they make without missing. They may record the better of two attempts.

STATION 6: BEAN BAG AND SCARF JUGGLE
STATION *Equipment:* Fifteen or more bean bags and fifteen or more chiffon juggle scarves

- Students may choose to juggle scarves or bean bags and may choose one, two, or three scarves or bags

to juggle. Students should record the number of tosses before dropping the scarves or bags. They may record the best of five attempts.

STATION 7: HULA HOOP STATION *Equipment:*
Five to eight hula hoops, 24-inch diameter for smaller children, 30- or 36-inch diameter for larger children; a stopwatch

- Have students hula hoop around the waist while a partner keeps track of time on the stopwatch. The better time of two tries should be recorded.

STATION 8: THROW AND CATCH STATION
Equipment: Balls of various sizes, weights, colors, and textures

- With a partner, have children stand 30 feet apart and throw and catch a ball of their choosing. Students should count the number of throws before dropping the ball. After two minutes, have students record the best attempt.

STATION 9: BALANCE STATION *Equipment:* A stopwatch

- Have students balance on one foot with arms across the chest. Partner will begin the stopwatch when the child is balanced in a still position and stop the watch when balance is lost. Record times on left foot and on right foot as the best of three attempts.

STATION 10: KEEP IT UP IN THE AIR *Equipment:*
Short-handled paddles, small foam balls, 36-inch hula hoops, a stopwatch

- Give students 60 seconds to keep the ball up in the air by striking it with the paddle while remaining inside the hula hoop. Record the greatest number of consecutive strikes in the 60-second time.

CHAPTER 3

Movement Components and Skill Development

The purpose of this chapter is to introduce you to underlying components of movement. Movement components are concepts that can be applied to any movement form. Descriptions of basic locomotor skills, nonlocomotor movements, and manipulative skills are included and accompanied by activities that you can use to develop these skills.

Objectives

After studying this chapter, you will be able to do the following:

- Identify basic movement components.

- Implement activities that assist with the development of locomotor, nonlocomotor, and manipulative movements.

- Understand the performance levels of the manipulative skills of throw and pass, catch, kick and punt, strike and serve, volley, shoot, roll, dribble with hands, and dribble with feet.

- Develop activities to be used in the classroom and gymnasium that assist with the development of basic movement patterns.

Mrs. Harris knows the cold weather is coming. The barometric pressure is changing, and her third-grade class is bouncing off the walls. She is in the middle of her morning reading lesson and realizes she has lost them. Her class seems to be somewhere else. Since tonight will be the third game in the World Series baseball tournament, she decides to take a short break and get the children moving.

Each child is asked to stand beside his or her desk and pretend to be holding a baseball. She starts playing a recording of "Take Me Out to the Ball Game," and the fun begins. First Mrs. Harris asks the students to underhand toss and catch the imaginary ball to themselves, sometimes catching it high and sometimes catching it low. She reminds them to watch the ball with their eyes and to catch it using their hands. Next she tells them they are playing center field and need to throw the ball to the catcher, therefore practicing the overhand throw for distance and accuracy. "Step with your opposite foot and reach for your opposite hip after you throw," she reminds them. The umpire, Mrs. Harris, announces, "Three outs! Switch sides." The players now take turns at bat. One, two, three—swing! All classmates swing simultaneously, rotating their hips as they step in the direction of the pitcher. They run in place pretending to round the bases for a home run. Repeat several times. Mrs. Harris continues the World Series event until the song ends.

Introducing the Movement Map

The **movement map** (see Figure 3.1) categorizes the underlying components involved when the body moves. *All* body movements may be described using the components listed in the movement map, including those performed during a sport or athletic game, while cleaning the house, or at work on the line in a factory. For instance, the running long jump requires the performer to run (locomotor skill), increase speed when running (speed of movement), arrive on the takeoff board (relationships with objects), jump (locomotor skill), stretch while jumping (nonlocomotor movements), and bend the knees when landing (nonlocomotor movements). As you can see, many components are used to complete one pattern of

5 **Relationships: How the body relates**

- ▸ *With apparatus:* near-far, behind/in-front-of/ alongside, arriving on, above-below
- ▸ *Matching movements:* mirroring-matching, meeting-parting, together-apart
- ▸ *Contrasting movements:* up-down, wide-narrow
- ▸ *Simultaneous and successive movements:* following-copying

4 **Qualities of Movement: How the body moves**

- ▸ *Time or speed of movement:* quick-sudden, slow-sustained, accelerating-decelerating, basic beat, rhythmic pattern
- ▸ *Effort of the force of movement:* strong-light, accent, firm-fine
- ▸ *Free flow:* movement that cannot arbitrarily be stopped once started; *bound flow:* stoppable-ongoing, successive-jerky

3 **Space Awareness: Where the body moves**

- ▸ *Personal or limited space*
- ▸ *General space*
- ▸ *Directions:* forward, backward, sideways, up, down
- ▸ *Levels:* high, medium, low
- ▸ *Size:* big, small
- ▸ *Pathways:* straight, curved, zigzag

2 **Body Awareness: What the body can do**

- ▸ *Transferring body weight*
- ▸ *Balancing or weight bearing*
- ▸ *Flight*
- ▸ *Shapes:* straight, wide, round, twisted, curled, angular
- ▸ *Focus:* direction of gaze

1 **Body Movements: Ways the body moves**

- ▸ *Locomotor* skills
- ▸ *Nonlocomotor* skills
- ▸ *Manipulative* skills

FIGURE 3.1   The Movement Map

movement. Options for moving the entire body or specific body parts or for manipulating equipment are included in this tool. The movement map divides all possible movement into five major categories:

1. Body Movements: ways the body moves
2. Body Awareness: what the body can do
3. Space Awareness: where the body moves
4. Qualities of Movement: how the body moves
5. Relationships: how the body relates

Body Movements (locomotor, nonlocomotor, and manipulative skills) are the framework upon which the other four movement categories are developed. In other words, for the learner to experience Body Awareness, Space Awareness, Qualities of Movement, and

Relationships, the first category—Body Movements—must be used. When students are exploring general space, in the Space Awareness category, they must somehow move within space—for example, using locomotor skills. Locomotor skills or nonlocomotor skills must be used to develop skills related to balance in the Body Awareness category. Young children learn best by exploring the various movement components outlined in the movement map. Older children learn to perfect movement forms with extended practice related to each specific skill. Each of the five movement categories is discussed in further detail in the following sections.

Body Movements: Ways the Body Moves

For the purpose of this text, **body movements** include a variety of movements that may be divided into three categories: (1) locomotor movements—when the body moves throughout space; (2) nonlocomotor movements—completed when the feet are stationary; and (3) manipulative movements—when individuals handle equipment. Combinations of various locomotor, nonlocomotor, and manipulative movements allow the body to move in many different ways. For example, you combine running with kicking to dribble a soccer ball.

LOCOMOTOR SKILLS

The eight basic **locomotor skills** are walk, run, gallop, slide, jump, hop, skip, and leap. **Locomotor movements** are defined as movements that propel the mover around an area. Age, balance, leg strength, and neurological development influence the development of these skills. For instance, if students have difficulty balancing on one foot, they may also find it difficult to hop on one foot and will probably find it challenging to ride a bicycle. Limited leg strength will also influence one's success when jumping, running, hopping, and leaping. Skipping and leaping are higher-functioning skills, as they require both sides of the brain to coordinate the movement. These eight locomotor patterns are defined as follows:

1. *Walk:* the transfer of weight from one foot to the other while maintaining contact with the ground with at least one foot at all times
2. *Run:* the transfer of weight from one foot to the other while experiencing at least a slight moment when neither foot is contacting the ground
3. *Gallop:* moving forward with the same foot leading
4. *Slide:* a sideways gallop

5. *Jump:* any combination of using two feet in the following patterns: two feet to two feet; two feet to one foot; one foot to two feet
6. *Hop:* takeoff and landing from one foot to the same foot
7. *Skip:* step, hop, step, hop—alternating feet
8. *Leap:* transfer of weight from one foot to the other foot while experiencing an elongated moment of flight with neither foot touching the ground

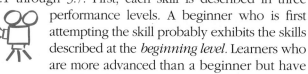

Each locomotor skill is analyzed further in Boxes 3.1 through 3.7. First, each skill is described in three performance levels. A beginner who is first attempting the skill probably exhibits the skills described at the *beginning level*. Learners who are more advanced than a beginner but have yet to master the skill display their skill at the *intermediate level*. The *advanced level* represents a student who has mastered the skill. After the **performance levels** are presented, teaching cues for each skill are provided. Also, two photos of each locomotor skill are provided (beginning and advanced levels). Quick Lesson 3.1 at the end of the chapter can be used to develop running skills.

NONLOCOMOTOR SKILLS

Nonlocomotor movements are defined as movements that are stationary or do not propel the mover around the area. The 14 **nonlocomotor skills** are bend, stretch, twist, turn, push, pull, rise, collapse, swing, sway, dodge, spin, shake, and balance. These skills may be used individually or in combination with locomotor skills and manipulative skills. For example, softball players may need to bend (nonlocomotor movement) to retrieve a ball before throwing the ball to a teammate. Learners should first attempt to master the skills individually and then combine them with other movements. Instant Activity 3.1 presents an exercise in collapsing. The 14 nonlocomotor movements may be defined as follows:

1. *Bend:* flexing any or all body parts
2. *Stretch:* extending body parts
3. *Twist:* rotating body parts in opposite directions
4. *Turn:* rotating the body around an axis
5. *Push:* directing a force or object away from the base of support
6. *Pull:* directing a force or object toward the body
7. *Rise:* moving the body or any parts of it to a higher level
8. *Collapse:* gradually relaxing the body or any parts of it in a controlled way while moving to a lower level
9. *Swing:* keeping the axis of support above the moving parts

10. *Sway:* keeping the axis of support below the moving parts
11. *Dodge:* quickly shifting one or more parts of the body away from a stationary or moving object or person
12. *Spin:* totally rotating the body on one body part on one spot
13. *Shake:* moving with vibration
14. *Balance:* moving in such a way that the body maintains a stationary position

MANIPULATIVE SKILLS

Manipulative movements are defined as movements in which the hands or feet handle equipment. **Manipulative skills** are divided into fine motor and gross motor skills. Fine motor skills involve the use of the hands and fingers and are instrumental in the success of penmanship, sorting small objects, zipping coats, buttoning shirts, tying shoes, and using scissors. A list of activities to develop fine motor skills is provided in Appendix A. Gross motor skills involve the large muscles in the body and are most often associated with individual activities and team sports—for example, dribbling in soccer, shooting in basketball, and serving volleyballs. Students who are encouraged to develop these skills during their younger years are usually more successful in gamelike situations during adolescence and adulthood. The 12 manipulative gross motor skills addressed in this book are as follows:

1. *Roll:* forcing an object or body to continuously turn over and over
2. *Throw:* using the hands to propel an object forward
3. *Catch:* using the hands to gather tossed objects
4. *Kick:* using the foot to impart force to an object
5. *Strike:* using an object or body part to impart force on another object
6. *Volley:* using the forearms (pass) or hands (set) to propel an object vertically
7. *Dribble with hands:* using the hands to repeatedly push a ball toward the ground
8. *Dribble with feet:* using the feet to repeatedly push a ball forward or sideways on the ground
9. *Punt:* dropping a ball from the hands (drop to self) and kicking it into the air to propel it up and forward
10. *Set shot:* using both hands to propel (throw) a ball up and forward (in curved pathway) toward a basketball goal
11. *Overhand serve:* using the dominant hand to strike a ball (above one's head) after the ball is tossed

INSTANT ACTIVITY 3.1
Collapse

Grades K–3
Equipment Needed

None

Activity

Push desks together in the center of the room and have the students stand scattered in the open space created around the perimeter. "As a break from sitting at our desks today, let's explore the movement concept of collapse. Stretch your right arm above your head. Stretch your left arm above your head. Stretch both arms above your head. Stretch really high. Feel the tension in the muscles as you try to stretch as high as possible. When I say go, let your arms collapse to your side. Go! What is the difference between a collapse and a bend?" (A collapse is giving in to gravity, just letting go.)

"This time, collapse your entire body (do not bend—just collapse). Try to sink your body straight downward, like you are feeling tired and cannot stand upright anymore, or like a three-scoop ice cream cone that is melting. Go!"

"This time, from your position on the floor, stand up and then collapse. At the end of the collapse, stretch out to a prone position on the floor on your right side. (Slide the upper body to the right while keeping the feet where they were.) Go!"

Repeat the above with the stretch to the left.

Repeat again with the stretch backward (end lying on your back).

"This time collapse but use a turn or twist on the way down. Go!"

"This time collapse in slow motion. Be sure I can see the letting go in the center of your body. It is not the same as bending. Go!"

into the air by the nondominant hand. The ball is propelled in a forward direction. The ball may also be struck with a racquet instead of the hand.

12. *Pass:* using both hands to throw a ball to a teammate

The skill levels of beginning, intermediate, and advanced for each of the 12 manipulative skills are provided in Boxes 3.8 through 3.20. Each aspect of the skill is analyzed in order to assist the child in performing a mature pattern in each skill, and photos of each skill (beginning and advanced levels) are provided.

(text continues on page 64)

BOX 3.1 Performance Levels for Walk

Body Actions	Beginner	Intermediate	Advanced
Foot	Toes turned outward or inward; flat foot	Toeing out or in is reduced; some heel-toe roll	Toeing out or in is eliminated; relaxed heel-toe roll
Leg	Short steps, wide base of support	Increased stride length	Relaxed elongated stride
Arm	Hooking across midline	Limited arm swing at side	Rhythmical arm swing with elbows slightly bent

TEACHING CUES

Cue Words	Description
1. Toes ahead	1. Point toes straight ahead.
2. Swing arms	2. Swing arms rhythmically in opposition to legs.
3. Heel-toe roll	3. Heel contacts the floor initially and then foot rolls forward to push off the toe.
4. Look ahead	4. Focus straight ahead.
5. Steady head	5. Keep head steady (no side-to-side movement).

Beginning walk technique

Advanced walk technique

BOX 3.2 Performance Levels for Run

Body Actions	Beginner	Intermediate	Advanced
Trunk	No trunk lean	Slight forward lean	Increased forward lean
Arm	Across and in front	Hooking	High in front and in back
Leg	Out to side and around	More definite bending of knee	Knees brought very high, heel brought up high to buttocks

TEACHING CUES

Cue Words	Description
1. Big steps	1. Strive for large stride length.
2. Bent elbows	2. Maintain 90-degree bend of upper and lower arm.
3. Pump the arms	3. Maintain bend in arm, swing arm and hand in an arc (from shoulder joint). Hands swing up to eye level and down even with the hips.
4. High knees	4. Thigh should be parallel to ground.
5. Look ahead; keep head steady	5. Focus straight ahead (chin up).

Beginning run technique

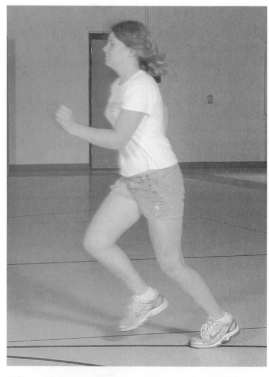

Advanced run technique

BOX 3.3 Performance Levels for Gallop and Slide

Body Actions	Beginner	Intermediate	Advanced
Gallop is forward and backward movement. Slide is a sideways movement.			
Trunk	No trunk lean	Limited forward lean	Slight forward lean
Arm	Little use of arms, hands by sides of body	Slightly out to side to aid balance	Arms swing forward at waist level on takeoff
Leg	Trail leg fails to remain behind and often contacts surface in front of lead leg (gallop), crosses over lead leg (slide)	Exaggerated vertical lift (gallop)	Trail leg lands adjacent to or behind lead leg

TEACHING CUES

Cue Words	Description
1. Step, close	1. Step with lead foot and bring other foot slightly behind lead leg (gallop), beside lead leg (slide).
2. Elbows bent and in	2. Keep elbows bent and close to sides of body.
3. Yee, ha, yee, ha	3. Repeat "yee, ha" verbally in a rhythmical pattern (slow, quick). Then perform gallop or slide while saying "yee, ha."

Beginning gallop technique

Advanced gallop technique

Beginning slide technique

Advanced slide technique

BOX 3.4 Performance Levels for Jump

Body Actions	Beginner	Intermediate	Advanced
Trunk	Vertical to slight forward lean	Slight forward lean, greater extension	Full extension
Arm	Limited	Initiate jump	Initiate jump, lead body to full extension
Leg	Range of little flexion to extreme flexion	Increase in crouch and leg extension	Complete flexion during preparation, full extension throughout jump

TEACHING CUES

Cue Words	Description
1. Squat	1. Bend knees as in preparation to sit down.
2. Arms back	2. Swing arms backward before swinging them forward.
3. Reach for the stars	3. Extend hands above head when leaving the floor.
4. Jump	4. Put it all together to see how long you can hang in the air.
5. Land soft	5. Bend knees upon landing to absorb force.

Beginning jump technique

Advanced jump technique

BOX 3.5 Performance Levels for Hop

Body Actions	Beginner	Intermediate	Advanced
Trunk	Body upright	Slight lean	Greater body lean
Arm	Flexed at elbows and held slightly to side	Move up and down vigorously and bilaterally	Move together in rhythmical lifting, used for force production
Leg	Nonsupport thigh parallel to surface	Nonsupport thigh at 45-degree angle to surface	Nonsupport thigh lifts with vertical thrust of support foot

TEACHING CUES

Cue Words	Description
1. Push up	1. Push upward to lift supporting foot off the floor; free foot, bent at knee, tight to body.
2. Land soft	2. Bend knees slightly on landing.
3. L arms	3. Maintain 90-degree elbow bend, elbows relaxed at sides.

Beginning hop technique

Advanced hop technique

BOX 3.6 Performance Levels for Skip

Body Actions	Beginner	Intermediate	Advanced
Trunk	No trunk lean	Slight trunk lean	Slight trunk lean
Arm	Hang by sides	Rhythmical arms	Rhythmical arms
Leg	Deliberate step-hop	Exaggerated vertical lift on hop	Low vertical lift on hop

TEACHING CUES

Cue Words	Description
1. Long, short, long, short	1. To practice arm movement, bend elbows, swinging alternately forward. Say "long, short." Each time "long" is said, move other arm forward.
2. Step, hop, step, hop	2. Step with one foot, then hop on that foot; step with other foot and hop on that foot. Continue. This is an uneven rhythm: slow (step), quick (hop).
3. Baby hop	3. Keep hopping foot low or close to the ground.

Beginning skip technique

Advanced skip technique

BOX 3.7 Performance Levels for Leap

Body Actions	Beginner	Intermediate	Advanced
Trunk	No lean	Little forward lean	Definite forward lean
Arm	No action	Used for balance	Definite opposition
Leg	Inability to push off in order to gain distance and elevation	Incomplete extension of legs during flight	Full extension of legs during flight

TEACHING CUES

Cue Words	Description
1. Push off strong	1. Bend supporting leg and push off up and forward to gain height and distance.
2. Drive arms	2. Use arms to drive body forward; 90-degree angle at elbow.
3. Reach	3. Reach forward with lead (nonsupporting) leg and opposite arm.
4. Land soft	4. Land on nontakeoff foot, bending knee slightly to absorb force.
5. Look forward	5. Focus forward; keep head steady.

Beginning leap technique

Advanced leap technique

After the performance levels are presented, teaching cues for each skill are provided, and finally, equipment considerations for increased success are suggested. The learner should first experience each movement component in a static position when the environment and task are stable. After mastering the skill in a static state, then the learner should be challenged to attempt each skill under varying conditions, such as with the body moving, the equipment moving, the targets moving, and so on (Gallahue and Ozmun 2002). Quick Lessons 3.3 and 3.4 (at the end of the chapter) may be used to develop the manipulative skills of kick, throw, and catch.

Appendix A contains activities that use (1) gross motor activities (including locomotor, nonlocomotor, and manipulative skills) and (2) fine motor activities. We suggest that upon initially attempting manipulative skills the learner first practice individually, then with a partner, and finally in small groups; therefore the activities listed in Appendix A are organized in this order. This sequence promotes maximal practice time for each student learning the skills and also considers the developmental level of the child. Activities in Appendix A are listed from simple to complex within each skill. Easier activities are listed first (individual), and as learners become more skilled, they should be challenged with the more difficult activities (partner and small group).

Appendix B contains assessment rubrics for the locomotor and manipulative skills. Teachers can use these rubrics to assess the child's achievement of the correct skill technique. The rubrics allow the teacher to look at performance techniques by analyzing specific body parts. The assessor then identifies the ability level of the performer on each specific movement component. Ask the student to perform the skill multiple times, preferably in an authentic gamelike situation, in order to obtain a valid evaluation of the skill ability. Peers or teachers may use these rubrics to provide students with immediate feedback, thus assisting in improving skill performance. For an in-depth discussion of rubrics, see Chapter 6.

Body Awareness: What the Body Can Do

As the body performs movements (locomotor, nonlocomotor, and manipulative), various body parts play different roles in the movement at different times. **Body awareness** describes *what* specific movements the body can perform or do while conducting various body movements. For instance, when children walk on a balance beam transferring their weight from right foot to left foot, they must combine the skills of walking and balancing. When throwing a ball, they must twist their trunk, a nonlocomotor skill, and step sideways, transferring their weight from the back foot to the front foot. Body parts can transfer the body weight, receive the weight or force, take flight, and form certain body shapes. Each of these elements is discussed in further detail.

TRANSFERRING BODY WEIGHT

When performing all locomotor skills, the body transfers its weight. Walking involves transferring weight from the right foot to the left foot. Performing a handstand requires a performer to transfer weight from the feet to the hands and then back to the feet. Forward rolls call for the weight to be transferred from the feet and hands to the back of the head, and back to the feet. A mature overhand throw involves transferring one's weight from the back foot to the opposite forward foot. In order to adequately perform a wide variety of skills, students should attempt to master the many ways the body can transfer weight.

BALANCING OR WEIGHT BEARING

Balancing the body challenges the student to hold the body in a controlled position. Various body parts may be used to bear the weight or create a balance. A one-foot balance could create a stork stand. Bearing weight on two hands and the head could form a tripod. A good balance progression is to walk on lines in the gym, low balance beams, and then high beams. Students should also experiment with both wide and narrow bases of support in order to discover the respective effects on balance. Many sport skills and recreational skills require a good sense of balance, such as riding a bike, walking on a log, or playing the position of center on a football team.

FLIGHT

Anytime the body is not in touch with the ground or not in touch with an object that is on the ground, it is considered to be in flight. Running, jumping, hopping, and leaping require the body to experience flight. Students use flight daily as they jump off of playground equipment, jump to catch a softball or

(text continues on page 79)

BOX 3.8 Performance Levels for Roll

Body Actions	Beginner	Intermediate	Advanced
Trunk	Exaggerated bend at waist before release	Bend at waist still pronounced	Lean forward (slightly from waist) at release
Arm	Straight arms, large pendulum-type swing, hands on both sides of ball	Slight elbow bend; one hand on top, one on bottom of ball	Bottom of ball held in dominant hand, forward swing while stepping with opposite foot
Leg	Straddle stance	Stride stance, limited knee bend	Stride stance, definite knee bend

TEACHING CUES

Cue Words	Description
1. Runner's stance	1. Stand with nondominant leg forward but weight on back (dominant) foot.
2. Grandfather clock swing	2. Balance ball in dominant hand, swing arm forward as step forward is taken.
3. Bend, step, smooth sailing	3. Bend knees and waist, step forward with nondominant foot, release ball gently on floor.
4. Look at target	4. Focus on target at all times.
5. Stretch forward	5. Follow through toward the target with the dominant arm.

Beginning ball roll technique

Advanced ball roll technique

BOX 3.9 Performance Levels for One-Handed Overhand Throw

Body Actions	Beginner	Intermediate	Advanced
Trunk	No rotation	Limited shoulder rotation	Hip, shoulder rotation good
Arm	No wrist action, push ball	Some wrist action	Elbow leads throw
Leg	No leg action	Step with same foot	Step with opposition

TEACHING CUES

Cue Words	Description
1. Straddle a line with side orientation toward the target, nondominant side closest to the target.	1. Keep one foot on each side of a line with ball held in the dominant hand.
2. Make a *T* shape with the body.	2. Hold arms straight at shoulder level.
3. Rock the *T*.	3. Rock sideways, transferring weight from right to left foot.
4. Make goal posts with the arms.	4. Bend elbows pointing fingers toward the sky.
5. Step and throw.	5. Step sideways toward the target with the nondominant foot and then throw.
6. Follow through, reaching for the opposite hip.	6. After releasing the object, move the throwing arm across the trunk and reach for the opposite hip.

EQUIPMENT CONSIDERATIONS

Learners should use an object that comfortably fits the size of their hand. Beanbags work well, as they do not roll after landing on the ground. Foxtails, scarves, foam balls, and Wiffle balls gain limited distance when thrown, therefore saving retrieval time. As their accuracy improves, the students should use tennis balls, softballs, or footballs.

Beginning overhand throw technique

Advanced overhand throw technique

BOX 3.10 Performance Levels for Catch

Body Actions	Beginner	Intermediate	Advanced
Head	Turns to side, fear reaction	Watches ball	Eyes follow path of ball
Arm	May or may not be extended	Traps ball against chest	Contact with hands, arms flex to absorb force
Hands	Stiff	Face one another	Cupped with fingers relaxed

TEACHING CUES

Cue Words	Description
1. Reach with hands and arms.	1. Extend arms toward the object to be caught.
2. Watch the object.	2. Focus eyes on object.
3. Hug the object after catching in the hands.	3. Pull object in to absorb the force.

EQUIPMENT CONSIDERATIONS

Beginning learners should use a scarf or trash bag to catch, as these objects float and increase the visual tracking time for the students. Next students should progress to a large, soft foam ball that may be embraced with the arms or hands. If the catch is missed, the object should not harm or scare the catcher. Progress to a smaller, harder ball as students improve.

Beginning catch technique

Advanced catch technique

BOX 3.11 Performance Levels for Kick

Body Actions	Beginner	Intermediate	Advanced
Trunk	Trunk is erect	Slight forward lean	Movement basically at the waist, bend slightly forward until kick, then slight backward movement
Arms	Held at sides and slightly raised, very limited	Move sideways to assist balance	Held slightly raised at sides and move in opposition to kicking leg
Leg/Foot	Stiff movement in upward-forward motion, contacts ball with toe, uses no approach	Limited extension on contact, uses instep, approach is limited	Increased extension and flexion, uses instep, uses full approach

TEACHING CUES

Cue Words	Description
1. Watch the ball.	1. Keep eyes on the ball.
2. Kick with shoelaces.	2. Contact the ball using the instep of the foot.
3. Bend kicking leg.	3. Step with nonkicking leg; bend kicking leg so foot is close to buttock.
4. Step-hop.	4. Step with nonkicking leg, contact the ball, while kicking leg is following through, hop once on nonkicking foot.

EQUIPMENT CONSIDERATIONS

The beginning learner should use a foam or lightweight ball in order to avoid injury to self or others. The ball should initially be stationary. As the pattern improves, the ball should be rolled toward the kicker.

Beginning kick technique

Advanced kick technique

BOX 3.12 Performance Levels for Strike

Body Actions	Beginner	Intermediate	Advanced
Trunk	Limited	Limited hip, trunk, and shoulder rotation	Rotate to the rear and then forward
Arm	Overhand motion anterior-posterior plane	Approaches oblique plane	Horizontal plane
Leg	None	None to limited step with same foot as arm striking	Sideways step in direction of striking motion

TEACHING CUES

Cue Words	Description
1. Mighty stance	1. Stand sideways to oncoming object.
2. Stare at the ball	2. Focus on the ball.
3. Swing level	3. Swing bat in horizontal plane.
4. Step and rotate hips as swing	4. Step sideways with nondominant foot, and swing bat forward, rotating hips and shoulders.

EQUIPMENT CONSIDERATIONS

The beginning learner should begin a striking pattern using the hand and then use a short implement such as a Ping-Pong paddle, a nylon hose paddle, or a two-liter bottle. The ball that is being struck should be large and lightweight, such as a beach ball or Slo-Mo ball in order to increase success. As learners improve, they should be challenged with longer implements and smaller balls. Some learners will be more successful if they move their hand closer to the striking surface (choke up).

Beginning strike technique

Advanced strike technique

BOX 3.13 Performance Levels for Volley/Set

Body Actions	Beginner	Intermediate	Advanced
Eyes	Failure to track	Limited tracking	Good tracking
Arm/Hand	Unable to contact ball with both hands simultaneously; contact ball well below face level	Extends arms, bend at wrists, inconsistent contact on finger pads; contact ball at eye level	Good arm extension, stiff wrists, consistent contact with finger pads; contact ball above head
Leg	No leg action	Limited flexion	Good flexion and extension

TEACHING CUES

Cue Words	Description
1. Watch, watch, watch	1. Keep eyes focused on the ball.
2. Look through window.	2. Index fingers and thumbs form triangle or window.
3. Bend/straighten arms	3. Bent arms straighten while contacting ball.
4. Bend at knees	4. Bend knees when preparing to contact the ball.
5. Straighten legs as you contact the ball	5. Extend legs in order to impart power to the hit.

EQUIPMENT CONSIDERATIONS

When learning to volley, students should use a balloon because it is lightweight and increases the amount of time available before needing to contact the balloon. The next level would be to use lightweight beach balls, Slo-Mo balls, or foam volleyballs. Trainer volleyballs provide the advanced learner with a larger ball that is also softer and lighter than regular volleyballs.

Beginning volley/set technique

Advaced volley/set technique

BOX 3.14 Performance Levels for Volley/Pass

Body Actions	Beginner	Intermediate	Advanced
Eyes	Failure to track	Limited tracking	Good tracking
Arm	Unable to contact ball with both arms simultaneously; vigorous arm swing	Limited to good arm extension, arm swing moderate; ball contact inconsistent on forearms	Good arm extension, no arm swing; ball contact evenly distributed on forearms
Leg	No leg action	Limited flexion	Good flexion and extension

TEACHING CUES

Cue Words	Description
1. Watch, watch, watch	1. Keep eyes focused on the ball.
2. Straight arms	2. Keep arms extended.
3. Forearm contact	3. Contact ball on forearms.
4. Bend at knees	4. Bend knees when preparing to contact the ball.
5. Straighten legs as contact ball	5. Extend legs in order to impart power to the hit.

EQUIPMENT CONSIDERATIONS

When learning to volley, the students should use a balloon because it is lightweight and increases the amount of time available before needing to contact the balloon. The next level would be to use lightweight beach balls, Slo-Mo balls, or foam volleyballs. Trainer volleyballs provide the advanced learner with a larger ball that is also softer and lighter than regular volleyballs.

Beginning volley/pass technique

Advanced volley/pass technique

BOX 3.15 Performance Levels for Dribble Using Hands

Body Actions	Beginner	Intermediate	Advanced
Eyes	Limited	Track ball constantly	Track ball when needed
Hand	Slaps ball	Palm contacts ball	Controlled pushing action initiated from fingertips
Ball placement	Close to body, high or low bounce	Height of bounce inconsistent	Waist-high bounce

TEACHING CUES

Cue Words	Description
1. Push, push, pads, pads	1. Push the ball downward, contacting the ball using the pads on the fingers.
2. At your waist, not your face	2. Dribble ball with enough force so it rebounds waist high.

EQUIPMENT CONSIDERATIONS

Beginning dribblers should use a junior-size ball, five to six inches in diameter. A lightweight foam ball with good bounce is less intimidating in case the ball should accidentally hit the face, legs, feet, or other body parts. As skill progresses, playground balls or junior-size basketballs may be used.

Beginning dribble (with hand) technique

Advanced dribble (with hand) technique

BOX 3.16 Performance Levels for Dribble Using Feet

Body Actions	Beginner	Intermediate	Advanced
Eyes	Failure to track	Watch feet and ball continuously	Look ahead
Foot/Leg	Stiff legs, dominant use of one foot	Uses toes to touch ball	Uses inside and outside of foot to control ball

TEACHING CUES

Cue Words	Description
1. Easy taps	1. Contact ball softly.
2. Catch with arch of foot	2. Use the inside of foot to contact the ball.
3. Cuddle the ball	3. Keep the ball close to both feet.

EQUIPMENT CONSIDERATIONS

Beginning dribblers should use a lightweight ball that is seven to eight inches in diameter. They should be challenged to push the ball and try to keep the ball close to their feet. Equal use of both feet should be encouraged. Normally soccer skills would be performed in a grassy area, thus slowing down the speed of the ball.

Beginning dribble (with feet) technique

Advanced dribble (with feet) technique

BOX 3.17 Performance Levels for Punt

Body Actions	Beginner	Intermediate	Advanced
Trunk	No lean	Minimal lean	Lean backward slightly at contact
Arm/hand	Pushes ball down or tosses high	Tosses ball	Drops ball
Leg/Foot	No forward step with opposite foot	Contact with toes at knee level or higher	Contact with instep at knee level or lower; hops on non-kicking foot after contact

TEACHING CUES

Cue Words	Description
1. Shoelaces	1. Contact ball with instep.
2. Big eyes	2. Watch the ball contact the foot.
3. Egg drop	3. Drop ball softly to kicking foot.

EQUIPMENT CONSIDERATIONS

Beginning punters should use a large round ball to punt. As the skill level improves, they should advance to a small ball and then to an oblong ball like a football or rugby ball.

Beginning punt technique

Advanced punt technique

BOX 3.18 Performance Levels for Set Shot

Body Actions	Beginner	Intermediate	Advanced
Trunk	No forward lean	Limited lean	Slight forward lean
Arm/Hand	Both hands on sides of ball; ball is carried behind head and both arms swing forward	Elbow points to the sides	Spread fingers, shooting hand behind ball and other hand on the side of the ball
Leg	No leg action to exaggerated knee bend	Limited knee bend	Bend knees slightly

TEACHING CUES

Cue Words	Description
1. *L* arm	1. Shooting arm makes the shape of an *L*.
2. Serving tray	2. Ball rests on shooting hand like a serving tray.
3. Good-bye	3. After releasing the ball, wave good-bye to the ball.
4. Squat and reach	4. Bend and extend legs when shooting.
5. Make a rainbow	5. Arch the ball when shooting.

EQUIPMENT CONSIDERATIONS

Initially the ball should be a foam junior-size ball. Hang a hoop from the rim to create a large target. Then lower the basketball goal when possible to increase success. As the ability increases, use a regular junior-size ball, then a women's-size ball, then a regulation men's ball, and gradually raise the goal height to ten feet.

Beginning set shot technique

Advanced set shot technique

BOX 3.19 Performance Levels for Overhand Serve

Body Actions	Beginner	Intermediate	Advanced
Trunk	No trunk rotation	Slight trunk rotation	Full trunk rotation
Arm/Hand	Poor toss, contacts ball below head level	Poor toss, contacts ball with palm when hitting and arm is not fully extended at contact	Toss ball slightly in front of body an arm's length above head; contacts ball with hitting arm extended above head and follows through toward target
Leg	No forward step	Steps forward with same leg as hitting arm	Steps with opposition to hitting arm

TEACHING CUES

Cue Words	Description
1. Toss up a chimney	1. Toss ball as straight up as possible.
2. Toss, step, reach, hit	2. Toss in front of serving shoulder, step with opposite foot, reach hitting arm above head and rotate backward, hit with heel of hand as rotating forward.
3. Heel to target	3. Point heel of hand in direction ball should land.

EQUIPMENT CONSIDERATIONS

Beginners could use a balloon to toss and overhand serve for increased success. Then progress to an oversized trainer volleyball and then a regulation-size trainer volleyball. It is not suggested to use a regulation volleyball with elementary school children.

Beginning overhand serve technique

Advanced overhand serve technique

BOX 3.20 Performance Levels for Two-Handed Ball Passes

Body Actions	Beginner	Intermediate	Advanced
Trunk	No forward lean	Minimal forward lean	Light forward lean
Arms/Hands			
Chest	Hands on sides of ball, arms move vertically upward and finish with a downward motion	Hands positioned on sides of ball to correct position, arms not fully extended toward target	Both thumbs down behind ball, fingers spread wide, arms extended toward target
Overhead	Hands on sides of ball; ball moved to exaggerated position behind head; hands release ball early, causing ball to have more vertical direction than necessary	Hands on sides of ball; however, hands do not point toward target on release of ball	Hands on sides of ball, arms lifted overhead to throw, and hands point toward target after releasing the ball
Bounce	Hands on sides of ball, arms move vertically upward and finish with a downward motion	Hands positioned on sides of ball to correct position, arms not fully extended toward target	Both thumbs down behind ball, fingers spread wide, arms extend down toward the floor, aiming ball to bounce three-fourths the distance between self and partner receiving ball
Leg	No step forward	Limited step forward	Aggressive step forward with one foot

TEACHING CUES

Cue Words	Description
1. Watch before passing	1. Look to see that the receiver is expecting the pass.
2. Step, push	2. Step forward with one foot, then push the arms toward the receiver.
3. Aim at target	3. Aim for partner's chest (chest pass and overhead pass), aim for the ball to bounce three-fourths of distance between self and partner (bounce pass).

EQUIPMENT CONSIDERATIONS

Beginners should use a Slo-Mo ball or a playground-size foam ball. Then progress to a junior-size basketball, a women's-size regulation ball, and finally to a regulation men's ball.

(Box 3.20 continues on page 78)

Beginning chest pass technique

Advanced chest pass technique

Beginning overhand pass technique

Advanced overhand pass technique

Beginning bounce pass technique

Advanced bounce pass technique

football, perform a layup in a basketball game, or run over hurdles. Students should have the opportunity to experience a wide variety of situations in which they are not in touch with the ground. Many injuries can be avoided when children have a good understanding of how to control their body when in the air and how to land safely. Children break arms and legs most frequently during recess when jumping or being pushed off playground equipment. To avoid such injuries, allow students to practice jumping forward, backward, and sideways off playground equipment while being supervised. It is a good idea to emphasize bending the knees when landing on the ground and reaching for the ground with bent arms. If the surface allows, a good activity is to jump, land, bend, and roll sideways.

SHAPES

The body can form many shapes that accommodate the positions needed to perform a wide variety of skills. There are six categories of shapes: (1) straight, (2) wide, (3) round, (4) twisted, (5) curled, and (6) angular. Young students love to explore how their bodies can make different shapes. Straight body shapes are used when spiking volleyballs. Twisted shapes are effective when stretching, and curled shapes are used when tumbling. Wide shapes are needed when playing defense in basketball. Challenge students to form a variety of shapes. For example, "show me how you can make a wide shape, a round shape, or a twisted shape"; "can you make a curled shape at a low level?"; "I will be looking for students who can make an angular shape that moves sideways."

FOCUS

In order to complete many skills, performers must focus on or gaze at an object, such as a ball or a person. For example, focus is important in playing defense and in maintaining balance in gymnastics and ice skating. Sometimes students need to focus on a variety of spots in the same or opposite direction while performing movements. Lessons that challenge the students to practice their focusing skills may also assist in the ability to balance and to read. Exercising the eye muscles assists with the development of tracking skills. Asking children to follow the light from a flashlight while holding their heads still is a good activity to practice focusing. Another effective tool is to write numbers or letters on a ball or balloon; ask students to look for the number or letter while they play catch.

Space Awareness: Where the Body Moves

Space awareness is defined as *where* the body moves, whether in personal or general space. Movement activity occurs within space (e.g., within the classroom or gymnasium). When movement is completed in an area large enough for one individual, it is defined as personal space. General space is a larger area that is used by several individuals or an entire class concurrently. Moving in personal or general space involves using different directions (forward, backward, sideways, up, and down), different levels (high, medium, or low), different pathways (straight, curved, or zigzag), and a variety of special sizes (large, medium, or small). In Chapter 7, Box 7.1 provides activities that address where the body moves.

PERSONAL SPACE

Personal space may be defined as space that is used while in a stationary or moving position in a very small area. It is space that no one else invades or occupies at the same time as another person. In a stationary position, children may make a wide shape with their body and then twist this shape; if they cannot touch anyone else or anything else, such as a wall or a bench, then they are in their own personal space. Students may learn to run in place, jump, hop, or balance in their own personal space so they don't bump into another student. Using equipment (e.g., hula hoops, beanbags, or balls) in their personal space challenges students to control their equipment. Personal space may be used for safety purposes so students do not get hit with someone else's jump rope. Personal space also assists with classroom management, as it keeps students from being in close proximity to one another.

GENERAL SPACE

All activity requires the use of space, and most activity requires the use of **general space.** If students are able to move without touching anyone or anything when moving around in a specific area (e.g., the gymnasium or playground), they are moving safely in general space. Pretending that they have a bubble around their body and they don't want to pop the bubble helps them understand that they must not come into contact with anyone or anything. Dribbling basketballs or soccer balls around general space provides students the opportunity to avoid other players, a skill that obviously carries over to many sport skills. Learning to move safely in general space helps prepare kids for tag games, for moving in a limited space in order to avoid collisions, and for learning how moving or hitting an object to an open space can provide many successful experiences.

DIRECTIONS

Moving throughout general space may be done in several different ways: (1) forward, (2) backward, (3) sideways, (4) up, and (5) down. All locomotor skills can be performed using these five directions. Learning to slide backward may be helpful when playing basketball. Leaping sideways assists students in avoiding contact with other players. Jumping up is needed when blocking volleyballs. Activities such as running in different directions in order to avoid being tagged or tackled and dribbling a basketball forward, backward, sideways and while moving the body up and down will assist in development of soccer, football, or basketball skills. Soccer players and tennis players must also have good command over change of direction. Students who can alter directions quickly under control are said to possess agility.

LEVELS

The three levels of movement—high, medium, and low—may be defined as follows: (1) high—the area above the shoulders, (2) medium—the area between the knees and shoulders, and (3) low—the area below the knees. Parts of the body can certainly move in all three levels. Equipment can be manipulated at various levels as well. Learning to jump and place hands at a high level will assist in the development of a mature jumping pattern. Throwing a ball to a partner at a medium level is the exact spot for a good pitch in a softball game. Catching a ground ball at a low level is another skill students will use on a regular basis. Manipulating objects at all levels assists with development of visual tracking skills and overall body awareness that will transfer into successful sport skills.

PATHWAYS

Whenever one moves through general space, an invisible pathway is made with the feet. There are three categories of pathways: (1) straight, (2) curved, and (3) zigzag. A straight pathway is created when the mover propels the body or an object in a linear direction or straight line. A curved pathway is created when the movement follows a continuous *S* pattern. When

straight pathways are connected, forming continuous *Z*'s, a zigzag pattern has been established. When playing tag games, hopscotch, soccer, basketball, tennis, bowling, and all other sports, pathways are constantly used. Not only should students be familiar with various ways to move their own body in different pathways, but they should also experiment with moving equipment in various pathways. Challenge students to dribble a ball at a medium level in a curved pathway, then at a low level in a zigzag pathway. Combining directions, levels, and pathways provides many game-like situations related to specific skills.

SIZE

Size refers to the dimension of space the mover is using—big or small. When football receivers move to a big, open space, they provide a greater opportunity for the quarterback to throw them the ball. A tennis player may choose to hit the ball in a small space, barely over the top of the net, in order to score a point. Young children should learn to move to big spaces, or elephant spaces, when playing tag games. Soccer players should run to big spaces in order for teammates to pass them a ball. On the other hand, small spaces, or those that are occupied by others, are not good choices for players to occupy.

Qualities of Movement: How the Body Moves

Three movement factors (time, effort, and flow) blend to make movement effective and give it quality. The factor of time refers to the speed of movement. Effort refers to the strength of the movement, and flow refers to how controlled the movement is. The three factors combine to produce infinite **qualities of movement.** In Chapter 7, Box 7.1, appropriate activities are provided that reinforce concepts related to how the body moves.

TIME OR SPEED OF MOVEMENT

There are five components of time or speed of movement: (1) quick-sudden, (2) slow-sustained, (3) accelerating-decelerating, (4) basic beat, and (5) rhythmic patterns. Quick-sudden and slow-sustained movements are fairly self-explanatory. Accelerating movements are those that increase in speed as they are performed, and decelerating movements are those that slow down as they are executed. The basic beat is constant rhythm that has a consistent amount of time between intervals. Rhythmic patterns, on the other hand, may vary in regard to the intervals between the beats.

Activities that provide students the opportunity to experience time or speed of movement will assist in the development of many skills. Knowing when to accelerate or decelerate is helpful in most sports in order to avoid contact with others or avoid contact with volleyball nets, soccer goals, or boundary lines. Having students accelerate and then decelerate in order to land on a spot on the floor is an effective demonstration of this skill. The ability to perform a layup is evidence that the student is able to follow the rhythmic pattern of step, step, hop. Quick Lesson 3.2 offers activities that focus on acceleration and deceleration.

EFFORT OR FORCE OF MOVEMENT

Strong to light, firm to fine, and accent are qualities that define effort of movement. Strong and firm movements identify those that require a greater amount of force than light or fine movements. A strong force on a volleyball serve is needed to get the ball over the net, whereas a light movement is needed to dink the ball softly over the net. Underhand tossing a softball to a partner is needed when the two partners are in close proximity to one another. However, an outfielder must use a lot of force to throw the ball to home plate. Locomotor, nonlocomotor, and manipulative skills may all be performed using different amounts of force. Accent places a strong force during a series of movements that may otherwise require a medium to light force. Dribbling a ball from a low level to raise it to a medium level may take extra accent or force to make the ball rise to the level needed.

FREE FLOW AND BOUND FLOW

By definition, free flow is movement that cannot arbitrarily be stopped once it is started. Once a ball has been thrown, it will continue to move until it is caught or until it comes in contact with something. When performing a flip, the performer cannot usually stop the movement in midair. Bound flow is movement that is stoppable. It may be ongoing, successive, or jerky movement, but bound movement may be stopped at any moment. When students are able to discern whether a movement may or may not be stopped (once it is started), they will undoubtedly make good choices before initiating such movement.

For example, a basketball player commits to leaving the floor when trying to block a basketball; after the player's feet are off the ground, he or she is committed to the air.

Relationships: How the Body Relates

Movement takes place not in isolation but in relation to the surrounding environment. Thus all movement involves a **relationship** with space, with body parts, with other movers, or with equipment. In general, three basic types of relationships exist: (1) body parts to other body parts, (2) individuals and groups to each other, and (3) individuals and groups to objects, equipment, apparatus, rules, and boundaries. Quality relationships need to be formed with others, objects, equipment, rules, and boundaries to produce mature motor patterns.

MATCHING MOVEMENTS

Matching movements are typically performed with a partner; however, it is also possible to match movements with a piece of equipment or with specific body parts. There are three matching movements: (1) mirror-match, (2) meet-part, and (3) together-apart. Mirroring involves facing someone and replicating the exact movement on the same side of the body, as if looking into a mirror. This skill is useful when guarding someone during a basketball game. Matching means to move your right arm as the partner's right arm moves, matching the same body part on the right or left side of the body. Meeting and parting are obviously moving toward another person or an object or moving away. Bringing body parts together and apart occurs when performing jumping jacks, completing a forward crisscross with a jump rope, and using both hands when catching a ball. Exploring these concepts will have a monumental effect on producing successful movements. Quick Lesson 3.2 uses the skills of meet and part.

CONTRASTING MOVEMENTS

Contrasting movements are sets of movements that are opposite to one another. Two examples of contrasting movements are up-down and wide-narrow. Like a teeter-totter, when one end is up, the other end is down. Students learning to jump inside a double dutch jump

Leaping different distances (widths) is an example of contrasting movements.

rope must know that when one long rope is up the other is down. Understanding this concept helps them understand when to enter the ropes. In order to jump over different widths, students must know that the wider the object to be jumped is, the further (with more force) the student must jump to get over it successfully.

SIMULTANEOUS AND SUCCESSIVE MOVEMENTS

Simultaneous, or copying, movements are used when double dutch turners or tinkling pole pounders (people sitting at the ends of the poles, beating out the rhythm) must work together simultaneously to move the ropes or poles. To demonstrate simultaneous movement, have two students jump off of a box or bench and land at the very same time. Successive movements, or following, are used when playing Follow the Leader or when approaching the net during a doubles tennis match, in which one person follows the other. Successive movements help students to develop spatial awareness and the various qualities of movement.

USING EQUIPMENT

As students use equipment, they must develop skills that allow them to relate to the equipment for safety purposes or for spatial purposes. Students move with equipment in the following ways:

1. *Near-far:* when dribbling a soccer ball one should keep the ball near one's feet, and yet when shooting a soccer ball try to kick the ball far from the goalie.
2. *Behind/in-front-of/alongside:* volleyball players might squat behind a blocking teammate, stand in front of the ten-foot spiking line, or move alongside the net.
3. *Arriving on:* double dutch jumpers try to arrive on an *X* taped on the floor located between the turners.
4. *Above-below:* soccer players try to throw the ball in above their opponent's head or below the defender's knees.

Students should gain the ability to relate their entire body to specific body parts or to equipment they manipulate by using the concepts mentioned above. Asking students to jump and land behind a line, hop to arrive in a hoop, strike with a gym hockey stick below the waist, or jog alongside a partner directs them to safe and effective skill implementation.

The Role of the Classroom Teacher in Promoting Skill Development

Research supports the important role of movement in educating both mind and body (Calfas and Taylor 1994; Barton, Fordyce, and Kirby 1999). According to one report, cognitive scientists are researching how students best learn (Summerford 2000). One compelling theme has emerged in this research—*movement is essential to learning.* Physical activity can affect the following development in students: (1) academic achievement, (2) social and emotional development, and (3) self-concept. All teachers should be concerned about educating the whole child. Therefore, it is essential that classroom teachers address children's needs for physical activity, just as music, art, and physical education teachers should assist with the student's academic learning.

The academic needs of students may be addressed in many ways via physical activity. Many physical activities use tracking or visual skills that are also necessary for reading. Activities that encourage use of the eyes, such as throwing and catching, striking, dribbling, kicking, and volleying, certainly exercise the eye muscles necessary for tracking and focusing. Such skills may be practiced in the classroom by using balloons, Wiffle balls hung from the ceiling, and high-density foam balls to dribble, strike, or volley. Fine motor skills, such as writing, typing, and using scissors, may be improved with the following activities: sorting buttons, using clothespins to move cotton balls from one container to the next, or spinning tops. (Refer to Classroom Learning Station 3.1 and Appendix A for more fine motor skills.)

Physical activity environments offer numerous opportunities to develop social and emotional skills. One of the most important qualities one must possess in order to be successful in life is being able to work with others. Partner, small-group, and large-group situations promote the concepts of teamwork and cooperation. Students should be taught to realize and appreciate that *all* people of different physical skill abilities should be respected and valued as human beings. Less-skilled classmates may provide the mental knowledge to solve a problem or create a strategy to challenge the opposing teams. The sportsmanship issue assists children in learning how to win graciously and lose with dignity.

Vestibular development may assist in the maturation of physical abilities and one's self-concept, as well as self-control. The **vestibular system,** which includes the inner ear, assists in a child's ability to balance and to maintain proper posture and age-appropriate muscle tone. Spinning activities such as riding merry-go-rounds and scooters and playing tag games that encourage stopping and starting assist in the development of the vestibular system. Children lacking vestibular functioning may have difficulties balancing, riding a bike, sitting properly in a chair, or quickly changing directions during game situations. For obvious reasons, the development of one's self-concept can be impeded by lack of such development.

Teachers are constantly concerned with the self-concept of their students. When students feel good about themselves, they are more likely to succeed academically, physically, and socially. Educators who assist with motor development will also have an indirect effect on students' self-concept. Students who are more adept at motor skills will undoubtedly be more likely to be accepted by their peers. Competence at motor skills can increase the ability to cooperate with classmates when performing specific skills or strategies and also opens the door to exploring various solutions when problem solving.

Summary

Movement is made up of many components: ways the body moves, what the body can do, where the body moves, how the body moves, and how the body relates. In order to increase students' motivation and success, activities that assist in the development of locomotor, nonlocomotor, and manipulative skills should be presented in a developmental progression from simple to complex. Locomotor and manipulative skills have been dissected into performance levels in order to better understand learners' movement abilities, so classroom teachers may assist in the attainment of mature motor patterns by designing activities for use in the classroom and gymnasium. When students attempt to perform various skills, their success is influenced by the size, weight, and texture of the equipment. Larger, lightweight balls and shorter, lighter paddles are examples of equipment modifications that assist in increasing success. Short and simple teaching cues (like those indicated in this chapter) also aid learners in moving from one performance level to the next.

Chapter Activities

1. Obtain three to four pictures of athletes performing various motor skills and analyze the movement patterns to see whether the participants are exhibiting the components of an advanced pattern.
2. Have each student find a partner and have one partner run for approximately 20 yards while the other assesses the running pattern, focusing on the movement of the legs, arms, and trunk.
3. For each of the academic areas of math, spelling, social studies, and science, create two different activities that integrate locomotor or manipulative skills with the subject matter.

4. Using all locomotor and manipulative assessment rubrics provided in Appendix B, assess the performance levels of an elementary age student.

Internet Resources

About.com: Learning Disabilities. Discusses the importance of motor skills.
http://learningdisabilities.about.com/od/gi/p/grossmotor skill.htm

Essortment. "Information and advice you want to know" about helping children with motor skills.
http://papa.essortment.com/motorskillschi_rgxx.htm

National Association for Sport and Physical Education. The professional organization that develops standards and supports quality sport and physical activity programs to promote healthy behaviors.
www.aahperd.org/naspe/

PE Central. Information about developmentally appropriate physical education programs for children.
www.pecentral.org

PELinks4U. P.E. news, articles, ideas for lesson plans and games.
www.pelinks4u.org

Bibliography

Barton, G. V., K. Fordyce, and K. Kirby. 1999. The importance of the development of motor skills to children. *Teaching Elementary Physical Education* 10(4): 9–11.

Calfas, K., and A. Taylor. 1994. The effects of physical activity on psychological variables in adolescents. *Pediatric Exercise Science* 6: 302–314.

Gallahue, D. L. 1996. *Developmental physical education for today's children*. Dubuque, IA: Brown & Benchmark.

Gallahue, D. L., and J. C. Ozmun. 2002. *Understanding motor development: Infants, children, adolescents, adults*. 5th ed. Boston: WCB/McGraw-Hill.

Graham, G., S. Holt/Hale, and M. Parker. 2007. *Children moving: A reflective approach to teaching physical education*. Mountain View, CA: Mayfield.

Mehrhof, J., and K. Ermler. 2000. *Two left feet and a beat*. Emporia, KS: Mirror Publishing.

———. 2001. *Physical essentials*. Emporia, KS: Mirror.

Summerford, C. 2000. *PE-4 me*. Champaign, IL: Human Kinetics.

QUICK LESSON 3.1
Olympic Runner

GRADES K–2

NASPE STANDARD 1 Students demonstrate competency in motor skills and movement patterns needed to perform a variety of physical activities.

LESSON OBJECTIVES

- Students identify and perform the advanced level of a running pattern.
- Students assess a partner's arm movement while the partner is running in place.
- Students assess a partner's knee lift while the partner is running in place.

EQUIPMENT NEEDED

- Pictures of runners (use those provided in this chapter or those in sports magazines), pencils, and paper
- Find pictures of runners who demonstrate mature arm and leg movement

PREPARATION TIME Fifteen minutes

KNOWLEDGE CONTENT Students will know that an advanced running pattern involves the following components:

- The trunk leans forward slightly.
- Arms move in a forward and backward direction.
- Knees are lifted high with heels coming close to the buttocks.
- Head looks forward.
- Large strides are taken.

CLASSROOM ACTIVITY

- Standing beside their desk in their own personal space, students practice swinging their arms in the front and back plane (as if they were running), keeping elbows close to the body with hands moving by the eyes and then by the hips.
- Jogging in place, students practice lifting their knees high while jogging.
- Students watch and assess a partner's movements while running in place.

  - The partner watches the arm swing and tells how the arms are moving.
  - The partner describes how high the knees are lifted when running.
  - The partner tells whether the runner's head is looking straight ahead.

ASSESSMENT

- Show students pictures of runners and ask them to comment on the runners' arm and leg movements.
- Give students a pencil and paper and ask them to draw a picture of a good runner. Have them concentrate on the legs and arms.
- Ask students to discuss what fast runners do with their arms, legs, and head in order to run faster.

SUCCESS FOR ALL Nonambulatory students could practice the arm movements slowly and fast. If possible, they could practice alternately lifting up each knee.

INTEGRATION WITH OTHER SUBJECT AREAS
To assist with developing a rhythmical pattern while running, combine language skills with locomotor skills, asking the student to say nursery rhymes, such as "One, Two, Buckle My Shoe," "Pease Porridge Hot," and "Humpty Dumpty" while moving their arms and lifting their knees.

GRADES K–2

NASPE STANDARD 2 Students demonstrate understanding of movement concepts, principles, strategies, and tactics as they apply to the learning and performance of physical activities.

LESSON OBJECTIVES

- Students demonstrate competency in performing various locomotor skills.
- Students demonstrate competency in meeting and parting from partner safely.
- Students apply principles of accelerate and decelerate.

EQUIPMENT NEEDED

- Four cones to mark the play area, two on each end 20 yards apart
- Class list for teacher to record students' locomotor skills

PREPARATION TIME Two minutes

KNOWLEDGE CONTENT Practicing the various locomotor skills will assist students in the following ways:

- Identifying the difference between galloping and skipping, jumping and hopping
- Demonstrating their ability to decelerate and accelerate safely

CLASSROOM TO PLAYGROUND ACTIVITY

Students line up across the play area facing a partner. Using the locomotor skill called by the teacher, they perform that skill toward their partner, meet the partner in the middle, touching the body part identified by the teacher, and then return to the starting line. For example, gallop and touch elbow to elbow, skip and touch wrists, slide and touch ankle to ankle. Emphasize decelerating as students approach their partner and accelerating as they return to their starting position.

ASSESSMENT As students perform the various locomotor patterns, the teacher will record which students are able to perform the skills of gallop, skip, jump, and hop (see rubrics in Appendix B and example below).

SUCCESS FOR ALL For nonambulatory students, a partner could do a variety of "meet and part" activities using only the upper extremities.

INTEGRATION WITH OTHER SUBJECT AREAS

After children meet in the middle and touch the appropriate body part, have them count to ten by twos and then return to their starting position. They could also spell their name or spelling word before returning to the starting position.

Hop Rubric				
STUDENT NAME _____				
	Still Learning	**Improving**	**Good**	**Superb**
Body lean	None	Slight	Adequate	Relaxed
Arm swing	None	Slight	Adequate	Powerful
Nonsupport leg	Frequently touches the ground	Extremely low or extremely high	Parallel to ground	Parallel and powerful lift

GRADES 3–6

NASPE STANDARD 3 Students participate regularly in physical activity.

LESSON OBJECTIVES

- Students demonstrate cardiovascular fitness.
- Students sustain moderate to vigorous activity while playing partner kickball.
- Students demonstrate kicking and fielding skills.

EQUIPMENT NEEDED Two bases and one ball per set of partners

PREPARATION TIME Two minutes

KNOWLEDGE CONTENT Student participation in moderate to vigorous activity promotes the following:

- The ability to demonstrate endurance while playing a game
- The ability to try one's best during a game situation
- A feeling that a cardiovascular workout makes one feel good

CLASSROOM TO PLAYGROUND ACTIVITY Divide the class into partners and have the partners place the bases 20 to 30 feet apart. One player is the pitcher and the other is the kicker. The pitcher rolls the ball to the kicker, who kicks the ball, runs to the other base, and tries to return to home base before the pitcher retrieves the ball and returns to the starting position. Each player kicks three times before the players switch positions.

ASSESSMENT The teacher discusses with students how they felt when they played the positions of kicker and pitcher.

SUCCESS FOR ALL This activity could be played on an asphalt play area so that a child in a wheelchair could be pushed by a classmate in order to round the bases. The child in the wheelchair could throw the ball instead of kicking it.

INTEGRATION WITH OTHER SUBJECT AREAS Students could graph the number of bases run by each student, or they could determine the percentage of bases completed in three kicking attempts.

GRADES 4–6

NASPE STANDARD 4 Students achieve and maintain a health-enhancing level of physical fitness.

LESSON OBJECTIVES

- Students use upper-body strength and abdominal strength while practicing throwing and catching skills.
- Students understand the importance of overall fitness when performing motor skills.

EQUIPMENT NEEDED Two cones spread about 20 yards apart and one foam softball for each pair of students

PREPARATION TIME Two minutes

KNOWLEDGE CONTENT Having students use upper-body muscles and abdominal muscles before performing an overhand throw helps them understand the following:

- That strong arm muscles contribute to more power when throwing
- That strong abdominal muscles contribute to more power when rotating hips when throwing

CLASSROOM TO PLAYGROUND ACTIVITY

Divide the class into partners. All students are on one side of the play area with one partner standing behind the other. The person standing behind has one foam softball. When that partner says "go," the other runs out to the middle of the area and stops. The stationary partner throws the ball to the runner, who catches the ball and runs back to stand behind his or her partner. Continue in this format performing the following activities:

- The students in front lie on their tummy with their feet close to their partner. When the partner says "go," they push up to a standing position and then run out to receive the throw.
- The students in front lie on their back with their head close to their partner's feet. When the partner says "go," they sit up and then run out to receive the throw.
- The students in front stand; on the "go" command they run to the opposite side and then return, running toward their partner and catching the thrown ball.

ASSESSMENT Peer assessment: The throwing partner provides feedback to the catching partner regarding the catcher's ability to get up off the ground quickly and run out to catch the ball.

SUCCESS FOR ALL Students in wheelchairs could wheel themselves out to the middle of the floor to receive the throw. When they throw, they may need to be closer to the catcher than the other throwers are. If the task is to lie on the tummy first, they could touch their tummy before going to receive the pass.

INTEGRATION WITH OTHER SUBJECT AREAS

The thrower could call out the name of a state, and the catcher would try to call out the capital city of the state identified while catching the ball.

CLASSROOM LEARNING STATION 3.1
Fine Motor Station

GRADES K–6

NASPE STANDARD 1 Students demonstrate competency in motor skills and movement patterns needed to perform a variety of physical activities.

LESSON OBJECTIVES

- Students demonstrate the ability to use fingers and hands with control.
- Students demonstrate the ability to manipulate small objects using fingers and hands.

EQUIPMENT NEEDED

- One spin top per student
- Assorted buttons for each student
- Clothespins and cotton balls for each student
- One set of jacks for each pair of students
- One set of marbles for each pair of students

PREPARATION TIME Five minutes

KNOWLEDGE CONTENT Practicing the fine motor skills will help students with the following:

- Writing abilities
- Cutting abilities
- Manipulating small objects

CLASSROOM ACTIVITIES Students will progress in pairs to stations where the following activities are performed:

- Spin a top using the right or left hand and jump, hop, or perform jumping jacks until the top stops spinning.
- Sort buttons according to size, color, and shape.
- Use clothespins to pick up and sort colored cotton balls.
- Play a game of jacks.
- Play a game of marbles.

ASSESSMENT Peer assessment: Partners will provide feedback regarding the partner's success in performing the skills.

SUCCESS FOR ALL If students are unable to perform jumping jacks, they could move their arms in a jumping jack pattern. If fine motor skills are limited, they could tell a partner which button belongs in a certain color, size, or shape pile. Students could use fingers to sort colored cotton balls if they are unable to manipulate a clothespin. Jacks could be played using a larger ball and beanbags to increase success of those with limited fine motor abilities.

INTEGRATION WITH OTHER SUBJECT AREAS
Spin the top and try to say the alphabet or count to 100 before the top stops spinning. Spell words while picking up jacks. For another jacks variation, the partner gives an addition problem and the player must solve the problem by picking up the correct number of jacks.

SPECIAL EVENT 3.1
Who Wants to Be a Millionaire?

GRADES K–2

NASPE STANDARD 2 Students demonstrate understanding of movement concepts, principles, strategies, and tactics as they apply to the learning and performance of physical activities.

LESSON OBJECTIVES

- Students practice locomotor, nonlocomotor, and manipulative skills.
- Students demonstrate knowledge of the correct movement forms.
- Students enjoy the challenge of correctly answering the questions.

EQUIPMENT NEEDED Poker chips, buttons, dried beans, or the like

PREPARATION TIME Two minutes

KNOWLEDGE CONTENT Students will demonstrate specific knowledge of all locomotor, nonlocomotor, and manipulative skills as they analyze the skills individually and use the skills in game situations.

CLASSROOM ACTIVITY The teacher reads age-appropriate questions regarding specific aspects of correct movement forms or relating to how these forms are used in various sports. Students raise their hand when they wish to answer the question. If they verbally answer correctly, they must also perform the skill correctly and then they win a poker chip, a button, or a dried bean. Each object is worth the amount designated by the teacher. Here are some sample questions:

- How many feet are used in a hop?
- How many feet are used in a jump?

- Which foot should lead during a gallop?
- A step and a hop combined describes which locomotor skill?
- Should arms cross in front of the body when running?
- When landing on both feet at the same time, what kind of locomotor skill is performed?
- What locomotor skill starts on one foot and lands on the other foot?
- When throwing the ball, should a thrower step forward with the same foot as the throwing arm?
- What body part should the arm reach for when following through after throwing a ball?
- How high should a ball bounce when dribbling a ball?
- Should players swing their arms when volleying a ball?
- Name a sport that uses a striking skill.
- Name a sport that uses dribbling a ball with the feet.
- Name a skill that made Michael Jordan famous.
- What skills do baseball players use?
- Should soccer players be able to kick with both feet? Why or why not?

ASSESSMENT Teachers will observe how well students are able to answer the above questions.

SUCCESS FOR ALL Students unable to verbalize their answers could write them on a chalkboard or demonstrate the correct answer.

INTEGRATION WITH OTHER SUBJECT AREAS
The questions could be written on poster boards and students could progress to each poster board, read the question, and write the correct answer on a sheet of paper.

CHAPTER 4

Exercise Concepts and Fitness Education

The purpose of this chapter is to introduce you to concepts of exercise and fitness education so that you can present them to your elementary school children in a basic and meaningful manner.

Objectives

After studying this chapter, you will be able to do the following:

- Describe and discuss the concepts of fitness education and wellness.

- Discuss the terms *physical activity* and *physical fitness* and explain the differences between them.

- List and describe health risk factors and what children can do to reduce them.

- List several benefits of exercise and physical activity.

- Describe the basic components of the cardiorespiratory system.

- Identify and discuss the five components of health-related fitness.

- Describe several exercise principles that should be followed to improve physical fitness.

- Discuss how you can promote healthy lifestyles.

P ete and Carol are elementary classroom teachers who teach at the same school. They both have vivid memories of performing strenuous fitness activities (e.g., push-ups and sit-ups) during their K–12 P.E. experiences, but their memories are very different. Carol was always an active child, playing outdoors whenever possible. She mastered physical skills quickly and enjoyed participating in group games and sports. She viewed the exercises as a challenge and took them on willingly. She was good at physical challenges and enjoyed being successful when performing fitness activities.

Pete, on the other hand, was the indoor type. As a child, he read extensively and interacted primarily with his parents, who were also indoor people. Pete rarely played games or sports, as he had trouble mastering the physical skills necessary to be successful. In school, Pete dreaded fitness activities. He couldn't do even one push-up and could do only a few sit-ups. He was embarrassed when he had to perform these types of activities in front of his peers. Pete learned to avoid fitness and exercise activities in his life, whereas Carol learned the benefits of physical activities and fitness and appreciated the value of including daily physical activity in her life.

What Is Fitness Education?

In several ways, an individual's attitudes and values are formed at a very early age. Children who enjoy fitness activities and exercise when they are young will more than likely carry these experiences over to later years and adulthood. A quality, developmentally appropriate physical education program would have served the needs of both Pete and Carol. Together, elementary school classroom teachers and physical educators can build such a program—one that will encourage all their students to value and be successful in fitness and physical activities.

In the new century, fitness, exercise, health, and wellness will take on added importance as the public deals with the impact of increasing health care costs and the advancing age of the population. Issues such as proper nutrition, the deadly consequences of

Jumping rope is a fun way for children to build cardiorespiratory endurance and muscle strength.

smoking, and the benefits of exercise for the prevention of chronic disease will be important topics to schoolchildren. However, fitness and exercise may have been dismissed by certain adults because of past unpleasant experiences in physical education or athletics. The individual who learns the benefits of physical activity and fitness through a well-organized and meaningful physical education program will quite likely develop an appreciation for the value of exercise in daily life. Experience with quality, daily, well-organized physical education with attention to fitness and movement activities goes a long way toward increasing the value of physical activity in the lifestyle of the individual.

Elementary school physical education that is meaningful and purposeful explores many movement forms (e.g., dance, fitness, fundamental movements, sport skills). That efficient and enjoyable movement should be a primary purpose of elementary school physical education is substantiated by the nature of the NASPE national standards for physical education (NASPE 2004). Physical education has a role in the development of a healthy, active, physically skilled child as well. In fact, Standard 3 (participates regularly in physical activity) and Standard 4 (achieves and maintains a health-enhancing level of physical fitness) directly target the need for physical activity as an objective for the physically educated person (NASPE 2004). Therefore, elementary school classroom teachers will become fitness educators as well as movement educators.

Fitness education is a component of movement education. It may be defined as that part of the curriculum that emphasizes the importance of physical activity and physical fitness to a healthy and productive quality of life. Fitness education includes the why and how of physical activity, physical fitness, and exercise. Fitness education is not just fitness testing or preparing for fitness tests. Whereas the movement educator might be interested in how a child moves a ball around a gym (correct technique and efficiency of movement), the fitness educator is interested in having the child improve the cardiorespiratory and musculoskeletal systems at the same time. The focus goes beyond the ability to throw, catch, hit objects with an implement, and create efficient body movement.

Fitness education emphasizes an ability to sustain a reasonable intensity of exercise so that the individual can perform daily activities as well as sport activities with a minimum of stress and effort. Fitness education usually targets the development of **health-related fitness,** which focuses on those aspects of fitness that are related to improving health and achieving an active lifestyle. The components of health-related physical fitness include cardiorespiratory function, body composition, muscular strength and endurance, and flexibility.

It is difficult to develop a lifelong appreciation for exercise and activity without the skill to enjoy many of the activities that improve fitness. Therefore an additional goal of fitness education is to integrate the learning of skill with an appreciation for fitness and exercise. Performance objectives that require speed, agility, strength, explosive power, and coordination are often combined with cardiorespiratory fitness and muscular strength and endurance to constitute **skill-related fitness.** To accomplish the goal of providing meaningful fitness education within the movement education unit, the classroom teacher will find it helpful to be familiar with terms and concepts involving physical fitness, physical activity, health, wellness, and exercise.

WELLNESS VERSUS HEALTH

Health has been defined by the World Health Organization as "physical, mental, and social well-being, not merely the absence of disease and infirmity" (WHO 1947, 1). Wellness goes one step further. **Wellness** is generally more of a holistic term, encompassing emotional, spiritual, and vocational wellness as well as the physical, intellectual, and social aspects. Physical fitness is a necessary component of physical wellness and health, although a high level of fitness does not guarantee total wellness, nor does it guarantee good health.

Health promotion is the current preferred term for "the science and art of helping people change their lifestyle to move toward a state of optimal health" (O'Donnell 1986). Research is beginning to show that positive health behaviors such as staying active during childhood may continue into adulthood (Malina 1996). If a healthy attitude can be developed in the elementary grades, it will likely track into adulthood.

PHYSICAL FITNESS VERSUS PHYSICAL ACTIVITY

An important component of wellness, **physical fitness** usually refers to an element of vigor and energy needed to perform moderate to vigorous levels of physical activity without undue fatigue. The American College of Sports Medicine defines physical fitness as "a set of attributes that people have or achieve that relates to the ability to perform physical activity" (ACSM 2000, 4). The physically fit person usually has the ability to sustain a higher level of exercise intensity for a longer period of time than someone who is not fit.

Cardiorespiratory fitness is an important aspect of physical fitness and is related to the capacity of the cardiovascular and pulmonary systems to deliver oxygen to the muscles and tissues. It may also be termed *aerobic fitness*. Research shows that higher levels of cardiorespiratory fitness are related to reduced risk of cardiovascular disease and other chronic diseases. The surgeon general's report released in 1996 confirmed the importance of physical activity in reducing the risk of chronic diseases, such as coronary heart disease, diabetes mellitus, hypertension, and some cancers, and stated that significant health benefits could be obtained by regular moderate physical activity, such as 30 minutes of brisk walking per day (USDHHS 1996).

It is important to remember that most discussions of aerobic fitness focus on adults. Since children are arguably the most active segment of the population, the point can be made that most children are not all that unfit and the goal of fitness education is to teach children the best ways to preserve their natural tendency for activity. Motivating the child to remain active and providing activities that promote physical activity and physical exercise are the best ways to nurture physical fitness. In short, the fitness educator must strive to keep the *physical* in physical education and movement education.

A better idea than trying to achieve a measurement of physical fitness in each child is to provide opportunities for ample physical activity at school and to encourage physical activity during nonschool hours. *Physical activity* is defined as any bodily movement produced by skeletal muscles that results in energy expenditure above the resting level (Casperson, Powell, and Christianson 1985). A major goal of elementary school physical education as defined in the NASPE standards is to encourage physical activity in such a way that students will want to participate regularly in physical activity. In this way children will embrace an active lifestyle and be started on their road to maintaining a health-enhancing level of physical fitness.

PHYSICAL ACTIVITY VERSUS EXERCISE

The terms *exercise* and *physical activity* may seem synonymous, but they are not. Whereas children usually engage in physical activity or play, adults usually exercise or work out. Recall from Chapter 1 that exercise is physical activity that is planned, structured, repetitive, and purposive, in the sense that improvement or maintenance of physical fitness is an objective (Caspersen, Powell, and Christianson 1985). Usually children don't exercise or work out; they play or do physical activity.

In an effort to determine whether children are anywhere close to meeting the goals set forth in the NASPE recommendations, a number of studies have attempted to quantify physical activity in children. These research efforts generally show that children are not able to accumulate a great deal of activity minutes when limited to their physical education classes. Activity during recess adds to the total, but if the activity during school is the only measure, most children would fall short. During a class, most elementary school students do not achieve the physical activity goal recommended by the surgeon general's report, and the class may meet only three times a week. However, children are naturally active. It may be that they get a good helping of physical activity during the day, although not all at

A walk during the school day can be a fun contribution toward the recommended 60 minutes or more of daily physical activity. Classmates hold hands with a child with special needs to help him keep his balance, enabling the entire class to enjoy a walk together.

once. Whereas adults generally consume their physical activity requirement in one helping during a well-thought-out exercise or workout session, children are more likely to benefit from an accumulation of activities (Pangrazi, Corbin, and Welk 1996).

The Council on Physical Education for Children (COPEC) has expanded recommendations for physical activity for children ages 5–12 (COPEC 2004). Sixty minutes of daily physical activity is the minimum amount recommended, with up to several hours of age-appropriate activity attained during most days of the week. Activity should be accumulated during the day, but with long bouts of continuous activity such as long-distance running not recommended for meeting these guidelines. Bouts of 15 or more minutes at a time (with brief rest periods several times during the day) are now preferred (COPEC 2004).

Exercise and Health Risk Factors

If you watch many popular television talk shows, you can't help but notice the attention given to lowering blood pressure, eating low-fat diets to lower cholesterol, reducing obesity, and of course giving up cigarette smoking. These are all meant to lower the risk of developing a chronic disease such as heart disease or diabetes. Conditions and behaviors that increase the risk of developing a chronic disease are called **health risk factors.** Increasing daily physical activity is now touted as a way to improve your health and lower your risk factors, and programs range from simple walking and resistance training to interesting regimens such as Tae-Bo. Improving your health by targeting different risk factors is important, since they have conclusively been linked with the development of several chronic diseases.

Chronic diseases such as coronary heart disease take a devastating toll on the health and well-being of the population. Coronary heart disease remains the leading cause of death in the United States, despite all the knowledge of what it takes to reduce its risk. The American Heart Association has identified the six primary, modifiable risk factors for the development of coronary heart disease:

1. High cholesterol
2. Hypertension (high blood pressure)
3. Smoking
4. Obesity
5. Inactivity, or sedentary lifestyle
6. Diabetes

Modifiable risk factors can be reduced by adopting a healthier lifestyle. Some risk factors, such as family history, race, age, and gender, cannot be changed. Occasionally a disease situation will cause a risk factor to be very difficult to change. For example, someone who is predisposed to having high cholesterol might be able to control it only with intensive management and drug therapy. For a large percentage of the population, however, risk factors such as high blood pressure and high cholesterol can be improved with attention to positive changes in lifestyle. Classroom Learning Station 4.1 (Coronary Heart Disease Risk Factors) at the end of the chapter provides a review of these risk factors.

Coronary heart disease, also termed *coronary artery disease,* begins early in life and progresses over time. The basic cause is a gradual accumulation of cholesterol deposits in the arteries that deliver blood to the heart. The deposits harden to form a plaque that may build up to the point that blood flow to the heart is reduced and the heart muscle does not receive enough oxygen, thereby causing chest pain, or angina. In severe cases, the artery becomes completely blocked, resulting in a heart attack. The artery clogging process begins early, maybe even in childhood, and continues slowly throughout life until it reaches a point where symptoms such as shortness of breath, weakness, chest pain, or dizziness begin to occur. By the time these symptoms appear, an artery may already be dangerously blocked, requiring medical interventions to treat the problem.

Coronary heart disease is usually thought of as a disease of the adult, but poor habits developed during childhood lead to increased risk as the child grows into adolescence and adulthood. Genetics can play a major role in the development of coronary heart disease, but it is not the only factor. A poor lifestyle exacerbates the process, putting individuals who smoke and those who have high blood pressure, high cholesterol, diabetes, or obesity at greater risk. Children as young as 12 years of age may exhibit risk factors for the development of heart disease (Berenson et al. 1988).

The elementary school teacher can implement classroom lessons to encourage the understanding of these risk factors and discuss how increased physical activity and other lifestyle modifications such as proper nutrition can help. One such activity that would be appropriate for older children is described in Quick Lesson 4.1 at the end of the chapter (How Arteries Become Clogged). Each of these risk factors is discussed briefly in the following paragraphs.

HIGH CHOLESTEROL

Cholesterol is a fatty substance that circulates in the bloodstream and is necessary for the proper functioning of the body. Excess cholesterol, however, can clog arteries. More important than the total cholesterol level is the amount of high-density cholesterol (HDL) relative to low-density cholesterol (LDL). HDL seems to have a protective effect against coronary heart disease and is usually termed the good cholesterol. Several studies have shown that physical activity can have a positive effect on cholesterol levels. Children can exhibit positive changes in this important risk factor as a result of a program that targets improved health and increased cardiorespiratory fitness levels. A total cholesterol level of less than 170 (mg/dL) is considered acceptable for children and adolescents. A level of 170 to 199 (mg/dL) is considered borderline, and a level at or above 200 (mg/dL) is high (NCEP 1992).

HYPERTENSION (HIGH BLOOD PRESSURE)

Blood pressure is a bit mysterious to many individuals not involved in health care. In fact, even adolescents and young adults may not be able to describe what blood pressure is or what their own blood pressure value would be if measured. Blood pressure is the force of blood against the walls of the arteries as the heart pumps blood to the body and is reported in millimeters of mercury (Hg) as systolic pressure over diastolic pressure. Systolic pressure, represented by the top number, represents the pressure when the heart contracts to push blood into the arteries. Diastolic pressure, represented by the bottom number, indicates pressure in the arteries during the resting, or noncontraction, phase of the heartbeat.

Hypertension in adults is classified as a systolic pressure greater than or equal to 140 mm Hg or diastolic greater than or equal to 90 mm Hg, confirmed by measurement on at least two separate occasions (ACSM 2000). Optimal values are below 120 for systolic and below 80 for diastolic. Blood pressure that stays between 120–139 mm Hg systolic and/or 80–89 mm Hg diastolic is considered to be prehypertension (NHBPEP 2004). Prehypertension is a relatively new term that substitutes for the former designation of borderline blood pressure. Prehypertension is blood pressure that could be described as high normal and indicates that lifestyle modifications are probably necessary to prevent the progressive rise in blood pressure that occurs with aging from reaching hypertensive levels.

Blood pressure standards for children are less definitive than those for adults. The blood pressure of children is normally lower than that of adults and steadily increases as children grow older. Blood pressure is also higher for taller children. Therefore, recommendations are based on height as well as age and gender. This approach prevents misclassification of children at the extremes of normal growth. The National High Blood Pressure Education Program (NHBPEP) has recently updated their guidelines and revised their blood pressure tables, which include the 50th, 90th, 95th, and 99th percentiles for blood pressure by gender, age, and height (NHBPEP 2004). Both hypertension and prehypertension are becoming significant health issues in children because of the strong association of high blood pressure with overweight and the increase in overweight children now being observed (NHBPEP 2004). In fact, hypertension has been detected in approximately 30 percent of overweight children (Sorof and Daniels 2002). A prehypertensive range is now identified for children as blood pressure between the 90th and 95th percentiles. Elevated blood pressure that persists on repeated measurement at the 95th percentile or greater for height, age, and gender is considered to be hypertensive. So that the elementary school classroom teacher can have

Blood pressure measurement can be used as a learning experience.

a further understanding of blood pressures in children, examples of prehypertensive ranges for children ages 5–12 are given in Table 4.1 for the 50th, 75th, and 90th height percentiles. Height percentiles are determined using the newly revised CDC growth charts. These are available at www.cdc.gov/growthcharts.

High blood pressure is a risk factor for stroke as well as for coronary heart disease. It is a *silent* killer because it often has no symptoms. High blood pressure may not be a significant problem in most children, but they still can be made aware of what the mysterious little cuff that goes around their arm is all about. High blood pressure and higher than desirable cholesterol levels have been found in unfit and overweight children (Kuntzleman and Reiff 1992; Ogden, Flegal, Carroll, and Johnson 2002; Sallis and McKenzie 1991; Sorof and Daniels 2002).

If time and resources permit, classroom teachers can use measuring blood pressure as a learning experience, not only to explain blood pressure but to check on their students' current blood pressure. It is important to be aware, however, that blood pressure equipment designed for adults will be too large for most children. Pediatric cuffs are needed to accurately determine children's blood pressures. School nurses, local medical professionals, Red Cross or American Heart Association volunteers, paramedics and firefighters, or exercise science students from a nearby university may be willing to volunteer their time to help measure children's blood pressures. Quick Lesson 4.2 provides information about measuring blood pressures. The American Heart Association can also be called upon to provide information and kits for measuring heart rates and blood pressures.

SMOKING

The negative effects of smoking should be emphasized during children's elementary schooling. Children can appreciate the impact of smoke on their breathing. The American Lung Association and the American Heart Association can provide learning materials regarding the negative aspects of smoking. A simple activity using a soda straw can show children the impact of blocked air passages on breathing (see Instant Activity 4.1).

OVERWEIGHT AND OBESITY

Overweight and obesity have become a national epidemic among children as well as adults in the United States. Obesity officially joined smoking, hypertension, high cholesterol, and physical inactivity as a risk factor for heart disease in 1998 (Eckel and Krauss 1998). The terms *overweight* and *obese* are usually defined by Body Mass Index (BMI), a weight-for-height method of estimating a desired weight for a certain individual. (BMI as a measure of body composition is discussed later in this chapter.) The BMI used to indicate obesity in children will depend upon the source. The Centers for Disease Control (CDC) does not use the term obese when describing body weight due to the sensitive nature of the term; therefore, children above the 95th percentile BMI are classified as being overweight with no designation for obesity (CDC 2005). The CDC reports that 16 percent of children ages 6–19 years were in the overweight category in 2002, an increase of 45 percent over estimates from similar population studies obtained in 1988–94 (CDC 2005). The American Obesity Association (AOA) defines obesity in children as a BMI at or above the 95th percentile for a child of that age and sex. A BMI equal to or greater than 85 percent up to but not including 95 percent is considered overweight (AOA 2002). Using the AOA criteria, approximately 30.3 percent of children ages 6–11 are overweight, which includes 15.3 percent defined by the AOA criteria as obese (AOA 2002). There is also increasing concern that overweight children risk becoming overweight and obese adults. Lack of activity and an increase in the amount of time spent watching television and playing video games are often blamed for the increased prevalence of obesity in children.

The importance of proper nutrition to reducing obesity and other risk factors such as high cholesterol and diabetes cannot be overlooked. Nutrition is arguably the most critical determinant of body composition, the relative ratio of body fat to lean muscle in an individual. Although overweight and obesity are the result of a myriad of factors including genetics, an energy

TABLE 4.1 Classification of Prehypertension (90th–95th Blood Pressure Percentile) for Systolic Blood Pressure (SBP) and Diastolic Blood Pressure (DBP) for Children at the 50th, 75th, and 90th Height Percentiles

Age	50th Height Percentile		75th Height Percentile		90th Height Percentile	
	SBP*	DBP*	SBP*	DBP*	SBP*	DBP*
GIRLS						
5 years	106–110	68–72	107–111	69–73	109–112	69–73
6 years	108–111	70–74	109–113	70–74	110–114	71–75
7 years	109–113	71–75	111–115	72–76	112–116	72–76
8 years	111–115	72–76	113–116	73–77	114–118	74–78
9 years	113–117	73–77	114–118	74–78	116–119	75–79
10 years	115–119	74–78	116–120	75–79	118–121	76–80
11 years	117–121	75–79	118–122	76–80	119–123	77–81
12 years	119–123	76–80	120–124	77–81	121–125	78–82
BOYS						
5 years	108–112	68–72	110–114	69–73	111–115	69–74
6 years	110–114	70–74	111–115	71–75	113–117	72–76
7 years	111–115	72–76	113–117	73–77	114–118	74–78
8 years	112–116	73–78	114–118	74–79	115–119	75–79
9 years	114–117	75–79	115–119	76–80	117–121	76–81
10 years	115–119	75–80	117–121	76–81	119–122	77–81
11 years	117–121	78–82	119–123	77–81	120–124	78–82
12 years	120–123	78–82	121–125	77–82	123–127	78–82

SOURCE: Adapted from the National High Blood Pressure Education Program Working Group on High Blood Pressure in Children and Adolescents, The Fourth Report on the Diagnosis, Evaluation, and Treatment of High Blood Pressure in Children and Adolescents, *Pediatrics* 114(2):555–576 (Aug 2004).

*Measurement in mm Hg; measured on three separate occasions. Blood pressures below these levels are considered normal. Blood pressures in these ranges are prehypertensive, and blood pressures above these levels are classified as hypertension for a child of that age, height, and sex.

intake in the form of calories from food that exceeds energy outflow in terms of exercise and physical activity remains the most probable cause. In other words, when an individual consumes more calories than needed for daily energy production, weight is gained. Daily energy needs can be increased by participating in regular physical activity, thus reducing the amount of weight gained.

The cause of overweight and obesity is not always too much food; sometimes it is the type of foods that American children eat. Snacking, choosing from vending machines, and eating fast foods add considerable fat to the diet. The explosion of increased overweight and obesity in schoolchildren has prompted some states to pass legislation prohibiting vending machine sales of snacks and sodas on school grounds. This effort is targeted at decreasing the daily intake of fat and calories. Besides being loaded with calories, fat in the diet contributes to other problems as well. Diets high in fats, especially the saturated fats, have been linked to coronary heart disease and Type 2 diabetes as well as obesity. The observed increase in childhood overweight and obesity is serious enough to have

received the attention of the federal government. In 2004, the Child Nutrition and WIC Reauthorization Act was signed into law. This legislation requires schools that receive federal funds for food service programs to adopt a wellness policy by the beginning of the 2006–07 school year that must include goals for nutrition education and nutrition guidelines for the foods available at the school on any particular day. Programs such as these are definitely a step in the right direction. More information regarding these government efforts can be obtained by accessing www.healthinschools. org/ejournal/2004/July1.htm. Obesity, overweight, and body composition are discussed with regard to diet and proper nutrition later in the chapter.

PHYSICAL INACTIVITY

The American Heart Association added physical inactivity to the list of primary risk factors when large population studies began confirming that a sedentary lifestyle was an important contributor to the development of several chronic diseases. Research has shown

INSTANT ACTIVITY 4.1
Impaired Breathing

Grades K–6

Equipment Needed

Nose clips and straws

Activity

Have students hold their nose (nose clips, if available, work well) and breathe through a narrow cocktail straw or a round coffee stirrer. Emphasize that this is what it would feel like if you couldn't get enough air when breathing. Then have students run in place for 30 seconds and try to breathe through the straw. Have them describe how they felt when trying to exercise while not getting much air. Discuss the types of situations in which a person might not be able to get enough air. This is a good opportunity to discuss the effect of smoking and pollution on breathing and also the effect of asthma.

---

that physical activity and exercise reduce the development of high blood pressure, obesity, and high cholesterol that increase the risk of coronary heart disease and are also helpful in the management of Type 1 and Type 2 diabetes. Additionally, programs that emphasize an active lifestyle including aerobic exercise have been successful in producing weight loss in children (Epstein et al. 1982, 1985). Studies also suggest that childhood physical activity habits will continue into adulthood (Raitakari et al. 1994). Elementary school teachers can help their students by emphasizing the value of physical activity as a means to improve health and reduce these risk factors. They must strive to emphasize the *physical* aspect of movement education.

DIABETES

Diabetes mellitus is a chronic disease in which the body does not produce enough insulin or does not properly use the insulin it does produce. Diabetes is progressive and has no cure, although it can be controlled. The American Heart Association reports that adults with diabetes are two to four times more likely to have heart disease or stroke than adults without diabetes (AHA 2002).

Diabetes is classified into two types. Type 1 was formerly called juvenile diabetes since it typically presents itself during childhood. In Type 1 diabetes the pancreas fails to produce insulin. Insulin, a pancreatic hormone, is used to facilitate the uptake of glucose into the cells of the body so that energy may be produced. The individual with Type 1 diabetes must receive insulin by exogenous means to survive. Type 1 diabetes most often occurs when the body's immune system mistakenly destroys the insulin-producing cells in the pancreas. Children with Type 1 diabetes are not usually overweight and in fact may experience weight loss. Daily physical activity improves the management of Type 1 diabetes; however, daily injections of insulin will still be required. Type 1 diabetes is a very different disease from the other type.

Type 2 diabetes (formerly called adult-onset diabetes) is caused by the body's inability to make enough insulin or to use it properly. It is more common in adults but is currently on the rise in young populations. The American Diabetes Association reports that children with Type 2 diabetes are usually overweight (80 percent or more are overweight or obese) (ADA 2000). Type 2 diabetes typically is diagnosed in children over the age of ten who are in middle to late puberty; however, as progressively more children become overweight in the population, the incidence of Type 2 diabetes is increasing in younger children (ADA 2000). Genetics again has an important role in the development of both Type 1 and Type 2 diabetes; however, poor diet, lack of physical activity, and increased obesity are major determinants of risk, especially in Type 2 diabetes. Type 2 diabetes may be controlled without daily insulin injections in many cases. Meticulous control of glucose by self-monitoring, diet and exercise adjustments, and perhaps medication, are required to keep Type 2 diabetes in check. Minorities of non-European ancestry, such as Americans of African, Asian, and Native American descent, are more at risk of developing Type 2 diabetes.

Children with both types of diabetes are encouraged to eat a healthy diet (especially decreasing calorie intake and limiting foods high in fat) and participate in daily physical activity.

To recap, the six major controllable risk factors for the development of coronary heart disease are high cholesterol, high blood pressure, smoking, obesity, inactivity, and diabetes. It is appropriate for elementary school children to be able to identify these risk factors, describe their negative impact on a person's health, and identify ways to lessen these risks. Classroom Learning Station 4.1 provides an activity to reinforce this important topic.

Daily physical activity can help prevent obesity and manage Type 1 and Type 2 diabetes.

The Human Body and Activity

Elementary school teachers need to understand how the cardiorespiratory system operates, how children perceive exercise, and how children respond to different types of activity.

THE ENGINE FOR ACTIVITY: THE CARDIORESPIRATORY SYSTEM

The heart, lungs, arteries, veins, and even smaller blood vessels make up the **cardiorespiratory system.** Basic information about the heart can be given to students as early as the first grade, although it must be simplified so that the young child can comprehend it. One way to help children understand how the heart works is to create a game such as the one presented in Instant Activity 4.2.

The Heart, Lungs, and Circulation Oxygen is a substance in the air that cannot be seen but is needed for life. Oxygen is taken up from the outside air during inhalation into the lungs and delivered via the blood to the muscles, where it is used to produce energy. At the muscle, carbon dioxide is formed as a byproduct of energy production. It is taken up by the blood at the muscle and transported back to the lungs, where it is removed during exhalation.

The heart is the blood (and oxygen) pump for the body. The right side of the heart (the right atrium and the right ventricle) is responsible for taking blood that has returned from the muscles and tissues of the body by way of the veins and sending it to the lungs so that more oxygen can be loaded. Oxygen from inhaled atmospheric air is delivered to the bronchial airways of the lungs via the trachea.

INSTANT ACTIVITY 4.2

The Heart Beating

· ·

Grades K–3
Equipment Needed

None

Activity

Children use their fist to represent the heart. Have them make a fist and position it about where they think it is on the body. Have them relax and then close the fist to simulate pumping blood. Point out that when the fist is closed it is like blood being forced out of the heart. As the fist relaxes, it is like the heart filling again with blood. The fist has to squeeze when blood is pushed out to the body; then it must relax to refill with blood. Each squeeze and release of the fist represents a beat. Have children demonstrate what happens with their fist as they walk, lie down, and run.

In the lungs, air moves from large passageways to smaller passageways to even smaller air sacs called alveoli, where a process called gas exchange occurs. As oxygen moves into the blood from the tiny air sacs (alveoli) in the lungs, carbon dioxide moves from the blood into the air sacs of the lungs to be expired during exhalation. Oxygen attaches itself to red blood cells within the blood and travels back to the left side of the heart. The left side of the heart (the left atrium and left ventricle) pumps this oxygenated blood through a large artery leaving the heart (aorta) into a system of arteries so that blood may be delivered to all the muscles and tissues of the body. Figure 4.1 is helpful for reviewing the circulatory system; Quick Lesson 4.3 is a good way to present this difficult concept to children.

Blood flows from the atria of the heart to the ventricles through valves. The valves open and close when blood flows from atria to the ventricles and from the ventricles to the lungs (right side) and to the body (left side). As the valves open and close, the sounds of the heart can be heard through a stethoscope. Children may listen to their heartbeat through a stethoscope. They can also count the number of times the heart beats per minute (**heart rate**) by using the stethoscope (see Instant Activity 4.3).

The heart acts as a pump, expelling about five quarts of blood each minute. The total amount of blood that

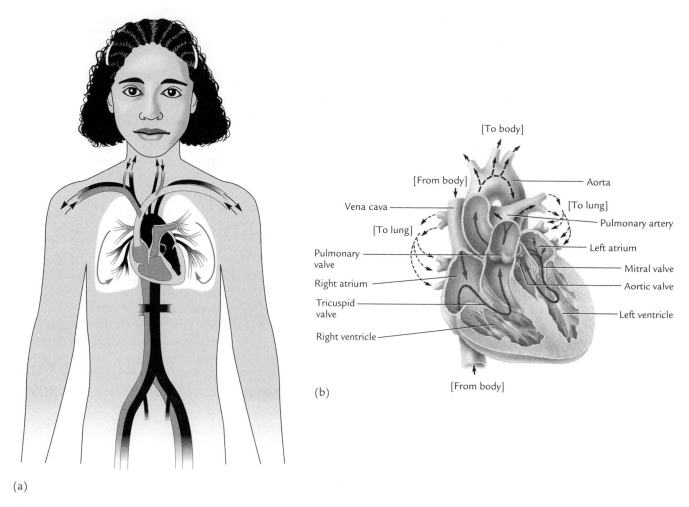

FIGURE 4.1 The Heart and Basic Circulation. Used, oxygen-poor blood enters the heart from the body through the vena cava. The right side of the heart pumps blood to the lungs, where blood picks up oxygen and discards carbon dioxide. Oxygen-rich blood flows back to the left side of the heart, where it is pumped through the aorta to the rest of the body's blood vessels. Valves in the heart prevent blood from flowing the wrong way.

can be pumped by the heart per minute depends on the amount that is pumped out with each beat (stroke volume) and the number of times the heart beats per minute. The well-conditioned heart will release more blood per beat, and its heart rate will be slower. The efficiency and capacity of the heart and lungs will vary depending on each child's individual abilities. The amount of physical activity in which the child engages will also affect the efficiency and capacity of the heart.

Physical Activity and Heart Rate Although many factors can influence heart rate, physically fit individuals usually have a lower resting heart rate, indicating that their heart is more efficient. Children's heart rates usually range from about 60 beats per minute to 80 or 90 beats per minute at rest and may increase to up to 200 beats per minute or more during vigorous

exercise. Children can be taught to monitor their own heart rate by taking a pulse rate. Each time blood is pumped out of the aorta, a pulse wave is created that travels through the arteries and can be felt if pressure is gently applied to certain points on the body. Generally the pulse is monitored at the carotid artery site (neck) or the radial site (wrist). Instant Activity 4.4 provides practice in taking pulses. Classroom Learning Station 4.2 (How to Determine the Heart Rate) provides instructions for taking a heart rate.

Physical activity and exercise cause the heart rate and breathing rate to increase. In someone who is not very fit, exercise causes the heart rate to reach high levels quickly and breathing to become rapid. In others it may take quite a bit of activity or a high intensity of exercise to elicit high heart rates. Instant Activity 4.5 provides a way to illustrate these concepts. The ability

INSTANT ACTIVITY 4.3
Listening to the Heart

Grades K–3

Equipment Needed

Stethoscopes (one for every two or three students) and alcohol wipes (for cleaning the ear pieces)

Activity

Each time the heart pushes blood from an atrium to a ventricle and from the ventricle to the body, valves of the heart open and close and make a sound. This sound can be heard with a stethoscope. Have children listen to the beat of the heart with a stethoscope. Have older children (grades 2–3) count the beats for six seconds. Start the count at zero and multiply by ten to get the heart rate for a minute. (You can just add a zero to your six-second count to get beats/minute.) Then have them run in place or march for a minute or two and listen again. They should hear a louder sound and more frequent beats. Discuss why the heart beats more rapidly with the exercise. This activity should be preceded by Instant Activity 4.2 if children have not previously reviewed the heartbeat concept.

to exercise at higher and higher intensities is increased with training. As the heart becomes more efficient, more physical activity can occur before becoming tired.

Perceiving Exercise Intensity   Children can learn to perceive how much effort they are putting forth to do an activity. Is the activity easy for them or is it difficult? Are they having to breathe hard to do the activity? How does their heart rate match up with the effort they are putting forth to do the activity? This concept is referred to as **perceived exertion.** Adults can become quite proficient at perceiving how hard they are working, and they rate their perceptions according to a scale called a **rating of perceived exertion (RPE).** Children can learn this skill as well.

The adult RPE scale is probably not appropriate for young children, but within limits children can perceive how much effort they are applying to the activity. For example, are they working really hard or just moderately hard? If they are working moderately hard, they can be expected to be able to exercise for a longer amount of time (continuous activity) than if they are working hard or very hard. This is important as

they determine how to pace themselves during activity. They can rate activity as very easy, easy, moderate, hard, and very hard as a beginning to perceiving their exertion. For young children, pictures with which to compare might work well. In fact, picture scales such as the children's OMNI scale of perceived exertion have been developed and validated for this purpose (Robertson et al. 2000). Quick Lesson 4.4 provides children with practice on perceiving intensity of activity.

Aerobic versus Anaerobic   Not all physical activities have the same effect on the body. With some activities you might be able to perform quite a while without taking a deep breath, whereas other activities cause you to become quite breathless and you have to slow down or stop. In most cases your response has to do with the intensity of the activity, or how hard you are working. If the exercise is moderate, you are able to do quite well. However, if the activity becomes very intense, you may or may not be able to continue. In many cases your ability to keep up with the activity will depend on how fit you are and how much activity you do on a daily basis. It also depends on the type of activity or exercise you're doing.

Exercise that is moderate enough that oxygen is delivered to the muscles at the same rate it is used is called aerobic. **Aerobic** means "with oxygen" and denotes an exercise intensity where you are able to have adequate oxygen delivered to the muscles. The activity is accomplished without stress and exhaustion. Brisk walking and jogging are of the aerobic type. The heart, although beating fast, is able to keep up with the oxygen requirement. The breathing rate, although increased, is also able to keep up with requirements. However, without being accustomed to this type of activity, a child will quickly become tired. Some individuals may be able to exercise continuously for 20 minutes or more, whereas others can barely go 5 to 10 minutes. Children who are better conditioned will be able to sustain aerobic activity for longer periods than those who are not.

The type of activity that can be sustained over a considerable period of time without undue physical fatigue is called moderate and is normally aerobic. Moderate activities include brisk walking, bicycle riding, and jogging, to name a few. The ability to do moderate activity for prolonged periods of time, such as running a mile, is not easily attained. The endurance necessary to perform an activity such as a mile run must be gradually built up over time. Children cannot be expected to run long distances at first, but with continued aerobic conditioning they can begin to excel at activities that require a prolonged effort.

INSTANT ACTIVITY 4.4
Determining Heart Rates

Grades 3–6

Equipment Needed

Note cards on which to record heart rates

Activity

Each time blood is pumped out of the heart a pulse wave is created that travels through the arteries and can be felt if pressure is gently applied to certain points on the body. Have children feel for their radial and carotid pulses. Determine the heart rate by counting the number of times the pulse is felt. Students record their heart rate on a note card. Then they run in place for a minute and take their heart rate again. Older children take the note card home and record their heart rate immediately upon rising in the morning. When children return with the cards, discuss the differences in heart rate in the morning as compared with those determined at school. Children can also take their heart rates after a game of tag or other vigorous game and compare those rates with their resting heart rate. The procedure for determining heart rates is presented in Classroom Learning Station 4.2.

INSTANT ACTIVITY 4.5
Heart Rate and Activity

Grades 3–6

Equipment Needed

Paper on which to record heart rates, stop watch or timing device

Activity

Heart rate increases with intensity of exercise. This phenomenon can be easily observed by having a child take a heart rate at rest, after doing moderate activity such as walking, then after a vigorous activity such as jogging or running. The heart rate should increase in each case as the heart works harder to pump blood to the muscles of the body. This activity can be done in a gym, outside on a playing field, or even in a classroom by desks.

Children should be able to determine heart rates (see Classroom Learning Station 4.2) before doing this activity. Students take a resting heart rate and record it on a paper. Then children march in place by their desk or walk around a marked course for about one minute. When the teacher stays "stop," the children locate the carotid or radial sites for palpating the pulse. On the "go" or "count" signal, students begin counting their heart rate. The first count should be a zero. The teacher should measure off six seconds and then say "stop." The children record the number and then add a zero to get the number of beats per minute.

The next activity is running in place with knees high or jogging for a minute. Again, stop and take a heart rate. Discuss with children why the heart rate increases during the exercise (more muscular activity, therefore more oxygen needed, therefore heart rate increases).

Even the most athletic and well-trained individual will not be able to exercise a long time if the activity is too intense. At some point during exercise, as intensities increase and the exercise gets harder to do, a point is reached where breathing increases in an effort to increase the amount of oxygen, but still either the heart cannot beat fast enough or the muscles become limited in their ability to use the oxygen. In this case energy for exercise is produced in a different manner—without oxygen, or **anaerobically.** Individuals cannot exercise anaerobically for as long as they can aerobically without quickly becoming tired. Children do not have anaerobic capacities that are as well developed as those of adults, so they become tired faster. Activities of high intensity (anaerobic) must be mixed with adequate rest periods or at least lower-intensity exercise (aerobic) so the child will not become tired and disinterested. High-intensity activities include sprinting, weight lifting, jumping (both vertically and horizontally), and many sport activities.

The ability to sustain high-intensity exercise is a very individual trait. Some children enjoy the challenge

and the feeling of working hard, becoming breathless, whereas others detest it. Activity that is at the higher end of the intensity scale is called vigorous. What is moderate activity for the conditioned child may be vigorous for the child that is not regularly active. Vigorous activity cannot be sustained for very long without periods of rest, especially in children or adults who are not accustomed to physical activity. So that an individual can exercise for a prolonged period of time, rest periods can be interspersed throughout the activity. A rest period gives the heart and lungs a chance to catch up on production of oxygen so that the body is again producing enough to meet the demand. The activity is termed intermittent due to the "stop, rest, and go again" nature of the activity and includes both aerobic and anaerobic components.

Continuous versus Intermittent Activity Prolonged activity such as running a mile or more is normally aerobic exercise for the individual who has been training for this activity. However, without adequate conditioning the moderate activity of jogging can quickly become a vigorous anaerobic activity requiring periods of rest. The ability to run or even briskly walk the mile is not an inherent ability to most individuals, especially children. The activity quickly becomes drudgery, and children will learn to dislike it. That dislike often continues past childhood into adulthood where the thought of exercising more than five minutes on a treadmill is enough to keep the person away from a fitness center or exercise program.

Prolonged activity without rest periods that is continuous in nature is designed to be moderate and aerobic, but individuals must pace themselves to keep it that way. This type of activity is often used with adults to develop the cardiorespiratory system and create a more efficient and healthier heart. For children, continuous activity may tax the heart and respiratory system past the aerobic stage and become anaerobic and vigorous. It is desirable for children to experience vigorous activity even if they can only go a short period of time. Once the activity lengthens past a few minutes, children become tired and disinterested. Continuous vigorous physical activity that is prolonged for more than several minutes is therefore not recommended for children 5–12 years of age. This would mean that a 15- to 20-minute continuous walk or jog would not be an age-appropriate activity for many elementary school children. A better idea is to break up the activity into shorter bouts with brief periods of rest (intermittent). Intermittent activity may still be thought of as moderate and aerobic, but children will be able to tolerate the activity better and hopefully enjoy the activity.

COPEC Guideline 1 recommends accumulating "at least 60 minutes and up to several hours of age-appropriate physical activity on all, or most, days of the week. The daily accumulation should include moderate and vigorous physical activity with the majority of the time spent in activity that is intermittent in nature" (COPEC 2004, 3). The accumulation of physical activity is a necessary revision to the COPEC guidelines since 60 minutes or more of physical activity is recommended but children rarely have the opportunity to meet this requirement all at once. Physical education classes may not extend beyond 30 minutes if at all and even then may meet only three days a week. Recess,

play periods, and after-school activity must be added to the total. Some children will be naturally active, while others will do only what is requested of them. Classroom teachers should plan on activity that is in bouts of about 15 minutes and is both moderate and vigorous with occasional rest and recovery periods to meet the COPEC guidelines.

THE APPARATUS FOR ACTIVITY: THE MUSCULOSKELETAL SYSTEM

An efficient heart is necessary for physical activity and exercise. However, you also need an efficient and adequate **musculoskeletal system** to move you around. The classroom teacher can teach students the muscles and bones that make up the human body. Classroom Learning Station 4.3 (Which Muscle Is Which?) will help children learn these anatomical terms. For a quick review of bones and muscles to use in the learning station, refer to Figures 4.2 and 4.3.

Musculoskeletal fitness is usually divided into three components: (1) muscular strength, (2) muscular endurance, and (3) flexibility. Although related, each is a little different from the other.

Muscular Strength The ability to create a large amount of force at one time is **muscular strength.** The ability to lift a heavy weight is the most common marker of strength. In fact, strength is usually measured by determining how much weight can be lifted in one repetition, often called a one-repetition maximum (1RM). The more a person can lift at one time, the more force that muscle can generate for that movement. Although having a lot of strength is probably not necessary for good health, all persons should have the strength to pursue recreational and daily activities.

Children demonstrate strength in many ways as they go about their daily activity. Trying to lift one another or pull one another, as in a game of tug of war, are two examples of such strength activities. Strength is necessary for success in many sports. The more strength a child has, the better able to hit a ball well, as in baseball; make a basket, as in basketball; or even throw a Frisbee. Differences in strength are easily observed on the playground. Some children can easily pull themselves up onto a climbing apparatus or horizontal bar, whereas others struggle. However, the stronger child in the first grade may not necessarily be the strongest in the fifth grade.

Children develop strength as they grow and mature. As the child grows, muscle tissue develops and strength is increased. Some children grow at a faster rate and are stronger than others. Others have a body type that

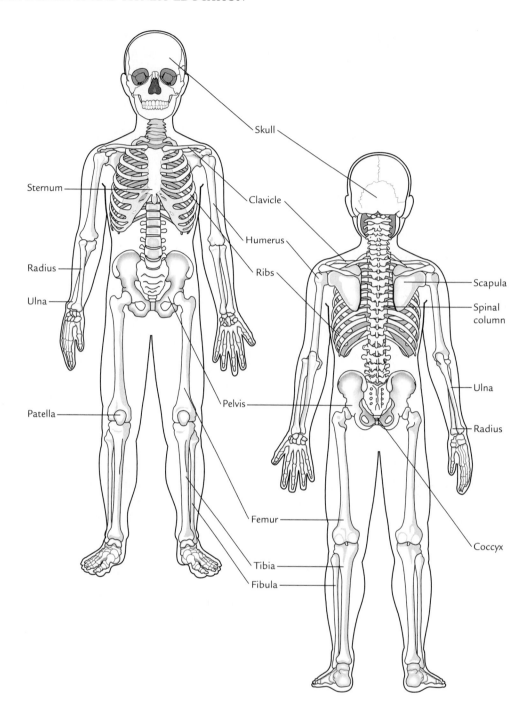

FIGURE 4.2 The Major
Bones of the Human Body

is more conducive to a muscular type of body. Physical activity will also cause muscles to develop more strength. Poor upper-arm strength and poor leg strength might affect some of the activities that a child might like to perform. Poor strength definitely affects success in some types of activities. Quick Lesson 4.5 will help to convey the concept of muscular strength.

Muscular Endurance Somewhat different from strength, **muscular endurance** is related to the ability of a muscle to perform a contraction repeatedly. The more endurance a muscle has, the longer it can continue to contract. A person may be able to lift a heavy weight only one time (strength), but a lighter weight could be lifted many times (endurance).

The ability to perform multiple crunches (sit-ups), to lift a weight 10 or 20 times, or to hold a heavy weight for an extended period of time is related to endurance. Abdominal endurance has been related to low-back function. The ability of the abdominal muscles to hold the body in correct alignment during the course of the day and during activity such as lifting is related to

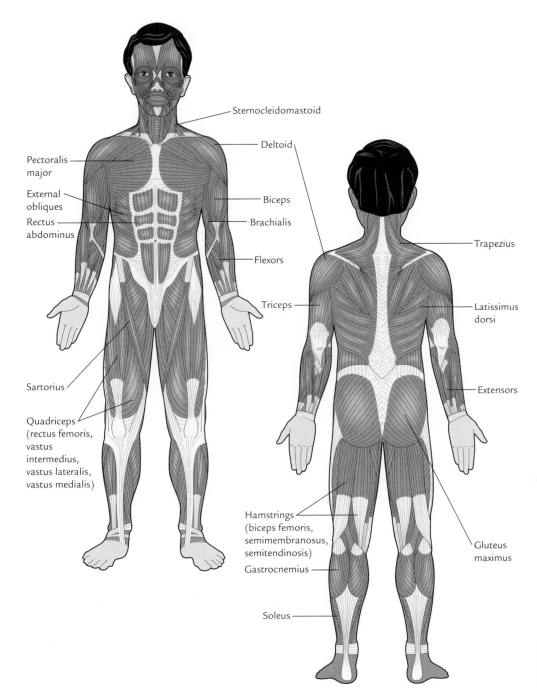

FIGURE 4.3 The Major Muscles of the Human Body

endurance. Upper-arm muscular endurance is necessary to perform exercises such as push-ups. Leg endurance is necessary to play running, squatting, crawling, and crab-walking games. A child needs muscular strength to do one pull-up, at least enough strength to pull the body up to the horizontal bar; but muscular endurance is needed to do several pull-ups. Quick Lesson 4.6 is helpful in presenting this concept.

Flexibility   The ability of a limb or body part to move through its complete range of motion is **flexibility.**

Range of motion involves movement of a body part around a joint. In the case of the hip joint, an individual can usually lift the leg to at least 45 degrees from a supine position (lying on the back) without bending the knee. Many people can lift the leg to a 90-degree angle without bending the knee, but only those with excellent flexibility in the back of the leg can pull their leg back over their head without the knee bending.

The ability to sit and touch the toes without bending the knees shows good flexibility in the lower back and hamstrings (the muscles in the back of the thighs). Poor flexibility in the low back and hamstrings has been linked to low-back pain in adults, although research confirming the relationship is far from conclusive (Nieman 1999). Quick Lesson 4.7 will help to convey this concept.

THE VEHICLE FOR ACTIVITY: THE BODY'S COMPOSITION

When you look at the children in your classroom, you will notice a variety of body types and sizes, from very small to tall, and from narrow to wide. You will also notice that some children appear to be muscular, others thin, still others overweight. Some of the variety in children's body types can be attributed to genetics. Large, tall parents tend to have tall children. In some cases, overweight children may have overweight parents. Because so many things determine the body type of a child, where one factor ends and the other begins is hard to determine.

Body Type Three major **body types** have been identified: (1) mesomorph (muscular), (2) ectomorph (thin, slight of build), and (3) endomorph (rounded, possibly plump) (Figure 4.4). Most individuals are a combination of the different types. However, the advantage a person with a mesomorph body type would have in an activity such as weight lifting or body building is obvious. Body shapes and sizes are due to genetics, lifestyle, and nutrition. A natural tendency toward the endomorph (rounded, plump) body type is exacerbated by overeating and inactivity. Children with an ectomorph body type may become too thin if they are undernourished. Children's weight provides only an estimate of their relative fatness or leanness. Some children may be naturally heavier without necessarily being fat. The terms *overweight, overfat,* and *obese* do not accurately describe the body's composition in many cases. To get a better idea of the leanness or fatness of a child, or of an adult for that matter, it is valuable to measure body composition.

Body Composition The relationship of body fat to lean body weight is **body composition.** Lean body weight is the weight of the nonfat components of the body and is primarily made up of muscle mass and bone. Several different methods are used to measure body composition. A procedure called underwater weighing determines body fat through a time-honored method of estimating the density of the body by how much the body weighs while submerged in water. Though accurate, this method is impractical for testing large groups such as schoolchildren.

(a)

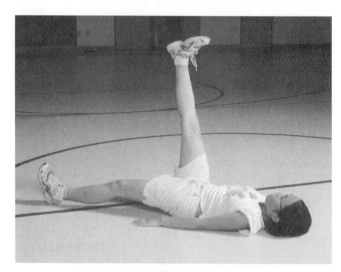

(b)

(c)

Flexibility varies from individual to individual. These children show (a) limited, (b) good, and (c) excellent flexibility of the hamstring muscle group.

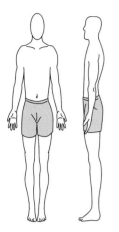
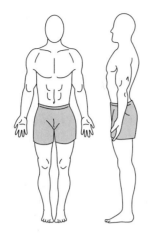
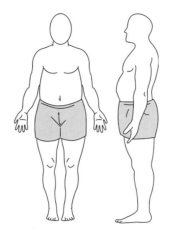

Ectomorph   Mesomorph   Endomorph   **FIGURE 4.4**   General Body Types

Estimating overweight by determining how much a person should weigh in relationship to height is the basis for the popular Body Mass Index, or BMI (weight/height^2). BMI values from 25 to 29.9 classify adults as overweight, and a value at or above 30 classifies the person as obese (regardless of age or sex). Since BMI depends on weight and height, determinations of overweight categories for children and adolescents are more complicated. Age and gender must also be taken into consideration; therefore, BMI-for-age is plotted according to sex-specific growth charts. Determining who is obese is also tentative. The CDC does not advocate the use of the term obese when referring to children, so a child who is in the 95th percentile or higher of BMI is considered overweight. Children who score at or above the 85th percentile but below the 95th percentile are termed *at risk of overweight*. Although quick and easy, this method does not account for differences in body composition among individuals. Muscular individuals may be categorized as overweight when actually they have a low percentage of body fat. Nevertheless, the Body Mass Index has gained acceptance as the preferred way to classify children and adolescents as overweight or at risk of overweight. Using Body Mass Index to determine overweight and risk of overweight is preferred for schoolchildren because of the ease of measurement and because height and weight are the only factors considered.

Another quick and relatively easy method of assessing body composition is to determine percentage of body fat using skinfold calipers. The method involves holding or pinching a fold of skin between the thumb and index finger, pulling it away from the body, and measuring the thickness of the fold with calipers. The skinfold thickness may be taken at several different sites, but the triceps (back of the upper arm) and calf (back of the lower leg) are traditionally used for children. The result is put into a standardized formula to determine percentage of fat. As in measuring blood pressure, the procedure is quick and easy to do, but it does take practice and knowledge of the correct techniques. Measuring body fat using the skinfolds will probably require the help of a physical educator or other professional versed in the use of the correct technique. Although the BMI method and the skinfold method are both relatively easy to do, determining body fat in children within the school setting may not be recommended due to the sensitive nature of the subject of obesity.

Improving Body Composition   Body type depends to a large extent on genetics, but body composition is influenced considerably by lifestyle factors. One goal of exercise and physical activity is to improve body composition. Exercise and activity increases muscle mass and decreases body fat in both adults and children. The best gains in muscle mass are usually with muscular strength and endurance types of activities. The best types of activities for loss of body fat tend to be the more prolonged types of activity. However, any increase in energy expenditure during the day has the effect of burning calories, a necessary goal if the objective is to reduce body weight and improve body composition.

Nutrition is extremely important in balancing caloric intake and energy expenditure. Whereas quite a bit of activity may be needed to expend 100 calories, a high-calorie snack food that has been replaced by a lower-calorie fruit might cut that 100 calories quickly.

A prudent recommendation for all Americans would be to reduce fat in the diet to 30 percent or less, with no more than a third of that from saturated fat. Protein should make up 10 to 15 percent of the daily calories, and carbohydrates should supply the rest.

Carbohydrates are the main energy food and should be the major dietary component. Carbohydrates are described as either complex, such as potatoes, breads, pasta, fruits, and vegetables, or simple and refined, which includes foods such as sugars. An adequate intake of complex carbohydrates as compared to simple, refined sugars is an important key to a good diet.

A good way to improve the diet is to reduce fats and refined sugars such as cakes, cookies, and potato chips and increase complex carbohydrates such as fruits and vegetables. The new food guide pyramid provides a guideline for approximate amounts of different types of food in the daily diet (www.mypyramid.gov). A pyramid specially designed for children is shown in Figure 4.5. The widths of the different shaded bands in the pyramid give a general guide as to portion sizes. The figure stepping to the top of the pyramid represents the importance of daily physical activity. The bands emphasize the need to increase consumption of grains, vegetables, and fruits and decrease consumption of oil, meat, and beans. In September 2005 the USDA released a computer game called "MyPyramid Blast Off" in an effort to increase interest among children for the concept. In the chapter Activities section at the end of this chapter, activity #6 gives details on the kids' pyramid and the new game. A complete discussion of nutrition is beyond the scope of this book. However, the interested classroom teacher can refer to the excellent nutrition textbooks by Melvin Williams (2002) and William McArdle, Frank Katch, and Victor Katch (1999) for more information.

Implementing Fitness Education in the Classroom

The classroom teacher can implement many fitness activities and demonstrations in the classroom. Access to a play area for class increases the opportunity for activity. The classroom teacher can add fitness activities as a small part of the daily lesson, as they are a good way to warm up to prepare for activity. However, knowledge of exercise principles is helpful in establishing a plan for presenting some of the fitness material.

EXERCISE PRINCIPLES FOR DEVELOPING FITNESS

Three broad **principles of training** are used for developing physical fitness, whether in adults or in children: (1) the overload principle, (2) specificity of exercise, and (3) progression or progressive resistance.

Overload   The **overload principle** simply states that to improve a fitness component you must do a little more work than you are accustomed to doing. The body—muscle, heart, respiratory system—will adapt to the increased workload. As the body keeps adapting to an increased requirement, a training effect occurs and the individual becomes able to do more work. The principle is easy to understand when you think of how it feels to begin an exercise program. When you start, it may be difficult to walk once around the neighborhood or around the block. As you begin to walk faster and farther, your body gradually adapts to this overload and the walk seems easier.

Specificity   The second principle is **specificity.** Training is very specific to the muscles and systems used for the exercise. Doing a multitude of 40- or 50-yard dashes will not improve a child's ability to run a half mile as much as running a few longer distances will. Exercise is so specific that muscles of a right-handed tennis player may be measured as larger in the right arm than in the left. Someone who is an excellent swimmer may not do as well when running.

Children must do some prolonged running to develop the ability to run longer distances. To develop speed, children must do some fast running. To improve the ability to do pull-ups, children must improve not only upper-arm strength but specifically the type of strength necessary to pull the body up against resistance (gravity). Surprisingly, a child who does push-ups every day to develop upper-body strength may be unable to do very many pull-ups, because different muscle groups are used to do pull-ups and push-ups. Therefore the best way to gain the strength to climb a rope—is to climb a rope.

This does not mean that children must continually practice pull-ups. It does mean that many different upper-body strength activities (that are fun) should be included in daily lessons. Playground climbing equipment is especially useful for this purpose. Climbing walls for children have become popular because they increase upper-body strength and conditioning, a major goal for the teacher, and because they are fun, a major goal for the child.

Progression   The third principle of training is **progression.** All children are encouraged to tax themselves at least a little so that a training effect occurs. They do not have to go to extremes, however, and patience is key. Adaptation does not take place quickly. The body needs time to adapt to an overload; therefore the increase in how hard you are working or how long you are exercising should be gradual. The best approach is to add a little more to an activity each time you do it.

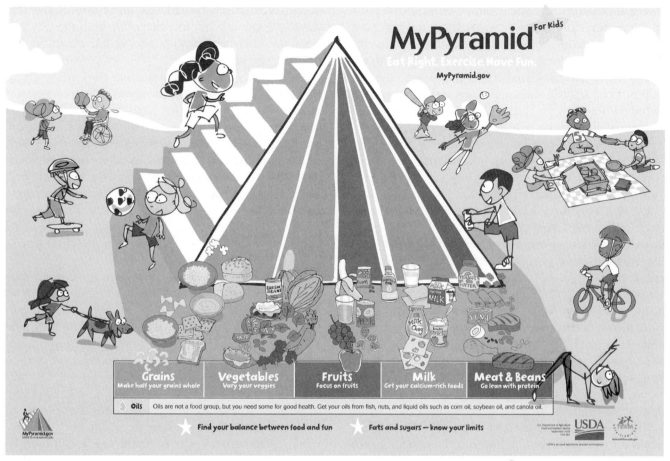

FIGURE 4.5 MyPyramid
Source: U.S. Department of Agriculture, Center for Nutrition Policy and Promotion (MyPyramid.gov).

For example, if the goal is eventually to do 50 crunches (curl-ups), do not try to do 50 the first time. Start with 10 the first week and gradually keep adding a few each week until you have worked up to the target. Trying to meet your goal without a gradual progression will cause soreness, frustration, and possibly even injury.

WARM UP AND COOL DOWN

Encourage children to warm up before activity and cool down afterward. A **warm-up** might include brisk walking, calisthenics, or any large muscle activity that increases the heart rate. The warm-up prepares the body for activity by increasing the heart rate, in turn increasing blood flow to the muscles. The muscles in turn warm up in response to the increased activity. The **cool-down** does the opposite. Gradually decreasing the intensity of the exercise begins the cool-down. Walking is a good way to finish the cool-down and help the child recover from the activity. The heart rate begins to slow down, breathing is less labored, and

the walking discourages blood from pooling in the lower extremities. Stretching and relaxation exercises can be done after the cool-down while the muscles are still warm. In fact, flexibility exercises should be done during cool-down when muscles are warm. Stretching and flexibility should not be used as a warm-up.

IMPLEMENTING FITNESS ACTIVITIES

The classroom teacher may develop activities, assignments, and attitudes that recognize the unique characteristics of different types of exercise and activity and provide instruction in how best to do them. The teacher must not assume that the child is proficient in an activity simply because it is easy or is done all the time. Even proper walking form should be taught; Quick Lesson 4.8 will help to illustrate this concept.

A variety of activities that encourage moderate to vigorous levels of physical activity must be presented. Running, skipping, chasing, dodging, and tagging activities can all be designed in various ways to produce a smorgasbord of games. These games increase children's energy expenditure and heart rate without the boredom of repetitious, tedious, unenjoyable exercise, such as calisthenics or the continual wait for a turn to participate. Fun is an important ingredient in fitness activities. In games and activities, waiting in lines and being tagged as *out* do not improve fitness. Games must be designed so that children are back *in* as quickly as possible.

Elementary school children may become bored with the type of activity that is acceptable and pleasing to adults. Running a mile would be especially boring for most children; therefore effort must be made to design physical activities that are more appealing to children's likes and dislikes and appropriate for their developmental level. The goal is not to practice running a mile but to do a variety of activities that will eventually enable children to have the endurance to run a mile. Games and activities that add up to a mile's worth of running are far superior to having children try to complete a continuous mile run. Activities must be discontinuous at first, with significant recovery periods. The amount of time in continuous activity can be gradually lengthened. Intensity of the exercise is not the critical factor, especially in the first stages of developing the endurance required for prolonged exercise.

The classroom teacher can use a variety of heart rate games to improve children's cardiorespiratory fitness. Heart rate games are those that are fun for the child, include everyone in the game, and have a goal of increasing the heart rate to a moderate or vigorous level and sustaining it for a period of time. Examples of heart rate games are provided in Quick Lesson 4.9. Older children (grades 4–6) can be taught to develop an exercise plan to increase their fitness level and should be introduced to the principles of physical training. Make the child's individual goals and objectives the focal point of the plan, and make it relatively simple to follow. Children regulate their exercise plans themselves. They should learn to record their own data, determine the activities they would like to do, and test themselves to see how their fitness level is coming along. This is a first step in teaching children how to plan their physical activity to achieve fitness objectives.

Various technological advances have made exercise and physical activity more interesting to many children. The use of heart rate monitors, if available, can augment activities where heart rate must be measured. Several of the heart rate activities presented in the Quick Lessons can be modified for use of a heart rate monitor. Heart rate monitors use a chest strap with a transmitter and a wristwatch type of receiver. Chest straps must be a child's size to be effective. This added technology provides a great opportunity for the classroom teacher to collaborate with the physical educator teacher who is knowledgeable about the use of heart rate monitors.

Pedometers are the current craze; they are worn on the hip and activated by movement. Simple pedometers measure how many steps an individual takes while the pedometer is worn. The simple pedometers are relatively inexpensive and are often given as prizes or as incentives to buy certain products. The more sophisticated pedometers calculate the distance and even calories burned by the activity. These instruments are intriguing to today's high-tech children and are easily incorporated into a fitness education lesson. By using the pedometer in a physical activity, children can count their steps and measure their activity. Goals can be established for attaining a certain number of steps per week as part of a movement education class. Special Event 4.1 at the end of the chapter can be modified using pedometers. Each step counts as 1/10 mile (10 steps = 1 mile), and the number of steps determines the mileage attained. The pedometers can be used during heart rate games (Quick Lesson 4.9) and other activities presented in the book to determine the amount of activity accomplished during the lesson.

Pedometers also make an excellent home assignment. Students can receive extra credit, stickers, or other rewards (but not candy) for achieving a certain number of steps. Pedometers can be used within a math lesson to determine distance covered with a certain number of steps. The lesson can be related to the sciences by calculating calories burned. Even weight loss expected with accumulation of certain distances can be determined. The uses of the pedometers are endless; however, remember that children should not compete with each other as to number of steps to be the "winner." Children should formulate their own personal activity goals and work to reach them. Pedometers can make activity fun and interesting and encourage children to be active.

FITNESS TESTING

In the 1950s, emphasis in physical education centered on performance-based objectives, such as how fast a student could run a 50-yard dash. **Fitness testing** was initiated in many schools with awards given to those children who met certain standards. The tests included measurements of attributes such as speed, agility, and motor skill. These were previously described as skill-related components of physical fitness.

The idea of assessing a child's performance on different tests has changed little through the years, but

---

BOX 4.1 Fitness Testing Programs for Grades 3–6

FITNESSGRAM

Description

The Fitnessgram is a health-related fitness test; it evaluates aerobic capacity, body composition, muscular strength, endurance, and flexibility.

Components

1. *Aerobic capacity:* select from the PACER, a 20-meter progressive shuttle run, a 1-mile walk or run, or a walk test.
2. *Body composition:* select from a skinfold test to measure percentage of body fat (measurements at the triceps and calf) or Body Mass Index (calculated from height and weight).
3. *Muscle strength, endurance, and flexibility:* use a curl-up test (abdominal endurance), trunk lift (trunk extensor strength and flexibility), push-up, pull-up, flexed arm hang or modified pull-up (upper-body strength), sit-and-reach (back and hamstring flexibility), and shoulder stretch (shoulder flexibility).

Further Information

For more information about the Fitnessgram fitness test, visit the Cooper Institute's website at www.cooperinst.org/ftgmain.asp.

THE PRESIDENT'S CHALLENGE PHYSICAL ACTIVITY AND FITNESS AWARDS PROGRAM

Description

The President's Challenge offers a choice of three areas: (1) active lifestyle, (2) physical fitness, and (3) health fitness.

Components—Presidential Active Lifestyle Award

- Students must be active for a minimum of 60 minutes a day, five days a week; or they must use a pedometer to measure 11,000 steps for girls, 13,000 for boys.
- Students must participate for six weeks to be eligible for an award.
- Students are encouraged to earn additional six-week recognition throughout the year.
- For the first time, in 2002–2003 adults are encouraged to become active role models and earn the Presidential Adult Active Lifestyle Award by participating regularly in physical activity on their own or with children.

Components—Presidential Physical Fitness Award

- Students' level of physical fitness is tested in five events: (1) curl-ups or partial curl-ups, (2) shuttle run, (3) endurance run or walk, (4) pull-ups or right-angle push-ups, and (5) V-sit or sit and reach.
- Awards given at three levels reflect performance and participation.

Components—Presidential Health Fitness Award

- Targeting health-related fitness, this program includes a five-item assessment: (1) partial curl-ups, (2) run or walk (distance depends on age group), (3) V-sit or sit and reach, (4) right-angle push-ups or pull-ups, and (5) a measurement of Body Mass Index.
- Awards given to those students who maintain a healthy level of fitness.

Further Information

For more information about the President's Challenge fitness tests, visit the website of the President's Challenge at www.indiana.edu/~preschal or at www.fitness.gov.

---

the purpose of the tests and the components that are included are very different. Although children are still assessed and compared with norms, the focus has changed to a health-related goal as opposed to a performance goal. Most current testing batteries use items considered to be essential components of health-related fitness and include measurements of cardiorespiratory fitness, muscular strength, muscular endurance, flexibility, and body composition. Simple standardized tests such as a one-mile run or walk to assess cardiorespiratory fitness and the number of sit-ups that can be completed in a minute to assess muscular endurance are included in the test battery. Which components are used depends on the test. Two popular testing programs, their

components, and contact information are provided in Box 4.1. A physical educator may be recruited to provide specific instructions and assistance if fitness testing is required in the elementary school.

The value of fitness testing in the schools is continually questioned. It takes time to do the tests, and results may reflect the effects of growth and maturation rather than fitness improvements. Children may be able to perform adequately on certain fitness tests because they are bigger and stronger than their peers, not because they are fitter. Studies have shown that even students who are not all that active may do well on the tests simply because of genetic factors (Welk and Wood 2000).

Variations in strength among children may reflect growth and maturation rather than fitness levels.

Most disturbing of all, some physically active children may not do as well on the tests as others who are more mature or genetically endowed, thus creating a negative attitude toward testing and perhaps even causing the active children to dislike activity. Additionally, children may not truly comprehend the purpose of some tests. A study of fourth- and fifth-grade children's perceptions of a mile run test showed that they had little understanding of why they were doing the test, and in fact they disliked it so much that some found ways to avoid taking it (Hopple and Graham 1995). Such testing would not foster the objective of having children develop an appreciation for physical activity or physical fitness. Testing of physical fitness in students at the elementary school level is probably not necessary in most circumstances, and the assigning of grades to fitness-level performance is not recommended.

A better idea is to emphasize the role that achieving an adequate level of physical activity has in children's lives. One way to do this is for children to accumulate participation points. Give children points for participating in certain activities. Once they have obtained a certain number of points, they may receive some type of award or reward. Creativity can be used to make the attainment of points an interesting activity in itself. One such activity is given in this chapter's Special Event (Are We There Yet?) at the end of the chapter. Children could also be given points for voluntarily participating in fitness testing, recording their scores, and charting their data. However, do not assign grades that are dependent on the scores. The object is to foster an appreciation for the activities, not to have children participating just to get a high score.

Participation points may also be given for minutes of activity. More participation points would correspond to more minutes of activity, resulting in an improvement in physical fitness.

The Role of the Elementary Classroom Teacher as a Fitness Educator

Elementary classroom teachers who are willing to undertake the development of an appreciation for activity in their students can play an important role in helping children remain healthy and fit. They can emphasize what activities are appropriate and necessary to meet physical activity requirements. Ideally, teachers will serve as positive role models and express positive attitudes toward fitness and physical activity. They should be prepared to teach the fitness education knowledge base and to work to maximally use the resources available to provide an appropriate fitness education curriculum.

A primary role of classroom teachers is to engage their students in physical activity whenever possible during the school day so as to develop behaviors that encourage children to be active. The information in this chapter, the NASPE guidelines, the surgeon general's recommendations, and perhaps assistance from a physical educator, will enable classroom teachers to be successful in providing a quality fitness education curriculum.

Summary

Elementary school classroom teachers who provide movement education to their students are in an excellent position to initiate and reinforce an appreciation for physical activity and healthy living. Classroom teachers should be able to explain the different concepts related to health, wellness, physical fitness, physical activity, and exercise. They can foster an understanding of health risk factors in their students and emphasize the value of physical activity, exercise, and proper nutrition in reducing the risk of chronic disease.

Classroom teachers should provide materials and activities that teach the basic workings of the heart, circulation, and musculoskeletal system. The effect of different types of activity on heart rate and perception of effort will help children learn how to pace themselves during exercise so that activity is enjoyable and beneficial. The classroom teacher can encourage good nutrition and increased energy expenditure as ways to improve body composition and reduce obesity.

Exercise principles for developing fitness can be presented gradually with simple concepts taught in the early grades. Emphasis must be placed on developing an appreciation for activity and providing opportunities for activity to take place. Finally, the classroom teacher serves as a role model for a healthy lifestyle as well as a facilitator for movement and physical activity.

Chapter Activities

1. Obtain the surgeon general's report on physical activity and health, available online at www.cdc .gov/nccdphp/sgr/sgr.htm. List some of the activities that you do that are included on the report. Estimate the time you spend in different types of activity each day. Would you classify yourself as active? Do you participate in any moderate exercise during the day? Do you participate in vigorous exercise during the day? How could you change your daily lifestyle to meet the surgeon general's recommendation for activity?

2. List some of the activities you like to do. For each activity, describe what components of fitness are primarily addressed. Rate each activity as anaerobic or aerobic. Are the activities moderate or vigorous? Are the activities continuous or intermittent?

3. What do you think the following activities would do to the heart rate? First take a resting heart rate; then predict what the heart would do during the following activities. Put the activities in order of what you expect the heart rate to be. Then do the activity and take a heart rate immediately upon stopping. Compare your predictions with what you found.

    Sitting
    Lying down
    Running in place for one minute
    Walking around the room
    Lifting a three-pound weight 20 times with your
      dominant arm

4. Determine how active you are daily. Record the activity you do during the day and determine the number of minutes you spend in moderate and vigorous activity. Would you meet the NASPE standards? Would you meet the surgeon general's recommendation?

5. Record your food intake for one day. Use the new food guide pyramid for adults to determine how your diet might be improved. This information can be obtained by logging onto mypyramid gov. What would you change to improve your diet?

6. After trying the food guide pyramid described in activity 5, take a look at the MyPyramid Blast Off game available at the same site. In this interactive computer game, kids can reach Planet Power by fueling their rocket with food and physical activity. You might want to see how you would do at reaching Planet Power. The instructions for downloading the game are on the website (www.mypyramid .gov/kids).

7. Discuss your comfort level regarding the need for elementary school classroom teachers to be fitness educators. Is that comfort level related to your experiences in physical education during your K–12 schooling? Explain your answer.

Internet Resources

The Center for Health and Health Care in Schools. Health information specifically targeted to policies, politics, and financing of health programming in schools. www.healthinschools.org

National Association for Health and Fitness, the Network of State and Governor's Councils. The website promotes health, fitness, and exercise programs and reports on statewide efforts for improvements in these areas. www.physicalfitness.org

Additional information is available from websites for many of the agencies and organizations discussed in this chapter, including the following:

American College of Sports Medicine
  www.acsm.org
American Heart Association
  www.americanheart.org
MyPyramid.Gov
  mypyramid.gov/kids
National Heart, Lung, and Blood Institute
  www.nhlbi.nih.gov
U.S. Department of Health and Human Services: Small Step Kids
  www.smallstep.gov/kids

Bibliography

American College of Sports Medicine (ACSM). 2000. *ACSM's guidelines for exercise testing and prescription.* 6th ed. Philadelphia: Lippincott, Williams & Wilkins.

American Diabetes Association (ADA). 2000. Type 2 diabetes in children and adolescents (Consensus Statement). *Diabetes Care* 23: 381–389.

American Heart Association (AHA). 2002. The heart of diabetes: Understanding insulin resistance.www.american heart.org/presenter.jhtml?identifier=11243

American Obesity Association (AOA). 2005. AOA fact sheet: Obesity in youth. www.obesity.org

Berenson, G. S., S. R. Srinivasan, T. A. Nicklas, and L. S. Webber. 1988. Cardiovascular risk factors in children and early prevention of heart disease. *Clinical Chemistry* 34: B115–B122.

Casperson, C. J., K. E. Powell, and G. M. Christianson. 1985. Physical activity, exercise, and physical fitness. *Public Health Report* 100: 125–131.

Centers for Disease Control and Prevention (CDC). 2005. Prevalence of overweight among children and adolescents: United States, 1999–2002. www.cdc.gov/nchs/products/pubs/pubd/hestats/overwght99.htm

Centers for Disease Control and Prevention, National Center for Health Statistics. 2000. CDC growth charts: United States. www.cdc.gov/growthcharts

Council on Physical Education for Children (COPEC). 2004. *Physical activity for children: A statement of guidelines for children ages 5–12.* 2nd ed. Reston, VA: National Association for Sport and Physical Education.

Eckel, R. H., and R. M. Krauss, for the AHA Nutrition Committee. 1998. American Heart Association call to action: Obesity as a major risk factor for coronary heart disease. *Circulation* 97: 2099–2100.

Epstein, L. H., R. R. Wing, R. Koeske, D. Ossip, and S. Beck. 1982. A comparison of lifestyle change and programmed aerobic exercise on weight and fitness changes in obese children. *Behavior Therapy* 13: 651–665.

Epstein, L. H., R. R. Wing, R. Koeske, and A. Valoski. 1985. A comparison of lifestyle exercise, aerobic exercise, and calisthenics on weight loss in obese children. *Behavior Therapy* 16: 345–356.

Health and Health Care in Schools. 2004. Congress gives schools two years to improve nutrition wellness. www.healthinschools.org/ejournal/2004/July1.htm

Hopple, C., and G. Graham. 1995. What children think, feel, and know about physical fitness testing. *Journal of Teaching in Physical Education* 14: 408–417.

Kuntzleman, C. T., and G. G. Reiff. 1992. The decline in American children's fitness levels. *Research Quarterly for Exercise and Sport* 63: 107–111.

Malina, R. M. 1996. Tracking of physical activity and physical fitness across the lifespan. *Research Quarterly for Exercise and Sport* 57: 48–57.

McArdle, W. D., F. I. Katch, and V. L. Katch. 1999. *Sports and exercise nutrition.* Philadelphia: Lippincott, Williams & Wilkins.

National Association for Sport and Physical Education (NASPE). 2004. *Moving into the future: National standards for physical education.* 2nd ed. Reston, VA: Author.

National Cholesterol Education Program (NCEP). 1992. Highlights of the report of the expert panel on blood cholesterol levels in children and adolescents. *Pediatrics* 89: 495–501.

National High Blood Pressure Education Program (NHBPEP) Working Group on Children and Adolescents. 2004. The Fourth Report on the diagnosis, evaluation, and treatment of high blood pressure in children and adolescents. *Pediatrics* 114(2): 555–576.

National High Blood Pressure Education Program (NHBPEP), National Heart, Lung and Blood Institute. 2004. *The Seventh Report of the Joint National Committee on Prevention, Detection, Evaluation, and Treatment of High Blood Pressure* (JNC7). U.S. Department of Health and Human Services (USDHHS). NIH Publication No. 04-5290. Washington, DC: USGPO.

Nieman, D. C. 1999. *Exercise testing and prescription: A health-related approach.* 4th ed. Mountain View, CA: Mayfield.

O'Donnell, M. P. 1986. Definition of health promotion, part II: Levels of programs. *American Journal of Health Promotion* 1(2): 6–9.

Ogden, C. L., K. M. Flegal, M. D. Carroll, and C. L. Johnson. 2002. Prevalence and trends in overweight among US children and adolescents, 1999–2000. *JAMA* 288(14): 1728–1732.

Pangrazi, R. P., C. B. Corbin, and G. J. Welk. 1996. Physical activity for children and youth. *Journal of Physical Education, Recreation and Dance* 67(4): 38–42.

Raitakari, O., K. Porkka, S. Taimela, R. Telama, L. Rasanen, and J. Viikari. 1994. Effects of persistent physical activity and inactivity on coronary risk factors in children and young adults. *American Journal of Epidemiology* 140(3): 195–205.

Robertson, R. J., F. L. Goss, N. F. Boer, et al. 2000. Children's OMNI scale of perceived exertion: Mixed gender and race validation. *Medicine and Science in Sports and Exercise* 32(3): 452–458.

Sallis, J. F., and T. L. McKenzie. 1991. Physical education's role in public health. *Research Quarterly for Exercise and Sport* 62: 124–137.

Sorof, J., and S. Daniels. 2002. Obesity hypertension in children: A problem of epidemic proportions. *Hypertension* 40: 441–447.

U.S. Department of Agriculture Center for Nutrition Policy and Promotion. 2005. *MyPyramid.* www.mypyramid.gov

U.S. Department of Health and Human Services (USDHHS). 1996. *Physical activity and health: A report of the surgeon general.* Atlanta: USDHHS, Centers for Disease Control and Prevention, National Center for Chronic Disease Prevention and Health Promotion.

Welk, G. J., and K. Wood. 2000. Physical activity assessments in physical education: A practical review of instruments and their use in the curriculum. *Journal of Physical Education, Recreation and Dance* 71(1): 30–40.

Williams, M. H. 2002. *Nutrition for health, fitness, and sport.* 6th ed. New York: McGraw-Hill.

World Health Organization (WHO). 1947. Constitution of the World Health Organization. In *Chronicle of the World Health Organization,* p. 1. Geneva: World Health Organization.

QUICK LESSON 4.1
How Arteries Become Clogged

GRADES 4–6

NASPE STANDARD 4 Students achieve and maintain a health-enhancing level of physical fitness.

LESSON OBJECTIVES

- Students understand the role of cholesterol in the development of blocked arteries.
- Students name various factors that increase cholesterol levels in the bloodstream.
- Students understand the effect that factors such as smoking have on the flow of blood in the arteries.
- Students demonstrate how poor nutrition can increase cholesterol levels in the bloodstream.

EQUIPMENT NEEDED

- Two playground ropes
- A pinny (mesh vest) for each child in the class; have two colors (preferably red and white)
- Scooters (one for every two or three children in class)

PREPARATION TIME Fifteen minutes

KNOWLEDGE CONTENT Foods that are high in fat and cholesterol contribute to the buildup of plaque in the arteries. As fat and cholesterol are deposited on the artery wall, a plaque, or bump, forms on the artery wall. As more and more fat and cholesterol is deposited, the plaque grows bigger and bigger until blood flow is slowed. If the artery becomes blocked by the plaque, blood cannot move through and the heart experiences pain because oxygen does not reach the heart muscle. In severe cases, the artery becomes completely blocked causing a heart attack.

CLASSROOM ACTIVITY Before doing this activity, children in the lower grades should have discussed arteries and blood flow (see Quick Lesson 4.3). Two ropes are set parallel on the floor to represent artery walls. Set the ropes about four feet apart. Have children put on their pinnies. One color represents blood cells going through the arteries (red pinnies), and the other represents cholesterol in the arteries (white pinnies).

Several children stand outside the rope at two or three places. The children outside the rope will try to tag the children going through on the scooters. Children are then asked to move through the channel made by the ropes. Children with white pinnies must stop and sit along the rope where they are tagged, while the

children with red pinnies are allowed to pass. Children with the red pinnies scoot through between the ropes with no trouble. Add one or two of those with the white pinnies. As the children with the white pinnies come close to the artery wall (the rope and the taggers), they are captured (tagged) and must stay next to the rope.

Each time the children pass through, one or two children with the white pinnies may or may not be captured. If they are captured and are sitting beside the rope, they now become taggers. Again, only the children with the white pinnies have to stop. The children with the red pinnies may pass through even if they are tagged. This represents blood flow with little cholesterol. It is difficult for the white pinnies to become captured since there are few of them in comparison to the red pinnies.

Now increase the number of white pinnies going through the artery to represent more cholesterol. As the number of white pinnies increases, more of them get captured. Eventually so many are captured that the red pinnies are blocked from going through. In other words, the artery has been clogged to the point that the red blood cells cannot go through.

After the activity is set up and the children understand the concept, relate different foods to the amount of fat flowing through the arteries. For example, if the teacher says "butter," then more of the children with white pinnies begin to go through. Other concepts can also be shown with the older children. Smoking constricts arteries; therefore in someone who smokes, the ropes can be brought closer together, making the flow even more difficult.

ASSESSMENT Discuss the impact of different situations on the flow of blood through the artery. The teacher can describe a situation and the child can explain what the effects will be (i.e., more cholesterol, slower blood flow, etc.). Have the students answer (in writing) the following questions:

- List at least five foods that are high in fat content.
- Why should you not eat lots of foods that are high in fat?

SUCCESS FOR ALL Assign partners to students who might have problems flowing through the ropes.

INTEGRATION WITH OTHER SUBJECT AREAS
You might integrate this lesson with a spelling lesson. Students could define and learn to spell words such as *artery, plaque, oxygen, cholesterol, nutrition,* and *constrict.*

QUICK LESSON 4.2
Measuring Blood Pressures

NASPE STANDARD 4 Students achieve and maintain a health-enhancing level of physical fitness.

LESSON OBJECTIVES

- Students define blood pressure and describe how it is measured.
- Students explain the relationship between blood pressure and health.
- Students observe how blood pressure is measured on a volunteer.

EQUIPMENT NEEDED Blood pressure equipment, including

- A sphygmomanometer (apparatus to measure blood pressure)
- Blood pressure cuffs (one adult, one pediatric)
- A stethoscope
- Alcohol wipes (to clean the stethoscope ear pieces)

PREPARATION TIME Ten minutes

KNOWLEDGE CONTENT Explain what blood pressure is and how blood pressures are taken. Demonstrate how to take blood pressures using a sphygmomanometer (blood pressure apparatus) on a volunteer. Explain that with the cuff pumped up, the blood cannot go through. As you release the pressure, the blood pressure will reach the point where it exceeds the pressure in the cuff and the blood will begin to pulse through. With a stethoscope on the brachial artery, you can hear the pulse as the blood passes through. The point at which you begin to hear the pulse is called the systolic pressure. This represents the pressure when blood is forced into the arteries from the heart. When systolic pressure is high, the heart has to work harder to force the blood out.

As the cuff pressure continues to be reduced, the point will be reached when blood flows through readily and no sound can be heard. This is the diastolic pressure. This represents the pressure in the arteries during the resting phase of the heart, when it is refilling with blood. The arteries have at least this amount of pressure all the time. In arteries that are blocked or narrowed in some manner, such as might be the case if the person is a smoker, the diastolic pressure is higher.

Desirable blood pressures are shown in Table 4.1. A school nurse or health care professional should take the blood pressures unless the classroom teacher has had previous experience. A complete description of the procedure for taking blood pressures is beyond the scope of this book.

CLASSROOM ACTIVITY This activity would primarily be presented as a demonstration. Seek the aid of a school nurse or other health professional to help take blood pressures. Exercise science or nursing students from a nearby university could also be recruited to help measure blood pressures in elementary school children. Take blood pressures only on children who volunteer. In some schools, permission from parents may be needed before children's blood pressures can be taken. Be sure to check the school policy before attempting this activity. Allow students to listen to their own pulse through the stethoscope.

ASSESSMENT This is an information-only type of demonstration. Emphasize the importance of desirable blood pressure to good health. Children may be asked to remember blood pressure as a component of good health. They could also be asked to know factors that might affect blood pressure, such as genetics, too much coffee or sodas (caffeine), and of course smoking.

SUCCESS FOR ALL For students with limited hearing, flick a light to the beat of the pulse as the blood pressure is taken.

INTEGRATION WITH OTHER SUBJECT AREAS This lesson could be integrated with music and dance by having the students dance to the rhythm of their pulse or beat musical instruments (drums, cymbals, blocks of wood, etc.) to the rhythm of their pulse.

QUICK LESSON 4.3
The Circulatory System

NASPE STANDARD 4 Students achieve and maintain a health-enhancing level of physical fitness.

LESSON OBJECTIVES

- Students describe basic circulation of the blood from the heart to the body, and from the body back to the heart and lungs (grades 2–3).
- Students understand that blood cells carry oxygen and that oxygen is delivered to all the muscles and tissues of the body (grades 3–6).
- Students describe the exchange of oxygen and carbon dioxide in the tissue and what happens in the lungs as carbon dioxide and oxygen are exchanged (grades 4–6).
- Students understand that the heart pumps blood throughout the body at a certain rate and that the type and intensity of physical activity affects that rate (grades 4–6).
- Students understand that the lungs take in air from the atmosphere through inhalation and expel carbon dioxide to the atmosphere during exhalation (grades 4–6).

EQUIPMENT NEEDED

- Four playground ropes
- Several cones
- Several red and blue playground balls
- Several carpet squares or towels

PREPARATION TIME Fifteen minutes to collect equipment and set up the course (representing the heart, lungs, and muscles)

KNOWLEDGE CONTENT The heart pumps blood to the body at a rate of about 40 to 100 beats per minute at rest and up to 220 beats per minute during exercise. The blood delivers oxygen to the muscles and tissues so that the work of the muscles and tissues can be done. The left side of the heart (the left atrium and the left ventricle) pumps blood that has picked up oxygen in the lungs through a large artery leaving the heart (aorta) into a system of arteries so that blood may be delivered to the body.

At the muscle, the oxygen is released from the blood cell to be used to produce energy for muscle contractions. The blood cell also picks up carbon dioxide, a product of the energy-producing reactions at the muscle. The carbon dioxide will be carried back to the right side of the heart by way of veins. When the blood in the veins reaches the right side of the heart (the right atrium and the right ventricle), it is then pumped to the lungs, where it picks up oxygen and dumps the carbon dioxide. Blood that is now oxygenated flows back to the left atrium, and the cycle begins again (see Figure 4.1).

CLASSROOM TO GYMNASIUM ACTIVITY Set up a course in the gym with ropes and cones representing the heart, lungs, and muscles. Red balls represent oxygen and blue balls represent carbon dioxide. Children walk through the course dropping off the red ball at the muscle and picking up a blue ball and carrying it back to the lungs. Represent resting heart rates by children walking. Represent exercise heart rates by children jogging. For older children, use blankets, towels, or carpet squares to represent cholesterol or plaque buildup so they can see the effect on the blood of the blockage (see Quick Lesson 4.1).

The circulatory system lesson should be relatively simple for grades 1 and 2. Have children trace the blood from the heart to the muscles, back to the heart, then to the lungs, and back to the heart. Children should understand that as the exercise intensity increases, the blood cells move at a faster rate through the system. The teacher can create different scenarios and have the children mimic what they think the rate of blood flow will be by adjusting their speed of movement.

Older children (grades 3 and 4) can begin to add more details to the course. They can use the balls representing oxygen and carbon dioxide. Children in grades 5 and 6 should understand how the blood flow alters with changes to the system. An example might be the effect of smoking on the arteries.

ASSESSMENT Children can be asked to illustrate what happens to the flow of blood as the activity changes. If the lesson is successful, children will be able to mimic blood flow by speeding up or slowing down with just a mention of the activity. Fast movement will occur through the course with activities such as galloping, skipping, and sprinting. Slow movement will occur with activities such as walking, crawling, and crab-walking.

SUCCESS FOR ALL Assign partners to students who might have problems flowing through the cones representing the heart, lungs, and muscles.

INTEGRATION WITH OTHER SUBJECT AREAS This lesson could be integrated into science lessons covering the structure and function of the body's organs.

GRADES 1–6

NASPE STANDARD 3 Students participate regularly in physical activity.

LESSON OBJECTIVES

- Students perform movements and exercise at different intensities and speeds.
- Students perceive how hard they are working during the different activities and learn to use a number scale to represent their effort.
- Students learn how to pace themselves during different intensities of activity.

EQUIPMENT NEEDED Space (outdoors or indoors) in which to walk, jog, and run; wall chart explaining perceived exertion

PREPARATION TIME Fifteen minutes to prepare a wall chart of the perceived exertion scale

KNOWLEDGE CONTENT Children can learn to perceive how much effort they are putting into a certain activity. A number scale called rating of perceived exertion can be used to predict a person's exertion level, with low numbers representing little exertion and higher numbers representing higher levels of activity. Knowing how hard you are working is a necessary skill when learning to pace yourself during activity. For an activity in which children must be active continuously for a period of time, pacing is required so that they don't immediately get tired and have to stop before completing the activity. The best example is pacing during a long run (more than 50 or 100 yards). Children must work at a moderate level to perform continuous exercise. They can work at a higher level when performing intermittent exercise, because they will be able to rest more often. Children can begin to think about how hard they are working at an early age. As they get older and have more movement experiences, they will become more adept at predicting their exertion levels.

CLASSROOM TO PLAYGROUND ACTIVITY While in the classroom, explain perceived exertion to the children using the wall chart you prepared. Then go to an activity area. The students follow the teacher's lead in doing a simple slow walk. The teacher then calls out "how hard are you working?" In unison the children call out a number that corresponds to an exertion level. Then the teacher does a faster activity and finally a jog or a run and asks again "how hard are you working?" Once children understand the concept, they are asked to perform at a certain level on their own. Vary the time and intensity of the activity from a moderate pace for five minutes to a fast pace for 15 to 30 seconds. Each child will perceive the different activities at a different level, but eventually the child will perceive walking as easy, jogging as moderate, and sprinting as hard work.

The number of levels of exertion presented to the students depends on the developmental level of the children in the class. For grade 1, use two levels of exertion, 1 representing easy and 10 representing hard. For grades 2–3, use three levels: 1 for easy, 5 for moderate, and 10 for hard. For fourth, fifth, and sixth graders, 1 means very easy, 3 means easy, 5 means okay or moderate, 7 means hard, and 9 to 10 very hard.

ASSESSMENT Children's perceptions vary widely as to how hard they are working. The teacher acts as a guide during the activity. When a 5 is requested, children (grades 2–5) should be doing moderate types of work. If they are walking or running fast, it is apparent that they do not understand the concept. The teacher then says something like "are you sure that is a moderate work level for you?" so that students will begin to equate the number with how they feel.

SUCCESS FOR ALL Students in wheelchairs or on crutches may perform with the group if the surface of the activity area is smooth (indoor gym floor or blacktop areas outdoors). When all students are performing the same physical activities, students with physical disabilities may reach higher exertion levels faster than other students do. Students with balance problems may be assigned a partner (of the same fitness level), and together they can walk or run while holding hands.

INTEGRATION WITH OTHER SUBJECT AREAS This lesson could be integrated with geography lessons in which students are walking or running across the country or around the world. Miles walked or run by individuals are accumulated to move the group across the country. As they arrive at certain geographical locations, children stay and visit to learn about the location (its history and peoples). Obviously, the class will move faster from one location to the next if the students are walking or running at higher exertion levels. Average class exertion levels could be calculated from one location to the next location.

GRADES 3–6

NASPE STANDARD 3 Students participate regularly in physical activity.

LESSON OBJECTIVES

- Students describe and demonstrate muscular strength.
- Students understand why adequate strength is desired.
- Students understand the relationship between strength and size.
- Students test their strength on a grip dynamometer (if available).

EQUIPMENT NEEDED

- Several sponge balls or tennis balls
- Hand grip dynamometer (if available)

PREPARATION TIME Ten minutes to collect equipment

KNOWLEDGE CONTENT Strength is related to the force generated by a muscle during a maximal contraction. Strength is measured by how much weight can be lifted one time (called a one-repetition maximum) or how much force can be applied to an object. To illustrate strength, a student must squeeze an object maximally for about three to five seconds or lift weight that can be lifted only once with maximal exertion. Since such lifting is not recommended for young children, squeezing is the appropriate choice.

Strength training to maximal exertion is not recommended for young children because bones are still growing and muscles are developing. Children in elementary school should not be asked to lift maximal weights; therefore the concept is presented by having the child squeeze a tennis ball or sponge ball. Although children will not know exactly how hard they squeezed, the concept is conveyed. A hand grip dynamometer (if available) can be used to measure the force (in pounds or kilograms) generated with a maximal squeeze on the grip, thereby providing a measurement of strength.

CLASSROOM ACTIVITY A hand grip dynamometer is recommended for this activity. An alternative would be to do the activity with a tennis ball, Nerf ball, or small foam ball. The purpose is to illustrate muscular strength. The concept is easier to understand if strength is measured, such as with the dynamometer. However, students can gain a general idea about strength using the other types of instruments.

Give each child a tennis ball or Nerf ball. Have children squeeze on the ball as hard as they can. Explain that the harder they can squeeze the ball, the stronger they are. If a hand grip dynamometer is available, have them test their grip strength by squeezing as hard as possible on the dynamometer. Children should not compete with one another. Rather, have them compare their current score with an earlier one to measure improvement. Older children can test themselves every semester to see if their score has improved.

ASSESSMENT The teacher must be careful not to turn this activity into a competition. Do not compare grip strengths among children. However, a discussion as to why some children are stronger than others is appropriate. As children grow, they naturally become stronger. Use the grip dynamometer only on occasion, so that children can compare their current score with a previous one.

SUCCESS FOR ALL Students who have limited hand function could squeeze the tennis ball between their knees (while seated).

INTEGRATION WITH OTHER SUBJECT AREAS To work on their writing skills, students could investigate how their favorite athletes work to improve muscle strength in order to perform their sport. Have students write a paragraph summarizing their findings.

QUICK LESSON 4.6
Muscular Endurance

GRADES 1–3

NASPE STANDARD 3 Students participate regularly in physical activity.

LESSON OBJECTIVES

- Students understand the concept of muscular endurance.
- Students are able to demonstrate muscular endurance.
- Students improve their muscular endurance through activities designed to work the muscle in such a way as to improve endurance.

EQUIPMENT NEEDED Exercise mats or a carpeted area on which to perform various exercises

PREPARATION TIME Five minutes

KNOWLEDGE CONTENT Muscular endurance is related to the ability of a muscle to contract repeatedly or to hold a contraction over a period of time. Lifting a heavy weight 1 or 2 times requires strength, but lifting a weight 15 or 20 times requires muscular endurance. Whereas pulling up to a bar once requires a certain amount of strength, consecutive pull-ups require muscular endurance.

CLASSROOM ACTIVITY First show students how to do an abdominal curl, or a crunch, properly. This can be done on individual mats on the floor in the classroom or gym or on a carpeted area. No other equipment is needed. Children lie on the floor on their back with the knees bent. The arms are crossed across the chest. The feet are not held or stabilized. Children then lift the head and shoulders off the mat in a slow, controlled motion to the count of three. Each child should be able to lift the head at least once. Endurance is the ability to lift the head more than once. Have children raise the head as many times as they can, but not more than five times, and then rest. Repeat five times and rest again.

The ability to raise the trunk repeatedly in this way is related to the endurance of the abdominal muscles to pull the upper body up off the mat. Explain to the children that they are building the endurance to do crunches, or abdominal curls. Once they have mastered doing five, have them try to do more. The performance of crunches is an individual activity. Have children do as many as they can, but no more than 5 or 10 the first

time. Work up to 20 or 30 as a goal. Emphasize that the abdominal muscles are important to good posture.

The same type of progression can be followed for other endurance exercises. The push-up develops upper-body endurance. Start this activity with only 1 or 2 repetitions to make sure that children have the strength to lift their body correctly. Then encourage children to do 3 or 4, then 10, then 20 as they progress through the grade levels.

ASSESSMENT Be careful not to turn this activity into a competition. Self-assessment is the best way to evaluate performance in this case. Children should have a reasonable target goal. Once they have reached that goal, have them set new goals. The activity must be progressive; that is, children spend a few sessions with a limited number of endurance exercises such as curls and gradually work up to the target. If children try to do too much at one time, they become frustrated and could even become sore and tired.

SUCCESS FOR ALL Some students may have difficulty doing even one push-up or abdominal curl. In the case of the abdominal curl, have students begin by lifting only the head off the mat. Once they have developed the endurance to lift the head five to ten times, have them try adding the shoulders. Children gradually increase the number of times they can raise the head and shoulders off the mat.

Another alternative is to have children contract the abdominal muscles while sitting in a chair. They contract the muscles for three counts and then relax. Children repeat this action until they tire or reach ten contractions. Once they are able to perform ten contractions without getting tired, they are ready to try an abdominal curl.

In the case of the push-up, use a modified position. The modified push-up is similar to the regular push-up except that it is performed from a knees-and-hands position rather than a toes-and-hands position. Explain to students that this is a modification, not a baby push-up or a girl's push-up. Students should be able to do 10 to 20 of the modified push-ups before moving to the regular push-up.

INTEGRATION WITH OTHER SUBJECT AREAS
Integrate this lesson into science lessons in which students are learning the location and function of the body's muscle groups.

QUICK LESSON 4.7
Flexibility

GRADES 1–3

NASPE STANDARD 3 Students participate regularly in physical activity.

LESSON OBJECTIVES

- Students describe and demonstrate flexibility.
- Students demonstrate several flexibility exercises.
- Students work on improving their own flexibility.

EQUIPMENT NEEDED Exercise mats or carpeted area

PREPARATION TIME Five minutes

KNOWLEDGE CONTENT Flexibility is related to the ability of a joint or joints to move through a complete range of motion. While flexibility may be somewhat genetically determined, it can be improved with a regular program of stretching. The flexible person can usually bend and reach farther and sustain positions that are difficult for the person who is not very flexible. Poor flexibility may contribute to injury and stiffness. Flexibility exercises are designed to move the body part through a complete range of motion about the joint.

CLASSROOM ACTIVITY This activity allows students to demonstrate flexibility. Each child is assigned a particular flexibility movement that he or she can then demonstrate to the class. Children do not have to be flexible to demonstrate the movement. They describe the movement, what body parts benefit from flexibility in that joint, and lead the class in doing the movement. Some children are more flexible than others. Explain that the best method to improve flexibility is stretching. To stretch a muscle, students must push the body segment until they feel a stretch. Then have them hold the stretch for 20 to 40 seconds. Stretching in this manner will improve flexibility at that particular joint.

A short walk, marching in place, arm circles, arm reaches, and similar calisthenic exercises should be done before stretching, or this lesson can be presented during cool-down when muscles are already warm.

The following stretches are recommended.

1. Stretch arms and trunk by raising the hands to the sky ("reach for the sky").
2. Stretch legs by leaning forward against a wall until a stretch in the back of the legs (calf) can be felt.
3. From a sitting position on a carpeted floor or mat, reach forward and try to touch your toes or ankles. As you reach, do not bounce. Try to hold the stretch for at least ten seconds. From this position, point the toes; then bring the toes back. Which muscles do you feel stretching?
4. From a supine position, bring one leg up (to a 90-degree angle or more) with a straight knee while the other leg remains on the floor. What muscle is this stretching? With the one leg in this position, pull the toe back, forward, and side to side. Do the same with the other leg.
5. From a supine position, pull one thigh to the chest (with the knee bent) while leaving the other leg on the floor. Pull both thighs to the chest. What muscle does this exercise stretch?
6. From a standing position, pull one arm across in front of the body with the other gently pulling on the elbow. Try this with the other arm.
7. From a standing position, put one arm over the head in a patting-the-back position. Tuck the other arm behind the back, reach up, and try to touch the fingers of the other hand. A child with good upper-body flexibility should be able to do this. Switch arms and do the same exercise with the other arm.
8. Sit on the mat with one leg crossing the other close to the body. Turn the body the opposite way of the leg that is crossed. Try to twist as far as possible in this position. What body part does this stretch?

ASSESSMENT Participation in the activities is the only form of assessment in this lesson. A child's flexibility should not be graded, since it is very individualized. Children should be able to recognize good and poor flexibility and discuss how poor flexibility might contribute to injury and chronic low-back pain. Students may chart their progress on these stretches during the semester.

SUCCESS FOR ALL Allow children in wheelchairs to try all the stretches. A teacher or student partner may be needed to help them maintain proper body position while stretching. For example, the partner may hold the child's legs out straight in front of him or her when performing the toe touches from a sitting position.

Assist any child who needs help in establishing the proper beginning position for the stretch. Proper body position is necessary to prevent injury while stretching.

INTEGRATION WITH OTHER SUBJECT AREAS
Integrate this lesson into science lessons in which students are learning the location and function of the body's muscle groups. Specific stretches are available for the various muscles of the body, and all muscle groups need to maintain their flexibility as students get older.

1. Reach-for-the-sky stretch

2. Calf stretch

3. Seated toe-touch stretch

4. Gluteus maximus and hamstring stretch

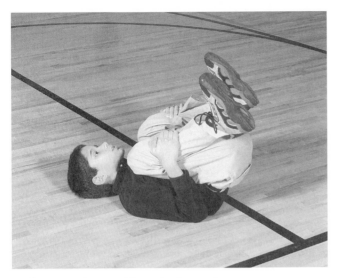

5. Gluteus maximus and lower-back stretch

6. Arm stretch

7. Shake hands stretch

8. Trunk-twist stretch

GRADES 1–3

NASPE STANDARD 3 Students participate regularly in physical activity.

LESSON OBJECTIVES

- Students demonstrate the proper way to walk for fitness.
- Students are able to walk for increasing periods of time.
- Students play different fitness games using walking as a mode of activity for the day.

EQUIPMENT NEEDED Walking area (perimeter of the classroom, indoor gym, or playground trail)

PREPARATION TIME Five minutes

KNOWLEDGE CONTENT Young children should be taught proper walking form, walking with the head up and the arms swinging freely. Pickup and placement of the feet should be accomplished without shuffling the feet or walking on the toes. Encourage children to walk with the toes pointed forward, not inward or outward. This may take some concentration since toeing in or out may have become natural for some children. Walking is a natural activity, yet some children appear stiff-legged or slouched when they walk. Have children practice proper walking technique as well as maintaining proper posture as they walk. Brisk walking is an excellent fitness activity, and walking with a partner is relaxing and fun.

CLASSROOM TO PLAYGROUND ACTIVITY

Before beginning the activity, mark out a walking course. If a gymnasium or all-purpose room is not available, the perimeter of the room can be used. A walking trail set up outdoors is an excellent alternative, weather permitting. Most classrooms are too small for a walking lesson, so some type of marked space should be acquired.

The teacher begins by demonstrating proper walking form. Children then duplicate the teacher's example by walking around the area. Have children walk with a partner and begin with a moderate pace. Remind students to avoid shuffling the feet and walking stiff-legged or on the toes. Use different commands to have the children walk at different speeds. They should be able to walk fast, keeping proper form as they walk.

Play a back-to-front game while walking. Children walk single file with six or seven children in a line. The child at the back has to pick up the speed to make it to the front of the line. Once in front, that child becomes the new leader. Have older children pick up the speed to a fast walk. This game can also be played with music. When the tempo of the music slows, the leader must slow; if it speeds up, the leader speeds up. When the music tempo changes or the teacher gives a signal, the child from the back of the line must move to the front. The children are encouraged to use proper walking form throughout the activity.

ASSESSMENT Place a check mark in the appropriate column of the rubric for each specified technique.

Student: _____   Skill: Walking   Grade Level: _____

TECHNIQUE	ALWAYS	SOMETIMES	NEVER
Head is up.			
Arms swing freely.			
Arms swing front to back (not across the body).			
Knees bend freely as lower leg flexes in a straight line with the knee.			
Foot rolls from heel to the ball of the foot (on each step).			
Toes point forward.			

SUCCESS FOR ALL Students in wheelchairs can participate by rolling in their chairs (on relatively smooth surfaces). Have students with walking disabilities (e.g., a student with cerebral palsy who wears walking braces) walk as long as they can and then continue by being pulled in a wagon by other students. If walking long distances, this student may be in and out of the wagon along the entire distance.

INTEGRATION WITH OTHER SUBJECT AREAS

This lesson could be integrated with math by having the students (in small groups) measure distances so they know how far they are walking. Distances (once around the classroom, playground or gym) could be measured in yards, then converted into feet, miles, etc.

QUICK LESSON 4.9
Heart Rate Games

NASPE STANDARD 3 Students participate regularly in physical activity.

LESSON OBJECTIVES

- Students exercise moderately in the classroom for 10 to 15 minutes intermittently, depending on grade level.
- Students try to maintain a heart rate that reflects moderate-to-vigorous intensity.
- Students improve cardiorespiratory endurance.

EQUIPMENT NEEDED

- A clock or stopwatch with a second hand
- Two pictures of basketball hoops to use as targets for jumping
- Optional: jungle pictures for the corner stations

PREPARATION TIME Fifteen minutes

KNOWLEDGE CONTENT Heart rate games are activities that include everyone in the game, have a goal of increasing the heart rate to a moderate to vigorous level for a period of time, and are fun. The purpose of these types of games is to elevate the heart rate during the activity and to intermittently keep the heart rate between moderate and vigorous for five to ten minutes or more. This type of activity is good for improvement of cardiorespiratory endurance, muscular endurance, and body composition. The intermittent exercise trains the heart to continually deliver blood to working muscle tissue at the rate at which the oxygen is used. As students become fitter, the length of time they can exercise increases the less they need to rest, and the heart becomes more efficient. The younger the child, the less the ability to exercise continuously, so heart rate games keep the child interested in being active while the game continues. Younger students (grades 1–3) can be expected to exercise continuously for about 5 minutes before they must rest, increasing to 10 or 15 minutes. Older students (grades 4–5) should be able to exercise continuously for 30 minutes or more, although that is probably more time than should be dedicated to one activity.

CLASSROOM ACTIVITY FOR GRADES 1–3

These activities are performed at the perimeter of the classroom with the desks pushed to the middle. The object is to have the students exercising continuously.

The activity is to go on a safari. The four corners of the room are set up as stations. At each station students do some type of activity that represents being on safari. Between stations the students do an activity that represents moving from place to place.

Station 1 represents the airport for the flight to the safari location (ask students where they will be going). Students jump five times straight up in the air as high as they can (to get on the plane). After jumping five times, the students move to the next station by pretending to be an airplane with a long wingspan. Motor noises are optional but are encouraged. Upon arriving at station 2 (the base of operations), students do push-ups or bend-and-squat exercises (loading their equipment). The first part of the safari is through dense brush, so they slither like a snake to station 3. At station 3 they are welcomed by the villagers, and all march wildly in celebration of their arrival. Students march in place swinging arms high for about a minute.

En route to station 4, children go through high grass. They lift the legs as high as possible and pretend to jump over the high grass, marching with high leg lifts from station 3 to station 4. At station 4 they are asked by the villagers to scare lions from the bushes. They jump in the air and clap their hands for about ten jumps to scare the lions. Now they are on their way home but must slide along a steep mountain trail. They do a slide step half the way back to station 1, where they pick up horses and gallop back to the starting point. At the starting point everyone does high fives because it was a great trip.

Be sure to have only about four children start the trip at a time. Everyone should be spread out at the different stations as the activity progresses. Don't forget to give occasional rest periods for the first few times the activity is done.

CLASSROOM ACTIVITY FOR GRADES 4–6

These activities are similar to the activity described above except the students are engaged in basketball practice rather than a safari. Students begin at station 1, which represents a basketball goal. They must try to dunk the ball with the right hand five times. Dunk the ball by jumping vertically and slapping a basketball hoop picture that is taped to the wall. Children then do a grapevine step to station 2. At station 2, they find a partner and jump as high as possible (five times), doing high fives (representing a center jump on the court). With their partner, children do slide steps (basketball shuffle) to station 3. One person pretends to be guarding the other. When at station 3, children dunk the ball with the left hand five times (another basketball hoop picture is needed at this station). Now students perform a basketball shuffle to station 4, where student and partner again do five high fives. Hopefully this group of students will need fewer rest periods than the first group, their activity will be more vigorous than moderate, and they will have some fun with it.

ASSESSMENT After each circuit, students stop and quickly take a heart rate. A clock or stopwatch is needed at the last station. Students whose heart rate falls below their target heart rate need to speed up on the next circuit.

SUCCESS FOR ALL Modify the station activities and the between-station locomotor skills as needed for particular students. For instance, students who cannot jump may lift light hand weights up and down (from shoulder height to above the head) as quickly as possible to increase their heart rate. If students cannot slither like a snake, they might crawl or move while seated on a scooter.

INTEGRATION WITH OTHER SUBJECT AREAS
This lesson could be integrated with creative writing by having the students write (and then perform) stories they have written (similar to the ones in this lesson).

GRADES 3–6

NASPE STANDARD 4 Students achieve and maintain a health-enhancing level of physical fitness.

LESSON OBJECTIVES

- Students name the six primary risk factors for heart disease.
- Students name several unmodifiable risk factors for heart disease.
- Students understand how to reduce modifiable risk factors and thereby lower their risk of developing heart disease as an adult.

EQUIPMENT NEEDED Poster board to make the large placards for the bulletin board display

PREPARATION TIME Five–ten minutes, if supplies are on hand

KNOWLEDGE CONTENT The primary risk factors for developing coronary heart disease are (1) smoking, (2) high blood pressure, (3) high cholesterol, (4) inactivity, (5) obesity, and (6) diabetes. Factors that are also important but cannot be modified include age, family history, race, and gender. Modifiable risk factors can be reduced by attention to improving lifestyle. The best way to prevent the deleterious effects of smoking is to refrain from starting the habit. High cholesterol levels can be modified with attention to proper nutrition and lowering saturated fat in the diet.

Lowering high blood pressure is accomplished by reducing stress, maintaining a healthy weight, and eating a healthy diet. Obesity is influenced by a myriad of factors including genetics; however, the most important factors are to improve nutrition, reduce fat in the diet, and eat a caloric intake that does not exceed the daily expenditure. Type 2 diabetes is associated with obesity in children; therefore, reducing obesity by improving the diet and increasing exercise will also reduce the risk of diabetes.

Finally, inactivity seems to be the easiest risk factor to improve. Children should develop a desire to be active as they grow into adolescence and adulthood. Although students cannot influence their genetics, age, gender, or race, reducing the modifiable risk factors will go a long way in avoiding the development of coronary heart disease in the future.

CLASSROOM ACTIVITY Children work together to develop this learning station. This station is put together during an art (or similar) time. Large placards are placed on a bulletin board in the learning station. One side of each placard will represent modifiable coronary heart disease risk factors. The other side represents nonmodifiable risk factors. Each of the risk factors is shown under the title placard representing the type of risk factor. Children are asked to bring a picture from a magazine or newspaper that illustrates that risk factor.

Assign each child a risk factor—modifiable or nonmodifiable—to put up on the board. Then children bring in a picture of a healthy behavior to put on the board. Ask each child to do a healthy behavior at home that would help reduce the risk factor they have been assigned. Children write down the healthy behavior; then at school they draw the behavior and also put it up on the board. Teachers use their creativity to develop the board in accordance with the theme.

ASSESSMENT Children's participation in the activity is the only form of assessment for this learning station.

SUCCESS FOR ALL For students with motor delays (fine motor skills), adapt the writing and cutting processes by having appropriate scissors and markers available, or have precut shapes and letters for them to use.

INTEGRATION WITH OTHER SUBJECT AREAS
Integrate this lesson with art by allowing the students to decorate the bulletin boards.

GRADES 1–6

NASPE STANDARD 3 Students participate regularly in physical activity.

LESSON OBJECTIVES

- Students describe the location of the carotid and radial sites for taking a heart rate.
- Students demonstrate the proper method for palpation of the carotid and radial arteries so that a heart rate can be determined.
- Students determine their heart rate for one minute.

EQUIPMENT NEEDED Clock or stopwatch with a second hand

PREPARATION TIME Five minutes

KNOWLEDGE CONTENT Two sites are usually used for determining the heart rate (see figure). The first, at the carotid artery, is at the neck. Using the first and second finger, children apply light pressure to the carotid artery located on the side of the neck. Children must not press very hard, because too much pressure could cause the heart rate to slow down.

The second site, at the radial artery, is at the wrist. The student palpates (feels for pulse) on the thumb side of the hand, in the wrist area on the inside portion of the arm. The radial pulse is palpated close to the thumb. Again, the student must be careful not to press too hard, because doing so could decrease the heart rate. Even young children can learn these skills if they practice. Encourage children to determine resting heart rates and even to stop during exercise to get a heart rate.

CLASSROOM ACTIVITY Have each student find the proper site for palpating the carotid or radial pulse. Ask students at random to describe the position for a correct measurement. Be sure that they are placing the fingers at the proper position, and remind them to press softly. Keep time and say "go" so that the children will begin counting with each beat. The first beat is counted as zero. The student counts until the teacher says "stop." If the heart beats on the stop signal, that beat is counted.

For grades 1 and 2, students first try to locate and feel the pulse. Make sure each student is doing the skill properly. Ask them to show where they are palpating. Then have them count for 15 seconds. A chart that converts a heart rate for 15 seconds to beats per minute is

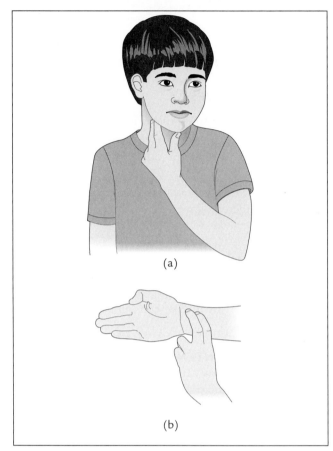

Sites for taking (a) carotid and (b) radial pulses.

helpful (see table). As children begin to learn numbers, they can refer to the chart to determine their heart rate. Older children may count for 30 seconds (and multiply by two) or for a minute.

For grades 4–6, a heart rate station can be set up in the room. The station includes a clock with a second hand or a stopwatch. Students work as partners. As one child keeps track of the time, the other counts her or his own heart rate. It's also helpful for the station to have a chart that converts beats counted for 15 or 30 seconds to beats per minute. As children become more proficient, they can try to take one another's heart rate.

To make the activity somewhat easier without the use of a chart, have students count for only six seconds. Add a zero and you have the heart rate.

ASSESSMENT Children monitor their own heart rate while the teacher also takes a heart rate to double-check. With practice children can become proficient at taking their heart rate.

Conversion Table: Heart Rate for 15 Seconds to Beats per Minute

Heart Rate (15 SECONDS)	Heart Rate (BEATS/MINUTE)
10	40
11	44
12	48
13	52
14	56
15	60
16	64
17	68
18	72
19	76
20	80
21	84
22	88
23	92
24	96
25	100
26	104
27	108
28	112
29	116
30	120
31	124
32	128
33	132
34	136
35	140
36	144
37	148
38	152
39	156
40	160

SUCCESS FOR ALL Have classmates help others to find the proper palpation location.

INTEGRATION WITH OTHER SUBJECT AREAS
Instead of using the conversion table, have students do mental math to calculate the number of heartbeats per minute (multiply the counted heartbeats by two, four, or six, depending on whether students counted for 30, 15, or 10 seconds).

GRADES 1–6

NASPE STANDARD 3 Students participate regularly in physical activity.

LESSON OBJECTIVES

- Students identify major bones in the human body.
- Students identify major muscle groups in the human body.
- Students describe one action for each muscle group in the body.
- Students identify the muscle responsible for a given movement.

EQUIPMENT NEEDED

- Diagram of the human body containing bones and muscles
- Short books or poems (with physical actions in them) for the station for grades 3–6

PREPARATION TIME Thirty minutes to find and enlarge the diagram of the human body

KNOWLEDGE CONTENT Bones form the structure for the human body. Bones join one another at the joint. Bones and muscles are the keys to movement in the human body. Among other functions, muscles connect bones, causing movement about a joint. The movements of eyelids are due to tiny muscles, just as movement of the arm is due to a larger muscle group.

Muscles use the oxygen delivered from the lungs to produce energy for contraction. When muscles contract, they shorten, thereby pulling two body segments closer together. When a muscle shortens, it is called a *concentric contraction*. A muscle can also lengthen while it is contracting. This is called an *eccentric contraction*. In some cases, a muscle is contracting but the force generated is not enough to overcome the resistance and the muscle length does not change. This is called an *isometric contraction*.

Muscles are arranged together to perform similar functions. For example, extending the knee is accomplished through the action of four individual muscles grouped together to form the quadriceps muscle group. Children should begin to learn the names of major bones and muscle groups as early as possible. The following list of bones and muscles may be helpful to the classroom teacher in developing this learning station. Refer to Figures 4.2 and 4.3 for help with the learning station.

Major bones (grades 1–2):

- Skull
- Humerus (upper arm)
- Radius (lower arm, thumb side)
- Ulna (opposite radius)
- Femur (thigh bone)
- Tibia (lower leg, large bone)
- Fibula (lower leg, small bone)

Add these bones for grades 3–6:

- Clavicle (collar bone)
- Scapula
- Sternum (breast bone)
- Spinal column
- Ribs
- Pelvis
- Coccyx
- Patella

Major muscle groups (grades 1–2):

- Biceps (front of arm, crosses the elbow joint): responsible for flexing (bending) the arm
- Triceps (back of arm, crosses the elbow joint): responsible for extending the arm
- Rectus abdominus (abdominals) (front of trunk): responsible for bending at the trunk
- Quadriceps (front of thigh): responsible for extending the knee
- Hamstrings (back of thigh): responsible for bending the knee and moving the upper leg back at the hip (hip extension)
- Gastrocnemius (calf muscle): responsible for pointing the toe and bending the knee

Add these muscle groups for grades 3–6:

- Pectoralis major (chest muscles): responsible for bringing the arms together at the chest, pushing
- Sternocleidomastoid (large muscle at the side of the neck): responsible for moving the head and neck
- Deltoid (large muscle on top, front, and back of the shoulder joint): responsible for arm movement at the shoulder
- Trapezius (large upper-back muscle): responsible for bringing the arms backward (rowing motion) and pulling downward

with all students. These suggestions can be used as a personal evaluation tool or as a checklist when observing other teachers.

- Use person-first language. See the child first and then the disability. Refer to children by their names, not their disability. Do you hear teachers say "My LD kid goes to the resource room in the afternoons"? Or do they use person-first language, saying "Tommy, my student with learning disabilities, goes to the resource room in the afternoons"?
- Let children be the experts on their own disability when possible. For example, if students wear special braces or use a walker or wheelchair, let them show other children how these devices work.
- Look for positive individual and unique personality characteristics in all children. Children with special needs also have individual personalities. Some are shy and reserved, whereas others could be stand-up comedians within their own classroom arenas.
- Celebrate all children's uniqueness. Ask children to share something unique about themselves. Look for the rising star in all students. There is a shining spot in each child if you are open to finding it. Ask students what they like or dislike and what their hobbies and interests are. Do you see bulletin boards or other evidence of individuals being highlighted in the classroom? Quick Lesson 5.1 provides an activity to showcase the "stars" in your classroom.
- Celebrate children's victories and accomplishments, no matter how small. The physical act of cheering and celebrating is a natural motivator—be a party waiting for an occasion to celebrate. Celebrating each child's victories conveys the message that *all* children in your classroom are valued. Consciously be aware that each child is celebrated every day. Try these fun celebrations:
  - Firecracker: Start with hands together in front of you. Shoot hands into the air with a firecracker sound. Clap hands at top. Hands come apart and float back down with an "ah" sound.
  - Wow: Using the fingers in both hands to form *W* shapes, place them on either side of your mouth. Form an *O* with your mouth and yell "wow!"
  - Ape hoot: Dance around like chimpanzees making their hooting sound.
- Talk to the special education teachers, physical education teachers, and classroom teachers who have worked with the child you are getting to know or with children who have similar disabilities (see Reality Tour 1 later in the chapter).
- When becoming acquainted with a child who has a disability, read the child's educational file, looking to identify strengths, weaknesses, health condition, academic level, social and emotional concerns, and medications needed. Prepare a quick reference card for yourself to keep in the classroom, highlighting any information you may need to access quickly.
- Read about the child's specific disability. Do not assume that the characteristics or behaviors of a disability are the same with every child with that disability. For example, not all children in wheelchairs have cognitive delays. Search the Internet with the name of the specific disability as the keyword.

Understanding and Accepting Diversity

As our world becomes increasingly diverse, it is important for teachers and children to understand and be comfortable with those who are different from themselves. These differences can come from many areas of diversity: race, religion, color, disability, national origin, gender, size, sexual orientation, or age.

The discipline of physical education supports this need for **understanding and accepting diversity** in its national standards. NASPE explains Standard 5 as follows:

[Students] exhibit responsible personal and social behavior that respects self and others in physical activity settings. The intent of this standard is achievement of self-initiated behaviors that promote personal and group success in activity settings. These include safe practices, adherence to rules and procedures, etiquette, cooperation and teamwork, ethical behavior, and positive social interaction. Key to this standard is developing respect for individual similarities and differences through positive interaction among participants in physical activity. Similarities and differences include characteristics of culture, ethnicity, motor performance, disabilities, physical characteristics (e.g., strength, size, shape), gender, age, race, and socioeconomic status (NASPE 2004, 14).

To help students achieve this standard of understanding and respecting the differences among people, teachers must first learn how to promote these skills. Think back on your own education. Did your school have appreciating diversity as a goal? If so, what was done to promote it?

A TEACHER'S FINGERPRINT

Each teacher comes with his or her own unique fingerprint. This fingerprint comprises an array of unique qualities that help define how you think, what you value, and what you do. Embedded in your fingerprint are the values you gained from your family, rituals, celebrations, and customs that seem second nature to you. This can be as simple as the established routine your family has at mealtimes. Does your family sit down at a table to eat together? Does your family eat in shifts? Does your family eat in front of the television? No one answer is right or wrong. Acknowledging that you come to the classroom with your own unique background or culture will help you better recognize and understand the differences among your students.

A CHILD'S FINGERPRINT

Students also come with their own unique fingerprint and background, just as teachers do. This is true for all students, whether or not they have a disability. Some aspects of a child's fingerprint are visible. When you observe a class even briefly, you can quickly see noticeable differences, such as variations in height, weight, dress, hair color, eye color, and skin color. As you continue to observe, you can see differences in students' social skills, academic skills, and participation levels. However, not all aspects of a child's fingerprint are visible in the classroom. Some cultural traits from home, such as a family's eating times and behaviors, structured study times, family structure, religion, and leisure activities may be discovered or revealed only by asking the student.

BLENDING FINGERPRINTS

Research suggests that the **teacher-student relationship** is one of the most important aspects of a child's educational experience (Baergen 2000; Grant and Sleeter 1998; Payne 1998). "For many students, a caring relationship with the teacher is a prerequisite to learning" (Grant and Sleeter 1998, 17). Teachers' mind-sets can determine whether they are capable of bonding with students who are different from themselves. Does your mind-set about students with disabilities lead to limiting possibilities or opening new doors? Teachers who choose to open new doors see that students' disabilities do not always limit the possibilities of what they can accomplish; disabilities merely present obstacles that can often be overcome with imagination and creativity. Teachers who are committed to developing relationships with all the students in their classroom will find a way to overcome obstacles.

Teachers can structure their classroom so that students learn about racial, cultural, family, gender, religious, and skill differences that make up each student's unique fingerprint. "One particularly useful way of beginning to talk about different backgrounds and cultures is through children's names. When children are asked to share the background of their full names, many exciting details of cultural background and history emerge" (Sapon-Shevin 1996, 259). For example, "My name is Ireta June Graube. My mother wanted a name that started with *I* because her mother was named Ida and one of her five sisters was named Irene. She made up the name Ireta because she could not find any other names that started with *I.* June is the name of a nurse that my mother liked that had taken care of her. The last name, Graube, is from German origin" (I. Graube, personal communication, July 23, 2001). Quick Lesson 5.2 gives additional ideas for ways classmates can get to know each other.

As students learn about each other, they can begin to see common ground and develop relationships and friendships. The following ideas can promote friendships in the inclusive classroom (Calloway 1999, 176–177).

- Be open and honest about disabilities. If children ask for information about a disability, respond with a simple, truthful answer.
- Use all of your resources. Involve your class in brainstorming sessions on how to adapt activities for children with disabilities. Be sure to include your child with a disability in this process in a respectful and dignified way.
- Make disability a comfortable concept. Provide representations of children and adults with disabilities through pictures, literature, dolls and figures, and dramatic play activities so that disabilities are shown to be a part of everyday life.
- Provide equal access for typically achieving peers. Allow all children supervised access to adaptive equipment when it is not in use.
- Explore a variety of differences and similarities among people. Emphasize the positive things that individuals can share with each other. Make being unique a benefit rather than a problem. See Instant Activity 5.1 for a sample activity to explore differences and similarities among your children.

Teachers' positive relationships with all students can be contagious, affecting the relationships between classmates. Teachers can promote relationships be-

INSTANT ACTIVITY 5.1
Similarities and Differences

Grades K–6

Equipment Needed

Prepared music

Activity

Play music as students move around the room performing different locomotor skills. Each time the music stops, have children find a new partner and tell the partner something that is similar and something that is different about themselves. Call out a new locomotor skill and start the music again. Repeat until students have been partners with each classmate. Younger students may be limited to telling their partner similar and different physical characteristics. Encourage students in the upper grades to think more in depth.

tween students by showing that each student makes a valuable contribution to the class. Box 5.1 shows how a student with a disability can contribute to a class.

Disabilities Require a Deeper Understanding

It is difficult, if not impossible, to understand the unique fingerprint or culture of students with a disability, or of their families, without going a step further and looking at life from their perspective—walking in their shoes—or riding in their wheelchair. Disabilities are often misunderstood because individuals with disabilities unwittingly break the norms of culture. They can be perceived much as a foreigner might be. The student with a disability may speak louder than socially accepted or may have physical movements that are unpredictable or constant and repetitive. Students with disabilities often break the invisible social barrier of proximity. These students may hug you when you were expecting them to say hi. They may be nose to nose with you in a conversation. Many people in society stare at students with disabilities or even

become uncomfortable or upset by their appearance or behaviors. Teachers need to get to know students and their families well enough that they can break out of any stereotypic reaction.

The following activities are designed to help you think about daily life from the perspective of someone with a disability, and from the perspective of a parent whose child has a disability. To do this activity, you will embark on a journey to discover the realities in the world of the disabled.

JOURNEY TO DISCOVER REALITIES

The realities of our world and culture are often very different from those of children with disabilities and their families. The purpose of discovering these realities is not only to inform but to challenge your attitudes and perspectives regarding children with disabilities. Do you truly know how you feel about disabilities?

What to Pack   On this journey you will leave the land of preconceived notions, stereotypes, and clichés. When you pack, leave behind feelings that people with disabilities need to be pitied. Leave behind attitudes that people with disabilities cannot do certain things. Leave behind notions that people with disabilities do not have real feelings. When you pack, do bring an adventurous spirit. Do bring an open mind and a loving heart. Do bring a willingness to look with new eyes.

Who Will Guide Your Journey?   On this journey you will need guides to help navigate your trip, much as you need a tour guide when visiting a foreign country. Your guides will be the parents or caregivers of children with disabilities as well as the children themselves.

Usually, you feel in control of your life with respect to the activities you choose to participate in and the people you choose to socialize with. But on this journey, in order to reach your destination, you must give up this secure sense of control. If you do not feel a bit lost, then you have not relinquished the navigational control and given it to the caregiver or child. Expect some disorientation while someone else steers.

Sensitivity Toward Your Guide   The parents or caregivers of children with disabilities and the children themselves can guide you on this journey to discover their perspectives and their innermost feelings. You must take care to be extremely sensitive to

BOX 5.1 Meet Deb

Deb is a nine-year-old girl in the third grade. She drives an electric wheelchair with the one hand she is able to control. Deb does not speak, but she communicates by smiling, not smiling, looking away, shaking her head yes or no, using picture cards, and using a computer with voice output. One of Deb's contributions to the class is informing children of the lunch menu each morning. She "reads" the menu to the class by touching pictures on her computer of the foods for that day and letting the computer name off each food item.

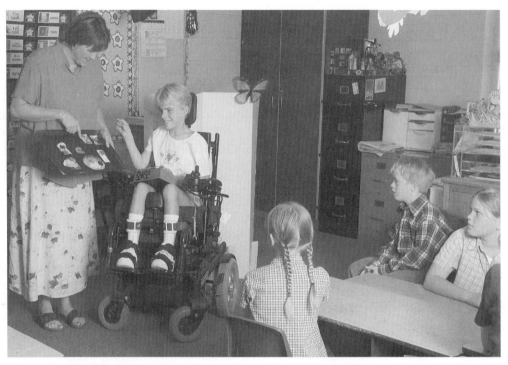

This student announces the daily lunch menu to her class by touching pictures on a computer.

your guides' perspectives and feelings. Letting caregivers express the realities of having a child with a disability can be painful. Their feelings are part of their reality, but they may be stored several layers deep. Retrieving and sharing these personal feelings with others has potential to bring their painful reality to the surface.

REALITY TOURS

Your journey of understanding will take you on three reality tours: (1) reflections from an experienced professional who has extensive experience working with children with disabilities and their families, (2) perceptions from the parent of a child with a disability, and (3) perceptions from a student with a disability. Each of the three tours examines issues regarding educating all children, future dreams of parents and teachers, and field trips. In Reality Tour 1, each topic is introduced by asking a question that addresses a certain issue from the professional's perspective. Reality Tours 2 and 3 also address questions related to these three issues, but the questions are individualized to represent the perspective of the parent and the child.

REALITY TOUR 1: THE PERCEPTIONS OF AN EXPERIENCED PROFESSIONAL

Educating All Children Are teachers open to accepting the responsibility to educate all children?

Peggy is a seven-year old girl with a mental disability and a seizure disorder. She has short, wavy blond

Some students with disabilities may break norms of personal space and speak to others in very close proximity.

hair and blue eyes. Her parents have been very supportive and involved in Peggy's educational program. Peggy enjoys teasing and has a grin that would make almost anyone laugh. Sometimes when Peggy does not get what she wants, she becomes very loud and throws a tantrum. After she calms down and visits with the teacher, she can often be heard saying, "But I was just a wittle bit woud." Peggy has difficulty pronouncing the *l* sound. Consistent behavior modification programs have helped Peggy decrease her behavioral outbursts.

Peggy can sing the alphabet song and point to the letters in her name. She can count to ten by rote and point to the numbers one, three, and five in isolation. Peggy can write the letter *P* of her name independently. She loves music and movement activities and enjoys songs that have actions to them.

Peggy made slow but steady progress for two years. This progress abruptly stopped, and sudden losses of skill and language took place five months ago. Peggy became ill and her doctors could not determine

what was wrong with her. She can no longer talk. Different medications have triggered aggressive behaviors in her.

Because of all of these changes in Peggy, especially the aggressive behaviors, Peggy's parents sent her to school very sporadically the first semester. She attended school only 17 days during the second nine-week period. We (Peggy's educational team) met independently and with the parents numerous times. Peggy's educational needs had changed drastically since the beginning of the year. She had lost her ability to communicate with us, and she had lost her ability to show us what academic skills she possessed. Her behavior was aggressive toward teachers and other students. What could we do to help Peggy educationally?

We recommended to Peggy's parents that she needed to be at school more, even though she was a totally different child than she had been before. Peggy's mom replied, "I don't think it is fair to send Peggy to school in her current condition. She's my responsibility, and we can keep her home and try to work on school things there. I don't want her to be a burden for you." We replied that it is also our responsibility to provide an appropriate education for Peggy. That education may not look like the same educational program she was receiving before, but it will be specially designed to meet Peggy's current needs. It looked as if Peggy's parents were relieved and thankful that the school still wanted Peggy to be there.

What must parents or caregivers feel if they are not sure they have the right to send their child to school? Should parents ever have to feel that their child is a burden to the school? Do school personnel make every effort to welcome all students? Do teachers reach out to parents who have students with disabilities? What if it was your child? Do teachers assure parents that they will be accepting of their children no matter what the circumstances are? Are teachers unconditional in their willingness to accept *all* children?

Future Dreams for Parents and Teachers Are teachers sensitive and understanding about the parents' hopes and dreams for their child?

Kade is a bubbly nine-year old boy with cerebral palsy. He is deaf and has had numerous health problems throughout his life. Kade started attending a special needs class when he was three years old. He was cute and lovable, and staff members were overflowing with ideas to try with him. They saw endless potential in Kade.

When Kade was three years old, his mother attended his Individual Education Plan (IEP) meeting with his educational team. She was cooperative and agreeable to the programs we wanted to try with Kade, but she did not have any suggestions herself. The following year, when Kade was four years old, his mother did not want to come to his IEP meeting. She did not want to discuss programs or anything that had to do with Kade's future. After much persuasion, she finally agreed to come to his IEP meeting. None of us knew what was going on.

Shortly into the IEP meeting, tears began to stream down Kade's mother's face. There was a long, silent pause. As Kade's mom tried to regain her composure, she told us that she could not bear to plan Kade's future because a doctor had told her when he was two years old that he would not live to be six. Our hearts ached for her, and tears welled up in all our eyes. How audacious it must have seemed and how painful it must have been for the teacher to ask this mother to project what she thought her son could accomplish in the next year, only two years away from what was possibly Kade's last year. Kade's mother asked the teachers to plan his program at school, but she just could not help us.

Although Kade's mother was very supportive of the school staff, she was not involved with the development of his IEP for the next two years. When Kade turned seven years old, his mother suddenly became very active in planning for his educational needs. Kade had beaten the doctor's odds, and that burdensome timetable was gone. In his mother's eyes, Kade now had a future. Can teachers begin to imagine how Kade's mother felt when she was told he would not live to be six? When parents or other caregivers do not respond the way teachers think they should when planning for their child's education, do we jump to conclusions? Do teachers wonder if they really care about their child? Do teachers take the time to really listen to their story?

Field Trips Does accessibility limit where teachers can take their students on field trips?

Logan is a second grader. She needs an electric wheelchair for mobility. Logan's class is going on a field trip to a local restaurant. They have been studying the food groups, ordering etiquette, and acceptable manners. Each student is prepared to order his or her meal and then visit with the other students at the table about the different food groups in the meal.

The bus unloads the class at the front of the building. The rest of the class enters the front door, which requires climbing three steps. Logan and the teacher wheel around to the side door to enter where there is a ramp. The class begins to follow the mazelike ordering line that weaves back and forth between two rails. Logan immediately can tell that her wheelchair will not fit between the rails. How will she get her turn to order? Logan had rehearsed her order at school and knew exactly what to say to follow proper etiquette.

Logan was the last student to order and could not figure out a way to get close enough to the counter to place her order. In frustration, the teacher just had Logan give her the order and she relayed it to the waiter. Logan drives her wheelchair back to the booths where the other children are sitting (four to a booth). Three girls call to Logan to come sit with them. Logan pulls up to the end of the booth and realizes her wheelchair will not fit between the booth seats at the end of the table. Logan had anticipated sitting at a table with her friends and left her wheelchair tray at school. How was she going to eat? Once again frustrated by the inconveniences of this restaurant for Logan, the teacher helped Logan hold her food in her lap.

As the students ate, they discussed the food groups present in their meal. Logan was so busy trying to eat from her lap that she missed the entire discussion. The field trip was a flop for Logan. How accessible are the restaurants in your community? Do you notice when stairs are required to enter a building? Do you notice if the bathroom door swings in or out? Doors that swing in do not generally allow room for a wheelchair to enter, or if they do, for the door to be closed after the person has entered. What message was Logan given on that field trip?

REALITY TOUR 2: THE PERCEPTIONS OF A CAREGIVER

The second part of your journey is to look at disabilities from the perspective of a parent or other caregiver whose child has a disability. This interview will give you significant insight into the caregiver's perspective. Remember to let the person you are interviewing be the guide and teach you. Be an active listener. Follow the work sheet in Figure 5.1 during the interview. Record the interviewee's answers so you can look back and regain that person's perspective.

REALITY TOUR 3: THE PERCEPTIONS OF A CHILD WITH A DISABILITY

The third part of your journey is to look at life from the perspective of a child who has a disability. Signed permission must be acquired from the child's parent or other caregiver before visiting with the child. Do not point out the disability to the child. Speak to him

Protocol to be read verbatim to the caregiver:

Thank you for agreeing to visit with me. I am becoming a teacher and want to learn more about children with disabilities. This class project is designed to help me learn about disabilities from the perspective of a caregiver whose child has a disability. We will choose a code name for you and put it on my work sheet. Your real name will be kept in strict confidentiality. In a later activity, the other students in my class and I will reflect on and share our experiences with the parents and other caregivers we have interviewed. At this time, only your code name will be referred to.

Some of these questions may be difficult, or even painful, for you to answer. Please answer the ones you feel comfortable with, and feel free to say that you would rather not answer a particular question. Again, thank you for giving me this learning opportunity.

Date _____

Code name _____

Description of child's disability _____

_____

Questions

1. Education. What do you think of your child's school? Do you think the education for your child is appropriate? What would be the perfect education for your child?

2. Future Dreams or Vision. What are your hopes and dreams for your child? What suggestions can you give teachers to help them be understanding and relate to the history your child brings to school?

3. Family Outings. Do you believe the restaurants in your town are accessible to your family? Describe what is involved in taking your child out to eat. What recreation/leisure activities are accessible to your family in the community?

FIGURE 5.1 Protocol and Work Sheet for Interviewing the Caregiver of a Child with a Disability

Protocol to be read to the child:

Hi. My name is _____. I am trying to learn more about kids. Would you be willing to answer some questions for me? I won't put your real name on my work sheet. You can help me choose a name to call you. Thank you for helping me learn more about kids.

Date _____

Parent's signature _____

Child's code name (let child choose name) _____

Questions

1. Education. What is your favorite activity at school? What is easy for you? What is hard for you? If you could change something at school, what would it be?

2. Future Dreams or Vision. What do you want to be when you grow up? What do you like to do outside of school?

3. Family Outings. What is your favorite food? Where do you like to eat out? Does your family do activities in the community? If so, what are they?

FIGURE 5.2 Protocol and Work Sheet for Interviewing a Child with a Disability

or her as you would to any other child. The work sheet in Figure 5.2 has been designed to guide you through Reality Tour 3.

Understanding and Adapting to Disabilities

Reality Tour 1 allowed you to look through the eyes of an experienced professional at issues that relate to students with disabilities. Reality Tour 2 gave you a glimpse into the life of a family with a child who has a disability. Reality Tour 3 took you up close and personal with a child who has a disability. Do you have a better understanding of the family's and the child's perspectives? This deeper understanding facilitates positive relationships between teachers and students.

Now we will focus on the requirements by law, inclusion, and the most common types of disabilities that students in your classroom are likely to have. The law requires that the physical needs of students be addressed. Disabilities are classified in five categories: (1) learning disabilities, (2) mental disabilities, (3) emotional disabilities, (4) sensory impairments, and (5) physical disabilities. In this section we'll look at each type of disability more closely. Classroom teachers can learn to adapt to and meet the needs of children with disabilities, keeping in mind that "individuals with disabilities, for the most part, can gain very similar benefits from physical activity and the accrued physical fitness as people without disabilities" (Seaman, Corbin, and Pangrazi 1999, 12). The report from the surgeon general (President's Council on Physical Fitness and Sports 1996) on physical activity and health states that "regular physical activity can help people with chronic, disabling conditions, improve their stamina and muscle strength, and can improve psychological well-being and quality of life by increasing the ability to perform activities of daily life."

REQUIREMENTS BY LAW

In 1975, the U.S. Congress passed the Education for All Handicapped Children Act (PL 94-142). In 1990 and 2004, this law was reauthorized and named the

Individuals with Disabilities Education Act (IDEA)
(PL 101-476), which mandated the use of the term *disability* instead of the formerly used term *handicapped*.
The significant components of IDEA are as follows:

- It guarantees a *free, appropriate public education* for all children with disabilities ages 3–21.
- *Due process* of law requires parent participation and involvement in the initiation, development, and implementation of their child's educational program.
- *Least restrictive environment* (LRE) requires students with disabilities to be educated with their nondisabled peers to the maximum extent possible.
- An *Individual Education Plan* (IEP) must be developed and implemented for each student with a disability.

The IDEA 2004 requires all public schools to have a system to locate, identify, and evaluate all students who might have a disability. This is usually referred to as a "child find." Parent permission must be obtained in writing before professionals can evaluate or assess a student. After formal assessment, an Individual Education Plan must be made before placement in a special program can occur. Parents must give written consent to the placement recommendations before the plan can be implemented.

Definitions The term *special education* means specially designed instruction, at no cost to parents, to meet the unique needs of an individual with a disability, including

1. instruction conducted in the classroom, in the home, in hospitals and institutions, and in other settings; and
2. instruction in physical education (300.26).

The term *child with a disability* means a child having mental retardation, a hearing impairment including deafness, a speech or language impairment, a visual impairment including blindness, serious emotional disturbance, an orthopedic impairment, autism, traumatic brain injury, and other health impairment, a specific learning disability, deaf-blindness, or multiple disabilities (300.7).

Requirements for Physical Education Physical education is the only specific area mentioned in PL 94-142 and retained in PL 101-476. IDEA defines physical education for individuals with disabilities as follows:

1. The development of
   a. physical and motor fitness;
   b. fundamental motor skills and patterns;
   c. skills in aquatics, dance, and individual and group games and sports (including intramural and lifetime sports); and
2. Occurring through special physical education, adapted physical education, movement education, and motor development [300.39(b)(2)].

INCLUSION

The term *inclusion* can have many interpretations. Tripp, Piletic, and Babcock define **inclusion** as "a philosophy of acceptance that supports placing students with disabilities in their neighborhood schools. Supplementary aids and services, or other supports, are brought to the student while in the general physical education class rather than having the student go to the services in a separate class" (2004, 8). Inclusion of each student should be made on an individual basis. This decision is made by the team in the IEP process.

Physical education services may be provided in a number of settings:

- The inclusive setting occurs when the student's physical education is delivered in the general physical education setting with typically developing peers. The student may or may not need additional staff support in this setting. Staff members that might support the teacher and student include adapted physical educators, aides, paraprofessionals, peers, physical therapists, orientation and mobility specialists, vision specialists, and special educators.
- A noninclusive setting occurs when the student receives adapted physical education in a separate setting from the general physical education class.
- A third setting may occur when students receive a combination of inclusion and noninclusion services. For example, the child participates in the general physical education class (with his or her peers) once a week, but also attends adapted physical education class twice a week.

The decision to include students in the general P.E. setting is not contingent on their skills matching their age level. Block and Horton point out that "one of the biggest misconceptions with inclusion is that students with disabilities have to follow the same content at the same level as their peers without disabilities. Children can work on the same content but at different levels matched to their physical, mental, and emotional abilities" (1996, 69–70). According to Lieberman and Houston-Wilson, "It is only when teachers are willing to analyze their curriculum, instruction, rules, equipment,

Students showshoeing in Adapted P.E. with and without snow.

and environment that children with disabilities will have a chance at full participation in general physical education" (2002, 2).

Quality inclusion "depends to a great extent on the environment the teacher creates. The atmosphere should be cooperative rather than competitive, and the teacher must model positive behavior" (Lieberman, James, and Ludwa 2004, 37–39). Quality inclusion considers the following points (Tripp, Piletic, and Babcock 2004, 6–7):

- "Students with disabilities must be actively engaged participants in meaningful learning experiences in the general physical education class, not just in the physical proximity or space. The best inclusive environments offer a variety of activities at different levels of difficulty so ALL students can be involved in learning."

- Decisions involving the inclusion of students with disabilities into the general physical education program must consider the safety of ALL students, including the students with disabilities. Often, safety concerns can be addressed with supplementary aides and supports, and such supplements should be tried before removing the child due to safety concerns."

See Figure 5.3 for a teacher checklist to ensure safe inclusion of students with disabilities.

An excellent inclusive and fitness activity is snowshoeing. One study demonstrated that for nondisabled students, snowshoeing is a safe, feasible, low-impact form of exercise. The study found that even though children move at much slower speeds during snowshoeing than while walking, they burn a significant amount of energy (Connolly, 2002). A pilot research study (Combs and Pitetti 2007), using heart rate monitors with students with disabilities while they snowshoed, showed participants spent almost double the time in their vigorous physical activity heart rate zone versus their moderate physical activity heart rate zone. Snow is not required to snowshoe, making it a bonus for students with disabilities who are sensitive to cold temperatures. Also, the learning curve is very short. If a student can walk, they can learn to snowshoe. Another perk for snowshoeing is the ability for all students to snowshoe regardless of their size. Being overweight is not a deterrent to participating with snowshoes. Snowshoeing is an excellent activity to use in inclusive settings whether it is in the regular physical education setting or in the recess setting. The ease of learning to snowshoe allows *all* students to participate actively.

Have You Done Everything Possible to Ensure the Safe Inclusion of Students with Disabilities?

1. Have you taken the time to get to know the students with disabilities?
   _____ Have you identified specific health/medical problems?
   _____ Have you learned about each child's specific disability and learning characteristics as they relate to safety in physical education?
   _____ Have you talked with each child's parents?

2. Have you gotten involved in the IEP process?
   _____ Have you attended IEP meetings?
   _____ Have you shared your concerns for physical education with team members?
   _____ Have you provided specific information about your program to team members?
   _____ Have you talked with a specialist who works with the child?

3. Have you determined each student's abilities through formal and informal assessment?
   _____ Have you observed the child in general physical education?
   _____ Have you noted the child's behavior as it relates to potential safety concerns?
   _____ Have you determined the child's fitness and motor abilities as they relate to potential safety concerns?

4. Have you examined the teaching environment for safety concerns?
   _____ Have you examined the environment for adequate movement space?
   _____ Have you established clear boundaries that all children can recognize?
   _____ Have you set up equipment in a safe manner for all children?
   _____ Have you examined accessibility of your environment, including lockers and playing fields?

5. Have you examined all of your equipment for safety concerns?
   _____ Have you recently checked equipment for adequate repair?
   _____ Do you have necessary adapted equipment for children with disabilities?
   _____ Do all children know the proper use of equipment?

6. Have you used safe teaching techniques?
   _____ Have you established safety rules, and have you made sure all children understand these rules?
   _____ Can you adequately supervise all areas, especially areas where children with disabilities are moving?
   _____ Have you modified instruction so that all children understand directions?
   _____ Have you planned activities that are progressive so that children are not participating in activities beyond their abilities?

7. Have you considered modifications to content to ensure safety?
   _____ Have you examined the need to present content at levels that match students' physical, mental, and emotional abilities to ensure safety?
   _____ Have you examined the need for an alternative curriculum to ensure safety?

FIGURE 5.3 Teacher Checklist to Ensure Safe Inclusion of Students with Disabilities

Source: J. E. Block and M. L. Horton. Include Safety in Physical Education: Do Not Exclude Students with Disabilities, *The Physical Educator* 53(2): 71 (1996). Copyright 1996 by Phi Epsilon Kappa Fraternity. Reproduced with permission of Phi Epsilon Kappa Fraternity in the format Trade Book via Copyright Clearance Center.

COLLABORATION

Teachers engage in **collaboration** when they work together to pool their resources for the benefit of students. When a child with special needs is included in the classroom, teachers play a key role on the IEP team. Classroom teachers can attest to how the multitude of services provided the child are working. They can provide perspective on whether more special education services are needed to help the child be successful. Classroom teachers have firsthand knowledge of the classroom atmosphere and the friendships or lack of friendships that the child has developed.

Classroom teachers are not expected to have in-depth knowledge about every possible disability that a student might have. The classroom teacher, physical education teacher, and special education teacher can work together to share information on a specific disability and learn what types of modifications might be needed to help the student be successful in all of his or her learning environments. The school nurse may also be a valuable resource for information about a specific disability or may be able to answer questions about health concerns or medications. Coordinating and communicating with this many professionals can be a challenge. Open communication and dialogue will benefit the teachers, support staff, and students.

LEARNING DISABILITIES

A **learning disability** is defined in the Individuals with Disabilities Education Act as "a disorder in one or more of the basic psychological processes involved in understanding or in using language, spoken or written, that may manifest itself in an imperfect ability to listen, think, speak, read, write, spell, or to do mathematical calculations, including conditions such as perceptual disabilities, brain injury, minimal brain dysfunction, dyslexia, and developmental aphasia. The term does not include learning problems that are primarily the result of visual, hearing, or motor disabilities; of mental retardation; of emotional disturbance; or of environmental, cultural, or economic disadvantage" [300.8 (c)(10)]. Learning disabilities are a universal problem that occurs in all languages, cultures, and nations (Lerner 1997). Box 5.2 introduces a student with a learning disability.

Many characteristics are associated with learning disabilities, but each child is unique and presents only some of these characteristics. The common characteristics are (1) disorders of attention; (2) poor motor abilities; (3) perceptual and information-processing problems; (4) failure to develop cognitive strategies

---

BOX 5.2
Meet Jacob

. . . .

Jacob is a seven-year-old boy with learning disabilities. He has short brown hair and is tall for his age. He wants to have friends but often unintentionally pushes peers away by getting right in their face when he talks to them or demanding that they play with him. Jacob has been likened to "an accident waiting to happen." He often falls over desks, runs into other kids and falls, and knocks other kids down when moving about the room. Jacob is in constant motion, whether it be shaking his legs while sitting, tapping his pencil on the desk, or rocking on his chair. Jacob will listen and stop moving when asked by the teacher, but the movement begins again within minutes. As Jacob stands for the flag salute, he places his left hand over his heart.

---

for learning; (5) oral language difficulties; (6) reading, written language, and mathematics difficulties; and (7) inappropriate social behavior (Lerner 1997).

Children with learning disabilities can experience difficulty in motor performance, which occurs for several possible reasons: (1) poor coordination in gross motor activity, (2) poor fine motor coordination, (3) poor body image, (4) clumsiness, and (5) perceptual motor problems. Difficulties in perception can be related to any of the six perceptual systems: (1) visual (sight), (2) auditory (sound), (3) tactile (touch), (4) kinesthetic (muscle feeling), (5) olfactory (smell), and (6) gustatory (taste).

Common perceptual motor problems can be evident in poor balance; inability to identify body parts, sizes, and shapes; and inability to discriminate between right and left. Perceptual motor problems can also be evident in poor spatial orientation affecting the ability to understand orientational directions and spatial relations of the body to other bodies and objects (Auxter, Pyfer, and Huettig 2001; Lerner 1997; Pangrazi 1998; Sherrill 1998). "Difficulty or a reluctance to cross the midline may be a factor that hinders motor skill learning and performance" (Woodard and Surburg 1999, 164). The midline is an invisible line running the length of the body, dividing the body into a right side and a left side.

Students with learning disabilities benefit from an instructional environment that is highly structured and consistent. Reducing the stimuli in the movement area or classroom can help the student with a learning disability focus on the instructor. This can be accomplished by keeping extra equipment out of sight, waiting to bring needed equipment out until you are ready to use it, lowering window blinds, and keeping the markings on the floor to a minimum. A wide-open movement area can be overwhelming for students with learning disabilities. Limit the space that will be used by cones, partitions, or some type of boundary.

Consistent routines help students with learning disabilities. Have a set routine for students to follow when entering the movement environment. All students enjoy having responsibility and jobs to do. Having an assigned job helps the student with a learning disability to focus and stay on task. Set up opportunities for the student to have a positive contact with you as soon as he or she enters the movement environment. For example, as the student enters, the first task is to find you, give you a high five, and tell you what the lunch choices are for the day. This initial positive contact can help the student remain calm when entering an environment without becoming overwhelmed by the size or the stimuli present.

MENTAL DISABILITIES

The Individuals with Disabilities Education Act places **mental disabilities** in the category of mental retardation. It states that "mental retardation means significantly subaverage general intellectual functioning, existing concurrently with deficits in adaptive behavior and manifested during the developmental period, that adversely affects a child's educational performance" [300.8 (c)(6)]. A wide continuum or degree of mental disabilities exists. Cognitive capabilities vary greatly along this continuum.

> Physically, this group presents significant variations in characteristics. At the mild end of disability, there may be few or no observable physical differences. Slight motoric immaturity or slowness to develop may be the only sign of developmental problems. As the level of disability increases, especially when there are biological or pathological causal factors present, there may be facial differences (e.g., Down syndrome), sensory disabilities (hearing or vision), and seizures or cerebral palsy resulting from brain injury. (Raymond 2000, 72)

Box 5.3 introduces a student with a mental disability.

BOX 5.3
Meet Jared

Jared enters the gym each day pretending to be a super action hero. He is slight in build and has long legs that wobble when he walks. He wants the teacher to guess which action hero he is that day. If you do not guess correctly on the first or second try, he becomes agitated and tells you the answer. Coaxing him to become an eight-year-old boy again and participate can be a challenge.

Jared can walk, run, and gallop. He cannot balance on one foot, hop, skip, or leap. Jared is generally eager to participate in all activities, especially if you refer to an activity as a game. Jared's sense of humor is beyond his years at times. Here is a conversation he has with his teacher:

> **TEACHER:** Today after warm-up and exercises we will play a game working on catching skills. Jared, do you want to do your warm-up or exercises first?
>
> **JARED:** I want to play the game with balls.
>
> **TEACHER:** First we need to do our warm-up and exercises. Which one do you want to do first?
>
> **JARED:** I want to play the game first.
>
> **TEACHER:** But when will we do our warm-up and exercises?
>
> **JARED:** When pigs pie.
>
> **TEACHER:** What do you mean by pigs, Jared?
>
> **JARED:** You know, when they pie in the sky (Jared is flapping his arms like a bird).
>
> **TEACHER:** Oh, you said "When pigs fly"! That's funny, Jared. We can't wait that long.
>
> **JARED:** I'll do my warm-up first.

Students with Down syndrome need to take precautions when participating in physical education and Special Olympics:

There is evidence from medical research that up to 15 percent of individuals with Down syndrome have a misalignment of the cervical vertebrae C-1 in the neck referred to as Atlantoaxial Instability or sometimes referred to as Atlantoaxial Subluxation. This condition exposes individuals with Down syndrome to the possibility of injury if they participate in activities that hyperextend or radically flex the neck or upper spine. Special Olympics require temporary restriction of individuals with Down syndrome from participation in certain activities that pose potential risk. This restriction may be lifted once an X-ray is produced showing no evidence of instability on the C-1 vertebrae. Students with Atlantoaxial Instability should not participate in physical education or Special Olympics in the following sports and activities: butterfly stroke and diving starts in swimming, diving, high jump, equestrian sports, artistic gymnastics, soccer, alpine skiing, and any warm-up exercise that places undue stress on the head and neck. (www.specialolympics.org, search Atlantoaxial Subluxation)

Students with mental disabilities follow the same developmental sequence as their nondisabled peers except the rate at which they learn is slower (Dunn 1997). Some of the common characteristics of students with mental disabilities include (1) having short attention span, (2) being slow to understand and follow directions, (3) being lovable and wanting to please, (4) exhibiting a delay in physical and motor skills, and (5) showing a delay in perceptual motor skills. Children with mental disabilities often have a wonderful sense of humor, enjoy teasing, and have great imaginations. A child's teasing can often be misinterpreted as disobedience. However, tease children in return and watch how they respond. If they continue to tease with you, they are not meaning to willfully disobey. You may need to teach children when it is acceptable to tease and when they need to follow directions immediately.

As you recall, many characteristics of students with learning disabilities are common in students with mental disabilities. Students with mental disabilities are often clumsy and lack balance. Students with mental disabilities often have the same perceptual motor delays as students with learning disabilities: (1) poor body image, (2) poor spatial relations, and (3) poor spatial relations of their body to other bodies and objects. "Students with mental disabilities often score lower than other children on measures of strength, endurance, agility, balance, running speed, flexibility, and reaction time" (Dunn 1997, 330).

Students with mental disabilities benefit from the same structured and consistent environment that students with learning disabilities do. Reduce extra stimuli in the movement environment. Teach by using demonstration and verbalization at the same time. Ask students to repeat directions back to you before they begin an activity. Be brief with directions. Give only directions that are necessary at the time, and stop to

Students with and without disabilities can enjoy square dancing.

add directions as needed. Students with mental disabilities generally progress at a slower rate than do students without disabilities. Acknowledge small gains in a skill and celebrate with the student.

Students with mental disabilities often need instant gratification from an activity. Affirm and praise approximations of a skill or a valid attempt. These students often respond to physical types of affirmation such as hugs, tickling, and high fives. When giving high fives, seize the opportunity to work on body parts and spatial awareness. Give high fives using elbows, shoulders, backs, knees, hips, bottom of shoes, and full body. Give high fives under your leg, behind your back, over your head, between your knees. The more creative you are, the more students will be motivated to work hard to earn them.

Students with mental disabilities need to work on the same types of activities as their peers without disabilities: motor skills, skill games, fitness, rhythmic activities, and leisure skills. Within these activities, you may need to implement a slower pace, fewer rules, or modified rules. Students with mental disabilities particularly enjoy music. Square dancing is an easy way to incorporate music, cooperation, skill concepts, and fun into a lesson. Music and creative expression has particularly been successful for students with Down syndrome. Teaching a "Language of Movement" (Jobling, Virji-Babul, and Nichols, 2006) allows students to incorporate body awareness, space awareness (low, high, near, far, under, over) and effort awareness (slow, quick, hard, gentle) into their creative dances.

EMOTIONAL AND BEHAVIORAL DISTURBANCES

The Individuals with Disabilities Education Act defines **emotional disturbance** as follows:

A condition exhibiting one or more of the following characteristics over a long period of time and to a marked degree that adversely affects a child's educational performance:

A) An inability to learn that cannot be explained by intellectual, sensory, or health factors.
B) An inability to build or maintain satisfactory interpersonal relationships with peers and teachers.
C) Inappropriate types of behavior or feelings under normal circumstances.
D) A general pervasive mood of unhappiness or depression.
E) A tendency to develop physical symptoms or fears associated with personal or school problems.

The term [emotional disturbance] includes schizophrenia. The term does not apply to children who are socially maladjusted, unless it is determined that they have an emotional disturbance. [300.8 (c)(4)]

Box 5.4 introduces a student with an emotional disability.

Children with emotional or behavioral disorders often do not do productive work or know how

---

BOX 5.4
Meet Julie

Julie is a nine-year-old girl who likes to please but also likes to have things on her own terms. She has long blond hair that is usually worn in a ponytail, and she is stocky in build. As the physical education teacher enters the door of the classroom, she is met with a hug from Julie that nearly knocks her over. Julie is reminded to hug softly so it won't hurt. Julie immediately begins telling the teacher "it is my turn to be the line leader because Morgan was the leader yesterday, and Leah was the leader before that and I am never the leader." The teacher reminds Julie to look at the rotation chart on the wall that determines who the leader is for the day. Julie looks and declares it to be John's turn to lead. On the way to the gym, the teacher and Julie have the following conversation.

> **TEACHER:** Julie, I missed you yesterday. I'm glad you're back. How do you feel?
>
> **JULIE:** I feel good today. I'm not sick anymore. Can we play a game today?
>
> **TEACHER:** Yes, we will play a short game if we have time at the end. We need to finish our fitness testing today.
>
> **JULIE:** My stomach has been hurting all day today. [cough, cough] I hurt my foot at recess this morning and won't be able to run. [cough, cough]
>
> **TEACHER:** Okay. After we finish fitness testing, if you are too tired, I'll understand if you want to sit out during the game.
>
> **JULIE:** I'm feeling better now.

---

to play, give and receive love, and have fun. Yet these four experiences—work, play, love, and fun—are nearly the essence of satisfying and meaningful existence. The teacher's primary task is to structure or order the environment for the student in such a way that work is accomplished, play is learned, love is felt, and fun is enjoyed—by the student and the teacher. (Kauffman 2001, 533)

Most students with emotional or behavioral disturbances display behaviors similar to those of other children: crying, tantrums, mouthing off, and fighting. What separates them from other children is that they display these behaviors more frequently and that less provocation is needed to trigger the behaviors (Forness 2001). Students with emotional or behavioral disturbances generally have some type of a Behavior

Plan. This plan needs to be collaboratively developed with all adults who work with the student. "Even when the behavior management plan is collaborative, the needs of a student or class vary and unforeseen situations arise (i.e., environmental issues), which is why it is important to temper consistency and structure with flexibility" (Lavay, French, and Henderson 2007, 46).

Students with emotional and behavioral disturbances often withdraw from activity, in turn causing poor physical conditioning and delayed motor skill development. These students often have a poor body image (Auxter, Pyfer, and Huettig 2001). The following points will help teachers promote a positive instructional environment for students with emotional disabilities.

- Choose tasks that are developmentally appropriate for the pupil (so that the student can usually succeed) and arrange appropriate consequences for performance (Kauffman 2001, 534).
- Build trust with the students.
- Always let the student start class with a "clean slate," regardless of the student's behavior in a previous session.
- Be fair, consistent, and patient.
- Set clear rules and explain why there are rules. Letting students help set the rules will help them buy into the rules when there is a problem.
- Set clear expectations and boundaries and stick to them. Following through with positive and negative consequences will help students to know that you are honest.
- Be a good role model and maintain self-control.
- Use continuous verbal feedback and praise.
- Show the student you are willing to communicate by talking and listening.
- State comments positively to reinforce the positive consequence of appropriate behavior or performance (e.g., the negative statement "you will not join the activity until your shoes are tied" will not reinforce the positive consequence of appropriate behavior as effectively as "you may join the activity when your shoes are tied").
- Set realistic expectations for students and push them to succeed. Watch for signs of frustration and know when to ease up.
- Warn students in advance when there will be a change in the routine.

SENSORY IMPAIRMENTS: VISUAL

According to the Individuals with Disabilities Education Act, **visual impairments** include both partial sight and blindness. "Visual impairment, including

BOX 5.5
Meet Evan

Evan is a five-year-old boy with visual impairments. He can see light and dark shades, but he cannot see figures. Evan walks with an adapted walker made from PVC piping, which allows it to be lightweight. Evan prefers to be independent and often throws his walker when attempting to walk. After he throws his walker, he tips over or sits down. Evan is lovable and likes to snuggle. He enjoys swinging and rocking activities. When he becomes upset, Evan often pokes his fingers in his eyes or flaps his hands in front of his face. Sitting in a teacher's lap and rocking is calming to Evan. Climbing is one of Evan's favorite activities. He does not understand the danger of climbing on top of tables and objects and must be monitored for safety.

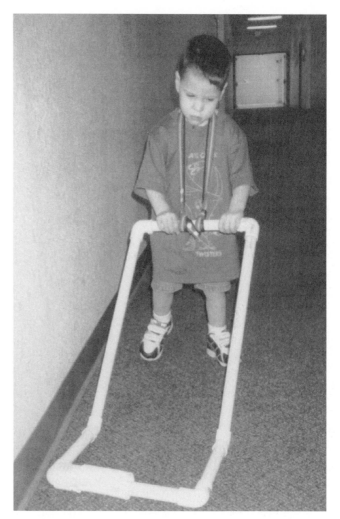

Adapted walkers can help increase mobility in students with visual impairments.

blindness, means an impairment in vision that, even with correction, adversely affects a child's educational performance" [300.8 (c)(13)]. Box 5.5 introduces a student with a visual impairment.

Children with visual impairments may be within normal limits of their age academically, or they may be delayed. Children with visual impairments receive input and learn primarily through their tactile and auditory senses. Always tell them your name when you are approaching them. Also tell them in advance that you are going to touch them.

Children with visual impairments often have stereotyped behaviors, such as rocking back and forth, pushing on their eyes, spinning circles, and waving their hands in front of their face. These children cannot read body language and social cues. Explain to other students that students with visual impairments may stand a little too close because they have difficulty judging distances.

Students with visual impairments need orientation and mobility training, which will help them gain a sense of where they are in relation to people and objects in their environment and learn to move around within that environment. Students with visual impairments are delayed in motor development. They are slow to walk and develop gross motor skills. "Limited movement and exploration, rather than blindness, is the cause of many of the resulting problems associated with visual

impairment" (O'Donnell and Livingston 1991, 287). The sooner you can get a child with a visual impairment to move, the more you increase the chances for that child to achieve physical fitness gains. Consult closely with your vision specialist in your district.

When children with visual impairments are navigating unfamiliar areas, gaits become mechanically less efficient, contributing to early fatigue (Sherrill 1998). Physically, individuals who are blind tend to possess higher levels of body fat and lower levels of cardiovascular endurance, muscular strength, and muscular endurance than their sighted peers do (Winnick and Short 1985). It is important to encourage individuals who are blind to participate in physical activity.

Make conscious efforts to be sure the classroom environment is safe for the student with visual impairments. Students will learn where desks, doors, computers, and other objects are in your classroom. Avoid

With a little help from her teacher, this student with impaired vision enjoys performing a dance.

When you are writing on the chalkboard, always say what you are writing verbally as you write. Use large print or use a black marker on a white board instead of the chalkboard to help the words stand out. As you point to objects in the classroom or use gestures, say their names out loud. Telling the students with visual impairments that the games are on "that shelf" (pointing) will not help them.

When helping a child with a visual impairment write, color, or complete fine motor activities, gently place your hand on top of the child's hand with a light touch. Completely covering the child's hand is like taking away the child's tactile form of vision. If the child can grip crayons or objects, move your support back to the wrist and elbow.

In a larger movement area, use auditory signals such as a whistle. Manipulation and ball-handling skills are difficult. Use brightly colored balls or balls that make noise. When moving, a student with visual impairment can be paired with a sighted student. The partners then hold hands to participate. The student with the visual impairment may prefer to hold the upper arm of the sighted student. Students with visual impairments enjoy dance and rhythms to express freedom of movement. Provide opportunities for free exploration and movement to music. Students with visual impairments often like to swing at recess. Swings can be a safety hazard. Attach bells to the vertical chains on a swing to alert students when they are entering an unsafe area. Teach students with visual impairments to stop when they hear the bells and wait for assistance to enter the swings.

Goal ball is a fun game designed for those who are visually impaired, and it is fun for all students to play. Because of the range of visual impairments among competitors, all students must wear a blackout mask to ensure that they are competing equally. Students with visual impairments will likely be better at goal ball than their blindfolded sighted peers because of their heightened ability to focus and use their auditory sense.

rearranging the room very often. Always tell the students with visual impairments when you have moved furniture, and show them where it now resides. Remind students to keep their desk and table chairs pushed in, and watch for unexpected obstacles such as trash cans and extension cords. Keep doors completely open or completely closed. Partially open doors can be a safety hazard.

Goal ball requires focused use of the auditory senses, and experience gives students with visual impairments an advantage over their blindfolded sighted classmates.

Goal ball is played using a ball containing a bell to indicate its location and direction to the competing players. Teams compete with three players on each side on an 18-meter-by-9-meter court. The lines are five centimeters in width and must have a texture for the players to feel. Competitors throw and aim the ball along the ground at great speeds toward their opponent's goal, which spans the entire width of the court. Spectators must be silent throughout the 14-minute game, allowing the competitors to intensely focus and concentrate on the sound and location of the ball. Cheering is allowed after a goal. Players can stand or lie on the floor to block the ball from reaching their end line.

SENSORY IMPAIRMENTS: AUDITORY

The Individuals with Disabilities Education Act defines **hearing impairment** as "an impairment in hearing, whether permanent or fluctuating, that adversely affects a child's educational performance but that is not included under the definition of deafness" [300.7 (c)(5)]. Deafness is defined as "a hearing impairment that is so severe that the child is impaired in processing linguistic information through hearing, with or without amplification, thereby adversely affecting a child's educational performance" [300.8 (c)(3)]. Box 5.6 introduces a student with a hearing impairment.

Children with hearing impairments can range from having normal intelligence to having difficulty academically. When hearing loss affects their ability to understand language, it can cause academic delays. The greater the hearing loss, the greater the language delays. Children with hearing impairments can become frustrated when multiple conversations are going on around them.

Children with hearing impairments cannot hear auditory warning signals such as fire or tornado alarms or bells. Assign a peer to help alert the student with a hearing impairment during these situations.

Some students with hearing impairment may have a cochlear implant. Visit with the student's parents to find out guidelines for participation in physical education. The school audiologist will also have more details on safety precautions for physical education. Objects that are potential electrostatic producing should be avoided. The physical educator should evaluate what equipment is being used and plan an alternate activity for the child if necessary. Examples of common equipment used in physical education that should be avoided are trampolines, gymnastic

---

BOX 5.6
Meet Shatory

Shatory is a six-year-old girl with significant hearing loss. She wears hearing aids and can hear some verbal direction if it is amplified. She is learning sign language and relies on signing for most of her communication. During free time, Shatory often chooses to play with the vibrating bumble ball. She takes the ball and moves across the room away from the rest of the children. Shatory moves the vibrating ball across her arms and legs and lies on the ball with it pressed against her stomach. She prefers to play alone but will agree to play with another child if an adult is directing the play.

---

mats, rope/climbing equipment, nylon parachutes, scarves, and balloons. Students with cochlear implants should not participate in contact sports (Pyfer and Castle 2004).

Students with hearing impairments may have difficulty with balance. Each child needs to be individually assessed. Most children with hearing impairments can learn skills at a normal pace, but research indicates that deaf children are often behind their hearing peers in physical fitness (Lieberman et al. 2000).

Effective communication is critical for students with hearing impairments. Some use sign language, so learn as much sign language as you can to better communicate with the child. Learning to sign will show the child you are genuinely interested in communicating with her or him. See Figure 5.4 for common signs used in a movement environment. The Classroom Learning Station at the end of the chapter provides an activity in which students use sign language to identify locomotor skills.

Always face the students when talking so they can better hear or read lips. Avoid lengthy explanations. Keep it simple. If you are outdoors, make sure the student's back is facing the sun. Avoid moving excessively while you are giving directions. Give visual demonstrations while you are giving verbal directions. Use visual hand signals to gesture to the class that students need to stop an activity or come over to you for directions. Flashing the lights in the classroom can signal a student with a hearing impairment to look up and find the teacher. Research has shown the effectiveness

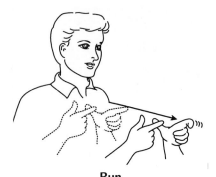

Run
Palm-in Ls move forward, index
fingers flicking in and out rapidly

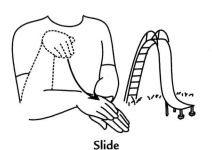

Slide
Right palm-down hand slides
down and outward over back of
left hand

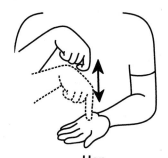

Hop
Inverted index fingertip on left
palm hops up to X several times

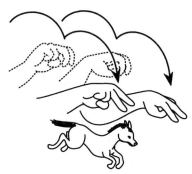

Gallop
Right behind left, bent-Vs leap
forward to open Vs; repeat

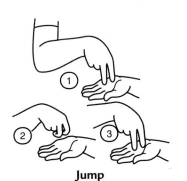

Jump
V-fingertips stand on left palm,
jump up to bent fingers and down
again

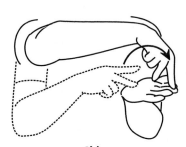

Skip
Middle finger of right K skips
upward to index finger on left flat
palm

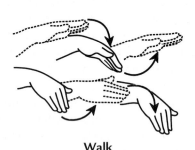

Walk
Palm-in flat hands alternately flip
up while moving forward

Stop
Side of right palm strikes left flat
palm

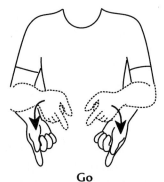

Go
G-hands face each other; roll out
to point forward

FIGURE 5.4   Common Sign Language Signs Used in a Movement Environment
Source: G. Gustason and E. Zawolkow, *Signing Exact English* (Los Alamitos, CA: Modern Signs Press, 1993).

of trained peer tutors working with hearing-impaired
students in a physically active setting. "The tutor training program consisted of teaching the peers how to
instruct, give feedback, and motivate the deaf student

using sign language. The peers were taught to communicate skills to stop and start an activity, give corrective feedback, and motivate the student to continue
engaging in physical activity. The benefit for the peer

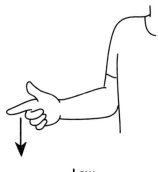

Low
Palm-left L drops slightly

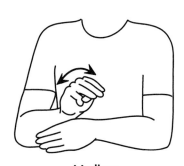

Medium
Right M rocks back and forth on
side of palm-in left B

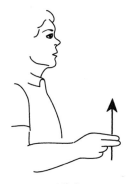

High
H-hand moves upward

Slow
Both hands palms-down, right
hand moves up back of horizontal
left hand

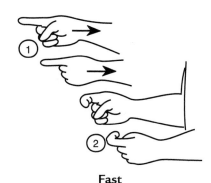

Fast
Indexes point forward, one ahead
of the other, jerk back to Xs

FIGURE 5.4   continued

tutor, as well as the deaf student, makes the use of peer tutors a desirable instructional strategy" (Lieberman et al. 2000, 35).

ORTHOPEDIC AND PHYSICAL IMPAIRMENTS

The Individuals with Disabilities Education Act defines **orthopedic and physical impairment** as "a severe orthopedic impairment that adversely affects a child's educational performance. The term [orthopedic impairment] includes impairments caused by congenital anomaly (e.g., clubfoot, absence of some member, etc.), impairments caused by disease (e.g., poliomyelitis, bone tuberculosis, etc.), and impairments from other causes (e.g., cerebral palsy, amputations, and fractures or burns that cause contractures)" [300.8 (c)(8)]. Box 5.7 introduces a student with a physical impairment.

Children with severe disabilities obtain the same benefits from physical activity as their able-bodied peers. Movement is the goal and can be defined, for example, as increasing range of motion in the shoulder or reaching to grasp a ball. Participation can enhance a student's functional life skills by improving strength, range of motion, and ability (Block 2000, in Lieberman, Lytle, and Irwin 2003).

It is impossible to generalize about the academic ability of students with orthopedic impairments. Some students with orthopedic impairments may be of average intelligence, whereas others have from mild to severe learning problems. Cerebral palsy is the orthopedic impairment most often found in public schools (Friend and Bursuck 1999; Sherrill 1998).

Cerebral palsy varies from mild (generalized clumsiness or a slight limp) to severe (dominated by reflexes, unable to ambulate except in motorized chair, unable to speak, and almost no control of motor function) (Sherrill 1998, 631). There are five major types of cerebral palsy: (1) spasticity, (2) athetosis, (3) ataxia, (4) rigidity, and (5) tremor. The most common type of cerebral

---

BOX 5.7
Meet Michael

Michael is a ten-year-old boy with spastic cerebral palsy. He relies on a wheelchair for mobility. Michael sports a flattop and has bright blue eyes that he uses for communication. He understands what is spoken to him but cannot use verbal language to reply. Instead, he communicates with eye gazes to the left or right to indicate yes or no. Michael smiles when he hears familiar voices of classmates but can be easily startled and upset when he hears unfamiliar voices in the room. Michael is cooperative and enjoys playing with other students if an adult is directing the play.

---

palsy is spasticity, which is caused by a lesion in the motor cortex resulting in impairment in voluntary motor actions. Mental impairment is more frequently associated with spasticity than with any other type of cerebral palsy (Dunn 1997, 196).

Students with spastic cerebral palsy have an increased hypertensity of muscle tone. Their muscles look and feel stiff. Students with spasticity react to the slightest stimulation with a muscular jerk (Sherrill 1998). The stimulation can be verbal, visual, or tactile. They appear to be startled even when you are not meaning to sneak up on them. Warn students with spasticity when a loud noise is going to happen or when you are going to touch them.

Spasticity affects posture and may cause the individual to walk with the legs rotated inward and flexed at the hip with the knees flexed and adducted. The muscle tightness causes the knees to cross over past midline and make a scissor-type motion called a scissor gait (Sherrill 1998). Some students with spastic cerebral palsy use a walker to help them balance. The degree of severity of the cerebral palsy depends on the different body parts involved:

1. Paraplegia—both legs involved
2. Hemiplegia—entire right side or entire left side involved
3. Triplegia—three limbs involved, usually both legs and one arm
4. Quadriplegia—all four extremities involved and usually the trunk

The instructional environment needs to feel warm and welcoming for a student with cerebral palsy or other orthopedic impairments. Students with cerebral palsy who are ambulatory need extra space to walk. They may be able to walk forward but find it difficult to sidestep through a narrow space. Students in wheelchairs need to have access to the entire room. This can be difficult in a crowded room, but with a little creativity teachers can arrange a room so it is inviting to all.

The physical therapist is a critical support staff member for students with cerebral palsy. He or she may provide exercises and stretches for the student to do. The physical therapist will suggest sitting positions and will often bring standers or other pieces of equipment to position the student with cerebral palsy. Under the guidance of the physical therapist, students with cerebral palsy in wheelchairs can be supported in a standing position, allowing the student to bear weight on his or her feet and experience movement from a different position.

Students with cerebral palsy and other orthopedic impairments need to experience all the activities the nondisabled students experience. Balance activities can be carried out on the floor rather than in a standing position if needed. Swimming is an excellent activity for students with cerebral palsy. They have more freedom of movement in the pool because of the buoyancy of the water and the lack of gravitational pull on their limbs.

GENERAL MODIFICATIONS

Some students may need modifications to participate in an activity whether they have a specified disability or not. Remember, for students to be included, all of them do not need to be working at the same level in a content area. Children can work at their different physical, mental, and emotional abilities. This holds true for all children. For example, within any given first-grade classroom, children have a wide range of eye-hand coordination skills. When you are working on eye-hand coordination skills, you must accommodate and challenge students at all levels of skill. Whether you are assessing a student with a specific disability or another peer in the class, the assessment of eye-hand coordination is the same. Wherever each of the student's skill levels falls, this is the appropriate level at which the students should work. Teachers need to be creative when thinking of ways to accommodate a specific student. Try to put yourself in the place of a student with a specific limitation, and problem-solve how you would participate. Use the thought-process of questions. Ask yourself: What is keeping the student from participating or being successful? Change or modify the portion that answers the question. The following four questions

(Block 2007, 128) will help determine whether your change or modification is appropriate: (1) Does the change allow the student with disabilities to participate successfully yet still be challenged? (2) Does the modification make the setting unsafe for the student with a disability or for peers? (3) Does the change affect peers without disabilities? and (4) Does the change cause an undue burden on the general physical education teacher?

The following **general modifications** and teaching strategies will help accommodate the skill level of all students in your class.

OBJECT CONTROL MODIFICATIONS

- Lower targets used for shooting and throwing. Depending on skill level, target suggestions are different-sized trash cans, hula hoops held at varying heights, pictures placed on the wall at varying heights, and basketball goals. A student in a wheelchair with limited arm movements may push the object off the wheelchair tray into a container.
- Students may use catapults to throw objects. Catapults are explained further later in this section.
- Use multiple types of balls, including varying the size, weight, softness, texture, and color. Larger, lighter, and softer balls like balloons, beach balls, or yarn balls are easier to catch and will help eliminate the fear of a harder ball being tossed to a student with delayed coordination. Wadding recycled newspapers into balls is a fine motor coordination activity that accommodates students with different hand sizes and those working on the skill of grasping.
- Play catch with stuffed animals. Ask students to donate stuffed animals or visit local thrift stores or garage sales to purchase them. Have animals of all sizes and shapes. Tie bells around their necks to add a sound. To add a strength component to catching, place a bag of sand inside some of the animals. Make a slit in the back seam, place the sand bag inside, and sew the seam shut.
- Use objects that make noise for students with visual impairments. Actually, all students enjoy noise-producing objects. Put small bells or coins in a balloon. The added weight will cause the balloon to descend a little faster, but it will still be slower than other objects. Place any size ball in a plastic grocery sack and tie it shut. The ball makes a noise when it is bounced or rolled. Equipment catalogs have numerous types of balls that make noise.
- Use soft balls for throwing to avoid injury resulting from errors in judgment regarding the velocity of the throw.
- Use multiple types of striking implements. Start with the hand and progress to shortened handles on implements. If the standard paddles and rackets are too large and heavy, or too small, make a lightweight racket. Lightweight rackets can be made by bending and shaping a coat hanger to form the racket head desired. Pull a pair of old pantyhose over the wire frame to form the racket. Wrap the handle with scrap foam to accommodate the student's hand size. Check with a business in your area that unpacks electronics wrapped in foam. They will be happy to donate scrap foam instead of throwing it away.
- Use Velcro straps to help students who have difficulty maintaining their grip on an implement.
- Hold objects stationary when students are striking them. Tie balloons or different types of balls on string and let them hang down for the student to strike.

BALANCE MODIFICATIONS

- Lower the center of gravity by bending the knees when performing balance activities.
- Vary the width and height of balance beams and extend arms for balance. A student may need a one- or two-hand assist to complete balance tasks. Varying widths of lines on the floor can be used to practice balance as well as a board on the floor or traditional balance beam. Students can stand on balance boards and rocker boards to work on balance. Walk on uneven surfaces outside to work on balance. Walk on flexible surfaces such as a large piece of foam or bubble wrap, which requires students to adjust their balance with each step.
- Keep maximum body parts in contact with the floor. A student with delays in balance can work on balancing on four body parts (e.g., two hands and two feet), or three body parts (e.g., one hand and two feet or one elbow and two knees).

ORGANIZATIONAL MODIFICATIONS

- Reduce the distance of the playing field.
- Reduce the speed of the game. Games can be played walking versus running.
- Modify rules of games.

Some students may need adaptations to existing equipment or special equipment to participate in movement activities during recess and physical education. The specialist in adapted physical education and the physical therapist can help you make the following kinds of adaptations.

Riding tandem bicycles or adapted bicycles is a great fitness activity and provides a leisure activity for students who are unable to ride a conventional bicycle. Students who cannot balance, support their upper body, pedal independently, or steer can still have the opportunity to ride a bicycle. Almost any individual

An adapted bicycle allows this student to experience cycling with the help of a teacher.

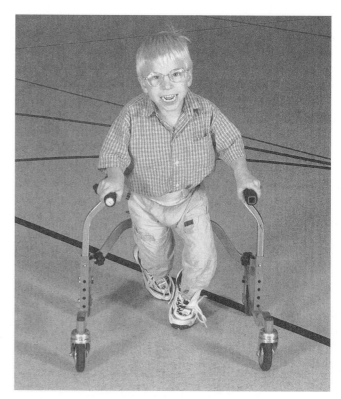

This student with cerebral palsy uses a walker to help him balance.

A tandem bicycle allows this student with a disability to bicycle with her friend.

with disabilities can use a three-wheeled bike with back supports, seat belts, and adapted pedals. The use of Velcro straps on the pedals allows the shoe to stay in contact with the pedal as it revolves around. When the bike is pushed, the pedals will revolve and allow the student to contribute at whatever level she or he is

able. Some students can help push the pedals, whereas others will let the pedals take their feet through the motion. An adult can help support the student, steer, and push the bicycle if needed. A tandem bicycle is ideal for students who have visual impairments or for students with physical disabilities. A nondisabled peer riding with a student with a disability can provide a fun recess activity.

Gait trainers and standers are special pieces of equipment that allow students to walk or stand when unable to do so on their own. The equipment allows students to be positioned to totally or partially bear their weight on their feet. The physical therapist will advise you on positioning for each student. Gait trainers and standers allow students to experience the world from an upright position. A student in a stander can be pushed by a peer and can participate in games and activities. The gait trainers can be adjusted in height to allow the student to wear in-line skates. Peers can help push the student and skate with them.

A catapult is a piece of equipment that acts as a throwing device for students who cannot throw on their own (Combs 1995). When the student pushes a lever, the piece of equipment you have placed on the catapult will be launched in the air. Catapults can also be designed to kick or push a piece of equipment, release an object such as an arrow aimed at an

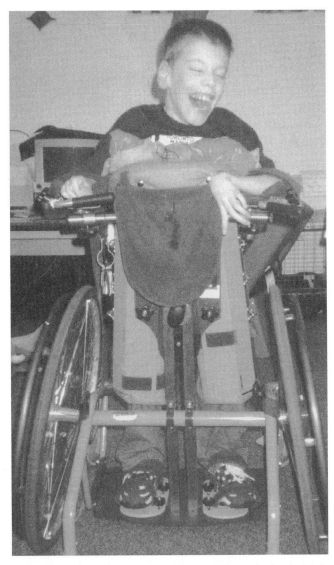

A stander allows this student, who has spastic cerebral palsy and needs a wheelchair for mobility, to experience new movements from a standing position.

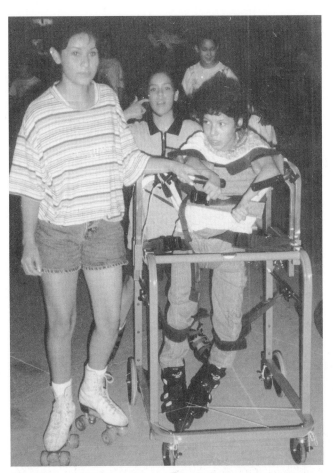

This student with cerebral palsy uses in-line skates with the help of a gait trainer.

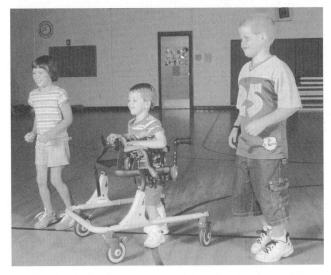

A gait trainer helps this student participate in a jogging activity with his classmates.

archery target, putt a golf ball, serve a Ping-Pong ball, shoot airplanes, and throw Frisbees. All students love playing with the catapult. Students can throw different sizes of balls and small stuffed animals. The catapult is especially fun to use around Easter. Students can launch plastic eggs, and the catching student can use an Easter basket to catch the eggs. The catapult can also be used outdoors to throw small water balloons. The catapult allows all students to be equally involved in the activity regardless of the type of disability they may have. Teacher supervision is necessary to ensure safety when using the catapult. See Box 5.8 for information on catapult designs.

Board games can be adapted so that all students can participate. Any board game that uses batteries can be adapted with a switch to allow students to push the switch to activate the game. The switch can be set to start with one push or require the student to hold it down continuously for activation. The assistive technology specialist, adapted physical education

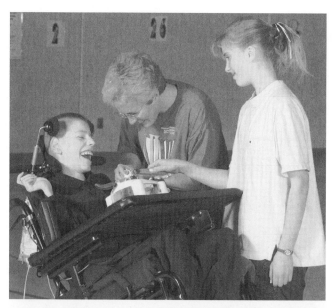

BOX 5.8
Catapult Designs

Designs for various catapults as well as other adapted equipment can be found on the Rockwell Collins Retiree Volunteer Program website with sponsorship through the Grant Wood Area Educational Agency, Cedar Rapids, Iowa: www.collinsclubs.com/rcrv. Scroll down to the "Completed Communities Projects," then scroll to games for persons with disabilities and look for catapult thrower designs. These plans are for individual use and are not to be used for production and resale. There is no guarantee that the website will continue to be published indefinitely.

Games such as Fleas on Fred (top) and Bed Bugs (bottom) can be adapted by attaching magnets to large tweezers.

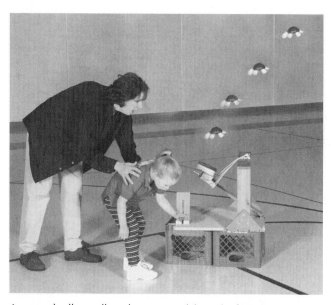

A catapult allows all students to participate in throwing activities.

specialist, occupational therapist, or special education teacher can provide and install switches for you.

Games that require students to pick up pieces with their fingers or use large tweezers to pick up objects can be modified with magnets. Small magnets can be placed on the object and on the tweezers, allowing the student to place the tweezers near the object and pick it up without manipulating the tweezers. The games Fleas on Fred and Bed Bugs are good examples of games that can be modified in this way. A switch can be used to make the dog and bed vibrate and jump around, and modified magnet tweezers can be used to lift the fleas off Fred's back and the bugs out of the bed.

Activities that are modified and take place outside of school should be encouraged. Most communities sponsor Special Olympics, providing physical and sporting activities for students with mental disabilities. The Joseph P. Kennedy Jr. Foundation instituted the Special Olympics in 1968. The Special Olympics motto reads "Let me win, but if I cannot win, let me be brave in the attempt." The mission of Special Olympics is as follows:

> To provide year-round sports training and athletic competition in a variety of Olympic-type sports for all children and adults with mental retardation, giving them continuing opportunities to develop physical fitness, demonstrate courage, experience joy, and participate in a sharing of gifts, skills, and friendship with their families, other Special Olympic athletes, and the community. (Kennedy 1985, 1)

BOX 5.9
Internet Resources

The following Internet sites have information on specific disabilities and sport and recreation opportunities for students with disabilities. The websites were active as of October 2008.

- **Achievable Concepts.** Products for adapted recreation and sporting equipment for people with disabilities and the aged: www.achievableconcepts .com.au
- **American Association for Physical Activity and Recreation.** Information and activities in the area of adapted P.E., adapted aquatics, senior activities, adventure, outdoor education, and recreation: www.aahperd.org/aapar
- **American Blind Skiing Foundation.** A nonprofit organization that provides an educational skiing program open to any blind or visually impaired person in the hope of providing both physical and psychological therapeutic value: www.absf.org
- **National Center on Physical Activity and Disability.** Resource for learning about specific disabilities and sports and recreation/leisure activities for persons with disabilities: www.ncpad.org
- **Palaestra.** A quarterly publication and premier resource on adapted physical activity: www.palaestra.com
- **PE Central—Adapted Physical Education.** Resources for adapting equipment and for activities, inclusion, parent support, assessment, and disability fact sheets: www.pecentral.org/adapted/ adaptedmenu.html
- **U.S. Paralympics.** A division of the U.S. Olympic Committee (USOC), formed in 2001 to increase support for American athletes with physical disabilities: www.usparalympics.com

---

An Internet search using the type of disability as the keyword will provide information on that type of disability along with sport and recreation opportunities for students with disabilities. The keyword "paralympics" will provide you with sites on sports for the disabled. Box 5.9 lists additional Internet resources.

Summary

Children come in all shapes and sizes and with all levels of abilities. The more experience you have with each type of student, the greater your comfort level will be when you are working with them. Firsthand experience working with a student who is different or has a disability gives teachers the opportunity to get to know the student, thus alleviating the fear of the unknown.

Teachers who understand their own background are better able to accept and understand the background their students bring to the classroom. Listening to students with disabilities and their parents helps you understand them. To truly understand how parents and children feel, attempt to step into their reality and hear their stories.

With a bit of extra effort and willingness on your part, students with disabilities can be accommodated in the elementary classroom and in the movement setting. The relationships you build with these students can be as meaningful as the relationships you build with your other students. Children are children; they all need love and acceptance.

Reach out and collaborate with other professionals who work with a student with a disability. A simple suggestion, idea, or piece of adapted equipment can make a huge difference in children's ability to fit in and be accepted by their peers. Give students the opportunity to experience what it might feel like to have a disability through simulation activities. Encourage students to reflect on their experiences, and use this opportunity to teach children to be empathetic, instead of sympathetic, and caring toward others who are different from themselves.

Chapter Activities

1. Contact a local special education teacher or adapted physical education teacher and find out what type of physical education services their students receive. Where on the continuum of services does this fall?
2. After completing the work sheet in Figure 5.1, write a one-page reflective summary about your experience.
3. Make a list of ten things you can do to help students who are different or disabled feel more comfortable in your classroom.
4. Conduct an Internet search and find three websites that have information on modifying activities for students with disabilities.
5. Contact your local Special Olympics organization. Find out what events are being held and volunteer a couple hours of your time to work at the event.

Internet Resources

See the sites listed in Box 5.9.

Bibliography

Assistance to States for the Education of Children With Disabilities and Preschool Grants for Children With Disabilities; Final Rule, 156 Fed.Reg. 46,540 (August 14, 2006). http://a257.g.akamaitech.net/7/257/2422/01jan20061800/edocket.access.gpo.gov/2006/pdf/06-6656.pdf.

Auxter, D., J. Pyfer, and C. Huettig. 2001. *Principles and methods of adapted physical education and recreation.* Boston: McGraw-Hill.

Baergen, J. F. 2000. *Shifting teacher paradigm in the multicultural classroom.* Unpublished master's thesis, Wichita State University, Wichita, KS.

Block, M. E. 2000. *A teacher's guide to including students with disabilities in general physical education.* 2nd ed. Baltimore: Paul H. Brookes.

———. 2007. *A teacher's guide to including students with disabilities in general physical education.* Baltimore, MD: Paul Brookes Publishing.

Block, M. E., and M. L. Horton. 1996. Include safety in physical education: Do not exclude students with disabilities. *The Physical Educator* 53(2): 71.

Calloway, C. 1999. Promote friendship in the inclusive classroom. *Intervention in School and Clinic* 34(3): 176–177.

Combs, C. 1995. Catapult for fun. *Kansas Association for Health, Physical Education, Recreation, and Dance* 66(1): 34.

Combs, C. A., and K. H. Pitetti. 2008. Heart rates soar in adapted snowshoeing. *Kansas Association of Health, Physical Education, Recreation, and Dance Journal,* Fall 80(2).

Connolly, D. A. 2002. The energy expenditure of snowshoeing in packed vs. unpacked snow at low-level walking speeds. *Journal of Strength and Conditioning Research* 16(4): 606–610.

DePauw, K. P., and G. Goc Karp. 1994. Integrating knowledge of disability throughout the physical education curriculum: An infusion approach. *Adapted Physical Activity Quarterly* 11: 3–13.

Dunn, J. M. 1997. *Special physical education: Adapted, individualized, developmental.* Boston: McGraw-Hill.

Forness, S. R. 2001. Personal reflections. In *Characteristics of emotional and behavioral disorders of children and youth,* ed. J. M. Kauffman, 35–37. Upper Saddle River, NJ: Prentice-Hall.

Friend, M., and W. D. Bursuck. 1999. *Including students with special needs: A practical guide for classroom teachers.* Needham Heights, MA: Allyn & Bacon.

Grant, C. A., and C. E. Sleeter. 1998. *Turning on learning: Five approaches for multicultural teaching plans for race,* class, gender, and disability. Upper Saddle River, NJ: Prentice-Hall.

Gustason, G., and E. Zawolkow. 1993. *Signing exact English.* Los Alamitos, CA: Modern Signs Press.

Jobling, A., and N. Virji-Babul, and D. Nichols. 2006. Children with Down syndrome: Discovering the joy of movement. *Journal of Physical Education, Recreation, and Dance* 77(6): 34–38, 53–54.

Kauffman, J. M. 2001. *Characteristics of emotional and behavioral disorders of children and youth.* Upper Saddle River, NJ: Prentice-Hall.

Kennedy, J. P. 1985. *Official Special Olympics sports rules.* Washington, DC: Joseph P. Kennedy Jr. Foundation.

Knipe, B., and R. Olberding. 1997. *Peer partners in physical education: Disability awareness.* Johnston, IA: Heartland Area Education Agency 11.

Kowalski, E., and T. L. Rizzo. 1996. Factors influencing preservice student attitudes toward individuals with disabilities. *Adapted Physical Activity Quarterly* 13: 180–197.

Kozub, F. M., P. R. Sherblom, and T. L. Perry. 1999. Inclusion paradigms and perspectives: A stepping stone to accepting learner diversity in physical education. *Quest* 51(4): 346–354.

Lavay, B., R. French, and H. Henderson. 2007. A practical plan for managing the behavior of students with disabilities in general physical education. *Journal of Physical Education, Recreation, and Dance* 78(2): 42–48.

Lerner, J. 1997. *Learning disabilities: Theories, diagnosis, and teaching strategies.* Boston: Houghton Mifflin.

Lieberman, L., and C. Houston-Wilson. 2002. *Strategies for inclusion: A handbook for physical educators.* Champaign, IL: Human Kinetics.

Lieberman, L. J., J. M. Dunn, H. van der Mars, and J. McCubbin. 2000. Peer tutors' effects on activity levels of deaf students in inclusive elementary physical education. *Adapted Physical Activity Quarterly* 17: 20–39.

Lieberman, L. J., A. R. James, and N. Ludwa. 2004. The impact of inclusion in general physical education for all students. *Journal of Physical Education, Recreation, and Dance* 75(5): 37–41, 55.

Lieberman, L., R. Lytle, and G. Irwin. 2003. Ideas for including a student with quadriplegia into physical education. *Strategies* 17(2): 21–25.

Making Sense of the New IDEA Regulations. 1999. *Federal Register* 64(48), LRP Publications.

National Association for Sport and Physical Education (NASPE). 2004. *Moving into the future: National standards for physical education.* 2nd ed. Reston, VA: Author.

O'Donnell, L. M., and R. I. Livingston. 1991. Active exploration of the environment by young children with low vision: A review of literature. *Journal of Visual Impairment and Blindness* 85: 287–291.

Pangrazi, R. P. 1998. *Dynamic physical education for elementary school children.* Boston: Allyn & Bacon.

Payne, R. K. 1998. *A framework for understanding poverty.* Baytown, TX: RTF Publishing.

President's Council on Physical Fitness and Sports. 1996. *Physical activity and health: A report from the surgeon general, 1996. Centers for Disease Control and Prevention (DHHS/PHS),* Atlanta, GA. Washington, DC: Author.

Pyfer, J., and N. Castle. 2004. Students with cochlear implants: Teaching considerations for physical educators. *Journal of Physical Education, Recreation, and Dance* 75(4): 28–33.

Raymond, E. B. 2000. *Learners with mild disabilities: A characteristic approach.* Needham Heights, MA: Allyn & Bacon.

Rizzo, T. L., G. D. Broadhead, and E. Kowalski. 1997. Changing kinesiology and physical education by infusing information about individuals with disabilities. *Quest* 49(2): 229–237.

Rizzo, T. L., and W. P. Vispoel. 1992. Changing attitudes about teaching students with handicaps. *Adapted Physical Activity Quarterly* 9: 54–63.

Sapon-Shevin, M. 1996. Celebrating diversity, creating community: Curriculum that honors and builds on differences. In *Inclusion: A guide for educators,* ed. S. Stainback and W. Stainback, 255–270. Baltimore: Paul H. Brookes.

Seaman, J. A., C. E. Corbin, and B. Pangrazi. 1999. Physical activity and fitness for persons with disabilities. *Research Digest Series* 3(5): 2–12.

Shapiro, D. R., and L. K. Sayers. 2003. Who does what on the interdisciplinary team regarding physical education for students with disabilities? *TEACHING Exceptional Children* 35(6): 32–38.

Sherrill, C. 1998. *Adapted physical activity, recreation and sport: Crossdisciplinary and lifespan.* Boston: McGraw-Hill.

Tripp, A., C. Piletic, and G. Babcock. 2004. *Including students with disabilities in physical education.* Reston, VA: AAHPERD/AAALF.

Winnick, J. P., and F. X. Short. 1985. *Physical fitness testing of the disabled: Project UNIQUE.* Champaign, IL: Human Kinetics.

Woodard, R. J., and P. R. Surburg. 1999. Midline crossing behavior in children with learning disabilities. *Adapted Physical Activity Quarterly* 16(2): 155–166.

QUICK LESSON 5.1
All-Star Bulletin Boards

GRADES 2–6

NASPE STANDARDS 5 AND 6

- Students exhibit responsible personal and social behavior that respects self and others in physical activity settings.
- Students value physical activity for health, enjoyment, challenge, self-expression, and/or social interaction.

KNOWLEDGE CONTENT

- Students respect others by giving compliments.
- Students show the ability to find good traits in all classmates.

EQUIPMENT NEEDED Magazines, scissors, glue, and a stapler. Physical education equipment catalogs are particularly good.

PREPARATION TIME Fifteen minutes

CLASSROOM ACTIVITY Divide the class into groups of three. Ask each group member to tell something that is good about the other group members or something that they are good at. Each member will receive two compliments. Ask each student to cut pictures out representing what they said about the members of their group. Let students post these pictures on a bulletin board and write the student's name that the picture represents.

ASSESSMENT Ask each student to take turns going to the bulletin board and informing the class what each of their group members are good at or something good about them.

SUCCESS FOR ALL For students with physical limitations, have adapted scissors available for use and remind students that a friend may help a group member if needed.

INTEGRATION WITH OTHER SUBJECT AREAS
To extend this activity into an integrated lesson using math skills, have students make a graph depicting how many students were good at similar activities.

QUICK LESSON 5.2
Getting to Know Your Classmates

GRADES K–6

NASPE STANDARD 5 Students exhibit responsible personal and social behavior that respects self and others in physical activity settings.

LESSON OBJECTIVES

- Students show respect for and acceptance of all classmates.
- Students discover similarities and differences among their classmates.
- Students practice imitating locomotor, activity, and sport skills.

KNOWLEDGE CONTENT

- Students should understand what respecting and accepting classmates looks like.
- Students should be able to demonstrate locomotor and activity skills and depict sports.

EQUIPMENT NEEDED None

PREPARATION TIME None

CLASSROOM ACTIVITY Each student stands by his or her desk. Ask the students to perform the following activities:

- Slide around the room and give a high five to three classmates that you did not play with at recess this week.
- Act out your favorite sport. If you see other classmates acting out the same sport, join together to form a group or team. When all groups are formed, ask each group to report what its favorite sport is and how many classmates are in the group.
- Act out your favorite activity in physical education class. If you see other classmates acting out the same activity, join together to form a group. When all groups are formed, ask each group to report what its favorite physical education activity is. Ask students in other groups to raise their hand if they also enjoy the activity of another group.
- Ask students to gallop around the room and shake hands with three other students who have a hair color different from their own.
- Ask students to march around the room and find all the students who have the same color eyes as their own.

ASSESSMENT Observe students to see how they relate to various partners and groups during the activity. Ask students to record the number of classmates in each group for each activity. Students can graph the information or draw pictures representing their groups.

SUCCESS FOR ALL Allow students with a disability to partner with another student. Partners perform the specific activities together as they move around the room.

INTEGRATION WITH OTHER SUBJECT AREAS
To extend this lesson into an integrated social studies or history lesson for grades 3 through 5, have students who formed the groups of favorite sports work together to research where that sport originated. Research the rules of the game and write a report that can be presented to the class.

CLASSROOM LEARNING STATION 5.1
Locomotor Sign Language

GRADES 3–6

NASPE STANDARD 5 Students exhibit responsible personal and social behavior that respects self and others in physical activity settings.

KNOWLEDGE CONTENT

- Students learn sign language for seven locomotor skills.
- Students know how to perform locomotor skills.

EQUIPMENT NEEDED Sign language signs enlarged from Figure 5.4 and mounted on posters placed around the room; slips of paper, one for each student, each with one of the seven locomotor skills (run, slide, hop, gallop, jump, skip, walk) written on it

PREPARATION TIME Fifteen minutes

CLASSROOM ACTIVITY Tell students they must play this game without talking. Ask each student to draw a slip of paper containing a locomotor skill. On the teacher's signal to go, students show the sign language sign for their locomotor skill and perform the skill with their bodies until they find a partner performing the same skill.

Once partners or groups are formed, students perform three different tasks with their locomotor skill.

1. Spell the word out loud three times.
2. Write the word on a partner's back.
3. Move around the room performing the locomotor skill and finding letters to form your word.

When partners or groups are finished, have students place the slips of paper back in the bowl and draw another slip to repeat the activity.

ASSESSMENT

- The teacher listens as students spell words out loud.
- Ask students to demonstrate the sign language for each locomotor skill with and without the poster to show how it is formed.
- The teacher observes students' form as they perform the locomotor skills.

SUCCESS FOR ALL Older students can write sentences that contain their locomotor word. Older students can brainstorm animals that might move in the pattern of their locomotor word.

INTEGRATION WITH OTHER SUBJECT AREAS
Integration of spelling, language arts, physical education, and sign language occurs throughout the activity.

GRADES K–6

NASPE STANDARD 5 Students exhibit responsible personal and social behavior that respects self and others in physical activity settings.

LESSON OBJECTIVES

- Students experience what it might feel like to have a certain disability.
- Students develop compassion for the struggles that some students with disabilities face.
- Students discover ways they might help a student with a disability in a physically active setting.

EQUIPMENT NEEDED For each simulation station, description cards explaining the simulation to be performed. Equipment needed for each activity is listed under each station.

PREPARATION TIME One hour to make description cards of each simulation

CLASSROOM ACTIVITY A simulation is an activity that allows students to momentarily experience what it might feel like to have a disability. Group reflection time after the simulation activities is critical. Students need to share their reflections on how it felt to have a specific disability. What was hard for them? What was easy? How did their classmates treat them? How might you differently treat a classmate with a disability after experiencing the simulation activities? Set up the simulation stations on the playground or in the classroom. The number of stations needed depends on the number of students participating and the number of students to be placed in each group. Place the equipment needed by the appropriate station.

STATION 1. SIMULATING A HEARING IMPAIRMENT Equipment: Recording of students' spelling list with loud music in the background, earplugs

- Play the prepared spelling list and have students write the spelling words.
- Have students wear earplugs (swimming earplugs work well). Give students verbal directions to go across the room, pick up an object, and bring it back to their desk.

STATION 2. SIMULATING A PHYSICAL IMPAIRMENT Equipment: Ace bandage, graham crackers, icing, wheelchair

- With an ace bandage, bind students' dominant hand to their body. Then give students some icing and graham crackers and ask them to spread some icing on a graham cracker and eat it as a snack.
- Have students sit in a wheelchair and push themselves forward and backward. Then have them try dribbling a basketball while staying seated in the wheelchair.

STATION 3. SIMULATING A VISUAL IMPAIRMENT Equipment: Blindfolds (made by placing colored cellophane or wax paper over the lenses of sunglasses), coloring pages, balls

- Students wearing blindfolds are given a coloring page and asked to color certain areas a specific color.
- Send students wearing blindfolds out to the hall to get a drink.
- Ask students wearing blindfolds to dribble a ball or to play catch with a partner.

STATION 4. SIMULATING FINE MOTOR AND LARGE MOTOR IMPAIRMENTS Equipment: Welding gloves or other large bulky gloves, coins, football, tape

- Ask students wearing bulky gloves to pick up and count various amounts of change. Ask for amounts that require several different sizes of coins.
- Have students tape the fingers and thumb of their dominant hand together and then have them play catch with a football.

STATION 5. SIMULATING A LEARNING DISABILITY Equipment: Large ball, marbles, tin can, 10 to 15 small objects, towel

- Have students lie on their stomach across a large ball. Their feet should not touch the floor. Students reach down and pick up marbles one at a time off the floor and drop them into a tin can. This activity simulates poor balance.
- Place 10 to 15 small objects under a towel. While students are watching, uncover the objects for ten seconds. Ask students to write down the names of the objects they saw. Give students a second chance

by uncovering the objects again, this time for five seconds. Ask them to write down what they missed on their first try. This activity simulates difficulty with short- and long-term memory (S. Levra-Wallace, personal communication, January 17, 2001).

STATION 6. SIMULATING CEREBRAL PALSY

Equipment: Three beanbags per student, a Nerf ball or a playground ball, masking tape lines on the floor

■ Have students place one beanbag between their knees and hold a beanbag under each elbow, keeping arms tight at their sides. Without dropping the beanbags, students gallop around space, do five push-ups, do five jumping jacks, and run and jump over the lines on the floor. Still holding the beanbags in place, students play catch with a partner using a Nerf ball or a playground ball (Knipe and Olberding 1997).

ASSESSMENT Students write a paragraph describing what it felt like to have a specific disability. Kindergarten students may describe their feelings orally.

SUCCESS FOR ALL Students with disabilities can be the experts, giving pointers and advice to the other students as they participate in the simulations. Grade levels could be combined to allow an upper and lower grade level to participate together using partners from each grade level.

INTEGRATION WITH OTHER SUBJECT AREAS

Integration of spelling, math, and physical education skills have been incorporated throughout the activity.

CHAPTER 6

Physical Education Curriculum

The purpose of this chapter is to (1) fully identify the characteristics of a quality elementary physical education program, (2) discuss who is responsible for producing a quality physical education program, (3) specify the physical education curriculum content, (4) provide a framework for and examples of writing objectives for the physical education lesson, and (5) discuss assessment theory and practice.

Objectives

After studying this chapter, you will be able to do the following:

- Articulate the characteristics of a quality elementary physical education program and determine whether a specific program exhibits those characteristics.

- Identify community and school personnel who are responsible for planning and implementing quality physical education.

- Critically review the physical education curriculum content of a specific school.

- Write lesson objectives.

- Write a lesson plan for a 30-minute movement lesson.

- Recognize and implement appropriate assessment practices.

Ms. Sanchez teaches fourth grade in a small K–12 school district. The district provides physical education for her fourth graders (taught by a physical education teacher) twice a week for 30 minutes. Ms. Sanchez and the physical educator work closely to integrate movement into the classroom and to integrate subject areas taught in the classroom into

the gymnasium. They meet regularly (once a month) to review each other's curriculum for that month and to plan specific integration activities (at least one activity each week).

In general, to integrate physical education into the classroom, Ms. Sanchez and the physical educator have agreed that Ms. Sanchez will teach activities in the classroom that prepare her students for what is coming next in the physical education class. Thirty-minute class periods are not long enough for the physical educator to teach content in depth. To teach as much material in as much depth as possible, Ms. Sanchez prepares her students in advance.

For example, next week the physical educator plans to teach students the folk dance "Gustaf's Skoal" (see Box 6.1 for the dance instructions). So this week Ms. Sanchez is teaching the parts of dance (the walk part and the skip part) with an emphasis on the students being able to walk and skip in time with the music. Students walk and skip to the music individually and with a partner in the general space of the classroom just to practice being in time with the music. With a partner, they practice skipping forward (with inside hands joined) and they practice skipping in a circle (with both hands joined).

Next week the physical educator will place the students in a square formation and teach the complete dance (also relaying background that the dancers are paying homage to King Gustaf of Sweden). Ms. Sanchez and the physical educator selected this dance because the fourth graders will soon be studying Swedish history, including the reign of King Gustaf. They are convinced that the integration of subject areas provides movement experiences that positively affect the lives of their students.

BOX 6.1 "Gustaf's Skoal"

. . . .

HISTORY

In this simple dance from Sweden, dancers pay homage to King Gustaf.

FORMATION

A square of four pairs of dancers begins in the formation shown in the diagram. All students face the center of the square.

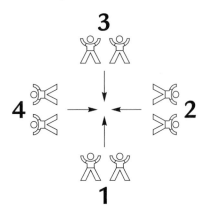

Pairs 1 and 3 are *head* pairs, and pairs 2 and 4 are *side* pairs.

INSTRUCTIONS

Part One (sedate walking music)

Measures 1–4: With inside hands joined and the free hand on the waist, the head pairs walk forward three steps, bow deeply on the fourth count, and then walk backward four steps. This action is performed in a very dignified manner.
Measures 5–8: Side pairs perform same action.
Measures 9–16: Repeat measures 1–8.

Part Two (spirited skipping music)

Measures 1–8: Side pairs lift their joined inside hands to make arches as head pairs (with joined inside hands) take four skips forward. As head pairs meet in the center of the square, they drop hands and join inside hands of the person they are facing as each person turns toward the side pair closest to them. With this new partner, they take four skips to move through the side arches. After going through the arch, partners drop hands, turn away from each other, and take four skips around the circle to return to their home position in the square. As dancers meet their original partner (at their home position), they join both hands and swing once around (in place) with four skipping steps.

These 16 skipping steps are performed in a lively, spirited manner and should be continuous (flowing without stops)—to the center, under the arch, around the square, and then swinging with the partner (with each action taking four counts).

Measures 9–16: The side pairs do the same actions just performed by the head pairs.

What Does a Quality Elementary Physical Education Program Look Like?

A quality elementary physical education program assists students in acquiring the skills, knowledge, and motivation to incorporate activity into their daily lives. The classroom teacher or physical education teacher (or both) develop a quality program through thoughtful, careful planning. The curriculum philosophy and content of the program are based on what students are to know and be able to do upon completion of the curriculum. Regardless of who plans and implements the curriculum, a quality program reflects the following characteristics.

PROGRAM CHARACTERISTIC 1: DEVELOPMENTALLY APPROPRIATE ACTIVITIES

As indicated in Chapter 2, movement content designed to accommodate the individual student's cognitive, psychomotor, and affective ability level is considered to be developmentally appropriate. No one standardized activity suits all students at the same time. A **developmentally appropriate movement activity** is one in which the frequency, intensity, duration, and type

Providing hurdles of different heights helps students of all development levels build movement skills and feel successful.

of activity accommodate the child's age; maturation level (cognitive, affective, and motor maturation); skill level (beginning, intermediate, or advanced); body size; fitness level; and previous movement experiences. For example, movement activities provided for K–3 children are simple (versus complex) and of short duration, since K–3 children are concrete thinkers with short attention spans.

A program that consists of developmentally appropriate activities leads to children performing at a high rate of success. The degree of success the elementary-aged child experiences is influenced by his or her ability to execute movement patterns effectively and efficiently. Thus achieving high rates of success means students work toward common standards of performances at individual rates and are recognized for their success at individual levels. The teacher designs activities that meet children at their particular developmental level thus providing a feeling of success that further challenges the child to progress to a more complicated task. For example, within the K–3 framework (short attention span and concrete thinking), children's individual display of these characteristics might be accommodated by allowing children to move from station to station based on when their interest begins to wane, and each station might have an activity and theoretical component to stimulate those ready for abstract concepts. In another example, the lesson is jumping over a low "hurdle." Two cones with sticks across are set up at varying heights. Students choose which hurdle to jump first. After successfully jumping a hurdle of a given height, students choose the next higher hurdle when they are developmentally ready.

PROGRAM CHARACTERISTIC 2: SKILL AND FITNESS IMPROVEMENT

As indicated in Chapter 4, lessons are designed to improve the motor performance and physical fitness of each child. The major emphasis is on developing motor skills and general body management, thus promoting more active participation in a variety of physical activities. Lessons also promote improved muscular strength and endurance, flexibility, agility, balance and coordination, cardiovascular and respiratory function, and knowledge and understanding of how these factors relate to lifelong health and physical fitness.

For example, the content of the lesson is for students, in general space, to run, leap, and turn to a signal (e.g., drum, cymbal, whistle). After the students have been physically active for a while, the teacher asks them to observe their breathing and heart rate. A brief discussion of cardiovascular fitness follows. For older children, hold the discussion after they have played a modified soccer game, and include an in-depth discussion of how the heart adapts (gets stronger) through strenuous physical activity.

INSTANT ACTIVITY 6.1 *Alphabet Jumble*

Grades K–6

Equipment Needed

Paper plates

Activity

At least two sets of the alphabet need to be written (in large print) on paper plates (one letter to a plate). Make extra plates with the vowels and more common consonants. On each plate, also write (in smaller letters) a physical activity that can be performed in the child's personal space. The class sits in a circle, and each child has a number of letters. Call out words (to be spelled) related to sports and fitness or use the week's spelling words. Appropriate class members, holding the appropriate letters, group together and spell the word by holding the letters in front of their chest. If sufficient letters are available to spell the word more than once, the group may do so.

After the word is spelled, students perform the physical activities written on the backs of the plates, beginning from left to right. Then the teacher calls out another word to be spelled.

Physical activities to be performed may include run in place 15 seconds, two sit-ups, two squat thrusts, two push-ups, skip in place 15 seconds, pretend to dribble a basketball, collapse to the floor and get up quickly, balance on one leg for 10 seconds, shake hands with someone, hold crab position for 15 seconds.

PROGRAM CHARACTERISTIC 3: PROMOTION OF PHYSICAL ACTIVITY

The primary purpose of physically educating children is to fulfill their current need to learn through movement and their future need to stay physically active throughout their lifetime in order to live long, healthy lives. Encouraging this lifelong physically active lifestyle takes more than just providing appropriate physical education lessons. It takes providing those lessons in a psychological environment where teachers respect students and their capabilities, use movement experiences to create feelings of success and fun, seek input from students regarding their needs and preferences, and stimulate children to be physically active outside of school time. Instant Activity 6.1 is an example of an activity that allows the students to be active in the classroom.

PROGRAM CHARACTERISTIC 4: FACILITATION OF LEARNING

The teacher serves primarily as facilitator, not as referee, official, or participant. The teacher circulates among students to provide leadership and feedback.

Teachers can facilitate learning by providing assistance and feedback when they are needed.

With careful planning and a little practice, teachers can become quite efficient in organizing students, equipment, and space (for more information on this topic refer to Chapter 7) so they are available to provide feedback to students. As students are involved in self-directed activity, the teacher moves about the room to facilitate learning.

For example, the content of the lesson is throwing and catching using an overhand throw. There are 20 students in the class. The teacher instructs the students to choose a partner (who has the same color of eyes), and each pair picks up a ball from a box (five boxes spread around the perimeter of the area). Two lines have been established, ten feet apart, using cones. The students are asked to face their partner, one on each line, and throw and catch back and forth to each other. (Appropriate mechanics of throwing and catching are explained and demonstrated. The lines have been established so that all balls are going in the same direction.) As students are successful, they may move further apart. They are encouraged to help each other accomplish the skill. The teacher moves about giving specific feedback and assistance where needed.

PROGRAM CHARACTERISTIC 5: MAXIMIZATION OF ACTIVE LEARNING TIME

The class is managed to provide maximum movement time. There are no spectators, no waiting in lines, no elimination games, and no boys and girls separated. Individual, partner, and small group activities are used to maximize active participation. When equipment such as a ball is used, each child or every two children (if throwing and catching) should have one ball. If the objective of the lesson is cardiovascular fitness, the students should all be participating in continuous movement.

For example, the lesson is the game of Kick-Steal. Students choose a partner (someone who has the same number of siblings), and each pair gets a ball (eight-and-a-half-inch soft sponge ball). The play is in a grassy area with two end boundary lines. One player kicks a ball starting in the middle of the field. The other player tries to steal the ball away with his or her feet. The object is for a player to kick the ball over the opposite end line. Each time the ball goes over the line, the partners start a new game. If the class has an odd number of students, one group of students may play two on one.

PROGRAM CHARACTERISTIC 6: INDIRECT COMPETITION AND COOPERATION

The emphasis of the activity is on cooperative rather than head-to-head direct competitive play. **Indirect competition,** where children are encouraged to improve individual achievement, is also desirable. Indirect competition is determined by achieving self-set goals or preset standards. **Direct competition** results in a winner and a loser, and the object is to impede the progress of another. In general, direct competition is inappropriate for elementary school children as their physical abilities and social skills have not yet developed to the point where they can properly handle the stress involved in direct competition. Instant Activity 6.2 is an example of a cooperative activity.

PROGRAM CHARACTERISTIC 7: INCLUSION OF MANY MOVEMENT FORMS

The yearly plan for physical education includes an appropriate distribution of fundamental movement skills, basic game skills, creative and rhythmic movement, body management skills and gymnastics, water skills, recreational activity skills, cooperative movement skills, and fitness. The percentage of time dedicated to each of these movement forms differs from grade level to grade level. Recommended time percentages based on grade level are specified later in the chapter.

PROGRAM CHARACTERISTIC 8: INTEGRATION OF ACADEMIC CONTENT

The physical education lessons integrate academic content whenever possible. Classroom teachers and physical educators integrate content from reading, writing, math, social studies, art, music, health, science, and technology. Integration of lessons helps children view knowledge in a more holistic manner. The activities described in the opening chapter scenario and Instant Activity 6.3 are examples of integration.

PROGRAM CHARACTERISTIC 9: ONGOING STUDENT AND PROGRAM ASSESSMENT

Ongoing student and program assessment is evident in planning documents and when observing physical education lessons. Assessment is part of the learning process in physical education and corresponds with the daily application of curriculum and instruction. Formative evaluation, or day-to-day indicators of progress, is best documented through authentic assessment. Authentic assessments such as portfolios, activity logs, contracts, checklists, and self-reports help the teacher in assisting the student. The assessment process is fully defined later in the chapter.

INSTANT ACTIVITY 6.2
Cooperative Musical Chairs

Grades K–6
Equipment Needed
Chairs and music

Activity
The object is to cooperate and keep every child in the game, even though chairs are removed as the music stops. The children have to team together, sitting on parts of chairs or on parts of one another, to keep everyone in the game. Instead of fighting for the sole possession of one chair, students work together so that everyone has a seat somewhere.

PROGRAM CHARACTERISTIC 10: COMPLIANCE WITH FEDERAL MANDATES

Several educational mandates need to be considered when designing an appropriate, effective, quality physical education program. **Title IX** of the Educational Amendments Act of 1972 calls for equal educational opportunities for boys and girls. In physical education, the law demands that all offerings be coeducational, except in some instances of contact sports (i.e., football, wrestling, lacrosse). This law has had a more significant impact on secondary school physical education programs, as most elementary physical education programs are usually coeducational. However, the spirit of the law should also be considered. To the extent that girls and boys are treated differently in physical education, equal opportunity does not exist. Equal opportunity should provide the basis for complying with Title IX, but research indicates that equal opportunity alone may not provide a physical education experience that is free of patterns of gender discrimination (Hannon and Ratliffe 2007; Nilges 1998). Examples of teachers treating students differently based on gender, from observations in the classroom or gymnasium, include the following:

- Interacting more often with boys than girls
- Praising boys for performance and girls for effort
- Using boys rather than girls to demonstrate
- Expecting different behavior and performance from boys and girls

INSTANT ACTIVITY 6.3 Target Toss Math

Grades K–6

Equipment Needed

Tagboard, beanbags, markers

Activity

Designate partners and give each set of partners a piece of tagboard, three beanbags, and magic markers. Have partners create targets (to aim at) by drawing shapes on the tagboard. In the targets write various numbers—low numbers for younger children (1–20) and high numbers for older children (50–200). Using appropriate symbols, write various math processes (addition, subtraction, division, and multiplication) in the spaces among the targets (shapes). Throw two of the beanbags into different shapes (that have numbers inside). Throw the third beanbag onto a math process. Then partners solve the math problem (either on paper or in their mind).

- Assuming a student's interest in certain sport activities based on gender
- Having gender-biased perceptions of and explanations for student behavior (Derry and Phillips 2004; Dunbar and O'Sullivan 1986; Garrahy 2001, 2003; Griffin 1985; Hills 2006; MacDonald 1990; Solomons 1980)

Another law, **PL 94–142,** and its 1990 amendments, PL 101–476, address the need for equal educational opportunities for children with and without disabilities. These laws state that children with disabilities have the right to a free and public education and must be educated in the least restrictive educational environment possible. This mandate has resulted in the concept of inclusion. Inclusion involves the placement of students with disabilities in the regular classroom and gymnasium as much as possible. The concept of inclusion is fully developed in Chapter 5 to provide you with the background and expertise needed to provide physical activity for the child with a disability. In addition, many of the lessons and activities in the text contain a "Success for All" section that suggests possible adaptations that allow students with disabilities to be included in the activity.

As an example of inclusion, consider a lesson that involves introducing the skills of passing and catching a six-inch playground ball. A student has vision problems and does not have the eye-hand coordination to catch the ball. You may pair this student with a buddy who tosses a beach ball back and forth, as the beach ball is larger and lighter and will approach more slowly.

Adjusting activities or equipment can help students with disabilities participate in physical education lessons with their nondisabled peers.
In the catch activity shown here, using a beach ball facilitates inclusion because it is larger and moves more slowly.

PROGRAM CHARACTERISTIC 11: APPROPRIATE INSTRUCTIONAL TIME

The Council on Physical Education for Children (COPEC) recommends that elementary school children accumulate at least 60 minutes of age-appropriate physical activity on most days of the week (COPEC 2004). This would include at least 30 minutes of physical education (instructional time) daily during school days. Since this recommendation often is not followed, the classroom teacher's commitment and ability to provide thoughtfully designed daily physical activity becomes vital to meeting children's physical activity needs. For example, a local school district chooses to provide elementary physical education twice a week with a physical education teacher. However, recognizing and valuing the need for daily physical activity, the school board creates a policy that all elementary school children shall have 30 minutes of daily indoor and/or outdoor physical education provided by the classroom teacher on days when the students do not see the physical educator. In addition, the school board mandates at least 30 minutes of quality recess time daily, thus meeting the accumulation guideline of 60 minutes of activity each day.

PROGRAM CHARACTERISTIC 12: QUALIFIED TEACHERS

Certified physical education teachers are the most desirable professionals to be hired by schools or school districts to provide a quality physical education program. They have intensive knowledge and training in designing developmentally appropriate physical education programs that meet students' physical, mental, and emotional needs. In addition, the certified teacher has specialized training in how to conduct movement activities in a safe manner. However, that is not to say that physical educators are the *only* professionals who can deliver safe, quality physical education. Many classroom teachers today plan and deliver quality movement experiences for their students. In elementary schools where the classroom teacher is responsible for the physical education taught to his or her students, the role of the physical educator evolves to that of a resource teacher who assists the classroom teacher in providing appropriate physical activity in both the physical education and classroom settings.

Who Is Responsible for Quality Physical Education?

The entire community plays a role in ensuring a physical education program that provides students with the knowledge, skills, and attitudes to live a long, healthy, and physically active life. Whether it is a parent, guardian, student, teacher, athletic coach, school administrator, or a community member who cares about young people, there is something he or she can do. Everyone should be aware of the status and quality of the physical education program in the schools. Teachers must use curricula based on the national and state standards for physical education and be strong advocates for their programs. School administrators and board members can require daily physical education for all students in grades K–12. They can create policy that provides additional time during the day, such as recess, for the students to be physically active. They can hire physical education teachers and provide staff development in quality physical education programs for both physical educators and classroom teachers.

When community members and school personnel value physical education for the benefits provided to students, programs will be viewed as an integral part of the school's efforts to address the movement needs of their students and to fulfill the mandates established within their local wellness policy. Physical education should be the primary vehicle for delivering quality movement time to students, with accessory time provided through recess, after-school programs, and integration of physical activity into the classroom. The physical educator should be the key person advocating for and monitoring progress toward the physical education objectives outlined in the school's wellness policy.

How to Build a Quality Elementary Physical Education Program

Movement at the elementary grade levels is the very essence of development as children learn cognitively, socially, and physically by moving in their environment. In other words, elementary school students learn through movement, and for this reason the quality of elementary physical education assumes special importance. Quality assurance begins with developing a written physical education curriculum that guides the teachers throughout the year. Without this blueprint (curriculum guide) for producing a quality physical education program, positive experiences for students are most certainly happenstance, because important skills, concepts, and attitudes may be overlooked.

Curriculum has been defined as all of the experiences of the learner in an educational setting. Formally, it is a prescribed course of study, usually clarified by a curriculum guide. In physical education, the course of study is based on education about and through movement, and the curriculum guide specifies the particular content to be mastered at each grade level. To ensure that each year the curriculum builds on the content taught in previous years, a scope and sequence is developed. The scope indicates the breadth and depth

of the content of the program, and the sequence indicates the order in which the program content will be taught from year to year, including the amount of time allotted to each standard and objective. The following steps are involved in building a curriculum:

- Selecting a guiding philosophy
- Establishing school-level program goals
- Determining grade-level program goals and benchmarks
- Developing the scope and sequence for the program content (yearly plan)
- Writing lesson plans that include lesson objectives (student outcomes), lesson content and organization, and student assessment
- Assessing students using formative and summative evaluations and other types of assessment, indicating student progress (grading), and assessing program effectiveness

Although classroom teachers may not be the ones who build (on their own) a physical education curriculum, they may collaborate with others to do so. Thus understanding the curriculum-building process (as described in this chapter) may be helpful.

SELECTING A GUIDING PHILOSOPHY

To develop a curriculum, a philosophy of education in general and physical education specifically should be adopted. The **philosophy of education statement** indicates the purpose of education (from the writers' viewpoint) and how educational practices would be implemented to meet the stated purpose. The philosophical statement indicates values and beliefs about physical education such as the following:

- The importance of movement to the elementary school child
- The primary goal of physical education
- The relative emphasis on skill versus fitness development
- The relative emphasis on cooperative versus competitive activities
- The role of physical education teachers and classroom teachers in meeting physical education program goals
- The need for daily physical education
- The need to design developmentally appropriate activities for each child
- The need to foster physical activity participation for a lifetime
- The place of physical education in the school wellness plan

---

BOX 6.2 Physical Education Philosophy

. . . .

PURPOSE

The purpose of this curriculum guide is to assist the physical education specialist and the elementary classroom teacher responsible for teaching physical education to the elementary school children (K–6) of Smithville, USA. It represents the thinking of school personnel and community members who worked closely on the school's wellness plan for meeting the nutritional and physical activity needs of the students.

BELIEFS

Since movement underlies nearly all of human accomplishment, physical education is an integral part of the total educational program. It offers a unique contribution in the development of knowledge, understanding, and positive attitudes about human movement. The degree of success children experience during play is influenced by their ability to execute movement skills effectively and efficiently. For the child, movement is the most frequently used means of nonverbal communication, expression, and learning. Through movement, impressions about self are learned. To become a fully functioning individual in the society, the child needs many opportunities to participate in a balanced, progressive, developmentally appropriate program of instruction in physical education.

The NASPE National Standards for Physical Education form the basis of the program. The standards indicate what a physically educated person should

know, value, and be able to do as the result of participating in a quality physical education program.

TEACHING METHODS

The movement exploration approach is the primary teaching method used. This child-centered approach encourages each child to develop an appreciation for movement. Movement experiences are designed so that each child is successful. Activities are developmentally appropriate in order to meet the psychomotor, cognitive, and affective needs of the students in a nonthreatening, noncompetitive environment.

PROGRAM CONTENT

Specific content includes locomotor, axial, and manipulative skills at the primary levels and a high emphais on fitness education and lifetime sport skills and rhythms at the intermediate level. The lessons are designed for maximum participation and a high percentage of time on task. Cooperative activities allow for the development of respect and responsibility for self and others. Ongoing assessments are used to assess student progress toward program objectives. These assessments are shared with the students and their parents. When possible, the assessments are authentic in nature, and a child's progress is monitored by comparing performance to norms or to the child's previous performance (not compared with other children's performance). Specific program content and evaluation tools are included in the next section of this guide.

The guiding philosophy may follow one of the current curriculum models designed for elementary physical education. Metzler (2005) describes four such models: movement education, skill themes, fitness concepts and education, and games-based education. The movement education model emphasizes learning the movement concepts and skills included in the movement map (Figure 3.1) through individual and partner activities. The skill themes model also teaches the movement map information; however, it organizes the information around the basic motor skills. The fitness concepts and education model teaches motor activities with an emphasis on fitness knowledge as well as the motivation to engage in fitness activities over a lifetime. The games-based education model focuses on participation in games to perfect movement skills

and game strategies. It is possible to have a different philosophy (or model) for different grade levels. For example, the curriculum philosophy might be congruent with a movement education model for grades K–2 or for a games-based model in grades 5–6.

Box 6.2 contains a typical physical education philosophy from a curriculum guide. This sample may be helpful to teachers as they develop the district's or school's unique physical education philosophy.

ESTABLISHING SCHOOL-LEVEL PROGRAM GOALS

Curriculum builders complete this second step of curriculum building by writing **school-level program goals** based on the developed philosophy (model),

BOX 6.3 Sample Program Goals with Corresponding Benchmarks

NASPE STANDARD 1

Students demonstrate competency in motor skills and movement patterns needed to perform a variety of physical activities.

SCHOOL-LEVEL PROGRAM GOAL

Students demonstrate competency in the basic locomotor skills, basic manipulative skills, simple dance forms, and basic tumbling skills.

GRADE-LEVEL GOALS AND BENCHMARKS (GRADES K–2)

- *Goal 1:* The student combines shapes, levels, directions, and pathways and arranges them into simple sequences.
- *Benchmark 1:* The student designs and performs a 32-count sequence of movement using at least two different shapes, levels, directions, and pathways.
- *Goal 2:* The student performs, with correct technique, successive forward rolls.
- *Benchmark 2:* The student correctly performs three forward rolls in succession.

GRADE-LEVEL GOALS AND BENCHMARKS (GRADES 3– 4)

- *Goal 1:* The student performs the basic locomotor skills with correct technique while playing basic games.

- *Benchmark 1:* The student can run into a turning long rope, jump 20 consecutive times, and run out without missing.
- *Goal 2:* The student accurately throws (using a mature throwing pattern) a football, softball, Frisbee, and basketball. Balls may be junior-sized and soft (Nerf).
- *Benchmark 2:* While playing catch, the student can successfully (accurately and with correct technique) throw to a partner five consecutive times.

GRADE-LEVEL GOALS AND BENCHMARKS (GRADES 5–6)

- *Goal 1:* The student performs basic locomotor skills in lead-up games.
- *Benchmark 1:* The student successfully dribbles a soccer ball while playing modified soccer.
- *Goal 2:* The student performs square dances in time to the music.
- *Benchmark 2:* The student successfully performs an entire square dance that includes the following figures: promenade, allemande left, swing your partner, swing your corner, circle left, and do-sa-do. Student must continuously move in time to the music with the correct foot shuffle. (Box 6.5, later in the chapter, shows a physical education lesson that includes a description of these square dance figures.)

---

the NASPE content standards, state standards (if available), and any unique local circumstances. The NASPE standards embody a specific philosophy of physical education and lead to program goals compatible with this philosophy. A particular school's physical education philosophy may not exactly match NASPE's philosophy, and that is to be expected because the school's philosophy is also based on local beliefs and conditions. But to the extent that the school's philosophy varies from that of NASPE, sound rationale should exist for those variations. In addition, since resources, facilities, and teacher expertise vary, the program content (activities) used to accomplish these program goals may look very different in schools around the country. However, evidence of the national standards is present in all well-planned quality programs.

School-level program goals are generally limited in number so that the program stays focused and the

assessment does not become burdensome. We recommend writing only one or two school-level program goals for each NASPE content standard.

DETERMINING GRADE-LEVEL GOALS AND BENCHMARKS

Once school-level program goals are established, writing more specific **grade-level goals** allows the program goals to be interpreted in light of the developmental needs of children of different ages and maturity. As each grade-level goal is written, a corresponding benchmark is developed. The **grade-level benchmark** describes the specific student behavior that indicates a student has achieved the goal. Box 6.3 provides an example of school-level program goals interpreted for specific grade levels with corresponding grade-level benchmarks.

DEVELOPING THE SCOPE AND SEQUENCE FOR PROGRAM CONTENT

Program goals are accomplished by having students participate in certain movement activities and learning experiences. So the next step in building the curriculum is to select the **scope of program content**—the depth and breadth of movement forms to be taught—and the **sequence of program content**—the order in which the forms are taught. Movement forms may be categorized in a number of ways. For our purposes, eight movement forms are defined and discussed: (1) basic movement skills, (2) basic game skills, (3) creative and rhythmic movements, (4) body management skills and gymnastics, (5) cooperative movement skills, (6) fitness and wellness concepts and activities, (7) water skills, and (8) recreational activity skills.

Basic Movement Skills   The **basic movement skills** include the locomotor, nonlocomotor, and manipulative skills underlying the movements specific to certain games and sports. *Refer to Chapter 3 for a list and definitions of the basic movement skills.* Every child should be provided with basic movement experiences that allow for maximum participation and the opportunity to progress at his or her own level of ability. In addition to the movement skills, movement concepts associated with the skills are taught. Movement concepts include the underlying components common to all movement (refer to the movement map presented in Figure 3.1). Using these movement components (body awareness, space awareness, qualities of movement, relationships, etc.), any physical skill or movement can be described and understood cognitively. The components allow educators to describe how to perform various physical skills. Students need to understand these movement components in order to develop efficient, effective movement patterns. The movement components are discussed and applied throughout the K–6 grades whenever motor skills are taught and practiced. Even students in grades K–2 can understand the movement components when exploring basic movement patterns. Appendix A (individual and partner sections) contains suggested activities to master the basic movement skills.

Basic Game Skills   When the basic movement skills are combined and used to play low-organized games or lead-up games to sports (e.g., basketball, volleyball, and baseball), the basic movement can be slightly altered because of how the game or sport is played. When used to play games, basic movements are then categorized as a different movement form: **basic game skills.**

For example, *striking* is a *basic movement skill* that young learners practice in a variety of ways (hitting a balloon off different body parts to self or hitting a volleyball underhand to a wall so it rebounds back for continuous hitting). *Striking* becomes a *basic game skill* when used to play games such as Keep-It-Up or Four-Square (see Appendix C). The basic game skills include throwing and catching; kicking; striking and volleying; bouncing and dribbling; chasing, fleeing, and dodging as applied to specific games. The basic game skills' portion of the curriculum continues to teach the four components of movement (body, space, effort, and relationships) and the fundamental movement skills (locomotor, nonlocomotor, and manipulative) as applied to specific game situations. Appendix A (small group activity section) contains suggested activities to master the basic game skills.

Creative and Rhythmic Movements   The **creative and rhythmic movements** include all kinds of rhythmic forms (fundamental movement to music, creative rhythms, square dance, folk dance, and manipulative activities to music such as jump rope, Lummi sticks, ribbons, and balls). Rhythmic activities are locomotor and nonlocomotor movements (Figure 3.1) performed in time to music accompaniment. These activities provide children an opportunity to develop their rhythmic abilities and to develop the body's ability to express ideas, concepts, and emotions through movement. This is a vital component of the curriculum as it is the primary area that deals with the expressive and communicative aspect of movement. Appendix E contains a progression of activities to teach fundamental movement to music, a suggested listing of folk and square dances appropriate for K–6 students, and suggested activities using manipulatives (e.g., balls, Lummi sticks). You can find the rhythmic activities included in the text in Appendix F (consult column titled "Movement Form").

Body Management Skills and Gymnastics   Activities largely concerned with the control of movement and the transference of body weight during movement fall in the category of **body management skills and gymnastics.** Content includes stunts, tumbling, and gymnastics activities with and without apparatus. Specific learning activities are listed in Appendix E. The knowledge base also includes movement concepts relevant to this type of movement. Appendix F contains a number of activities in this movement form (consult column titled "Movement Form").

Cooperative Movement Skills   **Cooperative movement skills** include tasks, games, and activities specifically designed so students must cooperate (in partners or groups) to accomplish the movement task or game goal. The performance of the physical skill or task is designed to develop cooperative skills such as teamwork, taking turns, listening to others, group decision making, problem-solving generation, being a leader or follower, respecting others, communicating effectively, and being able to reach goals as a group. Many cooperative activities are included in the text. (Consult Unit 2 in the lesson plan section for a complete cooperative activity unit, and consult Appendix F for the cooperative learning activities included in the text.)

Fitness and Wellness Concepts and Activities

Fitness and wellness concepts and activities include the knowledge base in fitness and wellness and any activities in the curriculum that are structured to improve children's fitness. Elementary school children need to understand the physiological benefits of physical activity, value physical activity, participate in physical activity, and know how to maintain fitness throughout their lives. Quick Lesson 6.1, Classroom Learning Station 6.1, and Special Event "Parents' Night" at the end of the chapter specify activities to improve fitness and learn the fitness and wellness knowledge base.

In general, for elementary school children, fitness activities are not different from the movement forms already mentioned. Elementary school students do not work out as adults do; rather, they reach fitness goals by participating in the other movement forms (water skills, rhythmic movements, basic movement skills, etc.). Chapter 4 contains the knowledge base and activities included in this movement form.

Water Skills

Water skills include swimming strokes, water games, water aerobics, diving, and water safety techniques. Usually the physical education program does not have access to a swimming pool, so to learn the physical skills, children are encouraged to engage in this movement form by participating in summer water activities sponsored by the community. For teachers who wish to promote water safety awareness (without the use of a swimming pool), the American Red Cross has available an education packet (*Longfellow's Whale Tales*) containing seven lessons for grades K–6. Teachers should contact their local Red Cross chapter to obtain this packet.

Recreational Activity Skills

Recreational activity skills include activities participated in for recreational purposes in the outdoors, such as canoeing, hiking, orienteering, biking, in-line skating, camping, fishing, and walking. Many elementary schools do include walking, biking, and in-line skating in the physical education program when space and equipment allow them to do so. However, children should also be encouraged to develop these skills outside of the school environment. If lack of equipment is an issue, try to find sponsors (local or national) who might provide the equipment. For example, through the Skate in School program, sponsored by NASPE and Rollerblade, schools can obtain grants to make in-line skating a part of their physical education program. The grant provides the school with 40 pairs of Rollerblade in-line skates, helmets, and 40 sets of knee pads, elbow pads, and wrist guards. Teachers should contact NASPE for information on how to apply for this grant (visit www.skateinschool.com or call 888-758-4386). At the local level, take advantage of community resources collaborating with businesses, industry, and agencies to provide services or equipment.

Scope and Sequence of Movement Forms

The eight movement forms just discussed are taught at all grade levels in order to achieve exposure to a balanced curriculum. However, the activities used to support the movement forms change at each grade level in order to be developmentally appropriate. And the percentage of time allocated to the eight movement forms within the curriculum changes as children mature and master the basic movement skills. Percentages of time generally allocated to each movement form are indicated in Table 6.1.

Most programs emphasize the first six movement forms. Ideally, the program would contain all

TABLE 6.1 Program Time Devoted to the Various Movement Forms

MOVEMENT FORMS	GRADES K–2 (%)	GRADES 3–4 (%)	GRADES 5–6 (%)
Basic movement skills	30	20	10
Basic game skills	10	20	35
Cooperative movement skills	5	10	15
Creative and rhythmic movements	25	20	15
Body management and gymnastics	20	20	15
Fitness activities	10	10	10
Recreational activity skills	0	0	0
Water skills	0	0	0

TABLE 6.2   Sample Yearly Plan for Grades K–2

Week	Movement Form	Lesson Focus
FIRST NINE WEEKS		
1	Basic movement	Locomotor skills
2	Rhythmic movement	Space awareness
3	Basic movement, manipulative	Throwing and catching
4	Body management	Fleeing and dodging
5	Basic game skill	Kicking
6	Cooperative movement	Partner stunts
7	Basic movement	Nonlocomotor skills
8	Rhythmic movement, creative	Force and flow
9	Basic movement	Striking and volleying
SECOND NINE WEEKS		
1	Body management	Body awareness
2	Cooperative movement	Group games
3	Rhythmic movement, creative	Dancing a story or poem
4	Basic movement	Dribbling (hands and feet)
5	Body management	Balancing
6	Physical fitness, flexibility	Animal walks
7	Basic game skills	Throwing and catching
8	Basic game skills	Locomotor skills
9	Rhythmic movement	Simple folk dances
THIRD NINE WEEKS		
1	Basic movement	Nonlocomotor skills
2	Basic movement	Striking and volleying
3	Body management, gymnastics	Tumbling
4	Physical fitness, strength	Stretch bands
5	Cooperative movement	Partner dance creation
6	Basic movement	Dribbling (hands and feet)
7	Basic game skills	Chasing, fleeing, dodging
8	Rhythmic movement	Creative dance
9	Body management, gymnastics	Tumbling
FOURTH NINE WEEKS		
1	Rhythmic movement	Simple folk dances
2	Physical fitness, endurance	Agility runs
3	Cooperative movement	Partner games
4	Basic movement	Throwing and catching
5	Basic game skills	Kicking
6	Rhythmic movement	Lummi sticks
7	Body management, gymnastics	Jumping and landing
8	Basic movement, manipulative	Parachute
9	Basic movement, manipulative	Hula hoops

the movement forms, as students need to acquire a broad movement repertoire. However, based on local circumstances (facility, equipment, community practices), forms are sometimes omitted (thus the zeros placed in Table 6.1). Obviously, omitting certain forms at the K–6 level can severely limit future achievement in those movement forms unless the community has strong programs in those forms and the children traditionally participate in those programs.

Table 6.1 represents the scope (depth and breadth) of the program content. The breadth is indicated by the movement forms listed in the first column, and

the depth is indicated at each grade level by the percentages in the right-hand columns. The depth, breadth, and sequencing of the program content are usually shown in a yearly plan. The **yearly plan** lists (by week) the movement form and primary content (focus) of the lessons. The lesson focus represents the primary lesson content selected from the previously mentioned movement forms (in the assigned percentages).

Sample sequences of program content (yearly plan) are shown in Table 6.2 (grades K–2), Table 6.3 (grades 3–4), and Table 6.4 (grades 5–6). The

TABLE 6.3 Sample Yearly Plan for Grades 3–4

WEEKS	MOVEMENT FORM	LESSON FOCUS
FIRST NINE WEEKS		
1	Cooperative movement	Orientation and games
2–3	Basic movement	Body awareness
4–5	Basic game skills	Throw, catch, shoot
6	Rhythmic movement	Creative dance
7	Physical fitness	Flexibility
8–9	Body management, gymnastics	Balance, weight transfer
SECOND NINE WEEKS		
1	Cooperative movement	Challenges
2–3	Basic movement	Space awareness
4–5	Body management, gymnastics	Stunts and tumbling
6–7	Rhythmic movement	Manipulative skills to music (Lummi sticks, parachute, ribbons)
8–9	Basic game skills	Dribble (hands and feet)
THIRD NINE WEEKS		
1	Cooperative movement	Games
2	Basic movement	Effort awareness
3	Physical fitness	Muscle strength
4–5	Basic game skills	Kick, strike (paddles)
6–7	Rhythmic movement	Square dance, jump rope
8–9	Body management, gymnastics	Balance, weight transfer
FOURTH NINE WEEKS		
1	Cooperative movement	Challenges
2–3	Rhythmic movement	Folk dance, jump rope
4–5	Body management, gymnastics	Stunts and tumbling
6	Basic game skills	Strike (bat), roll
7	Physical fitness	Cardiorespiratory endurance
8–9	Basic movement	Relationships with objects

movement forms listed in the second column of each table reflect the percentages indicated in Table 6.1. For instance, assuming 36 weeks in the school year, K–2 students spend 11 weeks on basic movement (30 percent), whereas fifth and sixth graders spend only 4 weeks (10 percent). In contrast, fifth and sixth graders spend 12 weeks (35 percent) on basic game skills, whereas K–2 students spend only 4 weeks. The third column in each table, the lesson focus, indicates the specific content within the movement form that the students should engage in during those weeks.

To use these yearly plans, movement educators would first select specific movement activities and experiences to teach the designated lesson focus and then fully develop the activities and experiences into physical education lesson plans (using the lesson plan elements indicated in the next section). The physical education lesson plan developed in the last section of the chapter is appropriate as a lesson for grades 5 and 6 based on the yearly plan just presented (appropriate during week 2 of the fourth nine weeks—square dance).

WRITING LESSON PLANS

From the yearly plan, a physical education **lesson plan** is written for each class period. The elements in the following lesson plan, which are listed below, provide a sample format for designing instruction with national standards, local program goals, and lesson objectives in mind. Remember that planning a lesson always begins by determining the lesson objectives and then selecting activities (from the specified movement form) to achieve those objectives.

- *Movement form:* Indicate the movement form being taught in the lesson focus.
- *Grade level:* Indicate the grade level of the students being taught.
- *NASPE standard:* State the NASPE standard (or standards) the lesson is designed to meet.
- *Benchmark:* State the program benchmark (or benchmarks) the lesson is designed to achieve.
- *Lesson objectives:* Indicate what the student will know, value, and be able to do after completing the lesson.

TABLE 6.4 Sample Yearly Plan for Grades 5–6

WEEKS	MOVEMENT FORM	LESSON FOCUS
FIRST NINE WEEKS		
1	Cooperative movement	Orientation and games
2–3	Basic movement	Body and space awareness
4–5	Basic game skills	Throw, catch, shoot, dribble (basketball skills)
6–7	Body management, gymnastics	Balance, weight transfer
8	Physical fitness	Muscle strength
9	Rhythmic movement	Line dances, jump rope
SECOND NINE WEEKS		
1	Cooperative movement	Challenges
2–3	Rhythmic movement	Folk dances, step aerobics
4–5	Basic game skills	Roll (bowling skills)
6	Physical fitness	Cardiorespiratory endurance
7	Body management, gymnastics	Stunts and tumbling
8–9	Basic game skills	Kick, punt
THIRD NINE WEEKS		
1	Cooperative movement	Games
2–3	Basic movement	Effort and relationships
4–5	Basic game skills	Strike, volley (volleyball skills)
6–7	Body management, gymnastics	Stunts and tumbling
8	Physical fitness	Flexibility
9	Cooperative movement	Partner dances
FOURTH NINE WEEKS		
1	Cooperative movement	Challenges
2–3	Rhythmic movement	Square dance, step aerobics
4–5	Basic game skills	Throw, catch, bat (softball and baseball skills)
6–7	Physical fitness	Muscle endurance
8–9	Basic game skills	Dribble (feet) (soccer skills)

- *Materials and equipment:* List all needed equipment (balls, ropes, paper, pencils, etc.).
- *Approximate time:* Indicate how much time is allotted to complete each activity.
- *Activity description:* Describe (in detail) the activities in which students will participate. As indicated in Chapter 7, this would generally include an introductory activity, a lesson focus activity, and a closing activity. A fitness activity is also included if none of the other activities develop any of the components of physical fitness. Most of the lesson time is spent on the lesson focus that contains activities from the movement form identified in the yearly plan for that particular lesson. This section also includes relevant teaching cues for the lesson activities, questions to ask students to check for understanding, and actions needed to alleviate safety concerns.
- *Success for all:* Indicate several activity alternatives or ways to adapt the activities that assist students who are not meeting the lesson objectives.

- *Class organization:* Indicate class formations needed to do the various activities and how you plan to move students into those formations.
- *Student assessment:* Indicate the event, activity, and instrument that will be used during the class activities to determine whether students are meeting the lesson objectives. These assessment events are formative in nature and used by the teacher to provide feedback to students during their performance as well as to adjust the learning activities to promote greater student learning.

For sample *physical education* lesson plans that contain these elements, consult the lesson described in the last section of this chapter and the lessons included in the final section of the text. Since the Instant Activities, Quick Lessons, and Learning Stations included in all the text chapters are *movement experiences for the classroom* (not full physical education lessons), some of the lesson plan elements just identified are not included.

For most of the lesson plan elements, the brief description just provided suffices to identify the information requested for that section. However, two of the elements need further specification: student assessment and lesson objectives. Student assessment is covered in depth in the next section of this chapter.

Lesson objectives may be written in three domains: cognitive, psychomotor, and affective. **Cognitive objectives** specify what a student will know intellectually. **Psychomotor objectives** indicate what the student will physically perform. **Affective objectives** indicate what the student values, believes, or feels as well as how the student is expected to interact with others. Lesson objectives in all three domains are written in performance or behavioral terms. They direct the student to do something that is observable. The lesson objective is a statement that begins by indicating who will do something: "The student will . . ." The verb in the statement indicates what the student will do, and the behavior specified is observable and measurable; for example: demonstrate, perform with 80 percent accuracy, show competence, identify, create, design, verbally explain, jump, run, shoot, dribble. "The student dribbles a basketball in a figure-eight pattern."

The last part of the lesson objective includes the assessment piece by indicating the criteria for judging whether the student has been successful. "The student dribbles a basketball in a figure-eight pattern twice around the four cones without losing control of the ball." In this example, two kinds of criteria are included: qualitative ("without losing control of the ball") and quantitative ("twice"). In general, both kinds of criteria are included in the lesson objective, as movement educators are concerned with not just how many times a students can perform a skill, but also the manner (technique) in which that skill is performed. Table 6.5 contains sample lesson objectives in the cognitive, affective, and psychomotor domains based on the goals listed in Box 6.3.

ASSESSING STUDENTS

Terminology used in the area of assessment continues to change as the educational reform movement alters the way assessment is viewed and defined. Today it seems that the term **assessment** includes the concepts of both measurement and evaluation. Thus assessment includes the collection of data (measurement) and the use of the data to make informed decisions (evaluation). For example, a lesson objective might indicate that students are to create three different shapes at each of three different levels. Assessment might involve creating an observation checklist that the teacher completes to collect data on student performance during class (measurement), and then using the data to plan future lessons, prepare students' progress reports, and determine program effectiveness (evaluation).

Quality assessment involves the processes of both measurement and evaluation. There is no reason to measure unless evaluation is going to occur; so why measure and evaluate? Assessment of students provides the basis:

- For knowing
  - what students have learned
  - what to teach next
  - whether students are meeting program goals and benchmarks
  - whether teaching methods are effective
- For reporting
  - summary information on program effectiveness to administrators and community members
  - individual student progress to students and parents
  - individual health status to students and parents
  - justifiable program needs (e.g., materials, equipment, teaching training) to administrators

Formative and Summative Evaluation Assessment is essential in determining whether the students are meeting the program goals, benchmarks, and lesson objectives. Within the educational reform movement, student assessment is emphasized not as a means of determining a grade, but rather as a means to determine whether learning occurred (Gallo et al. 2006). When used as a learning tool, the assessment process becomes formative in nature, occurs frequently, and uses the judgment of teachers, peers, and self to determine the student's level of success (NASPE 2004). **Formative evaluation** occurs frequently (within each lesson), helps students identify areas that need improvement, aids the teacher in planning, and is usually not used to provide a grade.

Summative evaluation occurs at the end of instruction, provides a summary of accomplishments, and is often used to determine a grade or prepare a progress report. Summative evaluation may occur at the end of a unit, midterm, or at the end of a grading period. Table 6.6 describes the characteristics of formative and summative evaluation in terms of when it occurs, who does it, what is being assessed, and why the assessment is occurring. Box 6.4 provides example formative and summative evaluation events indicating the characteristics of when, what, and why associated with that event.

TABLE 6.5 Psychomotor, Cognitive, and Affective Lesson Objectives

GRADE	PSYCHOMOTOR OBJECTIVES (WHAT STUDENTS CAN DO)	COGNITIVE OBJECTIVES (WHAT STUDENTS KNOW)	AFFECTIVE OBJECTIVES (WHAT STUDENTS VALUE) (HOW STUDENTS INTERACT WITH OTHERS)
K	Students travel in different directions, changing levels on the command of the teacher without touching other students.	Students recite the different directions and levels in which they may travel from place to place.	Students effectively express concepts through movement (water drip, tornado, etc.) so others in the class are able to guess the concept.
1	Students create three different shapes at three different levels.	Students verbally count the beat of a piece of music correctly for 32 counts.	Students verbally express a sense of self-satisfaction through expressive movement when questioned by the teacher as to their feelings.
2	Students, moving to music in different directions and at different levels, freeze in a self-designed shape when the music stops (three stops with three different shapes).	Students correctly verbalize the six space awareness elements (personal space, general space, direction, level, size, and pathway).	Students smile while moving to different types of music during one class period.
3	Students play "school" using the long jump rope, reaching the 12th grade without any jumping errors.	Students write (in their journals) the correct technique for jumping rope.	Students always take turns appropriately while playing "school" with the long jump rope during one class period.
4	Students throw and catch a Frisbee (with a partner) five consecutive times from a distance of ten feet.	Students analyze the throwing and catching technique of their partner and give correct feedback to improve their partner's performance.	Students select different partners (from among their classmates) in order to practice their throwing and catching skills without arguments occurring during one class period.
5	Students dribble a soccer ball the length of the playing field (without an opponent present) without losing ball control.	Students verbally describe at least one way to evade an opponent when dribbling a soccer ball in a soccer game.	Students obey rules and etiquette while participating in a modified soccer game for one class period.
6	Students perform a square dance without any movement mistakes while moving to the rhythm of the music.	Students score a minimum of 85 percent on a knowledge test covering the history of square dancing in the United States.	Students invite a classmate to be their partner for the next square dance using proper etiquette during one class period.

TABLE 6.6   Characteristics of Formative and Summative Evaluation

CHARACTERISTIC	FORMATIVE EVALUATION	SUMMATIVE EVALUATION
When	Given at frequent intervals. Given before or during instruction.	Given infrequently; usually at end of a large amount of instruction. Given after unit of instruction has ended.
Who	Given by self, peers, or teacher.	Given by teacher.
What	Tests specific skills or concepts. Ideally tests every concept and objective that has been taught.	Tests general concepts, skills, or terminal objectives. Tests only a sample from among the concepts, skills, or objectives.
Why	Determine specific skills, concepts, and objectives that students have or have not mastered (diagnosis). Provide immediate feedback to students on their learning performance. Predict probable performance on successive skills, program goals, and summative evaluation. Identify specific weaknesses in ongoing instruction (material and teacher procedures), allowing the teacher to remedy the instruction.	Determine students' grades based on final achievement. Revise subsequent instruction or redesign course or program. Predict students' probable performance in subsequent course. Determine program or course effectiveness. Identify final student achievement. Determine number of students who achieved program benchmarks.

Adapted with permission from the work of Dr. Hugh Baird for the Utah State Office of Education.

Obviously, both formative and summative evaluation processes must align assessment events with the program goals, benchmarks, lesson objectives, and learning experiences in order to be considered valid measures of student achievement. Both types of assessment processes should be present in the program to fully capture the range of evaluation purposes. And most important, the formative and summative evaluation processes should be planned when the curriculum is constructed—not as an afterthought. This allows assessment to be linked to program goals.

The student assessment element included in each lesson plan is a formative evaluation process in which the assessment event described provides a quick indication of student progress for the purpose of providing feedback to students in order to improve their performance. This feedback may also be used by the teacher to plan, or to alter already planned, learning experiences to meet students' needs. Sample formative assessment events (correlated with sample learning activities) are presented below.

- *Activity:* Students travel through general space, performing the locomotor skill called out by the teacher. *Assessment:* Using a checklist, the teacher assesses each student's mastery of the critical elements of the locomotor skills (teacher observation).

- *Activity:* Students throw and catch to each other, practicing the characteristics of a mature throw. *Assessment:* Concentrating on the critical elements of throwing—ready position, arm preparation, opposite side to the target, step with leg opposite the throwing arm, follow through, and accuracy of the throw—students give feedback to each other after five consecutive throws (peer observation).

- *Activity:* Students are taught the following muscles: biceps, triceps, and deltoid. *Assessment:* On a drawing of the arm and shoulder, students are asked to identify the biceps, triceps, and deltoid muscles (written test).

Types of Assessment   Although formative and summative evaluation processes occur at different times within instructional units for different purposes, the actual assessment events used within both processes may be very similar or exactly the same. For example, during jump rope instruction, every day the teacher completes a checklist specifying correct jumping technique, for the purpose of improving student jump rope

---

BOX 6.4 Formative and Summative Evaluation Events

WHEN ASSESSMENT OCCURS

Formative Evaluation

Example: Ms. Jones observes her class (using a checklist) once a week on the basic locomotor skills of skipping and galloping.

Rationale: Testing with such frequency indicates the teacher is determining student progress throughout the unit of instruction on locomotor skills and after teaching only one or two of them.

Summative Evaluation

Example: At the end of the unit on locomotor skills, Ms. Jones tests (by observation) the class to determine students' mastery.

Rationale: Evaluation occurs after all instruction is complete, and reports will be sent home to parents or guardians.

WHAT IS BEING ASSESSED?

Formative Evaluation

Example: Mr. Southall tests his students on the backward and forward roll.

Rationale: Evaluation occurs after instruction of a specific skill and measures every skill taught.

Summative Evaluation

Example: Mr. Southall tests his students on a floor exercise routine involving several tumbling moves.

Rationale: This evaluation tests competency in the whole unit of tumbling.

WHY IS ASSESSMENT OCCURRING?

Formative Evaluation

Example: When most of Ms. Stanley's students could not determine increase of heart rate after vigorous activity, she reorganized her lesson and retaught parts of it.

Rationale: This evaluation was used to assess, diagnose, and alter instructional methods, as well as students' skills, immediately.

Summative Evaluation

Example: After most of Ms. Stanley's fifth-grade students failed their test on determining target heart rate, she revised her lessons and rewrote the test for next year.

Rationale: The test results were used to revise instructional methods for subsequent classes.

---

performance. This is a formative evaluation process. At the end of the jump rope unit, the teacher uses the same checklist to determine final achievement for students based on their final jump rope technique. This is a summative evaluation process; however, the assessment event (teacher observation) and instrument (checklist) are the same as those in the formative process. Other appropriate types of assessment (in addition to teacher observation) include peer observation, self-evaluation, written tests or papers, student logs and journals, student projects, oral presentations, student performances, and student portfolios. The use of peer assessment is gaining in popularity as physical educators recognize the benefits of this assessment type. In large classes with many students moving at the same time, peer assessment allows learners to receive individual (and immediate) performance feedback. Significant planning must occur to structure a peer assessment event that connects the lesson goals with the information taught (Johnson 2004).

Recent developments in assessment theory and practice have significantly altered the terminology used to discuss assessment and the events considered to be appropriate. In the not-so-distant past, the primary means of assessment were teacher-made and standardized paper-and-pencil tests; thus traditional assessment activities excluded many of the assessment events named earlier. Today, however, the emphasis is on alternative assessment defined as any assessment that is not the traditional paper-and-pencil test.

The primary alternative assessment currently being used in the educational setting is **authentic assessment,** meaning that the assessment activity takes place in a real-life setting rather than in an artificial setting (Wiggins 1993, 1998). Thus, in physical education, when assessing movement skills, the teacher observes a student using a skill in a game or activity, as opposed to in the artificial setting of a standardized skills test. For example, the teacher observes the student's ability to throw and catch a softball while the student plays a softball lead-up game (real-life setting) instead of during a skills test or while the student is simply playing catch.

Authentic assessment is deemed to be a more accurate measure of the student's competencies than traditional assessments because with authentic assessments students must do more than recall or recognize facts they have learned. Authentic assessment calls for an in-depth understanding of what has been taught so the information learned is digested, analyzed, and synthesized in order to complete the assessment event. Thus students must use higher-order cognitive processes during authentic assessment events. If you observed students while they performed the entire "Gustaf's Skoal" dance and assessed their ability to walk and skip to the music, to begin movement for each phrase on time, and be in the correct position in the square at all times, that would be an authentic assessment.

To make authentic assessment activities valid, reliable, and objective, a **scoring rubric** is developed for each event. The rubric is used to judge the child's level of acquisition (based on the tasks specified in the assessment event). The rubric is usually developed in chart form. The chart indicates the criteria used to judge the performance or product and the rating scale used to judge level of achievement (based on the criteria).

The criteria may specify both qualitative (manner) and quantitative (number of times) aspects of the performance or product. The validity of the scoring rubric is assured by listing only the criteria emphasized during the instructional process. Objectivity is assured by specifying the rubric in sufficient detail that different teachers would give the same individual the same rating on the same performance. Reliability is assured by constructing a rubric such that the teacher would give performances (viewed on different days) by the same student (with no practice in between those performances) the same rating. Another way to increase the reliability of the student's score is to give the student multiple opportunities to perform and then average the scores to obtain the final score. This technique is especially appropriate when rating movement skills, as children tend to be very inconsistent when performing movement skills.

Figure 6.1 presents an assessment rubric for the folk dance "Gustaf's Skoal." Rubrics for all the locomotor and manipulative skills are included in Appendix B, and additional rubric examples (along with helpful hints for developing rubrics) can be found in *Creating Rubrics for Physical Education* (Lund 2000).

Folk Dance: "Gustaf's Skoal"

Student's name: _____　Date: _____

Criteria	Score
Walks in a stately manner (forward and back).	_____
Is in correct position on the floor at the start of each phrase.	_____
Skips in time with the music.	_____
Begins movement for each phrase on time.	_____

Total score _____

SCORING RUBRIC
0 = never
1 = sometimes
2 = usually
3 = always

FIGURE 6.1　Assessment Rubric for a Folk Dance Performance

Implementing Assessment in the Lesson　We know that teaching physical education lessons presents some challenges not present in classroom settings. Sometimes class sizes are larger than in the classroom setting. The gymnasium is larger and less confined in terms of space available and thus more difficult to supervise. In addition, physical activity performance is generally a "live, variable" event that occurs once versus a "taped, static" event such as a completed work-sheet or paper-pencil test. Taped, static performances can be assessed at a later date; whereas live, variable performances need to be assessed at the moment they occur. These conditions present unique circumstances in which the teacher must plan and implement not only instructional activities but also quality assessment activities. However, the use of authentic, embedded assessment events enables teachers to measure student performance in each lesson, if desired.

We have suggested that *formative student assessment* occur during each lesson. The assessment event for the lesson is planned when the lesson is formulated.

Student Name	Eyes focused ahead	Fingertips push the ball (versus slap)	Bounced waist high	Number of times lost control of the ball
Student 1				
Student 2				
. . .				
. . .				
Student 29				
Student 30				

Students are rated three times (thus they move across the floor dribbling at least three times).

Rating scale for technique assessment:
  Never
  Sometimes
  Almost always
  Always

FIGURE 6.2   Assessment Rubric for Dribbling a Basketball

Using the following steps to plan the assessment event in each lesson may be helpful:

1. Select the key one or two lesson objectives.
2. Write the objective in behavioral terms (as specified earlier in the chapter) so an observable definition of the behavior exists (e.g., students will dribble a basketball across the gymnasium using proper technique, with their dominant hand, without losing control of the ball).
3. Select the most appropriate observation activity (Johnson 2005). For example, with a class size of 30, set up six stations in the gymnasium. Students rotate stations upon signal from the teacher. Each student has a basketball. The stations might include the following:
   a. Stationary ball-handling skills: dribbling in place, in a circle, between legs, for example.
   b. Dribbling across the gym: this is the station where the teacher will assess the students on their ability to dribble.
   c. Dribbling around three cones placed in a row.
   d. Dribbling while walking (then running) on the center circle line painted or taped on the floor.
   e. Dribbling in place (on an *X* taped on the floor) while eyes are focused straight ahead (on an *X* on the wall).
   f. Dribble (in place) with a friend trying to keep "in time" with each other.
4. Find or create an observation instrument using the rubric system explained earlier in the chapter.

Practice using the instrument to become comfortable collecting the data. (Figure 6.2 contains an assessment rubric for dribbling a basketball.)
5. Test the observation instrument to establish reliability, if you created the instrument (Wright and van der Mars 2004). See if multiple observations (several days in a row) give you the same results. See if a colleague's observations agree with yours.
6. Teach the lesson, including the assessment event.
7. Use the assessment results to provide student feedback, determine student progress, and plan the next lessons.

Indicating Student Progress (Grading)   As indicated earlier, *summative evaluation events* are present throughout the program to identify the final achievement of each student. In general, most physical educators use this final achievement score to assign grades to students. However, we believe children of elementary school age should not receive grades in physical education, as grades do not provide any real information regarding what the student knows and values or how the student performs movement skills. Instead, we recommend that final achievement be recorded on a progress report that identifies specific skills, behaviors, and knowledge and indicates the level of mastery the student achieved. Figure 6.3 shows a progress report on various skills taught during a specific quarter. As shown in the figure, the skills are related to the NASPE standards and are judged by using rubrics.

Student _____ Grade ___ Quarter ___ Teacher _____

NASPE Standard 1: Demonstrates competency in motor skills and movement patterns needed to perform a variety of physical activities.

Skills Practiced	Assessment Scores*
Throwing	_____
Catching	_____
Short jump rope	_____
Locomotor movements	
Running	_____
Skipping	_____

NASPE Standard 4: Achieves and maintains a health-enhancing level of physical fitness.

Skills Practiced	Assessment Scores*
Short jump rope	_____
Curl-ups	_____
Horizontal ladder	_____
Mac the crab	_____

* The assessment rubrics for each skill practiced during the quarter should be placed on the back of the progress report. For example, a rubric for catching might be as follows. All the scores that apply are placed in the blank provided.

Score	Performance
7	Catches a variety of objects thrown at a high velocity
6	Transfers catching skills to game situations
5	Catches while moving
4	Catches a variety of objects
3	Catches a self-tossed ball
2	Catches a bounced ball thrown by a partner
1	Extends arms toward thrower but shows avoidance reaction

FIGURE 6.3 Sample Physical Education Progress Report

ASSESSING PROGRAM EFFECTIVENESS

The final step in building a quality physical education program involves determining to what extent the students achieved the program goals. This is accomplished by collecting data to determine how many students reached each benchmark. Data collection occurs throughout the year at appropriate times. At the end of each school year, the physical education teachers examine all the data to determine where the program is working well and where improvements are needed. This is a summative evaluation process in which the data collected are used to determine **program effectiveness** and to make changes in the curriculum or in the way the curriculum is delivered if students are not meeting the program benchmarks. This type of summative evaluation is appropriate to share with administrators and community members for the purposes of being accountable.

How to Use Existing District Curriculum Guides

The school district in which a teacher is employed should have an existing elementary physical education curriculum guide. If the curriculum guide does not exist, one should be developed through the collaborative efforts of the classroom teachers, physical education teachers, and representatives from the community (using the steps identified in this chapter).

CONTENT OF THE CURRICULUM GUIDE

At a minimum, the **curriculum guide** contains the district's or school's physical education philosophy, grade-level program goals and benchmarks, and program content. Many will also include yearly plans (scope

FIGURE 6.4 Sample Table of Contents in a Curriculum Guide

and sequence) for various grade levels. The table of contents of a typical guide is shown in Figure 6.4. Although this guide does not contain yearly plans, it does contain additional information regarding children's characteristics, motor development, and class management. The guide should also reflect the state standards for physical education (www.education-world.com/standards/state/toc/index.shtml/).

USING THE CURRICULUM GUIDE

Based on the curriculum-building steps identified in this chapter, movement educators may have to add information to an existing curriculum guide if essential pieces are missing. For example, if program goals are identified, but grade-level goals and benchmarks are missing, determining the grade-level goals and benchmarks will be necessary.

Most guides will *not* contain the daily lesson plans necessary for implementing the specified goals and content. In that case, generally, the classroom teacher collaborates with the physical education teacher to appropriately extend and reinforce the content and philosophy already established in the guide by writing appropriate lesson plans. A sample physical education lesson plan appears in Box 6.5 (pages 193–194). The sample lesson plan reflects a lesson appropriate to achieve grade-level goal 2 and benchmark 2 specified for grades 5 and 6 in Box 6.3. In addition, the lesson plan contains all the elements described previously in the chapter as belonging in a physical education lesson plan.

Summary

The NASPE content standards establish specific performance standards for grades K, 2, 4, and 6 at the elementary school level. The performance standards specify what students should know, value, and be able to do at these points of articulation in the elementary grades. Thus curriculum building begins with the end in mind.

At the local level, program goals are established using the NASPE standards, state standards, and local circumstances. Then grade-level goals and benchmarks are established. From the grade-level goals (outcomes), lessons are planned so students achieve the program goals by the time they move into the next grade level. Knowing program goals beforehand allows curriculum builders to align goals, instruction, and assessment with the final outcome in mind.

The following assessment principles can guide movement educators as they plan and implement assessment events:

- Use formative evaluations frequently (within lessons to improve student performance).
- Use summative evaluation to prepare student progress reports and judge program effectiveness.
- Use a variety of assessment types.
- Use authentic assessments whenever possible.
- Embed assessment events into instruction (in other words, practice what is to be learned in the same setting in which the skill or knowledge will be assessed).
- Use several assessment events to measure the same skill or knowledge (or use the same event on different occasions).
- Ensure that assessment activities align with program goals, benchmarks, lesson objectives, and learning experiences.

- Ensure that assessment instruments (checklists and the like) are valid, reliable, and objective indicators of the behavior being measured by designing and using rubrics to judge student performances and products.
- First determine why assessment should occur, and then plan the assessment event accordingly.

Chapter Activities

1. Make a list of items you might observe that would provide evidence that a program meets the 12 characteristics of a quality elementary physical education program.
2. Use the evidence statements developed in the activity above to observe a physical education program and determine whether the program meets the guidelines. Interview the physical educator and observe the teacher in action. Discuss your findings in a one-page paper.
3. Examine and critically analyze the written physical education curriculum guide of a school in your local area.
4. Using the NASPE standards (for the grade level you hope to teach), write a quick lesson (similar to those in the text) for a ten-minute physical activity period you could include in your classroom during a unit on U.S. history.
5. Develop a one-page statement that reflects your current philosophy about elementary physical education. You might continue to develop this statement throughout the semester as you learn more about physical education.

Internet Resources

American Association for Active Lifestyles and Fitness. Promotes active lifestyles for all individuals; website includes position papers on topics such as including students with disabilities in physical education.
www.aahperd.org/aapar

PE Central. Provides latest information about developmentally appropriate physical education practices and programs.
www.pecentral.org

PELinks4u. Contains general information on elementary physical education and great lesson plan ideas for integrating classroom subject content in a section titled "Interdisciplinary PE."
www.pelinks4u.org

Bibliography

Council on Physical Education for Children (COPEC). 2004. *Physical activity for children: A statement of guidelines for children ages 5–12*. Reston, VA: National Association for Sport and Physical Education, an association of the American Alliance for Health, Physical Education, Recreation, and Dance.

Derry, J. A., and D. A. Phillips. 2004. Comparisons of selected student and teacher variables in all-girls and coeducational physical education environments. *Physical Educator* 61(1): 23–35.

Dunbar, R. R., and M. M. O'Sullivan. 1986. Effects of intervention on differential treatment of boys and girls in elementary physical education lessons. *Journal of Teaching in Physical Education* 5: 166–175.

Gallo, A. M., D. Sheehy, K. Patton, and L. Griffin. 2006. Assessment benefits and barriers: What are you committed to? *Journal of Physical Education, Recreation, and Dance* 77(8): 46–50.

Garrahy, D. A. 2001. Three third-grade teachers' gender-related beliefs and behavior. *The Elementary School Journal* 102(1): 81–94.

———. 2003. Speaking louder than words: Teachers' gender beliefs and practices in third grade classrooms. *Equity and Excellence in Education* 36(1): 96–104.

Griffin, P. S. 1985. Boys' participation styles in a middle school physical education team sports unit. *Journal of Teaching in Physical Education* 4(2): 100–110.

Hannon, J. C., and T. Ratliffe. 2007. Opportunities to participate and teacher interactions in coed versus single-gender physical education settings. *Physical Educator* 64(1): 11–20.

Hills, L. A. 2006. Playing the field(s): and exploration of change, conformity, and conflict in girls' understandings of gendered physicality and physical education. *Gender and Education* 18(5): 539–556.

Holt/Hale, S. A. 1999. *Assessing motor skills in elementary physical education*. Reston, VA: NASPE.

Johnson, L. V. 2005. Choosing appropriate assessments. *Journal of Physical Education, Recreation, and Dance* 76(8): 46–47, 56.

Johnson, R. 2004. Peer assessments in physical education. *Journal of Physical Education, Recreation, and Dance* 75(8): 33–40.

Lund, J., and D. Tannehill. 2005. *Standards-based physical education curriculum development*. Boston: Jones and Bartlett.

Lund, J. L. 2000. *Creating rubrics for physical education*. Reston, VA: AAHPERD Publications.

MacDonald, D. 1990. The relationship between the sex composition of physical education classes and teacher-pupil verbal interaction. *Journal of Teaching in Physical Education* 9: 152–163.

Melograno, V. J. 2000. *Portfolio assessment for K–12 physical education*. Reston, VA: NASPE.

Metzler, M. W. 2005. *Instructional models for physical education.* Scottsdale, AZ: Holcomb Hathaway.

National Association for Sport and Physical Education (NASPE). 2004. *Moving into the future: National standards for physical education.* St. Louis, MO: Mosby.

Nilges, L. M. 1998. I thought only fairy tales had supernatural power: A radical feminist analysis of Title IX in physical education. *Journal of Teaching in Physical Education* 17: 172–194.

Solomons, H. S. 1980. Sex mediation of achievement behaviors and interpersonal interactions in sex integrated teams. In *Children in cooperation and competition,* ed. E. Pepitone, 321–364. Lexington, MA: D. C. Heath.

Wiggins, G. 1993. Assessment: Authenticity, context, and validity. *Phi Delta Kappan* 75: 200–214.

———. 1998. *Educative assessment: Designing assessments to inform and improve performance.* San Francisco: Jossey-Bass.

Wright, M. T., and H. van der Mars. 2004. Blending assessment into instruction: Practical applications and meaningful results. *Journal of Physical Education, Recreation, and Dance* 75(9): 29–34.

BOX 6.5 Sample Physical Education Lesson Plan

MOVEMENT FORM

Creative and rhythmic movement

GRADE LEVEL

Grades 5–6

NASPE STANDARD 1

Students demonstrate competency in motor skills and movement patterns needed to perform a variety of physical activities.

LESSON OBJECTIVES

- Students rhythmically perform the basic square dance shuffle in time with the music for at least 32 consecutive counts (psychomotor objective).
- Students perform the following figures correctly at least one time when called for during the dance (cognitive and psychomotor objective): promenade, allemande left, swing your partner, swing your corner, circle left, and do-sa-do.
- Students accept a variety of partners by holding hands with each new partner as requested by the caller.

MATERIALS AND EQUIPMENT NEEDED

- Music for "Oh Johnny" from Folkcraft Records and Tapes, P.O. Box 404, Florham Park, NJ 07932
- Record, tape, or CD player depending on source of the music

ACTIVITY DESCRIPTIONS AND CLASS ORGANIZATION

Introductory Activity (2 minutes)

As the students enter the gym, ask them to stand on the basketball circle in the middle of the gym (alternating boy-girl around the circle). Join the circle yourself. Tell students to join hands and begin performing the square dance shuffle step to the left (teacher sets the tempo by her or his speed). Shuffle step is a light running step with feet staying close to the floor. Next, cue the group to circle right. Then cue the group to the center and back (four times). Repeat entire sequence.

Lesson Focus and Physical Fitness (26 minutes)

Teacher steps out of the circle and walks around the circle designating couples (remembering that the girl stands to the right of her partner). Assuming the class composition is not equally boys and girls, have everyone who plays the part of a boy wear a scrimmage vest. The teacher distributes the vests while designating the couples.

The goal of the lesson is to teach the students how to perform "Oh Johnny." The instructions are as follows:

Measure 1
CALLER: "Oh, you all join hands and circle the ring."
Students join hands, and circle clockwise using shuffle step.

Measure 2
CALLER: "Stop where you are and give your partner a swing."
Students perform a two-hand swing—partners join both hands and circle once around in place.

Measure 3
CALLER: "Now swing that girl behind you."
Students perform a two-hand swing—boys join hands with girl on the left (corner) and do a two-hand swing.

Measure 4
CALLER: "Go back home and swing your own if you have time."
Students perform a two-hand swing with partner.

Measure 5
CALLER: "Allemande left with your corner girl."
Students perform allemande left with corner girl—boys grasp left forearms with the girls on the left and walk once around in place.

Measure 6
CALLER: "Do-sa 'round your own."
Students perform do-sa-do—with arms crossed in front of body, partners walk toward each other, pass by right shoulders, pass back to back, and walk backward to their original place.

Measure 7
CALLER: "Now you all run away with your sweet corner maid."

Continued

Students promenade with corner—with the girl on the left, boys and girls stand side by side, face counterclockwise, hold hands (skater's position, right to right and left to left), and shuffle around the circle.

Measure 8

CALLER: (Singing) "Oh, Johnny, oh, Johnny, oh!" Students stay with corner lady for a new partner and continue shuffle step (side-by-side position) until singing cues indicate to repeat the dance.

The teacher uses the following teaching progression:

- Students practice (on teacher's cue) shuffle step moving clockwise around the circle (all hands joined) without music.
- Teacher describes and demonstrates; then students practice two-hand swing with partner without music.
- Teacher describes and demonstrates; then students practice two-hand swing with corner (girl on the boy's left) without music.
- Students practice sequence of circle shuffle, partner swing, corner swing, partner swing (first with the teacher providing beat counts, then with the music).
- Repeat with the music until students can perform without mistakes.
- Teacher describes and demonstrates; then students practice the allemande left with corner girl.
- Teacher describes and demonstrates; then students practice do-sa-do with partner.
- Teacher describes and demonstrates; then students practice the promenade with corner girl.
- Practice sequence of allemande left, do-sa-do, and promenade (first with the teacher providing beat counts, then with the music).

- Repeat with the music until students can perform without mistakes.
- Walk through the entire dance with cues from the teacher (no music).
- Perform the entire dance with music.

Closing Activity (2 minutes)

Have the students sit down (while still in a circle). Teacher joins the circle and conducts a review of the square dance terms and figures performed. Students verbally describe the figures and define the terms.

SUCCESS FOR ALL

The dance can be made easier by slowing the tempo of the music and altering the movements (e.g., promenade with partner instead of corner so students are not changing partners or eliminate the allemande left and simply perform a do-sa-do with both partner and corner).

STUDENT ASSESSMENT

- Did the students define the terms correctly?
- Did the students correctly describe each figure?
- Were the students able to perform the dance twice without mistakes?
- Did students willingly partner with different students?
- Were all students able to shuffle in time with the music?

GRADES K–6

NASPE STANDARD 3 Students participate regularly in physical activity.

LESSON OBJECTIVES

- Students identify the benefits of an active lifestyle.
- *Kindergarten:* Students identify their likes and dislikes connected with participation in physical activity.
- *Grade 2:* Students experience participation in physical activity and express their pleasure in having done so.
- *Grade 4:* Students identify at least one physical activity that they participate in on a regular basis (formal or informal participation).
- *Grade 6:* Students identify opportunities in the school and community for regular participation in physical activity.

EQUIPMENT NEEDED Paper and pencil for each student or group of students

PREPARATION TIME Five minutes

KNOWLEDGE CONTENT The benefits of an active lifestyle include the following:

- Strong bones and muscles
- Strong heart muscle
- Improved coordination
- Improved movement skills
- Improved self-concept
- Feelings of well-being
- Feelings of fun and enjoyment
- Fun of being a moving person
- Feelings of success
- Decreased stress levels
- Fewer health risks

This content knowledge can be presented in varying degrees of depth based on the grade level of the children.

CLASSROOM ACTIVITY *Grades K–2:* Ask students to draw a picture of themselves playing outdoors doing a physical activity they like to do. On the back of the picture, the students answer the following questions (with one-word answers):

- What are you doing in your picture?
- How do you feel when you participate in this activity?

The teacher and students then discuss the above questions and the following additional questions.

- Why do you like the physical activity you drew?
- What other physical activities do you like to do?
- Why should you play actively outdoors? (Indicate the benefits that occur from regular participation in physical activities.)
- What feelings do you experience when participating in physical activities?

Grades 3–4: Ask students to work in small groups of two to three children and prepare a list of the physical activities they participate in on a regular basis (define for them "on a regular basis"). Be sure they include on their list the play activities they engage in (as well as the sport activities). Then each student writes a couple of sentences explaining why she or he participates in these activities and what health benefits are gained as a result of that activity. Discuss students' answers and add information about the benefits of regular participation (if the students neglect to mention any of the known benefits).

Grades 5–6: Ask students to work in small groups of three to four children. Half of the groups should prepare a list of the benefits of being physically active (the list should include physical, mental, and social benefits). The other half should prepare a list identifying opportunities within the school and community that allow students to participate regularly in physical activity. Have students write the lists on the chalkboard (or on easel paper that can be hung on the wall). Hold a class discussion to review all the benefits of being physically active and to point out the opportunities available for students to be active.

ASSESSMENT Students can write a paragraph describing at least three benefits of regular participation in physical activity. (Allow kindergarten students to describe the benefits orally.)

SUCCESS FOR ALL Ask students to take a fitness walk with a parent or other caregiver that evening. Be sure the students understand that a fitness walk is different from a leisure walk (faster speed over a longer distance). The next morning as students arrive in class, have them record (on a wall chart) how far they walked and with whom. The chart should not have the students' names on it. Just record the data without associating it with a particular student. Students in wheelchairs can take the fitness walk but will need to travel in an area that is wheelchair accessible. Students with limited vision can take the fitness walk with appropriate help from the person who accompanies them. If parents or caregivers are unavailable, students may walk with a sibling, grandparent, neighbor, or the like.

INTEGRATION WITH OTHER SUBJECT AREAS

To extend the sixth-grade lesson into an integrated lesson using art skills, have the students express, using an art medium of their choice, what they feel when they are successful movers.

To extend the fourth-grade lesson into an integrated lesson using math skills, take the activities and the reasons for participation identified by the students and make a survey instrument. Have the fourth graders administer the survey to all the fifth graders in your building (during class time). So now you have data on what activities the fifth graders participated in and why. Have the fourth graders graph the data from each fifth-grade class and interpret the activity patterns (amount of activity and which activities) of the fifth graders as a whole. The fourth graders could go back into the fifth-grade classrooms and present the data while talking about the benefits of an active lifestyle.

CLASSROOM LEARNING STATION 6.1
Exercise Bands

GRADES K–6

NASPE STANDARD 4 Students achieve and maintain a health-enhancing level of physical fitness.

LESSON OBJECTIVES

- Students improve muscle strength and endurance of the arm and shoulder girdle muscles.
- Students exhibit proficiency in various physical exercises.
- Students know the major muscles that make up the arm and shoulder girdle (biceps brachii, triceps, deltoid, trapezius, and pectoralis major). Although the latissimus dorsi is considered a muscle of the back, it too will be strengthened with the exercises in this lesson.

EQUIPMENT NEEDED
One small mat and three stretch bands of different thicknesses (since the strength of the resistance is controlled by the thickness)

PREPARATION TIME
One hour

KNOWLEDGE CONTENT

- Students understand that they can begin with a thin band, and by exercising every day they will be able to progress to the next thicker width.
- Students learn and name the specific muscles they are strengthening.

CLASSROOM ACTIVITY
The station consists of the following:

- A small mat (on the floor)
- Stretch bands of varying resistance so that students may select the one that is appropriate for them right now
- A wall poster listing the exercises or showing stick drawings of the exercises
- A diagram of the body's muscles (front and back views) on a laminated sheet of paper, taped to the mat

Student performs the following exercises while at the station. For all the exercises, grip the band firmly by wrapping it around each hand so the band is taut when the student is in the starting position. Hold each pull for a count of at least ten seconds. Do as many pulls as you can. When you can do ten repetitions (of a certain pull)

for ten seconds each, try moving up to a thicker band the next time.

- *Overhead pull:* Place arms straight overhead and pull the arms and hands away from the body (to each side).
- *Chest pull:* With elbows bent in front of the chest, pull across the chest away from the body (keep elbows bent).
- *Front pull:* Place arms straight out in front of the body and pull away from the body (to each side).
- *Sit and pull:* Sit on the band to provide resistance; hold both ends of the band in hands with elbows bent (placed up by the ears) and hands behind the head. Extend and flex the elbows (up to the sky then down to the back).
- *Elbow pull:* Hold band in right hand; pat right shoulder (on the back) with the right hand. At the same time, reach with the other arm and hand behind the back (from below) and grab the other end of the band. Tighten the band, then pull as if to straighten both elbows. Then switch sides.
- *Back pull:* Place hands behind the body at waist level (holding the band). Pull away from the body (to each side).

ASSESSMENT

- Record progress to increasing resistance levels.
- *Grades K–2:* Have students color the muscles (on a diagram exactly like the one on the mat) as you name the muscle. *Grades 3–4:* Ask students to write on a sheet of paper the names of the muscles that make up the arm and shoulder girdle. *Grades 5–6:* Assign partners and have them develop new exercises for the muscles being studied.

SUCCESS FOR ALL
The different resistance levels of the bands will allow students of varying strength levels to participate. Students needing further assistance may complete the learning station with a partner.

INTEGRATION WITH OTHER SUBJECT AREAS
Muscle identification may be integrated into science and anatomy lessons. Health lessons could be used to further the knowledge base of this lesson by studying the meaning of the terms *muscle strength* versus *muscle endurance* as well as studying the exercise principles of overload, specificity, and progression (see Chapter 4).

GRADES K–6

NASPE STANDARDS 3, 4, AND 5

- Students exhibit a physically active lifestyle.
- Students achieve and maintain a health-enhancing level of physical fitness.
- Students exhibit responsible personal and social behavior that respects self and others in physical activity settings.

LESSON OBJECTIVES

- Students complete the six stations with a parent (or other adult).
- Students perform designated activities with accuracy and proficiency.
- Students assist others as needed and treat everyone with respect.
- Students demonstrate knowledge of the concepts covered in each station.

EQUIPMENT NEEDED Depends on the content of the stations

PREPARATION TIME Significant time is needed to select the station content, prepare the stations, invite parents, and prepare the students.

KNOWLEDGE CONTENT The teacher selects fitness and wellness concepts and activities (from Chapter 4) that the students have studied. Here are some possibilities:

- Safe exercising techniques
- Exercise principles
- The food guide pyramid
- Health risk factors
- The cardiorespiratory system
- The musculoskeletal system
- Body composition

CLASSROOM TO GYMNASIUM ACTIVITY The teacher hosts a Parents' Night when parents or other caregivers and children in the class come to the gymnasium. The gym contains six stations reflecting the concepts and activities the children have studied. The children and their accompanying adults will complete the stations together. Three types of stations are prepared.

The first type of station allows children to show what they already know. For instance, they might complete a work sheet that covers something they have already studied. Or they might draw (out of a box) pictures of food (or actual food containers) and have to indicate which food group the food belongs to. Or they might show how flexible they are by performing flexibility exercises (which the adults can then imitate).

The second type of station allows children and adults to learn something new together. For instance, read a short children's book (e.g., *It Zwibble and the Greatest Cleanup Ever,* a children's book on pollution) and then complete a work sheet together.

The third type of station allows children and adults to be physically active together. For instance, step up and down on an aerobic step for two minutes; record heart rate before and after the activity. (Be sure to have low steps for the children and higher steps for adults.) Or find two other children and their accompanying adults and play a designated tag game (in a specific area of the gym).

The teacher begins the evening by explaining the purpose of the event and how it will proceed. The teacher should assign the first station, and then children and adults continue to rotate clockwise to complete all the stations. The teacher floats around the room watching for safety problems and interacting with the participants. At the end of the evening, call the participants together to summarize their experiences, complete a half-page assessment, and do a final group activity such as the Bunny Hop.

ASSESSMENT The teacher develops a questionnaire to assess the Parents' Night. Children and their accompanying adults complete the questionnaire together; however, have separate blanks for the children's and adults' answers. The following are questions that might be used.

- What did you like best about this evening?
- What did you like least about this evening?
- Would you come again if we held a similar event?
- If you answered yes to the previous question, what's the best evening for you to attend?

SUCCESS FOR ALL Allow adults to help as necessary if students are having difficulty with the activity; however, adjust the activities as much as possible so children have some level of independence.

INTEGRATION WITH OTHER SUBJECT AREAS Examples (in the activity section) already indicate station activities that integrate reading, writing, and health.

CHAPTER 7

Managing and Teaching the Physical Education Lesson

The purpose of this chapter is to present the mechanics of teaching physical education lessons. The mechanics involve teaching methods, class management techniques, and discipline strategies useful for decreasing class time spent on organizational tasks and increasing the amount of class time spent on lesson content. In addition, the effective implementation of the mechanics frees the teacher to provide feedback to learners while they are participating in activity.

Objectives

After studying this chapter, you will be able to do the following:

- Identify various teaching methods and strategies used to teach effective physical education lessons.
- Provide examples of performance feedback that are helpful to students in improving their motor skills, social skills, and physical fitness skills.
- Effectively organize students in a physical activity setting.
- Discuss effective class supervision techniques.
- Discuss discipline strategies and ideas that help students choose responsible behavior.
- Express the key elements for nurturing a caring classroom community.

Mr. Bing teaches second graders in a very small school district and is responsible for his students' physical education lessons, just as he is responsible for their math, science, and English lessons. He has the support of a physical education teacher who serves the entire school district. With assistance from the physical educator,

Mr. Bing constructed a yearly physical education plan that meets the local curriculum goals and the NASPE national standards. Because he believes in daily physical education for his students, Mr. Bing has scheduled 30 minutes of physical education into each day of school (with the support of the school administration).

Today Mr. Bing is in the middle of a week-long unit in which students are exploring where and how the body can move. The students are scattered throughout the gymnasium. When Mr. Bing says "Go," students perform the movement tasks outlined in Box 7.1. Students stop each activity when the whistle blows and listen for the teacher to announce the next task. Most tasks are performed individually, although occasionally students are directed to find a partner and then perform the task. While the students are performing, Mr. Bing walks around the room helping individual students, providing praise and feedback, watching for safety problems, and keeping all the students in his view at all times. At the end of class, Mr. Bing calls the students together and holds a brief discussion (one to two minutes) to review the movement components explored today (personal and general space, direction, level, size, focus, body shape, floor patterns, relationships with others, and force and time) and places those components within the context of the movement map presented in Figure 3.1.

Organizing and Teaching the Lesson Content

Teaching students in the movement setting involves elements not necessarily found in the regular classroom. Lessons are planned to encourage maximum *physical* activity for all the students, and many times that activity occurs in large, open spaces like the gymnasium

BOX 7.1 Sample Activities for Exploring Where and How the Body Moves (Grades K-3)

PERSONAL AND GENERAL SPACE

- Move one of your feet all around your personal space.
- With your hands as the base, move the rest of the body around in your own personal space.
- Standing still and then when lying down, stretch and find the limits of your personal space.
- Explore the general space of the room by touching each wall of the room (using a skip to move to each wall)—be sure not to bump into other movers.
- On the drumbeat, run, and continue running anywhere in the room *without touching anyone or anything*.

DIRECTION

- Skip forward eight skips, walk backward eight steps.
- Run in a small circle and then run a diagonal across your circle.
- Slide eight slides to the left and then eight to the right.
- Do the above with a partner, staying in rhythm with each other.

LEVEL

- In your personal space, reach as high as you can.
- Crawl forward at a very low level.
- Creep backward (not making a sound!).
- Walk at a high level and then at a low level.

SIZE

- Clap your hands with a large movement, then with a small movement.
- Turn, in your personal space, with a small movement, then with a large movement.
- Skip across the gym floor, first with small skips and then with big skips.
- Determine the least number of skips you can do and still get across the gym floor.

FOCUS

- Walk backward while focusing backward so you do not bump into anyone.

- Walk backward (slowly) while focusing forward.
- Wave to the teacher while looking at the teacher.
- Wave to the teacher while looking at the floor.

BODY SHAPE

- Lying on the floor, curl into as small a ball as possible.
- Now quickly change from a ball into a bat.
- With your body, make the first letter in your name.
- Make a strange body shape.

FLOOR PATTERNS (PATHWAYS)

- Walk a straight path forward, then a curved path forward.
- Gallop in a zigzag pattern.
- Slide in a small square pattern.
- Hop in a triangle pattern.
- Grapevine in a large square pattern (around the perimeter of the room).

RELATIONSHIPS WITH OTHERS

- With a partner, skip together around the room, staying in rhythm with each other.
- With a partner, one partner leads and the other follows (doing creative movements the leader chooses).
- With a partner, staying in personal space using non-locomotor movement, one partner leads and the other performs mirror image.

FORCE AND TIME

- Allow your arm to fall softly (like a feather).
- Allow your arm to fall quickly (like a rock).
- Walk like a floppy rag doll.
- Walk like a tin soldier.
- Tiptoe quietly across the floor.
- Stamp loudly, moving across the floor.
- Perform a creative karate sequence.
- Do the same karate sequence in slow motion.
- Fall to the floor quickly; then do it slowly.
- Walk quickly, then slowly.

---

and the playground. This is very different from a setting where students are placed in desks and spend a large part of the day seated at those desks. In addition, especially for upper elementary students, most physical activities take place either with partners or in groups (small or large), and students are free to socialize and move about the activity area as they work to accomplish lesson objectives. We believe these elements provide unique challenges for the movement educator in terms of teaching, managing, and disciplining students.

THE TYPICAL PHYSICAL EDUCATION CLASS

In order to identify those unique challenges, it may be helpful to know what happens in a typical physical education class—what do the students do? Table 7.1 shows what students typically do. The information clearly indicates that children in physical education classes (taught by physical educators) are spending minimal amounts of time engaged in motor skills (only 25 to 30 percent of the class time). Since time engaged in motor skills is directly related to the child's skill improvement, one challenge for movement educators is to create **active learning time (ALT)** by (1) reducing time students spend waiting their turn to perform; (2) limiting lengthy skill descriptions and demonstrations; and (3) decreasing managerial time through more effectively organizing students within the lesson. Active learning time (Siedentop and Tannehill 2000) consists of the time students are participating successfully in lesson activities that leads to achieving the lesson objectives. The keys to ALT are that the planned lesson tasks are relevant to content objectives, students are active, and students are successful in performing the lesson tasks. We suggest teachers strive for no student waiting time, 10 to 40 percent of student time engaged in either listening or management tasks, and 60 to 90 percent of student time as active learning time. Thus students will spend less time waiting to be active and less time engaged in managerial tasks.

Another challenge is to create more student **opportunities to respond (OTR)** within active learning time. Opportunity to respond (Siedentop and Tannehill 2000) measures the number of appropriate, successful task responses made by students. Building numerous successful student practice situations into each lesson significantly increases the degree of student learning. Also within the active learning time, students need to

be engaged in moderate to vigorous physical activity (MVPA) in order to improve their health. Current recommendations ask teachers to plan lessons where 50 percent of the class time involves students in MVPA. A review of the literature (Fairclough and Stratton 2006) indicated that elementary students in physical education classes averaged only 34 percent of class time in MVPA. The good news is that MVPA time was increased (up to 47 percent) when teachers planned and implemented lessons with objectives and content designed to increase MVPA time.

A third challenge is to increase movement time for *all* students in the class. Research indicates that girls and boys engage in about the same amount of movement time and MVPA time (Fairclough and Stratton 2006), but low-skilled students and those with disabilities are engaged in significantly less movement time than the other students (Siedentop and Tannehill 2000).

Yet another challenge is to create more opportunities to actively supervise students while they are performing physical skills. This active supervision consists of providing feedback to groups and individuals about their skill performance. The active supervision of the student's independent practice is crucial for learning to occur.

The final challenge is to effectively manage students' behavior problems. It appears that the environment (large space and free to move) leads to increased behavior problems not always exhibited in the classroom. These unacceptable behaviors must be dealt with immediately and efficiently in order to keep students on task and engaged in movement and to create a safe environment in this setting. This chapter deals with ways to teach students and manage lessons in order to successfully meet these challenges.

ORGANIZING THE PHYSICAL EDUCATION LESSON CONTENT

Management time tends to vary depending on the movement activity the students are engaged in. In general, movement time is the highest with fitness and dance activities and lowest with team sports (Siedentop and Tannehill 2000). Thus, as lesson content is selected, the teacher should consider whether the activities can be presented in a manner that maximizes active learning time for the students.

Another factor to consider is that students can organize more quickly if the lessons follow a set format. We suggest establishing a **lesson format** (30 minutes in length) in the following manner:

- *Introductory activity* (2 minutes): This activity lasts just a couple of minutes and allows students

TABLE 7.1 What Students Typically Do in Physical Education Class

What Students Do	Percentage of Class Time
Wait	20–30
Perform managerial tasks	15–20
Receive information	15–30
Engage in motor skills	25–30

Adapted and printed with permission of The McGraw-Hill Companies, Inc., from D. Siedentop and D. Tannehill, *Developing Teaching Skills in Physical Education,* 4th ed. (Mountain View, CA: Mayfield, 2000).

to become physically active immediately upon entering the activity area. When a student finishes this activity, he or she goes to a certain place in the gym and behaves in a certain manner, thus indicating readiness for the lesson focus. The activity begins with a minimum of instruction and incorporates gross motor movements to warm up the body (by increasing heart rate) for the rest of the lesson activities. For example, upon entering the gymnasium, students have a choice of jumping rope, running laps, or doing animal walks for two minutes. When the teacher indicates that two minutes are over (by holding up a red stop sign), students move into a circle formation in the center of the gym, sit on the black line that marks the center circle of the basketball court, and become quiet—ready to move on to the lesson focus.

- *Lesson focus activities* (20 minutes): The movement form for this part of the lesson is indicated in the yearly plan, and the activities (within the given movement form) relate directly to the day's lesson objectives. Most of the class time is spent on these activities.
- *Physical fitness activity* (5 minutes): These activities are especially designed to improve some component of physical fitness (muscular strength and endurance, flexibility, or cardiorespiratory endurance). If the physical activities built into the lesson introduction or focus are used to improve physical fitness, then the fitness part of the lesson is *integrated* into other parts of the lesson.
- *Closing activity* (1–2 minutes): This activity brings closure to the lesson. Mr. Bing, in the scenario that opened this chapter, closed the lesson with a verbal review of the material presented.

With a set format, such as the one mentioned, students begin to recognize the format (which forms a routine), and they quickly get the idea of what is coming next in the lesson. The sample yearly plans presented in Chapter 6 indicate the movement form and activity to be included in the lesson focus section of the lesson.

TEACHING THE PHYSICAL EDUCATION LESSON

Teaching methods describe ways to organize instruction and specify the roles that students and teachers will play during that instruction. In general, teaching methods tend to be placed into two distinct categories, direct or indirect, based on how much freedom the teacher gives the students in planning and implementing lesson activities and in evaluating

their performance within the lesson. **Direct teaching methods** occur when the teacher takes total responsibility for planning, implementing, and evaluating. The teacher directs when students begin the activity, where the activity occurs, and exactly how the activity is to be performed. Usually, all students are performing the same activities or movements at the same time, and the teacher serves as the expert during the lesson. The activity described in Box 7.2 is an example of teaching in a direct manner.

Indirect teaching methods allow students to be active in the planning, implementing, and evaluating phases of the lesson. Some indirect methods allow students almost total control to discover, explore, share, or create knowledge, whereas others simply give students more freedom to operate on their own in terms of when to begin activity, where to perform, whom to work with, and in what order to perform various activities. Because of this variation within indirect teaching methods, we propose that it's more helpful for the teacher to think of methods as being on a continuum from teacher directed to student directed. So a particular teaching strategy can be placed somewhere along the method continuum based on the student's role in the lesson versus the teacher's role. At the far end of the indirect side of the continuum, methods would allow students to be self-directing through the entire learning experience. Box 7.3 presents a lesson using a more indirect teaching method (same lesson activities as described in the direct lesson in Box 7.2). Box 7.4 contains examples of ways to involve students in the planning, implementing, and evaluation phases of the lesson (appropriate for elementary school children).

Particular teaching strategies (movement exploration, challenge activities, cooperative activities, problem solving, individual or partner practice) involve certain ways to teach. So each of these strategies has a somewhat *standard* implementation process, and based on the designated process, the strategy can be placed somewhere along the teaching method continuum. Figure 7.1 on page 205 names some specific teaching strategies and places them along the teaching method continuum. These particular strategies are delineated in this text because we believe they can be used effectively by movement educators to teach physical activities within the lesson content.

Implementing Specific Teaching Strategies To aid your understanding of the placement of each teaching strategy on the continuum, the implementation process for each teaching strategy is presented with reference to a box or end-of-chapter activity that contains sample lessons using the strategy.

> ## BOX 7.2 Direct Teaching Method Example (Grades 5-6)
> ## (Teaching Strategy: Direct Instruction)
>
> ### INTRODUCTORY PHYSICAL FITNESS ACTIVITY: RUNNING LAPS AND PERFORMING STRETCHES
>
> As the students enter the gym, they are verbally instructed to jog three laps around the perimeter of the gym and then sit on assigned Xs. Once students are seated, the teacher leads the students in ten stretching exercises. Each exercise is held for 20 seconds (counted by the teacher), and all the students do the same exercise at the same time.
>
> ### LESSON FOCUS: BASKETBALL DRIBBLING
>
> Each student, standing on his or her assigned X, has a junior-sized basketball. The teacher explains, demonstrates, and then leads the students through the following drills, in order.
>
> 1. In place, dribble continuously in the following ways:
>
>   With the right hand
>   With the left hand
>   From right to left hand
>   From right to left hand (under left leg)
>   Circling to the right
>   Circling to the left
>
> 2. Move forward from one sideline to the other (across the gym) while doing the following:
>
>   Dribble across with the right hand.
>   Return using the left hand.
>   Dribble halfway and switch from the right to the left hand.
>   Dribble across weaving in between four cones (placed in a line across the gym).
>
> 3. In partners, with one ball per pair of students, one partner dribbles against the other, who acts as a defensive player. Dribble across the gym without the defensive player taking the ball away. If the defensive player gets the ball, she or he becomes the ball handler and the original ball handler becomes the defensive player. Partners do not switch locations, so the new ball handler now moves toward the other sideline (not the original sideline).
> 4. In groups of four, with one ball per group, two offensive and two defensive players, dribble and pass, moving the ball from one sideline to the other. The goal is to reach the other sideline without the ball being stolen by the opponents. If opponents steal the ball, action moves toward the opposite sideline.
>
> The teacher leads each of the above activities by demonstrating the task (while all the students watch); then all students do the task. The teacher blows the whistle for the activity to stop, and a new task is demonstrated. This continues until all the tasks are completed, so each student is practicing each skill the same amount of time at the same time.
>
> ### CLOSING ACTIVITY: REVIEW OF DRIBBLING TECHNIQUE
>
> Students place basketballs back in equipment boxes as instructed and sit on their assigned X. The teacher reviews dribbling technique and tells students they performed well today. Students line up to walk to the classroom.

DIRECT INSTRUCTION (see Box 7.2 for example):

- **Direct instruction** is used for all grade levels to present information and provide initial practice of new motor skills.
- The teacher controls when, where, how, and with whom the lesson activities are performed.
- All students perform the same activities at the same time.
- The teacher serves as the expert and thus provides all instruction and feedback to the students.

INDIVIDUAL OR PARTNER PRACTICE (see Box 7.3, sections A and B, for example):

- **Individual or partner practice** is primarily used for independent practice on specific motor skills (after initial demonstrations and lessons on the motor skills have been completed).
- Task sheets or wall charts are used to keep students on task.
- Students select where and when to begin and end practice.

BOX 7.3 Indirect Teaching Method Example (Grades 5-6) (Teaching Strategies: Individual and Partner Practice; and Problem Solving)

INTRODUCTORY PHYSICAL FITNESS ACTIVITY: RUNNING LAPS AND PERFORMING STRETCHES

Students walk into the gym in a line formation, and the teacher assigns every two students to be partners. The teacher verbally instructs the partners to complete the activities on the wall chart as the introductory activities for the lesson. The wall chart lists ten stretching exercises and two laps around the gym (partners facing each other, holding both hands, performing a grapevine step—one lap should be done clockwise around the gym and the other one counterclockwise). Partners may choose to perform the exercises and laps in any order. They count their own 20 seconds as they hold each stretching exercise. Partners may place themselves anywhere within the gym space. The teacher provides prompts to keep the students on task and gives feedback on student performance. When finished, the partners go to the teacher to pick up a task sheet for completing the day's lesson focus activities.

LESSON FOCUS: BASKETBALL DRIBBLING TASK SHEET

Students are instructed as follows: Obtain a basketball from one of the equipment boxes. Find a space within the gym and practice the skills listed in section A of the task sheet. Perform the skills you have mastered already for a short period of time (just to warm up and review), and place a check on the sheet beside those skills. Then proceed to more difficult tasks. Practice each difficult task at least five times. Beside each difficult task, write the number of times you practiced it.

Section A

In place, dribble continuously. Then dribble in the following ways:

- With the right hand
- With the left hand
- From the right to the left hand
- From the right to the left hand (under the left leg)
- Circling to the right
- Circling to the left
- Moving from one sideline to the other (across the gym)

- Dribble across with the right hand.
- Return using the left hand.
- Dribble halfway and switch from the right to the left hand.
- Dribble across weaving in between four cones (placed in a line across the gym).

Section B

Find a partner (of similar skill level). Perform the following activity until each partner has crossed his or her sideline at least two times.

In partners, with one ball, one partner dribbles against the other, who acts as a defensive player. Dribble across the gym without the defensive player taking the ball away. If the defensive player gets the ball, she or he becomes the ball handler and the original ball handler becomes the defensive player. Partners do not switch locations, so the new ball handler now moves toward the other sideline (not the original sideline).

Section C

Find another set of partners (of similar skill level) and perform the following activity.

In groups of four, with one ball, two offensive and two defensive players, dribble and pass, moving the ball from one sideline to the other. The goal is to reach the other sideline without the ball being stolen by the opponents. If the opponents steal the ball, the action moves toward the opposite sideline.

Students make decisions about which skills to work on, for how long, and whom to work with. Teachers help students obtain partners (if necessary), help students stay on task, and provide feedback as they supervise the class.

CLOSING ACTIVITY: REVIEW OF DRIBBLING TECHNIQUE

Upon hearing the whistle, students are directed to place basketballs back in equipment boxes and then sit down. The students answer questions posed by the teacher to review dribbling techniques, and they congratulate each other for a job well done by doing high fives with their partners for the day. Students line up to walk to the classroom.

BOX 7.4 Sample Ways to Involve Students in Planning, Implementing, and Evaluating

PLANNING

- Students help establish program objectives.
- Based on specific objectives, students identify several units that could accomplish those objectives.
- Students select (from a list prepared by the teacher) which unit is taught next.
- Students determine the length of the unit.
- The teacher uses student survey data on activity likes and dislikes in determining the curriculum.

IMPLEMENTING

- Students determine when to start and stop activities, where to perform them, with whom, and in what order.
- Students work in pairs or groups to accomplish tasks, activities, or challenges.
- Students determine how long to practice tasks.
- Students use task sheets, wall charts, books, pictures, and videotapes as sources of information.
- The teacher provides activity choices that accomplish the fitness goal.

EVALUATING

- Students complete a self-evaluation skill checklist.
- Students write a portfolio entry on how well class members are respecting each other.
- Students decide when to progress to more difficult level, of tasks.
- Skilled students have tutoring sessions with less-skilled students during class time.
- Partners provide feedback to each other on skill performance during class activities (peer assessment).

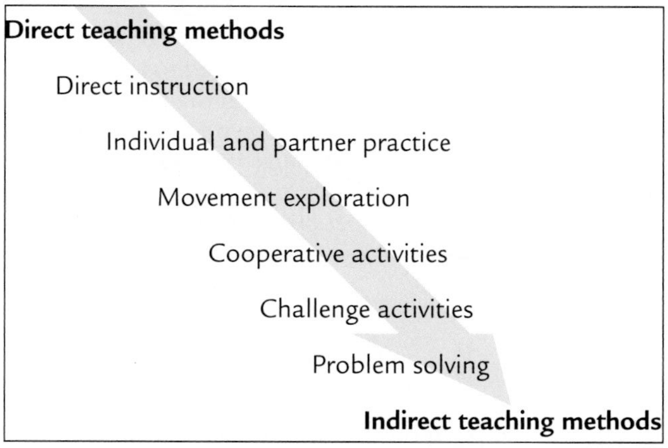

Direct teaching methods

Direct instruction

Individual and partner practice

Movement exploration

Cooperative activities

Challenge activities

Problem solving

Indirect teaching methods

FIGURE 7.1   Teaching Method Continuum

- Partners may evaluate each other's performance (using a check sheet that identifies the critical elements to be evaluated).
- Individuals may assess their own performance using a check sheet.
- Students work independently (according to the directions on the task sheet).
- The teacher monitors students to provide feedback and keep them on task.
- Practice can be set up so that certain activities are performed at stations distributed around the gym.

Generally students rotate from station to station upon the command of the teacher.

MOVEMENT EXPLORATION (see the scenario at the beginning of the chapter and Quick Lesson 7.1 at the end of the chapter):

- **Movement exploration** is primarily used with lower elementary children to explore movement possibilities.
- The teacher controls when, how, and with whom the lesson activities are performed (students are free to move anywhere in the general space while respecting the personal space of others).
- Students respond (individually) to teacher-posed questions that require exploratory, creative, or varied movement responses.

COOPERATIVE ACTIVITIES (see Instant Activity 7.1 for example):

- The goal in **cooperative activities** is for students to work together cooperatively (affective objectives) to learn lesson content.
- The teacher develops and assigns the activity and then monitors groups in their efforts to work cooperatively while completing movement tasks (Metzler 2005).

INSTANT ACTIVITY 7.1
Portraying Words and Phrases Through Movement

Grades 4–6

Equipment Needed

None

Activity

The class is divided into groups of four students. Give each student in the group a defined role (facilitator, harmonizer, resource manager, or recorder). Each group is given a word or phrase that they must portray through movement. Possible words are drip of water, tornado, popcorn popping, firecracker, melting ice cream, fire, smoke, snow, quicksand.

Students must determine what movement qualities are inherent in the word and then create a movement sequence portraying those qualities. The teacher might demonstrate this by doing a couple of simple examples (Joyce 1973, 172). "Everyone stand and with just one arm and hand show me how you would do a falling star. Wonderful! Some had the star sparkle by moving their fingers lightly, some made the star fall in a curve, some stars fell in a straight path, some fell slowly, others fell fast. The direction was down, the force was light, and it happened once and ended." "Now do a waterfall. How is a 'waterfall' different from a 'falling star'? They both travel in a downward path, but a waterfall is continuous, it is noisy, it is big and heavy, it splashes."

The teacher may provide a list of questions, such as the following ones, to help students discover the movement qualities of the word.

- How does the movement begin and end?
- Does the movement occur once or repeatedly?
- Is the movement big or small?
- What body shapes show the word?
- Is the force fast or slow, quick or smooth?
- What level or levels show the word?
- Is the word portrayed with locomotor or nonlocomotor movement? If locomotor, what is the pathway?
- What space is covered?
- What direction is the movement?
- What is the relationship with others (how to portray the word using all the group members)?

The group as a whole must show the movement sequence to the entire class, who then try to guess what word the group is portraying. Do not allow guesses during the performance—only afterward. If the class could not guess the word, discuss what movement qualities of the assigned word were not expressed that should have been. Groups may be allowed to reform and rework their performance based on the input from the audience. This activity may be extended to occur over a number of lessons so students can more fully portray the word or phrase and can interact with the same students for a longer period of time.

- Each student in the group has a clearly defined role (Cohen 1994):
  - The facilitator keeps the group on task and makes sure all members have an opportunity to contribute.
  - The harmonizer deals with interpersonal conflicts and helps the group reach decisions through compromise.
  - The resource manager knows what resources are needed (and where to obtain them) to complete the activity.
  - The recorder records the progress of the group and reports results upon project completion.
- The activity is designed so that all students must complete their work in order for the group to be successful.

- Students help each other complete the group task; however, students do not take over another student's role within the group.
- Groups are generally formed heterogeneously (Kirchner, 2005).
- Students are expected to listen to each other, ask questions, discuss, disagree, pose solutions, and make group decisions (Dyson and Grineski 2001).
- Activities occur over time so that students can achieve the cooperative nature of the assignment.

CHALLENGE ACTIVITIES (see Instant Activity 7.2 and Special Event 7.1 at the end of the chapter for examples):

- The goal in **challenge activities** is for a group of students to solve a movement challenge.

INSTANT ACTIVITY 7.2 New Ways to Bowl

Grades K–6
Equipment Needed

- Masking tape to make restraining lines
- Pencils and pads to sketch designs and keep score when playing the new game
- Two-liter pop bottles, balls, Frisbee, beanbags, hula hoops, cardboard boxes

Challenge

Each team designs a game based on bowling. Provide various pieces of equipment for the teams to use. Each team determines how to play the game and how to score the game. Once games have been designed, pair the teams so they can teach each other their new games. This challenge can be completed in a classroom, hallway, or gymnasium.

Rules for the Challenge

- Students must solve the challenge while operating as a team.
- The game developed must have as its goal the improvement of throwing/rolling accuracy.
- Students in the team must cooperate to self-assign their individual roles (organizer, encourager, and summarizer).
- The group must work as a team and be able to teach others.

One Possible Solution

Students might use a box and some bottles as arranged below. The object of the game is to slide the Frisbee into the box without hitting any of the pop bottles. You score five points for getting the Frisbee in the box. If the Frisbee hits a bottle (or tips it over), a point is deducted. The person with the most points wins.

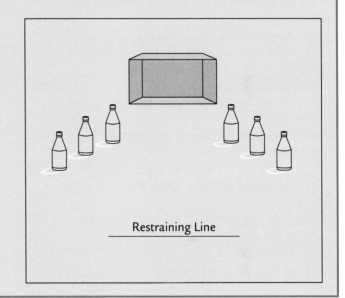

Restraining Line

- The emphasis is not on how quickly the students can solve the challenge, so allow students to come back and work on it at a later time if they do not finish within the time allotted in class.
- The emphasis is on successfully solving the challenge while also operating as a team.
- Each group is given a project description that lists the equipment available to be used, the starting position, the challenge, the rules, the consequences of breaking the rules, and questions to be answered.
- Roles may be assigned to the students in the group (Midura and Glover 2005):
  - The organizer uses the list of questions in the project description to make sure everyone in the group understands the challenge and the rules for solving the challenge.

- The praiser or recorder observes specific acts that should be praised and, when the challenge is completed, reports those acts to the entire class.
- The encourager provides praise during the solving of the challenge and encourages teammates to continue trying.
- The summarizer tells the teacher how the team solved the problem, what was fun, what was hard, and how the group worked as a team.
- The recorder recognizes, verbally or in writing, specific verbal statments that provided praise or encouragement during the group work.
- The teacher must avoid solving the challenge for the group, although hints may be provided to the organizer if a group is really having problems (be prepared to allow the students to struggle a little).

■ The teacher's role is to encourage the group to continue working and make sure attempts to solve the challenge are performed in a safe manner.

PROBLEM SOLVING (see Box 7.3, section C, and Classroom Learning Station 7.1 at the end of the chapter for examples):

■ The goal in **problem-solving activities** is for a small group of students to solve a movement problem.

■ This is a one-time activity (it does not occur over time).

■ This is usually a group activity (three to five students), with groups formed either heterogeneously or homogeneously.

■ More than one solution exists for solving the problem.

■ The teacher develops the problem and establishes the criteria to determine whether the solution is viable.

■ The assignment is carried out without direct input from the teacher.

■ Students figure out how to organize to complete the assignment and determine when they have a viable solution.

■ Project descriptions may be used to outline the activity for students.

Selecting Teaching Strategies The most important factor to consider when selecting the best teaching strategy for a particular lesson is the primary lesson objective. If the primary lesson objective is for students to reproduce specific motor skills, a more direct teaching method provides the opportunity to structure maximum repetitions for each student. If the primary lesson objective is to find creative solutions to a movement problem (as in challenge activities or creative rhythmic activities), either direct or indirect methods might be used. If individuals are creating solutions, a movement education (direct) approach could be used. If groups of students are to work together in creating solutions, then a problem-solving approach (indirect) is more appropriate. If the primary lesson objective is to have the students practice taking responsibility for their own actions and their own learning, then a teaching method that allows students much independence of action would be the best.

Another factor to consider when selecting the best teaching strategy is the previous experience students have with the lesson content. In general, initial exposure to a particular skill occurs through direct instruction, but once students have been exposed

to the content, continued practice on those skills is effective using more indirect teaching methods.

Teachers should have a repertoire of teaching methods they can select from and implement in various combinations depending on the purposes of the lesson (Prusak and Vincent 2005). This variety is needed to effectively achieve different lesson objectives (e.g., skilled motor performance, improved self-concept, appropriate social skills, increased physical fitness, and acquisition of the physical education knowledge base) (Mosston and Ashworth 2002). Typically, a variety of teaching methods are used in *each* lesson, as the different lesson parts (introductory activity, lesson focus, physical fitness activity, and closing activity) contain different student objectives.

Presenting Information Using Different Teaching Methods Teaching methods vary according to the source of information and instruction as well as the communication pattern used for delivering that information and instruction (Mosston and Ashworth 2002). In direct teaching methods, the teacher is the source of all information. Students communicate little with each other; instead, students communicate directly with the teacher, and the teacher provides the answers to students' questions. As teaching methods move toward the indirect side of the continuum, students communicate more with each other using sources of information other than the teacher. Students obtain (and share with each other) information from videos, books, task sheets, and wall signs. As independent learners, students rely less and less on the teacher as the source of all information.

As teachers move students toward becoming independent learners, they refer students to appropriate sources of information instead of providing the information themselves. For example, in a task teaching style, students are working at stations scattered throughout the gymnasium (practicing soccer skills). Each station has a wall sign indicating the tasks to be completed, and the wall sign also indicates where to find information on movement techniques. A student asks the teacher, "What am I supposed to do next?" The teacher directs the student to the task list on the wall and helps her use the task list if necessary (by asking probing questions, not just by providing the information). A student asks the teacher, "How do you perform a soccer dribble?" The teacher refers the student to the videotape (already set up at the station) that may be viewed as needed.

When using teaching methods where partners are to be sources of information for each other, students would primarily communicate with their partners. However, if a partner needed information from the teacher in order to fulfill the assigned role, he or she is usually permitted to communicate with the teacher. For example, using check sheets, partners provide feedback to each other (on their skill performance) while practicing dribbling a basketball in place and then across the gymnasium. One partner marks the check sheet while watching the other partner perform. Since partners are to provide feedback to each other, the teacher would not communicate directly with the performer but might very well communicate with the partner providing the feedback to help her or him evaluate the skill performance appropriately.

Most of the student-directed (indirect) teaching methods benefit from using written task sheets, wall signs, or project descriptions as ways to communicate and present information. This is true for several reasons. First, using both verbal and written task instructions allows the student to use several modalities to understand what is being requested. Second, when students are working independently, they need something to refer back to when they're uncertain as to what to do next. For young children, we suggest posting wall signs (with graphics for those unable to read well) that keep the children working on the appropriate skills. Older children are able to use individual (or group) task sheets and project descriptions. A sample task sheet, wall sign, and project description are shown respectively in Figures 7.2 and 7.3 and Box 7.5. Note that the task sheet in Figure 7.2 follows the motor learning principle of task progression and has students progress from performing simple skills to performing more complex skills. Additional information on task progressions (and examples) is provided in Chapters 9 and 11.

Most teaching methods or strategies also use **skill demonstrations** with verbal performance cues to communicate skill techniques to the students. Skill presentations, in direct teaching methods, usually consist of the teacher talking about how to perform the skill while also providing a live demonstration. The live presentation could be given by the teacher or by students. Students tend to listen more attentively to other students rather than to teachers, so using students to present information may be quite effective. Regardless of who presents the skill demonstration, it should follow the rule "model more and talk less" (Prusak, Vincent, and Pangrazi 2005, 24), thus allowing the students to concentrate on the visual image before them. In indirect teaching styles, the skill presentation might be on a videotape that is available to the students as needed or on a task sheet or wall sign showing drawings or pictures of correct skill technique. Remember to select a variety of students to give skill demonstrations (e.g., skilled versus still learning, female versus

male). Include skill demonstrations using models of similar sex, similar learning level, and similar ethnic background. Have several students provide skill demonstrations for the same motor skill. Using fourth grade girls as subjects learning to juggle, Meaney et al. (2005) found that model similarity positively impacted the girls' acquisition and retention of the motor task. Thus girls learned to juggle best when they observed skill demonstrations by other girls (versus boys) who were also learning the skill (versus girls who were already skilled performers).

Name of Student _____ Grade ____ Date _____

Perform the following tasks. You may enter the list at any point you choose. If successful, continue on to the next task. If not, go back up the list and select an easier task. Check off the tasks you have completed successfully.

1. Throw against the wall (without a target).
   ___ Hit the wall 5 out of 10 times.
   ___ Hit the wall 7 out of 10 times.

2. Throw a beanbag (overhand) at the large target on the wall from the 5-foot line.
   ___ Hit the target 5 out of 10 times.
   ___ Hit the target 7 out of 10 times.

3. Throw a beanbag (overhand) at the large target on the wall from the 10-foot line.
   ___ Hit the target 5 out of 10 times.
   ___ Hit the target 7 out of 10 times.

4. Throw a beanbag at the small target on the wall from the 5-foot line.
   ___ Hit the target 5 out of 10 times.
   ___ Hit the target 7 out of 10 times.

5. Throw a beanbag at the small target on the wall from the 10-foot line.
   ___ Hit the target 5 out of 10 times.
   ___ Hit the target 7 out of 10 times.

6. Throw a beanbag to a partner (5 feet apart).
   ___ Partner *does* move feet to catch.
   ___ Partner *does not* move feet to catch.

7. Throw a beanbag to a partner (10 feet apart).
   ___ Partner *does* move feet to catch.
   ___ Partner *does not* move feet to catch.

8. Throw a tennis ball to a partner.
   ___ Partner *does* move feet to catch.
   ___ Partner *does not* move feet to catch.

9. Throw a foam-core ball to a partner.
   ___ Partner *does* move feet to catch.
   ___ Partner *does not* move feet to catch.

Throwing Technique
- *Grip* a beanbag or tennis ball in the fingers of the throwing hand. Grip a football with the fingers spread so that the fourth and fifth fingers cross the laces.
- *Stand* with the feet shoulder-width apart, the back foot pointing toward the target, and the front foot on a 45-degree angle to the direction of the throw.
- *Face* the left shoulder (if right-handed) toward the target.
- *Cock* the ball behind the head at ear level (elbow bent, upper arm parallel to the ground). Point the opposite arm forward in the direction of the throw.
- *Step* forward with the back foot as the arm moves forward in a high, overhead motion and the body rotates to face the target.
- *Snap* the wrist when releasing the ball.
- *Follow through* with the throwing arm toward the target.
- *Focus* throughout the throw on the target.

FIGURE 7.2 Sample Task Sheet: Throwing Accurately, Grades 3–4

Do the following (in any order).
Work quickly, but with correct technique.
Do not interfere with others.

10 Jumping jacks

10 Curl-ups

20 Wall push-ups

10 Vertical jumps (against the wall)

Skip around the perimeter of the gym (twice)

When finished, sit around the black circle that is painted on the center of the gym floor.

FIGURE 7.3 Sample Wall Sign or Chart

The more direct teaching methods tend to use verbal instructions as a means to communicate any number of organizing events (e.g., what to do next, where to move to, when to move, how to get partners). Verbal instructions need to be short and concise in order to minimize management time, and of course, the length and content of the instructions need to match the cognitive and behavioral development levels of the students in the class. Instructions to kindergarteners (given their short attention span)

should last about 30 seconds and contain only one or two requests for action. Fifth graders can listen one to two minutes and remember multiple requests for action. In general, teachers tend to provide too much detail in lengthy instructions. Long explanations can be divided into parts and delivered over time between the students' active learning time (Pangrazi 2004).

Providing Feedback to Students

A critical element in all of the teaching methods and strategies is providing quality, timely **feedback** to students on their performance. Although children can (and do) practice and learn motor skills on their own without the direct supervision of an adult, they improve more rapidly and display more mature motor patterns with the help of a trained adult.

GUIDELINES FOR QUALITY FEEDBACK

Our discussion of congruent feedback specifically refers to positive and corrective statements made to students regarding their movement technique; thus, feedback centers on the technique used when performing, not on the result of the performance. For example, when students are throwing at a target, the teacher and student can observe the result (product) of the throw (whether or not the target was hit). The teacher observes the child's performance technique and the performance results to help determine which technique elements were performed correctly and which were performed incorrectly. The teacher then gives feedback to the student about movement techniques that will eventually lead to the desired results. When teaching young children, it is more important that they learn to perform skills correctly than that they obtain the desired result.

The brain's neural pathways are set up to use feedback; thus, learning is enhanced when teachers provide specific, frequent, and accurate feedback (Blakemore 2004). The following helpful hints and examples may help you provide quality, timely feedback to individual students.

Observe Carefully Obviously, no one performs perfectly on each trial. To be sure that an error detected is really one that is present most of the time, observe the student's performance a number of times before offering feedback. If you are not really sure what the

BOX 7.5 Sample Project Description

GRADES 1–2

The floor patterns (pathways), shown at right, are taped to the gym floor. With a partner, students find each movement pattern in the order numbered on their paper. The teacher prepares papers that contain different pattern orders so that students don't have to wait in line to perform an activity. When students find the pattern, they trace the pattern (two times) using the locomotor step listed.

GRADES 5–6, BASKETBALL UNIT

The teacher forms small groups of five students each. Each group is asked to design two offensive patterns in order to successfully score against another team. Groups proceed as follows:

- Discuss possible patterns.
- Draw (on the provided tablet) at least two patterns.
- Practice the two patterns on the court assigned to your group.
- Partner with another group (who will play defense) and run the offensive patterns.
- Evaluate the success of your efforts and make changes in the patterns if necessary.
- Continue trying patterns and perfecting them until they work (you can score).

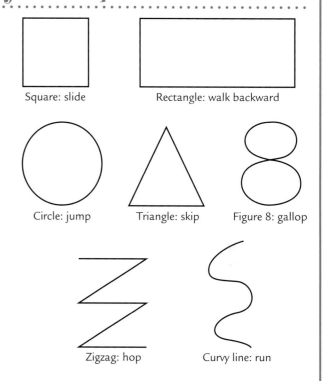

Square: slide   Rectangle: walk backward

Circle: jump   Triangle: skip   Figure 8: gallop

Zigzag: hop   Curvy line: run

---

student is doing wrong, say nothing. If sure the error is being consistently made, offer corrective feedback using your established teaching (verbal) cues and descriptions. Using consistent cues helps the learner remember correct technique.

Discuss Both Correct and Incorrect Technique

When observing students perform, they may be correctly demonstrating one or more technique points; however, they may not realize this. So in addition to providing feedback on incorrect performance, it is beneficial to indicate to learners what techniques they are performing correctly. When giving individual feedback to students, many physical educators begin and end the conversation by identifying what the student is doing correctly. In the middle of the conversation, one incorrect technique point is identified for the student to focus on and improve.

Focus on Improving the Most Important Error

In general, children cannot attend to lots of information,

so work on correcting only one error at a time. For example, you observe that while dribbling a basketball in place a student is making the following errors:

- Hunched over the ball (bent forward at the waist) instead of keeping the back straight
- Standing with locked knees instead of slightly bent knees
- Projecting the ball downward too close to the body so the ball contacts the learner's foot
- Projecting the ball downward with a hitting motion instead of a pushing motion
- Initially contacting the ball with the palm of the hand instead of the pads of the fingers
- Watching the hand contact the ball rather than looking up at surroundings and using peripheral vision to see the hand contact the ball

The teacher selects one of the above errors to bring to the learner's attention instead of trying to correct all of them at once.

The error you select should be the most important error. Most students will not *master* complex motor skills until after their elementary school years, so stay focused on improving fundamental errors first. In general, but not always, performance errors are ranked in importance as follows:

1. Body position
2. Focus point (where the learner looks while performing)
3. Movement actions that produce the force for the movement
4. Movements that come after the force production

Thus in the dribbling example just cited, the teacher would focus first on the errors in body position (the first two errors described). Corrective feedback for the body position errors might be as follows:

- "Keep your back straight (and head up) while your hand moves up and down to snap and catch the ball."
- "Flex your knees just slightly while dribbling."

Provide Consistent, Specific Feedback   Provide consistent feedback to the individual learner. In other words, if Suzie is told today to work on her body position, then tomorrow she should continue working on her body position. Do not work on body position today and then switch to another technique element tomorrow (unless, of course, Suzie has greatly improved her body position and is ready to work on correcting another error).

In addition, feedback statements should be specific rather than general (Kovar et al. 1992). For example, a fourth grader is playing catch with a partner, but the ball consistently does not reach the partner. Telling the student to throw the ball harder is too general. If the student knew how to throw harder, he or she would certainly do so. The teacher needs to tell the learner *how* to throw harder. For example, the power for throwing comes from transferring weight from the back foot to the front foot, rotating the trunk of the body, moving the throwing arm from behind to in front of the head (to full extension), and snapping the wrist as the ball is released. Thus several feedback statements are possible for increasing the length of a throw. Based on the learner's current performance, the teacher might say any of the following:

- "Be sure that as you step forward to throw, you also rotate your body to face your partner."
- "Be sure to snap your wrist as you release the ball."

- "Be sure as you begin the throw that your elbow is bent and the entire arm is extended backward, so you can move the arm forward as you throw."

Offer Immediate Feedback   Offer performance feedback to individuals during their practice sessions so they can try your suggestions immediately. Initially, you may want to allow students who are learning new skills to practice on their own (without teacher feedback) in order to establish a frame of reference in which to interpret the feedback that will come from the teacher.

INDIVIDUAL VERSUS GROUP FEEDBACK

In general, feedback is given to *individual* students as they perform in class, but sometimes giving feedback to a *group* of students is beneficial. When students are learning something new and most of the students are doing something fundamentally incorrect, it may be helpful to stop the entire class and instruct them how to correct the error.

SOURCES OF FEEDBACK

Sources of congruent feedback include the teacher, peers, and the performer. The suggestions provided on the preceding pages are relevant for when the teacher is the source of the feedback. In structured situations, peers can provide feedback to each other using checklists that refer to the performance technique being practiced. Providing peer-feedback situations helps students learn what correct performance looks like. For self-evaluation to be effective, teachers need to help learners feel the difference between correct and incorrect performance. This is accomplished by asking students questions that prompt them to examine the result (product) of their performance with how the performance felt. Eventually they can match the performance result with their performance technique to recognize the quality of their own performance without the assistance of others.

As you may recall, Chapter 3 contains descriptions of the motor skills children should learn. Along with the skill descriptions are feedback suggestions and verbal cues based on common errors beginning performers often make. At this time you may wish to review those feedback suggestions. For instance, Box 3.4 contains teaching (**verbal**) **cues** *for the jump: Squat, arms back, reach for the stars, jump, land soft.*

The feedback suggestions and examples provided in this section of the book all relate to the improvement

Specific individual feedback can help students learn motor skills more quickly.

of motor performance. However, feedback relative to all types of objectives is possible (motor skills, fitness skills, knowledge of physical education and fitness concepts, and social skills).

Organizing Students for Activity

Handling a group of 20 to 35 moving students in the gymnasium or playground setting is certainly a matter that movement educators think about and plan for. Four specific areas that educators need to think about are (1) establishing organizational routines, (2) transitioning from one activity to another, (3) supervising class activities, and (4) providing a safe environment.

COMMON ORGANIZATIONAL ROUTINES

If during each class period particular tasks that are not related to the academic content of the lesson must be completed, it is useful to establish a routine in order to minimize the time needed to complete the tasks. Useful **organizational routines** include establishing standard behaviors for entering and leaving the gymnasium, getting drinks of water and using the restroom during class time, responding to the teacher's signal when actively engaged in lesson activities, and obtaining and returning equipment.

Entering the Gymnasium   Students tend to misbehave less if immediately upon entering the gym they can be physically active (rather than having to sit quietly). So use their natural urge to move by structuring an introductory activity as indicated earlier in the chapter. *Before* entering the gymnasium, instruct students as to what they should do upon entering.

Leaving the Gymnasium   Ending the lesson with a closing activity not only pulls together the lesson for the learner but also establishes a routine that allows students to move efficiently from the gymnasium to the classroom. For example, a closing routine might have the students come together and sit down in a big circle. The teacher joins the circle, and while leading (by actions only) the students in stretching exercises the teacher briefly pulls the lesson together. The teacher might pull the lesson together by asking the students to verbally answer questions about the day's lesson or indicate what they will do during the next physical education lesson. Then students give high fives to the classmates on their right and left for working so hard today in physical education. Or you might instruct students to close their eyes and do deep breathing, then walk quietly to the door and line up so they can return to the classroom. If pushing and shoving occurs as the students line up, dismiss them to line up in smaller groups (by hair color, clothes color, birth months, etc.) or proceed to line up with movements other than walking (e.g., bear crawls, seal walk, or bunny hop).

Getting Drinks of Water and Using the Restroom

As much as possible (depending on the age and maturity of the students as well as the physical setting), students should be allowed to get a drink of water at any time during the movement parts of the lesson (if a drinking fountain is located within the gym). If the drinking fountain is located outside the gym, students should get drinks of water on their return trip to the classroom. Children need plenty of water before, during, and after exercise to replace body fluids lost through sweating. Even slight dehydration can make a student play less vigorously, and severe dehydration places the child at risk for heat cramps, heat exhaustion, and heat stroke. If bathrooms are located at the entrance door into the gym, students should be allowed to use the restroom as necessary (one student at a time). Obviously, the teacher needs to establish a routine for using the restroom (see the routine outlined in Box 10.6).

Responding to the Teacher's Signal

Another routine that can save precious minutes during each lesson is establishing *one signal* for getting students' attention. This signal is needed to move quickly between lesson activities, to provide group feedback, and to respond quickly in emergency situations. Most of the time, movement educators use a variety of signals (whistle, hand clap, loud voice, etc.) within the same lesson. However, using different signals harms the effort to keep management time to a minimum because students do not learn to respond quickly to these varying signals. *Consistency* is the key to establishing habits in students. For students to develop a habit (an automatic response), the cue to induce that response must be the same every time. We suggest using a short, sharp blow of a whistle because it is loud enough to be heard over gym noise and it is not a sound indigenous to any of the activities usually going on in the gymnasium. If children with hearing impairments are in the class, an additional (visual) signal must be used in conjunction with the whistle (e.g., green card for "go" and red card for "stop").

Obtaining and Returning Equipment

In general, it is best for students to obtain needed equipment *after* activity explanations and skill demonstrations have been completed, as students will play with the equipment (and not listen to instructions) if they have it in their hands. So *after* the explanations and demonstrations, students are instructed to obtain a needed piece of equipment and begin activity using the "when before what" principle (Prusak et al. 2005). For example, "When I say 'go', one partner (from each group

of two), please walk to the nearest equipment box, get a hula hoop, return to your partner, and begin the activity." The use of this principle allows students to hear what they are to do with the equipment before they actually have the equipment in hand. In the above case, before class the teacher placed three to four boxes containing the needed equipment around the perimeter of the gymnasium or along one side of an outdoor playing field. This method allows students to obtain and return equipment quickly. If only one distribution point is available (e.g., a box by the teacher), precious time is wasted distributing and returning equipment. Obviously, using this method of equipment distribution and collection necessitates teaching students how to behave during this process so that equipment is handled properly and students are not injured. To implement this equipment distribution approach, classroom teachers may need to have a classroom aide or helper get equipment ready in the activity area before the students arrive.

USING ROUTINES TO REDUCE MANAGEMENT TIME

We have outlined the use of a number of class management routines; however, just *establishing* routines does not automatically reduce management time. Management time decreases only if students learn to implement the routines quickly and appropriately. Teachers can do two things to help ensure that established routines really lead to decreased management time: (1) teach (and regularly practice) the proper response to the routine, and (2) be ready to move quickly into the next lesson activity. For example, students are taught what the attention signal (whistle) means and how they are expected to respond to it (Kovar 1991). The teacher might do that by saying that the whistle means *stop, look, and listen:*

1. *Stop* your present activity.
2. *Look* at the teacher.
3. *Listen* to the teacher.

With this three-pronged meaning, the teacher can verbally cue students after the whistle is blown. The proper response to the signal should be practiced on a daily basis until students respond quickly and appropriately. Practice the proper response in a variety of ways:

- While they are standing in a circle, have students perform various noisy activities (such as clapping their hands, bouncing balls, tapping Lummi sticks). The objective is for students to quickly stop the noisy activity (and control a piece of equipment), look at you, and listen for further instruction the moment they hear the signal.

- Play tag games in which all students are active. The objective is for the students to stop their body movement quickly and direct their attention to the teacher as soon as they hear the signal.

Practice the activities suggested above with the goal being to decrease the time it takes for students to *stop, look, and listen*. With a stopwatch, measure the time it takes for *all* the students to respond. Work to decrease the time, emphasizing that the goal is for *all* students to respond quickly. Once routines are learned and are being used on a consistent basis, periodic reviews and prompts will still be needed throughout the year to keep students responding appropriately. If students are using equipment, the teacher can use a four-pronged prompt by inserting *set* as the second action—*stop, set, look, and listen*—meaning students should place equipment down on the floor after stopping and before looking at the teacher.

In addition to practicing (and regularly reviewing) the routine, be ready to proceed immediately into the next activity. Keep the pace of the class moving along briskly. If the majority of the students have responded quickly and appropriately to the routine, then continue into the next activity. Do not wait for the stragglers; they will catch up, and they will learn that you are not going to wait for them (so they will pick up the pace). The use of routines can help increase the pace of the lesson. The increased pace should lead to fewer discipline problems, more time to teach, and more time on task for students. Box 7.6 reviews the effective implementation of routines and provides a list of management tasks for which the teacher may wish to establish routines.

TRANSITIONING FROM ONE ACTIVITY TO ANOTHER

Typical entire-class activity formations are displayed in Figure 7.4. Moving students (especially young children) is most efficient if these formations are taped, painted, or otherwise designated on the floor (using different colors for each formation). Then teachers can simply say, "Move to one of the red *X*s," and they have the students in a circle formation (equally spaced about the circle). Teachers could begin class with the students in any of these formations depending on the routine established for entering the gymnasium. A first-grade class might walk into the gym each class period and sit on assigned blue *X*s. Staying in

---

BOX 7.6

Establishing Routines

- Select routines (for management tasks).
- Use the routines consistently.
- Teach the routines to the students.
- Practice the routines.
- Review routines periodically.

MANAGEMENT TASKS THAT MAY NEED A ROUTINE

- Entering the gymnasium
- Getting drinks of water
- Using the restroom during class
- Responding to the teacher's signal
- Obtaining and returning equipment
- Behaving appropriately in emergency situations (including injuries)
- Leaving the gymnasium

---

that spot, each child performs the five activities listed on a sign at the front of the room (in any order). The activities are changed often; however, the "entering the gymnasium" formation stays the same over time.

The task of **transitioning** from one activity to another may or may not involve changing the activity formation. If it does not, then moving to the next activity simply involves getting students' attention (with the whistle) and providing instructions on how to do the next activity. For example, the first graders (mentioned above) who enter the gym and stand on the blue *X*s for their introductory activity may move into the second activity for the day (manipulative activities with Lummi sticks) without changing formation. As another example, fourth-grade students (in groups of three) have been throwing and catching foam-core basketballs using an overhand pass. The teacher wants the students to begin practicing a new pass (the bounce pass). The teacher blows the whistle to get students' attention (to *stop, set, look, and listen*), then provides instruction on performing the bounce pass and starts the students practicing the new skill.

If changing the lesson activity also entails changing the activity formation, then moving to the new activity becomes more difficult (and potentially more time consuming) unless the teacher is prepared with a plan for moving from one formation to another. For instance, suppose the first graders from our previous

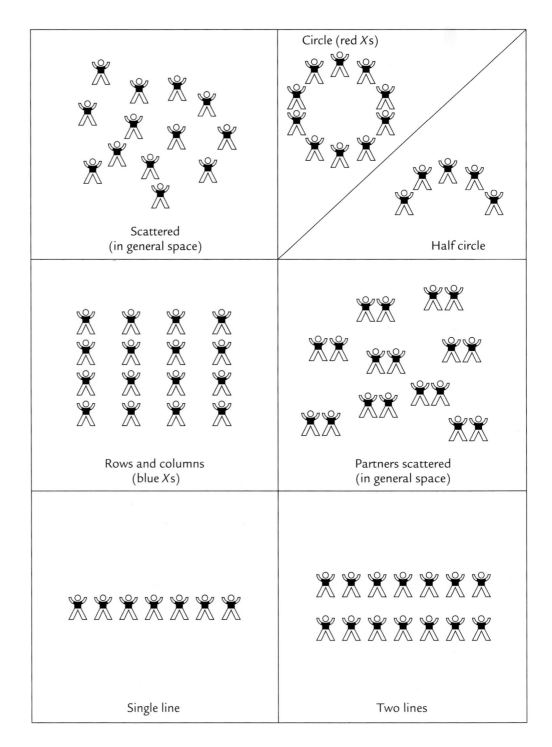

FIGURE 7.4 Class Formations

example needed to move into a circle formation after their opening activity in order to perform parachute activities. This transition is relatively easy if the red circle of Xs is painted on the floor. If you are not allowed to mark the floor, then use an existing circle (center circle on the basketball court) and have students move to some spot on the center circle. Using this technique, young children will tend to bunch together around the circle. To spread them out more

evenly, have them join hands and step backward until their arms are stretched tight out to the side. Then have them drop hands and begin the activity.

Moving from one activity to another becomes even more difficult if the transition involves altering the activity formation and the number of students in the group. For instance, how did the fourth-grade students from the previous example get into groups of three (scattered within the gym space) in order to

---

BOX 7.7 50+ Ways to Form Groups, Find Partners, and Line Up

COLORS

1. Something you wear
2. Shoelaces
3. Eyes
4. Favorite color
5. Socks
6. From the waist up or down
7. Shoe color
8. Stickers
9. Equipment

PETS

1. Type
2. Number of legs
3. How many
4. Favorite

SOMETHING YOU DID WHILE DRESSING

Button/snap/tie/zip/buckle

HOW YOU GOT TO SCHOOL

1. Walked
2. Bus
3. Car
4. Bike

FAMILIES

1. Number of siblings
2. Number of noses in the household
3. Number of people you live with

TRAVEL EXPERIENCE

1. Cities visited
2. Travel by train/plane/subway

MISCELLANEOUS

1. Birthday
2. Favorite food
3. Favorite sport
4. Favorite music
5. Sitting or standing
6. Height of students
7. Favorite TV show
8. Choose own partner
9. Answer to math problem
10. Spelling a word

CLOTHING

1. Wearing stripes
2. Plain color
3. Letters or numbers
4. Patterns
5. Collar/no collar
6. Sweater
7. Shoes that buckle, tie, slip on, use Velcro
8. Long sleeves/short sleeves

WORDS OR LETTERS

1. In name (first or last)
2. Initials
3. Beginning letter/sound
4. Number of letters in name

ADDRESS

1. Street number or name
2. Even/odd house numbers

SILLY THINGS

1. Curl your tongue
2. Wiggle your ears

---

practice the overhand basketball pass? If the students were in a line or a circle, and assuming there are 27 students in the class, the teacher could have them count off by nine. Then the ones are a group of three, the twos are a group, and so on. The groups are then asked to scatter within the gym space so they will not interfere with each other as they perform. This way of constructing groups works for older students, but not for younger students. For young children, the teacher could determine the group formations before class and quickly read off the names of the students in each group while moving around the gym space and

indicating where the group just named should stand. If students are in a line or circle formation, the teacher may create groups of four or five by walking down the line or around the circle and making every four or five people a group. If students are in rows, a row (or a column) may be designated a group.

Many ways exist to create groups, and numerous suggestions have been mentioned throughout the text on ways students can get partners. Consult Box 7.7 for additional suggestions. Many times, depending on the number of students in class that day and the groupings needed for the activities, the process will end with "extra" students. These "extra" students need to be quickly, and quietly, assigned to groups by the teacher. Be aware that groups containing "extras" may need help in understanding what to do given that the teacher's instructions for what to do will not exactly match their situation. Teachers need to plan for each activity transition and each group formation change in order to make the transition smoothly and quickly. In general, keep the number of times students must be reorganized to a minimum. Sometimes the order of activities can be changed to decrease the number of formation changes needed. Fewer formation changes should be used for younger students (i.e., movement in general space is what most K–2 lessons should entail). In addition, giving time parameters may be helpful, such as "you have 20 seconds to be in your groups" and "you have one more minute until activity ends."

When teaching in a circle formation, the teacher "joins" the circle, so everyone can see her and she can see each student for supervision and feedback purposes.

SUPERVISING CLASS ACTIVITIES

Active supervision in the physical activity setting is a difficult skill to master, but with practice you will be able to implement the techniques of active supervision automatically (so that during the lesson you can be concentrating on the lesson content). **Active supervision** means paying attention to where you (as the teacher) are located in the activity area in relation to the students, scanning for problems (e.g., safety issues, inappropriate student behavior, and students not on task), and keeping your eyes on all the students.

Position Yourself to Keep All Students in View

The first supervision technique used by physical educators is to take a position in the activity space so that all students are within their line of vision at all times. This is imperative for safety reasons. If students are scattered in the activity space, this means the teacher is positioned on the outside of the activity space, standing with his or her **back-to-the-wall** (so no student is behind them). It may be necessary to move inside the activity space to interact with students working there; however, those visits should be brief. If students are in one big circle, this means teachers position themselves in the circle with the students, not in the middle of the circle. Standing in the middle of the circle allows the teacher to see and speak to only half of the students. Standing in the circle allows a full view of all students, and it is easy for the teacher to move around the circle and make contact with individual students to provide feedback and instruction. If students are in rows and columns (see Figure 7.4), teachers usually stand at the front of the room facing

the students. The teacher can then walk the square around the students to reach all students for instructional purposes.

Move Around The second technique used is to move around the perimeter of the room (or around the class formation), keeping everyone in sight, rather than standing in one spot. Teachers tend to develop a favorite spot within the space, and then students situate themselves close to or far away from the teacher during their practice time. As teachers quickly learn, the students farthest away are usually the ones who need the most supervision! Thus, moving in different and unpredictable patterns throughout the class period allows the teacher to more effectively supervise the activities. For example, in the row and column formation discussed above, the students who misbehave the most will place themselves toward the back of the room. The teacher can overcome this by simply moving those at the front of the room to the back of the room. Once students have placed themselves in the formation, the teacher designates a new front of the room by making a different wall the front of the room and begins teaching from there. So now the students in the back of the room are in the front of the room. Moving around the room also helps the teacher view the performance of all students in order to provide corrective feedback as well as to assist students with visual or auditory disabilities.

Scan to Detect Problems Early The third technique used in active supervision is to scan the class frequently to detect problems as early as possible. The teacher scans periodically, all the while continuing

This classroom teacher demonstrates the "back-to-the-wall" supervisory principle when instructing physical activities.

other things such as lecturing, demonstrating, helping students, and providing feedback. The teacher scans for students who are off task, interfering with the learning of others, being disrespectful of others or the equipment, or behaving dangerously.

Watch Everyone All the Time The fourth technique used is when providing individual or small group feedback, teachers need to keep their eyes up and looking across the class to see what is going on with all of the students, not just the students currently being helped. Students will realize that the teacher is supervising all of them if sometimes the teacher provides feedback to an individual or group across the activity space. For example, while students are practicing, use a loud voice and give affirmative feedback to Ron and Becky, who are correctly playing catch, or give corrective feedback to Ralph and Janea, both of whom are throwing incorrectly.

Instill Safety into Every Lesson The fifth supervision technique used is to instill safety into each lesson. The teacher thinks about and plans for safety when preparing each lesson by examining the appropriateness of activities included in the lesson (based on the age and ability of the students) and by indicating specific safety procedures in the written lesson plan. Because safety in the movement setting is so important, an entire chapter (Chapter 11) is devoted to understanding the safety knowledge base and using that knowledge to recognize potential hazards and plan and implement safe lessons. For examples of instilling safety into each lesson, review the pedagogical elements (Instant Activities, Quick Lesson, etc.) in Chapter 11, because they illustrate how to weave safety issues and procedures into the planning of activities.

Helping Students Choose Responsible Behavior

In the previous section, we presented some techniques to help teachers supervise class activities. Another important part of the teacher's supervisory role is to monitor the behavior of students while they are engaged in class activities in order to establish a productive learning environment. Our approach for monitoring and improving student behavior is not based on the traditional idea of discipline that focuses on the teacher "keeping the students in line," but rather on **student behavior as a choice.** The traditional discipline approach is predicated on the fact that teacher manipulation of the environment will change student behavior. Most teachers who use this approach begin the year by establishing a long list of class rules that indicate to students what they can and cannot do. In addition, teachers specify the exact consequences (usually punishments) that accompany each breaking of a rule. For example, Sharon receives a check mark by her name the first time she talks without permission. On the second occasion she gets a time-out, and on the third occasion she has to take a note home to her parents and bring it back signed by them. For the following reasons, this approach does not help students learn to manage their own behavior (Kovar, Ermler, and Mehrhof 1992):

- Students and teachers become adversaries.
- Teachers are trying to control students' behavior when in reality only students have control of their behavior choices.
- Teachers take responsibility for everything that occurs in the class; students do not share in this responsibility.
- Teachers respond to student misbehavior with predetermined consequences that are not adjusted based on individual circumstances.

Students are not robots that teachers must control. Rather, students are thinking, feeling human beings who think about their environment and act (not just react) by choosing actions that suit their purposes. Students who repeatedly misbehave must be experiencing some benefit (Cimmins et al. 2007). For example, one student misbehaves because he likes to run the five laps he receives as punishment, another misbehaves to obtain the teacher's attention, and another misbehaves in order to receive a time-out from an activity she dislikes. Our approach to helping students choose responsible behaviors is based on the premise that students and teachers are partners in the learning process. This approach entails establishing a caring classroom community, teaching social skills to shape student behavior, and implementing discipline strategies that build self-management skills in students.

ESTABLISH A CARING COMMUNITY IN THE CLASSROOM AND GYMNASIUM

The relationship between the teacher and students is one key element in establishing a **caring community** in which students and teachers become partners in the teaching and learning process. This partnership is established and maintained in the following ways:

1. Develop ways to get to know your students on a more personal level than is normally the case. Become familiar with each student—his or her interests, family, background, personality, and so on (Jones and Jones 2004).
2. Develop ways to share your story with your students—your family, interests, background, and the like.
3. Make the classroom and gymnasium friendly places in the following ways:
   - Make the classroom and gymnasium physically attractive, inviting, and interesting places (Dodd 1997)—display student work and paint the walls with bright colors. In the classroom, place a beanbag chair in the corner (as an individual free-time reading space) and situate desks so they are not lined up in rigid rows. In the gymnasium, keep extraneous equipment in storage closets and display posters of boys and girls moving. Ask students to decorate the room.
   - Have students take ownership of their classroom by caring for the items in the room.
   - Praise students, on the spot, when appropriate. Send home positive notes to parents or make positive telephone calls to parents.
   - Value all students.
   - Greet students (individually) each day with enthusiasm and interest.
   - Share laughter with your students. Smile, laugh out loud, tell a joke (when appropriate), inject humor when tension is running high, exhibit humorous books or sayings in your classroom, and laugh at yourself—it shows you are human.
   - Recognize that teachers as well as students make mistakes.
   - Ask for student input and help. For example, if students complain about jumping rope, but they need a cardiorespiratory workout, ask how they would like to achieve this goal.

- Guide the students in setting their own class rules. Even kindergarten students can set appropriate rules (one to five rules, depending on the age of the children), such as "Put away the things you play with after you are finished playing," "Treat others nicely," and "Do not talk when someone else is talking." If possible, use language that complements the school's code of conduct, if one exists. Post these rules (in big letters) in several places in the classroom and gymnasium and refer to them as needed. Continue throughout the school year to reinforce the rules and reiterate why the rules lead to a productive learning environment.
- Give emotional support to students as needed.
- Have students take on responsibilities within the classroom and gymnasium.

4. Teach students to solve their own behavior problems in the following ways:
   - Help students to recognize desirable behavior (what behavior is appropriate versus inappropriate and why). For example, you institute the terminology "above-the-line behavior" and "below-the-line-behavior." Above-the-line behavior includes appropriate behaviors such as listening when others are talking, helping others, saying thank you, and waiting your turn. Below-the-line behavior includes inappropriate behaviors such as pushing, talking out of turn, and calling someone a name. You develop a poster (see Figure 7.5) and place it in the classroom where everyone can see it. Refer to the poster when particular behaviors are displayed and name the behaviors as above or below the line.
   - Use the steps of problem solving to help students find appropriate ways to respond to particular situations (recognize the problem, generate possible solutions, select the best solution, evaluate success of the solution, choose another solution if original solution is not working). Younger elementary school children can role-play possible actions and consequences. Older elementary school children can be assigned (on a rotating basis) to serve as class monitors who suggest and implement solutions to behavior problems that occur in the classroom.
5. Allow students to suffer the natural consequences of their actions. This teaches the cause-and-effect relationship between actions and consequences, and many times no other consequence (imposed from the teacher) is needed.
6. Do not take student misbehavior as a personal affront. In general, the student's response is not

Listening
Helping others
Saying "thank you"
Waiting your turn

Pushing
Talking out of turn
Calling someone a name

FIGURE 7.5 Behavior Poster

directed at you personally. You do not want to get into a power struggle with a student, as both of you will lose. So focus on the problem, not the student. Try to discover why the student responded as he or she did.

In a classroom/gymnasium community, students learn to work, play, and live together as a group. So the relationship between the teacher and students is not the only important relationship. Another key element in establishing a caring community is for students to establish caring, respectful relationships with one another. Students are encouraged to interact with each other, make their own choices, and work together in positive, supportive ways. This partnership between students is established and maintained in the following ways:

- Develop strong personal connections among the students.
- Use student-centered class activities and collaborative student projects to teach academic content material.
- Honor the experiences and contributions of each class member (Jones and Jones 2004).
- Establish ways for students to get along with each other (see Box 7.8).

- Encourage peer dialogue that is positive and supportive.

TEACH SOCIAL SKILLS TO SHAPE STUDENT BEHAVIOR

In addition to establishing a caring classroom and gymnasium community, teaching students appropriate **social skills** helps them choose responsible behavior. Teaching social skills has proved to be successful in positively shaping student behavior. Chapter 10 (in the section titled "Teaching and Assessing Social Skills in the Movement Setting") fully develops the process of teaching and evaluating social skills and places the teaching of those skills within the context of socializing students into the culture of the school and society.

IMPLEMENT APPROPRIATE SELF-MANAGEMENT TECHNIQUES

Teachers establish a basic classroom and gymnasium community that is caring and respectful and teach social skills to shape student behavior. In addition, teachers also need to respond to individuals who behave inappropriately at any given time. Using the approach that inappropriate behavior is simply an opportunity to help students learn to identify and solve their own behavior problems, the following **self-management techniques** represent current theory and practice.

Build a Student-Teacher Partnership Change the language from discipline and punishment to actions

BOX 7.9 Why Students Misbehave

INEXPERIENCE OR IGNORANCE

Sometimes students just simply do not know the lay of the land. They do not know the difference between a classroom voice and a gymnasium voice. They do not know they are always expected to walk (not run) in the school hallways. Clarifying expectations and practicing correct behavior may help these students.

PHYSICAL IMMATURITY

Often teachers expect students to behave in ways students are not physically capable of. For example, young children learn by touching, tasting, and doing. Asking them not to do those things only leads to frustration on the part of the student and the teacher. Teachers can revamp the environment or simply alter their expectations of the students.

EMOTIONAL IMMATURITY

Expecting young children to recognize appropriate behavior is probably unrealistic. They often laugh or act silly because those behaviors are perfectly normal for them. Teachers can help students recognize appropriate behavior and also reduce their expectations to allow some episodes of immaturity.

CURIOSITY

Students learn because they are curious. In situations where teachers expect that students will be curious, providing time for them to explore on their own (before settling down to the planned activity) is a good idea. For example, when introducing a new manipulative object, allow students to use it creatively before moving on to structured tasks with the object.

NEED FOR BELONGING

We all have the need to belong. Teachers provide this sense of belonging by creating a caring classroom community where everyone is respected and accepted.

NEED FOR RECOGNITION

We all have the need to feel special and to be recognized for the things we do well. Students and teachers should get to know each other (interests, abilities, background, etc.), and they should become partners in the teaching and learning process.

NEED FOR POWER OR CONTROL

We all need to have a sense of control over what is happening in our lives. Students feel a sense of control when teachers give them choices, allow them to solve problems, and give them real responsibilities within the classroom community.

ANGER RELEASE

Teachers can help students learn to control their anger and express it in appropriate ways. Time-outs may be used to allow students the opportunity to regain composure after an outburst of anger. Repair Shop (see Box 7.8) can be used to reestablish relationships between students after confrontations have occurred.

ENJOYMENT, ADVENTURE, AND FUN

Students (as well as teachers) like to have fun, and some fun in the classroom is appropriate and needed. However, students who are continually playing the class clown need to be taught how much is okay and how much is too much. And fun at the expense of others is always discouraged, as it is not consistent with a caring classroom community.

Adapted from M. E. Gootman, *The Caring Teacher's Guide to Discipline* (Thousand Oaks, CA: Corwin Press, 2001) and reprinted by permission of Corwin Press, Inc.

and consequences, from detention to afternoon appointment, and from class rules to class goals (Dodd 1997). These may be small changes, but they represent a shift in power, a transition from teacher dominance to student-teacher partnership.

Emphasize Student Behavior as a Choice "If you choose not to stay on task, then you choose to have a self-help time." Do not threaten to do something in response to what the student does. It is always the student's choice to behave appropriately or inappropriately.

Find Causes and Solutions for Behavior Problems
Discover why the student is disruptive, uncooperative, not completing homework, and the like. Box 7.9

presents some common causes of misbehavior and strategies for stimulating behavior improvement. Focus on trying to find a solution to the problem (with help from the child) instead of on punishing the student. Involve the student in stating the problem, identifying possible solutions, and selecting a course of action to remedy the problem. Help the student implement the course of action when she or he is next faced with a similar situation. Stand close to a student when you recognize a situation in which his or her behavior might break down, and encourage the student to implement the appropriate behavior (a we're-in-this-together approach). Or develop a special signal (known only to the teacher and the student) to cue this student to focus on appropriate behavior.

Try unobtrusive techniques. Ignore minor misbehavior, verbally or nonverbally signal a student who is misbehaving, remind about the rules just before doing something, and praise responsible behavior (Downing, Keating, and Bennett 2005). Also prompt correct behavior: "I like how Jeff is standing in his hula hoop waiting for instructions."

Be Consistent   Be consistent about which student behaviors are important. Pay attention to those behaviors and let other behaviors go unnoticed (as long as those behaviors are not interfering with the learning of others and are not posing safety problems).

Adapt Actions to Individual Students and Situations   Deal with individual students and individual situations. Each consequence should be specific to the child and to the situation. Do not make blanket statements about how certain misbehaviors will be handled. We advise against posting signs that indicate to the students what the specific consequences are for certain misbehaviors. The teacher needs flexibility in responding to individual student misbehavior. This approach means the teacher will not have to establish exceptions to the consequence rules for children with disabilities, as each child is treated as an individual with consequences based on the individual's needs, desires, and capabilities.

Create Consequences for Inappropriate Behavior
Create consequences (rather than punishments) that fit the inappropriate behavior. **Consequences** are related to the child's misbehavior, make the child accountable for his or her behavior, and keep the child's dignity. **Punishments,** on the other hand, are not remotely related to the misbehavior, place responsibility for correction in the hands of the teacher, and often humiliate the child (Gootman 2001). For example, a time-out may serve as a consequence or a punishment depending on the misbehavior to which it is applied. A time-out, given for the misbehavior of not completing homework, is considered a punishment because the time-out and the misbehavior are not related. However, a time-out given to a student who at the moment cannot control her or his anger is considered a consequence, since the time-out and the misbehavior are related. The time-out allows the child the opportunity to get her or his anger under control so that she or he can return to class activities without being a danger to others.

The four basic categories of consequences you can provide are as follows (Gootman 2001):

1. *You break it, you fix it.* For breaking physical objects, the student must fix it (tape the page back into the book) or pay for it (work after school in your room). For hurting someone's feelings, the student must apologize (verbally) and then offer to partner with this person in the next class activity. Establish a Repair Shop where students can fix relationships (see Box 7.8).
2. *Regain composure.* Establish a time-out spot where students go to regain control of their behavior. They return to class activities when they are ready to function appropriately.
3. *Loss of a privilege.* When students abuse a privilege, an appropriate consequence is for them to lose the privilege for a while.
4. *Reflection time.* Create a self-help desk, in addition to a time-out spot, where students go to reflect on their behavior and develop a plan for change.

In a caring community, the consequences you create for the students should have the following goals (Vitto 2003):

- Bring the teacher and student closer together (versus causing anger, resentment, and disrespect)
- Treat the student the way you as the teacher wish to be treated
- Model the social skills you want the student to possess
- Teach appropriate behavior
- Only minimally interfere with the flow of the lesson
- Give the learner the choice to redirect and then come back to activity
- Prove to be effective (eliminate undesired behavior)

Constructing viable consequences decreases inappropriate behavior while keeping the caring community atmosphere intact in the classroom and in the gymnasium.

Hold Class Meetings To address behavior issues or monitor progress in the gymnasium and classroom environment, hold class meetings on a regular basis (Flicker and Hoffman 2006). During the meetings, praise the good things that are happening and discuss the problems that still need to be solved. Students should evaluate their own behavior. Group progress could be recorded on a wall chart. Classmates might be taught to help each other make responsible behavior choices, and progress on this helping could be evaluated. Using a standardized structure for the meeting may increase the meeting's success. Lickona (1991) suggests the following format: Circle up (meeting held in circle formation), state purpose of the meeting, set the rules to be observed during the meeting, identify partners, pose the problem, provide personal thinking time, allow partners to talk about the problem, conduct whole-group discussion of the problem and solutions, and close the meeting to bring resolution to the problem.

Involve Parents and School Personnel Call a parent or other caretaker with the student present. The student talks first, and then the teacher talks to the parent. Visiting with parents or other guardians can help ensure that you are not misreading cultural differences and interpreting them as misbehavior (Gootman 2001). Another technique is to have the student write a letter to the parents or guardians describing the inappropriate behavior. A parent or guardian must sign the letter and the student must return it to the teacher.

Work with the school psychologist or behavior specialist in your building to personalize self-management techniques for specific students in the classroom. The specialist may be able to provide new ideas and fresh perspectives that will be helpful for the teacher to consider.

SHARED RESPONSIBILITY

In this section, many ideas and specific actions have been identified to help students choose responsible behavior. We again wish to emphasize that the ideas and actions are based on a philosophy where learning is a **shared responsibility** of the learners and the teacher. Thus the classroom and gymnasium become a caring community where "we are in this together." Teachers and students work together to establish a learning environment where students manage their own behavior and most of the class time is spent on learning instead of management. This philosophy takes a long-term view of helping the students. Rather than teachers trying to control student behavior (short-term, quick fix), they look to the future (long-term) and strive to induce self-management (forever fix).

However, implementing this philosophy and making it work are not easy. In fact, putting these techniques into practice is quite difficult! Community does not happen overnight (or maybe even in one semester). It takes time for students and teachers to adjust and grow into respecting each other and trusting each other's decision-making skills. It takes time for teachers to really believe the philosophy, thus changing their attitudes and actions toward students. And it helps tremendously if the entire school adopts this philosophy so it continues from teacher to teacher and from year to year.

Finally, we assume that teachers are examining their teaching methods and strategies continually to be sure they are not causing student behavioral problems. Teachers should often ask themselves these questions:

- Is this class activity meaningful? In other words, does the activity move the students forward on an important educational objective or does it just fill time?
- Is the activity at an appropriate developmental level for the students?
- Is the activity presented in an interesting way?
- Is the activity properly planned for?

Presenting relevant, meaningful, developmentally appropriate learning activities in an interesting manner goes a long way toward preventing student misbehavior.

Summary

Managing and teaching effective physical education lessons require much preparation and forethought. Most important to this effort is selecting and implementing teaching methods (direct and indirect) appropriate to the lesson objectives and capabilities of the students. Although teaching methods vary in ways of presenting information and communicating with the students, movement educators need to be prepared in giving skill explanations and demonstrations and in providing effective performance feedback to students.

To be able to focus on the teaching and learning of the physical education content, movement educators must be effective in organizing students for physical activity. This entails establishing common routines for managerial events that happen during each lesson, using those routines to reduce management time, planning how to move quickly from one activity to another, and actively supervising students to keep them on task.

Last, but not least, to focus on the teaching and learning of the physical education content, students must choose to behave responsibly. Teachers help students choose responsible behavior by establishing a caring classroom community, teaching social skills to shape behavior, and implementing student self-management techniques. The philosophy of a caring classroom and gymnasium community refers to both an attitude and a set of practices that do the following:

- Respect students for who they are
- Encourage them to be active participants in the learning process
- Allow them to learn from their mistakes (self-evaluation)
- Make the classroom a friendly place
- Use student-centered teaching approaches
- Help students take care of each other

Within that caring community, students are socialized (taught social skills) to use appropriate behaviors when interacting with others and their environment. In addition, discipline techniques encourage student self-management rather than control of student behavior by the teacher.

Chapter Activities

1. Given the following second-grade lesson content, write a lesson plan emphasizing the *organization* for teaching the lesson content:

   Introductory activity: Upon entering the gym, students immediately find a partner, join one hand (so they are now standing side by side), and skip around the gym perimeter two times.
   Lesson focus: Parachute activities
   Fitness activity: Stretching exercises with the parachute
   Closing activity: Talk about how to properly fold the parachute and put it away; then have the children do it.

2. Write your plan for nurturing a caring classroom community.

3. Write a two-page paper explaining your discipline philosophy. Include discussion of your reaction to the authors' philosophy for helping students choose responsible behavior.

4. Make a list of the class management routines you plan to implement in your classroom.

5. Write a lesson plan (for grades K–2) to accomplish the following lesson focus objectives:

   - Explore ways to creatively use a hula hoop.
   - Practice the hula hoop skills of throwing and catching with a partner and twirling the hoop around the waist.

Organize the lesson using the four-part lesson structure (intro activity, lesson focus, physical fitness activity, and closing activity). Select appropriate teaching methods. Provide possible feedback statements to be given to the students.

Internet Resources

PE Central. Information on developmentally appropriate physical education practices and programs.
www.pecentral.org
Human Kinetics. Can subscribe to print or email versions of *Teacher Education in Physical Education* (a practitioner's journal).
www.humankinetics.com/TEPE/journalAbout.cfm

Bibliography

Blakemore, C. L. 2004. Brain research strategies for physical educators. *Journal of Physical Education, Recreation, and Dance* 75(1): 31–36.

Crimmins, D., A. F. Farrell, P. W. Smith, and A. Bailey. 2007. *Positive strategies for students with behavior problems.* Baltimore: Paul H. Brookes Publishing Co.

Dodd, A. W. 1997. Creating a climate for learning: Making the classroom more like an ideal home. *National Association of Secondary School Principals Bulletin* 81(589): 10–16.

Downing, J., T. Keating, and C. Bennett. 2005. Effective reinforcement techniques in elementary physical education: The key to behavior management. *The Physical Educator* 62(3): 114–122.

Dyson, B., and S. Grineski. 2001. Using cooperative learning structures in physical education. *Journal of Physical Education, Recreation, and Dance* 72(2): 28–31.

Fairclough, S. J., and G. Stratton. 2006. A review of physical activity levels during elementary school physical education. *Journal of Teaching in Physical Education* 25: 239–257.

Flicker, E. S., and J. A. Hoffman. 2006. *Guiding children's behavior.* New York: Teachers College Press.

Glover, D. R., and D. W. Midura. 1992. *Team building through physical challenges.* Champaign, IL: Human Kinetics.

Gootman, M. E. 2001. *The caring teacher's guide to discipline*. Thousand Oaks, CA: Corwin Press.

Jones, V., and L. Jones. 2004. *Comprehensive classroom management*. Boston: Pearson Education.

Joyce, M. 1973. *First steps in teaching creative dance*. Palo Alto, CA: Mayfield.

Kirchner, G. 2005. *Towards cooperative learning in elementary school physical education*. Springfield, IL: Charles C. Thomas.

Kovar, S. 1991. Stop, look, and listen. *Kansas Health, Physical Education, Recreation and Dance Journal* 60(1): 15.

Kovar, S. K., K. L. Ermler, and J. H. Mehrhof. 1992. Helping students to become self-disciplined. *Journal of Physical Education, Recreation, and Dance* 63(6): 26–28.

Kovar, S. K., H. M. Mathews, K. L. Ermler, and J. H. Mehrhof. 1992. Feedback: How to teach how. *Strategies* 5(7): 21–25.

Lickona, T. 1991. *Educating for character*. New York: Bantam Books.

Meaney, K. S., L. K. Griffin, and M. A. Hart. 2005. The effect of model similarity on girls' motor performance. *Journal of Teaching in Physical Education* 24:165–178.

Metzler, M. W. 2005. *Instructional models for physical education*. Scottsdale, AZ: Holcomb Hathaway.

Midura, D. W., and D. R. Glover. 2005. *Essentials of team building*. Champaign, IL: Human Kinetics.

Mosston, M., and S. Ashworth. 2002. *Teaching physical education*. San Francisco: Benjamin Cummings.

Pangrazi, R. P. 2004. *Dynamic physical education for elementary school children*. 14th ed. San Francisco: Benjamin Cummings.

Prusak, K. A., and S. D. Vincent. 2005. Is your class about something? Guiding principles for physical education teachers. *Journal of Physical Education, Recreation, and Dance* 76(6): 25–28, 35.

Prusak, K. A., S. D. Vincent, and R. P. Pangrazi. 2005. Teacher talk. *Journal of Physical Education, Recreation, and Dance* 76(5): 21–25.

Siedentop, D., and D. Tannehill. 2000. *Developing teaching skills in physical education*. Mountain View, CA: Mayfield.

Vitto, J. M. 2003. *Relationship-driven classroom management*. Thousand Oaks, CA: Corwin Press.

QUICK LESSON 7.1
Movement Exploration with Beanbags

GRADES K–3

NASPE STANDARD 1 Students demonstrate competency in motor skills and movement patterns needed to perform a variety of physical activities.

LESSON OBJECTIVES

- Students practice manipulating an object (beanbag) individually and with a partner.
- Students explore (through physical activity with beanbags) the movement components (see Figure 3.1).
- Students improve their balance and coordination.
- Students improve their tossing and catching skills.

EQUIPMENT NEEDED A beanbag for each student

PREPARATION TIME None

KNOWLEDGE CONTENT

- Students understand the correct technique for tossing and catching the beanbag.
- Students can articulate the movement components.

CLASSROOM ACTIVITY Each student has a small beanbag and is standing by his or her desk. Ask the students to perform the following activities:

- Toss and catch to yourself with two hands.
- Toss as high as you can so that you can still catch the beanbag without moving from your spot on the floor.
- Toss and catch the beanbag with just your right hand, and then with just your left hand.
- Toss the beanbag with your right hand and catch it with your left; then toss with the left and catch with the right.
- Toss, clap once, and then catch the beanbag.
- Toss, clap twice, and then catch the beanbag.
- Toss, spin around in place, and then catch the beanbag.
- Toss, touch your shoulders, and then catch the beanbag.
- Toss, touch the floor, and then catch the beanbag.
- Toss the beanbag off your elbow and then catch it (off your knee, off your arm, off the instep of your ankle, etc.).
- Sit on the floor, toss and catch the beanbag (toss high and low).
- Balance the beanbag on various body parts (head, elbow, arm, shoulder) while walking around the room.
- Balance the beanbag on your knees or ankle instep and hop around the room.
- Toss beanbags for throwing accuracy (at a target on the wall, into a clothes basket or coffee can, from different distances, etc.).

If a space other than the classroom is available, most of the activities above can be performed while walking and running. The following partner activities can also be performed:

- Toss a beanbag back and forth with a partner—start close together and continue moving away from each other as long as you can successfully throw and catch the beanbag.
- Walk across the play space while tossing a beanbag back and forth to a partner.
- Run across the play space while tossing a beanbag back and forth to a partner.

ASSESSMENT Initially, with very young children, the activities are performed as a movement exploration. As students mature, the teacher can develop score sheets on which students record the number of times they can successfully perform each task (or the distance from which they can successfully hit a target). Keeping these records over time provides excellent evidence as to whether students are improving their throwing and catching skills.

SUCCESS FOR ALL For students who cannot consistently catch the tossed beanbag, use a scarf instead of a beanbag during the tossing activities. Since the scarf floats, it is easier to catch.

INTEGRATION WITH OTHER SUBJECT AREAS Math skills could be incorporated into this lesson. For example, K–3 students could do the following for many of the activities:

- Count the number of consecutive tosses caught.
- Add together the number of tosses caught (the "caught count") from several activities.
- Add together the number of tosses caught and then subtract the number of tosses missed (the "missed count") for several activities (using a tally system on a sheet of paper that is on each student's desk).

For older children, number the activities in the list to be performed and then create algebraic equations that the students must solve. For example, solve the equation $SS = (CC1 + CC2 + CC3) - (MC1 + MC2 + MC3)$, where SS equals the success score, CC1 equals the caught count from activity 1, MC2 equals the missed count for activity 2, and so on. Repeat the physical activities needed to solve the equation with the goal of maximizing SS. Design any equations you can think of. Another equation you might use is $SS = (CC1 - CC2 \times CC3) \div (CC4 + CC2 \times CC3)$.

CLASSROOM LEARNING STATION 7.1
Creating Bumper Stickers

GRADES 4–6

NASPE STANDARD 3 Students participate regularly in physical activity.

LESSON OBJECTIVES

- Students create bumper sticker sayings that promote a healthy lifestyle or present information about a healthy lifestyle.
- Students learn (or reinforce) the knowledge base on leading a healthy lifestyle.

EQUIPMENT NEEDED Manila folders (one for each student), tape, glue, construction paper, scissors, markers, and poster board

PREPARATION TIME One hour to collect needed materials and make the poster and student folders

KNOWLEDGE CONTENT Students should learn the knowledge base on leading a healthy lifestyle: what habits form a healthy lifestyle and what the benefits of a healthy lifestyle are. This knowledge base is covered in Chapter 4.

CLASSROOM ACTIVITY The following materials should be available at the learning station:

- The knowledge base in some form (on posters, in a text of the appropriate reading level, from students' class notes, etc.)
- Materials to be used to create the bumper stickers (scissors, tape, glue, construction paper, etc.)
- A folder with each student's name on it, into which the student places completed bumper stickers

Students, in groups of three or four, work at the learning station in their free time.

ASSESSMENT At some point, after all students have had a chance to work at the learning station, post the bumper stickers in the classroom. Hold a class discussion centered on the concepts displayed in the bumper stickers.

SUCCESS FOR ALL Have students with limited vision develop bumper sticker sayings by recording them however they would normally record information (on their own computer, with the aid of a helper, etc.). The knowledge base information should be available in large print or however the student normally "reads," for instance, via audiotape. A helper could design the actual bumper sticker according to instructions from the student.

For students with limited hand coordination, provide adapted tools or ready-made materials that allow them to maximize their efforts. For instance, construction paper pieces could already be cut. The student could use a stamp pad with various stamps to place designs on the bumper sticker (instead of free drawing as other students would do).

INTEGRATION WITH OTHER SUBJECT AREAS
This project could be integrated into a science unit in which students are studying human physiology. The teacher could specifically talk about what happens (physiologically) to the body during exercise (temporary effects) and the permanent effects of regular exercise on the body.

GRADES K–6

NASPE STANDARDS 5 AND 6

- Students exhibit responsible personal and social behavior that respects self and others in physical activity settings.
- Students value physical activity for health, enjoyment, challenge, self-expression, and/or social interaction.

LESSON OBJECTIVES

- Students are physically active during the school day.
- Students have fun participating in physical activity.
- Students treat their peers with respect.
- Students follow the rules established for each station.
- Students function independently and responsibly.
- Students include all group members as they complete each station.
- Students create solutions to the challenges posed at each station.

EQUIPMENT NEEDED Two buckets, various scoops (that will hold water), one stopwatch, 15 plastic crates (lightweight), ten tennis balls, one tug-of-war rope, and various items for the Fitness Course (jump ropes, cones, bamboo poles, beanbags, hula hoops, etc.)

PREPARATION TIME Two hours to collect materials and set up the stations

KNOWLEDGE CONTENT The teacher should clearly identify for the students why they are having a "challenge play day":

- To have fun
- To be physically active
- To practice respecting others
- To practice cooperation skills
- To use their creative abilities to solve the challenges posed
- To include all group members in creating solutions and performing the solutions

CLASSROOM TO PLAYGROUND ACTIVITY Set up the challenge stations on the playground. The number of stations needed depends on the number of students participating and the number of students to be placed in each group. Place the equipment needed by the appropriate station. For each station prepare a description card that explains the challenge, the rules,

and the penalties for breaking the rules (as indicated in this chapter). Allow team members to select their roles (organizer, praiser, encourager, summarizer, and recorder); however, each student's role must change when moving to the next challenge. Select challenges that allow the group to stay together for the day; so, for instance, all the challenges involve groups of six to seven students. The following are possible challenges:

- *Firefighter Drill:* Group members must move the water from one bucket to another bucket in the fastest, most accurate way. The other bucket is ten feet away. Draw or tape a line on the other bucket to mark the three-quarters full spot. Only a certain amount of water (one-quarter of the bucket) may be lost in the process. Provide a number of different scoops that will hold water. Provide a stopwatch so that team members can time their various solutions.
- *Fitness Course:* Group members must build a fitness course with certain specifications using the equipment provided (not all equipment needs to be used). Specifications might include the following:
  1. The course must contain at least three stations.
  2. Overall, the course must develop arm strength, leg strength, balance, agility, and coordination.
  3. Ways to travel between the stations must vary.
  4. The course is performed with a partner.
  When the group is ready, they complete the fitness course, and the teacher determines whether the specifications were met. (Variations: change any of the specifications to make the challenge more or less difficult based on the students' grade level. For instance, performing alone is easier than performing with a partner. K–3 students might simply be required to use a piece of equipment at each station instead of being sure they develop different fitness components.)
- *Tower Building* (for upper elementary grades): Team members must work collectively to stack lightweight plastic crates to a height just above their heads. Crates must be stacked so they are stable (not prone to falling). Then students put ten tennis balls into the top crate without letting the tower fall. (Emphasize the goal of not letting the tower fall so that this activity is safe.). Be sure this station is not close to any other equipment and that the ground is soft.
- *Spelling Names* (for lower elementary grades): Group members must spell the first name of each member of their group. A name is first spelled on the ground using jump ropes for the letters. The name is spelled again with their bodies. All group members must be part of each spelled name. The child whose name is being spelled plays the role of organizer at that

time. The teacher approves all completed spellings. (Variations: use a combination of bodies and ropes to spell names, spell both the first and the last names of each group member.)

ASSESSMENT The teacher moves around the station area and observes behaviors that indicate that students respect each other's ideas, work cooperatively, and involve all group members in solving the challenge. The teacher describes the behaviors (in writing—on a clipboard) and records the number of times they are observed. Use this information to end the play day by emphasizing the respectful, cooperative, inclusive behavior that was displayed as the students solved their challenges.

SUCCESS FOR ALL The teacher encourages groups to include group members with special needs and provides hints for how to do this as needed.

CHAPTER 8

Curriculum Integration in the Classroom

The purpose of this chapter is to identify and discuss how integrating movement with other curricular subject areas may benefit the elementary classroom teacher, physical educator, and student. The role movement plays in learning is substantiated by citing brain-based research, and its implications for teachers are discussed. Examples of ready-to-use movement activities and games are listed for various subject areas.

Objectives

After studying this chapter, you will be able to do the following:

- Describe the benefits of an integrated curriculum.
- Describe the role movement plays in learning.
- Design an integrated unit around a theme.
- Locate games and resources to incorporate movement activities into the classroom.

· ·

First-grade children, working in groups of three or four students, busily move about completing a task. One group of children can be seen executing a variety of locomotor skills, including walking, running, hopping on one foot, and galloping. A second group of children race around identifying and touching different-colored objects. A third group is lying on the floor using their bodies to spell out the word *red*. A fourth group is writing on a piece of paper. Are these children in physical education class, or are they in the elementary classroom? The answer could be either. These first-grade students are using different forms of movement and activity to practice their spelling words.

Benefits of Integrated Curriculum

People remember more when their bodies as well as their minds are active participants. According to research that indicates the importance of combining the senses in learning, people retain

- 10 percent of what they read;
- 20 percent of what they hear;
- 30 percent of what they see;
- 50 percent of what they hear and say at the same time;
- 70 percent of what they hear, see, and say;
- 90 percent of what they hear, see, say, and do (acting out, dramatizing, dancing, painting, drawing, constructing). (Fauth 1990, 160)

The terms *integrated* and *interdisciplinary* are often used interchangeably. *Interdisciplinary* is defined as "an educational process in which two or more subject areas are integrated with the goal of fostering enhanced learning in each subject area" (Cone et al. 1998, 4). In this chapter, the focus is on integrating physical education movement with other subject areas. "An attempt is made to arrange an active learning situation so that a fundamental intellectual skill or concept is practiced or rehearsed in the course of participating in the physical education activity" (Humphrey 1990, 70). **Curriculum integration** occurs in two ways: (1) movement is included in the classroom curriculum, and (2) academic subjects (classroom curriculum) are included in the physical education curriculum.

Students benefit from an integrated curriculum in many ways:

- Students benefit from an integrated curriculum when an academic concept is difficult to understand (Stevens-Smith 1999).
- Students benefit from increased information retention (Garcia and Garcia 1996).
- Students benefit by movement enhancing the understanding of abstract concepts such as shape, energy, space, and time (Cone and Cone 1999).
- Students benefit from an integrated curriculum when they are tired of sitting (Stevens-Smith 1999).
- Students benefit from information being presented in different learning styles.
- Students benefit by expressing their answers, thoughts, and ideas in a variety of ways other than traditional paper-and-pencil assessments.
- Students benefit when they see teachers working in different subject areas, teaching in different classroom space, and making similar points across subject areas (Cone and Cone 1999).

Another benefit of integration for students is that those who are not motivated about physical activity may be more interested in integrating activities that allow a measure of cognitive and physical success (Rauschenbach 1996). On the flip side, students who shine in physical education but are frustrated in other subject areas might better understand concepts encountered in a physical activity context.

CRITERIA AND PLANNING FOR INTEGRATION

Educators should consider integration a tool that is feasible and desirable in some situations but not all. Integrating activities across subject areas needs to have a purpose. "Two criteria must be met for appropriate integration: (1) activities should be educationally significant, ones desirable even if they did not include the integration feature, and (2) activities should foster, rather than disrupt or nullify, accomplishment of major goals in each subject area" (Brophy and Alleman 1991, 66).

When planning integrated learning experiences, the first question the physical educator must ask is "What learning objectives from the classroom unit will be enhanced through active learning experiences in the gymnasium?" (Westerhold 2000, 18). For example, if the classroom teacher is teaching about the human body, the game Circuit Training Through the Muscular System (Moen 1996), which is explained later in the chapter, could be played during the same time frame of presentation in the classroom. This same concept holds

Close collaboration between classroom teachers and physical educators is the key to successful integration and provides benefits for both students and teacher.

true for the classroom teacher. Classroom teachers can ask their students the following questions: "What concepts are being studied that could better be explained or experienced through a physical movement activity? What concepts are being studied that overlap with physical education terminology?" For example, the word *level* can have multiple meanings. In math, it can mean a horizontal line or plane. In physical education, there are different levels to travel: low, medium, and high. Ask students to name other meanings for the word *level*. As you discuss these different meanings, have the students physically demonstrate and act out each definition. Challenge students to demonstrate a combination of meanings (see Instant Activity 8.1).

Collaboration between physical education and classroom teachers is a key to successful integration. Integration has the potential to improve learning in the elementary classroom and physical education environment. The camaraderie developed through collaboration has a lasting positive effect on teachers as well as their students. Integrated activities that are more active can be used in the physical education class, whereas activities that are less active can be used in the elementary classroom.

Children's literature presents a wonderful opportunity for the classroom teacher, physical education teacher, dance teacher, and media specialist to collaborate and let the words move and dance off the page. "Through dance, children have the opportunity to respond to the literature in a way that recognizes their internal need to use movement as a means of

INSTANT ACTIVITY 8.1

Demonstrating the Different Definitions of the Word *Level*

Grades K–4

Equipment Needed

None

Activity

- Students move around the room in a physically low, medium, and high level.
- Students locate objects in the room that are horizontally level.

- Students move around the room in a low level while trying to maintain their backs in a horizontally level position.
- Students balance in positions that maintain different body parts in a horizontally level position.
- Students find a partner who is at eye level. They squat down while trying to remain at eye level.

Students move through the classroom at low and high levels.

expressing their meaning of the literary experience" (Cone 2000, 11). Children's imagination and reflective thinking skills are engaged as they plan and implement their creative movements to express the literature.

Teachers must take responsibility to present literature that does not contain cultural and gender stereotypes. Teachers' values and beliefs—both open and hidden—can be transmitted to children through their choice of literature (Bishop 1987). Choose a variety of literature pieces that represent all the cultures in your classroom. Ask students to bring special

books to share that represent their culture. Encourage students with a disability to share books about their disability and lead the class in a movement activity or dance. Depending on the age level, children can act out a page at a time or make an interpretation of the entire book when you are finished reading. Younger children tend to find it easier to create a dance or movement after each page. When selecting literature, visit with your school media specialist, who will have a wealth of information to share about books and will be eager to integrate activities (Flickinger, personal communication, 2005).

There are many ways to integrate literature and movement activities. These students are making shadows on a school wall as they interpret a story read by their teacher.

The following books are examples that work well for integrating literature, movement, and dance at different grade levels.

- *What Is the Sign for Friend?* by Judith E. Greenberg, might be chosen by a student with a hearing impairment. What movements and dances could represent friendships? How could sign language be incorporated in the dance? Let the students' imaginations run.
- *The Pea Patch Jig,* by Thacher Hurd, works well with students in grades 2–3. Children can experience the mischief a baby mouse gets into in a vegetable garden.
- *Ashanti to Zulu,* by Margaret Musgrove, works well with students in grades 4–5. Each letter of the alphabet is used to introduce the vastness of the African continent, the variety of African peoples, and the many African traditions. The beautiful illustrations in this book might prompt an integrative art project.
- *My Shadow,* by Robert Louis Stevenson, works well with K–2 students. Children illustrate and describe their relationship with their shadow in different situations. Read a page at a time and let the students interpret through dance, or read the entire book first.
- *Someone Special, Just Like Me,* by Tricia Brown, presents representatives of different disabilities. This book illustrates how children with disabilities enjoy lots of different things, which could include movement and dance.

For an extended activity integrating movement and literature, see Special Event 8.1 at the end of the chapter.

Sharing books about different cultures and different disabilities can promote inclusion as well as integration. These students with special needs use movement to interpret a book.

USING THE MULTIPLE INTELLIGENCES

In 1983, Howard Gardner, who coined the term *multiple intelligences,* named seven intelligences and later added an eighth. With his theory, instead of addressing intelligences as "How smart are you?" educators can ask

"How are you smart?" Although the bodily-kinesthetic intelligence is most closely related to physical activity, the use of all eight intelligences can give students an opportunity to best express themselves in the area of intelligence in which they are smartest. Students may find they relate to several intelligences.

In the United States, our schools and culture focus most of their attention on the linguistic and logical-mathematical intelligence. "Students with mild to moderate disabilities including students with learning disabilities often exhibit deficits in verbal/linguistic or logical-mathematical intelligences but show strengths in other areas" (Stanford 2003, 81). Teaching through all the intelligences can help level the playing field for all students. It is not necessary to incorporate all eight intelligences in every lesson or activity. Keeping track of when you incorporate an intelligence will help you balance your approach. The "instructional menus" (Campbell 1997) in Figure 8.1 will help you decide which intelligences can best be incorporated into a lesson or activity.

Graphic organizers are an example of an activity that can incorporate many of the intelligences. Graphic organizers promote thinking skills such as brainstorming, analyzing, comparing and contrasting, and sequencing (Mitchell and Hutchinson 2003). Table 8.1 gives an example of using each intelligence when teaching students to create a new game. Figure 8.2 shows brainstorming using a web with the topic of "locomotor skills." Draw a brainstorm web on large pieces of paper and place them around the gym walls. Place several crayons by each sheet. Fill in the middle bubble with "locomotor skills." Working in partners of two or three, ask students to demonstrate different locomotor skills and write the name of that skill in one of the empty bubbles on the web. A variation would be to have slips of paper in the middle of the gym floor with different locomotor skills written on them. Students choose a word and demonstrate that skill on their way to the wall. Partners spell out the word to each other as they copy it into the web.

Bodily-Kinesthetic Intelligence
The ability to control one's bodily motions and handle objects skillfully is **bodily-kinesthetic intelligence.** Students with this intelligence can use their bodies to express ideas and feelings, are coordinated, and like hands-on learning. Actors, dancers, swimmers, athletes, and instrumentalists are some of the people who may primarily display bodily-kinesthetic intelligence.

Linguistic Intelligence
The ability to use language in different forms—speech, reading, and writing—is

Linguistic Menu
Use storytelling to explain _____
Conduct a debate on_____
Write a poem, myth, legend, short play, or
    news article about _____
Create a talk show radio program about _____
Conduct an interview of _____ on _____

Logical-Mathematical Menu
Translate a _____ into a mathematical formula
Design and conduct an experiment on_____
Make up syllogisms to demonstrate _____
Make up analogies to explain _____
Describe the patterns of symmetry in _____
Others of your choice _____

Bodily-Kinesthetic Menu
Create a movement or sequence of
    movements to explain _____
Make task or puzzle cards for _____
Build or construct a _____
Plan and attend a field trip that will _____
Bring hands-on materials to demonstrate _____

Spatial/Visual Menu
Chart, map, cluster, or graph _____
Create a slide show, videotape, or photo
    album of _____
Create a piece of art that demonstrates_____
Invent a board or card game to demonstrate_____
Illustrate, draw, paint, sketch, or sculpt _____

Musical Menu
Give a presentation with appropriate
    musical accompaniment on _____
Sing a rap or song that explains _____
Indicate the rhythmical patterns in _____
Explain how the music of a song is
    similar to _____
Make an instrument and use it to demonstrate _____

Interpersonal Menu
Conduct a meeting to address _____
Intentionally use _____ social skills to learn
    about _____
Participate in a service project to _____
Teach someone about _____
Practice giving and receiving feedback on _____
Use technology to _____

Intrapersonal Menu
Describe qualities you possess that will help
    you successfully complete _____
Set and pursue a goal to _____
Describe one of your personal values about _____
Write a journal entry on _____
Assess your own work in _____

Naturalist Menu
Create observation notebooks of _____
Describe changes in the local or global
    environment _____
Care for pets, wildlife, gardens, or parks _____
Use binoculars, telescopes, microscopes,
    or magnifiers to _____
Draw or photograph natural objects _____

FIGURE 8.1   Multiple Intelligences Menus

Source: L. Campbell, Variations on a Theme: How Teachers Interpret MI Theory, *Educational Leadership* 55(1): 18 (1997). Used with permission.

TABLE 8.1 Teaching the Creation of New Games Through the Multiple Intelligences

INTELLIGENCE	ACTIVITY RELATED TO NEW GAME
Bodily-kinesthetic	Demonstrate the game to the class.
Linguistic	Define rules of game and equipment needed.
Logical-mathematical	Make analogies to other known games and strategies.
Musical	Create a musical jingle to promote your new game.
Spatial	Draw diagrams of the game and playing area.
Naturalist	Name objects in nature that could be used as substitutes for the equipment needed in the game.
Interpersonal	Work cooperatively in groups to design the new game.
Intrapersonal	Reflect on how this game relates to other games you are successful at.

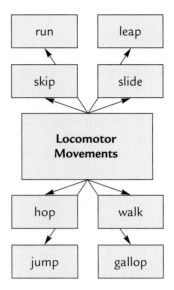

FIGURE 8.2   Brainstorm Web for Locomotor Movements

linguistic intelligence. Children with this intelligence typically do well in school. Spelling and memorizing come easily to them. Poets, authors, and speakers often have a strong linguistic intelligence.

Logical-Mathematical Intelligence   The ability to effectively use numbers, see patterns, and see things from a logical point of view is **logical-mathematical intelligence.** Those who possess strong logical-mathematical intelligence have logical, mathematical, and scientific abilities, which are especially valuable in problem-solving situations.

Musical Intelligence   The ability to use the core set of musical elements of pitch, rhythm, and timbre is **musical intelligence.** Students with strong musical intelligence remember melodies and make up their own songs. This intelligence is usually present in singers, composers, and instrumentalists.

Spatial Intelligence   The ability to create a graphic likeness of spatial information is **spatial intelligence.** People with spatial intelligence have a good sense of direction and can keenly perceive colors, lines, shapes and forms, and space, and the relationships that exist among these elements. Sailors, engineers, sculptors, painters, and architects are a few of the people who have spatial intelligence.

Naturalist Intelligence   The ability to understand, relate to, categorize, classify, and explain the things encountered in the world of nature is **naturalist intelligence.** Those with naturalistic intelligence are able to recognize plants, animals, and other parts of the natural environment such as clouds and rocks. The naturalist likes to farm, garden, hike, fish, dig for fossils, or handle animals.

Interpersonal Intelligence   The ability to notice and make distinctions among other individuals and, in particular, among their moods, temperaments, motivations, and intentions, is **interpersonal intelligence.** People in helping professions, politicians, and religious leaders often exhibit high levels of interpersonal intelligence.

Intrapersonal Intelligence   The ability to form an accurate model of oneself is **intrapersonal intelligence.** People who are strong in intrapersonal intelligence understand themselves and subsequently can use this information to guide their own behavior. People with intrapersonal intelligence are aware of their own strengths and weaknesses, are aware of their own moods, are self-disciplined, and have healthy self-esteem. Novelists, therapists, and psychologists typically exhibit strong intrapersonal intelligence.

Table 8.2 gives an example of using each intelligence when teaching students a unit on miniature golf.

BRAIN-BASED LEARNING

Brain research in the area of learning confirms that the learning process can be enhanced through physical activity (Jensen 2000b). However, critics in the area of

TABLE 8.2 Teaching Miniature Golf Through the Multiple Intelligences

INTELLIGENCE	ACTIVITY RELATED TO MINIATURE GOLF
Bodily-kinesthetic	Demonstrate and describe how body movements influence the direction of the ball. Describe what happens when you try swinging with only one hand or closing one eye.
Linguistic	Write the rules for miniature golf. Explain the rules to the class. Make a commercial advertising a miniature golf course.
Logical-mathematical	Help develop a miniature golf course in your gym or playground. Measure the distances and prepare a scale drawing.
Musical	Develop a musical skit that demonstrates the rules of miniature golf or the sequence of moves. Explain which instruments might represent the different sounds of golf.
Spatial	Using the scale drawing of the miniature golf course, use hoops, beanbags, and cones to build the course.
Naturalist	Help develop landscaping for the course.
Interpersonal	Interview someone who plays golf and report back to the class about why that person plays golf. Discuss the benefits of playing with a friend versus playing alone.
Intrapersonal	Discuss how self-talk and imagery can influence your play.

brain-based learning "warn educators to recognize the limitations of the fledging cognitive-neuroscience movement and its possible contributions to our profession. Although research findings provide limited support for the positive effects of brain-based learning, an avalanche of speculative 'brain research' assertions from educational consultants and professional developers has occurred" (Jorgenson 2003, 364). "Outside the research arena, many teachers report positive physical, academic, and social changes in students who participate in 'brain-based' activities" (Worrell, Kovar, and Oldfather 2003, 12).

Carla Hannaford, a neurophysiologist, confirms that "exercise juices up the brain, feeding it nutrients in the form of glucose and increasing nerve connections—all of which make it easier for kids of all ages to learn" (Hannaford 1995, 58). In Hannaford's book *Smart Moves: Why Learning Is Not All In Your Head* (1995), she explains that a movement-based approach to learning allows for greater brain growth in that both sides of the brain can be fully activated. The left side of the brain controls the right side of the body, while the right side of the brain controls the left side of the body. When teachers provide activities that are cross-lateral, the activities compel both sides of the brain to communicate.

Links Between Movement and Academics Three research studies showed correlations and links between academic achievement and physical activity. According to one study, students who received more hours of quality physical education per school year scored higher in English and language arts on the Massachusetts Comprehension Assessment (Tremarche, Robinson, and Graham 2007). Higher academic achievement also correlated with higher levels of fitness at each of the three grade levels measured (grades 5, 7, and 9) in research conducted by the California Department of Education (Satcher 2005). In another study, an after-school exercise program that delivered 40 minutes per day of vigorous aerobic exercise over 15 weeks resulted in improved planning abilities among overweight children at the Georgia Prevention Institute (Davis et al. 2007, 516). More research is needed on the relationship between physical activity and academic outcome.

Move More to Learn More There are many reasons why students should "move more to learn more." Integrating movement throughout the school day benefits students in the following ways:

- *Movement improves circulation.* Movement increases heart rate and circulation, and therefore arousal. Studies show increased performance following arousal activities (Tomporowski and Ellis 1986). After lunch, when arousal is low, have students hop around the room and give other students a high five as they spell each letter of their first name.
- *Movement increases the oxygen supply to the brain.* Stretching, which increases the cerebrospinal fluid flow to critical areas, is a productive movement activity. While it increases oxygen to key brain areas, stretching also provides an opportunity for the eyes and musculoskeletal system to relax

(Henning et al. 1997). After long periods of writing or reading, have students stand and stretch in a low and high position.

- *Movement regulates children's moods.* Data suggest that exercise is the best overall mood regulator (Thayer 1996, 129). When tensions are running high between students, stop and take a walk around the school playground and then resume your activity.
- *Movement encourages the body's natural motivators.* Gross motor repetitive movements stimulate the release of good chemicals (Jensen 2000b, 34). Each time you change subject areas in the classroom, have students jog in place for two minutes or complete 20 jumping jacks.
- *Movement reduces the amount of time spent sitting.* The typical student who sits much of the day runs the following risks: poor breathing, strained spinal column and lower-back nerves, poor eyesight, and overall body fatigue. Students expend much energy just to maintain a posture, even a bad one (Jensen 2000b, 35). When teaching concepts, allow students to stand and demonstrate with their bodies the concepts of big or small, tall or short, and quick or slow.
- *Movement discourages passive learning.* The brain learns best and retains most when the organism is actively involved in exploring physical sites and materials and asking questions to which it actually craves answers. Merely passive experiences tend to attenuate and have little lasting impact (Gardner 1999a, 82). Have students use their bodies to measure objects around the room and report the results during a math lesson. For example, report the length of a table in arm lengths, knuckles, or leg lengths.
- *Movement pins down thought.* A person may sit quietly to think, but remembering a thought requires that an action be used to anchor it. Students must materialize it with words. When students write, they are making connections with thought by moving their hand. Students may never need to read what they wrote, but the writing movement is necessary to build the nerve networks (Hannaford 1995, 98–99). As you read a story to students, have them write down the names of the main characters.
- *Movement anchors thought.* Talking is very much a sensory motor skill, requiring fine motor coordination of millions of facial, tongue, vocal fold, and eye muscles, as well as all the proprioceptors in the face. Talking allows students to organize and elaborate their thoughts. When students talk about what they have learned, the physical movements internalize and solidify it in nerve networks. After presenting new material, ask students to verbally share with a partner how the information relates to them personally (Hannaford 1995, 99). After reading a story, have students describe to a partner one of the story's main characters.
- *Movement generates interest.* Apathy in the classroom abates as sensory activation and active learning activities are increased (Jensen 2000a, ix). During spelling word practice, have students write the word, close their eyes, and spell the word out loud, and then move around the room and spell the word by touching each letter on visuals found in the room.
- *Movement maintains a mind-body state.* As a general rule, a purposefully planned activity lasting approximately ten minutes of every hour helps students maintain a productive mind-body state (Jensen 2000a, 27). Have students play charades to review main ideas or to dramatize a key point.

Brain Gym   Paul E. Dennison and Gail E. Dennison, researcher and teacher-dancer respectively, combined to develop a set of activities called **Brain Gym** (1989). These activities stimulate the mind and body to prepare a child to learn. Each Brain Gym activity addresses specific academic skills and behavioral or postural correlates. Brain Gym activities are categorized as follows: (1) midline movements, (2) lengthening activities, and (3) energy exercises and deepening attitudes.

Midline movements are movements that help stimulate both hemispheres of the brain at the same time. A movement on the right side of the body activates the left side of the brain, whereas a movement on the left side of the body activates the right side of the brain. Movements that use both sides of the body and cross the center midline help increase gross motor and fine motor coordination. An example of a Brain Gym midline movement is Cross Crawls. Cross Crawls is similar to walking in place with the arm and leg movements exaggerated. The student alternately moves the arm and leg on the opposite side while walking and swinging the arms. Arms can swing across to touch the opposite knee. Cross Crawls can also be done sitting. Academic skills enhanced by Cross Crawls are spelling, writing, listening, and reading and comprehension (Dennison and Dennison 1989).

The use of sign language is a fun way for students to incorporate activities that require them to cross their midline. Students can greet each other in the morning using sign language. Students can use the daily lunch count activity as a way to incorporate sign language.

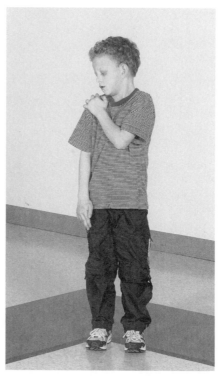
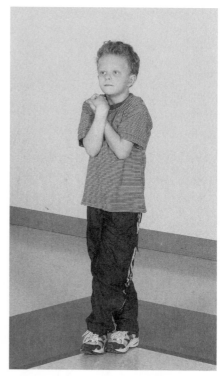

(a) Cross Crawls   (b) The Owl   (c) Hook-ups

Brain Gym activities stimulate the body and mind to help prepare a student to learn. The three sections of Brain Gym activities are midline movements such as Cross Crawls, lengthening activities such as the Owl, and energy exercises such as Hook-ups.

Figure 8.3 shows how to sign "Today for lunch we will have . . ." Students fill in the blank at the end of the sentence.

Lengthening activities compose the second category of Brain Gym activities. "Lengthening activities help students to develop and reinforce those neural pathways that enable them to make connections between what they already know in the back of the brain and the ability to express and process that information in the front of the brain" (Dennison and Dennison 1989, 16). Lengthening activities actually lengthen the muscles in the neck and shoulders, helping the muscles relax after long periods of sitting, reading, or close visual work such as solving math problems or working at a computer. An example of a lengthening activity is the Owl. To perform the Owl, grasp the muscle on one shoulder with your hand and turn your head toward that shoulder. Turn your head to the opposite shoulder and also drop the chin to the chest to relax. Breathe deeply during these movements. Repeat by grasping the muscle on the opposite shoulder. Academic skills enhanced by the Owl are listening comprehension, speech, mathematical computation, memory, and keyboard work (Dennison and Dennison 1989).

The third category of Brain Gym activities includes energy exercises and postures for deepening attitudes. "Energy exercises and postures for deepening attitudes help to re-establish neural connections between body and brain, thus facilitating the flow of electromagnetic energy through the body. These activities support electrical and chemical changes that occur during all mental and physical events" (Dennison and Dennison 1989, 23). An example of an energy exercise is Hookups, which connects the electrical circuits in the body. Hook-ups can be done sitting or standing. To get into position, cross your ankles and then extend your arms and cross your wrists. Interlock your fingers and pull your wrists back to your chest. While standing in this position for one minute, press your tongue to the roof of your mouth and breathe deeply. After one minute, uncross your legs and wrists and place your fingertips together while breathing deeply for an additional minute. Academic skills enhanced by Hook-ups are clear listening and speaking, test-taking, and keyboard work (Dennison and Dennison 1989).

Integrated Games and Activities

Students learn best when movement is involved. Use the following activities and games to collaboratively support learning in the classroom and movement

TO
Horizontal right index finger
approaches and touches
vertical left index finger

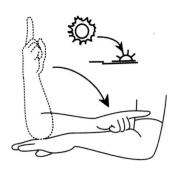

DAY
Right elbow on back of left hand,
right 1-hand drops down on
left arm

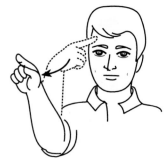

FOR
Palm-in right index finger on
forehead twists to palm-out

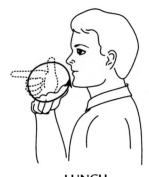

LUNCH
Thumb of L circles in and up
near mouth several times

WE
Palm-left W on right side of
chest circles to left side ending
palm-right

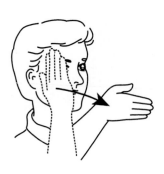

WILL
Right flat hand palm facing side
of head; arcs forward

HAVE
V-fingertips of both slightly
bent hands touch chest

FIGURE 8.3 "Today for Lunch We Will Have _____"
G. Gustason and E. Zawolkow, *Signing Exact English* (Los Alamitos, CA: Modern Signs Press, 1993).

setting. The name of the activity, grade level, skill area, equipment, and directions are listed for activities and games in the subjects of language arts, math, social studies and geography, science, anatomy and physiology, and health and nutrition. Additional games can be found by conducting an Internet search using the keywords "physical education games." Many websites have a link to integrated curriculum games. See "Internet Resources" at the end of the chapter for websites with information on equipment that can be used to integrate physical and cognitive skills, as well as multicultural experiences. Some available equipment includes alphabet beanbags, sign language beanbags, French and Spanish beanbags (for shapes, colors, and numbers), nutrition beanbags (with names of fruits and vegetables listed in foreign languages), alphabet puppets and carpet squares, letter and number vests, inflatable globe beach balls, eight-inch inflatable dice, United States puzzle, skeleton puzzle, soft Frisbees (with numbers in English and foreign languages), numbered soccer balls, and big jacks with numbers on the ends.

LANGUAGE ARTS

NAME OF ACTIVITY: Spell Around the Room

Grade Level: All

Skill Area: Spelling, cooperation, and fitness

Equipment: Alphabet letters on cards posted around the gym or classroom in random order, list of spelling words for that grade level.

Directions: Partners choose a word on the list. One partner spells the word out loud while the other partner runs and touches the letters on the wall to spell the word. One partner can touch the entire word or alternate letters with partner to spell the word. Continue until all words on the list are spelled.

Variations: Use names of sports (e.g., tennis, basketball, or soccer). As partners find letters to spell their words, pantomime the sport whose name you are spelling.

NAME OF ACTIVITY: Alphabet Balloons

Grade Level: All

Skill Area: Spelling, language arts, eye-hand coordination

Equipment: One balloon per student

Directions: Ask students to do the following:

- Tap balloon in the air, saying the alphabet in order, one letter for each tap of the balloon.
- Spell your first and last names, one letter per tap.
- Spell your age, one letter for each tap.
- Spell the color of your balloon, one letter for each tap.
- Spell spelling words, one letter for each tap.
- Spell the names of locomotor movements, one letter for each tap, and do the movement with your balloon.

NAME OF ACTIVITY: How Can I Get There?

Grade Level: K–2

Skill Area: Spatial awareness, language development

Equipment: None

Directions: Use this activity when naturally occurring situations in the classroom call for movement (i.e., lining up, changing centers, etc.). Ask students to move over, under, through, around, or between objects in the classroom as they move to the next location. To add difficulty, give combinations of directions (e.g., on your way to the next center, move under one desk and between two chairs).

NAME OF ACTIVITY: Punctuation Shuffle

Grade Level: All

Skill Area: Locomotor movements, punctuation

Equipment: None

Directions: Have students find a spot in general space. On a signal, the students move anywhere in the space using a locomotor skill designated by the teacher. On a stop signal, the teacher reads a sentence that ends in either a period or a question mark. The students form a period with the body (curl up in a tiny ball) or a question mark (lie down on the ground and make the form of a question mark).

Example question sentences: What time is it? Can you spell your name? What letter does dog start with? Who can run fast?

Example statement sentences: Count to ten. Draw with the red crayon. Stand up straight. Ride your bike tonight.

Source: J. H. Mehrhof and K. Ermler, *Physical Essentials: Kindergarten–5th Grade Physical Education Curriculum, Intermediate* (Emporia, KS: Mirror, 2001), 361.

NAME OF ACTIVITY: Letter of the Week

Grade Level: K–1

Skill Area: Letter recognition, computer use, low organizational games

Equipment: Computer with Internet access

Directions: Using the letter of the week being studied in class, have students select a game that begins with that letter. The website www.gameskidsplay.net has games listed in alphabetical order under the link "All Games." Help students read the rules for the game and use the activity as the warm-up that day.

NAME OF ACTIVITY: Jumping Words

Grade Level: All

Skill Area: Alphabet recognition, spelling, and cooperation

Equipment: Jump ropes

Directions: Ask students to form letters with their jump ropes. Walk around guessing the students' letters or work with partners to guess their letter. Students may use their bodies to help form the letters. Work in small groups to form words.

Variation: Shoe strings or yarn can be used in place of jump ropes for smaller areas.

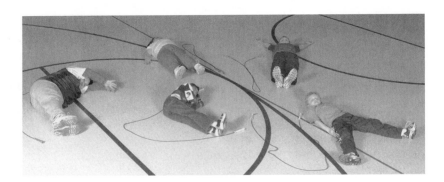

In Jumping Words, students use jump ropes and their bodies to form the first letter of their name.

MATH

NAME OF ACTIVITY: Double Dice

Grade Level: All

Skill Area: Cooperation, math facts, and fitness

Equipment: Two dice for each set of partners

Directions: Partners roll the dice. The numbers on the dice are added together (sum). Using the answer, one partner walks that many steps away from the other partner. The partner left behind copies the walker's movements to join back together, trying to reunite using the same number of steps. If both partners end up in the same spot, they score a point.

Variations: Multiply dice instead of adding them together. The first partner chooses a locomotor movement and the follower must do the same (e.g., walk, run, slide, gallop, hop).

NAME OF ACTIVITY: Fist Dribble

Grade Level: All

Skill Area: Dribbling while looking up, math skills

Equipment: Balls that dribble, one for each student

Directions: In partners, each student has a ball. Students start dribbling and hold up a fist. Partners take turns counting 1, 2, and 3, and then each student holds up fingers from 1 to 5. Students try to be the first one to yell out the number of fingers held up by the partner while maintaining the dribble.

Variations: Add or multiply the numbers held up by both partners and yell out the answer.

NAME OF ACTIVITY: Odds and Evens

Grade Level: 2–6

Skill Area: Math concepts, fitness, and social skills

Equipment: A deck of cards for each set of partners

Directions: Partners face each other each holding half the deck of cards. Decide which partner will be odd and which will be even. One partner flips a card over. If the number of the card is even, that person chases the partner across a designated line. If the number of the card is odd, the other partner is the chaser. Aces = Give your partner a compliment. Jacks = Give your partner a high five. Queens = Turn two circles in place and give your partner a double high five. Kings = Tell your partner that she or he is great.

Variations: Both partners lay a card down at the same time. Add or multiply the numbers on the cards to get the even or odd answer. If a face card and number card are laid down together, complete the face card task and then run or chase.

NAME OF ACTIVITY: Jump Rope Bingo

Grade Level: 2–3

Skill Area: Jump rope, fitness, number facts

Equipment: A blank Bingo card for each student, pencil, jump rope, and music

Directions: Students begin to jump rope to the music. When the music stops, the teacher asks a question the answer to which is a number. Students write the number in any box on the Bingo card. When the music begins again, the students begin to jump. This continues until the cards are full. The students will all get done at the same time. The teacher begins to read the answers to the questions asked. The students check off the number if they have it. When a student gets a Bingo, the game stops.

Hints: Try not to have the same number for the answer more than once. Laminate the cards and use washable markers. If you don't have enough cards, students can play in pairs or trios.

Here are some sample questions:

- How many *i*s are there in Mississippi? (4)
- How many continents are there? (7)
- How many planets are there? (8)
- What is the answer to $3 \times 5 - 4$? (11)
- How many beats to a measure in 3/4 time? (3)
- How many days are in February in a leap year? (29)
- How many inches are in a yard? (36)
- What is the answer to $27 - 8$? (19)
- How many letters does the word *Massachusetts* have? (13)

- What is the answer to 40 ÷ 8? (5)
- How many half-inches are there in a foot? (24)
- How many days are in a year? (365)

Source: J. H. Mehrhof and K. Ermler, *Physical Essentials: Kindergarten–5th Grade Physical Education Curriculum, Intermediate* (Emporia, KS: Mirror, 2001), 353–355.

• •

NAME OF ACTIVITY: Fruit Basket Upset Math

Grade Level: All

Skill Area: Locomotor skills, math

Equipment: None

Directions: Randomly place numbers 1 through 50 (or higher for upper grades) around the gym or walls of the classroom. Ask students to find a number and touch it. When the teacher says "go," students move to the next number in sequence using the locomotor skill called out. When the teacher calls out "Fruit Basket Upset," students listen for a new direction on how to find their number: count backward, count by twos, count by odd numbers, add the last two numbers touched and go to the answer, find your age.

Variations: Using manipulative objects, students toss and catch the number of times equal to the next number they are looking for.

SOCIAL STUDIES AND GEOGRAPHY

• •

NAME OF ACTIVITY: Presidential Race

Grade Level: 3–5

Skill Area: Running, tagging, dodging, spatial awareness

Equipment: A cutout of an image of each individual state, each with the number of that state's electoral votes written on it, and three presidential name tags

Directions: Ask for three volunteers to be the presidential candidates and to stand in the middle of the gym. The rest of the students are each assigned a state and are instructed to line up at one end of the gym. Each state name tag has written on it the number of electoral votes that state has in an election. The presidential candidates yell "the race is on!" and run toward the students wearing the state name tags. When one of those students is tagged by one of the presidential candidates, his or her state belongs to that candidate. The tagged student must then help that candidate capture more states. Each candidate will then add up the electoral votes gained to determine who will be the next U.S. president. Afterward, discuss electoral votes, populations, and the importance of each state in national elections.

Source: Adapted, with permission, from D. A. Stevens, 1994, "Integrated Learning: Collaboration Among Teachers," *Teaching Elementary Physical Education* 5(6): 7–8.

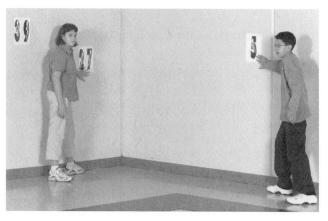

Students use both math skills and movement to play Fruit Basket Upset Math.

• •

NAME OF ACTIVITY: Walk Across Your State

Grade Level: 2–5

Skill Area: Map reading, math, and fitness

Equipment: Map of your state

Directions: Post a large map of your state in the classroom. Decide as a class what your route across the state will be. Mark it with a highlighter or a piece of yarn. Read the map to determine how many miles it is between major cities. Decide as a class (taking into account students' age level) what distance will equal a mile. For example, three laps around the playground could equal one mile. Encourage students to walk or jog the path outside and keep track of the number of miles accumulated. Let students move a marker along the map each time they have class miles to contribute. Set a class goal to make it across the state within a certain amount of time.

• •

NAME OF ACTIVITY: North and South Wind

Grade Level: All

Skill Area: Running, dodging

Equipment: Scarves or flags of two colors (blue and red)

Description: Have students find a spot in general space. Select several students to be the North Wind and give them a blue flag or scarf. Select several students to be the South Wind and give them a red flag or scarf. Explain to the students that the North Wind usually is a very cold wind and brings in weather such as snow and ice. The South Wind is usually a very warm wind and brings in warm weather. On a signal from you, the North Winds try to tag students. If the North Wind tags a student, that student must begin to move in a very slow motion. The student must continue moving slowly until tagged by the South Wind. When tagged by the South Wind, a student can resume moving quickly or at a normal pace. Change North and South Winds frequently.

Source: J. H. Mehrhof and K. Ermler, *Physical Essentials: Kindergarten–5th Grade Physical Education Curriculum, Intermediate* (Emporia, KS: Mirror, 2001), 371.

NAME OF ACTIVITY: I Have, Where Is

Grade Level: 4–5

Skill Area: States and capitals, state birds, famous people, and fitness

Equipment: "I Have" cards, state maps

Description: Post state maps around the gym in random order. Have each student find a partner. Give each pair a set of "I Have" cards. The pairs find a spot in general space. Have each pair indicate which person is number 1 and which is number 2. On a signal from you, the 1s pick up the first card and look at the clue (e.g., "I Have Topeka"). The pair guesses which state has Topeka and then number 1 runs to touch the state and comes back to number 2. While the number 1s are running to the state maps, the number 2s must spell the name of the state while doing ski-jumps. When number 1 returns, number 2 picks up the next card and the roles are now reversed. This process continues until all the cards are finished.

The information on the cards may vary depending on what is appropriate for the children's developmental level. For example, states and capitals might be appropriate for some students. State nicknames (or state birds or famous people) might be more appropriate for other students.

Source: J. H. Mehrhof and K. Ermler, *Physical Essentials: Kindergarten–5th Grade Physical Education Curriculum, Advanced* (Emporia, KS: Mirror, 2001), 370.

SCIENCE

NAME OF ACTIVITY: Newton's Laws

Grade Level: 3–5

Skill Area: Principles of force and motion, movement, eye-hand coordination

Equipment: Baseball bats, balls of three different weights (small and light, medium, larger and heavier), seesaw, swing, heavy rock, balloon

Directions:

1. Newton's first law: inertia
   [An object at rest tends to stay at rest and an object in motion tends to stay in motion with the same speed and in the same direction *unless acted upon by an unbalanced force.*]
   - Have students run with speed for a distance of 50 feet and then rest. Next have them run with speed for a distance of 50 feet, stopping and starting ten times along the way, and then rest. Finally, have them run with speed for a distance of 50 feet, changing direction sharply every ten feet, and then rest. Ask students, "At what

moments did you feel you had to exert more effort? Which run was the easiest? Which took the most effort?"

2. Newton's second law: Force = mass × acceleration [To move a heavy object it takes more force from you than if it was a light object.]
   - Have students use a lot of force to hit a baseball with a bat. Then have them use very little force to hit the same baseball with the same bat. Ask them, "Which time did the ball travel faster?"
   - Have students hit a small, light ball with a baseball bat. Then have them hit a larger, heavier ball with the same amount of force. Ask them, "Which ball traveled faster?"
   - Have each student balance with a classmate on a seesaw. Ask, "How many times can you go up and down in 30 seconds?" Add another person to each side of the seesaw, but only the original two can put their feet on the ground. Ask students, "Using the *same* amount of force, how long does it take for you to go up and down that same number of times? If you were to do it in the same 30 seconds, would you have to push harder?"

3. Newton's third law: For every force (action) there is an equal and opposite force (reaction).
   - Ask students, "Can you jump in the air without first pushing down into the floor?"
   - Have students sit quietly, suspended on a swing with a large rock in their lap. Then say, "Throw the rock in front of you (making sure no one is there!). What happens to you and the swing?"
   - Have students blow up a balloon and then release the air. Ask them, "What happens to the balloon as the air escapes? What is the relationship between the swing and the balloon?"

NAME OF ACTIVITY: Magnetic Field

Grade Level: 3– 4

Skill Area: Electricity and magnetism, creative movement

Equipment: Colored pinnies

Directions: Create a short dance sequence by having students move about the room as if they were all magnets with only a north pole. What would happen? They would repel each other, and as a result, the magnetic force would become so great as children approach one another that they could get only so close before they would move off in different directions. The students' movement selections should show choices in moving on different levels, in different directions, and at different speeds. They can also experiment with bringing specific body parts close together, showing greater tension as parts come closer together, and moving quickly away in different directions.

Pretend that the entire class is working in a magnetic field. Have each student choose whether she or he wants to be a north pole or a south pole. Use a signal or code for identifying poles; for example, a red band or pinny or thumbs up for north, a green band or pinny or thumbs down for south. Students should move around the room in different ways, such as hopping, skipping, sliding, crawling, and so on. As they approach another person, they will come closer and attach to each other by holding hands if they are opposite poles. They will repel and move away from each other if they are like poles. Once two poles attach, they must move around together while linked. Eventually the whole class will end up attached to each other.

Source: Adapted, with permission, from T. P. Cone, P. H. Werner, S. L. Cone, and A. Woods, 1998, *Interdisciplinary Teaching Through Physical Education* (Champaign, IL: Human Kinetics), 165–166.

• •

NAME OF ACTIVITY: Water Molecules

Grade Level: 2–5

Skill Area: Gases, movement

Equipment: Drum

Directions: Help children become aware that water is the only known natural substance that can be in the form of a liquid, a solid, or a gas. Discuss with students what percentage of the surface of the earth is water and what percentage of the human body is made of water. Then ask students to stand in a circle and move their bodies fluidly like water while you play the drum. While the children are moving (nonlocomotor), start slowing down the drum and ask what happens to water when it gets

Students jump up and down to demonstrate the movement of water molecules in this activity that integrates science and movement skills.

colder, and colder, and colder. Bang the drum once more and stop (this is the student's signal to freeze). "It turns to ice," they will say. Next say, "When I bang the drum once more, turn into an ice sculpture [bang]. Now make an ice sculpture on a different level [bang], and another level [bang]."

"Let's warm the ice. What will happen?" As you play the drum a little faster, the ice will melt into water molecules again (the children begin to move again). Keep playing the drum faster and faster, telling students that the water is getting hotter and hotter. Ask, "What do you think will happen to the water?" Briefly discuss evaporation as the children move about with more motion (they can add locomotion) to the faster drumbeat. Now cool them down again by slowing down the tempo as they become water again, ice again, vapor, water, and finally end in ice sculptures, which can melt into puddles onto the floor.

Reprinted with permission from *Minds in Motion* by Susan Griss. Copyright © 1998 by Susan Griss. Published by Heinemann, Portsmouth, NH. All rights reserved.

ANATOMY AND PHYSIOLOGY

• •

NAME OF ACTIVITY: Muscle Tag

Grade Level: All

Skill Area: Identifying muscles, fitness

Equipment: None

Directions: Assign several students to be "it." Those who are "it" chase and tag students on the muscle that is designated by the teacher. Change muscles each time you change chasers. When tagged, students need to freeze and raise their hand until another student comes over to them. Both students perform a stretch or strengthening activity for that particular muscle. Both students are then free to run again.

• •

NAME OF ACTIVITY: Speed It Up

Grade Level: All

Skill Area: Understanding heart rate, fitness

Equipment: Stopwatch

Directions: Discuss with students what happens to their heart rate when they exercise with greater intensity. Ask them to place their hand on their heart and decide whether it is beating fast or slow. For older students, they can actually take their heart rate. Ask students to perform different tasks and then feel their heart and decide whether it is beating faster or slower. Have students do one of the following activities: run across the gym or classroom, roll over two times on the floor, pretend to jump rope 25 times in place, watch a television show, play a video game, turn the rope for long ropes, and pretend to in-line skate across the floor. Give students enough time during the slower task to let their hearts slow down enough for them to recognize it.

● ●

NAME OF ACTIVITY: Circuit Training Through the Muscular System

Grade Level: All

Skill Area: Identification of skeletal muscles, activities to stretch and strengthen muscles

Equipment: Two large posters, one with anterior muscles and one with posterior muscles; pictures of individual muscles and exercise to be performed with that muscle, station numbers, Dyna-Bands, dumbbells

Directions: Using stations set up for circuit training, students learn the names and locations of major skeletal muscles and appropriate exercises to strengthen or stretch those muscles. Stations are set up with the posterior muscles on one side of the gym and the anterior muscles on the opposite side. Beginning with station 1 (gastrocnemius) just above the feet on the body's posterior side, stations are numbered consecutively, moving along the gym toward the head. For anatomical accuracy, anterior muscle stations are located directly across from their respective contralateral muscle whenever possible. For example, the gastrocnemius station is located directly across from the anterior tibialis station.

Station numbers and signs can be taped to a chair or taped on the gym wall. Each station has a sign with an individual muscle colored on it and a corresponding stretch or exercise for that muscle. Color muscles on the large posters to match the color of the muscles on the individual sheets. Use a different color for each muscle. Pictures of the stretch or strengthening activity may need to be added for younger students. Your physical education specialist, school nurse, physical therapist, or media specialist are all good resources for finding pictures of muscles. Students spend 30 to 45 seconds at each station and rotate on the teacher's command or when the music stops. Suggested station exercises:

1. *Gastrocnemius* (stretch). Standing with the back leg straight and the front leg bent, perform ten-count static, stretching one leg at a time with hands on a wall or on the bent front knee.
2. *Hamstrings* (stretch). Sitting with one leg straight and the other knee bent, perform ten-count static, stretching one leg at a time.
3. *Gluteus maximus* (strengthen). Kneel on all fours. Pull one knee toward nose, and then extend straight leg horizontally (no higher). Repeat with other leg, alternating legs.
4. *Trapezius and latissimus dorsi* (strengthen). Sit on floor with legs straight and extended in front of body. With hands by hips, arms straight, and fingers pointing toward toes, push up so that your bottom and legs come off the floor. Hold briefly, return to resting position, and repeat. For young children, place a

Circuit training boosts muscular strength as well as improving students' knowledge of the muscular system. These students are working at the biceps and triceps stations.

squeaky toy under the gluteus maximus so that the toy squeaks each time they return to the floor.
5. *Posterior deltoid* (strengthen). Holding a Dyna-Band in front of body with elbows straight, pull horizontally to sides of body (horizontal abduction). Repeat.
6. *Triceps* (strengthen). Holding a Dyna-Band behind the head and neck with elbows flexed, pull out to sides until arms straighten. Repeat.
7. *Biceps* (strengthen). Using dumbbells of appropriate weights, lift one at a time by flexing elbows. Weaker students can use both hands on one weight. Keep back straight, standing with back against a wall or another student's back.
8. *Anterior deltoid and pectoralis major* (strengthen). Perform a modified vertical fly. Holding a Dyna-Band in front of the body with elbows flexed, cross arms at the wrist, and push toward sides (laterally, left hand pushing toward right side, right hand pushing toward left side—horizontal adduction) as many times as possible.
9. *Rectus abdominus* (strengthen). Perform oil well situps. Using one ball for each set of partners, do a bent knee curl-up and pass ball to partner. Partner lies down, sits up, and passes ball back. Do as many as possible.
10. *Abdominal obliques* (strengthen). Lie down on the floor and put legs (from knees down) on a chair. Cross arms on chest, and perform as many twisting curl-ups, or crunches, as possible. Touch left elbow to right quadriceps and right elbow to left quadriceps. This can also be done with feet flat on the floor.
11. *Quadriceps* (strengthen). Do lunges. Step out with the right foot, bending the right knee until you feel

a stretch in right quadriceps. Bring right foot back, and then step out with left foot until you feel it in left quadriceps. Repeat.

12. *Anterior tibialis* (strengthen). Sit on a chair. Leaving heels on floor, lift up feet together as many times as possible. Put fingers on the anterior tibialis muscles and feel the muscles working. Young children can put a squeaky toy between their feet and make the toy squeak every time they lift their toes.

Source: S. Moen, Circuit Training Through the Muscular System, *Journal of Physical Education Recreation, and Dance* 67(2): 18–20 (1996). Reprinted with permission of the American Alliance of Health, Physical Education, Recreation, and Dance, 1900 Association Dr., Reston, VA 20191.

HEALTH AND NUTRITION

• •

NAME OF ACTIVITY: Junk the Junk Food

Grade Level: All

Skill Area: Distinguishing between healthy and unhealthy foods, pathways, and levels

Equipment: Laminated cards with pictures of food on each card (healthy and unhealthy)

Directions: Scatter the cards around the room facing down so the food cannot be seen. The teacher or a student calls out a pathway (e.g., zigzag, curved, straight) and a level (high, medium, low). Using the pathway and level named, students move to a food card and look at it. If it is a healthy food, the student picks the card up and progresses to a new card. If the student thinks it is an unhealthy food, she or he squats and freezes until tagged by another student. The student squatting explains why the food is unhealthy, and both partners run to a designated "junk pile" in the room or gym and discard the picture in the pile. When all pictures are gone from the floor, stop and celebrate as a class for junking unhealthy food.

Variation: For older students, name the food group the unhealthy food is in and name a replacement food in that food group that would be healthy.

• •

NAME OF ACTIVITY: Relaxation Walking

Grade Level: All

Skill Area: Relaxation

Equipment: None

Directions: At the end of a class period or when you are specifically teaching about relaxation, take your students on a relaxation walk. Students use imagery to relax as they listen to you tell a story. Make the story appropriate to the grade level. The following story works with younger students.

"Everyone find a nice cozy place to lie on the floor. Make sure you have enough room to move your arms and legs without touching another student. Close your eyes and take a walk with me in your mind. Let your muscles act like they are in the story and follow along. Let's pretend it is winter outside. You can hear the wind blowing through the trees, and snow is lightly falling from the big blue sky. Let's go play outside. Everyone put on your boots and coats and take a walk with me. The air is cool and crisp, and the snow sloshes under our boots. You are making tracks across the yard with your footprints. Let's build a snowman. Bend over and roll a snowball for the base of the snowman. The snow is wet and heavy. Roll another ball for the middle section. Tighten your muscles as you lift the heavy snowball up for his tummy. Roll the last ball of snow for his head. The snowman is almost as tall as you are. We've been outside for a long time. You're starting to get cold. Burr, your muscles are tense and tight. Let's go inside and warm up. As you walk into the house with your wet boots and clothes, the smell of chocolate chip cookies fills the warm air. Take off your boots and put on dry clothes. As you eat a cookie, stand by the fireplace and get warm. Pretend you are a snowman getting warmer and warmer. Your head starts to droop and your arms and legs go limp. You are melting closer and closer to the ground. Your snowman is melted, and you are a puddle of water lying on the floor. Your muscles are relaxed and loose. Thank you for taking a walk with me today. Open your eyes and sit up when you are ready."

Variation: Some students may need your assistance to relax. Circulate around the class and gently wiggle a leg or arm of a student who looks tense or tight. Whisper to the student that you are going to touch their arm or leg to check for relaxation.

DESIGNING THEME UNITS IN SUBJECT AREAS

A theme can provide a means for integration between subjects. The integrative activities are conducive to teaching through the multiple intelligences. Learners with all the different intelligences will have opportunities to shine. See Classroom Learning Station 8.1 at the end of the chapter for ideas on how students can generate themes. The theme of the Olympics provides a richness that naturally allows it to cross disciplines, thus encouraging integration. The spirit of an Olympic theme can encourage collaboration, sportsmanship, and good will. Examples are listed (Combs 1995) for ways the theme of the Olympics can be integrated across subject areas.

OLYMPIC MATH

■ Measure the distance of throwing events. Plot a graph to show class scores or a class average over several days' attempts.

■ The summer Olympic Games occur every four years. In Figure 8.4, fill in the year each city hosted

The Summer Olympic games are held every four years. Fill in the blanks to indicate what year each city was the host.

Year	Location
1896	Athens, Greece
_____	Paris, France
_____	St. Louis, Missouri, U.S.A.
_____	London, England
_____	Stockholm, Sweden
_____	Not Held (World War I)
_____	Antwerp, Belgium
_____	Paris, France
_____	Amsterdam, The Netherlands
_____	Los Angeles, California, U.S.A.
_____	Berlin, Germany
_____	Not Held (World War II)
_____	Not Held (World War II)
_____	London, England
_____	Helsinki, Finland
_____	Melbourne, Australia
_____	Rome, Italy
_____	Tokyo, Japan
_____	Mexico City, Mexico
_____	Munich, West Germany
_____	Montreal, Canada
_____	Moscow, USSR
_____	Los Angeles, California, U.S.A.
_____	Seoul, South Korea
_____	Barcelona, Spain
_____	Atlanta, Georgia, U.S.A.
_____	Sydney, Australia
_____	Athens, Greece
_____	Beijing, China
_____	London, England

FIGURE 8.4   Olympic Math: Host Cities of the Summer Olympic Games

T	A	B	L	E	T	E	N	N	I	S
W	A	T	E	R	P	O	L	O	W	N
E	V	Z	A	S	W	G	Q	I	A	L
I	U	C	D	F	N	K	M	I	V	L
G	K	A	W	I	A	M	R	B	S	A
H	C	N	X	J	I	T	A	C	G	B
T	F	O	H	N	S	D	I	N	S	D
L	B	E	G	E	M	T	I	K	O	N
I	M	N	U	I	S	C	P	Q	C	A
F	Z	Q	N	A	N	V	T	R	C	H
T	E	T	N	E	B	A	L	E	E	M
I	O	M	F	Y	R	E	H	C	R	A
N	Y	C	Y	C	L	I	N	G	Z	E
G	N	I	V	I	D	J	U	D	O	T

Table tennis, water polo, archery, judo, cycling, diving, weightlifting, canoe, soccer, team handball, boxing, swimming, equestrian, badminton, gymnastics, fencing

N	C	L	L	A	B	E	S	A	B	D
O	T	R	G	N	I	T	H	C	A	Y
L	V	L	L	A	B	T	F	O	S	Y
H	O	T	R	A	C	K	B	H	K	E
T	L	H	R	J	L	N	O	Q	E	K
A	L	S	O	U	F	O	D	K	T	C
T	E	M	W	L	T	O	G	E	B	O
N	Y	H	I	I	S	N	N	C	A	H
E	B	J	N	O	I	N	K	R	L	D
P	A	G	G	T	I	T	W	N	L	L
G	L	B	H	S	D	L	M	C	U	E
S	L	C	P	T	Y	B	I	A	R	I
T	A	E	K	W	O	N	D	O	T	F
T	B	W	R	E	S	T	L	I	N	G

Basketball, baseball, field hockey, pentathlon, shooting, rowing, tennis, track, volleyball, wrestling, yachting, softball, taekwondo

FIGURE 8.5   Summer Olympic Events Seek-a-Word

the Olympics. Make a chart for the dates of the winter Olympic Games. Make the chart on poster board and laminate it for use with washable markers or make individual work sheets.

OLYMPIC HISTORY

- Collaborate with your media specialist and physical education specialist to provide reading material on the Olympics. Study the early Greek Olympic Games and discuss what events were held. What events are held in the modern-day Olympics?
- Research and discuss the many symbols associated with the Olympic Games—doves, the Olympic rings, palm branches, the Olympic motto, the Olympic torch, the Olympic oath.
- Play *Olympic Jeopardy* with your students (see Quick Lesson 8.1 at the end of the chapter).

OLYMPIC SOCIAL STUDIES

- Locate Greece and the other host countries of the Olympic games on a map.

- Study different countries that athletes come from. What is their language? What is their culture like? What is the climate and weather like?
- Choose an Olympic hero and write a report about her or him. Share your findings with the class.

OLYMPIC LANGUAGE ARTS

- Add the name of Olympic events to the spelling list each week.
- Write a story about what sportsmanship means to you.
- Read books on the Olympics.
- Play seek-a-word (see Figure 8.5) to find the names of Olympic events. Laminate the puzzle on poster board for use with washable markers.
- Write reports on athletes.
- Make a list of verbs that describe the movements of different events.

OLYMPIC SCIENCE

- Study aerodynamics. Why do some objects fly longer than others? Olympic officials were forced

These students sign "I'm a winner" after each activity as part of an Olympic theme unit.

to redesign the javelin to make it less aerodynamic so it could not fly as far, therefore reducing the chance of injury to others. Conduct an experiment in aerodynamics. Have students choose three to five items of different sizes and weights to throw, such as toilet paper tubes, tennis balls, large playground balls, erasers, shoes or boots, paper airplanes, and straws. Let students make predictions about which item will fly the farthest and closest and predict the distance the object will fly. After students have tested the items, measure the distances and plot them on a graph. Let students discuss how accurate their predictions were.

OLYMPIC SIGN LANGUAGE

- Learn the Olympic oath in sign language (see Figure 8.6) and say and sign the oath each day.
- Learn to sign "I'm A Winner" (see Figure 8.7). Have students sign "I'm A Winner" after each attempt of an activity.

OLYMPIC FOREIGN LANGUAGE

- Learn to say "hi," "go," "stop," "run," and "very good" in different languages. Use these words when studying countries where those languages are spoken or playing games from those countries. Table 8.3 lists words from several countries.

OLYMPIC ART

- Study pictograms. Let students design their own pictograms for different Olympic events.
- Study flags from different countries and reproduce the flags using different art mediums.
- Study the Olympic rings and reproduce them.
- Design an Olympic bookmark.

OLYMPIC MUSIC AND DRAMA

- Collaborate with the music teacher to find Olympic music.
- Have students create dances to different Olympic music.
- Learn the national anthem from another country.
- Play charades, acting out Olympic events.
- Choreograph an opening ceremony for the class or school to participate in. Include a parade of nations and an Olympic torch run.

OLYMPIC PHYSICAL EDUCATION

- Laminate illustrations of different countries' flags that students have produced and cut them into puzzle pieces. Have relay teams race to put their flag puzzle together. Have flags displayed for students to look at and copy.
- Using colored hula hoops or laminated rings, conduct relay races to form the Olympic rings in the correct color order.
- Recite the modified Olympic oath in sign language each class period (see Figure 8.6).
- Participate in activities that symbolize the early Greek Olympic events—have students design chariot races.
- Participate in activities that symbolize modern-day Olympic events:
  Sprints: Laminate letters of the alphabet and spread them on the floor. Make several duplicates of the most commonly used letters. As individuals, small groups, or relay races, have students find letters to form names of Olympic events (e.g., sprints, distance, run, hurdles, shot put, discus, javelin, relays). Have a designated spot to set letters and words down.
  Hurdles: Place pieces of foam on the floor to serve as obstacles to jump over or run around during the alphabet sprints.
  Distance events: Make one lap around the gym equal 400 meters. Run distance events accordingly.
  Shot put: Use water balloons, weighted balls,

(text continues on page 253)

WE

Palm-left W on right side of chest circles to left side ending palm-right

PROMISE

Index from chin, to rest flat hand against top of left hand

IN

Fingertips of right flat-O enter left horizontal O

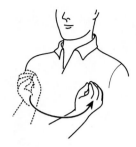

OUR

O-hand on right side of chest, circles to left

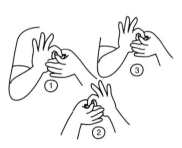

OLYMPIC

9-fingers link alternately three times in the form of a triangle

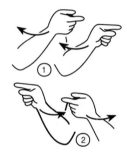

GAMES

G-hands, one palm-out, one palm in, swing back and forth, pivoting at wrists

TO

Horizontal index finger approaches and touches left vertical index finger

SHOW

Index on left palm, both move forward

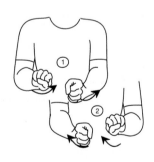

SPORTS..

S-hands swing side-to-side

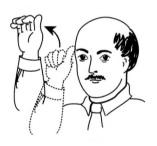

MAN ....

A on temple, then measure height with bent hand

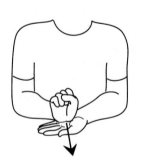

SHIP

S on palm, both move forward

AND

Palm-in horizontal 5-hand pulls to right, close to flat-O

FIGURE 8.6 Modified Olympic Oath in Sign Language

G. Gustason and E. Zawolkow, *Signing Exact English* (Los Alamitos, CA: Modern Signs Press, 1993).

FOLLOW
Right A follows left A,
both move forward left

THE
Palm-in T; twist to
palm-out

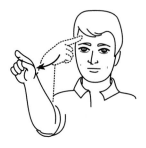

RULES
R on the fingers of left
vertical hand; then moves
down to the heel

FOR
Palm-in right index
on forehead twist to
palm-out

THE
Palm-in T; twist to palm-out

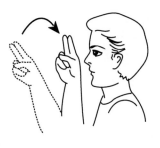

HONOR
Right H-hand arcs down
and back to near forehead

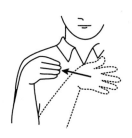

AND
Palm-in horizontal 5-hand
pulls to right, close to
flat-O

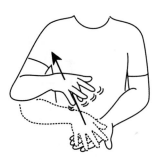

GLORY
Palm of 5 on palm,
right lifts off, fingers
fluttering

OF
Open hands approach and
link thumbs and index fingers

OUR
O-hand on right side of
chest, circles to left

COUNTRY
Palm-in Y rubs arm in
circle near elbow

Students put country flag puzzles together as part of an Olympic relay.

I'M
Palm-left I-hand on chest

A
Palm-out A moves slightly right

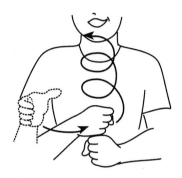

WINNER
Close right S on left S; spiral right S quickly upward

FIGURE 8.7 "I'm a Winner" in Sign Language
G. Gustason and E. Zawolkow, *Signing Exact English* (Los Alamitos, CA: Modern Signs Press, 1993).

TABLE 8.3 Words from Eight Countries

The phonetic pronunciation appears in parentheses, with the exception of England.

COUNTRY	GREETING	GO	STOP	RUN	VERY GOOD
United States (English)	Hello (hel loh)	Go (goh)	Stop (stop)	Run (run)	Very good (ver ee guud)
Germany (German)	Guten tag (gu ten tak)	Los (los)	Haltet (halt et)	Lauft (lauft)	Sehr gut (zer gut)
Sweden (Swedish)	God dag (good dag)	Gå (go)	Stanna (stah na)	Spring (spring)	Mycket bra (my kit bra)
Italy (Italian)	Ciao (chow)	Andate (ahn da tay)	Fermate (fer mah tay)	Correte (kor re tay)	Va benissimo (vah ben ee see mo)
The Netherlands (Dutch)	Goed dag (gud dag)	Klaar af (klahr off)	Stop (stop)	Lopen (lop en)	Zeer goed (zer gud)
Mexico (Spanish)	Hola (o la)	Anden (ahn den)	Paren (pah ren)	Corran (cor rahn)	Bien hecho (byen aitch o)
France (French)	Bonjour (bon joor)	Allez (ah lay)	Arrêtez-vous (ah reh tay voo)	Courez (koo ray)	Très bien (tray byeh)
England (English)	Wotcher (howdy)	Look slippy (get going)	Halt (stop)	Flit (move)	Smashing (terrific)

balloons filled with rice, or make papier-mâché shot puts of different weights.

Discus: Throw regular or foam Frisbees for distance.

Boxing: Borrow boxing gloves from students. Set up several boxing stations: (1) box balloons hanging from strings, (2) box loose balloons in the air, (3) box mats set along the wall, (4) box blow-up toys, (5) box beach balls, (6) box tetherballs, (7) dribble a playground ball using a boxing motion, and (8) perform shadowboxing.

Canoeing, kayaking, and yachting: Place a rubber raft or an air mattress on scooters. Take turns riding in and pushing boats. In the gym, make paper boats and blow them across the floor. Use toy boats for relay races using different locomotor skills. If you have access to a swimming pool, have toy boat races, floater races using hands as paddles, or rubber raft races.

Fencing: Use cardboard tubes to fence with each other. Tape a tack on the end of a dowel rod and fence with balloons taped to a wall. Use tubes to fence with swinging balloons and balls hanging from strings.

Shooting: Shoot water from squeeze bottles (drinking bottles or soap dish bottles) at targets. Shoot water to knock over a tower of objects. Shoot water to move balloons across the playground. Use air in empty squeeze bottles to push ballons across the floor to a target.

These are but a few ideas of how to integrate a unit on the Olympics. Let your imagination be your guide. Encourage students to help plan the unit and develop meaningful projects and activities. Invite local heroes to speak to your class or school. Inquire whether anyone has a parent or friend who has been an Olympic athlete or has been associated with the Olympics in any way.

Cultural Integration

As you collaborate with other teachers to integrate movement and the academic subjects, also work to integrate the study of cultures. Games from different cultures provide a rich history of how children from other places and peoples play together. **Cultural integration**—studying and learning games from other cultures—teaches students that all cultures are valued and that they can learn from all cultures. A good resource is the Passport to Play curriculum (www.passport2play.com), which is a cross-curricular program teaching games from different countries. It combines physical education, health, language arts,

geography, and art. There is also an emphasis on healthy eating habits.

DIVERSITY AND TECHNOLOGY

To integrate diversity and technology, have students develop a multicultural game website using a specific website (www.germantownacademy.org/Academics/MS/6th/MCGAMES/Index.htm) (Smith and Owens 2000). The students' website will have the following features:

- A directory of many games from different cultures
- Links to additional websites that have multicultural games
- Research tips that helped the students find and learn about the games on their website
- A unit overview that describes the steps students took to find the games and create the website
- The template the students used to produce their research findings

To find additional multicultural games, conduct an Internet search using the key words "multicultural games."

(Reprinted, with permission, from N. K. Smith and A. Owens, Multicultural Games: Embracing Technology and Diversity, *Strategies: A Journal for Physical and Sport Educators* 13(5): 18–21. Copyright 2000 by the American Alliance for Health, Physical Education, Recreation and Dance, 1900 Association Drive, Reston, VA 20191.)

DIVERSITY AND RESEARCH

Diversity and research can be combined to teach students how to "analyze, synthesize, and evaluate" games (Scharenberg 2001, 36–37). Games can help students use higher order thinking skills. During the analysis stage, students analyze games from other cultures to find the games' history, equipment, rules, and strategy. In the synthesis stage, students working in groups develop their own games. Each group's game needs to have a title, rules, equipment, players, strategy, criteria for winning and losing, history, and scoring. Make any necessary equipment available to students. After the development of their game, groups present a written report of their game and teach the game to their classmates.

The evaluation stage consists of evaluating other groups' games. One possibility would be to partner with a class from a different state or country to share and evaluate each other's games by videotape. Or you could also partner with younger and older students in your school. The students benefit from collaboration and teamwork. Refer back to Table 8.1 to see how this activity incorporates the multiple intelligences.

DIVERSITY AND ACADEMIC SUBJECTS

Integration of games and activities from different cultures can complement many subject areas. During history and social studies, introduce games that were played in the culture and time period being studied. During math, introduce games that emphasize unique scoring methods or incorporate math concepts. One example is found in *Multicultural Games* (Barbarash 1997). The game "How Many" originated in Tanzania. The game calls for three or more participants and is appropriate for children ages six and older. Equipment required is a large supply of counters, such as pebbles, corn kernels, or beads.

> How to play: Each player begins with the same number of counters (15 to 20 pebbles or beads). Be sure the size of the counters is appropriate to the age of the players. Number the players. Player 1 secretly chooses between zero and four counters to hide in his or her fist and then asks player 2, "How many?" Player 2 guesses how many are hidden. If the guess is correct, the hider gives the counters to the guesser. If the guess is wrong, the guesser pays a one-counter penalty to the hider. End the game at a prearranged time or when one player has all the counters. (Adapted, with permission, from L. Barbarash, 1997, *Multicultural Games* (Champaign, IL: Human Kinetics), 15.

When studying health, play games from different countries that emphasize strength building. The book *Games from Long Ago and Far Away* (Carr 2001) divides games into eight categories: (1) blindfold activities, (2) strength builders, (3) hopscotch, (4) jacks, (5) races and relays, (6) sports, (7) toss-throw-catch, and (8) tag.

Children in Puerto Rico play the game Rooster to build strength to maintain health. The game calls for two or more participants and is appropriate for children ages eight and older.

> How to play: All players stand inside a marked circle. Each player places a three-foot stick

The game Rooster, from Puerto Rico, helps build strength and balance.

behind the knees, squats down, wraps the arms under the stick, and clasps her or his hands in front of the shins. On the signal "Go!" players try to knock the other players off balance so they will either fall over or release their hands to stop themselves from falling over. (From Thomas J. Carr, *Games from Long Ago and Far Away: Ready-to-use multicultural P.E. Activities for Elementary Students*. Reproduced by permission of Pearson Education, Inc.)

For an art project, encourage students to study hopscotch patterns from different countries, reproduce these patterns, and learn the specific rules for each variation. *Hopscotch Around the World* illustrates hopscotch games in 19 geographical areas (Lankford 1992). As students learn about children and games from other cultures, they learn that one commonality they already have with all children is the language of smiles and laughter.

DIVERSITY AND DANCE

Students learn to respect each other when they have a better understanding of each other's cultural background. Dance and movement can be found in every country. Learning dances from different countries acquaints students with each country's unique aesthetics and shows them that each country is valued. One way to celebrate a country is to observe that country's Independence Day and learn its native dances. Students in your classroom who are from that country or have ancestors from that country can be the experts.

Invite parents and community members from the celebrated country to speak to your class and bring native clothing and artifacts to share.

The following list gives the dates on which different countries celebrate their Independence Day.

- January 6, Haiti
- February 16, Lithuania; February 27, Dominican Republic
- March 6, Ghana; March 20, Tunisia; March 25, Greece
- April 18, Zimbabwe; April 27, Sierra Leone
- May 15, Peru; May 25, Argentina and Jordan
- June 12, Philippines and Russia
- July 3, Algeria; July 4, United States; July 5, Venezuela; July 10, Bahamas; July 20, Colombia
- August 6, Bolivia; August 10, Ecuador; August 15, India; August 17, Indonesia; August 20, Senegal; August 24, Ukraine
- September 1, Vietnam; September 7, Brazil; September 15, Central American nations; September 16, Mexico; September 18, Chile; September 21, Armenia
- October 1, Nigeria; October 9, Uganda
- November 18, Morocco: November 22, Lebanon
- December 2, Laos; December 6, Finland; December 9, Tanzania; December 12, Kenya

Summary

The benefits of integrating movement into all subject areas are numerous. Research on brain-based learning confirms the need to integrate movement into the learning process. Students learn to make connections and understand concepts by investigating them in new and different ways. Allowing students to express themselves in the multiple intelligence that best suits them instills self-worth and understanding for students' unique talents.

Brain Gym activities provide teachers with ready-to-use activities to stimulate students' brains and prepare children to learn. Movement encourages learning by improving circulation, increasing blood supply to the brain, regulating moods, and generating interest by providing active learning activities. Collaboration between teachers not only benefits the teachers in their planning and sharing of knowledge but also benefits the students by modeling collaboration and teamwork.

Games and activities to reinforce learning can easily be introduced when studying different subject areas and exploring themes. Children's literature and movement provide a unique, creative outlet for students to interpret literature and express themselves. Integrating cultural activities helps students understand each other better and shows respect for the uniqueness of each student and country. Students can use technology, research, games, and dance to explore different countries.

Chapter Activities

1. List five benefits of an integrated curriculum.
2. List three reasons students benefit from moving. Write an activity that would help students accomplish each of the five benefits you listed in answer to question 1.
3. Choose a theme and make an outline of ways to integrate language arts, math, social studies, science, and history around the theme.
4. Choose an activity and list ways to present that activity incorporating all eight multiple intelligences.
5. Complete an Internet search using the key words "physical education games." Locate and learn the rules to three games that integrate movement with math, language arts, and science.
6. Complete an Internet search using the key words "multicultural games." Locate and learn the rules to three games from other countries.

Internet Resources

The following provide resources for integrating physical and cognitive skills and multicultural experiences.

LAKESHORE LEARNING MATERIALS
 www.lakeshorelearning.com
GOPHER
 www.gophersport.com
Wolverine Sports for Kids
 www.wolverinesports.com
US-GAMES
 www.US-GAMES.com
FLAGHOUSE
 www.FlagHouse.com
SPORTIME Physical Education
 www.sportime.com
U.S. TOY COMPANY
 www.ustoy.com

Bibliography

Barbarash, L. 1997. *Multicultural games*. Champaign, IL: Human Kinetics.

Bishop, R. S. 1987. Extending multicultural understanding through children's books. In *Children's literature in the reading program,* ed. B. E. Cullinan, 60–67. Newark, DE: International Reading Association.

Brophy, J., and J. Alleman. 1991. A caveat: Curriculum integration isn't always a good idea. *Educational Leadership* 49(2): 66.

Campbell, L. 1997. Variations on a theme: How teachers interpret MI theory. *Educational Leadership* 55(1): 14–19.

Carr, T. J. 2001. *Games from long ago and far away*. West Nyack, NY: Parker Publishing.

Combs, C. 1995. *The A,B,C's of Olympics: Activities, brains and competition*. Presentation at the Kansas Association of Health, Physical Education, Recreation and Dance (KAHPERD) Conference, Hays, KS.

Cone, S. L., and T. P. Cone. 1999. The interdisciplinary puzzle: Putting the pieces together. *Teaching Elementary Physical Education* 10(1): 8–11.

Cone, T. P. 2000. Off the page: Responding to children's literature through dance. *Teaching Elementary Physical Education* 11(5): 11–15, 34.

Cone, T. P., P. Werner, S. L. Cone, and A. M. Woods. 1998. *Interdisciplinary teaching through physical education*. Champaign, IL: Human Kinetics.

Davis, C. L., P. D. Tomporowski, C. A. Boyle, J. L. Waller, P. H. Miller, J. A. Naglieri, and M. Gregoski. 2007. Effects of aerobic exercise on overweight children's cognitive functioning: A randomized controlled trial. *Research Quarterly for Exercise and Sport* 78(5): 510–519.

Dennison, P. E., and G. E. Dennison. 1989. *Brain gym: Teacher's edition revised*. Ventura, CA: Edu-Kinesthetics.

Fauth, B. 1990. Linking the visual arts with drama, movement, and dance for the young child. In *Moving and learning for the young child,* ed. W. J. Stinson, 159–187. Reston, VA: American Alliance for Health, Physical Education, Recreation, and Dance.

Garcia, C., and L. Garcia. 1996. The value of integration: Activities that get children moving. *Teaching Elementary Physical Education* 7(3): 20–22.

Gardner, H. 1983. *Frame of mind: The theory of multiple intelligences*. New York: Basic Books.

———. 1999a. *The disciplined mind*. New York: Simon & Schuster.

———.1999b. Are there additional intelligences? The case for naturalist, spiritual, and existential intelligences. In *Education, information, and transformation: Essays on learning and thinking,* ed. J. Kane, 111–131. Upper Saddle River, NJ: Merrill.

———. 1999c. *Intelligence reframed: Multiple intelligences for the 21st century*. New York: Basic Books.

Garrahy, D. 2001. To integrate or not to integrate? That is the question. *Strategies* 14(4): 23–25.

Griss, S. 1998. *Minds in motion*. Portsmouth, NH: Heinemann.

Gustason, G., and E. Zawolkow. 1993. *Signing exact English*. Los Alamitos, CA: Modern Signs Press.

Hannaford, C. 1995. *Smart moves: Why learning is not all in your head*. Arlington, VA: Great Ocean Publishing.

Henning, R., P. Jacques, G. Kissel, and A. Sullivan. 1997. Frequent short breaks from computer work: Effects on productivity and well-being at two field sites. *Ergonomics* 40(1): 78–91.

Humphrey, J. H. 1990. *Integration of physical education in the elementary school curriculum*. Springfield, IL: Charles Thomas.

Jensen, E. 2000a. *Learning with the body in mind*. San Diego, CA: The Brain Store.

———. 2000b. Moving with the brain in mind. *Educational Leadership* 58(3): 34–37.

Jorgenson, O. 2003. Brain scam? Why educators should be careful about embracing "brain research." *Educational Forum* 67(4): 364–369.

Kutame, M. A. 1999. Teach your kids West African children's games. *Strategies* 13(2): 13–16.

Lankford, M. D. 1992. *Hopscotch around the world*. New York: Morrow Junior Books.

Mehrhof, J. H., and K. Ermler. 2001a. *Physical essentials: Kindergarten–5th grade physical education curriculum, advanced*. Emporia, KS: Mirror.

———. 2001b. *Physical essentials: Kindergarten–5th grade physical education curriculum, intermediate*. Emporia, KS: Mirror.

Merrefield, G. E. 1997. Three billy goats and Gardner. *Educational Leadership* 55(1): 58–61.

Mitchell, D., and C. J. Hutchinson. 2003. Using graphic organizers to develop the cognitive domain in physical education. *Journal of Physical Education, Recreation, and Dance* 74(9): 42–47.

Moen, S. 1996. Circuit training through the muscular system. *Journal of Physical Education, Recreation, and Dance* 67(2): 18–23.

Rauschenbach, J. 1996. Tying it all together: Integrating physical education and other subject areas. *Journal of Physical Education, Recreation, and Dance* 67(2): 49–51.

Satcher, D. 2005. Healthy and ready to learn. *Educational Leadership* 63(1): 26–30.

Scharenberg, C. 2001. Integrating PE across the curriculum. *Kansas Association of Health, Physical Education, Recreation, and Dance Journal* 71(1): 36–37.

Smith, N. K., and A. Owens. 2000. Multicultural games: Embracing technology and diversity. *Strategies* 13(5): 18–21.

Stanford, P. 2003. Multiple intelligence for every classroom. *Intervention in School Clinic* 39(2): 80–85.

Stevens, D. A. 1994. Integrated learning: Collaboration among teachers. *Teaching Elementary Physical Education* 5(6): 7–8.

Stevens-Smith, D. A. 1999. Physical education in the classroom . . . you've got to be kidding! *Teaching Elementary Physical Education* 10(1): 18–20.

Thayer, R. 1996. *The origin of everyday moods.* New York: Oxford University Press.

Tomporowski, P. D., and N. R. Ellis. 1986. Effects of exercise on cognitive processes: A review. *Psychological Bulletin* 99(3): 338–346.

Tremarche, P. V., E. M. Robinson, and L. B. Graham. 2007. Physical education and its effect on elementary testing results. *Physical Educator* 64(2): 58–64.

Wagner, K., and J. Paulseen. 2000, November. *Read and romp day.* Paper presented at the meeting of the Kansas Association of Health, Physical Education, Recreation, and Dance, Emporia, KS.

Westerhold, S. P. 2000. Bodies and brains in motion: Investigating the impact of an integrated curriculum. *Teaching Elementary Physical Education* 11(6): 17–21.

Worrell, V. J., S. K. Kovar, and S. Oldfather. 2003. Brain/body connection as it relates to physical education. *Teaching Elementary Physical Education* 14(1): 12–13, 26.

GRADES 2–6

NASPE STANDARDS 2 and 6

- Students demonstrate understanding of movement concepts, principles, strategies, and tactics as they apply to the learning and performance of physical activities.
- Students value physical activity for health, enjoyment, challenge, self-expression, and/or social interaction.

LESSON OBJECTIVES (FOR ALL GRADE LEVELS)

- Students see a connection between physical activity and academic subjects.
- Students show knowledge of Olympic facts and history.

EQUIPMENT NEEDED Paper to write answers on and one score pad per team, questions listed below, and *Jeopardy* music

PREPARATION TIME Ten minutes to divide class into groups and explain game

KNOWLEDGE CONTENT

- Students should understand how movement enhances learning.
- Students should know Olympic facts and history.

CLASSROOM ACTIVITY Divide the class into three teams. Older students can write responses and younger students can respond verbally. Team 1 chooses a category and goes first. Read the answer for which the teams must ask the correct question. Team 1 gets to go first. Play the *Jeopardy* theme music while waiting for the response. If the team's question is correct, team 1 gets three points. Then team 2 responds. If correct, team 2 gets two points. The same goes for team 3. For the next round, team 2 selects a category, responds first, and gets three points if correct. The other teams can also score two points on the same question. If the question is not correct, the team scores one point for the attempt. Have score sheets to write on at the other end of the classroom or gym for each team. After each answer and question, the entire team runs to the score sheet to record the score.

Two sets of *Olympic Jeopardy* (Combs 1995) questions and answers are listed here: (1) Olympic symbols and facts, and (2) Olympic summer events. Assign the students to make a set of questions for the Olympic winter events. The answer is listed first, followed by the correct question in italics. Remind students that they need to give their response in the form of a question (e.g., the correct response to question 1 is "What is the Olympic creed?").

Here are possible *Jeopardy* answers and questions for Olympic symbols and facts:

1. "The most significant thing in the Olympic Games is not to win but to take part. Just as the most important thing in life is not to triumph but the struggle. The essential thing is not to have conquered but to have fought well." *What is the Olympic creed?*
2. The five interlocked parts of this symbol represent five continents of the world. In every flag of the world there can be found at least one color of this symbol. *What are the Olympic rings?*
3. The colors of this symbol are blue, yellow, black, green, and red. *What are the Olympic rings?*
4. A symbol of peace, these birds are released at the opening ceremonies to remind all peoples that the Olympic Games are held in an atmosphere of peace. *What are doves?*
5. A branch from this tree is used as a symbol of peace or as a gesture of goodwill. *What is the olive tree?*
6. This music is played for the winner's country after each gold medal is won. *What is the national anthem?*
7. The meaning of the Olympic motto, "citius, altius, fortius." *What is "swifter, higher, stronger"?*
8. This is used to light the Olympic flame. *What is the Olympic torch?*
9. Olympic athletes make this promise to observe good sportsmanship. *What is the Olympic oath?*
10. The Olympic flame is lit during these proceedings. *What are the opening ceremonies?*
11. These are the six colors of the Olympic flag. *What are red, blue, green, yellow, black, and white?*
12. These people carry the flags of each country into the stadium. *What are members of each country's team?*
13. The five Olympic rings stood for this in ancient Greece. *What are the years between Olympic Games?*
14. This is what the five Olympic rings represent today. *What are the five continents?*
15. These are the five continents the Olympic rings represent. *What are Europe, Africa, Asia, Australia, and America?*
16. Citius, altius, fortius—swifter, higher, stronger. *What is the Olympic motto?*

17. Doves are sometimes released at the Olympic Games because they symbolize this. *What is peace?*
18. This country's athletes are the first to enter the opening ceremonies. *What is Greece?*
19. The athletes enter for opening ceremonies in this order. *What is alphabetical order?*
20. This person leads the athletes in reciting the Olympic oath. *What is one of the athletes?*
21. This is the prize for first place at the Olympic Games. *What is a gold medal?*
22. This is the prize for second place at the Olympic Games? *What is a silver medal?*
23. This is the prize for third place at the Olympic Games. *What is a bronze medal?*
24. This prize was given for winning at the ancient Olympic Games. *What is an olive wreath?*
25. The country in which the first Olympic Games took place in 776 B.C. *What is Greece?*
26. The year in which the first Olympic Games took place in Greece. *What is 776 B.C.?*
27. The number of years between the modern Olympic Summer Games. *What is four?*
28. This U.S. city has hosted two Olympic Summer Games. *What is Los Angeles?*
29. This is the essential criterion for a city to host the Olympic Winter Games. *What is snow?*
30. This was the mascot of the 1984 Olympic Games in Los Angeles. *Who was Sam the Eagle?*
31. Most Olympic Games have been held on this continent. *What is Europe?*
32. The Olympic Games in this city had a tiger for a mascot. *What is Seoul, South Korea?*
33. This country has hosted the most Olympic Games (seven). *What is the United States?*
34. This group of people was excluded from the ancient Olympic Games. *What is women?*
35. This city was the site of the ancient Olympic Games. *What is Olympia?*
36. These are the years of the next three Olympic Summer Games. *What are 2012, 2016, 2020?*
37. These beings were honored at the ancient Olympic Games. *What are Greek gods?*
38. Most Olympic athletes finish the games without one of these. *What are medals?*

Here are possible *Jeopardy* answers and questions for summer Olympic events and event facts:

1. A ten-event athletic contest consisting of the 100-, 400-, and 1,500-meter runs, the 110-meter high hurdles, the javelin and discus throws, shot put, pole vault, high jump, and long jump. *What is the decathlon?*
2. By points, distance, decision, or speed. *What are the four ways Olympic events are scored?*
3. This is the longest race in the Olympic Games. *What is the marathon?*
4. The number of miles in the marathon. *What is 26.2 miles?*
5. The season of Olympic Games that has the most events. *What is the summer games?*
6. The number of events in a pentathlon. *What is five?*
7. An Olympic event in which a pole (or poles) is used. *What is pole vault?*
8. The sport in which athletes perform a synchronized routine. *What is swimming?*
9. The number of events in a decathlon. *What is ten?*
10. These are two objects that a track and field athlete throws. *What are the discus, the javelin, and the shot?* (Name two of the three.)
11. This is an event in which both male and female gymnasts perform. *What are floor exercises? Or what is the vault?*
12. This is a nonteam event in which a hoop and a ball are used. *What is rhythmic gymnastics?*
13. This is a sport in which ten is a perfect score. *What is gymnastics? Or what is diving?*
14. This is an event in which a gymnast uses a horse. *What are men's and women's vaulting and men's pommel horse?* (Name one of the three.)
15. This is an event in which the athletes use a stick. *What is field hockey?*
16. This is the shortest distance of a track running race. *What is 100 meters?*
17. These are three swimming events. *What are butterfly, backstroke, breaststroke, and freestyle?* (Name three of the four.)
18. This race started the ancient Olympic Games. *What is the chariot race?*
19. These are three of the sports included in the ancient pentathlon. *What are long jump, javelin, foot race, discus, and wrestling?* (Name three of the five.)
20. These are the first two sports women played in the Olympic Games. *What are lawn tennis and judo?*
21. In this event, sets of arrows are shot at a target from varying distances. *What is archery?*
22. This is a team game in which players hit a pitched ball with a bat and run around bases to score. *What is baseball? Or what is softball?*
23. A team game in which athletes dribble and throw a ball through the opponent's hoop. *What is basketball?*
24. In this event, athletes hit each other with the painted part of the glove to score a point. *What is boxing?*
25. This event involves a water race in boats controlled by a single paddle. *What is canoeing? Or what is kayaking?*
26. This event involves riders who race distances ranging from 1,000 meters to cross-country courses. *What is cycling?*

27. In this water event, athletes enter the water from a springboard or high platform. *What is diving?*
28. A horseback event that includes dressage, jumping, and three-day combined. *What is equestrian?*
29. This event uses a foil, épée, and saber to touch the opponent's body to score points. *What is fencing?*
30. A team game in which a ball is guided by a stick into the opponent's net. *What is field hockey?*
31. This event consists of six events for men and four for women with both competing in vault and floor exercise. *What is gymnastics (artistic)?*
32. This event uses throws, chokeholds, and armlocks to defeat the opponent. *What is judo?*
33. This event consists of water races of 500 to 1,000 meters in flat boats propelled by single- or double-bladed paddles. *What is kayaking (canoe/kayak)?*
34. This event includes fencing, horseback riding, pistol shooting, running, and swimming in one day. *What is the modern pentathlon?*
35. This event consists of varied acrobatic moves with ball, hoops, clubs, and ribbons. *What is gymnastics (rhythmic)?*
36. This event involves a water race in which each competitor sculls with one oar. *What is rowing?*
37. In this event, competitors attempt to hit both still and moving targets, such as trap, skeet, and clay pigeons. *What is shooting?*
38. A team game in which the ball is put in the opponent's net by using body parts other than hands. *What is soccer?*
39. Water competition in butterfly, backstroke, breaststroke, and freestyle. *What is swimming?*
40. In this event, a pair of swimmers performs graceful turns and spins above and below the water's surface. *What is synchronized swimming?*
41. A game in which a ball is hit with a paddle across a net onto the opponent's side of a table. *What is table tennis?*
42. A seven-person team game played by throwing a ball into the opponent's net. *What is team handball?*
43. This group of events includes running, jumping, pole vault, shot put, discus, javelin, hammer throw, marathon, and decathlon. *What is track and field (athletics)?*
44. A team game in which the ball is hit to the opposite side of a high net so the opponent cannot return it. *What is volleyball?*

45. A team game played in water with players attempting to throw a ball into the opponent's net. *What is water polo?*
46. This event has competitors lift barbells using clean-and-jerk and the two-hand snatch. *What is weightlifting?*
47. This event includes Greco-Roman style, which allows only arm- and handholds above the waist, as well as freestyle. *What is wrestling?*
48. This event consists of four types of sailboats competing in two-hour races. *What is yachting?*
49. These three sports use a ball. *What are soccer, table tennis, team handball, tennis, volleyball, water polo, baseball, basketball, softball, field hockey?* (Name three of the ten.)
50. These two sports use water. *What are diving, swimming, synchronized swimming, water polo?* (Name two of the four.)
51. These two sports use a net. *What are field hockey, volleyball, tennis, table tennis, basketball?* (Name two of the five.)
52. A sport in which a birdie is hit back and forth across a net. *What is badminton?*
53. Four runners together make up this type of team. *What is a relay team?*
54. This event consists of a 100-meter race, hurdles, shot put, high jump, long jump, 800-meter race, javelin, and 200-meter race. *What is the heptathlon?*

ASSESSMENT Observe how students work cooperatively in groups. Record questions that are missed by teams and study those concepts and facts before playing again.

SUCCESS FOR ALL Allow students to work cooperatively to come up with the answer. Allow students to use notes, books, and other resources to find the answers. Show younger students a picture of the Olympic symbol if they do not know the answer.

INTEGRATION WITH OTHER SUBJECT AREAS
History, social studies, and language arts have been incorporated throughout the activity. To extend the activity into an integration lesson using art, have students draw and color the different Olympic symbols.

CLASSROOM LEARNING STATION 8.1
How Many in Our Theme?

GRADES 2–6

NASPE STANDARD 6 Students value physical activity for health, enjoyment, challenge, self-expression, and/or social interaction.

KNOWLEDGE CONTENT

- Students show an understanding of integrated subject matter.
- Students work cooperatively in groups.

EQUIPMENT NEEDED None

PREPARATION TIME Ten minutes to formulate topic list

CLASSROOM ACTIVITY

- Play with partners or divide into groups of two to four students each. Ask students how many things around the room integrate with the same topic or theme. Students walk around, searching the room, and make a list of ways different activities could be integrated into a topic or theme. For example, with the theme "dinosaurs," students could list "read about dinosaurs, measure dinosaurs in math, use a calendar to figure out when the last dinosaurs were alive, use the dictionary to look up words about dinosaurs, draw a picture of a dinosaur on the chalkboard."

After a set amount of time, have each group read its list to the class.

- *Variation:* Have students write the list in the form of questions without telling what their topic or theme was. Let the class guess what the topic or theme is from listening to their questions.
- *Variation:* Assign groups themes or topics before they begin. Sample topics include any sport, weather, different animals, space, famous people, heroes, and birds.

ASSESSMENT

- Ask students to share which aspects of the list they contributed.
- Ask students to share how their team worked cooperatively.
- Count how many ways the team found to integrate its topic.

SUCCESS FOR ALL If a group member is unable to verbally contribute answers or write answers, allow him or her to point to answers in the classroom or look at pictures to help contribute to the group.

INTEGRATION WITH OTHER SUBJECT AREAS
The activity itself is designed to formulate ways to integrate other subject areas.

SPECIAL EVENT 8.1
Read and Romp Day

NASPE STANDARD 6 Students value physical activity for health, enjoyment, challenge, self-expression, and/or social interaction.

LESSON OBJECTIVES

- Students see reading as a pleasurable activity.
- Students use creativity to interpret books and express themselves.
- Students work cooperatively in groups.

EQUIPMENT NEEDED Index cards with yarn tied on for each student listing the books read, and stamps or stickers to correspond with each book. Other equipment is listed with each station.

PREPARATION TIME Time to collaborate with the librarian and choose books and equipment. Preparation time in advance of the event to line up student or parent volunteers.

ACTIVITY Read and Romp Day is a collaborative effort between the physical education department and the library (Wagner and Paulseen 2000). It is organized so that children have the opportunity to move to different reading stations throughout the facility, listen to a volunteer read a story, and participate in a physical activity that corresponds with the book. The ten books selected here are for pre-K–1 students. Choose books that are appropriate for the age group participating.

Read and Romp can be incorporated into the classroom or physical education setting as a short activity or can be conducted as an event lasting several hours. Ask older students and parents to volunteer to read the books and help lead activities. Each station activity takes approximately 10 to 15 minutes, to accommodate the attention span of young learners. For older students, station activities could last longer. At each station, set a timer to go off when the designated time is up, use a whistle or buzzer, or designate volunteers to say "rotate" at the appropriate time.

The number of stations you set up will depend on the number of students participating and the number of students you wish to have at each station at any given time. The number of stations should not exceed the number of volunteers you have available. Stations can be set up around the gym or be spread out around the school. Work with the space you have. Books are selected in two ways:

1. Determine physical education equipment available, and then find books that match the themes of equipment or books that can use equipment in ways that the equipment is not typically used (e.g., yarn ball set on top of a large badminton birdie can make an ice cream cone).
2. Choose favorite books and find the necessary equipment or design activities that do not require equipment to illustrate the book.

Promote the Read and Romp event in school newsletters, notes to parents, and signs in the hallway. At the event, each child wears a card tied on yarn with the name of all the books in individual squares. As a child finishes a station, the appropriate square is either stamped with a rubber stamp or a sticker is placed in the square. Use a stamp or sticker that corresponds with or is related to the book (e.g., for a story about a bear, use a bear stamp). Even nonreaders can recognize the stamp or sticker and remember what the story is about. This allows students to talk about the books with their family, therefore promoting both physical education and reading.

The following resource also lists numerous literature resources that can be integrated into the physical education class and library class time. Colvin, V., and S. Rayburn. 2007. Read all about it: Physical educators and librarians team up in elementary schools. *Strategies* 20(3): 26–30.

BOOK AND ACTIVITY SUGGESTIONS

BUZZY THE BUMBLEBEE *by Denise Brennan-Nelson*

Equipment needed: Music is optional

Activity: Play Busy Bee. This game may be played with music or without. Start the children standing in a scatter position on the floor. Begin the music and ask them to move in a certain way (walk forward, walk backward, jump, hop, skip, gallop, roll, crab-walk, slide, march). When the music stops, the children freeze. Ask them to get together with a partner in a way that you designate when you say the words "Busy Bee" (back-to-back, hand-to-hand, toe-to-toe, side-to-side, elbow-to-elbow, knee-to-knee, handshake, high five).

Once children find a partner and stand the way they have been asked to, play the music again and change the locomotor movement. The music is then stopped, the children freeze, and you ask them to find their first partner and get together as they did before. After that, say "Busy Bee" and have them find a new partner in a new designated manner. Continue with this pattern, changing locomotor skills and adding more partners.

Read and Romp: Students toss and catch rubber chickens as their librarian reads *Chicken Tricks.*

Each time you ask students to find a certain partner, be sure to go through all the previous partners as well. This really helps young children remember who their partners were. Children love this game, and even very young children can remember quite a few partners. Sometimes it helps to have each child say the name of his or her partner on each skill. This helps with the memorization process.

CHICKEN TRICKS *by Meagan Lloyd*

Equipment needed: Rubber chickens

Activity: Students toss a rubber chicken to themselves or to a partner as the story is read. Ask students to catch the chicken in a tricky way.

THE GREEDY TRIANGLE *by Marilyn Burns*

Equipment needed: Two each of the following shapes drawn on index cards: circle, square, ellipse, oval, rectangle

Activity: Lay various shapes like a circle, a square, an ellipse, an oval, and a rectangle on the floor, and ask children to move around the different shapes in a designated locomotor movement. When you stay "stop," have children find the shape that is called out and make a circle around it. This is a fun activity to do to music. The students move while the music plays and stop when the music stops. Change locomotor movements often. Have more than one of each shape so that not all students are crowding around one card on the floor.

THE LETTERS ARE LOST *by Lisa Campbell Ernst*

Equipment needed: Hula hoops, cones, masking tape, flash cards, one set of alphabet cards per team

Activity: Organize the children into several relay lines. In front of each line place a hula hoop filled with alphabet flash cards (one set of 26 letters in each hoop). Using cones, designate a finish line and mark it with a piece of masking tape long enough to hold all 26 letters, or you may use a line that is already painted on the gym floor. The object of the game is to line up all the letters of the alphabet on the line. When a signal is given, the first person will find the letter A, pick it up, run down, and place it on the line. That person will then run back and give the next person a high five. The new runner will find the letter B, pick it up, run down to the line, and place it to the right of the A. This continues until the entire alphabet is placed in order on the line. Remember that very young children may not know all of the letters of the alphabet, so it would be helpful to have a volunteer hold up the flash card so that the students can match it.

PICKY MRS. PICKLE *by Christine Schneider*

Equipment needed: One serving spoon and dill pickle per team, colored cones

Activity: This is a relay using a very large serving spoon and a dill pickle. Organize the children into several relay lines. If possible, mark their starting place and destination with matching color cones. (It helps young children if they have a different color cone than the other lines. If you do not have different color cones, tape a piece of color construction paper around each cone.) Give the first person in each line a spoon. A volunteer will place a large dill pickle on the spoon. When a signal is given, each child walks down to his or her cone, walks around it, and comes back, keeping the pickle on the spoon. Continue until all children have had a turn. Be sure to have extra pickles on hand. A few are sure to need replacing after a few drops.

THE BUTTERFLY HOUSE *by Eve Bunting*

Equipment needed: Butterfly crackers, cheese, butterfly cookie cutter, orange Jello jigglers

Activity: This book can be read at the snack station. Butterfly crackers are topped with American cheese cut out with a butterfly cookie cutter. Orange flavored Jello jigglers can also be cut out in the shape of a butterfly.

A SQUIRREL'S TALE *by Richard Fowler*

Equipment needed: Music

Activity: Play the game Squirrels and Trees. This game is similar to musical chairs except no one is completely eliminated. Divide the children into groups of threes. Two children hold hands and are the tree. The third person is the squirrel. When the music plays, the squirrel leaves the tree and moves about the forest pretending to collect acorns. When the music stops, each squirrel hurries to get inside a new tree. What makes this game fun is having one or two extra squirrels who do not have a home. When the music stops, they attempt to find a tree, thereby leaving a different squirrel without a home. All squirrels, even those without a home, move around when the music plays. Change locomotor movements often to keep the children challenged.

FROM HEAD TO TOE *by Eric Carle*

Equipment needed: None

Activity: Have the children do the motions to the song "Hokey Pokey." This activity is perfect with the book, and young children enjoy doing the actions. Do the activity twice if time permits. If you can find different versions of this song, it is fun for children to hear the different ways it is performed.

MRS. HEN'S BIG SURPRISE *by Christel Desmoinaux*

Equipment needed: Plastic Easter eggs, foam Frisbee

Activity: If you have a large enough area to work with, play the tag game Throw Me the Egg. Have one child act as the tagger (using a foam Frisbee to tag with) and one act as the rescuer. A child tagged by a Frisbee must go down on one knee, squawk like a chicken, and call out "Throw me the egg!" The rescuer then comes by and throws the child the egg. If the egg is not caught, the tagged child is not free. The thrower and the tagged child must *not* pick up the egg if it is not caught. Only another student who is running by can pick up the egg and attempt to throw it to the child waiting to be rescued. The game continues in this manner, with the egg constantly being passed to new people. Stop the game often and change taggers and rescuers.

CAN'T YOU SLEEP LITTLE BEAR? *by Martin Waddell*

Equipment needed: Signing Teddy Bears or stuffed teddy bears

Activity: This is a sign language station. Check with your special education staff to see if they have access to the Signing Teddy Bears: Honey and Cookie. A person's arms go around each bear to act as the bear's arms. The hands are then used to sign. As the story is read, have two people whose arms are around the bears sign the conversation between the mother bear and the baby bear. When finished reading the book, teach the children how to sign "Read me a book please" and several other phrases. The Signing Teddy Bears are available from Modern Signs Press, P.O. Box 1181, Los Alamitos, CA, 90720.

ASSESSMENT Ask student and parent volunteers how groups worked cooperatively. Observe students participating as books are read. Afterward, ask students to tell what their favorite book was about and draw a picture to illustrate the story.

SUCCESS FOR ALL Allow students with special needs to work with a partner if needed. Anticipate which stations might need extra supervision and plan to have older students help with those stations.

INTEGRATION WITH OTHER SUBJECT AREAS

Math, reading, language arts, health, art, and physical education skills have been incorporated throughout the activity.

CHAPTER 9

Motivating Children to Be Physically Active

The purpose of this chapter is to present ideas and information the elementary classroom teacher and physical education teacher can use in motivating children to be physically active now and over their lifetime. Implementing the ideas presented will provide a nonthreatening, mastery-oriented gymnasium and classroom environment where students know that teachers care about them and their ability to remain fit and healthy over their lifetime.

Objectives

After studying this chapter, you will be able to do the following:

- Identify ways teachers, parents, and coaches can turn students on to physical activity.

- Discuss the key psychological variables relevant to increasing children's physical activity level.

- Understand the concept of maximum participation.

- Understand how your prior physical activity experiences affect your views and feelings today about physical activity.

- Develop your own approach for motivating children.

- Develop ways to discover your students' attitudes and perceptions about movement, physical activity, exercise, fitness, and physical education.

- Plan lessons that include task progressions for students with different movement abilities and task variations to stimulate interest.

Visualize a class of second graders participating in physical education by playing modified kickball on the school playground. The weather is sunny and warm; the classroom teacher is nearby, supervising and providing feedback to the students. The teacher believes strongly in providing activities that keep all the students actively engaged in movement all of the time. Thus the teacher has modified a regular kickball game to provide maximum opportunities for the students to kick, throw, field, and pitch the ball.

Groups, consisting of five students each, are scattered throughout the play area. Each group is playing its own game of modified kickball (pitcher, catcher, kicker, and two fielders). Each group has a playground ball and two bases—home plate and first base. All players rotate positions after each kicker has a turn at the plate. Four players (pitcher, catcher, and two fielders) play against the current kicker. The pitcher rolls the ball to the kicker, who kicks the ball into the playing field. The kicker must run to first base and return to home plate during his or her own turn at the plate in order to score a run. Fielders get the kicker out by stepping on first base (before the kicker gets to first base) or on home plate (before the kicker gets to home plate). Fielders must have the ball in their possession when stepping on first base or home plate for an out. In addition, to maximize student participation, both fielders must touch the ball before getting the ball to a base.

Moving around the perimeter of the playground, the teacher visits with each group, providing corrective feedback on skill performance and game strategies. Using proper supervision techniques, the teacher always faces the center of the playground while providing feedback in order to keep the entire class within his or her line of vision.

Modifying the game of kickball leads to maximum participation for all students. By moving around the perimeter, the teacher is able to keep the class within view and provide feedback.

Using Motivational Pedagogical Techniques

As stated many times in this book already, the goal of quality physical education is for *all* children:

- To be knowledgeable about movement performance
- To have the skills necessary to participate in a variety of physical activities
- To value participating in physical activity for the health benefits derived from that participation

In order to achieve the goals of quality physical education, teachers must use a pedagogy that motivates students to participate in physical activities now and in the future. Teachers and coaches should utilize teaching strategies that provide opportunities to be physically activity, promote perceived physical competence, foster enjoyment of physical activity, and encourage support from teachers and parents. Teachers plan and implement lessons in which all of the students are active participants all the time (as the teacher did in the scenario just described), so students have fun and improve their movement skills. Students who enjoy being skilled movers will participate in physical activities in situations where they have *choices* of participating or not, and they will choose to participate over

their lifetime. Turning students on to physical activity or supporting the natural tendency for children to be active does not happen automatically; teachers must structure the learning environment to make it happen.

Early motivational theories were very mechanistic in their approach to influencing the behavior of a child. Using conditioning techniques, the idea was to *force* children to do what was requested (such as be physically active) and give them rewards for doing it; thus over time, the children would develop a *habit* for doing the specific behavior. With this approach, physical educators believed that providing activities and exercise to children over their school years would produce an exercise *habit* that would continue into adulthood. Today the evidence is clear that such an approach has not worked.

A number of motivational theories and models for promoting physical activity exist today that attempt to explain why and under what conditions children choose to participate in physical activity (Hutchinson and Mercier 2004; Kamla, Davis-Brezette, and Larson 2006; Kilpatrick, Hebert, and Jacobsen 2002; Mandigo and Holt 2000; Roberts 2001; Shen, Chen, and Guan 2007; Standage, Duda, and Ntoumanis 2003; Stodden and Goodway 2007; Valentini, Rudisill, and Goodway 1999). These theories provide some direction on how physical education classes and classroom movement activities should be taught in order to motivate students to participate in physical activity. Three basic pedagogical elements are presented to help create a classroom environment that motivates students to participate:

1. Instill feelings of motor skill competency.
2. Build intrinsic motivation.
3. Involve students in their learning environment.

INSTILL FEELINGS OF MOTOR SKILL COMPETENCY IN CHILDREN

One primary motivational variable is a student's perceived level of physical competence. Evidence clearly indicates that teachers should strive to instill feelings of motor skill competence in their students. Researchers have found that students who view themselves as competent movers participate in more out-of-school physical activity, at higher intensity levels than those who view themselves as poor movers (Wallhead and Buckworth 2004). How students view their motor competency depends greatly on their past performances. Success in the past leads students to believe they will be successful in the feature (Kamla, Davis-Brezette, and Larson 2006). Adults feel the same way. Your personal insight probably tells you that your feelings about your own physical competence greatly affect your inclination to either participate or not participate in physical activity.

A central part of children's self-image involves the perceptions surrounding their performance competence within the physical realm. This is true for several reasons. First, movement is the primary way young children learn about themselves and their environment. The quality of their movement determines how much and what they learn. Second, when young children play, the play generally consists of some form of physical activity, so **motor skill competency** continues to be an important part of their lives. Once children are in the upper elementary grades, motor skill competency becomes even more important as children recognize the emphasis society places on the successful performance of motor skills in physical education, at recess time, and during after-school sport activities. Because physical ability is so honored and respected in our society, the presence or lack of that ability forms a part of each child's self-image. Thus the educator's job is to provide movement experiences that enhance children's perceptions of their physical abilities.

Numerous appropriate teaching practices instill perceptions of motor skill competency in children. We especially recommend six practices that strengthen students' confidence in their motor skill abilities and create a mastery-oriented learning environment:

1. Avoid embarrassment of children.
2. Respect differences in physical ability.
3. Maximize opportunities to practice skills.
4. Provide task variations.
5. Provide task progressions within lesson activities.
6. Focus on student learning and improvement.

Avoid Embarrassment of Children Evaluate, judge, correct and/or reward children's motor performance in private whenever possible. Any time public comparisons are made about children's motor performance, the low-skilled students will be embarrassed. Some examples of how to proceed include:

- Write skill test scores on an index card and hand the card to the student rather than verbally announcing scores to the entire class.
- Compare students' performance to a criterion level of performance or to their own "starting" skill level rather than to that of others in the class.
- Recognize improvement on an individual basis.
  - Award certificates to those who meet their individual fitness goals (established after pre-assessment determined current level of achievement), not just to those who achieve the 85th percentile on fitness tests. Comparing children's test scores to national or local norms serves only to further encourage those who probably need no encouragement and further discourage those who already dislike physical activities.
  - Award certificates to those who earn participation points.
- Form groups (or teams) needed during class time in advance during the lesson planning stage or use the random processes described in Chapter 7 when organizing students for activity. Never embarrass students by having student captains name their teammates one child at a time in front of the entire class. This can be a devastating experience for the children selected last.
- Ask students, before class, if they want to demonstrate skill performance that day.
- Practice skills in class formations where students cannot see everyone's performance. For example, use a scattered formation versus a circle (Alderman, Beighle, and Pangrazi 2006).

Children build skills and physical fitness through practice, so it is important to structure activities so that all students have many opportunities to be active. Having a piece of equipment for each child allows for maximum participation.

Respect Differences in Physical Ability Stress to students the importance of recognizing and respecting individual differences in physical ability. Teachers can model this idea by using some of the appropriate practices identified in this chapter and by establishing class rules that call for students to respect each other. In addition, if teachers plan lessons that include a variety of movement forms (dance, gymnastics, sport skills, adventure activities, cooperative activities, and swimming), students who shine in one form will not necessarily shine in another form. Thus, during different activities throughout the year, various students will have the opportunity to be the most skilled in the class.

Maximize Opportunities to Practice Skills and Participate Use movement activities that provide many skill repetitions for every child, because it is only through practice that children become more skilled. It is essential that children in early childhood master the fundamental motor skills so that in late childhood they can be successful using those skills in group physical activities, games, and sports. Mastery happens only through repetitive practice. Games that eliminate players from the action should not be part of the program or should be restructured to quickly allow eliminated players back into the games. Movement activities and games that have students waiting in line for a turn, such as relays, should also be restructured to allow all students to actively participate (or should be eliminated from the program) Note the chapter-opening scenario for how to restructure the game of kickball to meet the **maximum participation** requirement.

Have sufficient equipment available. For example, if students are practicing ball-handling skills, each student should have a ball when dribbling a basketball, a beanbag when throwing at a target, or a scarf when juggling. When enough equipment

is not available (e.g., basketballs), substitute other balls that can be dribbled, such as volleyballs and playground balls. Yarn balls can be substituted for beanbags when throwing at targets. Another way to overcome equipment limitations is to organize the activity into stations so only four or five basketballs would be needed for four or five students practicing at a certain station. Other stations would have different equipment provided for the students at that station.

Evaluate your ability to provide maximum participation. Keeping children active throughout the lesson is an easy concept to grasp, but it is not easy to implement. Evidence continues to grow every day indicating that many children are still waiting their turn to be active. An easy, informal way to determine whether all your students are generally active during a movement lesson is to have another teacher observe your class and record the activity level of selected students. Write your students' names on slips of paper and divide the slips into two piles: one for skilled students and one for less-skilled students. Fold the slips so you cannot see the names and draw a name from each pile. Have your colleague watch these two students during one lesson and record, once every 30 seconds, what each student is doing by placing a mark beside one of the behaviors listed in Figure 9.1. By counting the number of marks by each action, a rough estimate can be made regarding the activity level of the children in the class. Ideally, most of the marks would be placed by the action indicating that students were practicing a movement task. To ascertain whether children of high and low skill are equally active during the lesson, compare the number of ones to the number of zeros placed by the action "practicing a movement task." This same technique can be used to informally compare other groups (e.g., boys and girls, younger and older, African American and Euro-American).

Directions: Observe one skilled and one low-skilled child during the lesson. Every 30 seconds, record the activity each child is engaged in.

Practicing a movement task   _____

Watching someone else perform   _____

Waiting for a turn   _____

Waiting for something to happen in a game   _____

Listening to the teacher give directions   _____

Listening to the teacher give feedback   _____

Place a 1 on the line by the action if the skilled student is doing it, and place a 0 on the line by the action if the low-skilled student is doing it.

FIGURE 9.1   Observing Activity Levels of Selected Students

Another estimate of student involvement can be obtained by having a fellow teacher observe and record all the students in the class. Do this by having the fellow teacher scan the room every two minutes and simply count the number of students who at that very moment are actively participating in a manner you have specified. Average the two-minute counts for a rough estimate of the number of children who are usually on task.

Provide Task Variations   Practice skills using a variety of equipment, situations, teaching styles, and movement forms in order to keep students interested in practicing. Although children need many skill repetitions, those repetitions should not become boring. For example, *throwing and catching* may be practiced in the following ways:

- With many different objects (playground balls, softballs, basketballs, footballs, tennis balls, Frisbees, Velcro darts)
- In different situations (alone, with a partner, in small or large groups) as students' skills improve

- Using different teaching methods (e.g., direct, practice, problem solving)
- Using many movement forms (basic movement drills, games skills, cooperative skills, water game skills, and fitness activities)

This variety keeps children interested so they stay on task to obtain the skill repetitions needed to improve their skill performance. The practice repetitions (with accompanying corrective feedback from teachers or peers) allow students to master various movement skills.

As mentioned in Chapter 2, children need skill repetitions spaced throughout the school year so skills (e.g., dribbling a soccer ball) are practiced in small chunks of time spread over the entire year (distributed practice). Thus students are repeatedly exposed to skills (using task variations) during each school year. See Appendix A to find a variety of ways (activities) for students to practice various movement skills.

Provide Task Progressions   Use task progressions when building curricula to provide developmentally appropriate movement activities. As discussed in Chapter 2, classroom movement activities must be matched to students' cognitive, psychomotor, and affective ability level. A movement activity is considered *developmentally* appropriate if the frequency, intensity, duration, and type of the activity accommodate the child's age, maturation level, skill level, body size, fitness level, and previous movement experiences. For example, young children are not developmentally ready to play team games such as softball or soccer. In general, the physical education program should build *from simple to complex experiences* as children progress through each grade level. For example, first graders might experience striking skills in this order:

1. Explore striking balloons with various body parts.
2. Hit a balloon to self (with the hand) five consecutive times.
3. Hit a balloon back and forth to a partner.

Then in the second grade, the children might progress as follows:

1. Strike other soft objects with the hand (Nerf balls).
2. Strike a Nerf or rag ball off a batting tee with a soft bat.
3. Strike a tennis ball against the wall with a short racket.

These examples demonstrate increasingly complex tasks both within and between grade levels. Further

BOX 9.1 Jump Rope Skill Progression for First Graders Who *Cannot* Jump Rope

INDIVIDUAL ROPE SKILLS

The following activities help children with the arm motions needed to jump rope.

For the proper length of rope, the child should stand on the middle of the rope while pulling the rope ends up to his or her armpits. The rope should be neither longer nor shorter than the length necessary to reach the armpits.

Lasso High

With both rope handles in the right hand, swing the rope overhead (clockwise and then counterclockwise). Repeat with the left hand.

Lasso Low

With both rope handles in the right hand, swing the rope under both feet and jump as the rope reaches your feet. Repeat with the left hand.

Bird in Hand

With both handles in the right hand, do the following:

1. Circle the rope on the right side of the body.
2. Circle the rope on the left side of the body.
3. Alternate circling right, left, right, left.
4. Repeat with the left hand.
5. Circle the rope (as above) and jump every time the rope hits the floor.
6. Repeat all of the above with rope handles in the left hand.
7. Do all of the above to music (keeping time with the music).

Double Twirl

The arm action on these skills should simulate the action of turning an individual jump rope. With two ropes, both handles of one rope in the right hand and both handles of the other rope in the left hand, do the following:

1. Circle rope in right hand on right side (five times).
2. Circle rope in left hand on left side (five times).
3. Circle both ropes on appropriate sides at the same time (five times).
4. Repeat the above sequence until completed smoothly.
5. Repeat the above sequence turning the rope backward.
6. Repeat the sequence to music (keeping time with the music).
7. Repeat the sequence jumping every time the rope hits the floor.

LONG JUMP ROPE SKILLS

For the following activities, which are designed to help students work on their jumping rhythm, it helps to have skilled rope turners.

Swinging Bridge

The rope is swung in a low arc on the floor. Jump as the rope moves toward the jumper.

Cradle

Swing the rope in a back and forth movement. Jump the rope as it goes back and forth.

Rock the Cradle

Perform three of the above cradles, then turn the rope completely overhead and try to continue jumping.

---

examples demonstrating increasingly complex movement activities are provided in Appendix A.

Provide task progressions within lesson activities in order to adjust for children's varying levels of ability. Task progressions include a series of motor tasks (related to the skill being learned) designed to move the student from static practice to being ready for dynamic game play. Each task becomes more complex (and thus more difficult) by structuring and controlling the environmental conditions under which the student

must practice. Environmental conditions include factors such as (Palmer and Hildebrand 2005):

- Space (amount, shape)
- Defenders or obstacles (present/absent, number, location, mobility)
- Equipment (size, shape, amount, manipulation directly or indirectly by hands or feet)
- Targets or goals (placement, size)
- Number of team members

BOX 9.2 Jump Rope Skill Progression for First Graders Who *Can* Jump Rope

JUMP AND HOP

Turning the rope forward, do the following:

1. Jump on both feet.
2. Hop on the right foot.
3. Hop on the left foot.
4. Alternate hops and jumps.

Repeat the above sequence turning the rope backward.

JUMP AND SWING

Turning the rope forward, do the following:

1. Jump on both feet (several jumps).
2. Swing the rope to the right side (continue jumping during the swing).
3. Jump on both feet (several jumps).
4. Swing the rope to the left side (continue jumping).
5. Alternate jumps and swings in any pattern desired.

Repeat the above sequence turning the rope backward.

MOVE AND JUMP

Turning the rope forward, do the following:

1. Jump while moving forward.
2. Hop while moving forward.
3. Jump or hop while moving to the side.
4. Jump or hop while moving backward.

Repeat the above actions while turning the rope backward.

RUNNING

Run forward while turning the rope forward.

SIDE STRADDLE

Alternately jump the rope with feet together (as usual), then apart (side straddle). Repeat with the rope turning backward.

FORWARD STRADDLE

Jump the rope with forward straddles (right foot forward on the first jump and left foot forward on the next jump). Continue this pattern. Do not separate the feet too far.

SKIER

Jump the rope while landing on either side of a line on the floor. The lateral movement should be about one-half foot on each side of the line.

CRISSCROSS

Jump the rope (turning the rope forward), cross the arms as the rope comes overhead so the rope is jumped while the arms are crossed. You can continue jumping with the arms crossed, or you can uncross your arms after the rope is jumped once. You can also do this with the rope turning backward.
   Use good form while jumping:

- Jump on the balls of the feet (not flat-footed).
- Keep the body upright while jumping.
- Strive for a low jump (just high enough for the rope to slip between your feet and the ground).

Manipulating these conditions, the teacher designs movement activities for varying levels of student ability.

We have included a jump rope lesson for first graders to show an example of **task progression** (see Boxes 9.1 and 9.2). First graders generally have a large range of abilities in rope jumping (from a few students who can jump extremely well to some who cannot even jump the rope once). Providing only one

task for all the children to practice is not likely to meet children's varying needs. For some students the level of difficulty of that task will be "just right," but for some it will be too difficult and for others too easy. So the teacher must provide a number of tasks of varying levels of difficulty. Boxes 9.1 and 9.2 show task sheets that allow first graders to begin with any task they can perform and move down the task list as their skill improves. Classroom Learning Station 9.1 (bowling) at the end of this chapter provides another example of task progression (scoring methods and a task sheet that progresses from simple to complex). Chapter 7 (Figure 7.2) contains a task progression sheet for the skill of throwing, and Chapter 11 (Classroom Learning Station 11.1) provides a task progression for skills on the low balance beam.

Focus on Student Learning and Improvement

Create a mastery-oriented environment that supports student learning and improvement (Alderman et al. 2006; Solmon 2006; Weiss 2000). To create this environment, the teacher works in the following ways:

- Sets expectations for improvement (verbally)
- Designs class activities that lead to improvement (not just lead to participation)
- Gives students practice repetitions with an emphasis on the quality of the movement (not just an emphasis on the outcome of the movement) by providing:
  - corrective feedback related to movement quality
  - praise related to movement quality
- Views student mistakes as part of the learning process
- Gives praise/reinforcement for students' work efforts
- Helps students set and achieve meaningful goals based on their individual strengths and weaknesses
- Designs skill evaluations that track individual student performance over time in order for the teacher and student to view progress
- Emphasizes cooperative learning (versus competitive learning)

BUILD INTRINSIC MOTIVATION

Another primary motivational variable (in addition to perceived motor skill competency) deals with encouraging students to be intrinsically motivated to be physically active. Students have two primary sources of reinforcement when involved in class activities: themselves and those around them (teachers and other students). Sources of reinforcement from within the child are called **intrinsic motivators,** whereas sources of reinforcement from others are called **extrinsic motivators.** In general, teachers want students to be motivated intrinsically because that source of reinforcement is always available to the child. Extrinsic sources, such as prizes from the teacher, will not be present throughout the child's life. In addition, internal motivation is within the student's control, whereas external motivation is not. Research indicates that students receiving extrinsic rewards are *not* motivated to continue their participation in physical activity. This section explores six ways to build intrinsic motivation in your students:

1. Draw attention to students' positive feelings about movement skills.
2. Plan for student success.
3. Evaluate students appropriately.
4. Praise students for their accomplishments.
5. Link effort and ability so that children feel they are in control of whether or not they succeed.
6. Construct flow experiences for children.

Draw Attention to Positive Feelings

Children express feelings of intrinsic motivation in terms of experiencing a sense of accomplishment, having fun, feeling good because of skill improvement, and enjoying the excitement of the game. Teachers should draw attention to these feelings so students recognize and use their inner sources of motivation.

Having fun may be the most important intrinsic motivator of the ones mentioned above. Children who have fun while participating in physical activity are more likely to want to participate again and more likely to repeat their involvement in the activity. Having fun is a feeling children enjoy experiencing, and children seek out this feeling. According to research, fun is one of the most cited motives given by children for participating in sports and physical activities. In fourth-grade students who participated in a year-long running program, fun was a positive predictor of their motivation to continue running (Xiang et al. 2006). Some scholars (Petlichkoff 1992) have defined *fun* as the experience that occurs when the physical task balances the child's level of skill with the challenge of the task. This balance entails matching the task to the child's skill level so the child is neither bored (task is too simple) nor stressed (task is too difficult). In other words, if the child finds success and entertainment while performing movement skills, the child will have fun.

Making the task fun for each child in the class can be difficult, but it is more likely to happen if the motivation principles outlined in this chapter are considered when designing and implementing physical activity instruction. Instant Activity 9.1 contains a fun way to build arm and shoulder-girdle strength, and Classroom Learning Station 9.1 (at the end of the chapter) presents bowling activities that allow children to have fun while improving their throwing and rolling skills.

INSTANT ACTIVITY 9.1 Mac the Crab

Grades 4–6

Equipment Needed

Music for the "Macarena"

Activity

The object of this activity is to complete a modified version of the "Macarena" while in a crab position. First, teach the arm actions to the "Macarena" with the students standing in their personal space. After the students master this sequence of arm movements, then have them perform it while in a crab position. For another variation, have them perform the arm movements while in a push-up position. Children have the most fun if the teacher can obtain the original "Macarena" music (song was recorded by Los Del Rio).

Modified "Macarena" arm actions in standing position are as follows (each action takes one count of music):

1. Extend right arm straight out in front of the body, palm facing down—leave it there.
2. Repeat with left arm.
3. Turn right palm to face up.
4. Turn left palm to face up.
5. Place right hand on left shoulder.
6. Place left hand on right shoulder (arms are now crossed).
7. Place right hand on back of head.
8. Place left hand on back of head.

9. Place right hand on left waist.
10. Place left hand on right waist (arms will be crossed).
11. Place right hand on right hip (buttock).
12. Place left hand on left hip (buttock).
13. Repeat the entire sequence as many times as desired.

Obviously, when performing the arm actions in a crab or push-up position, one hand has to be on the floor supporting the body at all times, so the active arm does the "Macarena" action while the other arm is the supporting limb.

From Jill Best, elementary physical education teacher, Omaha, Nebraska.

Plan for Student Success Teachers can encourage an environment of inner motivation for children by planning for their success. Educators know that accomplishing a task successfully stimulates children to want to do the task again; thus it is very important to structure learning tasks so that *all students can feel successful.* Attainable, individualized objectives should be developed for students based on the program goals and students' current levels of performance. The proposed level of goal achievement is not the same for all students, and all students do not perform the same tasks as they work toward goal accomplishment. This type of approach allows all students an opportunity to succeed. Using task progressions, children are given appropriate movement tasks organized from simple to difficult, and they select the task that is maximally challenging that will also allow them to be successful (Mandigo and Holt 2006; Weiss 2000).

Classroom teachers and physical education teachers should also remember that students (especially young children) feel successful when they believe their effort was high (regardless of the actual ability demonstrated). In one study, third and fifth graders found success when they achieved the goal of the activity but also found success when they were trying hard (Dyson 1995). In their physical education curriculum, the students were less hesitant to attempt new, difficult, or risky activities if their teacher emphasized "trying their best."

Evaluate Students Appropriately Another way to encourage internal motivation is to evaluate students in ways that recognize their achievement. Today many physical educators challenge the traditional practice of judging success primarily in terms of achievement based on comparisons between and among students (Alderman et al. 2006; Hutchinson and Mercier 2004). If the final goal of physical education is for children and adults to lead healthy, physically active lives, then defining success in terms of who wins a game or who can run the fastest is not appropriate. It is worthwhile for physical educators to examine the similarities and differences between the goals of sport performance and the goals of lifetime participation and examine how best to achieve those goals. An emphasis on winning and losing may further the goal of sport performance, but achieving lifetime participation may require a more recreation-oriented approach.

Instead of peer comparisons of physical performance, success should be measured in terms of *individual improvement* in physical skills; fitness levels; knowledge about exercise, fitness, and movement; and activity levels. Success is defined in terms of mastering the task rather than performing better than others in the class. Assessment tools to measure individual success include activity contracts, diaries, and goal progress charts, as these indicate a student's progress over time. Figure 9.2 shows an individual evaluation sheet for jump rope skills that allows for evaluation throughout the school year; when completed it will clearly indicate the individual's improvement over time.

As much as possible, have students evaluate their own progress toward specific goals (Mowling et al. 2004) so they are invested in the learning process. Focus the self-evaluation on self-improvement (Alderman et al. 2006) so the student recognizes the connection between assessment and future practice.

Another evaluative process that affects students' motivation is the practice of grading students in elementary physical education. Letter grades do not provide any useful information for either the students or their parents. Certainly students should be evaluated (but not graded) on their progress toward program goals. As indicated in Chapter 6, physical education report cards at the elementary level should be progress reports that identify specific skills and behaviors to be mastered and then indicate the level of mastery the student achieved. Grades are an external source of motivation and in the long run will not provide adequate motivation for students to continue to engage in physical activity. Even in the short run, grades lessen intrinsic motivation by making children ignore the pleasure derived from their physical performance, feel anxious about receiving poor grades, and choose nonchallenging tasks (Harter 1978). Thus grades encourage students to be more concerned about passing than feeling the joy of movement or striving to do their best.

Student's Name _____

List five different jump rope tricks that you will demonstrate in your routine. When you demonstrate each trick, do it at least eight times. You will be evaluated three different times throughout the semester on the same five tricks (during units in which we are practicing jump rope skills and tricks).

Jump Rope Trick	Evaluation 1	Evaluation 2	Evaluation 3

* Indicates the skill was performed correctly for all eight jumps

+ Indicates the skill was performed correctly for some of the eight jumps

- Indicates the skill was not performed correctly

FIGURE 9.2   Individual Improvement over Time

Praise Students   Although **praise** is a form of extrinsic reinforcement, research indicates that it acts as an internal motivator. Praise given to the student by teachers, peers, and parents allows a child to feel a sense of accomplishment (which is an internal source of motivation). This sense of accomplishment stays with the child to shape future experiences. Effective praise is a powerful tool for developing a child's inner feelings of worth and accomplishment. Box 9.3 provides guidelines for effective praise and sample "praise phrases." The praise given should relate to student performance and provide specifics about that performance. Praise given to students should be warranted as well as specific, since constant "cheerleading" will eventually be ignored by the students. When the situation actually warrants praise, teachers should praise their students and encourage them to praise each other.

Link Effort and Ability   The beliefs children have about what causes them to succeed or fail when performing physical skills also contribute to their internal motivation. Using achievement motivation theory, learners may explain the quality (positively or

BOX 9.3   Guidelines for Effective Praise

Effective praise has the following characteristics:

- It is delivered immediately, yet without intruding on task-related behavior.
- It identifies specific aspects of behavior that were completed well (Brophy 1981).
- It provides information about why the behavior is important.
- It is well matched to the behavior being reinforced.
- It relates to a criterion or previous performance rather than comparing with other students (Brophy 1981).
- Effective praise attributes success to effort or ability or both (Brophy 1981).
- Effective praise includes expectations for continued success and improvement.
- Effective praise shows variety, sincerity, and enthusiasm (Brophy 1981).

Sample "praise phrases" for the teacher:

- Jason, your form on that shot was perfect—good job!

- Phillipe, you kept your elbow tucked in that time— way to go! Could you feel the difference in your arm position?
- Brigitte, thanks for following my instruction so well!
- Lop-Hing, you are doing an excellent job of assisting me today!
- The entire class worked hard at each station today, so I saw lots of skill improvement—good work, class!

Sample "praise phrases" for the students:

- Looking good!
- Yea, way to go!
- Nice shot!
- Good teamwork!
- Great pass!
- Nice soft landing!
- Good wrist snap!

negatively) of their performance by attributing it to one or more of the following attributes: effort, ability, luck, and/or task difficulty. **Effort** involves the learners' rating of how hard they tried to perform well in a given situation, while **ability** involves the learners' perception of how well, in general, they are capable of performing. Thus effort ratings may vary for each situation, and ability ratings may vary based on perceived competence in various movement forms (e.g., throwing and catching versus running long distances). Both effort and ability are internal to the learner and thus to a certain extent under her or his control. Luck involves attributing the quality of the performance to outside forces such as calls by referees or poor facilities. Task difficulty involves attributing performance to the perceived difficulty of the task (i.e., performed well because the task was easy or performed poorly because the task was too difficult). Elementary-age children do not generally use the attribute of luck to explain performance. They do use the attribute of task difficulty, and that is another reason why teachers must vary movement tasks to fit the developmental needs of each child.

In studying elementary-age children, researchers have found that students connect *effort* and *ability* and perceive that high levels of effort lead to improved skill. These children made no real distinction between ability and effort; thus level of ability is related to the amount of effort exerted. Children assume that practice will lead to improvement. It appears that elementary school teachers should attribute success or failure in performing movement skills to effort and ability. Children view themselves as able to control effort and, subsequently, ability; so attributing success or failure to effort and ability allows children to continue to control whether or not they will be successful. Viewing effort and ability as changeable and in their control allows children to be internally motivated.

By the time children are in middle school (age 11 or 12), they have developed a distinction between ability and effort. Ability is now judged in comparison with the ability of others. A performer must be good in relation to peers in order to have high ability. Children of this age may view ability as a stable condition. If so, then attributing failure to lack of ability will not motivate children to continue skill practice, as they believe they cannot change their ability level. Eventually, these children may decrease their efforts to improve and develop negative attitudes toward physical activity. On the other hand, attributing success to ability does increase motivation because children believe their ability level is stable; thus they will be successful in the future also.

Opportunities to practice skills may occur in the classroom.

Teaching effort attributions to children while they are young encourages them to work hard to develop adequate physical skills (ability). So the goal is that by the time they begin to view ability as a stable condition, they already have (and believe they have) sufficient ability to continue on the road to skill improvement (rather than dropping out of physical activity altogether). This conclusion applies to boys and girls, as no gender differences have been found in children's understanding of effort and ability in the physical activity setting.

Construct Flow Experiences For Children Having children participate in activities that provide a sense of enjoyment and exhilaration also builds internal motivation. One concept used to describe and study this sense of enjoyment and exhilaration is called flow. *Flow* is defined as "the state in which people are so involved in an activity that nothing else seems to matter; the experience itself is so enjoyable that people will do it even at great cost, for the sheer sake of doing it" (Csikszentmihalyi 1990, 4). Children obviously demonstrate the experience of flow when they engage in free play, but flow occurs just as well when children engage in activities that are goal directed, are bounded by rules, require certain skill levels, and involve a high energy investment (physical or mental energy). Getting into the flow during physical activity helps students enjoy the activity.

Research involving children's experiences in physical activity settings indicates that **flow experiences** are characterized by high levels of intrinsic motivation, self-expression, positive emotions, concentration, challenge, skill development, enjoyment, satisfaction, clear objectives, peak performance, positive mental states, and perceived success (Kimiecik 2005; Mandigo and

INSTANT ACTIVITY 9.2
Push-up Hockey

Grades 4–6

Equipment Needed

Beanbags

Activity

Students are paired together, and each pair has one beanbag. Students take a regular push-up position, facing their partner with two to three feet between them. The surface of the floor needs to be smooth (a carpeted surface will not work). One student, with the beanbag, begins the game. (If needed, students can play Rock, Paper, Scissors to determine who begins the game.) Students get into the push-up position, and one partner begins the game by sliding the beanbag across the floor to the opponent (thus supporting the body on one hand while sliding the beanbag). The object of the game is to slide the beanbag through the extended arms of the opponent before it can be intercepted (intercepting is done with one hand while supporting the body in the push-up position with the other hand). If the beanbag does pass through the opponent's arms, then the slider gets a point. After each point, the player scored against gets the bag to begin the game again. Players must stay in the push-up position in order to get points.

From Jill Best, elementary physical education teacher, Omaha, Nebraska

Thompson 1998). Knowing these conditions, it should be possible to structure physical activity lessons that meet the conditions that in turn provide flow experiences for the participants. Instant Activity 9.2 contains a strenuous fitness activity that is exhilarating and challenging for students (and thus may produce a flow experience). The "create and share" activity in Special Event 9.1 is built to contain many of the characteristics needed to produce a flow experience.

INVOLVE STUDENTS

Another primary motivational variable (in addition to perceived motor competency and intrinsic motivation) is involving students in the teaching and learning process. Presumably students are the most important element in the educational process, but educators rarely ask for their input, listen to their opinions, value their thoughts and feelings, or allow them to be involved in the planning process. We suggest three ways to emotionally, physically, and intellectually involve students in the teaching and learning process:

1. Listen to student voices.
2. Share control of the learning process with the children.
3. Provide children with a cognitive basis for being active.

Listen to Student Voices   Educators determine program goals and plan curriculum without ever consulting the students. Yet the physical education curriculum experienced by students is their own interpretation of the presented curriculum. In general, the experienced curriculum is not exactly the same as the presented curriculum. From this perspective, it seems logical that educators ought to discover and understand the experienced curriculum by seeking out their **students' voices**. Using student perception information, modifications can then be made to the presented curriculum in order to achieve program goals or to modify the goals.

In recent years, researchers have begun the process of listening to students' voices about their experiences in physical education (Carlson 1995; Dyson 1995; Graham 1995; Mowling et al. 2004; Portman 1995). These studies serve to demonstrate that students (even as young as five years old) can express their thoughts and feelings about their physical education experiences and that the thoughts and feelings expressed are important to consider when planning curriculum and implementing instruction.

Since students vary greatly in their interests, abilities, and attitudes, it makes sense for educators to ask their own students about their physical education experiences. One means of collecting information is to interview randomly selected students or talk with selected groups of students. Interviewing can provide in-depth understanding of students' perceptions, but it is time consuming and it is possible that students will not be totally honest if their own teacher is asking the questions. It is best to have another teacher in the school conduct the interviews.

The educator may also try more informal, less time-consuming collection methods, such as short, open-ended writing assignments completed in the classroom that ask students to write a paragraph answering questions such as those listed below. To keep the assignments short, use only one question per writing assignment.

- Why is physical education important?
- When do you feel most successful in physical education class?
- According to your P.E. teacher, why are you learning to _____?
- What was the most enjoyable part of today's P.E. lesson?
- What would you change about your physical education to make it better for you?
- What do you like about P.E. class? What do you dislike?
- What's your favorite P.E. activity? Why is it your favorite?
- What's your least favorite P.E. activity? Why?
- What do you most want to get better at during P.E. this year?
- Describe a physical activity that you are good at performing.
- Describe a physical activity that you are not good at performing. Why can't you do this activity?
- What part of your school day is most fun?
- What physical activities and sports do you participate in outside of school?
- Outside of school, whom do you exercise or play with? Why do you choose to exercise or play with these people?
- After school, would you rather watch television or go outdoors and play? Why?
- I like physical education class when my teacher does _____.
- I dislike physical education class when my teacher does _____.

Quick Lesson 9.1 at the end of the chapter outlines a classroom activity in which students express their views on the topics listed above, and Box 9.4 presents some answers to one of the questions from real fourth and fifth graders.

Children's perceptions (attitudes, thoughts, and feelings) about physical activity are all-important in determining whether they will choose to be physically active now and over their lifetime. Educators cannot ignore these perceptions but must strive to make those perceptions positive. Listening to students' voices and valuing their perceptions allow students and teachers to communicate about making the physical education class more effective in turning students on to lifetime physical activity. Listening to what children have to say and giving their opinions serious consideration empower them intellectually and emotionally.

BOX 9.4
Opinions of Real Fourth
and Fifth Graders

What would you change about your physical education to make it better for you?

MARGO: "Ask the kids what they want to do."

SUAD: "Bowl all the time."

PETER: "Have the rops (ropes) have more nots (knots) so I can climb higher."

AZEEM: "I would run more."

HAMID: "I wouldn't change anything."

CAROL: "I don't like Frisbee."

JESSICA: "Stop the rhythms."

JHARNA: "Have snacks."

EMILIO: "I wouldn't change anything because it's a challenge and I like challenges because it get me stronger."

MARIA: "Do it every day."

MIMI: "I would have it for longer periods of time."

Share Control Of the Learning Process Students can be physically and emotionally drawn into lessons when teachers **share control** with them. A small but very important way to share control is to allow children some *choices* within each lesson, such as where to perform a task, whom to perform a task with, and which activity to perform from a list of possible activities. Another way to share control is to give students a choice as to which activity they would like to focus on next. Perhaps the teacher can allow students to perform different activities (based on what each student likes), but all the activities are designed so the students will achieve the lesson goal (just in different ways). For example, to achieve aerobic fitness, students could select to participate in jogging, jumping rope, or doing step aerobics. Another way to share control is to have the students help the teacher determine the class rules they will follow for the year.

Most important, teachers should allow students to alter tasks to better fit their abilities whenever students are presented with a performance task that is too difficult or too easy for them. In one study of kindergarten children, all the children (at various times during class activities) altered the assigned tasks to make the tasks more challenging or more fun (Sanders and Graham 1995). Children indicated they liked participating in activities in which the teacher allowed a wide range

of acceptable responses to the assigned tasks. When the teacher had a very narrow range of acceptable behavior (such as everyone doing stretching exercises at the same time to the same count), the children experienced less fun and less challenge and appeared to be turned off to that activity. Thus, in performing stretching exercises, the students might stay on task longer (and enjoy the activity more) if partners could perform the stretches in the order they choose and on their own count.

Other instructional techniques allow students to respond in different ways. Movement education stimulates different responses by asking questions such as "show me how many ways you can jump rope" and "show me how many ways you can balance on two body parts." Challenge activities and cooperative activities (as defined and described in Chapter 7) also allow students the freedom to discover (in their own time and space) how to reach a determined final result in a variety of different and creative ways.

Another way for teachers to build more student control into a lesson while also providing for a wide range of response behaviors is to use indirect styles of teaching (styles that give students permission to make some decisions regarding lesson implementation). Indirect styles of teaching make the students active participants in the learning process and empower them to take responsibility for their learning. Students who are empowered are likely to view themselves as partners with the teacher in the learning process, partners who have input into the learning process and who are sources of knowledge. So with these styles the teacher (as expert) steps back and allows students to find, share, and create knowledge. Obviously, these styles of teaching support interactions between and among students so they can help each other learn the lesson objective. The Special Event at the end of the chapter uses a teaching style that is very student directed. A continuum of teaching strategies, progressing from teacher directed to student directed, is presented in Chapter 7.

Students who make decisions (within certain parameters) feel they have personal control since they are learning in an environment they helped create. Thus the primary benefit of shared control is having students who want to learn because they have been empowered to be partners in the learning process. Instant Activity 9.3 provides students an opportunity to determine the exact movements being performed.

Provide a Cognitive Basis for Being Active Our final suggestion for involving students involves them intellectually in understanding why they should be

Allowing students to choose equipment for a balance activity helps keep them involved.

physically active and how to develop a healthy lifestyle. This means children should know the health benefits of being active, and they should know how to structure exercise sessions to increase physical and mental fitness. Of course, this knowledge base needs to be expressed in terms children can understand given their cognitive developmental level. For example, at the kindergarten level, health benefits can be as simple as "being active makes you feel better." The health and fitness knowledge base (provided in Chapter 4) should be taught to students at each grade level (with adjustments for their cognitive level of functioning), but the depth of knowledge should be increased for each grade level as children mature cognitively. In addition, since elementary-age children are motivated by the concrete reality of "here and now," most of the reasons for being active should be grounded in the present, not in what will happen in the future. As children become older (junior and senior high school), the reasons for being active may be more future oriented.

PROMOTING PHYSICAL ACTIVITY

Thus far in the chapter, we have covered pedagogical strategies teachers might use to positively impact student interest and motivation in being physically active. However, in addition to pedagogy, teachers impact (for better or worse) students' motivation to be physically active through their everyday words and actions. This impact occurs daily as you go about the business of teaching in your school community. You need to promote physical activity at every opportunity because your students are watching (and noting what is important to you). Your students need to hear you "talk the talk" and see you "walk the talk." Your words and actions join the words and actions of others in the school to create an environment where being physically active is expected.

BE PHYSICALLY ACTIVE YOURSELF

In this environment, not only are your students involved in physical activity, but you also are an active participant in the world of physical activity. For instance, you walk/jog two miles three or four times a week. Or you walk around the playground at lunch time every day (and invite students to join you). Or you belong to a dance club that meets every week to practice. In addition to being physically active, we suggest that you (1) model enthusiasm and interest for your students, (2) join others in the school to support physical activity, and (3) collaborate with others in the community in their efforts to affect the activity levels of children.

MODEL ENTHUSIASM AND INTEREST FOR YOUR STUDENTS

In promoting physical activity, teachers, parents, and coaches should be models of the physically active adult. This involves not only being physically active themselves on a regular basis, but also talking often about their interest in and enthusiasm for physical activity, and occasionally participating in physical activities with the children during class time. These behaviors play a major role in shaping children's predisposition toward physical activity. Interestingly, research supports the contention that encouragement from adults (parents, teachers, and coaches) is just as important as actually participating in physical activities with children. Thus it is important that adults provide verbal encouragement to children to be active as well as directly facilitate their participation through behaviors such as being coaches, driving them to practice, and providing after-school physical activities.

JOIN WITH OTHERS IN THE SCHOOL

Remember that you are not alone in your efforts to keep students physically active. Given the school wellness policies already in place, it is likely that every teacher and staff member in your school will be your partner. You are now part of a much larger enterprise dedicated to producing healthy, active children.

INSTANT ACTIVITY 9.3 Follow the Leader

Grades K–6

Equipment Needed

None

Activity

Students form a circle. The circle could include the entire class, or the class could be subdivided into smaller groups. Play Follow the Leader. The leader must select a pose or movement that keeps everyone basically in place (but students can change levels while in place). Each student in the circle takes a turn at being the leader (designate that turns at being the leader progress around the circle in a clockwise or counterclockwise direction). Followers continue doing the pose or movement until the next leader shows them a new pose or movement. The teacher verbally indicates when it's the next leader's turn. Continue until everyone has been a leader.

The activity works best if students are allowed to plan what pose or movement they will do. So before playing, give the students a few minutes to select a pose or movement. Then indicate that even if the pose or movement they selected is done by someone else, they may still do that pose or movement.

For variation, Follow the Leader can be done to music. Play music that the students have selected (with the teacher's okay). The next leader must time the start of her or his pose or movement to match counts of the music. For example, students count the beats of the music, and every 16 counts the next leader does his or her pose or movement. (At first the students may need to count the music out loud, but eventually they can master silent counting.)

Another variation is called One Behind. The followers must stay one action behind the leader. This can be done with and without music also.

We encourage you to become an integral part of that enterprise by joining your school's efforts. Integrate fully what you do in the classroom with what is going on schoolwide. You could join the school's wellness committee or make a commitment to implement in your classroom the priorities established by that committee. Help build a school curriculum that teaches children the health benefits of regular physical activity. Or help the physical educator improve the school's playground so that age-appropriate equipment and play spaces are available. Or design a model for you and your colleagues to use for involving your students'

parents and families in the effort to increase activity levels. As you join various schoolwide efforts (or build your own schoolwide efforts), you will bring your students along with you. They will involve themselves in whatever you involve yourself.

JOIN WITH OTHERS IN THE COMMUNITY

As educators, physical education teachers and classroom teachers may need to join together the efforts of the school with family and community efforts to make a

An indirect teaching style can empower students by giving them more control over their activities. These students are actively engaged in station work that gives them flexibility in determining the order of their activity and when they start and stop each activity.

positive impact on children's involvement with physical activity. Promoting physical activity in youth may necessitate coordinating the efforts of various groups to accomplish the final objective of a physically active child who grows up to be a physically active adult. Hopefully, local wellness policies connect the school and community in ways that promote physical activity. Physical education is rightly recognized as the primary vehicle for promoting this objective, but other groups may also play a key role in furthering this objective. Classroom teachers can provide additional movement experiences for their children that will enhance their physical competence; family members can encourage and model being physically active; and community groups can provide access to facilities and programs that keep children active during nonschool hours.

Summary

Researchers do not yet know exactly what turns a child on or off to physical activity. Obviously, a combination of factors influences the child: attitudes and interests; motor self-confidence; attitudes and actions of parents and peers; and availability of physical activity experiences in the home, school, and community. This chapter has examined a number of variables that influence children: cognitive variables (attitudes and beliefs about physical activity and its benefits), affective variables (enjoyment and interest in physical activity), and the physical variable of perceived physical competence. The principles presented in this chapter for motivating children to be physically active were developed to enhance these cognitive, affective, and physical variables so that children are positively disposed to be physically active now and in the future. In summary, those principles are as follows:

- Maximize each child's movement time.
- Avoid embarrassment of children.
- Allow children to have fun.
- Respect differences in physical ability.
- Instill feelings of motor skill competency in children.
- Use developmentally appropriate movement activities.
- Listen to student voices.
- Provide task variations and progressions.
- Build intrinsic motivation in the students.
- Evaluate students appropriately.
- Share control of the learning process with the students.
- Ask students to put forth maximum effort.

- Praise students and link effort and ability.
- Provide successful class experiences.
- Construct flow experiences for children.
- Model enthusiasm and interest for your students.
- Provide a cognitive basis for being active.
- Join together with others in the school and community.

Chapter Activities

1. Observe an elementary physical education class and determine whether the rule of maximum participation is being observed. Use the observation instrument provided in this chapter to determine a rough estimate of activity time for each student.
2. Write a paragraph about your own experiences that do or do not dispose you to be a physically active person.
3. Write a short paper (two pages) discussing your feelings and beliefs about your level of motor skill competency.
4. Select one of the questions in the section on listening to student voices. Administer this question to a class of elementary students. Write a summary of your findings, including how the findings might help the movement educator design learning experiences.
5. Select one of the motivational concepts discussed in the chapter. List on a piece of paper all the strategies you might use to implement that concept in the teaching and learning process. Concepts such as intrinsic motivation, sharing control, and flow experiences might be selected.
6. Develop a lesson plan (15 minutes in length) to be used in teaching physical education. Within the plan, demonstrate individualizing levels of goal achievement and providing a range of movement tasks (from simple to complex) for students with different movement abilities.
7. Develop a lesson plan for the classroom that teaches one (or several) point(s) from the knowledge base on the health benefits of living an active lifestyle. Prepare the lesson for the grade level of your choice.

Internet Resources

The President's Council on Physical Fitness and Sports. The first site contains an article by James Whitehead, University of North Dakota, on physical activity and intrinsic motivation. The second contains an article on motivating children in physical activity.

www.fitness.gov/activity/activity7/intrinsic/intrinsic.html

www.fitness.gov/activity/activity2/digest_sept2000/ digest_sept2000.html

Bibliography

Alderman, B. L., A. Beighle, and R. P. Pangrazi. 2006. Enhancing motivation in physical education. *Journal of Physical Education, Recreation and Dance* 77(2): 41–45, 51.

Brophy, J. 1981. On praising effectively. *Elementary School Journal* 81(5): 269–278.

Carlson, T. B. 1995. We hate gym: Student alienation from physical education. *Journal of Teaching in Physical Education* 14: 467–477.

Csikszentmihalyi, M. 1990. *Flow*. New York: Harper & Row.

Dyson, B. P. 1995. Students' voices in two alternative elementary physical education programs. *Journal of Teaching in Physical Education* 14: 394–407.

Fry, M. D., and J. L. Duda. 1997. A developmental examination of children's understanding of effort and ability in the physical and academic domains. *Research Quarterly for Exercise and Sport* 68(4): 331–344.

Graham, G. 1995. Physical education through students' eyes and in students' voices: Implications for teachers and researchers. *Journal of Teaching in Physical Education* 14: 478–482.

Harter, S. 1978. Pleasure derived from challenge and the effects of receiving grades on children's difficulty level choices. *Child Development* 49: 788–799.

Hutchinson, G. E., and R. Mercier. 2004. Using social psychological concepts to help students. *Journal of Physical Education, Recreation and Dance* 75(7): 22–26.

Kamla, J., J. Davis-Brezette, and K. Larson. 2006. The social-cognitive approach to motivation in physical education. *Strategies* 19(5): 17–20.

Kilpatrick, M., E. Hebert, and D. Jacobsen. 2002. Physical activity motivation: A practitioner's guide to self-determination. *Journal of Physical Education, Recreation and Dance* 73(4): 36–41.

Kimiecik, J. 2005. Phat exercise: How young adults enjoy and sustain physical activity; Intrinsic motivation promotes exercise adherence, but how can it be instilled? *Journal of Physical Education, Recreation and Dance* 76(8): 19–22.

Lambdin, D., and J. Erwin. 2007. School wellness policy: Community connections. *Journal of Physical Education, Recreation and Dance* 78(6): 29–32.

Lee, A. M., J. A. Carter, and P. Xiang. 1995. Children's conceptions of ability in physical education. *Journal of Teaching in Physical Education* 14: 384–393.

Li, W. 2006. Understanding the meaning of effort in learning a motor skill: Ability conceptions. *Journal of Teaching in Physical Education* 25: 298–309.

Mandigo, J. L., and N. L. Holt. 2006. Elementary students' accounts of optimal challenge in physical education. *Physical Educator* 63(4): 170–183.

Mandigo, J. L., and L. P. Thompson. 1998. Go with their flow: How flow theory can help practitioners to intrinsically motivate children to be physically active. *Physical Educator* 55(3): 145–159.

Mowling, C. M., S. J. Brock, K. K. Eiler, and M. E. Rudisill. 2004. Student motivation in physical education: Breaking down barriers. *Journal of Physical Education, Recreation, and Dance* 75(6): 40–45, 51.

Palmer, S. E., and K. Hildebrand. 2005. Designing appropriate learning tasks: The environmental management model. *Journal of Physical Education, Recreation and Dance* 76(2): 48–55.

Petlichkoff, L. M. 1992. Youth participation and withdrawal. Is it simply a matter of fun? *Pediatric Exercise Science* 4: 105.

Portman, P. A. 1995. Who is having fun in physical education classes? Experiences of sixth-grade students in elementary and middle schools. *Journal of Teaching in Physical Education* 14: 445–453.

Pringle, R. 2000. Physical education, positivism, and optimistic claims from achievement goal theorists. *Quest* 52: 18–31.

Roberts, G. C. 2001. Understanding the dynamics of motivation in physical activity: The influence of achievement goals on motivational processes. In *Advances in motivation in sport and exercise,* ed. G. C. Roberts, 1–50. Champaign, IL: Human Kinetics.

Sanders, S., and G. Graham. 1995. Kindergarten children's initial experiences in physical education: The relentless persistence for play clashes with the zone of acceptable responses. *Journal of Teaching in Physical Education* 14: 372–383.

Shen, B., A. Chen, and J. Guan. 2007. Using achievement goals and interest to predict learning in physical education. *Journal of Experimental Education* 75(2): 89–108.

Solmon, M. A. 2006. Creating a motivational climate to foster engagement in physical education. *Journal of Physical Education, Recreation and Dance* 77(8): 15–16, 22.

Standage, M., J. L. Duda, and N. Ntoumanis. 2003. A model of contextual motivation in physical education: Using constructs from self-determination and achievement goal theories to predict physical activity intentions. *Journal of Educational Psychology* 95(1): 97–110.

Stodden, D. F., and J. D. Goodway. 2007. The dynamic association between motor skill development and physical activity. *Journal of Physical Education, Recreation and Dance* 78(8): 33–34, 48–49.

Valentini, N. C., M. E. Rudisill, and J. D. Goodway. 1999. Incorporating a mastery climate into elementary physical education: It's developmentally appropriate. *Journal of Physical Education, Recreation and Dance* 70(7): 28–32.

Veal, M. L., and N. Compagnone. 1995. How sixth graders perceive effort and skill. *Journal of Teaching in Physical Education* 14: 431–444.

Wallhead, T. L., and J. Buckworth. 2004. The role of physical education in the promotion of youth physical activity. *Quest* 56: 285–301.

Weiss, M. R. 2000. Motivating kids in physical activity. *President's Council on Physical Fitness and Sports Research Digest Series,* ERIC, 470-695.

Xiang, P., A. Chen, and A. Bruene. 2005. Interactive impact of intrinsic motivators and extrinsic rewards on behavior and motivation outcomes. *Journal of Teaching in Physical Education* 24: 179–197.

Xiang, P., A. Lee, and L. Williamson. 2001. Conceptions of ability in physical education: Children and adolescents. *Journal of Teaching in Physical Education* 20: 282–294.

Xiang, P., R. E. McBride, and A. Bruene. 2006. Fourth-grade students' motivational changes in an elementary physical education running program. *Research Quarterly for Exercise and Sport* 77(2): 195–207.

Xiang, P., M. A. Solmon, and R. E. McBride. 2006. Teachers' and students' conceptions of ability in elementary physical education. *Research Quarterly for Exercise and Sport* 77(2): 185–194.

GRADES K–6

NASPE STANDARD 6 Students value physical activity for health, enjoyment, challenge, self-expression, and/or social interaction.

LESSON OBJECTIVES

- Students recognize physical activity as a positive experience.
- Students express experiencing success while participating in physical education.
- Students recognize their favorite activities.
- Students report feelings of enjoyment while involved in physical activities.
- Students assess the importance of physical activity in their lives.

EQUIPMENT NEEDED Work sheet and pencil for each student

PREPARATION TIME One hour to select the question and place the question and graphics on the work sheet

KNOWLEDGE CONTENT The physically educated person needs to do the following:

- Associate positive feelings with participation in physical activity
- Try new physical activities
- Enjoy interaction with peers during physical activity
- Enjoy participating in physical activities
- Use physical activity as a way to express her- or himself
- Recognize personal success in the physical domain
- Support and recognize the achievements of others in physical activity
- Seek challenging physical opportunities
- Seek physical activity outside the school setting

CLASSROOM ACTIVITY In class, ask students to answer one of the questions in the "Listen to Student Voices" section of this chapter. The following figure is a sample work sheet for the students to use. Teachers can develop more work sheets with different questions (selected from the text) and enhanced with attention-getting graphics. Then hold a brief class discussion that recognizes students' opinions and, when possible, emphasizes any of the points listed in the knowledge content section.

ASSESSMENT Collect the students' answers and show them to the physical education specialist. The classroom teacher and the physical education teacher should use the information in the answers to plan the next steps needed to continue their efforts to produce physically educated students.

SUCCESS FOR ALL Do not always have students *write* answers to the question posed. To use the different intelligences your students possess, have them sing the answer, dance the answer, draw the answer on paper, or verbalize the answer to a partner.

INTEGRATION WITH OTHER SUBJECT AREAS When you have students sing their answer, ask the music teacher to coteach the class with you. Students could select popular songs for which the music teacher would probably have an instrumental version (without words), so students could make up their own words (which answer the question) to one verse of the song. Then students sing their songs (answers) to the class.

When you have students draw an answer, invite the art teacher to coteach the class with you. Perhaps with the art teacher's guidance you could select one art medium (e.g., drawing facial expressions). The students express their answer to the question by drawing a face with an appropriate expression. The art teacher would be able to present content knowledge helpful to the students as they work on their drawings.

What do you like about physical education class?

CLASSROOM LEARNING STATION 9.1
Bowling

GRADES K–6

NASPE STANDARD 1 Students demonstrate competency in motor skills and movement patterns needed to perform a variety of physical activities.

LESSON OBJECTIVES

- Students improve their bowling technique.
- Students improve their bowling scores (compared with their previous scores).
- Students improve their math skills by scoring a bowling game.
- Students have fun.
- Students engage in self-assessment in order to progress through the activity task sheet.

EQUIPMENT NEEDED Task sheets, score sheets, one plastic bowling set (ten pins and one ball with finger holes). If bowling set is not available, use a soft-core ball and empty plastic two-liter bottles. The task and score sheets follow below.

PREPARATION TIME Less than one hour to set up the station with needed materials.

KNOWLEDGE CONTENT The correct technique for throwing a bowling ball is as follows when using a four-step approach:

1. Hold ball (in right hand) in front of chest just slightly to the right side.
2. Step forward with the right foot (while extending the ball straight forward away from the body).
3. Step forward with the left foot (while the ball arm swings straight back past the body).
4. Step forward with the right foot (while finishing the ball arm swing).
5. Step forward with the left foot (while rolling the ball forward on the floor).

FIRST AND SECOND GRADERS First and second graders can keep score by simply recording the number of pins knocked down on each roll of the bowling ball. (Reset the pins after each roll.) As a next step, have the students record the number of pins knocked down for each of the ten rolls of the ball and then add for a total score (see the score frames for first and second graders in the scoring sample).

THIRD AND FOURTH GRADERS Third and fourth graders can be taught the concept of a frame: they get two chances (two rolls) to knock down all ten pins (see the score frames for third and fourth graders in the scoring sample). The number recorded in the Frame box is the total of both rolls. Introduce the concepts of a strike and a spare. A strike occurs when all ten pins are knocked down on the first roll of the ball. After a strike, the bowler does not get to roll a second time. A spare occurs when the second ball knocks down all the remaining pins.

FIFTH AND SIXTH GRADERS Fifth and sixth graders can play and score a regulation bowling game. Previously students were simply adding scores from the frames together to get a final score. But in regulation bowling, extra points are scored when the bowler gets a strike or a spare. After a spare, the bowler gets ten points plus the total of the pins knocked down on the next roll of the ball. After a strike, the bowler gets ten points plus the total of the pins knocked down on the next two rolls of the ball (see the game frames for fifth and sixth graders in the scoring sample). After rolling a strike, that frame is done (the bowler does not get to roll a second time).

CLASSROOM ACTIVITY The station should have the following items:

- A plastic bowling set (containing a ball with finger holes and ten pins), if available from the physical education teacher. If the bowling set is not available, use a playground or soft-core ball of an appropriate size. Empty soda cans or two-liter plastic bottles can be used as bowling pins. If cans are too noisy, tape or paint spots on the floor for the pins. Set the pins (or painted spots) as in regulation bowling (see figure).

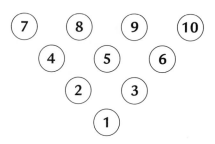

Bowling Pin Placement

Scoring Sample

Grades 1 and 2:

Frame	1	2	3	4	5	6	7	8	9	10
	[2]	[3]	[5]	[1]	[6]	[5]	[4]	[8]	[1]	[7]
Carlos	2	5	10	11	17	22	26	34	35	42

Grades 3 and 4:

Frame	1	2	3	4	5	6	7	8	9	10
	[5|1]	[3|3]	[1|4]	[2|6]	[0|6]	[4|3]	[2|4]	[7|0]	[2|2]	[9|0]
Yumi	6	12	17	25	31	38	44	51	55	64

Grades 5 and 6:

Frame	1	2	3	4	5	6	7	8	9	10
	[5|4]	[6|0]	[8|◣]	[3|◣]	[7|2]	[X]	[5|◣]	[X]	[6|1]	[2|◣|9]
Rajiv	9	15	28	45	54	74	94	111	118	137

Symbol key: X = Strike
◣ = Spare

- Blank scoring sheets appropriate to the method being used to score, along with a sample game that has already been scored
- Peer assessment sheet for evaluating bowling technique
- Task sheet containing bowling activities to be practiced

Blank forms for scoring and peer assessment as well as a sample task sheet (with progressive skill activities) appear at the end of this Classroom Learning Station.

Set up the learning station so the student is rolling the ball toward a wall (not into the center of the room) or toward a partner (standing behind the pins), who stops the ball immediately. If the wall has padding of some kind, the ball will not rebound so strongly. From the task sheet below, the students select which task is appropriate to practice. The tasks provide a number of possible bowling activities (from simple to complex). The teacher may need to help some students select appropriate tasks if they are not being successful.

This learning station could be a partner activity in which two students are at the station. Together they would take turns (after each frame) rolling at the pins, retrieving the thrown ball, resetting the pins, keeping their partner's score, and doing peer assessments of their bowling technique.

ASSESSMENT Students check their progress in three ways:

1. Comparing their game score to previous game scores
2. Determining how far down the task sheet they have progressed
3. Having a peer complete the Bowling Technique Peer Assessment sheet

SUCCESS FOR ALL All students should be successful because they can select tasks that are fun and challenging from a list of tasks designed to progress from simple to complex.

Note for first and second graders: You might set up only three to four pins (instead of ten) if students are spending most of their time resetting the pins instead of bowling.

INTEGRATION WITH OTHER SUBJECT AREAS

Math skills have been integrated throughout this learning station activity.

Task Sheet

Directions: Begin with any task that you can do well. Practice as indicated and move to the next task when you meet the criteria.

1. **Task:** Bowl with a Nerf ball using a one-step approach. The Nerf ball should be sized so the child can grasp the ball in one hand. Grasp the ball in the right hand and move the arm backward. Step forward (on left foot) at the same time as the arm swings the ball forward to roll it along the floor. Aim at the spots marked on the floor (spots should be in the same formation as the pins in a regulation bowling game, and if possible, the spots should be numbered). The distance between the bowler and the spots should be 10 to 15 feet.
   Criteria: When you can hit the #1 pin three times out of ten (using one step), you are ready to bowl a game. The game is rolling the ball ten times (resetting the pins after each roll). Keep score using score sheet #1.
   Criteria: When you score at least 30 in one game, you are ready for the next task.

2. **Task:** Bowl with a Nerf ball using a two-step approach. Step right foot, left foot forward (for right-handed person) with a Nerf ball in right hand. Move arm backward on the first step, and move arm forward (to roll) on the second step. Aim at spots marked on the floor (spots should be in the same formation as the pins in a regulation bowling game). The distance between the bowler and the spots should be 10 to 15 feet.
   Criteria: When you can hit the #1 pin three times out of ten (using two steps), you are ready to bowl a game. The game is rolling the ball ten times (resetting the pins after each roll). Keep score using score sheet #1.
   Criteria: When you score at least 40 in one game, you are ready for the next task.

3. **Task:** Do task number 2 above with a plastic bowling ball (with holes) and plastic pins.
   Criteria: When you can hit the #1 pin three times out of ten, you are ready to bowl a game. The game now includes ten frames (not just ten ball rolls). Keep score using score sheet #2.
   Criteria: When you score at least 50 in one game, you are ready for the next task.

4. **Task:** Do task number 2 above, but increase the distance to 20 to 25 feet.
   Criteria: When you can hit the #1 pin three times out of ten, you are ready to bowl a game. The game now includes ten frames (not just ten ball rolls). Keep score using score sheet #2.
   Criteria: When you score at least 50 in one game, you are ready for the next task.

Bowling Task Sheet for the Classroom Teacher to Use in Developing a Student Task Sheet

5. **Task:** <u>Bowl with a Nerf ball using a four-step approach.</u> Hold the ball (in your right hand) in front of your chest just slightly to the right side of the body. Step right, left, right, left. Foot steps and arm movements coordinate as follows:
   - Step right foot forward (while extending the ball straight forward away from the body).
   - Step left foot forward (while beginning the ball arm swing straight back past the body).
   - Step right foot forward (while finishing the back arm swing).
   - Step left foot forward (while rolling the ball forward on the floor).
   - Be sure to lower the body toward the floor (by bending the knees slightly) as the ball is released.

   Aim at spots marked on the floor (the spots should be in the same formation as the pins in a regulation bowling game). The distance between the bowler and the spots should be 20 to 25 feet.

   Criteria: When you can hit the #1 pin three times out of ten, you are ready to bowl a game. The game still includes ten frames (not just ten ball rolls). Keep score using score sheet #2.

   Criteria: When you score at least 50 in one game, you are ready for the next task.

6. **Task:** <u>Do task number 5 above with plastic bowling balls and pins.</u>
   Criteria: When you can hit the #1 pin three times out of ten, you are ready to bowl a game. Game still includes ten frames (not just ten ball rolls). Keep score using score sheet #2.

   Criteria: When you score at least 50 in one game, you are ready for the next task.

7. **Task:** <u>Bowl a regulation game using plastic bowling balls and pins.</u> Keep score as you would in a regulation bowling game, using score sheet #3.

Score Sheet #1

Frame	1	2	3	4	5	6	7	8	9	10
Carlos	2 / 2	3 / 5	5 / 10	1 / 11	6 / 17	5 / 22	4 / 26	8 / 34	1 / 35	7 / 42

Frame	1	2	3	4	5	6	7	8	9	10

Frame	1	2	3	4	5	6	7	8	9	10

Score Sheet #2

Frame	1	2	3	4	5	6	7	8	9	10
Yumi	5 1 6	3 3 12	1 4 17	2 6 25	0 6 31	4 3 38	2 4 44	7 0 51	2 2 55	9 0 64

Frame	1	2	3	4	5	6	7	8	9	10

Frame	1	2	3	4	5	6	7	8	9	10

Score Sheet #3

Frame	1	2	3	4	5	6	7	8	9	10
	5 4	6 0	8 ◣	3 ◣	7 2	X	5 ◣	X	6 1	2 ◣ 9
Rajiv	9	15	28	45	54	74	94	111	118	137

Frame	1	2	3	4	5	6	7	8	9	10

Frame	1	2	3	4	5	6	7	8	9	10

Symbol key: X = Strike

◣ = Spare

Bowling Technique: Peer Assessment

Performer's Name _____

Evaluator's Name _____

Today's Date _____

Directions: Answer the following questions about the performance of your partner. You will need to watch your partner perform many times in order to answer all the questions.

In the starting position, your partner
- holds the ball in front
  of his or her chest   yes ____   no ____
- holds the ball with two hands   yes ____   no ____
- is looking at the pins   yes ____   no ____

When stepping forward, your partner
- takes the first step with the right
  foot (if right-handed)   yes ____   no ____
- takes four steps toward the pins   yes ____   no ____
- swings the ball out from the body,
  and then backward   yes ____   no ____

When releasing the ball, your partner
- has the left foot forward (if
  right-handed)   yes ____   no ____
- swings arm forward (with the ball)   yes ____   no ____
- lowers body toward the floor so
  the ball hits the floor softly
  (no loud sound)   yes ____   no ____
- follows through by continuing the
  arm movement upward (after the
  ball is released)   yes ____   no ____

GRADES K–6

NASPE STANDARD 6 Students value physical activity for health, enjoyment, challenge, self-expression, and/or social interaction.

LESSON OBJECTIVES

- Students express themselves through movement.
- Students work with others to produce a final product.
- Students share a final product with the entire class.
- Students enjoy moving to music.
- Students accept the challenge of creating new movements.

EQUIPMENT NEEDED Audiotape or CD player

PREPARATION TIME If integrating with music and physical education, you will need a group meeting with those teachers of approximately one hour.

KNOWLEDGE CONTENT Students can do the following:

- Move different body parts
- Move in place or travel
- Travel different pathways
- Move by walking, running, skipping, leaping, sliding, hopping, jumping, or galloping
- Move on different levels
- Move in different directions
- Make big or small movements
- Move softly or strongly
- Move smoothly or sharply
- Move in unison or separately

Students realize that different music stimulates different feelings and movements.

Students should know the following terms and be able to identify them in the music:

- *Beat:* the underlying pulse heard in the music
- *Tempo:* the rate of speed of the underlying beat
- *Accent:* the emphasis placed on a beat to make it stronger or louder than others
- *Measure:* one group of beats made by the regular occurrence of the heavy accent
- *Phrase:* a group of measures representing a musical sentence or thought

CLASSROOM ACTIVITY Divide the class into groups of five or six children each. Their task is to create a

movement sequence (line dance) to music. The length of the sequence and other task requirements should be relative to the age of the children. Younger children need sequences that include more repetitions of the same movements. Since many popular songs have a chorus, older students can design movement sequences that include a chorus.

Use music selected by the students (and approved by the teacher).

Students will need time to design and practice their line dances. When perfected, the dances should be demonstrated to the class. If time allows, let groups teach their dances to the entire class.

All the dances could be presented so parents and other community members could see the creative abilities of their children. Dances could be presented at the halftime of an athletic event, at a community celebration, or at a local shopping mall.

ASSESSMENT After the project is completed, hold a class discussion to evaluate the following:

- How well the members of the groups worked together. If problems occurred during work time, identify those problems and how they were solved.
- How much the children enjoyed moving to music.
- The students' knowledge of the musical terms.

SUCCESS FOR ALL Remember that when constructing dances, not all students have to do the same movements. Some movements, but not all, should be in unison. Therefore, if some students do not possess the ability to perform certain movements, they simply select a different movement to do during those movement counts. If some students cannot move as fast as others, have them, for example, do a movement for four counts while others are doing it in one or two counts, or select a slower tempo for the music for the entire dance.

INTEGRATION WITH OTHER SUBJECT AREAS Invite the music teacher and physical education specialist to join your class for this project. The music teacher can work with students in identifying the underlying beat, groups of beats (measures), phrases (musical sentences), and accents found in the music. The physical education specialist can help the students use various space, force, time, and movement factors when selecting movements to be performed.

CHAPTER 10

Sociological Aspects of Children Moving

The purpose of this chapter is threefold: (1) to describe the socialization process in general and specifically as it applies to children in their role of being physically active; (2) to identify ways the socialization process can be used in teaching the social skills of sportlike behavior, fair play, responsibility, and respect; and (3) to discuss diversity issues (cultural, ethnic, gender, and disability) relative to the movement setting.

Objectives

After studying this chapter, you will be able to do the following:

- Briefly describe how children are socialized into behaving as society expects.

- Identify various agents within the society who are part of the socialization process, and describe each agent's role in shaping children's behavior and attitudes.

- Discuss socialization *through* and *about* movement.

- Discuss inclusion as a socialization issue.

- Identify ways the elementary classroom teacher can *socialize* children to be physically active.

- Identify ways to encourage respectful diversity in the movement setting.

- Identify and describe the influence of gender, ethnicity, and disability on the way children are socialized as to the role of physical activity in their lives.

- Discuss the impact of physical skill ability on the socialization of the child.

- Discuss the elements common in most models for teaching social skills.

- Design ways to teach and assess social skills in the movement setting.

Mr. Washington teaches sixth grade. Both he and the physical educator provide physical education for his students. For several weeks, they have been presenting lessons designed to improve the students' striking skills. Today Mr. Washington is continuing that theme using a problem-solving teaching method, so he assigns the problem-solving project described in Box 10.1 The teacher forms groups (composed of four students) with the intention of having students who do not usually work together in a group. Mr. Washington indicates that students must figure out how to organize themselves to complete the project.

This instructional design is deliberate because Mr. Washington believes students are responsible for their own learning, can learn to interact appropriately with others, and should value all the students in their class. While the students are working on completing the project, Mr. Washington moves from group to group, asking questions that help students think through the problem, providing helpful hints about possible organization techniques, and ensuring that students value input from everyone in the group.

Mr. Washington ends the lesson by having each group tell the class one movement principle group members discovered while completing the project and one interaction principle they found helpful while working together. As one student is speaking to the class, another student from the group will write the principles on a large wall sign—one sign for the movement principles and another for the interaction principles. In addition to the content being placed on the wall signs, in evaluating the students Mr. Washington wants to see that all four group members of each group participate in the closing activity.

BOX 10.1 Mr. Washington's Problem-Solving Project

GRADES 4–6

DIRECTIONS

- Each group of four students should collect two soccer balls, a tablet of paper, and a pencil.
- Move to one of the outdoor areas defined by having a soccer goal with two cones placed 20 feet in front of the goal.

QUESTION TO ANSWER

What kicking technique maximizes the speed of the kicked ball (beginning with a stationary ball and having been kicked along the ground instead of into the air)? Write your notes and final answer on the tablet.

HINTS TO CONSIDER

- As a stationary object is struck (kicked), it will move only if the force applied to it is sufficient to overcome its inertia. Maximizing the ball's speed (upon being kicked) involves maximizing the force production of the body's movement. Experiment with weight shift, ball approach, body rotation, length of backswing, and sequence of muscle actions as you kick the ball to determine the best technique.
- Should the kicking foot be firm or should it give with the kick? (Answer: It should be firm because the reaction of the soccer ball against your foot is just as great as the force that projected the ball.)
- Where on the ball should the foot contact the ball? Why? (Answer: The more nearly the ball is contacted in line with its center of gravity, the greater the amount of force that is transferred to the object in the direction it should travel; so contact the ball dead center.)
- How should the body be placed in relation to the ball as the kick is made? (Answer: To kick the ball straight ahead, the kicker should be directly in line with the ball.)

The Socialization of Children

The socialization that occurs in schools, classrooms, and gymnasiums is generally considered part of the "hidden curriculum" because much of the time the learning that takes place through socialization occurs without the direct guidance or awareness of the teacher. Whether or not the teacher consciously guides students in the areas of respect, friendship development, fair play, self-control, and cooperation, learning is occurring in those areas. Constantly throughout the day, as children interact with their peers and teachers, children are learning what is expected of them in various situations.

Sometimes what they learn is an appropriate behavior, but other times they learn an inappropriate behavior. Children try various behaviors to obtain what they want or need, and they continue to display behaviors that were effective for them in the past (regardless of whether adults view the behavior as appropriate or inappropriate). For example, students seeking attention from the teacher (or from classmates) may continually break class rules in order to obtain that needed attention. We believe the socialization process at work in the classroom and gymnasium is a worthy topic to understand in order to grasp the fundamental ideas necessary to use that process in an effective manner.

In general, sociologists examine human behavior and social development from a group perspective. They are interested in group behaviors and differences between or among groups rather than in individual behaviors or individual differences. They seek to understand society in a broad context by studying the presence and origins of group differences. How does the society view its members with disabilities? Do men and women (boys and girls) in the society think and behave differently? How do children learn the values and rules of the culture they live in?

THE PROCESS OF SOCIALIZATION

In the broadest sense, **socialization** is education. It is the process through which children acquire a sense of personal identity, learn what people in the surrounding culture believe, and discover how to behave according to the expectations of that culture (Henslin 2007). Through both explicit instruction and conscious and unconscious modeling, children are taught the values, norms, beliefs, and skills necessary to become fully functioning members of their culture. For example, examine the scenario that opened this chapter and find the beliefs, norms, and expectations that Mr. Washington was espousing (both explicitly and unconsciously).

Peer interaction plays an important role in socializing children; it gives students the opportunity to learn more about themselves and to mature both cognitively and socially.

For considerable time, scientists have debated whether individual and group behavior is a product of heredity (and thus is predetermined) or is a product of experience and learning, in which case behavior could be altered by changing the environment in which children are raised or in which groups operate. Sociologists today deal with the **heredity ("nature") versus environment ("nurture") argument** by agreeing that the socialization process involves both nature and nurture. The results of the socialization process depend on the interaction between the biological attributes of the child (nature) and the environmental variables present throughout the child's life (nurture).

Socialization is primarily concerned with the emergence of *self*—the individual's sense of identity (who am I?)—and self is defined and developed through social interaction. Our view of ourselves is primarily a reflection of how other people respond to us—how we think others see us, how we believe they judge what they see, and how we feel about those reactions. Through socialization, children acquire a sense of who they are and where they belong. Through socialization, children internalize cultural norms regarding how to feel, think, and act so that they can function effectively in that particular society. It is worthwhile for educators to understand the nature of the socialization process and how they might encourage children to learn appropriate social skills and develop healthy personal identities.

SOCIALIZATION AGENTS

A **socialization agent** is usually defined as any individual, group, or organization that influences a person's behavior or sense of self. This influence occurs by rewarding and punishing behavior, by providing instruction in social rules and social roles, and even by serving as a role model. The influence of the agent can be either positive or negative. For example, a parent who models caring behavior projects a positive influence, whereas an athlete (viewed on television) displaying violence projects a negative influence. For children today, some primary agents of socialization include family, peers, school, and the mass media (Henslin 2007).

Family   During early childhood, the family is the primary agent of socialization. The size and composition of the family unit affect the messages being delivered to the children. Family structures, socioeconomic status, ethnic culture, and amount of time parents spend with their children all affect the techniques used to parent and the messages sent to their children about work, school, family, peer and adult relationships, and so on. In addition, family structures continue to adapt to sociocultural contexts, thus developing new family structures. The two-parent, married family is becoming just one of a variety of functional structures. For example, grandparent-headed households containing children younger than 18 years old have increased by 65 percent from 1990 to 2000 (Lever and Wilson 2005). Today families consist of traditional structures, single-parent families, extended families, foster and adoptive families, gay or lesbian couples, step families, as well as people committed to each other but with no legal ties to each other (Kaslow 2001).

School and Peers   Although the family is the primary socialization agent during early childhood, the school environment and the child's peers play extremely important roles in the socialization of the child once the child begins to attend school. In our society, the basic function of school is to *socialize* the child into becoming an adequately functioning adult. The school consciously teaches academic content (including physical education content) to prepare students for further education and jobs. It also, consciously and unconsciously, teaches habits, skills, and values that enable children to function as social beings in our society; provides the forum in which children learn who they are; and allows opportunities for children to develop and sustain close relationships with others.

Within the school setting, interaction with peers provides opportunities for children to mature (cognitively and socially) and learn who they are. It is clear that children influence one another through modeling, talk, and social reinforcement. What is not clear is exactly how that happens. However, gender, age, ethnicity, social competence, social status, and the quality and stability of peer friendships are all conditions that affect the outcome of peer interactions.

The last section of this chapter identifies the social skills important for children to learn and presents ways to teach those skills in the physical education and classroom setting. Instant Activity 10.1 promotes group interaction and acceptance that may lead to friendships developing among group members.

The Mass Media In addition to family, school, and peers, the **mass media** (in the form of television, computer and Internet games, video games, Nintendo, etc.) constitute a particularly enticing socialization agent. The messages conveyed through the mass media are especially problematic in the areas of violence, gender and race stereotyping, and boy-girl relationships. Much of the time television portrays characters solving problems effectively through the use of violence, shows women and minorities in stereotypic roles, and conveys unrealistic messages about relationships between men and women. And video games are notorious for including violence against men and women and portraying violence as an effective solution to problems. Certain television programs (designed for children), such as *Mr. Rogers' Neighborhood* and *Sesame Street,* do encourage curiosity, "pretend" play, effective (nonaggressive) ways of dealing with peers, and acceptance of those different from ourselves. And certain video games are effective in building reading and math skills.

However, regardless of the programs being viewed or games being played, child experts recommend that young children watch a limited amount of television and spend a limited amount of time playing video

INSTANT ACTIVITY 10.1
Floor Patterns

Grades 2–6
Equipment Needed
Rope, string, or masking tape

Activity
Partners (for grades 2–3) or groups (for grades 4–6) work in the open area by their desks. Children use rope, string, or masking tape to make a pattern on the floor. Children must work cooperatively to design and make the floor pattern. You might specify that the design has to include straight and curved pathways and that the paths must cross or intertwine with each other, so a possible design might be as follows:

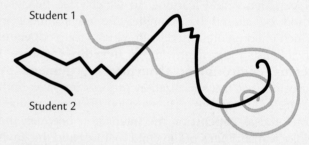

Student 1

Student 2

Once the design is drawn, the students must create a movement sequence to perform along their pathway. Moving along the intertwining pathway (all at the same time) will necessitate cooperation, communication, and respect.

The teacher encourages the building of friendships by making sure that group members create an environment in which members express thoughts and feelings; share honest, sincere, positive statements; allow all to be heard; and accept each other's differences.

or computer games—first because of the negative modeling that occurs, and second because sedentary activities such as watching television and playing video games take away from the time children might spend on other kinds of play activities. Children might otherwise play board games or pretend activities, read books, or help their parents cook. Children who use their minds and their imaginations in these ways develop a sense of mastery over their environment. Third, watching television and playing video and computer games decrease the time available for

INSTANT ACTIVITY 10.2 Hula Hoop Fun

Grades K–6

Equipment Needed

Hula hoops

Activity

With this activity, children practice their locomotor skills, develop balance, and learn to work with others in the group.

Place hula hoops on the floor around the classroom and assign two or three students to work at each hoop. Students will need to coordinate and communicate while jumping, hopping, and leaping around the hoop and in and out of the hoop so as to operate in a safe manner. Encourage group members to work out their own problems and give them time to do so.

Move the children around the hoop (both clockwise and counterclockwise) with tasks such as these:

- Jump in and out of the hoop ten times.
- Hop in and out of the hoop with your right foot as many times as you can until you get tired.

- Repeat above task with your left foot.
- Hop around the outside of the hoop on the right foot, then on the left foot, moving clockwise (then repeat, moving in a counterclockwise direction).
- Repeat the above task but jump instead of hop.
- Leap from outside to inside the hoop (for older children, leap across the entire hoop).

As children get older, increase the complexity of the tasks by combining movements. For example, move around the outside of the hoop repeating the following patterns:

- Five jumps, five right hops, five left hops, and five jumps
- Three jumps, leap to the inside, three jumps, leap to the outside, continue

Pairs or groups of older children can create their own patterns for moving around the hoop. Increase the complexity of developing their own patterns by setting the patterns to music so they must keep time to the music as they perform.

---

the child to be physically active through play activities such as climbing a tree, riding a bike, in-line skating, and playing tag with the neighborhood children. And as indicated in Chapter 4, this lack of physical activity is leading to an increase in childhood obesity. Increased time spent watching television and playing video games is contributing to an increased prevalence of obesity in children.

MOVEMENT AS A SOCIALIZATION AGENT

Having identified and discussed four well-accepted socialization agents (family, peers, school, and the mass media), we wish to propose another agent that we believe greatly affects children as they grow up in our society. That agent is the ability or disability to perform well in the performance of movement—especially in the movement forms relevant to children as they progress through their school years.

As discussed in the previous chapter on motivating children to be physically active, a central part of children's self-image involves the perceptions surrounding their performance competence within the physical

realm. Children who are physically skilled, thus enabling them to participate very effectively in games and sports, have better peer relations and higher self-esteem than those who are not physically skilled (Barbour 1996; Evans and Roberts 1987; Weiss and Duncan 1992). Much of children's play involves physical activities, and as children learn about their world through play, they also learn (and form opinions) about their own physical abilities. In addition, physical play with others is always observed by others. So children see each other's successes and failures—unlike in the classroom where academic abilities are less observable—and quickly begin to make judgments about their own (and others') physical competence. In the best of worlds, children come to believe that they possess high ability in a number of physical skills. Classroom teachers and physical education teachers would do well to help children develop their physical skills in order to enhance their opportunities to make friends and be accepted by others. Instant Activity 10.2 allows children to practice locomotor skills and improve balance while learning to work with others in a group setting.

Socialization about movement occurs in our society. The beliefs society instills in its members about movement are numerous. In fact, society uses movement to help children develop an appropriate gender-role identity (based on what society views as appropriate gender roles for men and women). Whereas *sex* is a biological term indicating male or female, *gender* is a social, cultural, and psychological creation (Henslin 2007). Your sex is inherited; however, your gender is learned as you are socialized into behaviors and beliefs that your culture says are appropriate for your sex. Thus society tells us who we are and how we are expected to behave relative to physical activity based on our sex. For example, society tells us the role of physical activity in our lives, who are appropriate activity partners, what are appropriate activities, and what is the importance of winning.

The Role of Physical Activity   Based on recent evidence of the health benefits derived from participating in exercise and sport, messages about the role of physical activity in our daily lives stress the need for all *adults* to be physically active (regardless of age, gender, and ability). However, society is just beginning to recognize and promote the *child's* need for regular physical activity. And the role of physical activity in the lives of various ethnic groups within our society must not be overlooked. Various ethnic groups have different beliefs as to the importance of physical activity and the types of physical activity that are appropriate for their members (Williams and Bedward 2001). Activity preference studies continue to show disparities in terms of activity preferences based on ethnicity (Kovar et al. 2001; Hill and Cleven 2005). For instance, ninth-grade students in California have significantly different preferences based on ethnicity—while 52.9 percent of Asians selected badminton, only 15.1 percent of African Americans did, and while 61.5 percent of Hispanics selected soccer, only 18.1 percent of African Americans chose soccer (Hill and Cleven 2005).

Appropriate Activity Partners   Society's rules are really quite complicated for determining how and when boys and girls (men and women) may play physical activities together. While in elementary school, boys and girls may participate together in physical education classes. Junior and senior highs separated boys and girls for many years (until Title IX had the apparent effect of putting them together). However, even today many high school physical education classes are places where boys and girls still do not play together in the spirit of Title IX (Napper-Owen et al. 1999). At elementary schools, girls and boys play on the same playground during recess, but they also do not, in general, play together across gender.

How and when people of different ethnic backgrounds may play physical activities together is also prescribed by society. Research presented in Chapter 12 indicates that not only do boys and girls not play together on the playground, but children from different ethnic groups also do not, in general, play together. In the study, this was especially true in situations where language was a barrier and when a small number of children from a different ethnic background were present in a large group from the majority culture.

Appropriate Activities   Society prescribes the physical activities appropriate for specific genders, ethnic groups, and religious communities to participate in. Girls are encouraged to play what society views as *less active* sports (e.g., volleyball, softball, dance, and figure skating) and to be more *ladylike* in their performance of physical activity. Girls are definitely not to participate in contact sports such as boxing or football. Boys are encouraged to play in a *rough and tumble* manner (Henslin 2007), and they are greatly respected for playing physical contact sports and almost *required* to be physically skilled in order to be considered *men*. Ethnic minority men are overrepresented in very rough sports (e.g., football and boxing) and underrepresented in the *gentlemen* sports that require significant financial means (e.g., golf, tennis, and sailing). Ethnic minority women are overrepresented in women's sports viewed traditionally as men's domain (e.g., basketball and track and field) and are underrepresented in the traditional women's sports (e.g., dance, gymnastics, and ice skating) (Smith 2007). Religious mores may also exclude participation in certain activities (e.g., dance) and restrict participation in other activities due to dress requirements (e.g., cannot wear shorts or pants).

The Importance of Winning   In general, our culture subscribes to the notion that it is unacceptable for skilled and nonskilled performers to play together. Primarily this view is maintained because the goal of most *adult* physical activities and sports is to win. The likelihood of winning increases substantially if the team is composed of skilled players. This belief has filtered into physical education programs (even at the elementary level) and poses major problems for movement educators to overcome as we want to de-emphasize winning and promote the acquisition of skill.

Changes in Societal Beliefs   Although society instills certain beliefs in its members, those beliefs can, and do, change over time. Our identity as moving human beings is always evolving. What boys and girls (men and women) were allowed to do just ten years ago is different

When movement education promotes values such as joyful interaction with others, rather than winning, students of all skill levels can have positive movement experiences.

from today. For example, girls no longer play half-court basketball. Slowly, acceptance of even those with disabilities into the movement setting is being achieved. In addition, as the supremacy of *winning* gives over to the other values of participating in physical activity (joy of effort, benefits of exercising, playing with others), children with low skill levels are being better served in physical education and sport settings. As new research and information becomes available, attitudes change. For example, the surgeon general's report has significantly altered how adults view the importance of physical activity in their lives. And the recent media focus on the ever-increasing incidence and negative impact of childhood obesity indicates that society is listening and ready to be supportive of what schools and communities can do to combat this epidemic through quality physical activity programs. Society's expectations change over time, and the expectations will continue to change as society evolves and adapts to the wishes of its members.

Learning Social Concepts Through Movement   In addition to learning *about* movement, children also learn **socialization through movement** by playing together. They learn about the concepts of cooperation, friendship, fairness, and doing what's right. They learn what social and moral conduct is acceptable or not acceptable in their society. This social development occurs whenever children play together (during free play or during instructional physical activity) and work together (in the elementary classroom). Classroom teachers teach social skills (e.g., respect, responsibility, safety) and encourage students to behave appropriately while at school (Darch and Kame'enui 2004). Physical educators also strive to develop certain social skills within their students. Most physical educators strive to teach the social skills identified in NASPE's Standard 5 (NASPE 2004, 39–41):

1. Following class rules and procedures
2. Using appropriate etiquette for the activity

3. Practicing physical skills in a safe manner
4. Behaving ethically
5. Interacting with others in a positive manner
6. Developing the skills of teamwork and cooperation

The last section in this chapter provides an in-depth discussion about teaching social skills to elementary school children in the movement setting. Instant Activity 10.3 provides children an opportunity to develop the skill of working with a variety of partners.

Socializing Children to Be Physically Active

Children's physical activity behaviors are of great importance based on the evidence indicating the physical, social, and psychological benefits to children of being physically active. However, knowing how important physical activity is to the developing child has not appeared to affect the way parents, teachers, and society in general structure the child's life. Children continue to be raised in neighborhoods where it is not safe to play outdoors. Parents drive their children to and from school. Children go to after-school programs where physical activity is limited by the available space. Schools continue to be places where children are inactive for long periods of time as they sit at desks and complete their academic work. It appears that society establishes structures (perhaps not consciously) that work to decrease the activity levels of children. So what can parents and teachers do to provide encouragement and opportunities for their children to be active? Let's look at how **parental influence** and teacher-parent partnerships can make a difference.

INSTANT ACTIVITY 10.3 Stretchies

Grades K–4

Equipment Needed

One stretchie for each child. Stretchies are strips of spandex material 2-1/2 inches wide and 2 yards long. The two ends are tied together in a knot to form a loop.

Activity

Have the children work in pairs and change partners often, and be sure that boys and girls work together. Ask the children to do the following activities:

- Use different body parts to make different shapes (use a different number of body parts and make round, narrow, wide, straight, twisted shapes).
- One partner makes a shape and the other partner copies it (stand beside partner and match the shape).

- One partner makes a shape and the other partner copies it (partners stand facing each other and pretend they are standing in front of a mirror).
- One partner ties him- or herself up with the stretchie and then the partner unties him or her.
- Make a balance and hold. Copy the balance that a partner makes.
- Partners share one stretchie and make various shapes.
- Partners hold one stretchie under their feet and try to hop or jump in place.

As the children perform, the teacher emphasizes the skills involved in getting along with a partner. Notice partners having trouble and suggest ways to resolve issues.

THE INFLUENCE OF PARENTS

Parents are certainly the most important influence when it comes to affecting children's activity levels. Research has found a strong relationship between the physical activity levels of parents and their children (Davison, Cutting, and Birch 2003; Freedson and Evenson 1991; Moore et al. 1991; Trost et al. 2001). The research also indicates that the salient factor in this relationship is the parental belief system (Brustad 1996; Kimiecik and Horn 1998). This research is the foundation for the following four techniques that parents can use to socialize their children to be physically active (Welk 1999):

1. *Parental encouragement:* Verbal and nonverbal forms of encouragement (direct efforts to get a child to play outdoors or reduce the amount of time spent watching television and indirect efforts to promote the child's interest and involvement).
2. *Parental involvement:* Direct involvement by the parent in the child's activity (taking a walk with the child, playing on the neighborhood playground equipment, building sand castles in the sandbox).
3. *Parental facilitation:* Efforts by parents to make it easy for children to be active (driving them to soccer practice, purchasing softball equipment, providing sport equipment for use at home).
4. *Parental role modeling:* Efforts by parents to be physically active themselves (walking to work, jogging daily, and working in the yard or garden).

Parental support appears to be especially important for the populations most at risk for inactivity (i.e., girls, youth with low perceived physical competence, and youth who are overweight) (Davison et al. 2006). These at-risk populations have the greatest need for parental support and show benefits when that support is given.

THE TEACHER-PARENT PARTNERSHIP

Although parents are a primary influence on children's activity levels, we believe that teachers and parents together can become an even stronger influence. We have already indicated a number of times that this book is about helping classroom teachers provide opportunities for their students to be active as much as possible throughout the school day. We have included many suggestions (and specific lessons and activities) for including physical activity in the classroom. We hope classroom teachers find these suggestions helpful. By using these lessons and activities, teachers not only encourage their students to be physically active but also provide the opportunities to do so. In addition, they become role models for including physical activity in daily life.

Teachers are encouraged to work with parents as partners to achieve the goal of regular participation in physical activity by their students. If necessary, educate parents as to their role in this effort and how they might implement the four techniques identified in the previous section. Advise parents about developmentally appropriate activities. Help families identify barriers to being active and potential ways to overcome the barriers. Education can occur through newsletters, presentations during parent-teacher nights, displays at sporting events, and/or "homework" that the student and parent complete together. Establishing a working relationship with parents is key for educational efforts to be effective (Council on Sports Medicine and Fitness 2006).

Physical educators become major partners with parents and classroom teachers in their efforts to produce physically active children. Physical educators are trained to design physical education programs to meet Standard 3 of the NASPE guidelines, which specifies that "children participate regularly in physical activity" (NASPE 2004, 27). Children's experiences in the home, in the classroom, and in physical education are critical to them choosing an active, healthy lifestyle.

Inclusion as a Socialization Issue

In general, the **dominant culture** (values, beliefs, and behaviors) in U.S. society today comes primarily from Anglo-Saxon thought and perspective. This culture contains attitudes and perceptions about people of certain socioeconomic status, with particular physical characteristics (skin color; body size, shape, and weight; gender; facial features), and from different ethnic backgrounds. To the extent that minority cultures do not have the same values, beliefs, and behaviors as the dominant culture, children from minority cultures have difficulty in identifying and conforming to the expectations set by the dominant culture; thus inclusion is a socialization issue. Society's perceptions and expectations must become broader and more flexible to meet the needs of children from minority cultures.

In addition, although the socialization process provides children opportunities (through interactions with peers and adults) to discover who they are and where they belong, that process must be very confusing for minority children. Finding a sense of identity, when the expectations of the dominant culture and the minority culture are not the same, must be very difficult for children. How do you find a place for yourself within the dominant culture and within your own ethnic culture? Perhaps you learn to manage life in multiple worlds. "To thrive, minority children must also learn to engage in the academic process communally, rather than individualistically; they must

By providing students with many opportunities to be active—both inside and outside the classroom—teachers can help promote lifetime physical activity.

also learn that to attain the highest levels of human functioning, they must remain embedded in familial and communal support systems while they participate in other worlds" (Stanton-Salazar 1997, 25).

Society's norms and perceptions are changing. That change is being driven primarily by dramatic increases in the Hispanic and Asian American populations who continue to grow at a much faster rate than the population as a whole. Sections of the United States are already "majority-minority" states, where minority populations make up a majority of the state's population (California, District of Columbia, Hawaii, and New Mexico). Texas is set to join these states soon as 49.5 percent of its population is minority (U.S. Census 2004). The continuing development of "majority-minority" cultures will certainly impact the socialization process and shape that process for many years to come.

The discussion thus far seems to speak only to ethnic minorities. However, the case just built for ethnic minorities is relevant and applicable to those who belong to the dominant culture but who are valued less (i.e., girls and women, persons with disabilities, lesbian and gay youth, and low-income families). Their struggle to gain access to the privileges and resources of the dominant culture is very similar to those of people from minority cultures. For example, Hills (2006) reports that girls struggle to both conform to and break out of the social barriers placed on them in regard to being feminine and participating in physical activity.

Girls continue to view their physical self in relation to societal norms of femininity so they value muscle tone and slenderness more than they value developing the physical skills needed to be physically active (Garrett 2004). To the extent that physical activity and femininity are viewed as not being compatible, girls lose the potential to benefit from participation in physical activity because they choose not to participate (thus excluding themselves based on cultural norms).

RESPECTING DIVERSITY

As an official institution of the dominant culture, schools tend to perpetuate the dominant values, beliefs, and behaviors. This tendency is problematic for minority children and children with disabilities because it places them at risk for not becoming viable members of the mainstream culture. It is problematic for boys and girls because, as limits are placed on the behaviors of each gender, it does not allow them to develop their full potential. Respecting diversity by being inclusive within the school setting is a difficult task; nonetheless, it is one worth striving for. When society's messages are harmful to children, educators must step forward and be agents of change. For instance, when a student in a wheelchair is told she cannot play football, educators will find ways to involve her in the play experience of football. For example, when boys are told they should play football instead of dancing, educators will provide dance role models and dance experiences for their male students.

Respecting diversity means that teachers are committed to using teaching practices that enable all children to learn and provide all children access to appropriate learning opportunities. This commitment begins with an examination of your own possible biases (instilled by our society) that might be affecting your teaching practices and curriculum. You might begin that examination by discussing with your peers in education the culture beliefs and practices with which you were raised. Possible discussion questions are:

1. How were our lives constructed by gender, race, and class socialization during childhood?
2. How have those perceptions and beliefs changed during our years of study in college?
3. How might classroom teachers perpetuate biases that may reproduce limitations of gender, race, and class?
4. How do gender, race, and class shape our teaching practices?
5. What tensions might arise from gender, race, and class issues in an elementary school setting?

After discussing how society has and continues to affect you, consider trying to obtain more insight into your own specific behaviors to determine any inherent biases. Knowing possible biases is the first step toward changing those biases. Ask yourself:

1. *Do I expect more of certain students?* This bias means, for instance, expecting girls to perform better academically while expecting boys to perform better in physical activities, or expecting African American boys to be better basketball players than other boys.
2. *Do I treat groups of students differently?* Examples of this bias would be segregating boys and girls in any of the ways identified in the next section of the text, using boys more often than girls to demonstrate physical skills, calling on Caucasian students more often than others when students raise their hands in class to respond to a question, or asking mostly Asian students to tutor others in class.
3. *Do I allow groups of students to behave differently?* Examples of this bias include allowing boys to be more active and expecting girls to sit quietly in the classroom, allowing boys to be more aggressive when playing on the playground, or disciplining African Americans more harshly than other students.
4. *Do I assume knowledge of an individual by ascribing a group characteristic to that individual?* This bias includes, for example, expecting a boy to lead the discussion on football, a girl to lead on the topic of dance, and a Hispanic boy to demonstrate soccer skills.
5. *Do I provide a curriculum that is not relevant to my students?* This bias includes doing only physical activities I like to do, or limiting the curriculum to physical activities of interest to the dominant Caucasian society.

Evidence clearly indicates that physical education teachers' practices are influenced by their beliefs on the difference between boys and girls (Hunter 2004; Martino and Beckett 2004) and what those differences say about physical activity participation. In addition, teachers' ignorance about social styles, traditions, and persistent negative media images of people from diverse ethnic backgrounds leads to inappropriate teaching practices and student discipline practices (McCadden 1998; Schwartz 2001). Our students deserve nothing less than a pedagogy that creates an open and fair learning environment. Each teacher must create that open and fair learning environment within their own classroom. Thus it behooves teachers to examine their beliefs and practices and learn new practices, if necessary, in order to develop students to their full potential.

Students, as well as teachers, must respect diversity. In the movement setting, NASPE indicates that children should "develop respect for individual similarities and differences through positive interaction among participants in physical activity" (NASPE 2004, 39). Those differences include characteristics of cultures and religions, ethnicity, motor performance, disabilities, physical characteristics, gender, race, sexual orientation, and socioeconomic level. Quick Lesson 10.1 and Classroom Learning Station 10.1 at the end of the chapter present activities that help children and teachers learn about each other's abilities and cultures.

PROVIDING QUALITY INSTRUCTION

Quality, responsible teaching in the movement setting demands that educators respect diversity and make available to all students the resources provided by the school. Thus, *in terms of ethnicity,* teachers must focus on four areas (Culp 2006; Torrey and Ashy 1997):

1. *Developing positive, nondiscriminatory attitudes and practices:* This entails knowing your own culture and learning more about other cultures. The Special Event (Grandparents' Day) at the end of the chapter provides one way to learn more about the cultures represented in your classroom. This also entails treating students in a similar manner—for example, not trying to "control" the behavior of African American males more tightly than while males.
2. *Developing a positive learning climate:* This entails making different cultures consistently apparent in the learning environment (post signs in several languages, pronounce names correctly, include photographs and music from diverse cultures, etc.). It also entails knowing and responding to common learning styles exhibited in different cultures. For example, a student's role in the Navajo society is to be a listener rather than to be an active participant.
3. *Enriching the curriculum:* Although the basic curriculum remains constant, be sure to include a variety of activities from many cultures around the world and recognize that some students work best in a cooperative environment whereas others like spirited competition.
4. *Expanding family involvement:* This entails seeking out parents to learn information about customs (e.g., eye contact, personal space, and physical contact), leisure activities, and behavioral expectations for their children.

In terms of providing quality instruction for children with varying motor and mental abilities, we suggest using a cultural and social minority perspective (Kozub, Sherblom, and Perry 1999) that assumes all children, regardless of ability level, have an inherent right to participate in physical education with their peers. This perspective views disability as another form of diversity or difference—not as something less. Implementing this approach needs to be learned and practiced; thus Chapter 5 covers this approach in depth.

In terms of providing quality instruction for children of both genders, we suggest eliminating segregation based on gender as a way to encourage positive interactions between girls and boys. "Gender segregation exposes boys and girls to differing social influences— not on the basis of the individual child's interests and aptitudes but on the basis of their sex alone. When boys and girls play separately, they miss out on opportunities to learn from and cooperate with each other. The maintenance of separate groups encourages an acceptance of gender stereotypes, suggesting that boys and girls are more different from each other than they really are" (Powlishta 1995, 65). Gender labeling increases children's gender stereotyping bias (Bigler 2005). It is hoped that physical education teachers and classroom teachers will eliminate the following types of behaviors in their classrooms:

- Lining up boys and girls into separate lines for purposes of walking to and from physical education classes, or to recess, or to any other activity
- Allowing girls to wear clothing that prohibits full participation in physical activity
- Holding competitions between girls and boys, for example, the boys competing against the girls while running races or holding a math contest
- Allowing students to self-select partners and groups containing only members of one sex
- Using terminology that links poorer performance with a specific gender ("girls" push-ups versus "modified" push-ups)
- Comparing boys and girls ("You throw like a girl")
- Controlling boys' behavior by threatening that they will have to work with a girl if they do not behave
- Using artificial distinctions such as greeting the children every day with "Good morning, boys and girls" (Just say "good morning")
- Using male terminology when referring to an entire group composed of both boys and girls ("Good morning, guys")

Instead of emphasizing differences, educators can emphasize similarities by forming mixed-gender work

INSTANT ACTIVITY 10.4
Stand Up, Sit Down

Grades K–6

Equipment Needed

None

Activity

For lower elementary children, assign partners and have the partners sit back-to-back and hook elbows. Have children tuck their feet closely to the body. Then have them stand up together by pressing against each other. Children practice standing up and sitting down ten times in a row. Have them switch partners often so children experience working with a variety of classmates.

For older children, expand the number of children in the group (from two to ten), and have them stand up and sit down as a group. Form new groups and repeat the task.

groups, using inclusive language ("Good morning, children"), and comparing social behavior and skill performances to standards (rather than to those of other individuals). Instant Activity 10.4 presents an activity (suitable for classroom or physical education) that encourages work with various partners (regardless of gender).

Teaching and Assessing Social Skills in the Movement Setting

The literature provides several theories and models and numerous strategies that can be used to teach social skills in the classroom and gymnasium. In this section, we present some general issues that need to be resolved, discuss the common elements found in many of the models, and present several models and strategies for teachers to consider. Finally, we also present some ways for teachers to assess children's social skills.

The first general issue to be resolved deals with the many terms used to describe and name the social skills important for children to learn. The list of terms is long and many times redundant. The redundancy probably occurs as educators choose terms based on

the age of the students and the understandability of the terms to particular groups of children. In order to facilitate the discussion in this chapter, the categorical scheme in Box 10.2 is used. The scheme places the commonly identified **social skills** (in the movement setting) into three broad categories: decision-making skills, interpersonal skills, and acceptance of personal responsibility. The social skills listed in each category are terms currently found in the literature. Teachers may use the terms most appropriate for their students and should clearly define the terms as needed for their particular situation.

The second general issue deals with the teacher's role in structuring a model to teach social skills. The teacher's role is twofold: (1) to know what kind of behavior she or he wishes to see in the classroom and gymnasium, and (2) to develop a plan for making certain that is the kind of behavior that occurs. Not all educators want exactly the same kind of behavior from their students, but it is very important that individual teachers explicate how they want their students to behave. Once teachers determine the important behaviors, they can develop a plan to teach those behaviors. This section of the chapter presents various models and strategies for teaching desired behaviors; however, we are not advocating one model over another. Different local circumstances may necessitate using different models and strategies and perhaps even altering the teacher-selected behaviors to be taught.

ELEMENTS CONTAINED IN MOST MODELS

Elements common to all the models are identified because in essence these elements seem to be essential in allowing the models to work successfully.

Social Interaction Is a Learnable Skill The first element common in the models is teachers who believe that social interaction behaviors are skills that can be taught and learned. With this belief, teachers view the acquisition of social interaction skills as a process that begins in the home and continues in the school. Thus teachers do not punish children for not having these skills, but rather develop strategies for moving children toward mastery of the skills. For example, while in a physical education class, a student breaks a piece of equipment by throwing it into the storage container (rather than placing it in the container). Instead of punishing the student ("Alan, since you cannot properly handle the equipment, you will not be allowed to participate in class

---

BOX 10.2   Categories of Social Skills

Decision-Making Skills	Interpersonal Skills	Personal Responsibility
Independence	Communication	Self-control
Resourcefulness	Manners	Respectfulness
Making choices	Sportlike behavior	Honesty
	Fair play	Helpfulness
	Teamwork	Empathy
	Cooperation	Caring
	Sharing	Compassion
	Encouraging	
	Listening	
	Friendship	

---

activities for the next ten minutes"), the teacher responds by having the student practice placing equipment in the container correctly five times consecutively. In addition, Alan is told to further discuss this issue with the teacher at the end of class, as he will have to figure out how to reimburse the school for the broken equipment. In this scenario, teachers plan and deliberately teach desired social skills to their students.

Children Are Responsible for Their Own Behavior   The second common element in the models is teachers who are ready to move control of the child's behavior from being the teacher's responsibility to being the child's responsibility. This involves the child learning to be self-regulated and self-controlled. However, in order for children to practice (and master) self-control and responsibility for their actions, the teacher must give up some control and responsibility. To become responsible, children must experience responsibility. To become self-controlled, they must experience situations in which they truly have control. For example, during physical education classes in the gymnasium, students may get drinks of water and use the restroom as needed without asking for permission from the teacher.

Although it is difficult at times to give control to the students, it is the appropriate thing to do, for in reality only the child controls his or her behavior. Teachers may think they control a child's actions, but the child's actions are choices made by the child. Evidence indicates that responsibility cannot be imposed upon or instilled in a child. Rather, teachers and parents can structure the environment so that *responsibility is*

activated. Current literature indicates that responsibility is activated in the following ways (Greenberg 1992):

- Responsibility is activated by an urge to contribute something to someone—a person, or one's own best self.
- Responsibility is an outgrowth of self-esteem, which in turn is an outgrowth of independence, competence, and initiative.
- Responsibility grows out of an ability to see other people's viewpoints and feel concern for them (empathy).

Children who come to school from homes where parents have already activated their responsibility will probably conform readily to teachers' expectations about them being responsible for their behavior. However, it should be noted that students having little previous experience in being responsible will probably resist the teachers' expectations. In those cases, teachers may slowly (over time) have to begin shaping small behavior changes that eventually lead the child into being responsible.

Physical educators, using Sport for Peace or other sport education teaching structures, have discovered increased student involvement and less off-task behavior. These types of structures provide students control of their learning experiences by building in student ownership of skill learning, team play, and team roles such as coach, scorekeeper, player, official, and statistician (Ennis et al. 1999; Hastie 1996, 1998). Teachers are learning that giving everyone a ball to practice with (instead of two balls per class) does not lead to chaos. It leads to involvement, improved skill performance, and willingness to participate in the future.

Children Are Valued Members of the Classroom Community The third common element is that teachers view their students as valued members of the class community. Students recognize they are valued when they are part of a classroom where they are given opportunities to be self-directed, asked to perform activities they view as meaningful, asked to participate in making decisions that directly affect them, and given caring attention from the teacher. For example, the movement educator allows the children to select the activities the class will engage in on each Friday during the month of February.

Children Learn Best Through Student-Centered Activities The fourth element common to most models for developing social skills is that they use a variety of student-centered, problem-solving, and cooperative learning activities. These types of activities allow students to make some decisions regarding their learning environment, encourage students to gain confidence in their ability to solve problems, and provide opportunities for children to interact with each other while learning. During these types of activities, children are actively involved in their learning and become committed partners with their classmates and teachers in the learning process. In addition, students are more interested in learning because they are using higher-order thinking skills such as problem solving, synthesis, discrimination, and analysis. How to design challenge and cooperation lessons or activities is outlined in Chapter 7, and Unit 2 at the back of the text contains 15 cooperative movement lessons.

Teachers Model Appropriate Behavior The final element common to models for teaching social skills is that they stress that teacher behavior in the classroom or gymnasium is just as important as student behavior. If teachers expect students to treat each other in certain ways (such as with respect, courtesy, and dignity), then teachers must also treat students that way. It would probably be helpful to encourage all personal interactions within the school to follow the stated expectations—teacher to teacher, teacher to student, student to student, teacher and student to principal, teacher and student to paraprofessional, and so on. This consistency in modeling the expected behavior can be a powerful tool in improving student behavior.

MODELS FOR TEACHING SOCIAL SKILLS

Several physical educators have developed models for teaching social skills based on a framework,

---

BOX 10.3
Seven Significant Resources of Successful People

1. Strong perceptions of personal capabilities: "I am capable."
2. Strong perceptions of personal significance: "I contribute in meaningful ways and I am genuinely needed."
3. Strong perception of personal influence over life: "I can influence what happens to me."
4. Strong intrapersonal skills: the ability to understand personal emotions, use that understanding to develop self-discipline and self-control, and learn from experience.
5. Strong interpersonal skills: the ability to work with others and develop friendships through communication, cooperation, negotiation, sharing, empathizing, and listening.
6. Strong systemic skills: the ability to respond to the limits and consequences of everyday life with responsibility, adaptability, flexibility, and integrity.
7. Strong judgmental skills: the ability to use wisdom and evaluate situations according to appropriate values.

From S. Glenn and J. Nelsen, *Raising Self-Reliant Children in a Self-Indulgent World.* Copyright © 2000 by H. Stephen Glenn and Jane Nelsen. Used by permission of Prima Publishing, a division of Random House, Inc.

---

developed through research, that says successful people possess certain skills and certain perceptions about themselves. These skills and perceptions are called **"significant tools"** (Glenn and Nelsen 1989, 2000). Box 10.3 contains the seven significant resources (perceptions and skills) that successful people possess. In this context, skills are things people can do (learned through practice), and perceptions are what people think of themselves after reflecting on past and current experiences.

Developing Capable People Adapting the "significant resources" concepts to their local circumstances, physical educators in Austin, Texas, implemented a model called Developing Capable People (DCP) for use with elementary school children (Kahan and McKnight 1998). The model includes three self-perceptions—"I am capable," "I am significant," and "I am influential"—and four skills—"maintains self-identify," "develops friendships," "maintains flexibility and integrity," and "maintains a code of ethics." Strategies used by the teachers to implement this model included having weekly DCP meetings with students, using teacher behaviors that support the development of capable people, and using a series of what, why, and how questions that allow teachers insight into student perceptions of their behaviors. The entire school used the same model, and one physical educator reported substantive improvements in student affect and student behavior in her classes after implementing the model.

Teaching Social Skills   Again based on the "significant resources" concepts, a physical educator in California developed a student-centered model for directly teaching social skills in physical education (Mercier 1993). The model included the following:

- Preventing students' negative behaviors
- Building trust with students in order to substitute appropriate behaviors for negative behaviors. For example, when a student calls another student a derogatory name, the teacher intervenes and asks, "How else might you handle this situation that would show respect for others, but still communicate your anger or issues?"
- Teacher modeling of behaviors that build trust (rather than behaviors that "tear people down"). For example, when students are lining up to walk to the gymnasium, instead of saying "Follow directions, don't push in line, and don't make faces," the teacher says, "When you walk in line without pushing, we are all safer. I would like you all to be safe. How can you help to make yourself and your classmates safer?"

These strategies were implemented while students were engaged in physical education lessons that use a cooperative teaching approach. A unique feature of the model was its ability to tie into the physical education framework specified by the state of California.

Developing Personal and Social Responsibility
Don Hellison, a professor and researcher at the University of Illinois at Chicago, has been espousing the teaching of responsibility through physical activity for over two decades. He developed (and continues to perfect) a **model for teaching personal and social responsibility** within the movement setting. The model is designed to help students take responsibility for their well-being and become more sensitive and responsive to the well-being of others. Hellison's original model specified five levels of development (irresponsibility, respect, participation, self-direction, and caring) that placed students along a continuum from being irresponsible to being very responsible. The levels described student behaviors viewed as typical to that level. The levels were viewed as being cumulative, so in general, students progressed through the levels (from 0 to 5) as they became more socially adept. This approach was easy for students to understand and focus on. Students also found it easy to complete self-evaluation based on the levels. For example, "I operated at a level three today." Hellison's model has been used in this manner by many practitioners. However, the original model had limitations. Hellison has therefore enhanced it by adding:

- A new level showing that students could operate responsibly "outside the gym"
- A new dimension to the levels so they are now considered goals (with corresponding components)

The revised model allows teachers and students to focus on the thoughts, feelings, and actions for which students need to take responsibility in school and at home (see Box 10.4; Hellison et al. 2008). Using the levels as goals, teachers can plan lessons to specifically teach certain responsibilities (components). Hellison believes that in order to effectively set the stage for teaching social responsibility, teachers must operate to (1) integrate responsibility goals into lessons, (2) teach for transfer from the classroom to outside the classroom, (3) empower students, and (4) interact with students in a way that respects each student's strengths, gives them a voice, and builds their ability to make good decisions.

Hellison also identified several strategies he found helpful in teaching responsibility to students in the movement setting (Box 10.5; Hellison 2003). He suggests that in *each* lesson teachers:

- Begin with an *awareness talk.*
- End with *individual reflection time* or a *group meeting,* thus keeping the students focused on the social outcomes expected from the lesson.
- Incorporate individual *counseling time* as needed before, after, or during the lesson.

Developing Classroom Interventions   Classroom teachers are also active in developing effective intervention programs designed to improve students' social skills. One such success story involved an intervention program that continued for a four-month period (Bertone et al. 1999). The children (in kindergarten and

---

BOX 10.4
Hellison's Responsibility Goals and Components

LEVEL 1   Self-Control: Respect for the Rights and Feelings of Others

- Control yourself (in speech and actions)
- Include others
- Resolve conflict peacefully

LEVEL 2   Self-Motivation: Effort and Participation

- Motivate yourself
- Try new tasks and skills
- Stay on-task

LEVEL 3   Self-Direction

- Work independently
- Set progressive goals
- Reflect on goal achievement
- Resist peer pressure

LEVEL 4   Helping Others and Leadership

- Show compassion toward others
- Be sensitive toward others
- Use your inner strength

LEVEL 5   Transfer to Other Areas of Life

- Be a role model for younger kids
- Try using the components in settings outside the gym
- Reflect to see if use of components is effective

Adapted by permission from Hellison, D., T. Martnek, and D. Walsh. 2008. Sport and responsible leadership among youth. In *Positive youth development through sport*, ed. N. L. Holt, 49–60. New York: Routledge.

---

displayed on the wall, classroom discipline plan developed jointly by teachers and students, and inspirational music played during introductory activities).

- Integrating social skills instruction into the curriculum (emphasized lessons on self-control, manners, listening, respect, taking turns, and sharing taught one time per week in 30- to 40-minute sessions).
- Using cooperative learning activities to cultivate prosocial behavior (taught the roles of cooperative groups, formed groups heterogeneously, and used team-building activities at the beginning of the project).

Developing Your Own Model   Thus far in this chapter, many strategies have been identified for teaching social skills so the teacher can select from among them based on a number of factors. Different strategies work in different situations. Teachers need to discover what works for them based on their views and personality and the unique environment in which they work (characteristics of the children, school, and community). Remember that models and strategies developed for use in the gymnasium may well be applicable to the classroom, and those developed for the classroom may work in the gymnasium. Many times, finding what works requires a trial-and-error approach.

For teachers who are not quite ready or who do not wish to commit to a total program focused on teaching personal and social responsibility, it is possible to implement a few strategies within the classroom that will increase the students' responsibility level. We offer two suggestions:

- Use any or all of the techniques listed in Box 10.6. Although designed for the elementary gymnasium, the strategies apply just as well to the elementary classroom.
- Use any of the many activities in this text that indicate NASPE Standard 5 is being met. You can easily find those activities by consulting Appendix F.

second-grade classrooms, second-grade physical education classes, and primary-age trainable mentally handicapped classes) improved their social skills in response to the intervention program. They demonstrated a marked decrease in negative behaviors as well as increases in cooperation, staying on task, listening, and sharing with others. The program included the following:

- Structuring a classroom environment that cultivated prosocial behavior (prosocial posters and sayings

ASSESSMENT OF SOCIAL SKILLS

Just as students' knowledge about movement and their ability to perform movement are appropriate areas to assess, so is the students' ability to display appropriate social behavior and skills.

Student Self-Awareness   The most important type of assessment is self-assessment used primarily to give students an opportunity to reflect on their own behavior

---

BOX 10.5 Hellison's Strategies for Implementing the Responsibility Goals

AWARENESS TALKS

Brief talks by teachers or students (or even just one-sentence comments) that keep the developmental levels fresh in students' minds.

REFLECTION TIME

Brief time during which students evaluate (orally or in writing, publicly or in private) their own behavior during a particular class period.

GROUP MEETINGS

Group meetings are scheduled whenever necessary, and during the meeting students voice their ideas, opinions, and feelings for the purpose of solving problems that have arisen. During these meetings,

students should practice group decision making and compromise.

COUNSELING TIME

Brief one-on-one meeting with students held before, after, or during class (while other students are involved in activity). The purpose is simply to touch base and have an opportunity to talk specifically about issues relevant only to that student. Counseling time should occur with all students, not just with those displaying behaviors at the lower developmental levels.

Adapted, with permission, from D. Hellison, 2003, *Teaching Responsibility Through Physical Activity,* 2nd ed. (Champaign, IL: Human Kinetics), 41–54, selected text.

BOX 10.6 Techniques for Teaching Responsibility

- Allow students the freedom to use the restroom whenever it's necessary. Design a reusable hall pass (one for the girls and one for the boys) that hangs by the classroom door. A student may take the pass, go to the restroom, and replace the pass upon returning.
- Allow students to get a drink from water fountains located within the gymnasium whenever they are thirsty—but only one person at a time (no line may form in front of the fountain).
- Have students pick up and return equipment instead of handing equipment to them one at a time. Of course, they will need instructions on how to do this.
- Have students begin an activity as soon as they enter the gym by reading the posted activity and beginning on their own.
- Allow students to alter activities to meet their individual needs.

- Use peer teaching and peer assessment when possible.
- Have students evaluate their own work, behavior, and attitudes.
- Make time-out progressive: (1) First disruption, the student decides whether a time-out is needed. (2) Second disruption, the teacher mandates a time-out, but the student returns to the activity when ready to do so. (3) Third disruption, the teacher mandates a time-out, and the student cannot return to the activity until the teacher permits the student to do so.

Source: M. Parker, J. Kallusky, and D. Hellison, High Impact, Low Risk: Ten Strategies to Teach Responsibility, *Journal of Physical Education, Recreation, and Dance* 70(2): 26–28 (1999). Reprinted with permission of the American Alliance of Health, Physical Education, Recreation, and Dance, 1900 Associations Dr., Reston, VA 20191.

---

at a certain time. Children can reflect on their behavior with a variety of *quick* assessment methods. Young children may need to use visual and verbal assessment methods, whereas older children can also use written methods (either checklists or short-answer statements). Also, young children may be better able to reflect on

their behavior during a single event rather than over an entire day. For instance, at the end of an activity, first graders might reflect silently on their behavior and then go touch a visual (taped to the wall) that represents their level of behavior. As another example, at the end of a particular activity, kindergarten children

Name _____

Date _____

Directions: Check all the blanks that apply to your behavior in class today.

My Self-Control

____ I did no name-calling.

____ If I got mad, I tried to have self-control.

____ I didn't interrupt when somebody else was talking.

____ My self-control was not that good today.

My Involvement

____ I listened to all directions.

____ I tried all activities.

____ I played even when I didn't feel like it.

My Self-Responsibility

____ I followed all of the directions.

____ I did not blame others.

____ I was responsible for myself.

My Caring

____ I helped someone today in P.E.

____ I said something nice to someone in P.E.

____ I did not help anyone at all.

Comments:

_____

_____

_____

_____

_____

_____

FIGURE 10.1 Self-Responsibility Checklist.

Source: N. Compagnone, Teaching Responsibility to Rural Elementary Youth: Going Beyond the Urban At-Risk Boundaries, *Journal of Physical Education, Recreation, and Dance* 66(6): 58–63 (1995). Reprinted with permission of the American Alliance of Health, Physical Education, Recreation, and Dance, 1900 Associations Dr., Reston, VA 20191.

might raise their hands to respond positively when asked the following questions:

- Do you believe you and your partner got along well during the activity? How do you know whether you got along or not?
- Did you talk to a classmate while the teacher read the book?
- Did you return toys to where they belong after doing activities at station 4?
- Did you say something nice to a classmate?

Second graders might respond verbally to questions such as these:

- Tell us one thing you did to help your partner during our last activity.

Name _____

Date _____

Directions: Check "Yes," "no," or "sometimes" for each statement listed based on what you did in class today.

	Yes	No	Sometimes
I worked well during group time today.			
I helped someone in class today.			
I helped get out or put away equipment.			
I encouraged my classmates to do well.			

FIGURE 10.2   Social Responsibility Checklist

- When you help someone else, how does that make you feel?
- When the teacher asked you to get a partner, how did you decide whom to choose?
- Tell us one thing you did today showing that you cooperated with others.

Third, fourth, fifth, and sixth graders could answer similar questions in writing (either in class or as a homework assignment). Since writing assessments are more private than verbal assessments, additional kinds of questions such as these can be asked:

- How many of your classmates do you like to have as a partner?
- Why do you not like to be partners with some of your classmates?
- Did you get angry today? If yes, did you express your anger in an appropriate manner? Describe how you expressed your anger.

Students can make journal entries on a regular basis in a social skills journal. This is a great way to observe changes over time in individuals, since all their work is right there to be viewed whenever another assignment is completed.

Checklists also provide a quick way for older elementary children to assess their behavior. When using a checklist, select behaviors to include in the list based on the social skills being taught and the skills you expect to be displayed that day (or during a specific activity). For instance, using Hellison's levels of responsibility, a physical educator developed a self-responsibility checklist for his fifth-grade students (see

Figure 10.1; Compagnone 1995). A simpler checklist for second or third graders is shown in Figure 10.2. Teachers should read the instructions to the students, and perhaps provide sample behaviors for each statement. Although these checklists were developed for the gymnasium, many of the behaviors specified also apply to the classroom setting.

Documenting Changes   In addition to having students assess their own social behavior in order to develop self-awareness, the teacher may be interested in documenting changes in student behavior. This can be accomplished by having a colleague (teacher, principal, paraprofessional) tally the positive and negative behaviors they see while observing the class. The observed behaviors are predetermined by the teacher based on what social behaviors have been taught and reinforced. If having a colleague in the classroom would distract the children too much, the class could be videotaped and the teacher could tally the behaviors by viewing the videotape.

If the teacher wishes to measure behavior throughout the semester and compare tallies over time, be sure the observations are taken when the children are engaged in similar activities (i.e., activities that prompt the same kinds of behaviors and promote the same level of physical intensity and physical freedom). For example, if the first observation occurred while the children were in a cooperative activity, do not make the second observation while the teacher is lecturing. A sample observation instrument is shown in Figure 10.3.

Positive Behaviors	Tally Marks
Helped a classmate	
Listened while others talked	
Followed directions	
Displayed cooperation	
Complimented a classmate	
Negative Behaviors	
Talked out of turn	
Made inappropriate comments	
Did not follow directions	
Was uncooperative	
Was disrespectful to others	

Date of observation _____

Name of observer _____

Number of students observed _____

Amount of time students were observed _____

Describe the activity students were engaged in:

_____

_____

_____

_____

_____

_____

_____

_____

_____

FIGURE 10.3   Classroom Behavioral Observation

It may be time consuming to document changes in children's social behaviors, and teachers may view the documentation as unnecessary because they already *know* the intervention program is working, as they can see every day in the classroom that the students are more respectful and caring. However, formal documentation of the program's effects can be quite useful for purposes of public accountability. Figure 10.4 shows a sample checklist the teacher can complete and send to parents as a report on their child's progress in the area of learning necessary social skills.

Summary

Socialization is the process through which children acquire a sense of who they are and where they belong, learn what is expected of them as members

---

Riverwood Elementary School
Physical Education Behavior Report

Name _____   Date _____

Educational research has shown that when a teacher spends class time managing discipline problems, less teaching and less learning occur. Therefore, when disruptive behavior is nonexistent in a class situation, greater student achievement is likely to result.

I am glad to inform you that during physical education class your child consistently exhibits the following exemplary behaviors:

_____   **Listens to the teacher**

_____   **Is courteous to others**

_____   **Is on task**

_____   **Follows directions**

_____   **Plays safely**

_____   **Is eager to participate**

_____   **Treats equipment with care**

Your child is doing a wonderful-terrific-dynamite job in physical education, and I am proud of him/her. You are to be commended for preparing your youngster to function so well. I am a more effective teacher because of your efforts.

Vicki Worrell
Physical Education Teacher

FIGURE 10.4   Sample Physical Education Behavior Report

of their culture, and come to espouse the ideals, values, beliefs, and attitudes of their surrounding culture. Socialization occurs through the interaction of children with various agents in the society (primarily family, peers, school, and the mass media).

Our society socializes children *through* and *about* movement. Society tells us who we are and how we are expected to behave relative to physical activity.

These expectations vary based on gender, ability, disability, and ethnic background. When society's messages are harmful to children, educators must step forward and be agents of change. Quality, responsible teaching in the movement setting demands that educators make available to *all* their students the resources provided by the school, regardless of the students' gender, physical ability, disability, or ethnic background. Quality movement experiences are beneficial for all children.

Through movement, society teaches children the concepts of cooperation, friendship, fairness, and competition. Using various models and strategies, these social skills can be learned by students, so it is worthwhile for classroom teachers and physical education teachers to design ways to teach these skills to their students.

Chapter Activities

1. Write a paper one to two pages in length discussing how you view yourself as a *moving* human being. How has your view influenced your life? What might be the most healthful view to have?
2. Examine how your ability or lack of ability to perform physical skills has affected your life thus far. How might your ability (or lack of ability) affect your health in the future?
3. Examine how your gender or cultural background has affected the way you have interacted with society.
4. List the most important socialization agents in your life. Identify how these agents have affected you.
5. Sketch a model (for your classroom or for an entire school) for teaching the social skills you want your students to learn and master. Include key concepts and skills the students would learn as well as methods and strategies used by the teachers to teach the key concepts and skills.

Internet Resources

Family Education. Site maintained by Family Education Network where parents can obtain information about the school–parent relationship.
www.familyeducation.com/home/

The President's Council on Physical Fitness and Sports. Articles on motivating children to be physically active.
www.fitness.gov/digest900.pdf

National Network for Child Care. Article on children without friends and the reasons for peer rejection.
www.nncc.org/Guidance/dc31_wo.friends2.html

Journal of Sport and Social Issues. Contains articles on the latest research, discussion, and analysis of contemporary sport issues.
jss.sagepub.com

Bibliography

Barbour, A. C. 1996. Physical competence and peer relations in 2nd-graders: Qualitative case studies from recess play. *Journal of Research in Childhood Education* 11(1): 35–46.

Bertone, L., J. Boyle, J. Mitchel, and J. Smith. 1999. *Improving prosocial behavior through social skill instruction*. ERIC, 434-296.

Bigler, R. S. 2005. 'Good morning, boys and girls.' *Teaching Tolerance* (28): 22–23.

Brustad, R. J. 1993. Who will go out and play? Parental and psychological influences on children's attraction to physical activity. *Pediatric Exercise Science* 5: 210–223.

———. 1996. Attraction to physical activity in urban schoolchildren: Parental socialization and gender influences. *Research Quarterly for Sport and Exercise* 67: 316–323.

Centers for Disease Control and Prevention. 1997. Guidelines for school and community programs to promote lifelong physical activity among young people. *Journal of School Health* 67(6): 202–219.

Compagnone, N. 1995. Teaching responsibility to rural elementary youth: Going beyond the urban at-risk boundaries. *Journal of Physical Education, Recreation and Dance* 66(6): 58–63.

Council on Sports Medicine and Fitness and Council on School Health. 2006. Active healthy living: Prevention of childhood obesity through increased physical activity. *American Academy of Pediatrics* 117(5): 1834–1842.

Culp, B. 2006. Classroom management for diverse populations. *Strategies* 20(1): 21–24.

Darch, C. B., and E. J. Kame'enui. 2004. *Instructional classroom management: A proactive approach to behavior management*. Upper Saddle River, NJ: Pearson Prentice Hall.

Davison, K. K., T. M. Cutting, and L. L. Birch. 2003. Parents' activity-related parenting practices predict girls' physical activity. *Medicine & Science in Sports and Exercise* 35(9): 1589–1595.

Davison, K. K., D. S. Downs, and L. L. Birch. 2006. Pathways linking perceived athletic competence and parental support at age 9 years to girls' physical activity at age 11 years. *Research Quarterly for Exercise and Sport* 77(1): 23–31.

Duke, M., and S. Nowicki. 1996. Helping the kid: Strategies to help the socially awkward children in your class. *Instructor* 105: 56–57.

Ennis, C. D., M. A. Solmon, B. Satina, S. J. Loflus, J. Mensch, and M. T. McCauley. 1999. Creating a sense of family in urban schools using a "Sport for Peace" curriculum. *Research Quarterly for Exercise and Sport* 70(3): 273–285.

Evans, J. R., and G. C. Roberts. 1987. Physical competence and the development of peer relations. *Quest* 39: 23–35.

Freedson, P. S., and S. Evenson. 1991. Familial aggregation in physical activity. *Research Quarterly for Sport and Exercise* 62: 384–389.

Garrett, R. 2004. Negotiating with a physical identity: Girls, bodies and physical education. *Sport, Education and Society* 9(2): 223–237.

Glenn, H. S., and J. Nelsen. 2000. *Raising self-reliant children in a self-indulgent world: Seven building blocks for developing capable young people.* Roseville, CA: Prima Publishing.

Glenn, H. S., and J. N. Nelsen. 1989. *Raising self-reliant children in a self-indulgent world.* Rocklin, CA: Prima Publishing.

Greenberg, P. 1992. How to institute some simple democratic practices pertaining to respect, rights, roots, and responsibilities in any classroom (without losing your leadership position). *Young Children* 47(5): 10–17.

Hastie, P. A. 1996. Student role involvement during a unit of sport education. *Journal of Teaching in Physical Education* 16: 88–103.

———. 1998. The participation and perceptions of girls within a unit of sport education. *Journal of Teaching in Physical Education* 17: 157–171.

Hellison, D. R. 2003. *Teaching responsibility through physical activity.* Champaign, IL: Human Kinetics.

Hellison, D., T. Martnek, and D. Walsh. 2008. Sport and responsible leadership among youth. In *Positive youth development through Sport,* ed. N. L. Holt, 49–60. New York, NY: Routledge.

Henslin, J. M. 2007. *Essentials of sociology.* Boston: Allyn and Bacon.

Hill, G. M., and B. Cleven. 2005. A comparison of students' choices of 9th grade physical education activities by ethnicity. *High School Journal* 89(2): 16–23.

Hills, L. A. 2006. Playing the field(s): An exploration of change, conformity and conflict in girls' understandings of gendered physicality in physical education. *Gender and Education* 18(5): 539–556.

Honig, A. S., and D. S. Whitmer. 1996. Helping children become more prosocial: Ideas for classrooms, families, schools, and communities. *Young Children* 51(2): 62–70.

Hunter, L. 2004. Bourdieu and the social space of the PE class: Reproduction of doxa through practice. *Sport, Education and Society* 9(2): 176–192.

Kahan, D., and R. McKnight. 1998. Personal responsibility in the gymnasium. *Strategies* 11(3): 13–17.

Kaslow, F. W. 2001. Families and family psychology at the millennium. *American Psychologist* 56: 37–46.

Kimiecik, J. C., and T. S. Horn. 1998. Parental beliefs and children's moderate-to-vigorous physical activity. *Research Quarterly for Exercise and Sport* 69(2): 163–175.

Kovar, S., K. Ermler, J. Mehrhof, and G. Napper-Owen. 2001. Choosing activity units to promote maximum participation: Creative physical education curricula. *Physical Educator* 58: 114–124.

Kozub, F. M., P. R. Sherblom, and T. L. Perry. 1999. Inclusion paradigms and perspectives: A stepping stone to accepting learner diversity in physical education. *Quest* 51: 346–354.

Lever, K., and J. J. Wilson. 2005. Encore parenting: When grandparents fill the role of primary caregiver. *The Family Journal* 13(2): 167–171.

Martino, W., and L. Beckett. 2004. Schooling the gendered body in health and physical education: Interrogating teachers' perspectives. *Sport, Education and Society* 9(2): 239–251.

McCadden, B. M. 1998. Why is Michael always getting timed out? Race, class and disciplining other people's children. In *Classroom discipline in American schools: Problems and possibilities for democratic education,* eds. R. E. Butchart and B. McEwan, 109–134. Albany, NY: State University of New York Press.

Mercier, R. 1993. Student-centered physical education: Strategies for teaching social skills. *Journal of Physical Education, Recreation, and Dance* 64(5): 60–65.

Moore, L. L., D. A. Lombardi, M. J. White, J. L. Campbell, S. A. Oliveria, and R. C. Ellison. 1991. Influence of parents' physical activity levels on activity levels of young children. *Journal of Pediatrics* 118: 215–219.

Mullen, J. K. 1994. *Count me in: Gender equity in the primary classroom.* Toronto: Green Dragon Press.

Napper-Owen, G. E., S. K. Kovar, K. L. Ermler, and J. H. Mehrhof. 1999. Curricula equity in required ninth grade physical education. *Journal of Teaching in Physical Education* 19(1): 2–21.

National Association for Sport and Physical Education (NASPE). 2004. *Moving into the future: National standards for physical education.* St. Louis, MO: Mosby.

Parker, M., J. Kallusky, and D. Hellison. 1999. High impact, low risk: Ten strategies to teach responsibility. *Journal of Physical Education, Recreation, and Dance* 70(2): 26–28.

Parker, M., and J. Stiehl. 2005. Personal and social responsibility. In *Standards-based curriculum development,* eds. J. Lund and D. Tannehill, 130–153. Boston: Jones and Bartlett.

Pica, R. 1993. Responsibility and young children: What does physical education have to do with it? *Journal of Physical Education, Recreation, and Dance* 64(5): 72–75.

Powlishta, K. K. 1995. Gender segregation among children: Understanding the "Cootie Phenomenon." *Young Children* 50(5): 61–69.

Schwartz, W. 2001. School practices for equitable discipline of African American students. ERIC, 455-343.

Smith, L. 2007. Black female participation languishes outside of basketball and track. *Chronicle of Higher Education,* June 29, 2007, A34.

Solomon, G. B. 1997. Fair play in the gymnasium: Improving social skills among elementary school students. *Journal of Physical Education, Recreation, and Dance* 68(5): 22–25.

Stanton-Salazar, R. D. 1997. A social capital framework for understanding the socialization of racial minority children and youths. *Harvard Educational Review* 67(1): 1–40.

Torrey, C. C., and M. Ashy. 1997. Culturally responsive teaching in physical education. *Physical Educator* 54(3): 120–127.

Trost, S., L. Kerr, D. Ward, and R. Pate. 2001. Physical activity and determinants of physical activity in obese and non-obese children. *International Journal of Obesity and Related Metabolic Disorders* 25: 822–829.

U.S. Census Bureau News. 2004. Press release. www.census.gov/Press-Release/www/releases/archives/population/002897.html.

Weiss, M. R., and S. C. Duncan. 1992. The relationship between physical competence and peer acceptance in the context of children's sport participation. *Journal of Sport and Exercise Psychology* 14: 177–191.

Welk, G. J. 1999. Promoting physical activity in children: Parental influences. ERIC, 436-480.

Wheeler, E. J. 1994. Peer conflicts in the classroom. ERIC, 372-874.

Williams, A., and J. Bedward. 2001. Gender, culture and the generation gap: Student and teacher perceptions of aspects of national curriculum physical education. *Sport, Education and Society* 6: 53–66.

QUICK LESSON 10.1
Scooters as Wheelchairs

GRADES K–6

NASPE STANDARD 5 Students exhibit responsible personal and social behavior that respects self and others in physical activity settings.

LESSON OBJECTIVES

■ Students experience being in a wheelchair by moving on scooters.

■ Students identify the elements in the physical environment (in the classroom and on the playground) that present problems for those who sit in wheelchairs.

■ Students better understand the difficulties people experience as they move through our physical world in wheelchairs.

EQUIPMENT NEEDED One scooter for each child

PREPARATION TIME None

KNOWLEDGE CONTENT Moving about while sitting cross-legged on a scooter simulates being in a wheelchair in a number of ways. Make sure students are aware of these similarities:

■ It makes children use their arms as a means of propulsion.

■ It makes children shorter (compared with the objects in their physical environment such as desks, door handles, water fountains, etc.).

■ It places children on rollers that in general can negotiate only surfaces similar to those a wheelchair can negotiate.

Students will express what they learn by answering the questions listed in the next section.

CLASSROOM TO PLAYGROUND ACTIVITY

1. Ask children to sit on their scooters cross-legged by their desk.
2. Take them for a "walk" (in a single file). They must remain on the scooter the entire trip, using only their hands (pushing on the floor or ground) to propel themselves. *Safety tip: Do not run over your own or others' fingers.*
3. Walk through the classroom. Is it too crowded for the wheelchair? Can they reach the chalkboard?
4. Walk down the hallway. Can they reach the door knob to get out of the classroom? Can they get a drink from the water fountain? Is the floor a good surface to roll on?
5. Walk to some steps. Can they go up the steps?
6. Retrace your path down the hallway to a ramp and go up the ramp. How difficult is it to go uphill?
7. Go outdoors to the play area. What playground surfaces allow a wheelchair to function easily? Try pavement, grass, and gravel. What equipment could they play on?
8. Return to the classroom. Are the children tired? How do their arm muscles feel? Did they use more energy than they would have on the usual kind of walk? Did this walk take longer?

ASSESSMENT For grades K–3, hold a class discussion about what children learned from the experience. For grades 4–6, ask students to write a paragraph telling what they learned on their "wheelchair" walk. Match their comments with the objectives of the lesson.

SUCCESS FOR ALL Students' arms will become very tired during this activity. Allow those with tired arms to temporarily pick up their scooter and walk in line with the class. When their arms have recovered, they are to continue moving on the scooter. Students with cerebral palsy with very limited arm action and strength may be pushed on the scooter by a helper.

INTEGRATION WITH OTHER SUBJECT AREAS
This lesson might be integrated into a history lesson in which students are studying innovations (like wheelchairs) that have changed people's lives.

CLASSROOM LEARNING STATION 10.1
Tell Me Something About You

GRADES K–6

NASPE STANDARD 5 Students exhibit responsible personal and social behavior that respects self and others in physical activity settings.

LESSON OBJECTIVES

- Students examine their own abilities, likes, and dislikes.
- Students learn about their classmates.
- Students understand how everyone in the class is different.

EQUIPMENT NEEDED Work sheet and materials with which to decorate the learning station area

PREPARATION TIME Minimal (15 to 45 minutes), depending on whether the teacher alters the work sheet in the text and how extensively the teacher wishes to decorate the learning station area and the area where the work sheets will be posted

KNOWLEDGE CONTENT The knowledge students learn is contained in the work sheets completed by each student.

CLASSROOM ACTIVITY At a learning station located in the classroom, have each child complete the following work sheet. Upon completion, the child posts the sheet on a wall or bulletin board designated for this purpose. The children are to read and study these sheets.

ASSESSMENT At some point, the teacher gives students a quiz on the information on the work sheets (emphasizing how much they know about each of their classmates). Provide a prize for the student who knows the most. During this activity, discuss respecting the differences between individuals.

SUCCESS FOR ALL For students who cannot write on the work sheet (because of a disability), use their usual writing method to obtain the information (typing or talking into a computer).

INTEGRATION WITH OTHER SUBJECT AREAS Once you know all this information about the students, try to remember it and refer to it when appropriate in the classroom. For instance, you are studying the ecology of a farm and you remember that several of your students live on farms. So you can refer to that and use the firsthand information they may provide on the topic.

Work Sheet:

Tell Me Something About You

- My name is _____
- I like to be called _____
- My favorite game of sport is _____
- My favorite TV program is _____
- After school, I usually _____
- One thing I do *fairly well* is

  _____

- One thing I do *very well* is

  _____

- One thing I do to help at home is

  _____

- A book I like very much is

  _____

- If I could visit any place I wanted to, it would be

  _____

- A food I especially like is _____
- When I grow up, I want to be a _____
- Members of my family are

  _____

- I have a pet at home, and it is a _____

  My pet's name is _____

- I do not have a pet at home, but if I did it would be a _____

  My pet's name would be _____

GRADES K–6

NASPE STANDARD 5 Students exhibit responsible personal and social behavior that respects self and others in physical activity settings.

LESSON OBJECTIVES

- Students learn about their heritage.
- Students learn how the world has changed from the time when their grandparents were born.
- Students learn about prejudice and discrimination.
- Students learn how their experience of school is different from that of their grandparents.

EQUIPMENT NEEDED Extra chairs in the classroom so the grandparent can sit by their grandchild, and perhaps a bleacher pulled out in the gymnasium so the grandparents can sit down when they prefer not to participate in the day's activities

PREPARATION TIME One hour total—writing and sending invitations home with the children, and finding the extra seating needed

KNOWLEDGE CONTENT The specific content will vary based on the cultures represented in class and the experiences of the grandparents who attend.

CLASSROOM ACTIVITY Invite grandparents to join the class for half a day (make it the half of the day during which the class has physical education). The grandparents participate in the day's activities with their child. During each of the day's activities, involve the grandparents in "telling their stories." For example, ask questions such as those listed below for the lessons indicated.

DURING SOCIAL STUDIES

- Where were they born? What year?
- Where were their parents born?
- How many siblings do they have?
- What was going on in the world when they were born?
- What generation American are they?
- Which holidays did they celebrate when they were children? How?
- What chores did they perform as children?
- Have they experienced prejudice or discrimination? If so, please describe.

DURING PHYSICAL EDUCATION

- Did they have physical education when they went to school?
- What activities did they play as children? Whom did they play with? When did they play?
- Did boys and girls play the same activities?

AFTER RECESS

- What activities did they do during recess?
- What playground equipment was available?
- How many recess periods did they have?
- Did they play outdoors?

AT THE END OF THE DAY

- How is school now different from how it was when they attended?
- What subjects did they study?
- Which cultures were represented in their school?
- Did they walk to school?
- Did they bring their lunch to school? If so, what was a typical lunch?

ASSESSMENT For grades K–3, in a class discussion conducted the next day, ask students to identify the traditions of the cultures represented in the class.

For grades 4–6, as homework, ask students to write a paragraph comparing the traditions of the cultures represented in the class. Be sure they include comparisons of play activities.

SUCCESS FOR ALL Allow any older adult to serve as a grandparent if some children cannot bring a real grandparent.

INTEGRATION WITH OTHER SUBJECT AREAS
The lesson is already integrated with social studies. You could integrate geography by showing on maps where your students' ancestors originally came from. You could integrate science by talking about the inventions that were or were not present when their grandparents were young children—or how inventions (cars, telephones, etc.) have changed over time.

CHAPTER 11

Creating a Physically Safe Movement Environment

The purpose of this chapter is to identify and discuss the unique safety concerns and legal issues relevant to situations in which children are involved in physical activity. General concepts are presented to help you think about safety as applied to particular physical activities and situations. In addition, specific recommendations are provided to help you plan for and conduct physical activity in a safe manner in classroom, playground, and gymnasium settings.

Objectives

After studying this chapter, you will be able to do the following:

- Identify safety concerns when children are engaged in physical activity.

- Discuss the legal issues involved in the movement setting.

- Understand the concept of negligence as applied to movement settings.

- Determine the appropriateness of various physical activities in particular movement settings.

Ms. Werner is a fifth-grade classroom teacher in a large school district. The fifth-grade students receive 30-minute physical education lessons, taught by a specialist, only twice a week. She knows that her students should be active every day and also recognizes that physical fitness is difficult to develop if students do not have physical education at least three times a week for 45 minutes. So she plans and conducts at least one 45-minute physical education lesson for her students each week. In addition, she strives to provide short activity periods (10 to 20 minutes in length) for her students to supplement the afternoon recess they have every day.

Today, probably midmorning, she plans to take the children on a 15-minute fitness walk (around the playground perimeter). Although it is winter, there is no snow on the ground, the sun is shining, the wind is not blowing, and by midmorning the temperature should be above 40 degrees.

Because Ms. Werner often provides outdoor activities for her children in cold weather, they have learned to come prepared for that experience. Most of the students will either be wearing or have in the classroom coats, hats, gloves, pants, and tennis shoes. If not, Ms. Werner has extras that they may wear. When they go outdoors for the walk, Ms. Werner will lead the first time around the playground in order to establish the pace of the walk and to be sure the path is clear of objects (sticks and debris) and ruts. After the first round, students become leaders, and Ms. Werner walks and talks with various students throughout the 15 minutes.

Ms. Werner and her students really like these fitness walks. She has increased the pace throughout the year so the students know they are improving, and they have come to enjoy getting to know Ms. Werner and each other better through this "walk and talk" program.

Safety Is Your Concern

The scenario you just read illustrates how every time you plan and conduct physical activity for your students, your concern for their safety is paramount. Your school's legal counsel might indicate that teachers ought to be concerned about their students' safety in order to reduce the likelihood of becoming involved in a legal action. However, we suggest that the primary reason physical education and classroom teachers work to create a safe movement environment is to prevent injuries to the students under their care. In the scenario, Ms. Werner wanted her students to have a safe fitness walk; thus she knew the weather conditions, the proper attire for her students, and the importance of checking the trail for hazards. You have the responsibility to provide for students' physical as well as psychological and academic needs. This responsibility is quite similar to the responsibility parents have to care for their children; thus educators strive to prevent physical injuries to students and to create a safe environment (both physically and psychologically) within the classroom and school. Obviously, a major concern of educators, especially at the elementary school level, is to properly care for their students simply because they are human beings who deserve the best care you can give them!

GENERAL LEGAL CONCEPTS

Tort law provides the basis for awarding compensation to individuals for losses suffered as a consequence of the actions of others. Tort law covers both intentional acts and unintentional acts that result in harm to others. It also covers situations of omission, in which a teacher should have done something to prevent injury but did not do so. For example, a teacher allowed Jarod to participate in gymnasium activities in bare feet because he had forgotten his tennis shoes. Injury resulted when Jarod tripped and fell. In this case, an act of omission occurred, as the teacher, instead of taking no action, should have taken action and stopped Jarod from participating in his bare feet. In another example, while in a physical education class, Karen, an overweight student, indicated she could not successfully climb the rope. The teacher insisted that Karen try to climb the rope. Karen fell after climbing one-quarter of the way up and broke her foot upon landing on the mat. In this case, an intentional act (insisting Karen try to climb) resulted in student injury.

Most litigation (claiming negligence) in movement settings involves the unintentional acts or acts of omission of teachers as they go about performing their regular job duties. "**Negligence** is the failure to act as a reasonably prudent person would act in the same or similar circumstances" (Hart and Ritson 2002, 1). In order to prove in a court of law that a teacher was negligent, five factors must have been present in the situation: (1) duty, (2) breach of duty, (3) injury occurred, (4) causal relationship, and (5) foreseeability.

Duty   A **duty** exists between students and teacher because of their unique relationship. A duty, recognized by law, requires that the teacher conduct his or her job responsibilities with a certain **standard of care** that protects others (students) against foreseeable harm and unreasonable risk of injury. In the movement setting, that duty includes four basic responsibilities: (1) the duty to provide adequate and proper instruction, (2) the duty to supervise, (3) the duty to maintain equipment and facilities in safe conditions, and (4) the duty to provide proper first aid. In the duties just mentioned, the teacher has the responsibility to exercise reasonable care to protect students from harm, including recognizing foreseeable harm and taking steps to negate or minimize that harm.

Breach of Duty   A **breach of duty** constitutes unreasonable conduct in that the teacher failed to give the prerequisite standard of care. For example, a teacher allows her or his fifth-grade students to play a competitive game of regulation soccer. Some of the students were novice players, whereas others played on competitive community teams. Teams were not assigned based on size, weight, or ability, and the danger of possible injury was not assessed by the teacher. The standard of care is measured by what a reasonable, prudent, trained, experienced teacher would do in the same circumstances. Reasonable care varies from case to case because circumstances in given situations are never exactly the same.

Injury Occurred   An injury or loss occurs to a particular person when the teacher failed to give the appropriate standard of care. In the example above, a forward on one team collided violently with the other team's goalie, and the goalie suffered a concussion that resulted in a hospital stay.

Causal Relationship   The teacher's action or inaction was the immediate cause of the injury to another person. Continuing with the same example, a **causal relationship** might be established if the forward was a tall, heavy fifth grader with much soccer experience and the goalie was a small, light fifth grader with little soccer experience. Sometimes the teacher's action intersects with others' actions that might cause an injury. For instance, perhaps the fifth-grade forward was mad at the goalie for something that happened previously in the day, and thus intentionally collided with the goalie. Then both the forward player and the teacher are immediate causes of the injury.

Ensuring activity surfaces are safe, selecting appropriate equipment, and pairing students and choosing activities based on skill—all of these are part of a reasonable standard of care.

Foreseeability   The teacher must have been able to predict (**forseeability**) the likelihood of an injury occurring given the situation in question in order for negligence to occur. In this example, teacher preparation programs and information available from national organizations indicate the dangers of not matching students or teams for size and ability. The standard of care in this case says the teacher should have been able to foresee the likelihood of injury and should have made adjustments in the teaching of the lesson. Those lesson adjustments should have been noted in the original lesson plan prepared by the teacher.

To summarize, courts have clearly indicated that teachers have a "duty" to provide their students a reasonable "standard of care." In the movement setting, that standard of care means that classroom and physical education teachers must conduct instructional lessons, supervise their students, and maintain equipment and facilities based on what a prudent, reasonable, up-to-date teacher would do in the same circumstances. Although this chapter specifically addresses legal issues in the context of children being involved in physical activity, the concepts and issues covered in the chapter are also relevant to classroom teachers as they go about their regular duties of teaching and supervising students each day.

RISK MANAGEMENT PLANS

Programwide or schoolwide **risk management plans** are designed to reduce the number and severity of injuries as well as the likelihood of litigation arising from those injuries (Stewart 2000). Your school or physical education department may have a risk management plan that addresses safety issues specific to the movement setting. If so, you should be familiar with the content of that plan in order to implement the policies and procedures identified therein.

RULES FOR STUDENT CONDUCT

Establish **student conduct rules** that specify how children should behave with peers, in certain activity areas, with particular equipment, and in both indoor and outdoor physical activity settings. If classroom and physical education teachers construct the rules of conduct together, they will be providing the same information to the students. This helps to ensure that no mixed messages are given to the students and allows the children to remember only one set of rules (not two sets!).

Whether performing physical activity in the classroom, gymnasium, or outdoor areas, the rules of conduct need to be simply worded (so children understand them), general in nature (so the rules can be applied to many situations), and limited in number (from one to five depending on the age of the children). At least one of the rules should make reference to safety. Figure 11.1 shows possible sets of rules. The rules are posted and reinforced during each class period. Students are told how to apply the rules in general to all movement experiences and to the specific activities in each lesson. For example, to be safe in most activities, children should never chew gum or candy or wear jewelry while participating. Children should participate with activity shoes on (never in dress shoes or just in socks). Games that teach children specific safety rules can be developed. Instant Activity 11.1 teaches children to control their bodies while moving around in general space, and Special Event 11.1 at the end of the chapter teaches children how to play games in a safe manner.

CARING FOR INJURIES

Even under the safest conditions, participation in most physical activities involves the potential for injury. Since movement educators lead students in performing

Example #1:	Play hard.	
	Play fair.	
	Hurt no one.	
Example #2:	Respect others.	
	Respect equipment.	
	Safety at all times.	
Example #3:	Be polite.	
	Be positive.	
	Be safe.	

FIGURE 11.1 Student Conduct Rules

INSTANT ACTIVITY 11.1

No Touch

Grades K–6

Equipment Needed

Music

Activity

Children are in the classroom. Play music. Ask them to move around the room to the beat of the music, using designated locomotor skills (walk, jog, leap, skip, jump, hop, slide, and gallop), attempting not to touch another person or object in the room. If children touch each other, they stand back-to-back, count to ten, and return to the game. The focus of this activity is to teach children to move appropriately in general space to prevent injuries and to gain space awareness and body awareness skills.

For grades 4–6, move around the room using complex motor patterns (grapevine, two-step, schottische, waltz, etc.).

activities that have a potential for injury, we strongly recommend that classroom and physical education teachers have certification in administering first aid, for several reasons. First, the injury is most likely to occur in the presence of the movement educator, so he or she will be the first person who can respond to the injury. Second, if the injury is life-threatening, the knowledge and skill of the first responder may partially determine the ultimate outcome of the situation. Third, many schools do not have a full-time nurse available, so other personnel must have the first-aid training. The logical personnel to have the training include physical educators and classroom teachers.

Most school personnel who receive first-aid training take the training from the American Red Cross (www.redcross.org). The American Red Cross specifies certain procedures for handling first-aid care; however, some school districts have developed their own procedures or have adopted care procedures from other agencies (such as their state health agencies). As a teacher, you must use the procedures that are officially adopted by your school district. Obviously, districts should provide in-house training when they have adopted the first-aid procedures of a particular agency. If at this time you do not think you would be able to properly handle the situations listed in Box 11.1, you might consider enrolling in a first-aid course or obtaining first-aid certification from a training agent. Providing first aid without proper training and/or certification places the teacher and school at risk for being negligent and may further injure the student by providing inappropriate care.

School districts have forms for reporting injuries and usually specify the minimum amount of time that can lapse between the injury and the filing of the injury report. Completing the report form as soon as possible allows the details to be easily remembered. Teachers should know and follow the school's policies and procedures regarding treating and reporting injuries. Figure 11.2 shows a typical **injury report form.** We suggest that teachers keep a copy of the completed injury report in their files. For future reference, it is also beneficial to keep all excuse notes and parental notes that reflect health problems students are experiencing. Students who receive serious injuries should obtain a note from their doctor explaining when they are ready to return to physical activity.

The school district should provide adequately stocked first-aid kits for teachers to use. You should review American Red Cross publications for the contents of a general-use first-aid kit (e.g., American Red Cross 2006) and consult with the school nurse and physical educator for any additional items needed because of the special needs of your students or because of typical injuries that occur when students are involved in physical activity.

Finally, in caring for injured students we recommend that teachers call parents immediately (with the approval of the school administration) to communicate

---

BOX 11.1
Injury Situations
. . . .

Bleeding	Shock
Frostbite	Not breathing
Epileptic seizure	Head trauma
Knocked-out teeth	Heat stroke
Sprains and strains	Unconsciousness
Fractures	Lack of heartbeat
Asthma attacks	Allergic reaction

Elementary School, Somewhere, Kansas

Name _____ Sex _____ Birth date _____

Date of injury _____ Time of injury _____

Describe the accident/injury in your own words:

_____

_____

_____

_____

_____

_____

_____

_____

_____

Additional Information

Sent to school nurse by _____

First-aid treatment given by _____

Name of person notified _____

Student: ___ remained at school

___ went home

FIGURE 11.2   Sample Student Injury Report Form

---

what happened and express their concern for the student's welfare. Contact with the parent should be made *before* the student arrives home after school and should occur even if the injury appears to be minor. It is the parent's responsibility (not the teacher's) to decide whether the child needs to see a doctor, so immediate notification is essential. It is also extremely important that teachers communicate to the parents the true circumstances surrounding the accident to aid the parents in deciding whether medical attention is needed.

Selecting Curriculum Activities

As mentioned previously, participation in most physical activities involves the potential for injury. Teachers need to recognize that potential and take steps to reduce risks before students participate in the activities. The first important element in reducing risks is for the teacher to critically examine the movement activities that are to be included in the curriculum.

DANGEROUS ACTIVITIES

Well-trained physical educators include in the curriculum only activities that are reasonably safe given the particular circumstances that exist in the instructional setting. Activities can be examined to determine whether, given the situation, they are inherently dangerous or potentially dangerous. An inherently dangerous activity cannot be structured so as to make it safe, whereas a potentially dangerous activity can be conducted safely with proper planning and appropriate instructional processes (Gray 1995).

Since all physical activities have some potential for accidents to occur, thoughtful planning and prudent judgment must prevail. Teachers examine each activity

and the situation in which it would be taught to be certain that no inherently dangerous activities are included in the curriculum. In addition, for each potentially dangerous activity that the teacher would like to include in the curriculum, steps must be taken to reduce or eliminate the possibility of harm. If the risks cannot be reduced to an acceptable level (potential severity or likelihood of injury outweighs the value of participating in the activity), then the activity should be excluded from the curriculum. For example, in-line skating is a potentially dangerous activity. Under proper conditions (i.e., with safety equipment for each student, properly fitting skates, trained teachers, and a large skating area), the risk of injury from in-line skating can be minimized. However, if the proper conditions cannot be met, the activity should not be offered in the curriculum.

There are a number of common activities that are potentially dangerous and require special consideration. Tumbling activities are potentially dangerous, and we recommend that classroom teachers refrain from teaching tumbling activities because they are not trained enough to do so. Activities should never include the child as the target (e.g., dodgeball), and when partners or groups are throwing balls (or other objects) to each other, teach children not to throw until the receiver is looking directly at them (and thus knows the object is coming). Using bats is especially dangerous, so have enough activity space to create room between the batters and other students, and teach batters to let the bat drop to the ground on their follow-through (not "throw the bat" or let the bat fly through the air behind the batter). In order not to cause injury, exercises and stretches (e.g., sit-ups and toe touches) must be performed with correct technique. For example, sit-ups are performed with knees considerably bent to protect injury to the back. For the same reason, standing toe touches should be performed with the knees slightly bent. Stretches and exercises included as suggested activities in this text show proper technique. If in doubt about the correct technique, consult a physical educator.

ACTIVITIES RELATED TO LESSON OBJECTIVES

Activities included in the lesson certainly need to be related to the objectives of the lesson, as well as to the curriculum approved by the local Board of Education. In fact, this relatedness to the lesson objectives is the first filter through which an activity is passed when considering whether to include it in the lesson. If an activity does not relate to the lesson objectives, it should not be included. If the activity can be used to achieve a lesson objective but is potentially unsafe, the teacher needs to determine the advisability of including the activity in the lesson.

AGE-APPROPRIATE ACTIVITIES

The second filter through which an activity is passed considers whether the activity is appropriate based on the age and abilities of the students. The school district's physical education curriculum guide (described in Chapter 6) may be helpful in determining whether the district considers an activity appropriate. If the guide suggests the activity for the grade level you are teaching, it is further evidence that the activity is judged to be safe.

However, curriculum guides tend to list activities that are age appropriate and do not indicate *how* an activity is to be taught in a safe manner. So under these circumstances, we recommend that you visit with an experienced physical education teacher to be sure the implementation of the activity will be safe in your situation. For example, the curriculum guide may indicate that track and field events are appropriate activities for fifth- and sixth-grade students, as many of the elementary schools in the district are located close to outdoor tracks maintained by middle schools in the district. Without those facilities, some of the track and field events might not be safe to teach to your elementary students. If your school is not close to an outdoor track, the activities might not be safe for you to conduct on the playground you do have available.

In addition to the district's curriculum guide, information presented in Chapter 2 that outlined the developmental stages of children (cognitive, social, physical, and motor) is helpful in determining whether specific activities are age appropriate for your students.

ACTIVITIES FOR STUDENTS WITH DISABILITIES

Because we emphasize in this text the importance of using activities that *all students can participate in together,* the final filter through which to pass the activity is its appropriateness (with or without modifications) for students with disabilities. Safety should not be used as an excuse for denying children with disabilities the opportunity to participate in physical activities with their classmates.

Throughout this chapter, safety in the movement setting is approached from the viewpoint that classrooms, gymnasiums, and playgrounds contain students with and without disabilities. Thus the information provided addresses the needs of both groups. And in a previous chapter, specific adaptations (in equipment, facility, and instructional methods) for children with disabilities were outlined. But perhaps some general statements about the safety of children with disabilities are necessary given that a heightened standard of care may apply for students with disabilities (Bettenhausen 2002).

Remember that in movement settings, children with disabilities can be a risk to themselves and also to others. Thus the teacher plans a safe environment for all children. For example, when playing tag games in a class where a child is in a wheelchair, the teacher must protect the child in the wheelchair (smooth outdoor surface) and the other children (large enough play area to avoid running into the wheelchair).

Teachers should discover whether their school districts have special forms that must be completed by parents or guardians before children with disabilities can participate in physical education. If so, use these forms to collect needed information on what the child can and cannot do, what behavior to expect from the child, and how to respond to the child's needs.

One final important point: Do not overprotect children with disabilities, but do take reasonable, prudent precautions to allow safe participation in the lesson's activities.

Clear instruction in skills and performance feedback can help increase safety during movement activities. Here the teacher is showing correct hand positioning in the overhead volley to help students avoid finger injury when they practice.

Current "Best Practices" in Safety

Once activities are included in the curriculum, the next element in reducing risk is to conduct the activities in a safe, appropriate manner. We highlight here several **best practices:** using up-to-date instructional methods, using appropriate task progressions, using proper supervision techniques, and providing safety knowledge to the students.

UP-TO-DATE METHODS OF INSTRUCTION

Classroom teachers and physical education teachers have the responsibility to stay informed about the latest teaching techniques, methods, and procedures through professional development activities such as these:

- Reading professional journals (e.g., *Strategies* and *Journal for Physical Education, Recreation, and Dance*)
- Reading position statements of national organizations
- Reading articles on professional websites (e.g., www.pecentral.org and www.aahperd.org)
- Talking to other professionals
- Attending conferences and in-service workshops
- Taking college courses
- Observing "master" teachers

Current best practices in instructional methods relevant to safety dictate that teachers be aware of a number of standard operating procedures.

Health Status of the Students Know the health status, health problems, and disabilities of students before you ask them to participate in physical activity. It may be easy to identify students with obvious needs (on crutches, in a wheelchair, etc.) while other students' needs go unnoticed (asthma, diabetes, epilepsy, allergies, etc.). The teacher may learn about students' health problems, history, and disabilities by reviewing the students' medical records on file at the school, asking the school nurse to share the medical and special needs information she possesses, and participating in individual education plan meetings held for students with disabilities (Block and Horton 1996) The teacher also needs to know the specific medications students are taking and the possible side effects of those medications, as well as who will be self-medicating (e.g., with inhalers to treat asthma or with food to control sugar levels) in the classroom and on the playground. It is likely that you will have students with asthma, diabetes, and/or allergies in your classroom as these ailments are common in children today.

Warm-up Activities Provide adequate warm-up activities before asking students to perform skill or fitness activities, and plan warm-up activities that meet students' needs. Vary warm-up activities often so students do not become bored, and if possible, relate the warm-up activity to the movement that will be the primary lesson content. For example, if basketball skills are the lesson focus, have students warm up by running around the perimeter of the gymnasium while dribbling a basketball. All students may not necessarily participate in the same warm-up activities. For example, if the children are warming up by jogging a few laps around the school, a child with asthma may be allowed to alternate between walking and jogging. Quick Lesson 11.1 at the end of the chapter provides stretching activities that can be performed after warming up with a walking activity.

Instructions to the Students Provide sufficient instructions to the students before they are asked to perform (either a skill activity or a change of location within the space). The verbal instructions to the students should use language appropriate for the age, ability levels, and special needs of the students and should be supplemented when appropriate with demonstrations, written material, and pictures. In some cases, it may be necessary to physically assist a student in following the given instructions.

Each class period, instructions outlining safety procedures specific to the activities in the day's lesson are presented to the students, and the instructions regarding how to perform specific motor skills must be technically correct based on the latest available knowledge in the field. In addition, provide correct performance feedback to students regarding their skill performance, as incorrect performance may lead to injuries. This feedback must be individualized to each student; do not just make general comments to the entire class.

Selecting Partners or Groups Carefully consider how to select group members or partners for the purpose of practicing skills and playing games. Partners and group members may be selected by students or assigned by the teacher. Students' selection of their partners or groups usually results in friends being together, so you will end up with groups and partners of the same gender and same ethnic background. Friends being partners may not be safe in certain cases. For example, the stunt Partner Get-Up (described in Lesson 2.15 at the end of the book) should be performed with students of the same size and weight. In addition, self-selection of groups and partners may not be appropriate if you want to mix your students so everyone gets to know each other. In that case, you will need to assign students to groups and partners, or use student selection techniques that lead to students' selecting from outside their usual friends (such as partner with someone who has the same color shirt as you, the same birthday month, the same number of siblings). In addition to considering the social goals of group membership, teachers will also want to consider whether the lesson goal is to practice skill in a competitive or noncompetitive (developmental) setting. In developmental settings or in team settings where the students' most important instructional goal is to successfully operate as a team member, students can usually be mixed into groups regardless

of their height, weight, skill proficiency, experience, or health status. However, these factors become critical in a competitive setting and must be considered when assigning groups and partners. For example, height and weight are a factor when sixth graders are practicing or playing three-on-three soccer. Because of possible contact during play that could result in injury, students on each team should be matched on height and weight. In this situation, students might also be grouped based on skill proficiency if the teacher is trying to challenge students of all skill levels in the class. However, matching students based on skill proficiency can be difficult. You cannot assume that students skilled in one activity (e.g., rope jumping) will be skilled in another activity (e.g., ball throwing). Since skill proficiency is task specific, pretesting students on the particular skill in question provides more information about a student's ability (relevant to the task of selecting partners or groups) than does information from a general motor skill test or a fitness test. For example, if the teacher wants to match partners of similar ability so that the students can practice partner jump rope skills, a pretest consisting of the teacher observing the students' jump rope skills would be appropriate.

Competition Versus Practice In general, provide skill practice in a noncompetitive setting. There is a vast difference between performing in a developmental (practice) setting versus a competitive setting. Activities appropriate in the developmental setting may not be appropriate in a competitive setting. For example, practicing the basic locomotor skills in forward, backward, and sideward directions in a movement exploration activity (developmental setting) is quite appropriate and relatively low risk (as long as students are not moving at full speed). Performing locomotor skills (especially running) in a backward direction at a fast speed or in a race (competitive setting) is definitely high risk and thus is an inappropriate activity. Activities included in the competitive setting should be low-risk activities, as well as activities that the students are proficient in performing.

TASK PROGRESSIONS

To ensure the physical as well as psychological safety of children, they should never be forced to perform a skill or activity against their will. This does not mean a teacher cannot encourage students to overcome their fears or to stretch their capabilities. It simply means there is a fine line between encouragement and forcing, and the educator must walk that fine line carefully in order to prevent physical or psychological injury.

In general terms, to teach effectively as well as to prevent injuries, teachers use **task (skill) progressions** to provide lessons that enable students to progress from performing simple skills to performing more complex skills. This statement seems easy to understand; however, the implementation is quite complex and difficult for several reasons. First, it assumes that the teacher knows the current ability level of each student. Circumstances do exist in which teachers do not know the ability level of their students, such as when a teacher takes a position at a new school, when a substitute teacher must be called in, or when a new student arrives in an already existing class.

For elementary grade students without health problems or disabilities, observation of the students (while they perform) is the most efficient way for the teacher to gain knowledge of their skill abilities. Observation occurs to judge the students' functioning in physical fitness (cardiorespiratory endurance, muscle strength and endurance, and flexibility) and skill development (space and body awareness, speed, coordination, and balance). Until that observation and judgment can occur, teachers need to be particularly careful of what they ask their students to do.

For students with health problems or disabilities, additional precautions need to be taken until the teacher fully understands the problem or disability and can make instructional modifications to ensure the safety of the students. For example, for children with asthma, the teacher would need to know that continuous exercise might cause an exercise-induced asthma attack. Thus the cardiorespiratory fitness level of those students may not be assessed through traditional observation or standardized fitness tests.

Second, children within a class will not be at the same level of motor development, nor will they possess the same level of skill development. A particular lesson activity will not be appropriate for all of the students. Developmentally appropriate activities, as mentioned many times in the text (see Chapter 2), are designed based on the physical, cognitive, and psychomotor capabilities of the children. To the extent the lesson content provides a match between the lesson activities and the capabilities of the children, the lesson participants are at less risk for injury. Adjusting each lesson activity to fit the wide range of students' abilities becomes the ultimate goal of the teacher. For example, in a throwing lesson, children are participating in one of three activities based on their skill development and experience. Some children (with motor delays) are throwing yarn balls at a target on the wall, others are throwing tennis balls and catching the ball as it rebounds off the wall, while still others are playing catch with a partner. Other examples of adjusting lessons appear in various chapters of the text, and Instant Activity 11.2 allows students opportunities to practice their balance (with skills listed in order of difficulty).

Third, physical education professionals have not developed well-accepted hierarchical listings of activities (from simple to complex) to be used to develop a particular task such as balance. Each movement educator develops his or her own hierarchical listing. Thus Appendix A contains task progressions for classroom teachers to use in designing appropriate lessons.

Fourth, whether students are ready for particular movement activities also depends on their communication skills and level of social development (not just level of motor and skill development). Some students may be able to act appropriately when not directly supervised whereas others may not. Some students may be able to work in a large group setting whereas others may not. Adjustments may need to occur in groupings used and level of teacher supervision based on students' social capabilities and communication skills. A list of questions to guide the teacher in discovering the current status of students in terms of their social and communication skills is provided in Figure 11.3 on page 334. These questions need to be answered by professionals who have had previous experience with the student (parents, other classroom teachers, therapists, teacher aides, etc.). These observations may be helpful in planning lesson activities for various students.

Professionals need to be aware of these four issues (just discussed) as they develop task progressions for students in their classes and take steps as indicated to address those issues. In addition, task progressions used in each lesson should be specified in the teacher's lesson plans. Classroom Learning Station 11.1 provides a task progression for the low balance beam for students in kindergarten through third grade.

SUPERVISION TECHNIQUES

Basic supervisory techniques were presented in Chapter 7 (in the section titled "Supervising Class Activities"), so this section focuses on supervision specifically as it relates to student safety. As indicated previously, teachers scan for students who are off task, interfering with the learning of others, being disrespectful of others or the equipment, or behaving dangerously. Unsafe behavior that is observed must be stopped immediately. Students should never be allowed to endanger the safety of others in the class. Teachers should be sure to scan more frequently during the lesson activities that have the most potential for injury.

INSTANT ACTIVITY 11.2 Body Balance

Grades K–3

Equipment Needed

Music

Activity

Students are standing beside their desk in the classroom. Have the students jog in place to music for one minute. Stop the music and have the students perform the first balance task indicated below. Between each balance task, jog another minute in place. Notice the balance tasks include just static balance tasks (performed in place, like a statue), not dynamic balance tasks (moving from place to place). When performing static balance tasks, children should focus (look at) on one spot straight ahead of them. This is the key to holding static balances for any length of time. Hold each balance as long as possible, and be sure to repeat balances so that both the right and the left leg are used as the supporting leg.

Balance Tasks

- Balance on four body parts (in a push-up position).
- Balance on three body parts: (1) two hands and one leg; (2) two legs and one hand.

- Balance on two body parts (one hand, one leg).
- Balance on buttocks (*V*-sit position), with arms out to the sides of the body for balance.
- Stand on one foot (flat-footed), use arms for balance, place free foot so it is touching the calf of the supporting leg.
- Same as above except stand on tiptoe on the supporting leg.
- Stand on one foot (flat-footed), place arms on hips, place free foot so it is touching the calf of the supporting leg.
- Same as above except stand on tiptoe on the supporting leg.
- Stand on one foot (flat-footed), arms on hips, with the free leg held out in front of the body.
- Same as above except stand on tiptoe on the supporting leg.
- Stand on one foot (flat-footed), arms to the side for balance, with the free leg extended to the back (swan balance).

The drawings below can be used as visual aids for the students while performing this activity.

1. Balance in push-up position

2. Three points of support

3. Two points of support

4. Balance on buttocks (V-sit)

5. Flat-foot, hands free to balance

6. Tiptoe, hands free to balance

(continued)

INSTANT ACTIVITY 11.2 Body Balance (continued)

7. Flat-foot, hands on hips

8. Tiptoe, hands on hips

9. Stand on right foot, left foot forward; stand on left foot, right foot forward

10. Tiptoe, hands on hips

11. One point of support (swan)

Scanning for unsafe behavior is a very difficult technique to master. Inexperienced teachers find it almost impossible to perform the scanning while also paying attention to other matters. With sufficient practice the scanning becomes automatic. This "practice makes perfect" situation indicates that classroom and physical education teachers need to practice their supervision techniques, and at least part of the practice should occur in real movement settings within the schools.

Regarding safety issues, the exact teacher behaviors that constitute *adequate* supervision vary based on the number of children in the class as well as the children's age, skill level, special needs, communication skills, and social responsibility level. In general, a second-grade class needs to be supervised more closely than a sixth-grade class, less-skilled students need more active supervision than highly skilled students, and a class containing large numbers of students needs more active supervision. The student who is less socially responsible requires more supervision. Thus the teacher might allow sixth graders to step into the hallway (out of the gymnasium) to get a drink of water during class, but a second grader would not be allowed that privilege. Teachers should be particularly "aware of children who have impulsive tendencies, children who can be aggressive, and children who wander away from the group," as these students need extra supervision (Block and Horton 1996, 67).

As a general rule, whether the class is being held indoors or outdoors, the teacher never leaves the area or students being supervised. However, following this rule becomes problematic in certain situations. For

<u>Communication Skills</u>

- Does the child understand simple verbal directions?

    ___ yes ___ no

- If you answered "no," do you have suggestions to facilitate communication?

    _____

    _____

- Can the student convey his or her wishes or needs to me?

    ___ yes ___ no

- If you answered "no," do you have suggestions regarding how I might know what the student wants or needs?

    _____

    _____

<u>Behaviors</u>

- Do you think the child understands rules of simple games?

    ___ yes ___ no

- If you answered "no," do you have any suggestions so that the child can play safely?

    _____

    _____

- How does the child handle conflict, such as being on the losing team?

    _____

    _____

- Does the child ever get aggressive? If so, what do you do when this happens?

    _____

    _____

- Does the child have a hard time paying attention and staying on task? If so, what do you do when this happens?

    _____

    _____

<u>Reinforcers</u>

- What activities, objects, and people does the child like?

    _____

    _____

- What activities, objects, and people does the child dislike?

    _____

    _____

FIGURE 11.3 Questions to Help Determine a Student's Level of Social Development and Communication Skills
Adapted from M. Block and M. Horton, Include Safety in PE: Do Not Exclude Students with Disabilities. *Physical Educator* 53(2): 58–72 (1996).

instance, when a student is injured (or becomes sick) during a class, what is the teacher to do? The teacher should not leave the area with the injured student, nor should the teacher allow another student to take the injured student into the building (or down the hallway) to the nurse's office.

We recommend that teachers have on their person (in a fanny pack) basic first-aid supplies so that first aid can be given immediately to the injured student. The fanny pack should also contain a cell phone so the teacher may call the school office for assistance (or use the intercom system if class is being held indoors). Office personnel may either (1) call the paramedics (for life-threatening injuries) while the teacher stays with the class and the injured student or (2) send the school nurse to the playground (or gymnasium) to treat the injured student and bring her or him indoors. If a school nurse is not available, the office personnel should send someone to supervise the class so the movement educator can provide medical treatment in a private setting (assuming the movement educator is certified to administer first aid).

We also recommend that teachers determine (before they get into an injury situation) how they plan to handle their supervisory responsibilities while also giving immediate first aid to an injured student. Students should be taught what to do when a classmate is injured. A possible response might be that the students are to stop all activities, come together within the view of the teacher, sit down, and wait patiently until the teacher has attended to the injured student.

Teachers are well advised to know the supervisory policies and procedures set forth by the school district in which they are employed. It is imperative for the teacher to follow these policies and procedures at all times. For instance, most schools will have specific procedures for handling blood and other body fluids, as well as procedures for how to handle specific situations (e.g., head injuries and seizures). The teacher's supervisory role occurs not only during class activities but any time the teacher is directly responsible for the students (walking in the hallway to and from activity areas, supervising students getting off and on buses, and the like).

INSTANT ACTIVITY 11.3 The Krinkle Slide

Grades 3–6

Equipment Needed

Krinkles, Koosh balls, or beanbags (one per student), masking tape

Activity

The class is divided into two teams who are facing each other with two center lines down the middle (see figure). There should be at least one Krinkle, Koosh ball, or beanbag per student. These objects are placed along the center lines. On a signal, everyone comes forward to their respective center line and picks up an object, attempting to slide it and tag the opposing team on their feet. *For safety reasons, when everyone comes forward, no running is allowed.* Students may walk fast.

For safety reasons, all of the objects must slide on the floor when entering into the opponent's space. Objects must be slid from behind your respective center line. Objects that stop between the center lines are left in that area for the remainder of the game.

If hit by a ball or beanbag, a student must sit down in a pike position. In the pike position the student "hip walks" to the "Krinkle Kingdom," which is located at the back of their own playing area, and then the player may return to the game.

This game can be played in the classroom if enough space is available to move the desks against the wall to create an open space in the middle of the room. The center lines can be drawn with masking tape.

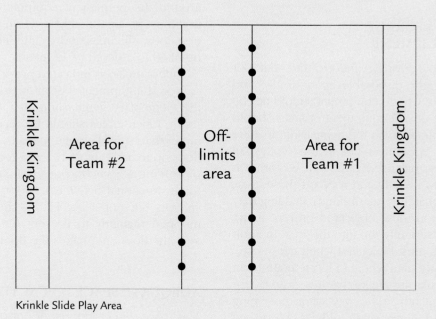

Krinkle Slide Play Area

STUDENTS' SAFETY KNOWLEDGE

In each lesson plan that includes movement activities, the teacher and students benefit if the lesson plan specifies possible risks and actions taken to minimize those risks. This information reminds the teacher (or substitute teacher) of safety concerns while getting ready to teach the lesson, so that safety procedures are actually implemented into the lesson. It also provides the teacher with the opportunity to identify foreseeable risks during the planning stage of instruction (rather than during the implementation stage). As indicated earlier in the chapter, the safety rules established for a particular situation need to be taught to the students and enforced by the teacher. Instant Activity 11.3 allows the teacher to establish and enforce rules and allows the students to practice complying with the rules. In addition to the students knowing how to behave appropriately in the movement setting, students should also know when and how to report broken or damaged equipment.

Adequate Physical Environments (Indoors and Outdoors)

In order to prevent injuries to students, teachers must maintain the physical environments where children perform physical activity. Teachers monitor indoor and outdoor equipment and activity spaces and consider the weather conditions when having lessons outdoors (or even indoors on hot days if there is no air-conditioning in the gymnasium). In addition, someone in the building is probably charged specifically with maintaining playground equipment and spaces. Teachers should know who that individual is in order to report unsafe conditions. Physical educators are usually the staff members responsible for the equipment and spaces in the gymnasium. Maintenance records should be kept on file and accessible for others to view.

MAINTENANCE, STORAGE, AND USE OF EQUIPMENT

Movement educators inspect indoor and outdoor equipment (fixed and disposable) periodically and just before each use. Unsafe equipment should not be used, and access to unsafe equipment or areas should be prevented. Unsafe areas in the gymnasium include those areas where equipment not in use (volleyball standards, bleachers, balance beam, etc.) is stored. It may be necessary to identify and rope off these areas to remind students that they are off-limits. Padding may need to be placed on these objects to prevent injury when students inadvertently run into the area. In addition, climbing ropes must be locked when not in use.

The teacher should plan where to locate equipment needed for a particular lesson so that it is close by for easy distribution but not in the way when not being used in the lesson. Equipment should also be placed so that the arrangement does not entice students to play with it at inappropriate times. In general, it is best to place equipment (in boxes or in hula hoops) in several places scattered around the perimeter of the gymnasium. This allows the teacher to distribute the equipment without all the children converging on one spot to obtain needed equipment.

Equipment should be used for its intended purpose, and equipment used during instructional lessons should vary in size and hardness based on the age, ability level, and special needs of the children. For example, when throwing and catching, children with poor eye-hand coordination can use foam balls, and a student with limited vision can use a ball (that is soft in texture) with a beeper inside. When on the playground, children should use only the permanent equipment that is designed for their age group.

Most activities performed in elementary physical education will not require children to wear protective equipment; however, protective equipment should be purchased and used when necessary. For example, helmets, knee pads, and elbow pads should be worn for in-line skating. The protective equipment should fit the students properly, and should be disinfected after each use to stop the spread of communicable diseases.

MAINTENANCE OF ACTIVITY SURFACES AND SPACES

Outdoor grassy areas need to be mowed on a regular basis and must be free of holes or indentations that students might step into, thus injuring themselves. Cement and blacktop areas, dirt areas, loose-fill areas around the permanent equipment, and the walking trail must be smooth and level on the surface. In addition, loose-fill areas under climbing equipment should be filled to a depth of 12 inches.

Indoor areas, as indicated previously, should be free of stored equipment if at all possible. For instance, if the elementary gymnasium also serves as the lunchroom, lunch tables should be recessed into the walls rather than stored along the walls. The walls (from the floor up to a height of 10 to 15 feet) should be free of protruding objects (to prevent injury and to be usable for instructional activities). Floor surfaces should be smooth but not slick. Floors should be swept and mopped regularly to prevent dirt buildup that damages the floor and makes the floor slick.

ADEQUATE SPACE FOR ACTIVITIES

The space (either indoors or outdoors) in which activities are conducted should be large enough to accommodate all children. The amount of space needed to ensure a safe environment varies based on the age, ability, and special needs of the students in the class. For example, more space is needed to accommodate a student in a wheelchair. More space is needed when children are using striking instruments (bats, golf clubs, hockey sticks, etc.). The space the teacher wants to use for the lesson needs to be accessible for all the children in the class. If inaccessible areas exist, talk to school administrators about how to make them accessible. Space is also needed between the activity area and any obstructions such as walls or equipment.

This space is a buffer or safety zone where students may go to tie shoes, catch their breath, or manage their equipment changes or needs.

A July 2001 NASPE position paper (*Guidelines for Facilities, Equipment, and Instructional Materials in Elementary Education*) provides additional insight into facility and equipment issues related to elementary physical education. The paper also provides in-depth equipment lists for elementary physical education. This position paper is available on the NASPE website (www.aahperd.org/naspe) from the pull-down menu titled "Publications," then "Position Papers." This publication contains size recommendations for various movement spaces (outdoor physical education spaces, recess space, and indoor gymnasium space).

REPORTING UNSAFE CONDITIONS

School districts usually have a policy regarding how to notify the physical plant personnel that an unsafe condition exists somewhere on the property. Small school districts may simply have the teacher ask the custodian to take care of the unsafe condition, whereas larger school districts may have a form to be completed and submitted to the physical plant office. Teachers should protect themselves by keeping a copy of the form they submit or by making their request to the custodian in writing. They should also follow-up to be sure the problem has been corrected. In addition, it is wise to know who (within the school system) is responsible for setting up off-limit zones around unsafe conditions.

ADAPTING TO WEATHER CONDITIONS

Weather conditions are also a factor to consider when discussing the physical environment. Moisture (rain or melting snow) may cause ground or equipment surfaces to be slippery and thus unsafe. Lightning is very dangerous, so children should be taken indoors when storms threaten that may contain lightning.

Extreme cold and heat may also be dangerous. At high temperatures, students may develop sunburns, heatstroke, or heat exhaustion. High temperatures accompanied by high humidity simply make the conditions worse, and in general, physical activity should be less vigorous for a shorter length of time. During hot weather, allow students to drink water as they wish or provide frequent, designated times when everyone must drink water. Remember, water is the best beverage to drink. Also provide frequent rest periods in the shade or shorten the length of the outdoor activity period. In cold weather, students need to have body parts covered to prevent frostbite, and the length of the outdoor activity period may need to be adjusted depending on the temperature.

In some parts of the country, teachers need to consider the air quality in deciding whether to be active outdoors. In those cases, follow the standards set by the school, and be mindful of health issues specific to your students that could be impacted by breathing contaminated air.

Summary

Planning for a safe movement environment involves selecting appropriate curriculum activities based on program goals and lesson objectives. Then the activities must be taught using current "best practices" in the field of physical education. In addition, the physical environment where the activities are taught must be adequate for safely conducting the activities, and the teacher must be able to properly care for injuries once they occur.

Because teachers have a duty toward their students, it behooves them to implement the suggestions in this chapter. The policies, procedures, and actions outlined here provide the basis for what "a prudent, reasonable, up-to-date teacher" would do in similar circumstances. In addition, the recommended actions help the teacher guard against causing injury to students.

Chapter Activities

1. Based on what you learned about safety in this chapter, what would you recommend the movement educator do in the following situations? Identify possible safety concerns and determine an appropriate course of action.

   - Ebony forgot her gym shoes, and she wants to participate in the lesson activities barefoot (rather than in her dress shoes).
   - Jason, a second grader who is overweight, does not want to jog the half-mile the rest of the students will be performing next in the lesson.
   - During your fifth-grade class (playing three-on-three outdoor soccer), a student, Nischant, is seriously injured. He is lying unconscious on the field after running into his opponent, who is a

much larger, more skilled member of the class. How do you handle the current injury situation, and what have you learned about grouping your students during future activities?

- Your third-grade class wants to participate in tumbling activities.
- Debbie comes to class with her long hair not tied back out of her face. During activities, her hair continually falls in her face and obstructs her vision.
- The teacher wants to use regulation softballs when the second-grade class practices throwing and catching.
- Tony has an asthma attack after participating in a strenuous running activity. The teacher was not aware Tony had asthma and thus did not plan appropriate activities for Tony.
- The teacher wants to use the horizontal bars located on the playground for class activities, but she remembers that several weeks ago the bars were placed off-limits because they needed repair.
- During a particularly rainy fall season, the teacher becomes concerned that he will not have time to test his sixth-grade class in the mile walk-run test (outdoors). He usually tests the students after several months of training, but the training has been limited this year because of the rain.
- During recess, jump ropes are available for the students to use to improve and practice their jump rope skills. Today a group of students is using the ropes to lasso each other.

2. Answer the following questions based on information learned in this chapter.

- At the beginning of the school year, the teacher was determining the rules of conduct for her second-grade class. If you were that teacher, what would be included on your list of class rules?
- At the beginning of the school year, the teacher wants his sixth-grade class to participate in determining what the rules of conduct will be for this school year. Describe a process the teacher might use to determine and implement the class rules.

3. Prepare a lesson plan to teach one of the games outlined in the Special Event at the end of the chapter. Be sure to consider all the safety concerns identified in the chapter.

4. Prepare a lesson plan to teach a different game outlined in the Special Event. Your class contains one student who has vision problems and one who has coordination problems (a "clumsy" child). Be sure to indicate how you will accommodate the children with special needs and how you will ensure a safe environment in which to play the game.

5. After accepting a job offer at Sunflower Elementary, you discover that the school does not have a curriculum guide for elementary physical education. Why might you want to remedy this situation?

Internet Resources

PE Central. Site for health and physical educators providing information—lessons and assessment activities—about developmentally appropriate physical education for children.
www.pecentral.org

American Alliance for Health, Physical Education, Recreation and Dance; National Association for Sport and Physical Education. Contains position paper on facilities, equipment, and instructional materials for elementary physical education.
www.aahperd.org/naspe

Bibliography

American Red Cross. 2006. *First aid/CPR/AED for schools and the community.* Yardley, PA: Staywell.

Bettenhausen, S. 2002. School liability: Student to student injuries involving students with disabilities. ERIC, 476-381.

Block, M. E., and M. L. Horton. 1996. Include safety in physical education: Do not exclude students with disabilities. *Physical Educator* 53(2): 58–72.

Gray, G. R. 1995. Safety tips from the expert witness. *Journal of Physical Education, Recreation, and Dance* 66(1): 18–21.

Hart, J. E., and J. Ritson. 2002. *Liability and safety in physical education and sport: Practitioner's guide to the legal aspects of teaching and coaching in elementary and secondary schools.* ERIC, 470-729.

Seidler, T. L. 2006. Planning and designing safe facilities. *Journal of Physical Education, Recreation, and Dance* 77(5): 32–37, 44.

Stewart, D. 2000. Schools and the law: A preventive risk management perspective. *International Journal of Educational Reform* 9(4): 342–348.

GRADES 3–6

NASPE STANDARD 1 Students demonstrate competency in motor skills and movement patterns needed to perform a variety of physical activities.

LESSON OBJECTIVES

- Students practice motor skills in safe game situations.
- Students learn safety rules that must be observed while playing games.
- Students are physically active for the purpose of developing physical fitness.
- Students are rewarded for studying hard all week.
- New games are introduced so students can incorporate them into their recess play.

EQUIPMENT NEEDED Depends on the games selected. For the games described in this special event, the equipment needed to play the game is indicated with the game description.

PREPARATION TIME Fifteen minutes to select games and collect equipment

KNOWLEDGE CONTENT The students must learn the rules for playing each game (described herein). Suggested games include Hit the Club, Prison Ball, Kick Back, Five Passes, Dribble Tag, Dribble Drop, Soccer Softball, and Hoopla Hoop Basketball.

Be sure to teach the safety rules that must be observed while playing each game. These rules are identified within each game description.

PLAYGROUND ACTIVITY Play one or more of the suggested games. Younger children will need to change games more frequently than older children. Play for a total of at least 15 to 20 minutes, if possible.

The teacher should provide corrective skill instruction while children are playing the games in order to improve their motor skills.

ASSESSMENT The teacher could develop and use a checklist or rating scale to evaluate a specific motor skill being performed in any of the games.

Children could rate their perceived exertion as described in Chapter 4, Quick Lesson 4.4.

The teacher may observe whether students play any of the new games at recess time.

SUCCESS FOR ALL Select or modify games so children with disabilities will be able to participate with

their classmates. For example, in Hit the Club, a sound could be placed by the bowling pin (e.g., a ticking clock) so a visually impaired student could take aim at the pin. A student in a wheelchair could roll the ball with his or her arm (instead of kicking the ball).

THE GAMES

HIT THE CLUB

Equipment: One playground ball and one bowling pin per group
Formation: Groups of two
Description: One partner is lined up at one end of the play area, and a club (bowling pin) is placed at the opposite side of the area (distance should vary depending on students' skill level). The other partner stands behind the club and retrieves the ball after it is kicked. The object of the game is to try to knock over the club by kicking the ball. Partners take turns kicking and retrieving the ball. Each group keeps track of the number of times they knocked the club down during the allotted game time. Each time period, they try to improve their score.
Safety: If children are kicking the ball,

- Teach them how to kick the ball so it rolls along the ground (instead of going into the air).
- Teach them to control and aim their kicks, not just kick as hard as they can.
- Use sponge balls so a child hit by a ball will not be hurt.

PRISON BALL

Equipment: Three soft sponge balls per group
Formation: Groups of eight to ten players on a grassy area
Description: Players form a circle holding hands. Players try to kick the ball through the legs of others. Hands may not be used to stop the ball, and players who kick balls that rise above waist level must sit out of the game for one minute.
Safety: Same as in Hit the Club

KICK BACK

Equipment: One football for each group
Formation: Groups of two, open field, two goal lines
Description: Three steps in front of one of the player's goal lines, the player punts the football to the partner. The partner attempts to catch the ball in the air. If the ball is caught in the air, that player takes three steps toward the other player's goal line before punting the ball back. If the ball hits the ground, the receiver kicks

back from where the ball is stopped. A point is scored whenever the ball is successfully kicked over the opponent's goal before the defender can catch it or stop it.
Safety:

- Students should have some skill in punting and catching a football before playing this game.
- Provide a large enough play area so students are not running into each other as they punt and catch.
- Use sponge footballs so injury will not occur if a punted ball hits a child.

FIVE PASSES

Equipment: One football, different colored pinnies for each team
Formation: Five players on a team, on a large grassy area
Description: Players from two teams are scattered on the field. Moving anywhere on the field, the team tries to make five consecutive passes to the five players on their team without losing control of the ball. This scores one point. No player may take more than three steps when in possession of the football. Taking more than three steps is called traveling, and the ball is awarded to the other team. There is no penalty if the ball hits the ground; however, if the ball is recovered by the team who previously had possession, their five-pass sequence is interrupted and they must begin anew.
Safety: This is a noncontact game, so players must keep their bodies under control and not make contact with opposing players while trying to intercept passes.

DRIBBLE TAG

Equipment: One ball for each student, hard surface area
Formation: Students scattered out in general space
Description: Each student has a ball (that bounces as it is dribbled like a basketball). Everyone is "it." Everyone must dribble a ball constantly, and everyone tries to tag other players with their free hand. A person who has been tagged three times walks (without dribbling) to the edge of the playing area, dribbles the ball in place 20 times, and then returns to participating in the game.
Safety: Students must tag others lightly and must maintain control of their bodies so they are not running into other players.

DRIBBLE DROP

Equipment: One ball for each student, boxes or crates placed on a hardtop area
Formation: Students scattered out in general space
Description: All children dribble a ball (like a basketball) around the boxes. When they get close to a box, they shoot (drop) the ball in. If it does not bounce out they get a point. The object is to get as many points as possible before the signal to stop.
Safety: Students must have their bodies under control so they are not running into each other.

SOCCER SOFTBALL

Equipment: One soccer ball, three cones, one home plate
Formation: Five players
Description: One student goes to home plate to kick a pitched ball (rolled along the ground). One student is the pitcher, one is the catcher (trapper), and the other two are out in the field to retrieve the kicked ball. All the players are playing against the kicker. The first person kicks the rolled ball and then runs all the way around the cones, returning home without stopping at any of the cones. Using soccer skills (no hands), the fielding students must retrieve the ball and get it home to the trapper as quickly as possible. The runner scores a point for each cone passed before the trapper traps the ball on home plate. Players rotate all positions until everyone has kicked. The player with the most points wins. The game can be repeated any number of times.
Safety: Players are not to block the progress of the runner around the cones or over home plate as they strive to move the ball toward home plate.
Note: The game rules for all the games above are adapted from the Broward County Public Schools (Florida) Elementary School Physical Education Curriculum and Instruction Guide.

HOOPLA HOOP BASKETBALL (BASKETBALL LEAD-UP GAME)

Equipment: Two hula hoops, Nerf basketball, two ropes
Formation: Two teams with six players each (a goalie, two outlet players, and three forwards)
Description: Attach a hula hoop to both basketball rims with two ropes. The hula hoop goal hangs down so that players may toss the ball through it. The object of the game is to pass the ball from player to player so that one of the forwards can score by tossing the ball through the hula hoop. The goalie has unlimited movement in the key area and can try to block a shot, get the rebound, or intercept the ball. Once the goalie has the ball, she or he will pass the ball to one of the outlet players. The outlet players try to pass the ball to one of the forwards for a possible score. Teams earn one point for each score. The ball is given to the opposing team's goalie after a score. A player with the ball is allowed to take three steps before passing or shooting the ball. The ball may be passed to teammates by throwing or rolling. All players can try to intercept the ball. Balls going out of bounds go to the other team. While forwards can either pass the ball or try to score, they are not allowed in the key area. Only the opposing goalie is allowed in the key area.
Safety: No body contact is allowed during the game, so players must have their bodies under control.
Note: Hoopla Hoop Basketball is from P. Gecoya, Hoopla Games, *Great Activities* 6(1): (1987).

CHAPTER 12

Recess as Quality Movement Time

The purpose of this chapter is to provide an in-depth discussion of recess within the school as an educational process, describe activities that could be used to encourage students to be active during recess, and provide helpful hints on making recess a profitable movement time for students.

Objectives

After studying this chapter, you will be able to do the following:

- Discuss the role of recess (free play) in the educational process.
- List the benefits students derive from playing during recess time.
- Identify typical playground behaviors.
- Identify the impact of gender, ethnicity, age, and disability on the dynamics of children playing together.
- Identify the types of spaces and equipment needed to provide quality recess experiences.
- Observe playground behaviors and draw conclusions regarding the quality of that recess play.
- Establish rules of conduct for the playground.
- Suggest actions a classroom teacher could take to improve the quality of the recess period.

Mrs. Nguyen teaches third grade in a large multicultural school district. She is an avid runner and uses that form of exercise to keep herself healthy and fit. She is very interested in using physical activity to help her students become physically educated and to enhance their social skills. To this end, she coordinates with her school's physical education teacher to provide numerous opportunities for her students to be physically active each day.

However, she had never really given much thought to the role recess periods might play in her efforts to socialize and educate her students—that is, until last summer, when she completed a course at the local university. She was aware of the release the recess periods provided for her students, but she had not viewed these periods as important educational opportunities that she might influence for the betterment of her students. The new school year begins in two weeks. She has mapped out a tentative plan to investigate how she might better use recess as an educational experience for her students. The plan involves three steps.

The *first step* is to *change her role.* Mrs. Nguyen will, as in past years, have the classroom aide supervise the morning and afternoon recess periods (20 minutes in length) for her students. Nonetheless, she intends to take direct responsibility for the recess periods instead of ignoring that part of her students' educational experience. She knows her aide takes excellent care of her students during recess. The aide never stands around and talks to other teachers. Instead, she actively watches for safety problems, intervenes when student behavior is inappropriate, moves around the play area to view all the children, and has learned the names of all the children on the playground at that time (her students and another class of third graders). Her aide will continue with the direct supervision under her leadership. Perhaps together they can prevent the spillover of events that happen during recess (fights and disagreements) into the classroom.

The *second step* is to *collect some basic information.* Although recess time is one of her planning periods, Mrs. Nguyen plans to observe her students during recess on a number of occasions. She will use this time to do the following:

1. Discover whether her children mirror the general playground behavior discussed in the summer class she completed, paying specific attention to the cultural composition of various play groups
2. Make a list of the activities her students engage in during recess and also indicate who plays these activities
3. Discover whether the composition of play groups and play activities is, in general, permanent in nature
4. Determine whether equipment (or the lack of it) has an impact on the activities engaged in
5. Compare her available recess equipment with the desired equipment (from a list obtained in the summer course)
6. Map who plays with whom and identify students who are isolates

The *third step* is to *develop a plan,* based on the data collected, for improving the educational benefits of the recess period for students. The plan might include the following:

1. Introducing new recess activities
2. Changing the dynamics of the interactions among students
3. Stimulating physical activity
4. Developing acceptance of others and quality friendships through play
5. Teaching conflict resolution skills
6. Implementing a structured recess program similar to those Mrs. Nguyen read about in the summer course

Mrs. Nguyen knows this is just the beginning of her search for a more educational recess period. But she believes her students will eventually benefit greatly from her work in this area, and she is looking forward to this new challenge.

The Roles and Benefits of Recess in the Educational Process

A brief overview of recess as profitable learning time for children occurred in the last section of Chapter 1. That section introduced the need for children to experience free play time (recess) as a part of the school day that supplements the recommended daily physical education class (NASPE 2004).

Children should have many opportunities during the school day to interact with their friends and be physically active (practicing their motor skills). Before the school day begins, after it ends, and during set recess periods (morning, afternoon, and lunchtime), children should be **free to play** on the school playground with supervision (but not unnecessary interference) by adults. "Quality physical education and recess are components of the elementary school educational experience that enable students to develop physical competence, health-related fitness, personal and social responsibility, and enjoyment of physical activity so that they will be physically active for a lifetime" (NASPE 2006, 2). In compliance with the Reauthorization Act of 2004, most school wellness policies support the need for daily recess periods that stimulate children to be physically active.

PHYSICAL EDUCATION VERSUS RECESS

Physical education and recess are quite different in terms of purpose, content, and structure; therefore it seems fitting at this time to reflect again, briefly, on the definitions of physical education and play. Although both physical education and recess time are very important elements of the child's curriculum, they do *not* fulfill the same educational needs. Physical education (like art, music, social studies, reading, etc.) is instructional time within the school curriculum in which students learn about movement (cognitive goals), practice their physical skills (psychomotor and fitness goals), learn to value the importance of being active (attitudinal goals), and work with all their classmates (social goals). Children participate in class activities directed (and planned) by the physical educator or classroom teacher in order to accomplish various educational goals.

During recess students are free to select with whom they wish to play and what they want to do (within certain broad limits). They can play games or sports, play on the equipment, or just talk with their friends, and adults will not interfere unless someone is in physical danger. The literature on play generally agrees that play behavior is intrinsically motivated, spontaneous, self-generated, pleasurable (not serious), variable from child to child and from one situation to the next, and not controlled by adult-imposed rules (Frost and Jacobs 1995; Krasnor and Pepler 1980). Since the activities children engage in during recess possess the characteristics just described, what children do at recess can be called play.

BOX 12.1
The Arguments in Favor of and Against Recess

AGAINST

- Recess takes time away from academics.
- Recess encourages aggressive behavior.

IN FAVOR OF

- Recess fosters attention by providing a mental break from classroom studies.
- Recess improves learning through distributed practice of classroom subjects.
- Recess boosts academic achievement through peer interactions.
- Recess stimulates cognitive functioning.
- Recess contributes to social and moral development.
- Recess leads to healthier children.
- Recess develops movement skills.

ARGUMENTS AGAINST PROVIDING RECESS

Arguments for not providing recess (free play) for children during the school day are usually centered around two ideas—time away from academics and the encouragement of aggressive behavior. Box 12.1 presents a summary of the arguments (for and against recess) discussed in this section.

Takes Time Away from Academics   Recess takes time away from academic work. Today's educational environment emphasizes the need for students to concentrate on and master the basic skills of reading, writing, and arithmetic. In order to accomplish this, schools are eliminating recess, establishing longer school days, and lengthening the number of days in the school year. This approach appears to value the cognitive development of children more than their social and physical development. As yet there is no evidence that taking the actions described would actually improve academic performance. In fact, evidence to the contrary is mounting. Five large cross-national studies comparing schools in the United States, China, Taiwan, and Japan indicate that simply increasing the length of the school day does not benefit the students academically unless teachers alter the way they

teach (Stevenson 1992). In addition, another study found that allocating more curricular time (total of 14–26 percent) to physical activity led to more rapid academic learning per unit of classroom time, so that students receiving more physical activity time (and less classroom time) matched or exceeded the academic learning of the other students (Shepard 1997).

Encourages Aggressive Behavior   The second argument against providing recess is that it encourages aggression and antisocial behavior. This approach also devalues the social and physical development of the child. Rather than finding solutions to social problems that occur on the playground, advocates would simply delete the recess period from the school day. This approach ignores the fact that someday, as part of the workforce, students will have to get along with their peers, and it denies the reality that students learn many appropriate, effective social skills by practicing them on the playground. Much anecdotal information supports the contention that students are aggressive on the playground, but empirical evidence indicates that aggression on elementary and middle school playgrounds is very uncommon, accounting for less than 2 or 3 percent of the children's total behavior (Boyle et al. 2003; Pellegrini 1995).

ARGUMENTS IN FAVOR OF PROVIDING RECESS

Children receive a number of benefits from having a regular recess time. These benefits provide the basis for the belief that recess enhances children's health, academic performance, classroom behavior, and social and physical competence.

Fosters Attention Through Variety   Evidence appears to be building to support the argument that children benefit from recess because of their mental need for variety and periodic diversion. Children become less attentive to academic lessons as a function of time because academic work becomes less novel and play (recess time) offers the chance for novelty (Jensen 1998). Thus inattentiveness in the classroom is the result of children's boredom with the academic setting. A diversion, such as recess, increases students' attention levels once the students are back in the classroom (Holmes et al. 2006; Jarrett et al. 1998; Ridgeway et al. 2003). Researchers have discovered that children liked going outdoors to play because it provided a break from lessons, and they could have fun, relax, and play with friends (Blatchford, Creeser,

INSTANT ACTIVITY 12.1
Hi Five

Grades K–6

Equipment Needed

None

Activity

At the beginning of the year, use this activity to encourage students to learn each other's names. Students spread out down the length of the gymnasium (down both sides of the gymnasium). Students then face each other from across the gym so each student has a partner across the way. Teacher gives the command, "High," "Medium," or "Low." On that command, all students walk forward to meet the student directly across from them. They meet in the middle of the area. As they meet, they introduce themselves, give each other a high, medium, or low five sign (by slapping hands at the designated level), and then pass by to the other line. The teacher then instructs one line to move to the right or left (the distance of one person). The odd person goes to the end of the line so he or she has a partner across the way. Repeat the process until all students meet each other. As the process is repeated, change how the students move to the center (skip, hop, jump, gallop, etc.). For older children, have them dribble a ball toward each other and exchange balls as they meet in the middle and call each other's names.

From Jill Best, elementary physical education teacher, Omaha, Nebraska.

and Mooney 1990). To provide a classroom break that includes physical activity, do Instant Activity 12.1 or play jacks (as described in Appendix C).

Improves Learning Through Distributed Practice The second argument for providing regular recess breaks proposes that playlike periods (not just break times) are important for young children (Pellegrini and Bjorklund 1996). This argument is based on the principle that children (and adults) learn better and more quickly when their efforts on a task are distributed over time with frequent short breaks rather than when their efforts are concentrated into longer periods of time. Conceptually, **distributed practice** supposedly reduces the cognitive interference that results from prolonged periods of concentrated work (Pellegrini and

Bjorklund 1996, 1997); and empirically, research does indicate that distributed practice has positive effects on both learning and attention (Toppino, Kasserman, and Mracek 1991). In this argument, recess is more than just a recreational activity. It is also an activity that fosters attention skills. Research results support the distributed effort argument that children's attention to a task is best when the work is spaced with breaks separating task effort (Pellegrini and Bjorklund 1996; Pellegrini, Huberty, and Jones 1995; Pellegrini and Davis 1993). Based on research evidence that the brain operates on a cycle of 90–120 minutes, Jensen (1998) suggests a guideline for the length of direct instruction: no more than the child's age in minutes. For example, 10 minutes for a 10-year-old child. These direct instruction periods need to be interspersed with physical movements and/or a change in academic activities such as moving to group work.

Stimulates Academic Achievement Through Peer Interaction The cognitive impact of children playing is studied in terms of whether cognition is facilitated through the social interaction with peers that occurs during play. This research line is based on Swiss psychologist Jean Piaget's **equilibration theory,** which proposes that peer interactions facilitate cognitive conflict and subsequent reequilibration (Piaget 1970). An empirical study did indeed find that peer interactions on the playground were significant, positive predictors of first-grade achievement, whereas interactions with adults were negative predictors of first-grade achievement (Pellegrini and Bohn 2005).

Although these findings are consistent with theory, we suggest that more studies are needed using different samples, larger samples, and different measures of peer-adult interactions. The study also reported that girls' games were significantly correlated with achievement. This finding is consistent with Piaget's belief that game playing has a cognitive component and playground games like jump rope and hopscotch (with grids made by the children) involve the use of cognitive processes. In summary, current evidence suggests a positive relationship between interactions with peers during recess time and academic achievement.

Stimulates Cognitive Functioning Through Physical Activity Supporters of brain-based teaching and learning (Jensen 1998) indicate that brain functioning research clearly shows a link between physical activity (movement and exercise) and thinking. They contend that movement changes the brain structure and functioning particularly in the region of the cerebellum where neurons connect to all parts of the brain's cortex. Evidence indicates that regions of the brain control multiple mental and physical capabilities (Calvin 1996). For example, stroke patients who have difficulty speaking also cannot perform hand and arm movement sequences. Thus engaging in physical movements (e.g., throwing darts, playing tag or hopscotch, kicking balls) seems to use the same areas of the brain that we use to problem-solve, plan actions, and sequence actions (Calvin 1996). Thus brain functioning can be enhanced through both physical exercise and mental exercise.

Current explanations for how exercise and physical activity influence cognitive functioning include three mechanisms (Etnier et al. 1997):

1. Increases in blood flow to the brain (as a by-product of physical activity) resulting in more nutrients going to the brain
2. Increases in levels of norepinephrine and dopamine (neurotransmitters) in the bloodstream resulting in better memory functioning
3. Changes in brain structure resulting in more effective brain functioning

These mechanisms are difficult to study directly; however, research using indirect methods of study supports the contention that exercise and physical activity can improve cognitive functioning (Etnier et al. 1997).

Although the research is not conclusive in this area, it certainly suggests that academic learning and movement ought to occur "hand in hand" in the elementary school in order to maximally activate the brain's development and functioning (Taras 2005; Tremarche, Robinson, and Graham 2007; Vail 2006).

Stimulates Social and Moral Development   Play has been recognized for many years as an important element in social development. Through play, children learn about justice, fairness, cooperation, friendship, loyalty, and social rules (Frost and Jacobs 1995; Gallegos 1998; Jarrett and Maxwell 2000). They also learn to express their own point of view and understand others' viewpoints, and as their social skills improve, so does their self-esteem. Play also encourages a sense of control because of the self-directed behavior inherent in play. This sense of control is important to the emotional development and mental health of children (Landreth 1993). To improve your students' cooperative skills, use Instant Activity 12.2 and recess games included in Appendix C such as hopscotch, Keep-It-Up, modified soccer, and half-court basketball.

It is also believed that play is related to moral development. Moral development theory suggests

INSTANT ACTIVITY 12.2
The Human Knot

Grades K–6

Equipment Needed

None

Activity

Divide students into groups of five or six (making sure different cultures are represented in each group). Students form a circle and randomly grasp the hands of different people across the circle. This forms the human knot. The goal is to "untie" the knot by stepping through, moving around, and so forth until you have a circle without knots. As the knot is untied, hands may not be released. If a hand is released, the entire group must begin again! The challenge is for each group to be successful.

Hint: Do not grab the hands of the person standing next to you.

From New Games Foundation, *The New Games Book* (Garden City, NY: Doubleday, 1976).

that children gain exposure to different opinions by interacting with their peers and thus become better able to make moral decisions that are less egocentric in orientation (Kohlberg 1971). Play provides the child opportunities to have the social interactions with peers necessary for the child to practice "getting along with others" and to learn the consequences of various actions. In general, the evidence currently available supports the contention that recess behavior is generally a positive predictor of children's, especially boys', social development (Pellegrini 1995), and that children, especially boys, use their physical game abilities to achieve social competence and adjust to early schooling (Pellegrini et al. 2002).

Leads to Healthier Children   Previously, this book has fully explored the need for children to be physically active for at least several hours a day. However, we reiterate (because it is so important) that the physical inactivity of children today is a major health threat for this nation. This inactivity coupled with poor nutrition contributes to obesity, high blood pressure, and high cholesterol in children. Recess can provide significant school time for students to experience high levels of physical activity.

Typically, most children spend the majority of their recess time engaged in physical activity. In terms of the percent of recess time that children are active, researchers reported children spent 59 percent of their recess time engaged in some type of physical activity and 21 percent of the time in vigorous physical activity (Pellegrini and Smith 1998). Using pedometers to monitor activity level, another group found that boys spent 78 percent and girls spent 63 percent of their recess time in some type of physical activity (Beighle et al. 2006). In terms of the number of the students who are active during recess, one study (Zask et al. 2001) observed children in 18 primary schools and found that 51.4 percent of the boys and 41.6 percent of the girls were engaged in moderate to vigorous physical activity while 14.7 percent of the boys and 9.4 percent of the girls were engaged in vigorous physical activity. These data strongly suggest that recess offers an opportunity where most children are active enough to achieve health benefits. Daily recess periods composed of physical activity can counteract weight gain, promote muscular strength and endurance, increase motor coordination, and stimulate higher levels of self-esteem—all leading to healthier children. Thus recess should be part of each school day for all children. In addition, since increased recess time correlates with increased physical activity levels by children after school (Dale, Corbin, and Dale 2000), and levels of physical activity (moderate and vigorous) by children are significantly higher during longer recess periods (Zask et al. 2001), perhaps schools should consider lengthening the recess periods to increase the health benefit derived by the children.

Develops Movement Skills   A final argument (developed by the authors of this book) for providing regular recess breaks is that these breaks provide practice time for children to become skillful movers. Even if, in the final analysis, recess does not enhance children's cognitive-social development, it does serve the movement needs of young children. In terms of physical development, play provides an opportunity for children to move in many different ways. Accomplishing physical challenges is fun and intrinsically rewarding.

To the extent children are physically active during recess, their motor skills and fitness levels may improve. As fitness levels improve, children feel better and have more energy. As motor skills improve, children perform better in various sport and game activities, leading to increased personal satisfaction, self-confidence, and friendships with peers.

Research confirms that physical competence is highly valued by children's peers, so being physically

Recess provides important opportunities for children to practice motor skills.

competent leads to social recognition. "Physical competence affects a child's choice of activities, the level of physical challenge he is willing to assume, and the peers with whom he interacts" (Barbour 1996, 43). Children with high physical competence engaged in more kinds of play and attempted more new activities than children with low physical competence. Children with high physical competence played primarily with children of similar physical ability. Based on this evidence, the improvement of children's physical skills should be a priority for classroom and physical education teachers. Classroom teachers can develop organized recess units that tie in with current class activities to afford students the opportunities to work toward skill competence. Teachers might also promote events during recess such as the American Heart Association's "Jump Rope for Heart" to increase activity levels and improve skill performance.

Much still needs to be studied and learned about the relationship between play and the child's development (social, cognitive, and physical development). But the preponderance of theory and empirical evidence supports the contention that play has an essential role in the child's development. Although research continues to find connections between the effects of play experiences and various social-cognitive characteristics, the physical dimension is studied less. It should not be!

An essential part of the self-worth of adults is dependent on their view of their physical bodies and their movement capabilities. The initial feelings about physical self-worth occur in young children during play; thus it is very important to recognize and begin studying the contributions play (during recess) makes to the physical development of the child.

In conclusion, research overwhelmingly supports the value of recess for elementary school age children

(Jarrett 2002; Pellegrini and Bohn 2005). "Outdoor recess is the single avenue that provides students with the irreplaceable and unparalleled opportunity to refresh their brains, exercise their hearts and muscles, choose their own activities, make friends, work out problems, and have fun. Recess is the fourth 'R,' because it helps children learn the other three" (Waite-Stupiansky and Findlay 2001, 23–24).

Setting the Stage for Quality Recess Experiences

In American schools, principals and teachers are responsible for establishing recess policies for their individual schools or districts. In a 1989 national survey conducted by the National Association of Elementary School Principals (NAESP), 87 percent of the school districts had the power to make their own local policy decisions regarding recess (Pellegrini 1995). With this local control comes the responsibility to do what is best for the students. Thus school personnel must make recess policies for their school based on the educational benefits to be derived from the experience with the understanding that these educational benefits occur in a number of domains (cognitive, social, and physical). In today's environment, those recess policies will be part of the local school's wellness policies in place under the directive of the Reauthorization Act of 2004.

Having determined that recess is an essential component of the elementary school curriculum, how might school personnel set the stage for quality recess experiences? In this section, we suggest four specific ways to enhance children's recess experiences:

1. Overcome obstacles that prevent play experiences
2. Select the amount and timing of recess within the school day
3. Identify appropriate recess spaces and equipment
4. Prepare for typical recess behavior

OBSTACLES THAT PREVENT PLAY EXPERIENCES

Given that children derive benefits from playing, continuing to provide opportunities for children to play seems to be an appropriate action for school personnel, especially in light of the fact that society deprives today's children of many play opportunities that existed for children in the past.

Factors That Limit Play Opportunities   Poverty, changing cultural values, inadequate space to play, and too much emphasis on work (versus play) in elementary and preschools are all factors that contribute to children's play deprivation (Guddemi and Jambor 1993). Additional factors that prohibit play experiences include the following:

- Adults who schedule their children's day and leave no time for free play
- Play spaces (public parks and school playgrounds) that are inappropriately designed and poorly maintained
- Schools that are shortening or eliminating recess periods
- Parents who are afraid to allow their children to play outdoors unsupervised (even in neighborhood parks or neighbor's yards)
- Cities that do not include play spaces for children when building new neighborhoods (Frost and Jacobs 1995)

Teachers as Advocates for Adequate Play Time
Society must address each of these factors in order to remedy the lack of play time for children, but for the purpose of informing classroom teachers, the most important factors are those in the control of the school. Schools need to provide adequate play time for elementary school children, appropriate (well-maintained) play spaces and equipment, and trained recess personnel to structure quality recess time. In addition, classroom teachers should be advocates for quality play experiences. Possible teacher advocacy actions include the following:

- "Talk to colleagues and administrators about the importance of play (get their support),
- "Use the outdoors as an extension of your classroom activities,
- "Avoid taking away outside time as a punishment for misbehavior, and
- "Find out about parks and play spaces in your community" (Patrick 1996, 20).
- Involve your local Parent Teacher Association (e.g., ask the association to update or buy new playground equipment and ask the association to participate in National Recess Week, which is sponsored by the National PTA. The national organization is involved in a Rescuing Recess campaign. Consult their website for details—www.pta.org).
- Consult play-advocacy websites to find the latest play information as well as play materials and ideas (www.playeveryday.org and www.ipausa.org).

It is important to view recess as an educational experience that children *need* rather than simply something the child does if time happens to be available in the school schedule. In this view, teachers *never* deny recess to a child as a means of punishment or as a time to complete academic work.

THE AMOUNT AND TIMING OF RECESS

Current arguments stressing the importance of recess to the developing child do not offer educators much concrete guidance as to the optimal length of recess, number of recess periods, or timing of recess periods so as to enhance the child's social, cognitive, and physical development. From a policy perspective, these questions are important. Armed with answers to those questions, educators could design recess periods that maximize health benefits, increase attention on post-recess tasks, and minimize boredom on the playground.

How Much Recess Time Do Children Currently Have? Several sources provide some basic data regarding the amount of recess within the school day. First, the 1989 NAESP survey mentioned earlier provided data from 47 state superintendents of schools. Ninety percent of the school districts had some form of recess, and in those districts 96 percent held recess once or twice a day. In general, recess periods lasted from 15 to 20 minutes.

The second body of evidence comes from 12 school districts in one county of upstate New York reporting that recess time ranged from 0 to 65 minutes, with a mean of 19 minutes for children in grades 1–6 (Newman, Brody, and Beauchamp 1996). The study further indicated that various factors affect the amount of recess provided by a school. Teachers in rural locations provided the most recess time, followed by suburban teachers and then urban teachers. Medium-sized schools provided the most recess time (average 20.5 minutes), and large schools the least time (9.41 minutes). Schools containing only grades K–4 provided more recess than schools containing grades beyond the fourth grade. Teachers who agreed or strongly agreed with positive statements about the educational benefits of recess provided more recess time for their students.

Several authors examined other cultures producing academically sound students to determine their pattern of play versus academic work. Chinese, Taiwanese, and Japanese children have an eight-hour school day that includes numerous opportunities for students to interact socially. The day includes frequent recess, long lunch periods, and after-school activities. The longer school day allows more time to be devoted to these nonacademic activities. In general, *one-quarter of the school day* (two hours) was devoted to these nonacademic activities (Pellegrini and Bjorklund 1997; Stevenson 1992).

The amount of recess time varies greatly within schools in the United States. However, if students attend school from 9:00 A.M. to 4:00 P.M. (seven hours) with a half-hour lunch recess and two 15-minute breaks (one in the morning and one in the afternoon), *only one-seventh of the day* is spent in nonacademic work. In addition, most elementary schools do not sponsor after-school activities for children. Asian elementary schools provide their students with more play time than American schools do and still manage to produce educationally sound students. This evidence directly refutes the current practice in the United States, where many schools are decreasing recess time in order to spend more time on academic subjects.

How Much Recess Time Should Children Have? Although amounts of recess time reported in the literature provide data as to "what is," the data provide minimal help to the educator about "what should be." Thus the information is not very helpful to administrators and teachers when they must make policy decisions regarding amounts of recess time.

The evidence from Asian schools suggests that increased recess and break times (appropriately placed throughout the school day) would benefit children both cognitively and socially (Pellegrini and Bjorklund 1997; Stevenson 1992). Researchers observed preschoolers (27 European American Children) and found that post-recess attention was greatest with a recess period lasting 20 minutes, followed by a 10-minute and then 30-minute recess period (Holmes et al. 2006). In addition, research already cited indicates that short, frequent recess periods encourage children's attention to academic tasks (especially for boys). Thus some empirical evidence does support the scheduling of frequent, short recess periods.

NASPE issued a recommendation that children ages 6–11 should participate in at least one hour (and up to several hours) of physical activity each day (NASPE 2004). This activity should occur in periods lasting at least 10–15 minutes and should include moderate to vigorous activity levels. NASPE's recommendation does not specify how much of the total activity time should come during in-school versus out-of-school time. However, recess, as well as physical education, is considered a way of providing this needed activity time during school hours. Most model school wellness policies and NASPE's recent (2006) position paper on recess also recommend that elementary school children should have at least one daily 20-minute period of recess, preferably outdoors to encourage moderate to vigorous physical activity levels. Assuming children have 30 minutes of *daily physical education* and need 60 to 120 minutes of *daily physical activity,* significant additional in-school time and out-of-school time needs to be provided. Scheduling morning and afternoon recess periods (20 minutes in length) and a noon recess period (20 minutes) would provide, at a minimum, a total activity time of 90 minutes and thus would meet the NASPE recommendation.

APPROPRIATE RECESS SPACES AND EQUIPMENT

Via observation of children's behavior on the playground during recess, it is apparent that children do different activities on different parts of the playground. For example, they play games on the grassy areas and hard court surfaces, and they play on slides, swings, and jungle gyms in the equipment area. Children also use the same part of the playground differently based on their ages and gender. For example, a contemporary playscape area situated in a pine forest might be used to play "house" or "cops and robbers."

Playground Equipment and Spaces As yet researchers do not know the specific effects that playing in certain spaces and on certain equipment have on children's behavior, self-esteem, or peer relationships. So educators have little empirical evidence to guide them in selecting spaces and equipment to meet the students' cognitive, social, and physical needs. Classroom teachers and recess supervisors should have significant input to their administrators regarding what equipment is present on the playground. New equipment should be added to stimulate children's interests, and unsafe equipment should be removed. Recess supervisors are in the best position to determine whether the equipment and spaces are safe and are providing educationally sound play opportunities for students.

Much research still needs to be completed before recommendations are forthcoming as to spaces and equipment that children ought to experience on the playground. The differences in where children play appear to support the need for schools to have a variety of playground equipment and spaces for children

to choose from on the playground. However, safety also needs to be considered. Equipment with a poor history for safety should not be placed on the playground even though children would enjoy playing on it. For example, merry-go-rounds are usually not included on playgrounds anymore.

We advocate having available the following play areas and equipment:

- Outdoor play spaces that include traditional play equipment consisting of fixed structures (such as swings, jungle gyms, and horizontal ladders with appropriate surfaces underneath, tetherballs, slides, etc.), grassy play areas, fields marked for various sports (soccer, baseball and softball, football, etc.), dirt areas, and blacktop areas for basketball, Four-Square, and hopscotch
- Outdoor play spaces that include contemporary structures such as stone culverts, open tents, railroad ties, tree areas, and the like
- Outdoor play spaces that include a variety of materials the children can use to build their own play spaces. Intuitively, it seems that more creative play might occur on contemporary structures and with building materials. There is some evidence to indicate that is so, but it is not conclusive. Children's creativity should be allowed to bloom during recess; thus spaces and equipment that allow creativity need to be provided. Some examples include allowing children to build a fort when it snows in the winter, make a house out of cardboard boxes, create house floor plans by drawing in the dirt, and create chalk drawings on cement.
- A walking trail around the perimeter of the play area to have cardiorespiratory fitness activities. Placing stations along the trail, where children can do muscular strength and endurance exercises, turns the trail into a circuit fitness course.
- Indoor play spaces include gymnasiums and multipurpose rooms where physical education is not normally taught so the area is available for use by the classroom teacher when the weather prohibits playing outdoors.

Play spaces and equipment should be age appropriate (i.e., designed with the physical, social, and mental developmental levels of the children in mind) (Bowers and Gabbard 2000). For example, a horizontal ladder designed for K–2 children would have smaller rungs (smaller in diameter), the rungs would be spaced closer together, and it would be a shorter distance from the ground than a horizontal ladder designed for children in grades 4–6. A basketball goal would be set lower than the standard height for K–2

TABLE 12.1 Checklist of Outdoor Recess Equipment (for a class of 25 students)

EQUIPMENT	QUANTITY
Balls	
Balzacs	2
Basketballs (junior high size)	2
Footballs (junior high size/regular and foam)	2
Foam balls (large and small/3 of each size)	6
Playground balls	
Soccer balls	2
Spider Balls	
Tennis balls	6
Volleyballs (trainer sized)	2
(Basketballs, footballs, soccer balls, and volleyballs can be purchased as Nerf balls. Grades K–3 should play with the Nerf versions of these balls. Upper grades should have some Nerf balls for the students who fear getting hit with regular balls.)	
Beanbags	12
Carts (to take equipment to and from the playground)	1–2
Chalk (to mark on cement areas)	2 boxes
Foxtails	6
Frisbees	6
Hula hoops	6
Jump ropes (long)	4
Jump ropes (short)	8
(A jump rope needs to be sized according to the height of the child, so each classroom should have ropes of varying lengths for the heights represented in the class.)	
Scoops (with balls)	4
Stick-A-Bals	4
Traffic cones (to mark court boundaries on grassy areas)	10
Volleyball net and standards	1 set
Hacky Sack balls	6
Spin Jammers	6

children, and the basketball itself would be smaller than regulation size.

Equipment for Indoor and Outdoor Recess A list of *basic equipment for outdoor recess,* which classroom teachers should have in their classroom (or at least have access to from the physical education teacher), appears in Table 12.1. A list of *basic equipment for indoor recess* appears in Table 12.2. Some equipment appears on both lists, as it can be used in both settings. Equipment sizes and textures are also indicated so children of various ages and ability can play with developmentally appropriate equipment. These lists reflect equipment needed for students to have quality *recess time.* Additional types and quantity of equipment would be needed to conduct quality *physical education lessons.* A comprehensive equipment list for elementary physical education can be found in the NASPE position paper: *Guidelines for Facilities, Equipment and Instructional Materials in Elementary Education* (NASPE 2001). If the equipment list contains equipment with which you are unfamiliar, consult with the school's physical educator for an introduction to the equipment and ways to use it.

Equipment carts should be purchased for each classroom. The carts provide storage when the equipment is not in use and allow easy movement of the equipment between the classroom and the playground. Classroom teachers can ask the physical educator for equipment catalogs from which to order the carts and needed equipment. The Peaceful Playgrounds program (www.peacefulplaygrounds.com) recommends that at least one piece of equipment should be available for every ten children on the playground.

TYPICAL RECESS BEHAVIOR

This section on children's playground behavior provides a view of what children typically do during

TABLE 12.2 Checklist of Indoor Recess Equipment (for a class of 25 students)

EQUIPMENT	QUANTITY
Balloon volleyballs and beach balls	4
Catchballs	4
Chinese jump ropes	
MagikRopes	8
Dice (large, for throwing on the floor)	2
Jacks (sets with balls)	4 sets
Juggling scarves	8
Jump Bands	8
Lummi sticks	4 sets
Marbles (for older children)	4 sets
Parachute	1
Spin Jammers	6
Stretch bands	8
Tinikling poles	2 sets
Tops	6
Cups (for stacking)	50
Beanbags	12
Hacky Sack balls	6

recess; thus preservice classroom teachers will have some idea what to expect once they have the responsibility to supervise children on the playground. *But this description of what happens on the playground does not imply that the recorded behaviors are preferred behaviors.* It is still the responsibility of school personnel to monitor playground behavior and shape that behavior in the direction predetermined and preferred by the school personnel (O'Brien 2003).

The empirical knowledge base on what actually happens on school playgrounds during recess is quite limited, especially considering that recess has been a part of the educational process since public schools were first instituted. A number of researchers have confirmed the factors (inherent in children) that influence **recess behavior.** Gender, age, race, disability, and the socioeconomic status of children affect their play behavior, with gender and age being the most strongly documented variables.

Gender Differences   Boys are more physically active than girls on the playground for all grade levels and engage in more vigorous physical activity such as rough-and-tumble play. **Rough-and-tumble play** is defined as a physically vigorous set of behaviors (such as hit at, jump on, run after, chase, and play fight) characterized by positive affect and playful facial expressions (Pellegrini and Blatchford 2000). After rough-and-tumble play, children tend to continue associating with each other and playing

together. Generally, during rough-and-tumble play children alternate between being in the dominant versus subordinate role. Rough-and-tumble play accounts for approximately 5 percent of preschool children's play, about 10–15 percent during late childhood, and approximately 5 percent again during adolescence (Pellegrini and Blatchford 2000). Rough-and-tumble play is different from aggression. Aggression generally occurs in the context of disputes over property (equipment or spaces), and the number of aggressive incidents does not vary as children get older.

Boys engage in significantly more aggressive behaviors during recess than girls do, with girls displaying more relational aggression and boys displaying more overt (instrumental) aggression (Boyle et al. 2003; Crick and Bigbee 1998). **Relational aggression** involves children ostracizing their peers or withdrawing their friendship from peers (Crick 1995). **Overt aggression** consists of behaviors that hurt others such as hitting, kicking, or threatening to do so (Crick 1995). Two types of overt aggression are specified: instrumental aggression and bullying. When overt, hurtful behaviors occur for the purpose of obtaining a desired object, territory, or privilege, it is called **instrumental aggression.** When overt, hurtful behaviors repeatedly occur for the purpose of intimidating others, it is called **bullying.** Bullying behaviors include name calling, taunting, threatening, excluding, stealing, vandalizing, slandering, and physically assaulting others. Bullying occurs almost twice as often on the playground than in the classroom (Craig, Pepler, and Atlas 2000). Both types of overt aggression are inappropriate behaviors and must be handled immediately by the recess supervisor for the physical safety of the children involved. Action to be taken is usually specified by the school's playground regulations. Although relational aggression does not place students in physically dangerous circumstances, it too is not appropriate recess or classroom behavior. Both forms of victimization (overt and relational aggression) are precursors to children's loneliness and school avoidance (Kochenderfer and Ladd 1996) and predict interpersonal adjustment problems (Crick and Bigbee 1998) for both girls and boys (Crick et al. 2006).

Increasing numbers of state lawmakers are passing laws to force school districts to deal with bullying in the schools. Obviously, bullying has no place in a school that emphasizes inclusion and playground friendships. Like other inclusion intervention strategies, we recommend that bullying intervention programs also focus on the entire school. The Olweus Bullying Prevention Program (Olweus and Limber 2000) is the most widely recognized, comprehensive

Boys and girls tend to play in same-gender groups and to engage in activities that they've been socialized to consider gender appropriate. Girls' play tends to be more cooperative, whereas boys' play is more likely to be centered around competitive team sports.

intervention program to deal with bullying. Other successful whole-school approaches typically have the core features included in the Olweus Program. Those core features are (Smith et al. 2005):

1. The program involves the entire school (teachers, students, and parents).
2. Teachers teach anti-bullying curricula in their classrooms.
3. Peer-helpers or befriending strategies are used with adult help.
4. Parents receive information about the school's anti-bullying program and actively participate in activities.
5. Community stakeholders become involved in the school's anti-bullying activities.
6. Specific interventions are targeted to children in bully/victim situations.

A good place to begin increasing your knowledge base in bullying is to read "Bullying in School: An Overview of Types, Effects, Family Characteristics, and Intervention Strategies" (Smokowski and Kopasz 2005). Then review several websites that contain bullying information and prevention programs (e.g., www.stopbullyingnow.hrsa.gov, www.usdhhs.org, and www.caper.com.au). This information will be beneficial when helping to develop your school's approach to bullying.

Boys and girls, while playing during recess, learn gender-role behaviors. Gender-role behaviors are socially constructed and as such reflect the teachings of society. On the playground, children are active agents in exploring norms related to gender—sometimes accepting and reinforcing gender stereotypes and at other times pushing the envelope of those specified roles and norms (Boyle et al. 2003). Many of the behaviors included in this section on typical playground behaviors reflect society's view of what equipment girls and boys should play on, what sports and games are appropriate for boys versus girls, and how active girls and boys should be. This socialization may be why, when asked, girls prefer to play indoors and boys prefer to play outdoors. As indicated in Chapter 10, teachers need to respect student choices yet move them in new directions (against society's teaching), especially when society's teaching limits the potential of either gender.

Boys' play tends to focus on coordinating peers around a competitive team game or sport, whereas girls' play tends to be cooperative (Jarrett et al. 2001; Pellegrini and Smith 1993). Groups predominately composed of girls most often accept boys of any skill level who are seeking to join their activity, whereas girls typically have to be highly skilled to join an all-boy group (Boyle et al. 2003). When groups contain both girls and boys, the group operates more similar to boys' groups than girls' groups (Smith and Inder 1993). In general on the playground, more instances of boys excluding girls occur than vice versa.

Girls and boys tend to play in same-gender groups until puberty. Since play styles of boys and girls are different, children may prefer to play in same-gender groups (Alexander and Hines 1994). It is also possible that girls avoid playing with boys because they have difficulty influencing boys (Maccoby 1990).

Obviously, teachers can encourage boys and girls to play together. If teachers wish to do that, we encourage them to plan the interactions. For example, one day boys are encouraged to join the pretend play of the girls, and on another day, the girls are encouraged to join the boys' soccer game. Careful planning is necessary to make sure that the new situations are physically and emotionally safe for both the boys and the girls. However, also remember that the value of recess comes from children selecting their own playmates and activities; thus, teacher interference should be limited.

Changes with Age   Activity levels decrease as children get older, and as they get older children choose to play outdoors less frequently. Some people suggest that as children get older they might have less need for outdoor play experiences. However, it is difficult to determine whether children decrease their activity level as they get older because they need less activity (in terms of biological development) or because they have been exposed to continual socialization that encourages them to be more sedentary. In some cases, this socialization actually *forces* children to be inactive (including school and home settings that do not allow time for outdoor play). No empirical evidence is available on the issue, but probably the decrease in activity levels is the result of both biological and sociological factors. If so, the socialization process needs to encourage children to continue to be active, as the evidence is overwhelming that inactivity leads to health problems and early death. Thus this book helps classroom teachers in their efforts to increase the amount of physical activity within the child's school days and encourage an active lifestyle outside of school time.

Boys and girls engage in a wide variety of activities on the playground. However, as children get older the range of activities engaged in appears to stay constant for girls but narrows for boys because of their interest in organized games and sports (Dahmes 1993). Observations of fourth-grade recesses (Boyle et al. 2003) indicated that the majority of the boys were playing a team sport (soccer, kickball, baseball, or touch football) while the girls were involved in a

Inclusion on the playground: Students of different cultural backgrounds have the opportunity to enjoy play activities together during recess.

wide variety of activities (rope jumping, swinging, jungle gym, walking and talking, playing all-girl team sports as well as playing on the boys' sport teams). With increasing age, the play activities of both boys and girls increases in organization and complexity. Thus classroom teachers can teach games of increasing complexity as students get older.

Inclusion Issues   Since children are more active in large environments, compared with small ones, it is important that recess be outdoors most of the time.

Rejected children, boys and girls, play in smaller groups than do popular children, and they play with younger children or other unpopular children (Ladd 1983). Rejected children spend less time in prosocial interactions and more time in agonistic and unoccupied behaviors than do children of popular or average sociometric status (Ladd 1983). **Prosocial interactions** are relationship-enhancing interactions such as engaging in social conversations or cooperative play. **Agonistic interactions** are behaviors such as arguments or rough-and-tumble play. While rejected children often display hostile behavior toward other children, **neglected children** display withdrawing behaviors, which makes them invisible to their peers (Kim 2003). Both rejected and neglected children need help improving their social skills. Using the suggestions presented in this chapter, teachers should implement strategies to include rejected and neglected children in recess activities.

Children from different ethnic backgrounds may play together when traditional minority groups are adequately represented in the school population and when language barriers are not present. Teachers in ethnically diverse schools should strive to remove language barriers and encourage integration of play groups.

Students with disabilities generally do not play with children who are not disabled. Professionals are concerned that students with disabilities are hindered by not being accepted or integrated into the recess activities of students without disabilities (McClure and Kinnison 1999; Ochoa and Olivarex 1995; Siperstein, Leffert, and Wenz-Gross 1997). Research indicates that elementary students with disabilities receive less favorable sociometric ratings than their older counterparts, have considerably lower sociometric status than nondisabled students, and evidence more immaturity, aggression, and personality problems than their nondisabled peers (Ochoa and Olivarex 1995). Teachers should encourage the integration of students with special needs into play groups consisting of students without special needs. In addition, teachers should investigate whether the playground design results in areas that are not accessible and/or functional for students with disabilities, which in turn leads to the inability of those students to play and interact with others (Shepherd, Burnett, and Zody 2003). For example, children using wheelchairs or crutches may need curb cuts, special surfaces, transfer stations, ramps, or crawl tubes to gain safe access to playgrounds. For students with limited vision and mobility, the occurrence of "high traffic areas" around slides and swings should be minimized. Slides and climbing apparatus can be modified by changing the height, slope, or design to accommodate children with disabilities.

Helping Children Construct Quality Recess Time

Instead of debating whether recess has any educational benefits for elementary school children, educators should be concerned about and studying how to help children construct quality recess time. Several suggestions are presented here for classroom teachers who are committed to establishing a recess time that is fun as well as educational for their students.

RULES OF CONDUCT

First, school personnel must establish **rules of conduct** for the playground. Students and parents ought to be involved in the process of establishing the rules of conduct. Students can even be involved in monitoring conduct compliance (see the "Recess Programs That Work" section at the end of this chapter). The playground rules need to be taught to the children with reminders provided on a regular basis. (Upon their arrival, be sure to inform new students of the playground rules.) School personnel should review the rules at least once a semester to be sure they are appropriate and effective. At any time throughout the year, the rules can be changed if they become ineffective. The playground rules should specify rules for interacting with peers, with the playground equipment, and with the playground spaces. Box 12.2 presents an example of typical playground rules, and Quick Lesson 12.1 at the end of the chapter provides an example of how to teach those rules to young children.

A SAFE ENVIRONMENT

Playground safety is an area of concern for all schools. The goal is to maximize play value while decreasing the risk of injury (Hudson, Thompson, and Mack 2001). Establishing and enforcing a code of conduct is the first step toward having safe interactions between children on the playground.

Safe Equipment and Play Areas   In addition to safe interactions, the permanent and disposable equipment used must be in working order and the spaces played in must be maintained properly. Each recess period, the supervisor should walk the playground area with the intent of finding any safety hazards and dealing with them before someone is hurt. The most common hazards are insufficient depth of ground cover under and around the equipment (as over time the rain and wind scatter and decrease the padding originally placed under the equipment), outdated equipment, rusting equipment, tightness of chains and fasteners that prevent clothing being caught, and entrapment of body parts in equipment spaces between 3.5 and 9 inches in width (Bowler 2003; Hudson, Thompson, and Olsen 2005). An in-depth discussion of maintaining equipment and facilities can be found in Chapter 11.

Disposable equipment used during recess, such as balls, bats, and Frisbees, should be made of a soft material—soft enough that injury will not occur if a player is hit with the equipment. Older children (fifth and sixth grades) can use regulation balls to play sport activities (e.g., soccer, football, and basketball), except allowing children to play with regulation baseballs and softballs is not recommended. Regulation hardwood or metal baseball and softball bats should *never* be allowed on the playground.

Appropriate Training for Recess Supervisors
As a further safety concern, recess supervisors need training in order to fulfill their supervisory role on the playground. According to a 1989 NAESP survey, data

---

BOX 12.2 Typical Playground Rules

RULES FOR INTERACTING WITH PEERS

- Take turns on equipment when others are waiting in line.
- Treat others with respect.
- Have your body under control while playing.
- Include others if they ask to join you.
- Invite others to join you or your group.

RULES FOR INTERACTING WITH PLAYGROUND EQUIPMENT

Swings

Students are allowed to

- Swing back and forth
- Swing with only one person in the swing
- Wait outside the sandy area if waiting to use the swings

Students are not allowed to

- Swing from side to side or twist the swing
- Jump out of a swinging swing

Slide

Students are allowed to

- Sit while going down the slide
- Wait at the bottom of the ladder for your turn
- Go up the ladder after the other person begins to slide down
- Climb the poles on the side of the slide

Students are not allowed to

- Stand on the slide
- Hang body parts over the side while sliding down
- Climb up from the bottom of the slide

Merry-go-round

Students are allowed to

- Stand or sit holding onto the bars
- Sit on top of the bars
- Keep body parts inside the equipment

Students are not allowed to

- Drag body parts
- Jump off while equipment is in motion

RULES FOR INTERACTING WITH PLAYGROUND SPACES

- Soccer may be played only on the west side of the playground in the marked area.
- Tag games must be played in the grassy area in front of the school.
- Touch football may be played only on the playground's east side.

---

on supervisory practices for recess periods indicated that teachers were supervisors in 50 percent of the cases and teacher aides supervised in 36 percent (Pellegrini 1995). Of the aides, 86 percent received no formal training for supervising recess. Whether recess supervisors are classroom teachers, teacher aides, or parent volunteers, they need training, as shown by data indicating that as little as four hours of supervision training helped school staff reduce the rate of minor injuries on the playground by about 50 percent (Bruya 1998). The training should be provided by the school district and should include the following:

- How to check the playground space for hazards
- How to check permanent equipment for wear
- How to actively scan the playground while children are playing to notice dangerous, harassing, or aggressive behavior

- How to monitor the playground when several classes and several supervisors are present (e.g., where to stand so the entire playground is being watched)
- How to establish "positive sight lines" that allow children to be viewed at all times (e.g., through vegetation and into equipment tubes)
- How to handle weather emergencies and natural disasters
- How to handle accidents that happen on the playground
- Knowing the school's policies and procedures for dealing with accidents
- Obtaining current Red Cross First-Aid Certification
- Wearing a fanny pack that contains necessary first-aid supplies and a cell phone
- How (and when) to complete written injury reports

- How to handle children's misbehavior and enforce school rules
- How to encourage conflict resolution between students
- What kinds of games and activities are appropriate for the developmental level of children of various ages and abilities
- Knowledge of the primary responsibilities of the recess supervisor as identified in the school's playground supervision plan (versus the role of other school personnel)

Children of Different Ages Another safety matter concerns the well-being of younger children when playing near older students who are stronger and faster. In general, it is best to have similar age groups on the playground at a given time or to isolate certain areas of the playground for children in particular grades when, for example, first graders must share the playground with fifth graders. It is best to have separate playgrounds for children 2 to 5 years old (preschool) and children 5 to 12 years old (K–6). If preschool programs are housed in the elementary school building, a separate playground should be specifically designed and supervised for that age level, as the physical needs and capabilities of preschool children are drastically different from those of elementary school children. Some professionals even advocate for three separate playground areas covering grades K–2, 3–4, and 5–6 (Olsen et al. 2002).

Appropriate Teacher-Child Ratios Safety is also an issue when determining how many children should play in a space of a certain size and, in addition, how many recess supervisors are needed to monitor a certain number of students. Obviously, the number of supervisors needed depends on the number of children, the size and layout of the play space, and the amount and kind of equipment on the playground. In general, the more children, play space, or equipment present on the playground, the more monitoring is necessary from an increasing number of recess supervisors. But even small playground spaces may require a number of supervisors if the spaces are not contiguous or within the supervisor's view at all times.

Research appears to show that the teacher is less effective in monitoring children's behavior and less likely to influence the direction of children's behavior when the child-teacher ratio is high (Ladd and Price 1993). It also appears that the number of aggressive behaviors children exhibit increases when play spaces become larger without corresponding increases in the number of recess supervisors (Price and Dodge 1989). The courts have found **teacher-child ratios** of 1 to 90 and 1 to 40 legally acceptable, depending on various circumstances (layout of the playground, age of the children, etc.) (Van der Smissen 1990). Professionals in the field recommend a ratio of 1 teacher to 40 students (Bruya and Wood 1998). The National Program for Playground Safety recommends the ratio be the same as that in the classroom. Having at least two supervisors on the playground at all times allows one supervisor to attend to an injured student while the second supervisor manages the rest of the children (Olsen et al. 2002).

Additional information on playground safety can be obtained from the National Program for Playground Safety (NPPS), which is housed at the University of Northern Iowa in Cedar Falls, Iowa (800-554-PLAY, www.uni.edu/playground). The NPPS was initiated by the Centers for Disease Control and Injury Prevention in 1995. Its literature is particularly helpful in determining proper supervision methods, age-appropriate designs for playgrounds, proper surfacing for particular playground areas, and equipment maintenance procedures. In addition, a report card on how safe playgrounds are (produced by the NPPS) is available, which indicates current safety issues and how to resolve those issues (Hudson, Thompson, and Olsen 2005).

RECESS AS FREE PLAY

Although it is tempting to want total control over the playground, we encourage school personnel to allow recess to consist of free play—meaning that the children (not the adults) structure the play. Thus children are free to choose activities and select playmates without interference from teachers (within the playground rules of conduct). This is the only time during the school day when children are given the freedom and responsibility to control their own destinies. This freedom may be important for developing physical and social skills during play. In addition, the freedom makes children responsible for their own self-control and self-discipline, which when handled appropriately leads to increased self-esteem and self-confidence.

STIMULATING PHYSICAL ACTIVITY

We encourage recess supervisors to stimulate children to be physically active during recess. The most basic (and proven) way to increase physical activity levels is to increase the availability of equipment

BOX 12.3 Strategies for Stimulating Physical Activity During Recess

- Provide appropriate equipment and play spaces.
- Challenge students to practice skills they are learning in physical education (have the physical educator teach some specific recess activities that focus on inclusion, low organization, and maximal activity levels).
- Challenge students to find a new game appropriate for use at recess time (using varied sources—the library, the Internet, or other people).
- Ask students who are just standing around if they would like to do the following:
  - Play a new game (and then teach them a new game)
  - Select and use a piece of equipment from the traditional and innovative equipment available on a cart
  - Walk with you around the perimeter of the play area
  - Join a game already in progress (help students ask if they can join the activity)

- Help groups establish and enforce fair rules for games and sports.
- Identify and reinforce expected recess behaviors so students know that teasing, fighting, name-calling, and the like are inappropriate behaviors that will not be allowed.
- Encourage play groups to include students who ask to join the group.
- Recognize if certain students are loners (never playing with anyone) and then take steps to help them overcome whatever obstacles keep them from joining in.
- Observe what's happening on your playground (who is playing what games with whom, who are the activity leaders, who's left out, who always fights, who plays fairly) and use that information to improve the activity levels of the children.

(Jago and Baranowski 2004; Verstraete et al. 2006). Box 12.3 contains additional strategies for stimulating children to be physically active during recess. Being physically active simply means the child should be engaged in some productive movement (such as playing hopscotch or jacks, tossing and catching a ball, playing with hula hoops, or playing "house"). It does *not* mean that students must be engaged in physically exerting activities (such as running, jumping rope, or playing soccer).

Activities for All Students The recess supervisor should be ready to suggest activities to students who are just standing around visiting or watching others play. The literature indicates that social prompts can lead to increased activity levels by children (McKenzie et al. 1997). The supervisor may also need to show children how certain equipment is typically used, although allowing creative uses is encouraged as long as the creative activity is not dangerous. The recess supervisor should particularly encourage children with a disability to be physically active. This may require visiting with the physical education teachers to find activities and equipment that are appropriate for the given students with disabilities. In addition, at the beginning of the school year (and when new students arrive), be sure students know each other's names. Students could wear name tags for several days if that is helpful. Instant Activity 12.1, which was presented

earlier, provides an opportunity for students to be active while also learning their classmates' names.

Quality Games and Activities Appendix C contains descriptions of quality recess activities that can improve children's gross motor skills, fine motor skills, and physical fitness levels. Each activity description includes playing rules, space and equipment needed, safety considerations, benefits of the activity, and grade level of children who will experience success when performing the activity.

Traditional and Innovative Equipment In order to stimulate physical activity, it is helpful to have plentiful amounts of equipment and a variety of traditional and innovative equipment available for the children to use. Refer again to Tables 12.1 and 12.2 for recommended amounts and kinds of equipment. Obviously the lists were developed for a typical classroom of students. The equipment provided for a specific group of students should be tailored to their wants and needs based on discussions of equipment they would like to have available and on the history of what equipment they use the most. In addition, we suggest the innovative equipment pieces be available on a rotating basis so each month only certain pieces are placed on the equipment cart. Thus seemingly new pieces of equipment appear on the cart each month and stimulate students' interest.

The recess supervisor's primary duty is to supervise the play behavior of the children to ensure a safe playground. The secondary duty of stimulating children to be active needs to be accomplished while also providing appropriate supervision. Thus teaching a new game to some students, distributing new equipment, or walking the playground perimeter with a group of students must occur quickly so as not to interfere with the supervisor's primary duty.

CALMING ACTIVITIES

On days when children are not able to settle down upon returning to the classroom, we suggest that **calming activities** be used to bridge recess time and the return to academic work. Some evidence indicates that *vigorous* play may interfere with subsequent attention in the classroom. Studying nine-year-old boys and girls, researchers found that students were less attentive and fidgeted more while completing an achievement task after vigorous play at recess, and that they were more attentive when recess contained sedentary play behavior. They concluded that perhaps children need changes (breaks) from academic work but that the changes should be settling, not exciting (Pellegrini and Davis 1993).

However, since vigorous physical activity is important for children's motor development, physical fitness, and weight control, other solutions should be found. Several possible solutions come to mind:

1. End recess with a calming activity either on the playground (before the students enter the building) or once the students are back in the classroom.
2. Change the time of recess within the day's schedule to place it before a classroom activity that does not require the students to immediately sit quietly upon entering the classroom.

Calming activities might include stretching exercises, relaxation techniques, calming musical transitions, or free time that gives the students five minutes to prepare themselves for the next concentrated academic task. All of these calming activities can help children tune in to their own inner capabilities to regulate their own behavior.

ENCOURAGING INCLUSION

Recess provides one of the few opportunities for children to learn to appreciate, respect, and cooperate with peers from a variety of backgrounds; thus teachers and administrators should encourage children from different cultural backgrounds to play together (Pellegrini and Bjorklund 1996). Is it possible that the playground could be a space for breaking down cultural barriers? If so, it will probably take more than simple encouragement to make it happen.

We suggest that school personnel make a concerted effort to answer the question "What behaviors would you need to see on the playground in order to say that the children were culturally tolerant?" Once those behaviors are identified, specific intervention strategies can be developed to move the children in that direction. And of course, systematic assessments would allow school personnel to determine how much progress is being made and to revise the intervention strategies accordingly. Special Event 12.1 at the end of the chapter helps students explore their own and their classmates' cultural roots.

Focusing on Diversity and Inclusion   Recess supervisors and classroom teachers would do well to focus on inclusion during recess time and encourage students to take responsibility for creating and fostering friendships. Students appear to have two types of problems on the playground: inclusion and conflict (Doll and Murphy 1996). Inclusion problems encompass behaviors such as having to play alone and not being allowed to join others in their games. Conflict problems include behaviors such as fighting, arguing, and teasing. Investigators found relationships between student reports of recess problems (inclusion and conflict problems) and measures of peer acceptance and mutual friendships.

Children's reports of conflict problems were unrelated to measures of peer acceptance and mutual friendships; however, *children's reports of play enjoyment were related to the absence of inclusion problems.* The degree to which children are included in their classmates' play appears to be the most relevant predictor of long-term social competence and immediate social acceptance. The research results suggest that adult efforts to affect students' overall social adjustment ought to concentrate on fostering inclusive peer cultures, not on preventing and mediating peer conflicts (Doll and Murphy 1996).

Fostering Playground Friendships   The importance of being included suggests that classroom teachers should develop courses of action for improving peers' acceptance of each other on the playground and for encouraging students to take responsibility for their playground behavior. Implementing intervention

> ## BOX 12.4   Strategies for Fostering Playground Friendships
>
> - Implement cooperative group challenges (see Instant Activity 12.2 for a sample group challenge).
> - Have students role-play how good friends act with each other.
> - Discuss how it feels to be left out of a recess activity and how students can include others in various playground games.
> - Teach various ways for students to include someone in an activity when he or she asks to be included. Refer to Classroom Learning Station 12.1 at the end of the chapter for an activity that teaches specific inclusion techniques.
> - Discuss how to make new friends. (Consult the three-week friendship curriculum in Kieff 2005/06).
> - Reward those who include others in their activity or game.
> - Discuss how to treat new students and establish specific class behaviors that include new students in already existing class groups. For example, have students form hospitality groups that take turns welcoming and orienting new students.
> - Make specific requests to various popular children, asking that they include rejected or neglected children in their activities. The request should be very specific in nature and limited in its time frame so the popular student is more likely to respond favorably.
> - Monitor the teasing that occurs on the playground. Teasing in fun may be positive, but hurtful teasing should not be condoned, and teasing that is harassment must be stopped immediately.
> - Monitor the aggressive behaviors (both relational and overt) displayed on the playground and implement intervention strategies as necessary.
> - Teach young children conflict resolution skills, which teach children to generate their own solutions to problems. In the process, children are practicing language skills and divergent thinking skills.

strategies may be necessary in instances where children continually display aggression or harassment or continually exclude others from playing. Intervention strategies should focus on a whole-class approach, not just on trying "to fix" those students who are rejected/neglected on the playground, because it is the social construction by the group that must be changed over time (Wohlwend 2004).

Interventions may be necessary because children's playground behaviors influence their acceptance in their peer group. Children who play cooperatively with peers gain peer acceptance, and those who establish (early on) arguing behaviors establish negative peer status. In addition, children who play cooperatively with peers and are popular at the outset of the school year tend to continue this behavior and be popular the rest of the school year (Ladd and Price 1993; Kim 2003). Thus classroom teachers would do well to learn, early in the school year, what is occurring on the playground and take corrective actions if necessary to improve how children interact on the playground. Consult Box 12.4 for strategies that foster playground friendships and Instant Activity 12.3 for an activity that allows classmates to work together and learn each other's names. Also consult Appendix C, as many of the recess activities described there require students to interact effectively with their peers.

ACTIVE INDOOR RECESS PERIODS

If possible, indoor recess periods should occur in spaces large enough for students to play in (i.e., in multipurpose rooms or lunchrooms). However, in reality most schools do not have these types of spaces available, so indoor recess occurs in the classroom. If students must stay in their classrooms for indoor recess, classroom teachers can plan for this eventuality. Select from the many classroom activities included in this textbook and be ready to lead the students in those activities on short notice. See Quick Lesson 12.2 at the end of the chapter for an indoor recess activity.

Recess Programs That Work

We offer several examples from the literature of programs that have worked in particular elementary schools to make the playground a fun, safe place to play.

NEWTON, NEW JERSEY: TEACHING PROSOCIAL SKILLS

Kathleen McDermott, a third-grade teacher in Newton, New Jersey, implemented the teaching of prosocial skills for the playground to the children in her primary school (McDermott 1999). She believed classroom

INSTANT ACTIVITY 12.3 Learning Names

Grades K–6

Equipment Needed

Beanbags (1–10)

Activity

The objective is for students to learn the names of everyone in class. Form several small circles of students (3–5 students in a circle). One person has a beanbag. That person says his or her name and then tosses (underhand toss) the beanbag to someone else, who catches it. The person who tossed the bag sits down. The process continues, tossing only to those standing.

The last person standing tosses to self. When everyone is sitting down, begin again.

Variations that make the game more difficult include (1) adding more beanbags so several students are calling out their name and throwing the bag at the same time; (2) adding different kinds of tossing objects (always soft objects); (3) having students repeat, in order of the tosses, everyone's name after everyone is sitting down; and (4) having small groups join to create larger groups when everyone in the smaller group knows everyone's names.

From Jill Best, elementary physical education teacher, Omaha, Nebraska.

---

teachers should intervene early in playground violence by teaching specific skills that help children learn a broad array of behaviors for resolving their conflicts. She identified five key elements important in teaching prosocial skills for use on the playground:

1. Give children a repertoire of acceptable games to play.
2. Give children tools for organizing the games.
3. Provide support on the playground by noting when children are having problems so you can intervene, model the correct behavior, and then leave the game so the children can continue the game alone.
4. Keep the environment in line with children's needs by having sufficient play equipment and adequate boundaries for the games being played.
5. Use the class meeting framework to discuss recess problems, develop solutions, and celebrate successes.

WARREN, RHODE ISLAND: PLAY FAIR

Mark Chuoke and Bill Eyman instituted a recess program called Play Fair at an economically diverse school in Warren, Rhode Island (Chuoke and Eyman 1997). The recess program was part of a total school effort to "build a sense of community" within the school. To facilitate community, Chuoke and Eyman believed that one must ask questions rather than make statements because questioning encourages group members to hold dialogues (rather than to hold arguments) and

to brainstorm their own solutions to the issues at hand. So one day they asked students what they thought about recess. The students identified many problems, "including bullying, exclusion from games, teasing, and conflicts resulting from competitive games" (Chuoke and Eyman 1997, 54).

Chuoke and Eyman suggested the students try a program called **Play Fair,** which was structured to make recess more fun, less competitive, and more inclusive. So how did Play Fair operate? A section of the playground was identified (with cones) to become the Play Fair area. In this area, noncompetitive games were played, under the direction of a Play Fair squad of five or six trained students. The squad selected the games to be played, monitored the games so they remained noncompetitive, and, if necessary, reminded players of the games rules. Students on the playground were not required to play in this area; they did so voluntarily. Squad members specifically invited students to play if the students were alone or appeared to be doing nothing. The Play Fair program was quite successful. Students regularly played in this noncompetitive area, problem behavior between students decreased significantly, and squad members who were once bullies were now active in making sure that rejected or neglected children were drawn into the games.

DERBY, KANSAS: PEER MEDIATORS

Personnel at Tanglewood Elementary in Derby, Kansas, use **peer mediators** (fourth and fifth graders) during noon recess periods to help students resolve issues that arise. Mediators are trained by a social worker in resolving conflicts. They wear orange vests while on duty and carry a clipboard on which they record a brief description of the conflict and how it was solved. Unless a child is in physical danger, the recess supervisor refers all student conflicts to the mediator on duty. The mediator does not solve the conflict but helps the individuals involved to reach their own solution. Formal assessment of the program occurs each year, and the results continue to show declines in the number of conflict incidences reported during recess. It is important to note that the peer mediator program is part of a broader school program in which all students are instructed in the strategies of conflict resolution (such as win-win solutions, "I" statements, etc.).

WELLS, MAINE: PLAYGROUND LEADERS

Kathy Calo and Pam Ingram implemented a **Playground Leader** program at a K–4 school in Wells, Maine (Calo and Ingram 1994). Fourth graders were trained to direct activity stations during recess periods. The goals of the program were "(1) to provide a wide variety of activities for students to engage in during recess, (2) to lessen recess-related injuries by providing safety-conscious activities, and (3) to provide an opportunity for a group of trained students to practice leadership and problem-solving skills" (Calo and Ingram 1994, 2). Each spring semester the Playground Leader program is evaluated using feedback from the fourth-grade leader participants and a review of recess-related injuries maintained by the school nurse. Feedback from the leaders has been consistently favorable over the years the program has been in existence.

LUSAKA, ZAMBIA: SPECIAL FRIENDS

John Ronning and Dabie Nabuzoka implemented an intervention that substantially increased the interaction between primary school children with intellectual disabilities and their peers without disabilities on the playground (Ronning and Nabuzoka 1993). The increased interactions occurred in the experimental setting and continued later (one-month and six-month follow-up) in the natural setting. A **"special friends"** approach was used with two children without disabilities being assigned to one child with a disability. The children without disabilities were responsible for initiating the interactions and including the child with a disability in their play activities. Short meetings (5–10 minutes) were held with the children without disabilities to do the following:

- Provide information about specific disabilities
- Emphasize how it "feels" not to be included
- Provide feedback on how well they are performing their responsibilities (praise and corrective feedback)
- Encourage discussion of how to include their special friends in various play activities

Ronning and Nabuzoka told the other children without disabilities (those not experimentally selected) that they could attach themselves as special friends to children with disabilities so they could also participate, and many children did participate in that manner.

BAR NUNN AND CASPER, WYOMING: PLAYGROUND MEETINGS

Paula Knudson and Darlene Wilson implemented **playground meetings** with their students at their respective elementary schools (first grade in Bar Nunn, Wyoming, and third grade in Casper, Wyoming). Knudson held the playground meetings immediately following the afternoon recess; Wilson was already holding a class meeting each morning, so she incorporated the playground discussion into that meeting. The purpose of the playground meeting was to allow students to discuss their playground problems, concerns, and experiences and then develop possible solutions. In directing the meeting, the classroom teacher clarified, commented, perhaps taught a new concept, and finally asked the children for their help in solving the problem.

Both teachers found the meetings to be very productive even though Knudson was not a recess supervisor. They learned much about the social dynamics of their classes and discovered that what happens on the playground during recess can affect the rest of the child's day. At the end of the year, students indicated they had learned how to get along better and were having more positive playground experiences. Sociometric data on the first graders indicated their circle of playmates had expanded (Thompson, Knudson, and Wilson 1997).

We wholeheartedly agree with Knudson and Wilson that classroom teachers need to talk with their students about their recess experiences. The method used does not have to be playground meetings, but some method needs to be implemented. You can ask all kinds of questions. "What activities are fun or not fun? What problems are occurring on the playground? What play equipment do you not have access to that you would like to have? Why? Whom do you play with on the playground? How could you include others in your games?" Whether the elementary classroom teacher is supervising the recess period or not, the students are experiencing recess, and what happens during recess can have a large impact on what happens in the classroom. Let students tell you what is happening so you can help them structure recess periods that are positive, educational experiences.

If asked, most classroom teachers would say that the role of the recess supervisor was to ensure the safety of the students during the recess period. We agree that is the primary role of the recess supervisor, but the expanded role we have developed in this chapter will surely lead to healthier children, safer playgrounds, and a school with a sense of community.

Summary

For elementary school children, schools need to provide adequate play time (recess), appropriate (well-maintained) play spaces and equipment, and trained personnel to structure quality recess time. Play is an essential element in children's development, and schools (in addition to parents and other community agencies) have a responsibility to provide children with play periods. No evidence exists that decreasing recess time and increasing academic time leads to improved academic performance. However, evidence does exist that limiting recess time during the school day decreases students' attention levels and decreases their participation in physical activity outside of school.

Children benefit from having a number of opportunities to be physically active while interacting with their peers during play periods before, during, and after school. The benefits of participating in quality recess time include the following:

- Improved motor skills
- Taking a break from academic work
- Improved attention upon returning to the classroom
- Improved social skills (e.g., respect, cooperation, fairness, and friendship)
- Facilitating cognition through social interaction with peers
- Feeling better as a result of being physically active

- Learning that actions have consequences

Play spaces should be available both indoors and outdoors with adequate space for the number of children who will occupy the space at one time. A variety of age-appropriate standard and creative play equipment should be available and should be maintained in proper working condition.

Confirmed factors that influence children's behavior on the playground include gender, age, race, and disability, with gender and age being the strongest influences. Although children typically behave in certain ways, the typical behaviors are not necessarily the preferred behaviors. Educators have the responsibility to monitor playground behavior and shape that behavior in the direction predetermined and preferred by the school personnel.

Educators can help students construct quality recess time by establishing and enforcing rules of conduct for the playground, providing a safe play environment, allowing recess to be unstructured play, stimulating children to be physically active, encouraging inclusion, and planning for active indoor recesses when going outdoors is not possible.

Chapter Activities

1. Obtain the literature on playground safety available from the National Program for Playground Safety (800-554-PLAY, www.uni.edu/playground). Use this information to help you complete number 2 below.

2. Develop a plan for establishing quality recess time.

3. Observe playground behaviors at a local school. Compare your observations with the findings reported in this chapter. Draw conclusions as to whether quality recess play was occurring.

4. Observe several recess periods at a local school and draw a map of the space and equipment provided for the students. Based on what you learned in this chapter, is this the space and equipment you would want to have on your school playground? Record the types of activities taking place in the various spaces and on the various equipment pieces and note who (age, gender, disability, race) does the activity. Summarize your findings and indicate what you learned from this experience.

5. Read the following scenarios and recommend actions the classroom teachers might take to ensure that recess time is a quality educational experience. Write a one-paragraph response for each scenario.

- During recess, a fourth-grade child fell off the jungle gym (eight feet high) and landed on his feet. He complains of pain in one foot. What should you do?
- It is during the winter season. You want to take your students outdoors (on a cold day) during recess to walk around the playground for 15 minutes. What things should you consider in order to make this outing safe? What things should you consider in order to make the walk a fitness experience?
- During recess you notice the same group of girls who always spend recess time talking to each other while sitting on the merry-go-round. What, if anything, might you do to encourage the girls to be more physically active?
- During recess, a group of boys always plays soccer. A student (new to your classroom) stood on the sideline and watched the game for several days. The group has not invited the new student to join them, nor has the new student specifically asked to join the group. What would you (as the teacher) do in this situation?
- During recess, a group of boys and girls tend to play basketball at the one hoop that is available on the playground. In general, the students play well together, but for several consecutive days two of the boys (on opposing teams) have gotten into a fistfight toward the end of the recess period. What would you (as the teacher) do in this situation?

Internet Resources

Action for Healthy Kids. Is a partnership of over 50 organizations and government agencies that helps schools find ways to help improve students' health and readiness to learn.
www.actionforhealthykids.org

American Association for the Child's Right to Play. Contains information and materials to promote the importance of recess for children.
www.ipausa.org

Child and Adolescent Psychological and Educational Resources. Contains resources on bullying, stress, and well-being.
www.caper.com.au

National Clearinghouse for Educational Facilities (NCEF). Created in 1997 by the U.S. Department of Education, NCEF is a free public service providing information on planning, designing, funding, building, improving, and maintaining schools.
www.edfacilities.org/rl/playgrounds.cfm

National Program for Playground Safety (NPPS). Housed at the University of Iowa, NPPS was initiated by the Centers for Disease Control and Injury Prevention in 1995.
www.uni.edu/playground

Peaceful Playgrounds. Contains information on playground construction and the many choices of play activities available on playgrounds and field areas.
www.peacefulplaygrounds.com

Stop Bullying Now. Campaign designed to stop bullying. Contains web-based, animated stories.
www.stopbullyingnow.hrsa.gov

The Partnership for Play Everyday. Is a partnership of various associations to increase the spaces and quality of play for children and youth.
www.playeveryday.org

U.S. Department of Health and Human Services. Contains information on bullying prevention.
www.hhs.gov

Bibliography

Alexander, G. M., and M. Hines. 1994. Gender labels and play styles: Their relative contribution to children's selection of playmates. *Child Development* 65: 869–879.

Barbour, A. C. 1996. Physical competence and peer relations in second-graders: Qualitative case studies from recess play. *Journal of Research in Childhood Education* 11(1): 35–46.

Beighle, A., C. F. Morgan, G. Le Masurier, and R. P. Pangrazi. 2006. Children's physical activity during recess and outside of school. *Journal of School Health* 76(10): 516–520.

Blatchford, P., R. Creeser, and A. Mooney. 1990. Playground games and playtime: The children's view. *Educational Research* 32: 163–174.

Bowers, L., and C. Gabbard. How safe is your playground? Risk factor two: age-appropriate design of safe playgrounds. *Journal of Physical Education, Recreation and Dance* 71(3): 23–25.

Bowler, T. 2003. Hazards and safety within playground facilities. *American Association for Leisure and Recreation,* fall newsletter, p. 2.

Boyle, D. E., N. L. Marshall, and W. W. Robeson. 2003. Gender at play. *American Behavioral Scientist* 46(10): 1326–1345.

Bruya, L. R. 1998. *Supervision on the elementary school playground.* Unpublished master's thesis, Gonzaga University, Spokane, WA.

Bruya, L. D., and G. S. Wood. 1998. Achieving a safe ratio on the playground. *Parks and Recreation* 33(4): 74–77.

Calo, K., and P. Ingram. 1994. *Playground leaders.* ERIC, 376-984.

Calvin, W. H. 1996. *How brains think: Evolving intelligence, then and now.* New York: BasicBooks.

Chuoke, F., and B. Eyman. 1997. Play fair—and not just at recess. *Educational Leadership* 54(8): 53–55.

Craig, W. M., D. Pepler, and R. Atlas. 2000. Observations of bullying in the playground and in the classroom. *School Psychology International* 21(1): 22–36.

Crick, N. R. 1995. Relational aggression: The role of instant attributions, feelings of distress, and provocation type. *Developmental Psychology and Psychopathology* 66: 313–322.

Crick, N. R., and M. A. Bigbee. 1998. Relational and overt forms of peer victimization: A multiinformant approach. *Journal of Consulting and Clinical Psychology* 66(2): 337–347.

Dahmes, V. M. 1993. *A descriptive study of multicultural elementary student playground behaviors and their relationship to gender, age, race and socioeconomic status.* ERIC, 369-521.

Dale, D., C. B. Corbin, and K. S. Dale. 2000. Restricting opportunities to be active during school time: Do children compensate by increasing physical activity levels after school? *Research Quarterly for Exercise and Sport* 71(3): 240–248.

Doll, B., and P. Murphy. 1996. *Recess reports: Self-identification of students with friendship difficulties.* ERIC, 406-629.

Etnier, J. L., W. Salazar, D. M. Landers, S. J. Petruzzello, M. Han, and P. Nowell. 1997. The influence of physical fitness and exercise upon cognitive functioning: A meta-analysis. *Journal of Sport & Exercise Psychology* 19: 249–277.

Frost, J., and P. Jacobs. 1995. Play deprivation: A factor in juvenile violence. *Dimensions of Early Childhood* 23: 14–17.

Gallegos, K. 1998. Inclusion, responsibility and fair play can also be learned outside the classroom. *Thrust of Educational Leadership* 28(1): 13.

Guddemi, M., and T. Jambor. 1993. Introduction. In *A right to play,* ed. M. Guddemi and T. Jambor, v–vii. Little Rock, AR: Southern Early Childhood Association.

Holmes, R. M., A. D. Pellegrini, and S. L. Schmidt. 2006. The effects of different recess timing regimens on preschoolers' classroom attention. *Early Child Development and Care* 176(7): 735–743.

Hudson, S. D., D. Thompson, and M. G. Mack. 2001. Safe playgrounds: Increased challenges, reduced risks. *Dimensions of Early Childhood* 29(1): 18–23.

Hudson, S. D., D. Thompson, and H. Olsen. 2005. How safe are school and park playgrounds? A progress report. *Journal of Physical Education, Recreation and Dance* 76(1): 16–20, 28.

Jago, R., and T. Baranowski. 2004. Non-curricular approaches for increasing physical activity in youth: A review. *Preventive Medicine* 39(1): 157–163.

Jarrett, O. S. 2002. Recess in elementary school: What does the research say? ERIC, 466-331.

Jarrett, O. S., B. Farokhi, C. Young, and G. Davies. 2001. Boys and girls at play: Games and recess at a southern urban elementary school. In *Play and culture studies,* vol. 3, *Theory in context and out,* ed. S. Reifel, 147–170. Westport, CT: Ablex.

Jarrett, O. S., and D. M. Maxwell. 2000. What research says about the need for recess. In *Elementary school recess: Selected games and activities for teachers and parents,* ed. R. Clements, 12–120. Boston: American Press.

Jarrett, O. S., D. M. Maxwell, C. Dickerson, P. Hoge, G. Davies, and A. Yetley. 1998. Impact of recess on classroom behavior: Group effects and individual differences. *Journal of Educational Research* 92: 121–126.

Jensen, E. 1998. *Teaching with the brain in mind.* Alexandria, VA: Association for Supervision and Curriculum Development.

Kieff, J. (2005/06). Let's talk about friendship: An anti-bias unit on building classroom community. *Childhood Education* 82(2): 98K–98M.

Kim, Y. A. 2003. Necessary social skills related to peer acceptance. *Childhood Education* 79(4): 234–238.

Kochenderfer, B. J., and G. W. Ladd. 1996. Peer victimization: Cause or consequence of school maladjustment? *Child Development* 67: 1305–1317.

Kohlberg, L. 1971. "From is to ought": How to commit the naturalistic fallacy and get away with it in the study of moral development. In *Cognitive development and epistemology,* ed. W. Mischel, 151–232. New York: Academic Press.

Krasnor, L., and D. Pepler. 1980. The study of children's play: Some suggested future directions. *New Directions for Child Development* 9: 85–94.

Ladd, G. 1983. Social networks of popular, average, and rejected children in school settings. *Merrill-Palmer Quarterly* 29: 283–307.

Ladd, G., and J. Price. 1993. Play styles of peer accepted and peer rejected children on the playground. In *Children on playgrounds,* ed. C. Hart, 130–161. Albany: State University of New York Press.

Landreth, G. 1993. The emotional healing benefit of play. In *A right to play,* ed. M. Guddemi and T. Jambor, v–vii. Little Rock, AR: Southern Early Childhood Association.

Maccoby, E. E. 1990. Gender and relationships: A developmental account. *American Psychologist* 45: 513–520.

McClure, C., and L. R. Kinnison. 1999. Recess in elementary schools: Implications for children who have disabilities. ERIC, 427-482.

McDermott, K. 1999. Helping primary school children work things out during recess. *Young Children* 54(4): 82–84.

McKenzie, T. L., J. F. Sallis, J. P. Elder, C. C. Berry, P. L. Hoy, P. R. Nader, M. M. Zive, and S. L. Broyles. 1997. Physical activity levels and prompts in young children at recess: A two-year study of a bi-ethnic sample. *Research Quarterly for Exercise and Sport* 68(3): 195–202.

National Association for Sport and Physical Education (NASPE). 2001. *Guidelines for facilities, equipment and instructional materials in elementary education.* Reston, VA: National Association for Sport and Physical Education, an association of the American Alliance for Health, Physical Education, Recreation, and Dance.

———. 2004. *Physical activity for children: A statement of guidelines for children ages 5–12.* Reston, VA: National Association for Sport and Physical Education, an association of the American Alliance for Health, Physical Education, Recreation, and Dance.

———. 2006. *Recess in elementary schools.* Reston, VA: National Association for Sport and Physical Education, an association of the American Alliance for Health, Physical Education, Recreation, and Dance.

Newman, J., P. J. Brody, and H. M. Beauchamp. 1996. Teachers' attitudes and policies regarding play in elementary schools. *Psychology in the Schools* 33(1): 61–69.

O'Brien, L. M. 2003. The rewards and restrictions of recess: Reflections on being a playground volunteer. Paper presented at annual meeting of the American Educational Research Association, Chicago. ERIC, 478-468.

Ochoa, S. H., and A. Olivarex. 1995. A meta-analysis of peer rating sociometric studies of pupils with learning disabilities. *Journal of Special Education* 29(1): 1–19.

Olsen, H. M., S. D. Hudson, and D. Thompson. 2002. Child's play. *American School Board Journal* 189(8): 22–24.

Olweus, D., and S. Limber. 2000. *Bullying Prevention Program.* Boulder, CO: Center for the Study and Prevention of Violence.

Patrick, T. 1996. *Play: An important component of preventative behavior management.* ERIC, 400-951.

Pellegrini, A. D. 1995. *School recess and playground behavior.* Albany: State University of New York Press.

Pellegrini, A. D., and D. F. Bjorklund. 1996. The place of recess in school: Issues in the role of recess in children's education and development. *Journal of Research in Childhood Education* 11(1): 5–13.

———. 1997. The role of recess in children's cognitive performance. *Educational Psychologist* 32(1): 35–40.

Pellegrini, A. D., and P. Blatchford. 2000. *The child at school.* New York: Oxford University Press.

Pellegrini, A. D., K. Kato, P. Blatchford, and E. Baines. 2002. A short-term longitudinal study of children's playground games across the first year of school: Implications for social competence and adjustment to school. *American Educational Research Journal* 39: 991–1015.

Pellegrini, A. D., and C. M. Bohn. 2005. The role of recess in children's cognitive performance and school adjustment. *Educational Researcher* 34(1): 13–19.

Pellegrini, A. D., and P. Davis. 1993. Confinement effects on playground and classroom behavior. *British Journal of Educational Psychology* 63: 88–95.

Pellegrini, A. D., P. D. Huberty, and I. Jones. 1995. The effects of recess timing on children's playground and classroom behaviors. *American Educational Research Journal* 32(4): 845–864.

Pellegrini, A. D., and P. K. Smith. 1993. School recess: Implications for education and development. *Review of Educational Research* 63(1): 51–67.

———. 1998. Physical activity play: The nature and function of a neglected aspect of play. *Child Development* 69(3): 577–598.

Piaget, J. 1970. Piaget's theory. In *Carmichael's manual of child psychology,* ed. P. Mussen, 1:703–732. New York: Wiley.

Price, J. M., and K. A. Dodge. 1989. Reactive and proactive aggression in childhood: Relations to peer status and social context dimensions. *Journal of Abnormal Child Psychology* 17: 455–471.

Ronning, J. A., and D. Nabuzoka. 1993. Promoting social interaction and status of children with intellectual disabilities in Zambia. *Journal of Special Education* 27(3): 277–306.

Shephard, R. J. 1997. Curricular physical activity and academic performance. *Pediatric Exercise Science* 9(2): 113–126.

Shepherd, D., J. Burnett, and J. Zody. 2003. The importance of playgrounds as developmental opportunities for children with disabilities. *Kansas Association of Health, Physical Education, Recreation, and Dance* 74(2): 48–52.

Siperstein, G. N., J. S. Leffert, and M. Wenz-Gross. 1997. The quality of friendships between children with and without learning problems. *American Journal on Mental Retardation* 102(2): 111–125.

Smith, A. B., and P. M. Inder. 1993. Social interaction in same and cross gender pre-school peer groups: A participant observation study. *Educational Psychology* 13: 29–42.

Smith, J. D., J. B. Cousins, and R. Stewart. 2005. Antibullying interventions in schools: Ingredients of effective programs. *Canadian Journal of Education* 28(4): 739–762.

Smokowski, P. R., and K. H. Kopasz. 2005. Bullying in school: An overview of types, effects, family characteristics, and intervention strategies. *Children & Schools* 27(2): 101–110.

Stevenson, H. W. 1992. Learning from Asian schools. *Scientific American* 267(6): 70–76.

Taras, H. 2005. Physical activity and student performance at school. *Journal of School Health* 75(6): 214–218.

Thompson, S., P. Knudson, and D. Wilson. 1997. Helping primary children with recess play: A social curriculum. *Young Children* 52(6): 17–21.

Toppino, T. C., J. E. Kasserman, and W. A. Mracek. 1991. The effect of spacing repetitions on the recognition memory of young children and adults. *Journal of Experimental Child Psychology* 51(1): 123–138.

Tremarche, P. V., E. M. Robinson, and L. B. Graham. 2007. Physical education and its effect on elementary testing results. *Physical Educator* 64(2): 58–64.

Vail, K. 2006. Is physical fitness raising grades? *American School Board Journal* 193: 30–33.

Van der Smissen, B. 1990. *Legal liability and risk management for public and private entities.* Cincinnati, OH: Anderson.

Verstraete, S. J. M., G. M. Cardon, D. L. R. De Clercq, and I. M. M. De Bourdeaudhuij. 2006. Increasing children's physical activity levels during recess periods in elementary schools: The effects of providing game equipment. *European Journal of Public Health* 16(4): 415–419.

Waite-Stupiansky, S., and M. Findlay. 2001. The fourth R: Recess and its link to learning. *Educational Forum* 66(1): 16–25.

Wohlwend, K. E. 2004. Chasing friendship: Acceptance, rejection, and recess play. *Childhood Education* 81(2): 77–82.

Zask, A., E. van Beurden, L. Barnett, L. O. Brooks, and U. C. Dietrich. 2001. Active school playgrounds—Myth or reality? Results of the "Move It Groove It" project. *Preventive Medicine* 33(5): 402–408.

QUICK LESSON 12.1
Four Activities Using Permanent Playground Equipment

GRADES K–3

NASPE STANDARD 5 Students exhibit responsible personal and social behavior that respects self and others in physical activity settings.

LESSON OBJECTIVES

- Students verbally indicate the rules for playing on the swings, slide, and merry-go-round.
- Students play on the equipment (indicated above) according to the rules for interacting with peers and interacting with the equipment (see Box 12.2).
- Students physically experience the motions of swinging, sliding, and twirling.

EQUIPMENT NEEDED Equipment on the playground (swings, slide, jungle gym, and merry-go-round)

PREPARATION TIME Five minutes

KNOWLEDGE CONTENT The knowledge the student needs to learn depends on the specific rules your school has established. For this lesson explanation, we are using the rules indicated in Box 12.2.

CLASSROOM TO PLAYGROUND ACTIVITY

Lesson 1: Swinging

Scatter students throughout a grassy playground area to do the following movement exploration activities:

- "Show me how many body parts you can swing." Arms and legs.
- "Can you perform a whole body swing while standing on the ground?" No.
- "But you can do a full body swing while on a swing or hanging (with hands) from a jungle gym bar."
- "How does it feel to swing free on a swing or jungle gym? Express that feeling as you move around this grassy area. Go. Stop. Do not interfere with others as you move."
- Review the rules for properly using the swings located on the playground and for swinging safely on the jungle gym. Have a group of students demonstrate proper safety.
- "How should you land when dismounting from the jungle gym? You should land on two feet, bending the knees to absorb the force and using your arms to balance." Students can practice landing by performing standing long jumps in a grassy area. Then they can practice landing from the jungle gym.

Lesson 2: Sliding

Scatter students throughout a grassy playground area to do the following movement exploration activities:

- "Show me how you can slide" (anywhere in this grassy area). "Slide to the left." "Slide to the right." "Be sure to have your body under control—meaning you do not contact others as you move in the area."
- "A slide is a locomotor movement (meaning it takes you from place to place) in which you step to the side (with the foot on that side of the body) and then draw the other foot to the foot you just stepped on." "Slide quickly." "Slide slowly." "Slide two slides to the right and pretend to catch a hit baseball traveling along the ground toward you. Pretend to throw the ball back to the pitcher. Repeat this to the left. Be sure to slide with knees slightly bent."
- "Baseball and softball players slide to catch batted balls traveling along the ground (as we just did). Repeat this action to the right and left."
- "Another type of sliding can be done on a slide." Review sliding as performed on a slide and cover the safety rules. Have a group of students demonstrate proper safety on the slide.

Lesson 3: Twirling

Scatter students throughout a grassy playground area to do the following movement exploration activities:

- "Twirl around while standing in one spot. Twirl to the right and then to the left—still standing in one spot. Twirl slowly. Twirl quickly."
- "How do you feel right now after twirling several times?" Dizzy.
- "Dancers get rid of the dizzy feeling by focusing on a spot in front of them, and then as their body twirls, they turn their head *quickly* (on each twirl) to refocus on the spot. Then they can do many twirls (turns) in a row. Focus on something (me, a tree, or a piece of equipment), and try to do this while twirling four times."
- "Twirl three turns to the right while moving to the right in a straight line. Repeat to the left. Be sure to focus on a spot to the right and turn your head quickly to refocus."
- "What piece of equipment on the playground can give you a similar sense of dizziness?" The merry-go-round. Review the safety rules for the merry-go-round. Indicate that a constant focus can again help reduce or eliminate the dizzy feeling. Have a group of students demonstrate proper behavior on the merry-go-round.

do something observable and also specify the criteria for judging whether the student has been successful. In the lessons in this section, the criteria for judging success are written in the objectives or are specified in the assessment section.

The closing activities in the physical education lessons are of two types: movement activity versus discussion activity. Discussion activities consist of "technique talk," "concept cues," "behavior blurb," "respect rap," "fun feelings," or "challenge chat."

Because Unit 4 is designed for the classroom, the lessons in this unit are formatted similarly to the Quick Lessons that are provided in each chapter. These lessons do not contain the four lesson parts (introductory activity, fitness activity, lesson focus, and closing activity); rather, they contain only lesson focus activities.

Movement Forms: Basic Movement Skills, Basic Game Skills, and Rhythmic Movement Skills

. . . .

FIFTEEN LESSONS, GRADES K–2
Virginia Hammersmith, Bostic Traditional Elementary, Wichita, Kansas

Lesson 1.1 Locomotor Movements

NASPE Standards 1, 4, and 5

Lesson Objectives

- Students will correctly perform the basic locomotor skills.
- Students will be continuously active (to build cardio-respiratory endurance) during the lesson activities with little rest time between activities.
- Students will perform the locomotor skills in time to music.
- Students will find partners or groups without help from the teacher.
- Students will practice fleeing, chasing, and dodging skills.

Equipment Needed

CD player (or record or tape player) and music of your choice, suitable for performing locomotor movements

Activity Descriptions

Introductory and Fitness Activity: Squat Tag

Everyone is "it." However, a person cannot be tagged if he or she is in a squat position. If tagged, a person goes to the sideline, does five jumping jacks, and then reenters the game. Play several times. (Squat position is defined as follows: student's knees are bent so that his or her bottom is at least at knee level.)

Lesson Focus: Locomotor Movements

Have the students move around in general space (without touching each other). Have students perform the following movements:

Walk like an old man (slow, bent over).
Walk like a young person (fast, upright).
Run to win a sprint race (fast).
Jog and then leap over a pile of leaves.
Jump like a rabbit.
Crawl like a snake.
Crawl like a seal.
Gallop like a horse.
Walk like a duck.
Jump like a kangaroo.
Walk like an elephant.
Walk like a lame dog.
Jump like a frog.

Have the students move around in general space while the music is playing. Students move based on how the teacher says to move (walk, run, leap, hop, jump, skip, gallop, or slide). When the music stops, everyone has to find a partner and on your direction stands in one of the following designated ways:

Back-to-back
Toe-to-toe
Hip-to-hip
Knee-to-knee
Head-to-head
Fingers-to-fingers
Palms-to-palms
Elbow-to-elbow

Continue as above (moving to the music). When the music stops, students again stand according to your instruction (in the ways just listed above) but in groups of three, four, five, and so on.

Closing Activity: Slowdown

To slow students' heart rates before returning to the class-room, ask them to walk (at a moderate pace) around the gym once, then sit on any X spot on the gym floor and take ten deep, slow breaths in and out.

Student Assessment

Using a checklist, determine and mark for each student the locomotor skills the student can perform correctly (without music and in time with the music). (See Chapter 3 for descriptions of the locomotor skills and Appendix B for assessment rubrics for the locomotor skills.)

Success for All

If the majority of the students are adept at performing the basic locomotor skills, the lesson focus can be designed so the students move in patterns that combine the basic locomotor skills with other rhythmic elements. For example:

- Walk a square on the floor and run across it diagonally.
- Hop a zigzag pattern.
- Hop with a partner (staying in the same rhythm).
- Skip in a circle (forward, then backward).
- Slide with a partner.
- Gallop four times leading with the right foot, then four times leading with the left foot. Repeat.

Classroom Activity: People Finder

People Finder is appropriate for K–6 grades, particularly at the beginning of the school year when students are learning their classmates' names. For children who cannot read, the teacher can read the questions and have the children ask three different students before going on to the next question. Instructions and a work sheet are included below.

People Finder Work Sheet

Name_____

Directions: Find someone who matches the description and have them sign their name on the appropriate line. An * means the person you ask must perform the skill (not just *say* they can perform the skill). Each classmate may sign your paper only one time.

Find someone who can jump rope backward.* _____

(Designate a place in the room where this demonstration may occur so others are not hit by a turning rope.)

Find someone who walks to school. _____

Find someone who can skip.* _____

Find someone who likes to fish. _____

Find someone who can gallop.* _____

Find someone who can slide.* _____

Find someone who likes to play hopscotch. _____

Find someone who likes to go in-line skating. _____

Find someone who can perform a grapevine step.* _____

Find someone who enjoys swimming. _____

Find someone who can hop for 30 seconds.* _____

Find someone who has been bowling. _____

Find someone who likes P.E. _____

Lesson 1.2 Locomotor and Nonlocomotor Movements

NASPE Standards 1, 4, and 6

Lesson Objectives

- Students will enjoy performing a rhythmic activity.
- Students will perform locomotor and nonlocomotor movements.
- Students will perform actions in time with a singing rhythm (thus improving their coordination).
- Students will manipulate a parachute as a group (to increase arm and shoulder strength).

Equipment Needed

Parachute, as well as music and player for Mulberry Bush (if desired)

Activity Description

Introductory and Fitness Activity: Parachute

With the children spaced around the parachute (standing), have them lift the parachute (while facing its center), hold it with an overhand grip, and do the following activities. The activities can be repeated using an underhand grip.

- Shake the parachute slowly (like waves on the ocean).
- Shake it quickly (like ripples of water).
- Lift the parachute as high as possible; then try to pull it down quickly (all the way to the floor). Repeat this several times so everyone is lifting and pulling at the same time.
- Do the previous activity; however, as the parachute is pulled downward, children kneel on the edge of the parachute to trap the air inside. See how long the air will stay inside.
- Do the previous activity; however, on the downward pull, children step forward (inside the parachute), sit down, and pull the chute behind their backs to the ground. If enough air is trapped inside, all the children will be able to see each other.
- Lift the chute as high as possible. At the highest point, the children release the chute and watch it float to the ground.

Lesson Focus: Mulberry Bush

Children remain around the parachute, but change their grip on the parachute. Have the children face clockwise around the parachute and grip the parachute with the hand that is next to the parachute. Sing the chorus and verses with the following actions. Have the children perform the actions while singing.

Chorus:

> Here we go round the mulberry bush
> (Hold parachute and circle clockwise.)
> The mulberry bush, the mulberry bush
> (Hold parachute and continue circling clockwise.)
> Here we go round the mulberry bush
> (Hold parachute and continue circling clockwise.)
> So early in the morning.
> (Drop parachute. Each child turns a circle in place.)

Verses (use "getting-ready-for-school activities"):

> This is the way we stretch ourselves (reach for the sky),
> Stretch ourselves, stretch ourselves,
> This is the way we stretch ourselves,
> So early in the morning.

Repeat the first verse and stretch by touching toes.

> This is the way we wash our face,
> Wash our face, wash our face,
> This is the way we wash our face,
> So early in the morning.
> This is the way we brush our teeth,
> Brush our teeth, brush our teeth,
> This is the way we brush our teeth,
> So early in the morning.
> This is the way we comb our hair,
> Comb our hair, comb our hair,
> This is the way we comb our hair,
> So early in the morning.

Continue singing more verses: put on our clothes, tie our shoes, eat our toast, drink our juice. Sing the chorus after each verse. Pick up the parachute to walk in a circle during each chorus. Allow the children to create a different theme and determine the activities within the verses. The activity can be performed with or without the music.

Closing Activity: Fun Feelings

Children sit in a circle and the teacher leads a brief discussion on enjoying the experience of moving to a rhythm (with and without music). What did moving to a rhythm feel like? Express that feeling on your face.

Student Assessment

The teacher should visually monitor the students to determine whether all students can move in rhythm to the Mulberry Bush song (with or without music). Note the percent of "happy" versus "other" facial expressions during the closing activity.

Success for All

If children with special needs cannot perform the lesson activities, alter the activities to accommodate the students' needs. For example, a student in a wheelchair can do the parachute activities if the rest of the students kneel while performing. (Be sure to do this on a mat so as not to damage children's knees.) If some children are not developmentally ready to participate in groups of four members (Mulberry Bush), have them perform with the teacher.

Classroom Activity: Desk Aerobics

Desk aerobics can be performed at children's desks using any type of music with a steady beat. You may use the steady beat for background or make the activities more difficult by asking the children to do the activities in time with the beat. Each child should stand to the open side of the desk.

Standing

- With right foot on the chair seat and left foot on floor, touch the left toe with the left hand; hold for ten seconds.
- Repeat with left foot on chair and right foot on floor, touching the right toe with the right hand.
- While holding on to the desk (facing the desk), kick the right leg backward ten times.
- Repeat with left leg.

- Sideward lunges, ten times (while facing the desk).
- Forward lunges, ten times (with side of body to the desk).

Sitting (facing toward open side of the desk)

- Raise both legs up to a 90-degree angle; hold for ten seconds.
- Raise and lower left leg (straight leg at knee joint) ten times.
- Repeat with right leg.
- With feet flat on floor, open legs wide (at the hip joint) and then close; repeat ten times.
- Lift legs off the floor (straight at the knees) and scissor kick at the ankles for ten seconds.
- Lift legs and hold them up while circling the ankles for ten seconds.
- Lift legs and hold them up while pointing the toes and flexing the ankles for ten seconds.
- Drop body over forward, slap the floor, come up, and clap; repeat ten times.
- Lift the right knee to the chest and pull it in tight; hold ten seconds.
- Repeat with the left knee.
- Push-ups (place hands on desk seat and lift bottom off the seat by pushing with the arms), ten times.

Sitting (facing the back of the desk with legs straddling the desk)

- Kick (right, left, right, left).
- Kick both legs up at the same time, ten times.
- Push-ups (place hands on the back of the desk, let chest fall to the back of the desk, push the chest back and forth), 20 times.

Lesson 1.3 Manipulative Skills: Beanbags

NASPE Standards 1 and 5

Lesson Objectives

- Students will perform physical activities in general space without interfering with others during the lesson.
- Students will perform locomotor skills.
- Students will manipulate a beanbag (to improve eye-hand coordination).
- Students will be able to hit a wall target at least two out of ten tries, using correct technique, and toss into a wastebasket at least two out of ten tries (to improve throwing and catching skills).

Equipment Needed

At least one beanbag for each student, any piece of music and music player

Activity Descriptions

Introductory Activity: Beanbag Toss

While music is playing, partners toss and catch the beanbag. When the music stops, the person with the beanbag is "it" and attempts to tag his or her partner. The person who is "it" continues to try to tag the partner until the music starts again. If the person successfully tags the partner before the music starts, they begin tossing and catching again.

Lesson Focus: Manipulative Skills—Beanbags

Each child has one beanbag and is standing in general space. Have students do the following:

- Balance the beanbag on different body parts (top of hand, knee, top of foot, elbow, head, shoulder, etc.).
- Walk around the room balancing the beanbag on different body parts.
- While performing various locomotor patterns (run, skip, hop), balance the beanbag on various body parts.
- With everyone standing on the gym sideline, slide the beanbags (underhanded) across the gym floor and retrieve your own beanbag.
- Play "Got Ya." Each person has a beanbag. Children are scattered in the playing area. Children slide beanbags across the floor and try to hit another person on the feet. If your beanbag hits someone's feet, yell "Got Ya!" Everyone remains in the game and continues to play.

- Toss with one hand (underhand) to self and catch. Then toss with two hands (short toss, then high toss).
- Toss to self and catch from right hand to left hand (and then from left to right).

Arrange four or five students around one wastebasket. Have them do the following:

- Toss (underhand) into wastebaskets from various distances.

Arrange students around the perimeter of the gym (students facing the wall). Have them do the following:

- Throw (overhand) at targets on the wall from various distances.

Assign partners and determine throwing distance. Have students do the following:

- Throw and catch with a partner (overhand throw, two-hand catch).

Closing Activity: Technique Talk

Students sit in a circle, and the teacher reviews the mechanics of throwing and catching.

Student Assessment

Use visual observation to determine whether students are moving in general space in a responsible manner. Have students record the number of tosses that go into the wastebasket from various distances and the number of times they hit the wall target when throwing overhand. In addition, while students are throwing at wall targets or playing catch, the teacher can use the following checklist to evaluate the throwing technique of each child:

- The child is stepping forward with the opposite foot.
- The child is looking at the target when throwing.
- The child is moving the arm backward and then forward when throwing.
- The child is following through toward the target after releasing the beanbag.

Or you can use the rubrics in Appendix B to assess throwing and catching.

Success for All

All students do not need to be performing the same activities at the same time, so distances from targets can be adjusted based on the developmental level of the children. The teacher (or class aide) may play catch with some students in order to ensure successful catching.

Classroom Activity: Beanbag Stunts

Each child has one beanbag and is standing by her or his desk in the classroom. Practice the following self-stunts; be sure to perform all the stunts tossing with the right hand and then with the left.

- Toss to self, clap once, catch.
- Toss to self, clap twice, catch.
- Toss to self, clap ten times, catch.
- Toss to self, turn around 360 degrees, catch.
- Toss to self, touch the floor, catch.
- Toss high, catch high.
- Toss high, catch low.
- Toss to self, catch on back of the hand.
- Toss to self, catch on knee.
- Toss to self, catch behind the back.
- Toss upward and catch while the body is off the floor.

Lesson 1.4 Kicking and Dribbling: Soccer

NASPE Standards 1 and 3

Lesson Objectives

- Students will be able to dribble continuously for five minutes (to improve cardiorespiratory endurance).
- Students will be able to dribble, with correct technique, around a line of cones at least once without losing control of the ball (to improve soccer dribbling).
- Partners will be able to kick the soccer ball back and forth to each other at least twice without losing control of the ball using correct technique (to improve kicking and trapping skills).

Equipment Needed

Soccer ball for each student and 24 cones (boxes, bases, etc.) to dribble around

Activity Descriptions

Introductory and Fitness Activity: Dribbling

Students dribble (using the inside-of-foot dribble technique) around a designated playground area without interfering with others. If soccer goals are present on the playground, they can run around the goals. Each child has a soccer ball. Remind the children to use correct technique: contact the ball with the inside of the foot, tap the ball just enough to keep it under control, keep the eyes up to watch where you are going.

Lesson Focus: Cone Dribbling, Pin Kickball, Kickers and Trappers

Cone Dribbling Set up as many stations as possible (given the number of cones available) with three to four cones placed in a straight line. Try not to have more than three or four children per station. Use other objects in place of cones, if cones are not available. Children dribble (weaving right, left, right, left, etc.) through the line. The goal is to keep control of the ball while keeping the head up.

Pin Kickball Each child has a ball and will kick the ball at her or his target (cone, bowling pin, or the like). Vary the distance between the kicker and the target based on children's abilities. Line children up on one line and the cones on another line. Children kick at the cone directly across from them and retrieve their own ball after the kick. Then they bring the ball back to the line and kick

again. How many times (out of ten tries) can each child hit the target? Use the inside-of-foot kick. Practice kicking both with the dominant and with the nondominant foot. For safety reasons, you may need to have students kick and retrieve on your signal.

Kickers and Trappers Every two children will need one ball. Partners stand facing each other. Children take turns kicking the ball to their partner. When receiving the kick, the child must trap the ball. Emphasize that the ball must be under control (trapped) before they can kick it back to their partner. Children cannot touch the ball with their hands. Practice trapping both with the dominant and with the nondominant foot. To perform the sole-of-the-foot trap, the player gets in line with the ball, lifts one foot, brings the sole of the foot down on the top of the ball, and traps it between the ground and the foot. The child then removes the foot quickly to kick the ball to the partner.

Closing Activity: Technique Talk

Have students sit in a group on the gym floor and watch a kicking and trapping demonstration by two of the students in the class. Review the major kicking and trapping performance techniques during the demonstration.

Student Assessment

The teacher may use a checklist to evaluate the performance technique and performance results of each child on the following skills: inside-of-foot dribble, inside-of-foot kick at a target, and sole-of-the-foot trap. The teacher should also visually observe (and prompt, if necessary) to make sure students remain active during the fitness dribbling activity.

Success for All

Based on the performer's ability, distances to targets can be increased or decreased, and the size of the target can also be adjusted. Obviously, larger targets are easier to hit.

Classroom Activity: Word Recognition

Have the students complete the following work sheet. After circling the words, practice spelling them.

Word Recognition

Name _____

Draw a circle around the words that name the skills performed when playing with the soccer ball.

DRIBBLE	STRIKE	PASS
KICK	JUMP	HIT
TRAP	CATCH	SLIDE
THROW	PUNT	RUN

Lesson 1.5 Kicking and Dribbling: Soccer

NASPE Standards 1, 2, and 3

Lesson Objectives

- Students will participate continuously in three activities designed to keep their heart rates elevated (to improve cardiorespiratory endurance).
- Students will be able to move the ball downfield, dribbling and kicking, and then shoot for a goal, scoring a goal two out of ten tries (to improve soccer dribbling, kicking, and trapping skills).

Equipment Needed

One soccer ball for each student and four soccer goals (or cones to designate goals)

Activity Descriptions

Introductory and Fitness Activity: Dribbling and Passing

Students dribble and pass back and forth as they progress around a designated area (playground area or perimeter of the gym). Emphasize controlling the soccer ball. Use inside-of-foot and outside-of-foot passes and traps for this warm-up activity.

Lesson Focus: Dribble Scramble, Bull's-Eye, Soccer Keep Away

Dribble Scramble   Each child has a soccer ball. All the children are dribbling throughout a designated area. The goal is to control your own ball sufficiently so that it does not touch another ball or another person. If a touch occurs, both children go outside the area. In the outside area, children continue to practice dribbling (moving around the outside of the designated area). Start the game again when only a few are left inside the designated area.

Bull's-Eye   Designate teams consisting of six members each. Each child on the team has a soccer ball. Each team has a target (a soccer goal or an area designated by cones). Two lines are drawn (designated with cones): the starting line and the kicking line. Team members stand 15 to 20 feet away (on the starting line) from the goal. Groups of three members dribble forward (each player with his or her own ball) and kick for a goal from the kicking line. The purpose of this drill is to practice kicking for a goal without stopping the dribble. Keep track of the number of goals made by the team. Players retrieve their balls (whether they make or miss the goal) and go back to the starting line. The next three members of the team proceed to try to hit the goal.

Soccer Keep Away   Designate groups consisting of three players with one ball for each group. Using dribbling, kicking, and trapping skills, two of the players try to keep the ball away from the third player. Players may travel anywhere within the designated area; however, all groups will be in this area. So players must watch not only what their group is doing but also what others close to them are doing (as no contact should be made with other groups). Frequently during this game, the teacher uses a signal to change which group member is in the middle trying to take the ball away.

Closing Activity: Technique Talk

Have students sit on the floor in a circle formation. Ask them to share with the group the performance techniques and strategies that led to successful performance.

Student Assessment

The teacher should assist children during these games by providing verbal feedback on skill performance to individual players. These games are fast-paced and will not allow the teacher time to supervise and complete a written evaluation at the same time. Students should remember how many goals they scored in Bull's-Eye.

Success for All

When playing Bull's-Eye, group the children by ability and place the kicking line closer to the goal for lower-skilled players. Also group by ability for Soccer Keep Away so the children within each group have similar skills.

Classroom Activity: Blob Tag

This tag game is designed to improve soccer skills. Clear the classroom desks to one side of the room or to the perimeter of the room so an open space is created. Or play the game in the hallway. You will need a plastic milk jug for each child. The jugs are filled with two inches of playground sand and placed on the floor. You will need a rubber band for each child, who will hold it until it is needed.

Designate two players to be the Blob. These players stand at one end of the open space. Other players are scattered within the space. Each player has a jug and a rubber band. The Blobs place their rubber band around the middle of their jug so all other players can see who the Blobs are. The game begins and the Blobs attempt to kick their jugs into the jugs of the other players. A player whose jug has been hit puts a rubber band around his or her jug and becomes part of the Blob. The Blob continues to grow until all players become Blobs.

Stress the need for keeping the head up while dribbling the jug so as not to run in to others. Stress that a short, controlled dribble (kick) is much more effective than a long kick in getting away from the Blob. Remind students to use the inside-of-foot kick to push the jug along the floor.

Obviously, the students should practice dribbling the jugs in the space and have some skill in doing this before playing Blob Tag.

This game was developed by Bob Jackson, an elementary physical education teacher at Earhart Environmental Magnet School in Wichita, Kansas. Used with permission.

Lesson 1.6 Manipulative Skills: Hula Hoops

NASPE Standards 1, 4, and 6

Lesson Objectives

- Students will manipulate a hula hoop (to improve coordination). See assessment section for specific performance criteria.
- Students will perform the basic locomotor skills.
- Students will have fun playing with hula hoops.
- Students will move continuously from one activity to another (to build cardiorespiratory endurance).

Equipment Needed

One hula hoop for each student

Activity Descriptions

Introductory and Fitness Activity:
Stuck-in-the-Mud Tag

Designate several children to be "it." The "its" have sponge balls in their hand; they tag other players with the ball. If tagged, players are "stuck in the mud" and must stand still in place. To become unstuck, another player must come by and pull them out of the mud (with a handshake pull).

Lesson Focus: Hula Hoop Fun

Children are scattered throughout the play area. Each child has a hula hoop. Have children perform the following activities *with the hoop placed on the floor beside them:*

- Walk around the hoop, gallop around the hoop, skip around the hoop, and then slide around the hoop.
- Jump in and out of the hoop while moving around it.
- Hop in and out of the hoop (with the right foot then the left).
- When the music plays, children move in free space (using any locomotor skill), and when the music stops, children find the closest hoop and stand in it—only one child to a hoop.
- Play a tag game. Designate several children to be "it." They will roam the free space between the hoops. Other children begin by standing in one of the hoops (have about six hoops on the floor for a class of 24 students). The teacher indicates when children must leave the hoop they are in and move to another one ("ready, set, go"). Children can be tagged only when *not* in a hoop (so the hoop is a safe spot). Tagged children become "it." This game can be played with fewer and fewer hoops. Be sure to teach children how

to share the hoop and how to get lots of children into one hoop safely before playing with only two hoops.

With children still scattered throughout the area, have them perform the following activities *with the children manipulating the hoop:*

- Twirl the hoop around the waist (you must teach children how to move hips around so the hoop stays at waist level).
- Twirl the hoop around an arm (right and then left arm).
- Twirl the hoop around the neck.
- Twirl the hoop around a foot, with the hoop twirling parallel to the floor (you must teach children how to hop over the hoop with the nontwirling foot as the hoop circles).
- Spin back (second grade)—Scoot or throw the hoop out in front of the body (along the floor) (the hoop is perpendicular to the floor). Using the wrist, spin the hoop back toward you (just as it is released from the hand). It will travel out away from the child and then come back.
- Jump rope—Use the hoop as a jump rope and jump rope in place. Turn the hoop forward and then backward.
- Balance the hoop in place (perpendicular to the floor), let go, try to run through the hoop before it falls over.

With children in lines so they can move across the play area, have them perform the following activities:

- Hula Hoop Cars—Hold the hoop as if it were the steering wheel of a car. Drive the car across the play area (students could use different locomotor skills as they drive).
- Walk or run across the play space with the hoop rolling by your side. Keep the hoop rolling by pushing the hoop with your hand (slide hand forward on the hoop as it moves around beside you). Do this with the right hand, then with the left.

Closing Activity: Enjoyment

Sitting in a circle, discuss the fun and enjoyment of playing with hula hoops.

Student Assessment

Assess whether each student can do the following coordination skills (answer yes or no):

- Can the student twirl the hoop around the dominant arm for 30 seconds?

- Can the student twirl the hoop around the waist for 30 seconds?
- Can the student twirl the hoop around the foot (completing three jumps with the nonhoop foot)?
- Can the student roll the hoop the entire length of the gym floor while running beside it?
- Can the student jump rope with the hoop for five consecutive jumps?

Success for All

Since most of the activities in the lesson are performed individually, students should pace themselves and not become frustrated trying to keep up with everyone else in class. Developmentally delayed students may benefit from the teacher performing with them when doing the locomotor skills.

Classroom Activity: In and Out Hoop Relay

Designate teams of five or six players. Team members stand in single file holding hands with teammates on either side of them. Designate one of the end players as the leader for that team. Each team has one hula hoop. The hoop is hanging over the free arm of the leader as the activity begins. The goal is to have each team member pass through (step through) the hoop as it comes down the line without breaking their handhold. The hoop may be steadied with a player's hand as long as the player does not let go of the next player's hand.

First and second graders may be able to perform this as a relay. When the last player steps through the hoop, that player goes to the front of the line, becomes the leader, and starts the hoop moving through the line again. This action is repeated until all the team members have been leaders. Do not compete against other teams; however, each team can compete to improve its own time.

In and Out Hoop Relay: Students try to pass the hoop down the line without breaking their handhold.

Lesson 1.7 Ball Handling: Basketball

NASPE Standards 1 and 4

Lesson Objectives

- Students will be able to throw at a target on the wall and hit the target four out of ten tries, using correct technique.
- Students will be able to catch the ball rebounding from the wall three out of ten tries, using correct technique.
- Students will be able to dribble with the dominant hand for 15 seconds, using correct technique.
- Students will be able to perform the introductory activity twice for two minutes each time (to build cardiorespiratory endurance).

Equipment Needed

Balls that bounce—one for each student

Activity Descriptions

Introductory and Fitness Activity: Sideline Sprints

Divide the students into groups of three. Each group of three lines up in a single file behind one sideline of the gym. On the teacher's signal, the first member of the group sprints across the gym, touches the sideline, returns to the group, and touches that sideline. When the second sideline is touched, the next player may go. Continue. Stop whenever the children become tired. This is a cardiorespiratory endurance activity. So throughout the year, this warm-up activity can be done, and as the year progresses, the students should be able to continue the activity for a longer period of time.

Lesson Focus: Passing and Dribbling

Have students perform the following passing activities:

- *Wall Passing:* Each student has a ball (junior-size basketball, foam ball, or the like). Students are spaced around the perimeter of the gym, facing the wall. Perform passes against the wall (chest and bounce passes). Focus on the target (*X* taped on the wall for chest pass or *X* taped on the floor for bounce pass), step as you throw, and make the arms follow through. Concentrate on hitting the targets and catching the ball when it returns.
- *Partner Passing:* Perform the chest and bounce passes with a partner.

Have students perform the following dribbling activities (each child has a ball) while seated on the floor:

- Roll the ball around the body (clockwise).
- Roll the ball around the body (counterclockwise).

- Dribble on the right side (with the right hand) using a low dribble.
- Dribble on the left side (with the left hand) using a low dribble.
- Dribble on right side with left hand.
- Dribble on left side with right hand.

Have students perform the same sequence as above while kneeling. Then have them perform the same sequence while standing (add dribbling between the legs). Finally, have students dribble around the room (without interfering with others) so they must look up and use their peripheral vision to view the ball dribbling.

While students dribble around the room, give commands for them to stop (but continue dribbling in place), go, change direction, change dribbling hand (without stopping the dribble).

Closing Activity: Creative Dribble

Have the students dribble their balls to the equipment box that is farthest away from them and deposit the ball into the box. Students may be creative—use different pathways to get to the box, different speeds, and the like.

Student Assessment

For second graders, post the dribbling sequences on the wall, so the children can continue performing the sequences while the teacher is assessing performance technique and results. For the ball-handling objectives, (1) record performance results and (2) use the rubrics in Appendix B to assess performance technique (for throw, catch, and dribble).

Success for All

Use balls of different sizes and textures to adapt to children's different skill levels. Use smaller balls for children with smaller hands. Use foam balls for those who are afraid of the ball. In general, assign partners of like ability. However, assigning a mentor (with excellent abilities) to a child with special needs could provide an opportunity for both children to grow—be sure to prep the mentor for the experience.

Classroom Activity: Dribbling Sequences

Each child has a ball and stands by his or her desk in the classroom. Have children perform the dribbling sequences (sitting, kneeling, and standing) that were done in the physical education lesson.

Lesson 1.8 Throwing, Catching, and Volleying

NASPE Standards 1 and 5

Lesson Objectives

- Students will be able to throw, catch, and volley balloons and beach balls. (See specific performance criteria in the assessment section.)
- Students will be able to perform the lesson activities without interfering with others.
- Students will be able to work appropriately with a partner and select a new partner quickly.

Equipment Needed

Yarn ball for each student; large balloon or beach ball for each student

Activity Descriptions

Introductory and Fitness Activity: Partners

Designate partners. Partners are holding hands (one hand). Beginning with these designated partners, students hop, skip, gallop, and the like around the area until the teacher calls "partners." At that time, partners drop hands and each child links up with a new partner. Students must link with a different partner each time. Students can also be given the opportunity to join with another set of partners to move in a small group.

Lesson Focus: Throwing, Catching, and Volleying

Have students perform the following volleying activities (first with balloons, then with beach balls, then with foam balls, then with volleyballs):

- Toss to self and catch (concentrate on tossing accurately enough that you do not have to move to make the catch).
- Toss to self, volley to self, and then catch.
- Toss and catch with a partner (underhand toss).
- Volley back and forth with a partner (overhand, two-hand volley). See how many volleys can be performed before the object hits the floor.

Have students perform the following throwing and catching activities:

- Overhand throw with beach ball (two-handed) and catch (two-handed) with a partner
- One-handed throw and catch (two-handed) with a partner with a yarn ball
- Play "Snowball": Designate two teams, with one team on each side of a volleyball net (adjust height for children's ability level). Throw yarn balls over the fence (net) into the neighbor's backyard (use overhand, one-hand throw). Begin with each child having a yarn ball that's thrown as soon as the game starts. Continue throwing the balls over the net as fast as you can retrieve them and throw them back. When the teacher blows the whistle, the team with least number of snowballs in their backyard wins.
- Play "All Run": Designate groups of three. One member of the group has a ball (yarn, foam—something soft) and is the thrower. The other group members stand with hands joined around the thrower. The thrower tosses the ball overhead and catches it. On the toss, the other team members drop hands and run away from the thrower. When the thrower catches the ball, she or he yells "stop" and the runners freeze. The thrower then tries to hit one of the runners (below the waist). If the hit is successful, the runner becomes the thrower. If not, the thrower remains the thrower.

Closing Activity: Respect Rap

Students sit in a circle. Discuss how well the students selected new partners quickly and performed without interfering with others.

Student Assessment

For second graders, determine (and record) answers to the following questions:

- In the game of "All Run," were all students able to throw accurately enough to hit a runner?
- In the game of "Snowball," were all students able to throw over the net successfully at least five times?
- Can each child toss to self and catch in place for three consecutive times?

Success for All

Vary the object that is volleyed (balloon, beach ball, foam ball, or volleyball) based on the child's ability. All children do not have to be volleying the same object at the same time. Progress students (on an individual basis) to new objects whenever they are ready.

Classroom Activity: Moon Throw

Push the desks to the center of the room to create long, open spaces down the sides of the length of the room. Place hula hoops along one length of the room—hoops are "standing up," leaning against the wall. Children line up on the other side facing the hula hoops. Each child has two beanbags. On the teacher's signal, the children all throw (one-hand, overhand throw with dominant hand) at the hoop targets at the same time—throw one beanbag and then the other. Students retrieve the thrown beanbags and get ready to throw again (on signal). Students do not have to find their previously thrown bags; they can just pick up any two bags and return to their throwing spot.

However, students do need to watch and see where the bag hits, as one point is scored for each beanbag that hits inside a hoop. Students record their own score after each set of two throws. Keep a running total for ten throws. Challenge the students to better their own score during the next ten throws.

Moon Throw: Students throw beanbags on cue toward hoops leaning against the wall.

Lesson 1.9 Ball Handling: Basketball

NASPE Standards 1 and 4

Lesson Objectives

- Students will be able to correctly throw, catch, and dribble a basketball.
- Students will be able to perform the introductory activity for three minutes (to build cardiorespiratory endurance).

Equipment Needed

One basketball (junior-high sized; soft in texture, e.g., Nerf basketball) for every two students

Activity Descriptions

Introductory and Fitness Activity: Sideline Sprints
See Lesson 1.7.

Lesson Focus: Throwing, Catching, Dribbling, and Shooting

Line Dribbling Partners stand together in single file on one sideline. Each partner has a ball. One partner dribbles across the gym and back again while the other partner dribbles in place. Then partners switch roles. Continue. The goal is to have both partners dribble across the gym and back again without either losing control of the ball.

Passing Game Partners stand about ten feet apart, facing each other. Pass the ball back and forth. If both are successful in catching the ball, one partner takes a step back. Throw and catch again. Continue until someone misses; then partners begin again ten feet apart. (Do this sequence with different types of throws: chest pass, overhead pass, and bounce pass.)

Shooting Game Just like the Passing Game, except partners are shooting (not passing) back and forth. Stress good shooting technique (one-hand set shot).

Basket Shooting Assign two to three sets of partners to one shooting station (line taped on the floor four feet from a basket—any kind of plastic basket). One partner shoots four times consecutively while the other partner retrieves the ball. Switch roles. Continue.

Closing Activity: Technique Talk
Students sit in a circle. Discuss correct shooting technique.

Student Assessment

- Post several score sheets around the gym and allow partners to place a tally mark on the sheet every time they dribble back and forth across the gym without losing control of the ball (Line Dribbling).
- Provide verbal feedback to each set of partners (on skill technique) during the Passing Game and Shooting Game.
- During Basket Shooting, use the rubric in Appendix B to assess skill achievement on shooting technique.

Success for All

Distances dribbled may be shortened or lengthened. In Basket Shooting, lines may be taped at different distances from the baskets and students choose the line to begin on.

Classroom Activity: Ball Fun

Standing beside their desk, students each have a ball. Have them perform the following activities:

- Move your body around the ball (placed on the floor) without touching the ball (move around on three, two, or one body part, move slowly, move fast).
- Pick up the ball and move it around: waist, head, both feet, in and out of feet in a figure eight.
- Balance the ball on your head, knee, elbow.
- Roll the ball, on the floor, around your feet in a figure eight.

With a partner (each set of partners has only one ball), perform the following activities:

- Stand back to back and move the ball—around both waists, over head, and back through your partner's legs.
- Place ball between partners and walk.
- Sit down several feet apart, face each other with legs spread in a *V*. Roll the ball back and forth (left hand, right hand, both hands).
- Sit down several feet apart, face each other with legs together straight out in front. Roll the ball back and forth. Catch the ball by pointing toes and feet toward the oncoming ball; allow the ball to roll up your legs and then catch with both hands.

Lesson 1.10 Ball Handling: Basketball

NASPE Standards 1 and 4

Lesson Objectives

- Students will improve their performance technique on basketball dribbling and shooting skills.
- Students will be able to perform the introductory activity for three minutes (to build cardiorespiratory endurance).

Equipment Needed

One basketball (junior-high sized; soft in texture, e.g., Nerf basketball) for every two students

Activity Descriptions

Introductory and Fitness Activity: Gym Dribble

Students dribble around the gym once using the right hand, then again while dribbling with the left hand.

Lesson Focus: Dribbling and Shooting

Cone Dribbling   Designate groups with three members. Groups stand behind the sideline (in single file). Each group is facing three cones placed across the gym floor. Each group member in turn dribbles around the cones (up and back). This is not a race or a relay. The emphasis is on controlling the dribble, not on speed. Introduce the concept that when you move around the cone to the left, you should be dribbling with the left hand, and when you move to the right of the cone, you should be dribbling with the right hand. Thus the dribbling hand switches throughout the time the performer is moving through the cones. Members not dribbling through the cones may be dribbling in place for additional practice.

Follow the Leader   In the same groups of three members, designate a leader. Leaders dribble anywhere in the general space and the other group members follow. Leaders (and followers) must look up so as not to run into other groups.

Shooting Game   See Lesson 1.9.

Basket Shooting   See Lesson 1.9.

Closing Activity: Technique Talk

Students sit in a circle. Discuss correct dribbling technique.

Student Assessment

Continue completing the rubrics for assessing dribbling and shooting for each student.

Success for All

During Cone Dribbling, students with special needs may not be required to switch hands. They may also be allowed to simply dribble up one side of the cones and back on the other side (rather than weaving through the cones).

Classroom Activity: Spelling Toss/Throw

Designate groups with four members each. Each group has four beanbags or foam balls. Groups are scattered around the perimeter of the classroom (desks are shoved to the inside). On the wall by each group is a chalkboard, felt board, or large piece of paper upon which the alphabet is written. Each letter of the alphabet is large and has a square drawn around it. The students are going to spell words that are called out by the teacher. Teams spell the word by tossing (underhand toss) the beanbag or throwing (overhand throw) the foam ball and hitting the correct letters on the wall or board. Since there are four members in each group, select four-letter words to spell. Group members stand in front of their board and try to hit their respective letter (first person aims at the first letter of the word, etc.). All members are tossing at the same time. When team members have successfully hit the appropriate letter, they can move to the next word (given to them by the teacher). (Teams are not competing against each other!)

Lesson 1.11 Ball Handling: Bowling

NASPE Standards 1 and 4

Student Objectives

- Students will develop fleeing, chasing, and dodging skills in the introductory activity.
- Students will increase their heart rate during the introductory activity.
- Students will be able to demonstrate the correct rolling technique common to rolling a bowling ball.
- Students will be able to successfully work in groups of three.

Equipment Needed

One ball for each child. The ball needs to roll smoothly along the floor and needs to be small enough for the child to be able to handle with one hand.

Activity Descriptions

Introductory and Fitness Activity: Balloon Pop

Each child has a balloon tied to a foot. Children try to break each other's balloons. The object is to be the last one left with your balloon not popped. In addition, inside the balloons is a piece of paper with an activity written on it. When the child's balloon gets popped, she or he must perform that activity.

Lesson Focus: Bowling Skills

Form Bowling   Without balls, children practice the rolling motion. Have them pretend a ball is held in the dominant hand (right hand). Swing the right arm backward. Then step forward (on the left foot) at the same time as the right arm swings forward to roll the pretend ball along the floor. Be sure the arm follows through straight toward the target (the wall). Be sure the knees bend when releasing the ball so the ball is not dropped to the floor. Pretend rolling ten times.

Target Bowling   Each child has a ball (that can be handled with one hand). Children line up opposite a wall (about ten feet from the wall). At the base of the wall, the teacher has placed X's (with masking tape) as a target for the students to roll at. Students roll the ball (as described above) at the target opposite them. Once the target is hit five times, the student may take two steps backward. Students continue moving backward after the target has been hit five times. If the target has not been hit five times, the child stays at the current distance.

Pin Bowling   Designate groups of three members. Each group of three has one bowling ball (or Nerf ball, beach ball, or playground ball) and five to ten pins. Place the pins about ten feet in front of a wall (leaving enough room that a group member can retrieve the ball after it's bowled at the pins). Have children stand about 10 to 15 feet in front of the pins to bowl at the pins. Of the group members, one is bowling the ball, one is retrieving the bowled ball, and one is resetting the pins. After each bowled ball, the roles rotate (the retriever becomes the bowler, the bowler becomes the pin setter, and the pin setter becomes the retriever). You can establish rounds that might include ten throws, and children keep score by rounds to see if they can do better each round (Classroom Learning Station 9.1 has a usable score sheet for this task). Children are competing against their own group's score, not other groups' scores.

Closing Activity: Behavior Blurb

Students sit in a circle. Discuss how effectively they worked in groups of three. How do they know they worked effectively?

Student Assessment

Use the rubric in Appendix B to record children's ability to perform the rolling technique correctly.

Success for All

- Alter distances from targets and pins in order to ensure success.
- Make targets larger or smaller in size depending on the students' skill level.
- Help children who are having trouble learning the rolling technique by standing behind them, holding their throwing hand in your hand, and rolling the ball with them.

Classroom Activity: Target Bowling

Move the desks to the middle of the room. Children stand next to the desks, facing toward the wall. Perform Target Bowling as described in this lesson. Use Nerf balls, as they rebound off the wall with less force, or use beanbags if space to chase balls is limited.

Lesson 1.12 Volleying and Striking

NASPE Standards 1, 4, and 5

Lesson Objectives

- Students will be able to correctly perform the skills of volleying and striking.
- Students will be able to perform activities without interfering with others.
- Students will be able to observe the rules for playing "Take It Back."
- Students will increase their heart rate during the introductory activity (to improve physical fitness).

Equipment Needed

Items to play "Take It Back" (beanbags, small balls, rings, scarves, Frisbees, etc.). Balls to strike and serve, one for each student (beach, foam, playground, volleyball).

Activity Descriptions

Introductory and Fitness Activity:
Take It Back

Students are divided into teams of three. A center area is full of beanbags, small balls, rings, scarves, and the like. Teams are arranged around the center area like spokes on a wheel. The object of the game is for players to obtain as many objects as they can from the center area and bring them back to their own team (within a certain amount of time). On the teachers' signal, everyone runs to the center and takes one object at a time back to the home area (have a hula hoop to serve as the home area for each team). However, once play begins, players may also take objects (one at a time) from other teams' home areas. The winner is the team who has the most objects when the stop signal is given. Play again, but reorganize teams first.

Lesson Focus: Volleying and Striking

Underhand Strike   Each child has three balls (beach, foam, playground, or volleyball). Using an underhand strike (like an underhand serve in volleyball), students hit the three balls into an archery net (or stage curtain) so the balls will just drop and not bounce back at them. After everyone has hit, everyone retrieves and lines up to hit again. Continue as long as desired.

Underhand Serve   Students will underhand serve over tennis nets. Have at least two tennis nets set up. Each student has a ball. Everyone hits across the net at the same time; then everyone retrieves at the same time. Retrieve any ball (not the ball you previously had). Continue as desired.

Overhand Strike   Each child has a ball (beach, foam, playground, or volleyball). Children are lined up facing a wall (about seven feet from the wall). With an overhand striking motion (like an overhand volleyball serve), children hit and aim at a spot marked on the floor. The teacher marks the spot so that if a ball hits the spot, it will come up, hit the wall, and rebound back to the student. When the ball returns, the student catches the ball and then hits again. Continue as long as desired.

Volleying   Designate partners. Half the class remains at the tennis nets and volleys (balloons, then beach balls) to each other. The other half of the class is volleying against the walls to themselves. Switch roles.

Closing Activity: Technique Talk

Students sit in a circle. Discuss correct technique for underhand serve and overhand strike.

Student Assessment

Use the rubrics in Appendix B to assess children's ability to perform the overhand strike correctly.

Success for All

- Have visually impaired students work with partners.
- Assist those children (with manual help) who are having real difficulties performing successfully.
- Allow students to use the object that best fits their developmental level.

Classroom Activity: Volleying

Push the desks to the middle of the room. Have students volley balloons (or foam balls) (1) to themselves, (2) to a partner, (3) in groups of three, and (4) against the classroom walls.

Lesson 1.13 Manipulative Skills: Rope Jumping

NASPE Standards 1, 4, and 6

Lesson Objectives

- Students will make at least three shapes with the rope.
- Students will walk the rope forward without falling off.
- Students will perform each basic jump rope pattern five consecutive times.
- Students will maintain increased heart rate during the entire class period (to improve physical fitness).
- Students will improve motor coordination by practicing their jump rope skills.
- Students will improve dynamic balance by practicing their jump rope skills.
- Students will accept the challenge to work independently on their rope skills.

Equipment Needed

One individual jump rope for each student

Activity Descriptions

Introductory Activity: Rope Play

Each student has an individual rope. In their own space, have them perform the following:

- Make a straight line with your rope and walk that line (forward and backward).
- Jump down one side of the rope and back up the other side.
- Make a circle with your rope; walk that circle forward and backward.
- Make a new shape with your rope; walk that shape.
- Make the first letter of your name with your rope.
- Make another letter.

Lesson Focus and Fitness Activity: Jumping Rope

Consult Boxes 9.1 and 9.2 for jump rope activities appropriate for K–2.

Closing Activity: Challenge Chat

Students sit in a circle. Discuss students' ability to work productively as independent learners. Was that a challenge? Was it easy or hard to work alone? Did you stay motivated to work hard? What would help you stay motivated?

Student Assessment

- Record names of students who can or cannot make at least three shapes with the rope.
- Record names of those students who could walk the rope forward without falling off.
- Record names of students who can perform the basic jump rope pattern for five consecutive times.

Success for All

Not all students must be performing the same lesson focus activities at the same time. Students not yet able to perform the basic jump rope should be working on lead-up activities (see Box 9.1).

Classroom Activity: Jump to Music

Have students stand beside their desk and perform the following sequence to music (without jump ropes):

- Jump eight times (in place).
- Hop on the right foot eight times (in place).
- Hop on the left foot eight times (in place).
- Jump forward eight times (don't run into the classmate in front of you).
- Jump backward eight times.
- Jump four times (in place) turning to the right.
- Jump four times (in place) turning to the left.

Repeat as many times as the music allows.

Use music that has a definite beat. After students know the pattern, perform to music with a faster tempo.

Lesson 1.14 Rhythmic Skills: Lummi Sticks

NASPE Standards 1 and 5

Lesson Objectives

- Students will enjoy performing a rhythmic activity.
- Students will be able to tap Lummi sticks in rhythm with the music.
- Students will listen carefully to the music (auditory training).
- Students will be able to tap a rhythmic pattern in concert with a partner.

Equipment Needed

Two Lummi sticks per child. If Lummi sticks are not available, rhythm sticks (12 inches in length) can be made from one-inch dowels. A drum or tambourine is needed and also an audiocassette player. The music needs to be in 4/4 time.

Activity Descriptions

Introductory and Fitness Activity: Marching

Children listen to the drumbeat produced by the teacher. Holding a Lummi stick in each hand, they march in place and tap sticks together in time to the drumbeat. First the drumbeat is slow; then gradually its speed increases.

Now students march in general space, tapping sticks as if they were drummers in a marching band. March forward, backward, sideways, and in different patterns. March and twirl sticks like a baton twirler.

Play Follow the Leader with the sticks. Students form a large circle, with students facing clockwise around the circle so they can move around the circle. Each child leads for 30 seconds in turn around the circle. Time is monitored by the teacher, who when the time for one student is over calls out the name of the next student in line. The student leader determines two things: which locomotor skill to use while moving around the circle (walk, run, jump, hop, skip, gallop, or slide) and whether sticks are tapped in front, above head, to the right, or to the left.

Lesson Focus: Lummi Sticks

Each student has two sticks and is sitting cross-legged in general space.

- Have students listen to the rhythm being tapped by the teacher and then have students repeat the rhythm.
- Demonstrate and repeat several times.
- Use hands to tap out the rhythm.
- Tap the sticks on the floor in a sequence—in front of you four times, to the sides four times, behind you four times.
- Tap the sticks together in the air four times; tap the end of your sticks together, alternating your palms up and down four times.
- Cross your arms in front of you and tap sticks to the floor.
- Tap a practice sequence—tap in front, tap to sides, cross and tap floor.
- Tap a set sequence—four taps in front, four taps to sides, cross and tap floor four times.
- Flip each stick over, in turn, and catch it.
- Tap a practice sequence—tap front, together, flip, and catch.
- Tap a set sequence—four taps front, four taps together, flip, and catch in the right hand, flip and catch in the left hand.

Have students find a partner and sit cross-legged, face-to-face. Listen to the music being played. Tap out the rhythm pattern in time to the music.

- Tap the floor in front four times; tap your own sticks together.
- Tap your partner's sticks in the air; trade sticks with your partner.
- Cross hands and tap sticks to the floor; tap your own sticks together.
- Tap your partner's sticks in the air; trade sticks with your partner.
- Then flip each stick in turn and catch.

Closing Activity: Collective Spirit

Children all stand. They must circulate in general space, tap sticks with five class members, and then return their sticks to one of the equipment collection sites.

Student Assessment

Through visual observation, determine whether all students can tap sticks in time with the music and drumbeat.

Success for All

- Slow down the beat of the music or drum if students cannot stay in time.
- During performance of the sequences, allow students to perform only those skills they have already perfected.
- Allow partners to create their own sequences.

Classroom Activity: Creative Sequences

Have students select a partner. Partners develop and perfect the performance of a Lummi stick sequence—eight measures of 4/4 time. Allow the class to select the music. Once its sequence is perfected, each group can perform in front of the class (or during a parents' night event).

Lesson 1.15 Rhythmic Skills: "Kinder-Polka"

NASPE Standards 1 and 5

Lesson Objectives

- Students will enjoy performing a rhythmic activity.
- Students will be able to perform a dance ("Kinder-Polka") in rhythm with the music.
- Students will listen carefully to the music (auditory training).
- Students will be able to perform a movement sequence to music with a partner.

Equipment Needed

"Kinder-Polka" music (tape or CD) and player

Activity Descriptions

Introductory Activity: Fast, Slow, High, Low

Have the students move around in general space (without touching each other). Have them explore the movement elements of fast, slow, high, and low by asking them to perform in the following manner:

- Move your entire body very fast while moving in general space.
- Move your entire body very fast while standing in one place.
- Move your entire body very slowly.
- Move your hand very fast. Do the same with the head, eyelashes, nose, shoulders, hips, and legs.
- Move these same body parts very slowly.
- Move your entire body very slowly while moving at a high level, then moving at a low level.
- Move in general space (with a run, skip, or gallop), first at a slow speed, then gradually increasing to a fast speed (acceleration).
- Do the opposite: move fast; then gradually slow down (deceleration).
- Choose a position and shape at a low level; then choose a different position and shape at a high level. Remember those positions. Move fast from your low position to your high position. Move slowly from your high position to your low position.

Lesson Focus: "Kinder-Polka"

"Kinder-Polka" involves the basic steps of step-close, stamping, clapping, and step-turning. Use the following teaching sequence:

- Have students learn and practice each dance step individually.
- Have students practice sequences of consecutive dance steps individually.
- Have students practice each dance step with a partner, partners facing each other.
- Have students practice sequences of consecutive dance steps with their partner.
- Have students pair off and form a single circle of couples, with partners facing (holding hands) and perform the entire dance.

The dance steps are sequenced as follows:

- Step-close, step-close toward the center of the circle; stamp your foot in place three times.
- Step-close, step-close away from the center; stamp your foot in place three times.
- Repeat entire pattern.
- Slap knees; clap hands; clap partner's hands three times. (With both hands, slap your knees once, clap your own hands once, then clap your partner's hands three times.)
- Repeat this clapping pattern.
- Hop on the left foot, and reach the right heel forward; then shake your pointer finger three times at your partner (this is called the scolding pattern).
- Repeat the scolding pattern with your left heel forward and left pointer finger.
- Turn in place (four steps).
- Face your partner and stamp your feet three times.)

Repeat entire dance.

Closing Activity: Challenge Chat

Students sit in a circle. Discuss the following questions: Was this dance challenging? Why? What parts were easy and which were hard to learn?

Student Assessment

While students are performing, record whether each student can perform the first dance pattern (step-close sequence) correctly in time with the music.

Success for All

It is not likely that students will learn this dance in one lesson. Break it down into parts. Teach the parts without music, then to music (first individually, then with a partner). As the parts are perfected, begin to combine the parts into a sequence.

The teacher needs to be able to cue the students as to what movement is coming next.

Classroom Activity: "Kinder-Polka"

If desks are in rows in the classroom, have students stand facing their desk. Practice the dance steps using the same teaching progressions as indicated in the physical education lesson.

Movement Form:
Cooperative Movement Skills

· ·

FIFTEEN LESSONS, GRADES 3–4

Susan Oldfather, Caldwell Elementary, Wichita, Kansas

Lesson 2.1 Being Successful

NASPE Standard 5

Lesson Objectives

- Students will identify what today's youth need to be successful. (*Note:* You may want to consult Box 10.3, "Seven Significant Resources of Successful People.")
- Students will cooperate and work as a team.
- Students will gather data about their knowledge of their needs.

Equipment Needed

Chalkboard, chalk, "Bunny Hop" music and music player

Activity Descriptions

Introductory and Fitness Activity: Clothespin Tag

Each child has two or three clothespins pinned to the back of his or her shirt. Have students try to pull other students' pins off. When you get one, pin it on the front of your shirt. No one may take the pins off the front of your shirt.

Lesson Focus: Phrase Craze and "Bunny Hop"

Phrase Craze   Write the following statements on the chalkboard:

- "To be successful a person must do many things."
- "To continue to be successful I must receive many things."

Designate teams of four members each. On your signal, the first person from each team moves to the board and creates one word using the letters in the statements. The words need to be related to what kids need to be successful. After the student writes a word, he or she returns and the next student goes. Continue for a few minutes and then add up the number of words the entire class created. Count one point scored for each appropriate word. Then in the same groups, toss a ball and say something that makes each of us successful. If using language balls, the child may say a word (an attribute or asset) that begins with the letter they are touching on the ball.

"Bunny Hop"   Students remain in the same groups. The teacher demonstrates and students individually practice performing the "Bunny Hop." The goal is for the group to then perform this rhythmic activity successfully as a group, moving around the room in single file. Students in the group help each other learn and master the movements. You can use any music in 4/4 time; however, the

"Bunny Hop" music is very motivational for the students. The actions are as follows:

ACTION	COUNTS
Hop and touch the right heel to the floor (slightly to the right of the body), *two times*.	1–2
Hop and touch the left heel to the floor (slightly to the left of the body), *two times*.	3–4
Repeat the above two patterns, but hop and touch only *one time* on each side.	5–8
Jump forward once.	1–2
Jump backward once.	3–4
Jump forward four times.	5–8
Repeat all of the above.	

When performing in single file, students hold on to the waist of the student in front of them. The leader's hands are placed on her or his own waist (on top of the other student's hands).

Closing Activity: Respect Rap

Students sit in a circle. Discuss behaviors displayed as students helped their group members learn the "Bunny Hop." How effective were those behaviors? What could they do better next time?

Student Assessment

- Use words written on the chalkboard to determine student knowledge—plan successive lessons based on that data.
- Use a rubric to score teamwork behaviors during both lesson focus activities.
- Have students evaluate themselves and the group.

Success for All

- Have students go to the board in pairs (so individual students feel less pressure to perform in public).
- Use a variety of ways of moving to the chalkboard.
- Help students help each other.

Classroom Activity: "Shoemaker's Dance"

This dance can be used to supplement the physical education lesson goals of teamwork and success. Describe how a shoemaker made a pair of shoes (before modern machines began making shoes). What would a shoemaker have to do to make a good (successful) pair of shoes? Some of the actions of the shoemaker are in the following dance. Designate partners and have them stand facing each other. The class is in a double circle formation. This dance is from Denmark. It can be performed to any music in 2/4 time with the teacher providing the verbal cues; however, the specific music for the dance enhances the learning experience.

ACTION	VERBAL CUE	MEASURES
Clench fists and circle forearms in front of chest (circle away from body).	Wind, wind, wind the bobbin	1
Clench fists and circle forearms in opposite direction (toward the body).	Wind, wind, wind the bobbin	2
Pull elbows back forcefully twice.	Pull, pull (pulling the thread)	3
Clap hands three times.	Clap, clap, clap	4
Repeat the first three patterns.		5–7
Instead of clapping three times, Tap three times (tap fists together as if driving pegs into the sole of the shoe).	Tap, tap, tap	8
Partners join both hands and skip counterclockwise around in a circle.	16 skips	9–16

Lesson 2.2 Coordination

NASPE Standards 2, 4, and 5

Lesson Objectives

- Students will perform map-reading skills (to improve directionality).
- Students will keep their heart rate in their training zone throughout the lesson (to improve fitness).
- Students will perform Eraser Run (to improve agility).
- Students will perform the grapevine step (to improve coordination).
- Students will work as effective team members during the Eraser Run.

Equipment Needed

Spots on the floor in a grid formation (poly spots or painted spots), wooden cubes, parachute. Poly spots are rubberized vinyl cut in circle shapes that can be placed anywhere on the floor to mark locations.

Activity Descriptions

Introductory Activity: Eraser Run

Designate teams of four members. Teams stand in single-file lines behind a line (the gym sideline). The first team member has an eraser. Another eraser is placed on the floor directly in line with each team about 30 feet away. The first team member runs to the other eraser, exchanges erasers (placing the one in his or her hand on the floor and picking up the one on the floor), runs back to the team, hands off the eraser to the next teammate. Team members continue performing this pattern (until stopped by the teacher's signal) to see how many round trips they can make in two minutes. Repeat several times.

Lesson Focus and Fitness Activity: Coordinate Coordination and Parachute Grapevine

Coordinate Coordination   Use the spots as the coordinates (horizontal, vertical, and diagonal). Put *V1, V2, D1, D2, H1,* and *H2* on the wooden cubes. Students may be paired or each can move alone. Roll the cube and move to the coordinate that is rolled. For example, a child who rolls *V2* moves vertical two spots. After each move, students perform a predetermined movement. For example, if you moved horizontally, you do push-ups; if you moved vertically, you do jumping jacks; and if you moved diagonally, you do sit-ups. The children all roll at the same time, moving and performing the exercise until the teacher cues them to roll again.

Parachute Grapevine   The goal of this activity is to teach and practice the grapevine step. Children are scattered around the parachute, holding the chute with an overhand grip. Demonstrate first and then have them perform the following sequence:

- Shake the parachute (slowly, quickly).
- Make the parachute a merry-go-round by sliding left, then right.
- Do the merry-go-round with a sliding pattern: slide eight times to the left, then eight times to the right; slide four times to the left, then four times to the right; slide two times to the left, then two times to the right.
- Do the merry-go-round with a modified slide: instead of bringing the trailing foot to meet the lead foot, cross the trailing foot behind the lead foot. So the pattern is side-step, cross behind, side-step, cross behind, and so on.
- Do the above pattern moving to the right, and then to the left.
- Do a different modified slide: cross in front instead of behind. So the pattern is side-step, cross in front, side-step, cross in front, and so on. Do this to the right and then to the left.
- Do a grapevine step:
  - Step to the side (right step to right side).
  - Cross over with the left foot to the back of the right foot (still moving to the right).
  - Side-step again with the right foot to the right.
  - Cross over with the left foot in front of the right foot (still moving to the right).
  - Repeat the entire pattern.

Closing Activity: Concept Cues

Students sit in a circle. Discuss the concepts of horizontal, vertical, and diagonal. Relate the concepts to various physical movements.

Student Assessment

- Teacher observation of social skills and appreciation of other team members.
- Teacher observation to determine whether the concepts of horizontal, vertical, and diagonal are understood.

Success for All

- Pair children with special needs with students who can help them understand the concepts and move correctly.

■ Move as a family (the entire class moves as one).

■ Use a variety of physical movements.

Classroom Activity: Grapevine Circle

Push the desks to one side of the room. Designate groups of four members each. Each group forms a circle by holding hands. Perform the following dance to any popular music in 4/4 time. Select contemporary music with a moderate tempo, and once students master the movements, then perform to music with a faster tempo.

ACTION	COUNTS
Grapevine to the right. On count 8, stamp the left foot instead of finishing the grapevine step.	8
Grapevine to the left. On count 8, stamp the right foot instead of finishing the grapevine step.	8
Drop hands and circle to the right (individually in place).	4
Circle to the left (individually in place).	4
Perform a movement selected by the group.	8
Repeat the above pattern.	

Lesson 2.3 Partner Teamwork

NASPE Standards 4 and 5

Lesson Objectives

- Students will be able to work effectively with a variety of partners.
- Students will keep their heart rate in their training zone during the lesson activity (to increase physical fitness).
- Students will be able to follow the instructions for the "Quack You Up" activity.
- Students will be able to remember which stations they have completed in order to complete each station only once.

Equipment Needed

Plastic eggs and ducks (or any other object that you can use under cones), ten cones

Activity Descriptions

Introductory and Fitness Activity:
Beanbag Partners

Designate partners. While the music plays, partners toss back and forth (underhand or overhand). Each partner has a beanbag and both tosses occur at the same time. When the music stops, both students drop their bags to the floor and on command do as the teacher indicates: jump back and forth over the bag (forward/backward or left/right), leap over the bag continuously, hop over the bag (with right foot or left foot). When the music starts again, partners go back to tossing and catching.

Lesson Focus: "Quack You Up" Activities

Change partners. If 30 students are in the class, place ten cones scattered throughout the gym area. Inside each of ten eggs (plastic Easter eggs), place the title of an activity and put the egg on top of a cone. Under the cone, place a duck with directions on its belly. Number each cone from one to ten and place a set of partners at each cone. At the cone, partners open the egg and see what the activity is and then check out the rubber duck for directions. They put back the duck and the egg, perform the activity, and move to the next available cone. They do not complete the stations in any particular order; however, they need to remember which ones they have already completed. (The teacher may provide a way for them to record which ones they've done, or they may be asked to remember.) Students need to return the egg (with activity inside) and the duck to their original positions for the next partners. The duck may specify the number of times to do the activity or specify other conditions for performing the activity.

Sample egg activities and duck directions:

EGG ACTIVITY	DUCK DIRECTIONS
Jumping jacks (inside hands joined)	Ten times
Modified sit-ups	As many as you can
Squat thrusts	Ten as fast as you can
Run (inside hands joined) and touch every wall in the room	As fast as you can
Wall push-ups	Three sets of ten
Crab-walk	Length of the gym
Make funny faces at your partner	Three different faces
Jump rope (with pretend rope)	For two minutes
Grapevine step (one hand joined)	Length of gym floor
Modified floor push-ups	As many as you can

Closing Activity: Challenge Chat

Students sit in a circle. Discuss how they remembered which stations they had completed (location in the gym, number on the cone, etc.). Discuss the ability of partners to work together effectively.

Student Assessment

- Teacher observation of students' ability to follow instructions
- Teacher observation of partners working together
- Teacher observation of partners making the station ready for the partners who will come next
- Peer assessment (during ending activity) of how students worked with their partner
- Monitor heart rate at least twice during the lesson (take ten-second heart rate counts)

Success for All

Select egg activities and duck directions that are appropriate for all students, or place several alternative cones in the gym area. Students can self-select to go to these cones as a replacement for cone activities they are unable to perform.

Classroom Activity: Human Letters

Designate groups of three members each. *Copy the pages of human letters in Appendix D,* mount them on construction paper, and laminate them for greater durability. Then cut around the square for each letter so you end up with a deck of cards. The group leader draws a card from the deck. The other group members have to use their body to make the letter the way it is on the card. The leader determines (evaluates) whether group members have performed correctly and provides feedback to group members who have performed incorrectly. The card is placed back in the deck. A new group leader draws another card and the activity continues.

Game developed by Rick Pappas and printed with permission.

Lesson 2.4   Partner Punt, Pass, and Kick

NASPE Standards 1, 2, and 5

Lesson Objectives

- Students will be able to dribble proficiently with feet.
- Students will be able to successfully perform a punt (as in soccer) or clear kick one out of five tries.
- Students will be able to recognize colors and numbers.
- Students will be able to work with an assigned partner.

Equipment Needed

Poly spots of different colors, cones of different colors, playground or soccer balls

Activity Descriptions

Introductory and Fitness Activity: Dynamic Balance

Children, scattered in general space, perform the following activities on command. Have them perform on a soft surface (on grass or on an indoor mat). Always land with feet together.

- Jump and land in a squat position.
- Jump and do the splits in the air (spread legs wide to the sides) before landing.
- Jump and spread legs wide (front to back).
- Jump and clap hands in front and back of body before landing.
- Jump and make a quarter turn in the air before landing (also do half turns and full turns).
- Do a seal walk (progressing anywhere in general space—do not interfere with others). On signal, find a partner and do a high five (while in seal walk position). Repeat to develop arm strength (finding a different partner each time). Students can do high fives with the right or left hand.
- Jump and touch your knees while in the air.
- Jump and touch your toes while in the air.
- Jump and clap your hands under your legs.
- Do a crab-walk (progressing anywhere in general space). On signal, find a partner and do a high five with your foot. Repeat to develop arm strength. Find a different partner each time. Students can do high fives with the right or left foot.

Lesson Focus: Partner Punt, Pass, and Kick

Color Dribble   Dribble the ball with your feet around or near a specified color cone; then dribble to the same color of spot. On cue, move to a different cone and spot. Repeat several times. Continue to move the ball in between cues.

Goalie Kick and Punt   In soccer, the goalie can "clear" the ball from the goal area by either kicking or punting the ball. This drill allows students to practice those skills. Have students stand in two lines, facing each other, 20 feet apart; partners are directly across from each other. Partners take turns being the goalie. The student who is not the goalie rolls the ball to the goalie. The goalie controls the ball and makes a strong "clearing" kick back to the partner (five consecutive times). Then partners change roles. Do the same drill again, but have the goalie "clear" with a punt back to the partner.

Partner Dribble and Pass   Partners move down the field, dribbling and passing to each other. One partner begins dribbling while the other runs alongside (actually slightly ahead). On a signal from the teacher, the person dribbling passes to his or her partner. Continue dribbling and passing (on signal) the entire length of the field. When students become somewhat proficient in this drill, add a defensive player who tries to take the ball away as the two partners are moving the ball down the field.

Closing Activity: Technique Talk

Students sit in a circle. Discuss the technique for performing a clear kick and punt. Discuss what constitutes a good clear kick or punt.

Student Assessment

- Teacher observation to determine how long students can maintain seal walk and crab-walk positions
- Teacher observation checklist (with scoring rubric) to record skill proficiency in punting and kicking (see Appendix B)
- Teacher observation to determine whether students respected their partners

Success for All

- Be sure cone colors are visible for color-blind students.
- Use beeper balls when performing the lesson focus activities with visually impaired students.
- Make the cone activity more difficult by placing numbers on each cone and using math problems (addition, etc.) to determine which number of cone to dribble toward.

■ Make numbers on cones large enough for visually impaired students to see them, or provide a partner for these students.

Classroom Activity: Animal Movement Cards

Push desks to the middle or to one side of the room. In the space provided, have the children move as the following animals: alligator, bird, chicken, duck, elephant, frog, gorilla, hippopotamus, iguana, jellyfish, kangaroo, lion, moose, newt, opossum, penguin, quail, rabbit, seal, tiger, unicorn whale, vulture, wolf, xenu, yak, and zebra. *Copy, mount on construction paper, and laminate the animal pictures in Appendix D.* Show the animal picture as the cue for the students to perform.

Developed by Rick Pappas and printed with permission.

Lesson 2.5 Group Juggling

NASPE Standards 1 and 5

Lesson Objectives

- Students will be able to perform juggling skills while in groups of six students (to develop cooperation).
- Students will be able to improve their group juggling time (to improve hand-eye coordination).

Equipment Needed

Various objects for tossing, foam balls, scarves, pinnies

Activity Descriptions

Introductory and Fitness Activity: Ball Tag

Name several students to be "it." Have them wear pinnies so everyone knows they are "it." Give six students who are *not* "it" a ball (it could be a football, basketball, or any other ball as long as it is a foam version). If you get tagged by someone wearing a pinnie, stop running and raise your hands. One of the students with a ball calls out your name and throws the ball to you. If you catch it, you are back in the game. If not, you stay put until someone else with a ball calls your name. If a ball is on the ground, any player who has not been tagged can pick it up and run with it.

Lesson Focus: Juggling

Group Ball Juggle Form groups of six students each. Each group stands in a circle formation. Try to keep the objects in your group moving. First start with two objects; then add objects as group members improve their skill. The objects must be tossed underhand and follow the same pattern each time. The items need to move continuously; this is not a game of catch. Toss a variety of objects (hoops, Frisbees, balls, rings, individual-sized milk cartons, etc.). Time how long the group can juggle without letting an object drop to the floor. Work to improve the group's score.

Scarf Juggle Review individual scarf skills (each student has one scarf). Have students do the following:

- Toss to self, catch underhand, toss right, catch left, then toss left, catch right.
- Same as above except catch overhand (grab scarf with a downward, overhand motion that snatches the scarf from the air).

Group Scarf Juggle Designate groups of six students each. Each group stands in a circle formation. On a signal from the teacher, each child tosses a scarf up, then takes a step (one space) to the right and catches the scarf thrown by the person on the right. Continue until you get back to your own scarf (called a round). Try to improve the number of times the entire group successfully catches during each round. Do rounds using only left hand, only right hand, or right and left hand in order. Do rounds designating the type of catch (underhand or overhand).

Closing Activity: Behavior Blurb

Students sit in a circle. Students verbally identify the behaviors that demonstrate cooperation in a group setting.

Student Assessment

- Conduct a class discussion to determine whether students know the behaviors that demonstrate cooperation.
- Allow peers to assess the group's ability to cooperate (use a scoring rubric).

Success for All

- Alter group size in the group juggles to make the tasks easier or more difficult.
- Perform the activities sitting down, in chairs, standing on the floor, or on old tires.

Scarf juggling: Students can build hand-eye coordination by practicing a variety of juggling moves.

Classroom Activity: Juggling

Move the desks to the center of the room and place children around the perimeter. Each child has two scarves. Have students practice the same skills as in the physical education lesson. In addition, have them practice the following skills:

- Toss high, touch the floor, then catch the scarf.
- Toss low and catch before the scarf hits the floor.
- Toss high and clap as many times as you can before you have to catch the scarf before it touches the floor.

- Toss high, turn around in place, then catch the scarf.
- Toss two scarves at the same time, catching with the same hand that tossed.
- Juggle two scarves (toss two scarves, one after the other, and catch each scarf with the hand that did not toss it). The pattern is toss, toss, catch, catch. Continue that pattern.
- Juggle three scarves.

Lesson 2.6 Fitness Fun

NASPE Standards 1, 4, and 5

Lesson Objectives

- Students will be able to maintain an increased heart rate throughout the lesson (to improve fitness levels).
- Students will be able to dribble a tennis ball with the foot in a competitive situation (to improve foot-eye coordination).
- Students will demonstrate respect for their teammates.
- Students will calculate their team's score using mental addition (to improve math skills).
- Students will be able to perform the locomotor skills.

Equipment Needed

Tennis balls, hoops, bowling pins and balls, funny hats and masks

Activity Descriptions

Introductory Activity: Loco Locomotor Skills

Make copies of the Loco Locomotor hats in Appendix D. Mount them on heavier paper or poster board (you could also laminate them for greater durability). Make a band that will go around your head out of construction paper or other heavy paper. Glue or staple the band to the hat so it will stay on your head. Tell children that when they see you wearing the hat, they are to perform the locomotor skill that is indicated.

Developed by Rick Pappas and printed with permission.

Lesson Focus and Fitness Activities: Tennis Ball Take and Team Bowling

Tennis Ball Take   The class is divided into five or six teams (with three to four members on each team). Each team is at a hoop. On the teacher's signal, the first player runs to the middle of the play area and brings back a tennis ball using only her or his feet. That player high-fives the next person in line, who then does the same. This continues until all of the tennis balls are taken. Count the team's tennis balls for your first score, return the balls, and try again to beat your own team's score.

Team Bowling   Designate new teams of four members each (or have students group themselves into new teams). Have each team set up the bowling pins (as in a regulation game) for their group. Each team has one ball. Three team members then line up single file behind a sideline (facing their bowling pins). One team member stands by the team's bowling pins (to retrieve the rolled ball). On the teacher's signal, players with the ball (one on each team) roll the balls toward the pins. The player who just rolled runs to replace the player who was behind the pins. That player also counts the number of pins knocked down and resets them. That player also announces the number of pins knocked down, as each player must keep a mental running score total for their team. The person who started behind the pins retrieves the ball and runs it back to the player next in line, who then rolls the ball. This action continues for a designated period of time. The goal is to see how many pins can be knocked down by the team within the time limit. Repeat to see if the team can improve its score. Each player records (on paper) the team total he or she mentally calculated for each time period.

Closing Activity: Concept Cues

Students sit in a circle. Review how to accurately take an exercise heart rate and how to calculate heartbeats per minute from a ten-second count.

Student Assessment

- For dribbling with feet, use the rubric in Appendix B.
- Use the teacher observation checklist for respecting others on your team.
- Monitor heart rate at least twice during the lesson (using a ten-second count).
- View mental math records to determine who might need further practice.

Success for All

- Challenge children to perform locomotor skills backward, in specific patterns, or with a partner (if just moving forward is too easy).
- Use other items besides tennis balls to retrieve during Tennis Ball Take.
- Award a variety of point values to the different equipment in Tennis Ball Take so students complete mental math in order to determine their score.
- Increase or decrease the time for Team Bowling depending on the mental math skills of the students.

Classroom Activity: Carpet Squares

Scatter 25 carpet squares throughout the room (one for each child in the class). *Copy, mount on construction paper, and laminate the Carpet Square pages in Appendix D.* Randomly place a numbered page on each carpet square. Children (alone or in small groups) read the activity sheet, do the activity, and then move to the next square. Have them move from one to two, two to three, and so on. Begin the rotation by assigning each child or group to a different carpet square (one child or group per square).

Developed by Rick Pappas and printed with permission.

Lesson 2.7 Basketball Teamwork

NASPE Standards 1, 2, 4, and 5

Lesson Objectives

- Students will be able to correctly shoot and pass a basketball.
- Students will be able to cooperate with team members.
- Students will maintain an increased heart rate during the first half of the lesson.
- Students will be able to describe the correct technique for passing and shooting.

Equipment Needed

Basketballs (junior-high size, regulation hardness or Nerf), basketball goals (lowered, if possible), and hula hoops

Activity Descriptions

Introductory and Fitness Activity: Math Shapes

Copy, mount on construction paper, and laminate the math shapes (triangle, square, pentagon, hexagon, heptagon, octagon) in Appendix D. Each shape page also indicates the number of sides for each figure and a locomotor skill. Scatter the laminated figures on the gym floor. Designate partners. Partners may begin at any figure. Partners touch the same number of walls in the gym as there are number of sides in the figure. Partners move to the walls using the locomotor pattern designated on the laminated page. After beginning, partners find the figure with the next higher number and continue the process until they have touched walls for each of the laminated pages.

Developed by Rick Pappas and printed with permission.

Lesson Focus: Basketball Teamwork

Dribble, Pivot, and Pass Designate groups of three members each. Members of the group stand in a single file behind the sideline. The first team member has a basketball, dribbles forward to a designated line, stops, pivots to face team members, passes back to the next team member, and then returns (runs) to the end of the team's line. The next team member repeats the pattern. Continue as needed to practice dribbling and passing skills.

Snatch Basketball Divide the class into four teams. Put two teams on a line at one end of the gym and the other two teams on a line at the opposite end of the gym. Give each player a number. Each team member is numbered starting with 1 until each has a number. Four basketballs or playground balls are in a hula hoop in the middle of the room. The teacher calls a number. The player with that number runs to get a ball, dribbles to one of the two basketball hoops in the gym, and shoots for a basket. All four players continue to shoot until at least one of them makes a basket. At that time, all four players return the balls to the hoop, and run to their spot in line.

Closing Activity: Technique Talk

Students sit in a circle. Discuss the correct technique for passing and shooting a basketball.

Student Assessment

- Teacher observation can determine which students are not consistently able to make a basket when shooting.
- Using a scoring rubric (see Appendix B) for dribbling, assess the skill level of each child.
- In their journal, while in their classroom, have students describe the technique for passing and shooting.

Success for All

- Call two numbers, make a pass with your teammate, and then make one basket and return to your spot.
- Call a number, make a pass to each person in your team's line, make a basket, and return.
- Instead of calling numbers, give the children mental math problems whose answer indicates which student goes.
- Allow those with less developed skill levels to shoot at a lower basket or with a smaller ball.

Classroom Activity: Trash Can Shoot

Move the desks to one side of the room. Set up at least four trash cans at which children can shoot sheets of paper that they have wadded up into a ball. Before wadding up the paper, have students write their name on the paper. Everyone shoots ten wadded balls. Retrieve balls and see who makes the most baskets. Have students write in their journals describing the correct technique for shooting and passing a basketball.

Lesson 2.8 Team Spelling

NASPE Standards 1 and 5

Lesson Objectives

- Students will be able to correctly spell words they create by using letters jumbled from a sentence.
- Students will be able to recognize words that can be jumbled from a sentence.
- Students will be able to perform a grand right and left (to improve coordination).
- Students will be able to dance with various partners.

Equipment Needed

Letter sets; a chalkboard or a dry erase board; record, audiotape, or CD with "Bingo" music; and a music player

Activity Descriptions

Introductory and Fitness Activity: "Bingo" (Dance Mixer)

Children stand in a single circle holding hands. Designate partners. One partner wears a pinnie and stands to the right of the partner not wearing a pinnie. Children sing the words to "Bingo" while performing.

For the grand right and left, partners turn to face each other and join right hands. They walk past each other (with right hands still joined), then give the left hand to the next child being met. Continue passing right, left, right, and so on. On each pass, yell the letters B-I-N-G-O. When "O" is yelled, the person you're facing is your new partner. Be sure the partner wearing the pinnie is standing to the right of the partner not wearing the pinnie. Then repeat the dance.

Lesson Focus: See and Spell

Divide the class into small groups of three or four at the most. Write a sentence or statement on the board. Put letters and other objects with letters on them randomly on the floor. Specify what locomotor pattern children should use. On the teacher's signal, one person from each team moves in the specified locomotor pattern and picks up one letter, returns to the team, high-fives the next person, and that person goes to get one letter. This continues until the teacher gives the cue to stop. Teams are trying to spell words that can be spelled by using letters jumbled from the sentence on the board. After the cue to stop, count the number of words that your team spelled. Try to improve your team's score. Go again.

Closing Activity: Respect Rap

Students sit in a circle. Discuss how respect for others is shown while doing group and partner rhythmic activities.

Student Assessment

- Have each team record the words spelled on a sheet of paper so that after class the teacher may assess the number and quality (number of letters in the word and correctly spelled words) of the words spelled.
- Using a scoring rubric, observe how team members work together during See and Spell.
- Observe who can and cannot correctly perform the grand right and left at least once around the circle.

Success for All

- Walk (instead of skip) for the dance mixer "Bingo."
- Instead of locomotor patterns, move on scooters in different ways during See and Spell. The body can

"BINGO" (DANCE MIXER) ACTION	MEASURES	"BINGO" WORDS TO SING
Skip right eight times.	1–2	A big black dog sat on the back porch and Bingo was his name.
Skip left eight times.	3–4	A big black dog sat on the back porch and Bingo was his name.
Skip (four times) to center of circle, bringing arms up overhead.	5–8	B-I-N-G-O
Skip (four times) back out, bringing arms down.	9–10	B-I-N-G-O
Repeat skip in.	11–12	B-I-N-G-O
Repeat skip out.	13–14	And Bingo was his name.
Grand right and left.	15–16	B-I-N-G-O (yell loud)

be in different positions: kneeling, sitting, prone, or supine. Students can move using force from feet, hands, or both.

- Place letters on tables or milk crates for See and Spell.
- Place restrictions on the See and Spell game, such as the words spelled have to contain four or more letters, or have students spell the weekly words they are learning in their classroom.

Classroom Activity: P.E. Bingo

This is played like regular bingo with bingo cards and pieces for placing on the card when your number is called. *Student bingo cards and P.E. pieces may be copied, laminated, and cut from forms in Appendix D. The teacher also has a set of cards (see Appendix D).* Each teacher card contains a number and a physical challenge. The teacher mixes the set of cards and begins calling the number and the challenge as they appear on each successive card. If the number is on a student's card, and the student can successfully perform the challenge, the student may place a P.E. piece on the appropriate square. Students yell out "bingo!" just as in a regular bingo game. Each student will need a beanbag and a scarf to perform the physical challenges. To increase concentration and scanning skills, allow students to watch more than one bingo card at a time.

Developed by Rick Pappas and printed with permission.

Lesson 2.9 Jump Rope Rhymes

NASPE Standards 1, 4, 5, and 6

Lesson Objectives

- Students will be able to jump rope continuously (to improve coordination).
- Students will be able to respect the contributions of all team members.
- Students will be able to create jump rope rhymes.
- Students will be able to maintain an increased heart rate during the entire lesson.

Equipment Needed

Bamboo poles, jump ropes, notebook paper, and pencils

Activity Description

Introductory and Fitness Activity: Tinikling Workout

"Tinikling," a bamboo dance popular in India and the Philippines, involves hopping over and between bamboo poles. Place six sets of bamboo poles in a circle like the spokes of a wheel; space them equally around the circle. Have a place card at each set of poles that cues students what to do at that station (see figure on page 420). Students begin at any set of poles, perform the movement specified—at their own pace—and then move counterclockwise to the next set of poles. Continue until all movements are completed. Students can repeat the activity several times in order to develop physical fitness. When students need a partner, they partner with someone else who is ready to do the same station. Six sets of poles are included in each circle. The number of circles needed depends on the number of students in the class. Enough circles should be present to maximize student participation. Stations include the movements shown in the figure.

Straddle Jump   Face the center of the circle, standing inside the poles, jump twice inside the poles, then jump once outside the poles (straddling them). Repeat ten times.

Cross-Through   Face the center of the circle, right side to the left pole. Hop between the poles on the right foot, hop between the poles on the left foot, hop out of poles with left foot (ending up on the other side of the poles). Now go back through (hop left, hop right, hop left) to where you began. Repeat ten times.

Walk Around   Face the center of the circle, right side to left pole (see figure). Beginning with the right foot, walk

three steps forward, cross through (left, right, left), walk three steps forward again (right, left, right), cross through (left, right, left). Repeat entire walk around five times. The cross-through is performed as described above, except on the last walking step (before each cross-through), pivot toward the poles so the left, right, left hops can be performed between the poles (now facing away from the center of the circle). On the second cross-through, the performer faces toward the center of the circle again.

Straddle Jump with Partner   This is the same as the individual straddle jump except one partner begins facing away from the circle center. So partners are facing each other with hands joined. Partners must coordinate to perform the same movements at the same time.

Cross Through with Partner   This is the same as the regular cross-through. Partners begin by facing each other on opposite sides and ends of the poles (see figure). Partners should be performing together. To coordinate, one partner will need to say "ready, go."

Walk Around with Partner   This is the same as the individual walk around. Partners begin in the same positions as for the partner cross-through (see figure).

Lesson Focus: Let's Go Jumping

Divide the class into teams of four or five members. Give each group four or five short ropes, one sheet of paper, and one pencil. The teacher places a list of topics (i.e., multiplication, addition, weather, holidays, etc.) on the board. Each group selects a topic. The goal is for each group to come up with a rhyme about the selected topic while jumping rope as they create the rhyme. The group will write down the final version of the rhyme. Each group will perform at least one rhyme for the entire class.

For example, this rhyme was created when the selected topic was math:

> We like numbers, quarters, halves, and wholes.
> Learning math is one of our goals.
> Adding, subtracting, multiplying, divide—
> Order of operations is our guide.

Closing Activity: Challenge Chat

Students sit in a circle. Discuss the qualities that made some rhymes more creative than others.

Student Assessment

- The rhyme is read to the class and then performed by the group.

- During the Challenge Chat, students were able to determine the qualities that made some rhymes more creative than others.
- Observe each student's jump rope technique (using a scoring rubric).
- Rate the ability of each team to listen to its members and make collaborative decisions.

Success for All

- Do the lesson focus activity with long ropes.
- Allow groups to create their own topic in the lesson focus activity.
- Perform the introductory activity to music.

Classroom Activity: Tinikling Workout

Place two strips of tape in the classroom aisles between desks. Strips should be the length of the aisle and about two feet apart if possible. Also place several strips in the free space at the front of the room. Have students (individually) practice the straddle jump and cross-through at the lines by their desk. Allow students to move to the lines in the front of the room to practice the walk around.

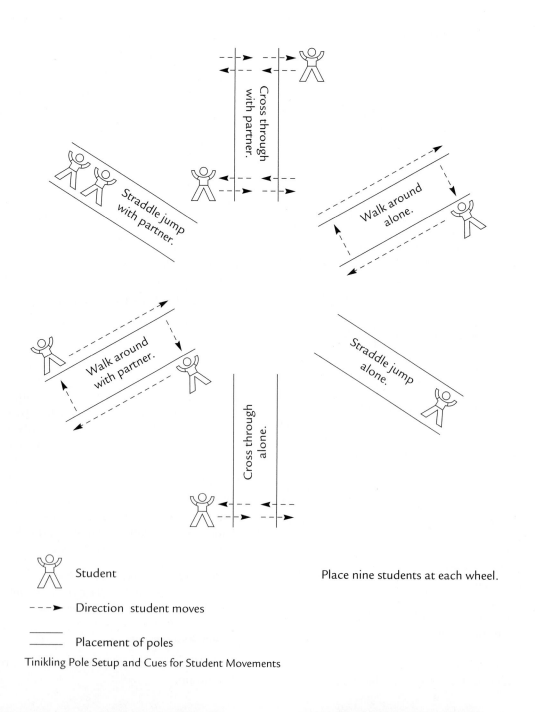

Straddle jump with partner.

Cross through with partner.

Walk around alone.

Walk around with partner.

Straddle jump alone.

Cross through alone.

Student

- - - → Direction student moves

_____ Placement of poles

Place nine students at each wheel.

Tinikling Pole Setup and Cues for Student Movements

Lesson 2.10 Station Rotation

NASPE Standards 1, 4, and 5

Lesson Objectives

- Students will maintain increased heart rate during the introductory activity (to improve physical fitness).
- Students will be able to jump rope (without missing) while saying the alphabet (to develop hand-eye coordination).
- Students will be able to cooperate with group members while performing station activities.
- Students will be able to pin clothespins to the rim of a can (to develop fine motor skills).

Equipment Needed

Short and long jump ropes, clothespins, cans, playground balls

Activity Description

Introductory and Fitness Activity: "Bingo" (Dance Mixer)

This is a repeat of an activity completed in Lesson 2.8. Consult Lesson 2.8 for specifics.

Lesson Focus: Station Rotation

Use the following stations to promote cooperation and respect, hand-eye skills, and improved physical fitness. Designate groups of six students each. Groups rotate every five minutes (upon a signal from the teacher). Be sure that enough equipment is at each station so all students are participating (not waiting their turn).

1. *Short Jump Ropes:* Say your alphabet while you are jumping.

2. *Clothespin the Can Man:* Hook the clothespins to the top rim of a can. How fast can you clip? Remember to use both hands.
3. *Shoot and Spell:* Pick a word from the teacher's list posted on the wall. Shoot a playground ball to a basket, and for each basket made you earn a letter. How many words can you spell?
4. *Egg Beater:* Cross two long jump ropes at the middle so they are perpendicular to each other. Four students turn the ropes as a team while another student tries to jump both ropes in the middle.

Closing Activity: Respect Rap

Students sit in a circle. Students identify the respectful, cooperative, and helpful behaviors they displayed while performing the station work.

Student Assessment

The teacher records the number and kinds of cooperative skills displayed by group members during the station activities.

Success for All

- Add more stations.
- Any station activity can be altered for the individual needs of the students in the class.

Classroom Activity: Jacks

Have a set of jacks (regular size or large size) for each student. See Appendix C for how to play jacks.

Lesson 2.11 Lummi Stick Partners

NASPE Standards 1, 4, and 5

Lesson Objectives

- Students will be able to maintain an increased heart rate during the introductory activity (to promote cardiorespiratory fitness).
- Students will demonstrate respect for their partner during Partner Tag and Lummi Stick Partners (to enhance teamwork between partners).
- Students will be able to perform a simple Lummi stick routine in time to music (to improve hand-eye coordination and fine motor skills).

Equipment Needed

Playground balls or other objects that can be thrown, music, music player, Lummi sticks (set for each student)

Activity Description

Introductory and Fitness Activity: Partner Tag

Designate partners. Partners toss an object back and forth to each other. On the teacher's signal, the one that has the object tries to tag the other person. On the cue "freeze," they continue tossing. Have students change partners if time permits. You could use music as the cue; then partners would throw when the music is playing and tag when the music has stopped.

Lesson Focus: Lummi Sticks

Lummi Stick Warm-up   Have a set of sticks for each student. Have the students do the following:

- Tap (repeat) the sound patterns the teacher makes.
- Tap the floor.
- Tap sticks together above your head.
- Tap sticks together under one lifted leg.
- Tap sticks together behind both legs.

- Do a simple routine:
  —Tap sticks together in front of body (two times).
  —Tap sticks together above head (two times).
  —Tap left shoulder (two times).
  —Tap right shoulder (two times)
  —Repeat.
- Set the routine to music.

Lummi Stick Partners   Teach and have the students perform any of the Lummi stick routines on a purchased album, audiotape, or CD such as "Lively Music for Lummi Stick Fun."

Closing Activity: Respect Rap

Students sit in a circle. Discuss how to work with partners of varying ability levels (respecting difference in the ability levels of others).

Student Assessment

- Observe to determine whether students can tap Lummi sticks in time with the music while performing a specific sequence of movements in correct order.
- Observe student behaviors during partner work.

Success for All

- Use specific passes while playing Partner Tag.
- Throw different objects for Partner Tag.
- Designate partners with similar abilities for Partner Tag and for the Lummi stick routine.
- Sets of partners could practice the Lummi stick routine without music.

Classroom Activity: Lummi Sticks

Teach a different Lummi stick routine from "Lummi Stick Fun."

Lesson 2.12 Taking Turns

NASPE Standards 1, 4, and 5

Lesson Objectives

- Students will be able to articulate strategies for effectively playing Flag Tag (to promote strategic thinking).
- Students will be able to honor the rules for playing Flag Tag and Four-Square (to encourage good sportsmanship when taking turns).
- Students will be able to play Four-Square without continually chasing the ball (to improve striking skills in a game that can be played during outdoor recess periods).

Equipment Needed

Flags (enough for each student to have two), playground balls, and tape or chalk to mark four Four-Square courts (if class contains about 24 students)

Activity Descriptions

Introductory and Fitness Activity: Flag Tag

Everyone has two flags, one attached to a Velcro belt around the waist and the other in one hand. Have students try to pull other students' flags while at the same time not getting their flag pulled. Players hold pulled flags in their hand. If players lose a flag and have an extra one in their hand, they can place it on their belt. Players try to collect as many flags as possible. Students are still in the game even if they lose both of their original flags.

Lesson Focus: Four-Square

Make Four-Square courts on the gym floor with gym tape, or use chalk to draw the courts on the playground (if not already permanently marked). Directions for making the squares and rules for playing Four-Square can be found in Appendix C.

Closing Activity: Respect Rap

Students sit in a circle. Discuss how to fairly take turns in various games that students play during recess.

Student Assessment

Using a scoring rubric, determine whether students take turns as the rules specify and whether they do so in a sportsmanlike manner.

Success for All

- Use larger balls (beach balls or playground balls) for students not competent at catching.
- Add objects in the squares to change the bounce of the ball (beanbags, rings, etc.).
- Play Four-Square with different types of balls, as they bounce differently (e.g., volleyball, basketball, playground ball, foam ball) and different sizes of balls.

Classroom Activity: Lummi Sticks

Designate partners or groups of three members each. Each student has a set of Lummi sticks. Have each group create its own routine (with or without music).

Lesson 2.13 Rhythm Time

NASPE Standards 1 and 4

Lesson Objectives

- Students will be able to complete at least one sentence strip correctly in a smooth manner (to improve cross-lateral movement and large-muscle coordination).
- Students will be able to perform the "La Raspa" pattern at least once in time with the music (to enhance rhythm and movement skills and to improve large-muscle coordination).
- Students will be able to dance with an assigned partner.

Equipment Needed

Sentence strips with arrows drawn on them, music or a metronome to keep the beat, "La Raspa" music, music player

Activity Descriptions

Introductory and Fitness Activity: Which Way Do I Point?

On construction paper or strips of butcher paper, draw a series of arrows pointing in different directions (see figure): up, down, left, and right. These are called sentence strips. Make different sentence strips (with different arrow patterns) and post them on the walls around the gym. Children use their arms and hands as pointers, pointing in the direction the arrows indicate. The trick is to shift the pointers (hands and arms) in a smooth, even manner (with no hesitations); thus using a metronome or music helps keep the students in rhythm. Do the arrow sequence in order and continue repeating until the music stops. Rotate so eventually all students have completed all the strips. Then do the strips again and add a jumping pattern (jump, bounce, jump, bounce), like jumping a long rope. Keeping with the jump pattern, again use your pointers to follow the arrow sequences. Try to point in the direction opposite the arrows while *not* performing a jumping pattern. Then try to point in the direction opposite the arrows while performing a jumping pattern.

Lesson Focus: "La Raspa" (Folk Dance)

- Teach students to perform the Bleking step individually, then with a partner. One Bleking step (to the right) is as follows: Hop on left foot while extending

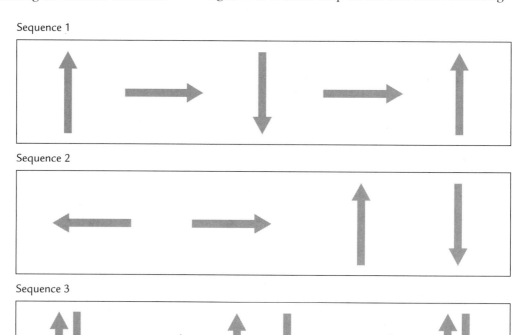

Arrow Sequences on Sentence Strips for "Which Way Do I Point?"

right heel to the front, hop on right foot while extending left heel to the front, hop on left foot while extending right heel to the front.

- Review the right elbow swing: Partners perform a right elbow swing by joining right elbows and skipping around in a circle (pivoting in place). Doing the same movement with the left elbows joined is a left elbow swing.
- Designate partners and have them stand facing each other. Partner sets may be scattered throughout the room. Perform "La Raspa" (a folk dance from Mexico).

ACTION	MEASURES
One Bleking step. Repeat three times, alternating lead foot.	1–4
Repeat above sequence three more times.	5–16
Right elbow swing	17–20
Left elbow swing	21–24
Repeat right and left elbow swings.	25–32
Repeat all of the above until the music ends.	

Closing Activity: Concept Cues

Students sit in a circle. Discuss why "Which Way Do I Point?" is so difficult.

Student Assessment

- Observe and record who can follow the arrows and stay in an even tempo during introductory activity.
- Using a scoring rubric, observe the performance of "La Raspa."
- Observe partners' ability to work effectively together to learn "La Raspa."

Success for All

- Use strips with two arrows for the introductory activity.
- For the introductory activity, point with Lummi sticks or other objects.
- For "La Raspa," partners hold hands during the Bleking steps.
- For "La Raspa," at times place students who have excellent rhythm skills with partners who may need help.

Classroom Activity: "La Raspa"

Have students partner with someone who sits next to them in the classroom. Partners stand in the aisle by their desks to perform.

Lesson 2.14 Large Group Fun

NASPE Standards 1, 4, and 5

Lesson Objectives

- Students will be able to list the names of the presidents of the United States and the order in which they served.
- Students will be able to maintain an increased heart rate during the introductory activity (to improve physical fitness).
- Students will be able to work cooperatively to successfully perform the Caterpillar Walk and Skin the Snake across the play area.

Equipment Needed

Pictures of each president (with name and number), activity and exercise cards

Activity Descriptions

Introductory and Fitness Activity: Warm Up with the Presidents

Find pictures of all the presidents of the United States. Under each picture, write the president's name and succession number; for example, under Truman's picture you would write "Harry S. Truman, 33" (because he was the 33rd president). Laminate the pictures for increased durability. Place the pictures in a large circle around the perimeter of the gym. By each picture place the name (or picture) of an exercise to be performed. Place students at the various stations (a station being a picture and an exercise) to begin the warm-up. Students perform the indicated exercise the number of times to match the president's succession number (e.g., since John Tyler was the tenth president, the activity by his picture would be repeated ten times). Students progress around the stations moving counterclockwise until they have completed all the stations. Students may move to the next station whenever they have completed the previous one. (Exercises might include arm circles, jumping jacks, walk like an Egyptian, hop on one foot, heel clicks, jump in place, treadmill, coffee grinder, straddle stretches [hold each for ten seconds], jump rope, seal crawl, ankle circles, modified push-ups, bent-knee sit-ups, squat thrust, skipping around the inside of the circle, running the inside of the circle, etc.)

Lesson Focus: Large Group Fun

Caterpillar Walk Divide the class into two groups. Within groups, designate partners. Partners stand facing each other in a double line. Partners join hands and hold them high overhead (as in London Bridge). Begin at one end of the gym. The last couples (the two partner sets standing closest to the gym wall) walk under their team's arms to become the first couple. Immediately following the last couple, the next couple walks through, and so on. The "caterpillar" moves quickly and cooperatively until the entire line has reached the opposite wall. This activity can be repeated to move back down the gym floor again (to the original wall).

Caterpillar Walk: Pairs of students move through the tunnel created by their classmates' arms, moving the "caterpillar" across the playground or gym.

Skin the Snake The class remains divided into two groups. Each group can have 20 to 25 students if necessary. Members of each group stand in a single file with legs spread apart. Members reach between their legs to join hands with the player in front of them (with the right hand) and the player behind them (with the left hand). You are ready to begin when everyone (except

Skin the Snake: With hands joined, students do a backward straddle walk as the person at the end of the line lies down. When all students are lying down, the pattern reverses, with students standing up and performing a forward straddle walk.

the players at the end of the lines) has both hands joined. On the teacher's signal, the last player in line lies down on her or his back. The person in front of that player backs up, walks by straddling the first player's body, and lies down behind the first player. This continues with the entire team doing a backward straddle walk (with hands still joined) until the first player in line is lying on the floor (or grass). After having lain down completely (with head touching the floor), the first player gets up and begins a straddle walk forward, pulling everyone else up so eventually all players are back in their original position.

A. Fluegelman, ed., *The New Games Book* (San Francisco: Headlands Press, 1976).

Closing Activity: Concept Cues

Students individually complete a work sheet on which the presidents' photos are displayed. Students are to name the president and indicate his succession number.

Student Assessment

- Assess students' physical fitness during the warm-up activity by stopping periodically to take pulse rates to determine how many students are in their training zone.
- Written assessment during the lesson's ending activity (face recognition of presidents and knowledge of succession number)
- Observe and record group members' cooperative behaviors.

Success for All

- Vary the exercises in the introductory activity.
- For the introductory activity, assign partners to students who might not be able to follow the directions.
- During the Large Group Fun activities, it is the responsibility of the group members to help all students successfully perform the activity. Group members determine when help is needed and how to provide it.

Classroom Activity: Lummi Stick Circle

Push the desks to the center of the room. Have students sit (crossed-legged) in a large circle around the desks. Each student has a set of Lummi sticks. Have students perform the following activities (all students are doing the same thing at the same time):

- The teacher taps various patterns on the floor with a stick or sticks and then students tap the same pattern.
- Do the "Shoemaker's Dance" with Lummi sticks, first without music (just with verbal cues from teacher), and then with the music:
  - Wind the bobbin (roll sticks in front of body).
  - Pull the thread (pull sticks back to the side).
  - Clap, clap, clap (right stick taps top of left stick).
  - Tap, tap, tap (left stick taps top of right stick).
  - Skips (hammer own shoes with sticks).
- Create and perform patterns (to verbal cues):
  - Tap sticks together four times in front of you around in a circle (counts 1–4), tap the floor four times (counts 5–8), then tap shoulders four times (counts 9–12). Repeat many times. Perform to music.
  - Designate partners and allow them to create patterns the entire group can perform. Then perform the patterns.
- Create and perform patterns in which children pass sticks around the circle:
  - Using only one stick per student (placed in right hand), tap the floor (count 1); pass stick to the right (count 2); with the left hand, take the stick that is being passed to you (count 3); move the stick from the left hand to the right (count 4). Keep repeating the sequence as the sticks move counterclockwise around the circle. Emphasize everyone staying in rhythm. All the taps (count 1) should occur at once. Have the students count beats with you.
  - Repeat the above sequence except pass the sticks clockwise instead of counterclockwise.

Lesson 2.15 Follow the Bouncing Ball

NASPE Standards 1, 4, and 5

Lesson Objectives

- Students will be able to bounce and catch two balls at the same time (right to right and left to left) at least five consecutive times (to increase proficiency in hand-eye coordination).
- Students will be able to bounce and catch (with no mistakes) during at least one rhyme (to promote rhythmic patterning).
- Students will be able to practice partner bounce-and-catch skills without becoming frustrated (to promote partner cooperation).
- Students will maintain an increased heart rate during the introductory activity.

Equipment Needed

Balls (tennis or racket), music or a metronome to keep the beat, and flag belts

Activity Descriptions

Introductory and Fitness Activity:
Catch the Dragon's Tail
Designate teams with four members each. Team members are in a single file, all facing the same direction, holding on to each other's waist. Place a tail in the last player's back pocket (or tucked in the waistline of pants, or use a belt with a flag on it). The dragon's head (the first player in line) must try to catch its own tail. The remaining team members try to prevent the dragon from catching its own tail. (Be sure to stress safety—students must remain standing during this tag game.)

Lesson Focus: Ball Progressions

Ball Progression with One Person

1. Bounce and catch one ball, right hand, *palm up.*
2. Bounce and catch one ball, left hand, *palm up.*
3. Bounce and catch one ball, right to left, left to right.
4. Use a rhyme:
   Diddle diddle dumpling, my son John.
   Went to bed with his trousers on.
   One shoe off and one shoe on.
   Diddle diddle dumpling, my son John.
5. Bounce with right, catch with left, pass to right.

6. Bounce with left, catch with right, pass to left. Use this rhyme:
   Hickory dickory dock,
   The mouse ran up the clock.
   The clock struck one,
   The mouse ran down.
   Hickory dickory dock.
7. Bounce two balls at the same time, right to right and left to left.
8. Bounce two balls at the same time, right to right and left to left, with a rhyme:
   Jack and Jill went up the hill
   To fetch a pail of water.
   Jack fell down and broke his crown
   And Jill came tumbling after.
9. Bounce and catch two balls in one hand.
10. Bounce and catch two balls in one hand, with a rhyme:
    Baa, baa black sheep,
    Have you any wool?
    Yes sir, yes sir, three bags full.
    One for my master,
    One for my dame,
    One for the little boy
    Who lives down the lane.
11. Bounce and catch three balls.

Ball Progression with Two People

1. Bounce and catch right to right.
2. Bounce and catch left to left.
3. Bounce right to left and pass to right.
4. Bounce left to right and pass to left.
5. Bounce right to left; pass around the back to right.
6. Bounce left to right; pass around the back to left.
7. Repeat sequence with two balls (one for each partner).
8. With two balls each, bounce right to left and pass to right.
9. Bounce left to right and back to left.
10. Pass right to left; pass around the back to right.
11. Pass left to right; pass around the back to left.
12. Pass both balls at the same time; one partner must toss high and the other low so the balls do not collide in midair.

Another rhyme to try:

Humpty-Dumpty sat on a wall,
Humpty-Dumpty had a great fall.
All the King's horses and all the King's men
Couldn't put Humpty-Dumpty together again.

Closing Activity: Technique Talk

Students complete a self-assessment checklist on their ball-handling skills as demonstrated in the activities today.

Student Assessment

- Using a scoring rubric, observe students' ball-handling skills.
- Students assess their own ball-handling skills using the same rubrics the teacher used.

Success for All

- Use playground balls.
- Toss and catch with beanbags.
- Have students move through the skill progression as their abilities allow.

Classroom Activity: Partner Stunts

Push the desks to one side of the room. Designate partners. Have them perform the following partner stunts. Be sure to emphasize safety and indicate how partners are to protect each other. If the classroom movement area is too small, these activities would best be performed on a grassy area outdoors, so when children fall, they will not get hurt.

- *Partner Walk:* Partners should be approximately the same weight and height. Partners face each other and grasp forearms. One partner stands on the feet of the other partner. Partners then walk forward. Try walking backward. Partners switch positions and perform walk again.
- *Partner Hop:* Partners stand side by side, place inside arms around each other's waists, lift both inside feet, and hop around the area. Variations (shown in the photos): Partners stand back-to-back; both lift the right leg backward so partner can grab the ankle, hop around the area. Partners stand facing each other. Both lift the right leg up (with knee bent), and the partner holds the lifted leg. Hop around the area.
- *Balance Sit:* This is an individual stunt; however, if your partner assists you while you learn, you'll learn to do it in a shorter amount of time. Stand and hold both arms straight out in front of you at shoulder level. Extend your right leg straight out in front of you and balance. In this balanced position, slowly lower your body by bending your left knee, until you

Partner Walk: Students walk forward and backward while one partner stands with feet on top of the other partner's feet.

Partner Hop: Partners stand facing each other with right legs lifted up. Partners hold each other's lifted leg and hop around the area.

Variation on the Partner Hop: Students stand back-to-back, grab each other's left ankle, and hop around the activity area.

are sitting on your left leg. Be sure to keep your back straight as you lower your body. Go up and down as many times as you can. As you are learning, use your partner to maintain your balance.

- *Jump from Knees:* This is an individual stunt, but have your partner assist you in learning it. Kneel on the grass (or mat) and place body weight on your knees, shins, and the arches of your feet. Try to keep your back straight and head erect as your arms swing forward and up. Using the arm momentum, lift your feet from under you and place them on the grass; then stand up.

Balance Sit: Students try to keep their balance as they lower themselves from a standing position with back straight and arms and one leg extended.

Jump from the Knees: Using the momentum from a forward arm swing, the student moves from a kneeling to a standing position.

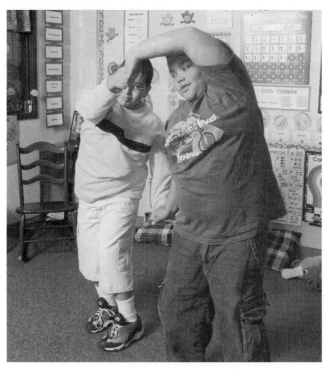

Wring the Dishrag: Holding hands overhead, students turn a circle in place.

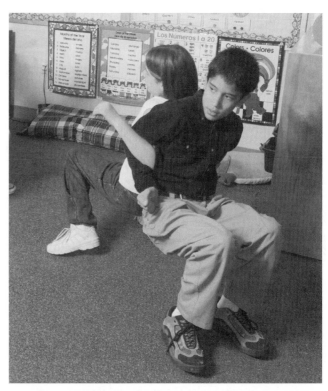

Partner Get-up: Sitting back-to-back with elbows hooked, partners stand up together.

■ *Wring the Dishrag:* Partners stand facing each other (fairly close to each other), holding both hands. Hold hands overhead, turning a circle in place (one partner turning to the right and the other to the left). Hold hands loosely as hands may need to turn to be comfortable while completing the circle.

■ *Partner Get-up:* Partners sit back-to-back, hook elbows, and pull knees up to their chest. Place feet shoulder width apart and slightly in front of body. Lean into your partner, push with your feet, and stand up together. Once up, sit down. Continue going up and down. Find another set of partners and do this with four people.

Movement Form: Basic Game Skills

FIFTEEN LESSONS, SOCCER AND FRISBEE, GRADES 5–6
Cindy Chrisman, Isley Elementary, Wichita, Kansas

Classroom activities to correlate with this unit are placed in each lesson plan; however, an additional activity of journal writing may be appropriate. Students make short entries in their journals based on assignments from the teacher. Teachers may use the information gleaned from the entries to better understand the students and better prepare lessons for them. Possible topics for journal entries include the following:

■ After watching a soccer game on television, describe your reactions to the game.

■ Would you like to play soccer outside of the school setting? Why or why not?

■ Do you prefer to play soccer as a competitive game or a recreational game? Why?

■ Do you prefer to play soccer with certain of your classmates? Why or why not?

■ What soccer skills can you perform well? How do you know you perform them well?

Lesson 3.1 Soccer Skills: Circle Kickball

NASPE Standards 1, 4, and 5

Lesson Objectives

- Students will maintain their heart rate in their training zone during the introductory and fitness activities (to improve physical fitness).
- Students will be able to dribble the ball (the length of the field) without a defensive player taking the ball away.
- Students will be able to pass and catch with a partner using correct passing and trapping techniques.

Equipment Needed

Twelve soccer balls (foam or regulation)

Activity Descriptions

Introductory Activity: Partner Tag

Students select a partner of equal ability. One person from each pair will then go stand on a predetermined line. The other students will go find their partner and stand approximately three to four feet in front of her or him. Both lines need to be facing the same direction. On the teacher's signal, the person in back tries to tag the person in front (partners can run anywhere in general space). Be careful not to run into others who are also trying to escape their partner. Partners switch roles and play again. Play each time for about 30 to 45 seconds. Do this activity three or four times.

Fitness Activity: Teacher-Led Exercises

- Twenty-five jumping jacks
- Three toe touches (three times, hold for ten counts)
- Twenty scissors jumps: jump with one foot forward and the other foot in back; then jump and switch. The two jumps together count as one scissors jump (one count).
- Five crunches: lie on your back on the floor, cross arms over chest, and raise head and shoulders off of floor.
- Fifteen push-ups.
- Locomotor skills for five minutes (skipping, galloping, marching, walking, sliding, and jogging). Students can perform the skills with music in the background, if you have music available. Do about 30 seconds of one locomotor skill, then do another. You can go in whatever order you choose.

Lesson Focus: Soccer Skills

Dribbling the Ball Designate partners. One partner moves the ball in a controlled manner with the feet, by either tapping or pushing the ball. Students move the ball over the soccer field and change directions to avoid opponent (their partner). Ideally the ball is contacted with the inside of the foot and kept close to the body to help maintain control. Partners switch roles on the teacher's signal.

Trapping and Passing Trapping is used to stop the ball for whatever reason. Simply pick up your foot and use the full surface of your foot to trap the ball between your foot and the ground. This technique will stop a rolling ball or a ball bouncing below knee level. For passing, use the inside of the foot for best accuracy. This technique can be used for long as well as short distances. The nonkicking foot should be planted next to the ball. The kicking foot should have the toe pointed out so the inside of the foot is actually making contact and moving the ball. Knees should be bent slightly. Partners stand facing each other 20 feet apart, pass to each other, trap the ball with foot, then return the pass to the partner. Continue.

Circle Kickball Designate groups of four or five members each. Each group has a foam soccer ball or regulation soccer ball, depending on the ability of students in the group. Each group forms a circle and places one person in the middle. The object is for the circle players to pass the ball to each other without the person in the center touching the ball (with his or her feet). If the person in the center touches the ball, then the person who passed goes to the center and the center person comes out to the vacant spot on the circle. Emphasize passing to someone not close to the defensive player (the player in center of circle). Emphasize that players must stop (trap) the pass so the ball does not roll out of the circle.

Closing Activity: Technique Talk

Students sit in a circle. Discuss the technique for successfully dribbling the ball so a defensive player cannot take it away.

Student Assessment

- Take ten-second count of heartbeats during the introductory and fitness activities to ascertain whether students are working in their training zone.
- Evaluate passing and trapping skills while partners are practicing (use a checklist with a scoring rubric).

Success for All

- Use foam soccer balls or regulation soccer balls based on the ability and comfort level of students.
- During Circle Kickball, if a student in the middle does not quickly touch the passed ball, rotate someone else into the middle.

- Allow students in wheelchairs (who have use of arms and hands) to perform soccer skills as if they were playing hockey—so these students would be dribbling, passing, and trapping with a shortened hockey stick.

Classroom Activity: Blob Tag

Refer to the Classroom Activity for Lesson 1.5 for a description of Blob Tag.

Lesson 3.2 Soccer Skills: Goalkeeping

NASPE Standards 1, 2, 4, and 5

Lesson Objectives

- Students will be able to maintain an increased heart rate during introductory and fitness activities (to improve physical fitness).
- Students will be able to successfully steal (tackle) the ball from the opponent at least once while playing Take Away.
- Students will be able to successfully block the thrown balls at least 50 percent of the time.
- Students will be able to work as instructed with their partner during Stop That Ball.

Equipment Needed

Four cones, 12 to 15 jump ropes, 25 soccer balls (foam or regulation)

Activity Descriptions

Introductory Activity: Hospital Tag

Everyone is "it." When you get tagged, you have to cover that area of your body with your hand. You can be tagged twice and still play as long as you can cover both areas that have been tagged. On the third tag you are frozen. Play several times, as the game does not last long.

Fitness Activity: Half and Half

You will need four cones and jump ropes for half of the class members. Have half of the class do a locomotor skill around the four cones, and half of the class jump rope; then switch. Do this rotation four or five times with different locomotor skills each time around the cones.

Lesson Focus: Soccer Skills

Review Drills   Students select a partner, scatter throughout the area, and review the skills of dribbling, passing, and trapping.

Take Away   You will need a foam or regulation soccer ball for each player. Designate five or six players as defensive players. All the other students will have a ball and can begin dribbling in a designated area. The defensive players will try to take the balls away from (tackle) the offensive players. When a defensive player succeeds, that player becomes an offensive player and the person who lost the ball becomes a defensive player. Tackle by approaching the offensive player from the front. When the ball is loose in front of the offensive player, quickly drag the ball to the side, move to that side, and dribble away from your opponent.

Stop That Ball   The goalie stops shots at the goal by catching, blocking, deflecting, or trapping the ball. The goalie needs to stay low to the ground and have the ability to change directions quickly, as balls may roll in or be kicked in at a higher trajectory level. Designate partners. The partner with the ball throws the ball ten times to the other partner, who is the goalie. The goalie is to stop the thrown ball by catching it (if thrown high), trapping it (if traveling along the ground), or blocking it (if thrown at body height). The partner should throw a variety of passes (high, low, to the side) so the goalie can practice the different stops. Then partners switch roles. When students have mastered this activity with thrown balls, have the partner kick balls that must be stopped.

Closing Activity: Technique Talk

Students sit in a circle. Students describe how to stop the ball (as a goalie), depending on how the ball is traveling toward the goal.

Student Assessment

Evaluate goalkeeping skills during Stop That Ball (with a scoring rubric and checklist).

Success for All

- Use foam balls when first practicing goalie skills.
- Have more-skilled throwers make tosses to less-skilled players during Stop That Ball so the less-skilled players can be successful.

Classroom Activity: "How To" Speeches

At the beginning of the soccer unit in physical education, have partners prepare a speech (three to four minutes long) on one of the following soccer skills they will be learning and practicing (dribbling, passing, trapping, tackling, shooting for the goal, punting, throw-in, penalty kick, blocking, and goalkeeping). The speech will be presented to the class on an assigned day (based on when the skills are being introduced in the physical education unit). The speech explains and demonstrates how to perform a soccer skill. This activity will reinforce information presented in physical education class.

Today, in the classroom, allow the partners to begin developing their speeches.

Lesson 3.3 Soccer Skills: Moving Downfield

NASPE Standards 1, 4, and 5

Lesson Objectives

- Students will be able to maintain increased heart rate during the introductory and fitness activities (to develop physical fitness).
- Students will be able to move the ball down the field successfully without and with defensive players trying to stop forward progress.
- Students (in groups of three) will be able to pass the ball back and forth as teammates in order to move the ball down the field.
- Students will include all their teammates in play when divided into teams.

Equipment Needed

Cones, soccer balls, music for line dances

Activity Descriptions

Introductory Activity: Go Home

Class is divided into groups of at least five members each. Groups line up behind their leader at various places scattered around the designated area. Place a cone by each leader, and the cone is home. When the teacher directs the students to move, they perform a specified locomotor skill (chosen by the teacher). Students may move anywhere in general space while performing the locomotor skills. When the teacher calls out "Go home!" all players run to their cone and line up behind their leader. Repeat.

Fitness Development: Sideline Tag

Divide the class in half. Have predetermined lines or areas for students to go to, and form two straight lines facing each other. One line is team A, and the other is team B. Choose one person from each side to go to the middle; they are "it." When the teacher yells "go," team A runs to B's line and vice versa. Runners try not to get tagged by the "it" players as they run across to exchange places. Those who get tagged also become "it." They stand in the middle with the other "its" for the next exchange. The group in the middle grows, and the outside lines get shorter as the game goes on. Play until there are five or six people left on a side. Then begin again with two new people in the middle.

Lesson Focus: Soccer Skills

Circle Kick Need foam or regulation soccer balls, one for each group of five players. Each group forms a circle. The object is to kick the ball out of the circle past the players in the circle. The ball must stay below shoulder level. Players may stop the ball from exiting the circle by trapping or blocking the ball; they cannot catch the ball with their hands. Start with one ball until the students get the hang of the game; then add a second ball to make it more challenging. Circle players are not only kicking but keeping track of where the balls are in order to keep them from going out of the circle.

Forward Ho! You will need several goal areas placed on the playground area. Students (forwards) are going to practice moving the ball down the field toward a goal area (see figure). First, have three forwards traveling downfield passing the ball back and forth. When they reach the goal, one forward shoots for a goal. Players retrieve the ball (whether a goal was scored or not) and return to their starting line. The next three forwards progress down the field. Repeat this several times, so each group of three receives many practice trials. Second, repeat this drill, but have a goalie stationed by the goal. The goalie tries to stop the shot for goal by catching, blocking, or trapping the ball. Third, repeat the drill with two defensive players guarding the forwards as they move downfield. Fourth, repeat the drill with three defensive players.

Closing Activity: Respect Rap

Students sit in a circle. Discuss the importance of including everyone when practicing skills or playing games (regardless of skill level).

Student Assessment

- Using a rubric, evaluate blocking and trapping skills during Circle Kick.
- Using a rubric, evaluate students' ability to pass to other forwards in order to move the ball down the field during Forward Ho!

Success for All

- Select offensive (forwards) and defensive players of similar abilities to practice against each other.

Position of Players and Goals in Forward Ho!

- Make sure everyone has a chance to block and trap the ball during Circle Kick.

Classroom Activity: Line Dance Development

It is difficult to work on soccer skills in the classroom with children who are beyond the lower elementary grades; thus many of the classroom activities in this unit focus on the underlying movement element in soccer: eye-foot coordination.

Push the desks to one side of the room. Designate groups of five members each. Each group designs dance movements (for a line dance) of 32 counts in length to popular music (approved by the teacher). The trick is that the dance steps must always involve movements of both the feet and the arms, thus working on coordination. Students will probably use multiple days to develop their dance movements.

Assuming 25 students are in the class, five dances will be created. Throughout this unit (on five different occasions), designated groups will teach their dances to their classmates. Today, in the classroom allow students time to begin developing their dances.

Lesson 3.4 Soccer Skills: Dribble, Dribble

NASPE Standards 1, 3, 4, and 5

Student Objectives

- Students will be able to maintain an increased heart rate during the fitness and lesson focus activities (to develop physical fitness).
- Students will be able to perform the basic locomotor skills correctly.
- Students will be able to operate respectfully in several large group activities.
- Students will be able to dribble, pass, and tackle successfully in gamelike drills.

Equipment Needed

One soccer ball for each student (foam or regulation)

Activity Descriptions

Introductory Activity: Leapfrog

Have all students form a large square within the play area. They should be spaced about four feet apart. Students place hands on knees, bend knees, and tuck chin to chest. Starting with one of the corners, as the teacher calls out the child's name, that child begins leapfrogging over those in front, continues to leapfrog over all the players in the square, then stops and takes a place in line so others may jump over her or him. To leapfrog, place hands in the middle of the bent-over person's back and spread legs to the side to clear the body of the person you are jumping. As soon as the first player clears the person in front of him or her, the next player in line begins to jump over those in front. This continues until everyone in class has jumped over everyone in class.

Fitness Development: Fitness Challenges

Alternate locomotor skills with exercises. Have students skip for 30 seconds, then have them get in push-up position and do as many push-ups as they can in 20 seconds, go back to a locomotor skill for 30 seconds, then exercise for 20 seconds, and so on. Additional exercises might include jumping jacks, squat thrusts, heel clicks, coffee grinder, seal crawl, crab-walk, and crunches.

Lesson Focus: Soccer Skills

Dribble Mania With one ball per player, all players dribble throughout the area and try to avoid hitting other balls that are being dribbled. The focus is on control. Make the playing area smaller, thus demanding more control by the players. After most students are pretty good at this, have them try to kick away another player's ball (while also maintaining control of their own ball). Players who lose their ball are out and must now practice dribbling outside the designated playing area until the game is over. Play quick games and repeat for the number of times desired.

Soccer Keep Away Designate groups consisting of three players each, with one ball per group. Using dribbling, kicking, and trapping skills, two of the players try to keep the ball away from the third player. Players may travel anywhere within the designated area; however, all groups will be in this area. So players must watch not only what their group is doing but also what others close to them are doing (as no contact should be made with other groups). Frequently during this game the teacher uses a signal to change which group member is trying to take the ball away. Begin in a large playing area, but as the students become more skilled, make the area smaller (to force the need for more control).

Closing Activity: Behavior Blurb

Students sit in a circle. Discuss the difficulty of playing in a controlled manner within a space that is full of people. What techniques work to control play in the games you participated in today?

Student Assessment

Evaluate dribbling using a checklist with a scoring rubric (see Appendix B for a sample rubric).

Success for All

- Place players of similar ability within each group (for Keep Away) to motivate the better players.
- Make heterogeneous groups (based on ability) for Keep Away, and have the best player in each group serve as a mentor for that group. Be sure to provide instruction to the mentors regarding their role and responsibilities in this situation.

Classroom Activity: Work on Speeches

Continue work on speeches from Lesson 3.2. Work must be finished today.

Lesson 3.5 Frisbee Throws

As noted at the beginning of the lesson plans, physical education units for grades 5–6 usually focus on a specific activity within one movement form. However, spending 15 consecutive days on soccer can become boring for some students. Generally, another activity is introduced into the unit to keep students interested. So every Friday during this soccer unit, Frisbee skills are presented and practiced.

NASPE Standards 1, 4, and 6

Lesson Objectives

- Students will be able to throw the Frisbee accurately (to a partner) at least 50 percent of the time using the backhand throw.
- Students will be able to catch the Frisbee successfully at least 33 percent of the time.
- Students will enjoy a change of pace.

Equipment Needed

Four to six beanbags of two different colors, 12 to 15 Frisbees, and music and music player

Activity Descriptions

Introductory Activity: Music Listen
Students do locomotor skills to music. When the music stops, they freeze and wait for the teacher to specify the next locomotor skill. Use walking, skipping, galloping, sliding, jogging, grapevine step, skipping backward, running, and so on.

Fitness Development: Beanbag Tag
You will need four to six beanbags, three each of a different color (e.g., three blue and three green). Give the beanbags to six different students; these students are "it." Explain to the class that if they get tagged by the blue beanbag, they are frozen, and if they get tagged by the green beanbag, they are unfrozen. The players that have the beanbags cannot tag each other. Students who have a beanbag cannot try to hide it; they have to carry it in their hand for all to see. Play as many times as necessary to allow most of the students to be "it" and to develop cardiorespiratory endurance.

Lesson Focus: Frisbee Skills

Backhand Throw and Catching   The backhand throw is the most common of all Frisbee throws. You will need at least one Frisbee for every two students. The thumb is on top of the Frisbee and the index finger is along the edge with the other fingers wrapped underneath the Frisbee. To throw the Frisbee, the arm has to move in a sideways motion across the body. At the point of release you need to snap or flip the wrist toward your target and try to keep the Frisbee flat at the same time.

Catching the Frisbee is done with the thumb on one side of the Frisbee and the fingers on the other side, trapping the disk between the thumb and fingers. Have students form two lines 15 feet apart, facing each other. The students across from each other are partners. Students practice throwing and catching the Frisbee at different levels. Have them concentrate on throwing accurately to their partner. Move the lines farther apart if students can throw accurately from 15 feet. Change partners and practice throwing and catching again.

Closing Activity: Fun Feelings
Students sit in a circle. Students express which of the activities performed today they liked best and why.

Student Assessment

No formal assessment is required.

Success for All

- The teacher can help students catch by being the one who throws to them.
- Throwing skills can be practiced without having to catch by having the students throw at targets on the wall (or on the building, if outdoors).
- The teacher can place a hand over the student's hand and help the student throw to give the feel of how to release the Frisbee.

Classroom Activity: Work on Line Dances

Continue work on dances from Lesson 3.3. Work must be completed today.

Lesson 3.6 Soccer Skills: Throw-ins and Punting

NASPE Standards 1, 3, 4, and 5

Lesson Objectives

- Students will maintain an increased heart rate during the introductory and fitness activities (to develop physical fitness).
- Students will be able to punt the soccer ball, using correct technique, at least five times.
- Students will be able to describe how to perform a successful throw-in.
- Students will be able to perform a correct throw-in at least five times while playing Target Throw-in.

Equipment Needed

Exercise cards, 12 to 15 soccer balls

Activity Descriptions

Introductory Activity: Partner Free-Hand Tag

One set of partners is "it" while all other students are playing independently at this time. Partners hold hands. On a signal from the teacher, they try to tag other students with their free hand. The first student tagged joins the partners, now making it a trio. When two more have been tagged, one pair must break off. Now you have a trio and a pair who are "it." Keep playing until all are tagged. Play a number of times.

Fitness Development: Circuit Activity

Construct several large cards with activities like crunches, jumping jacks, push-ups, frog jumps, toe touches, bend and stretch, jump rope, crab-walk, bear walk on them. Place at least ten of the cards around the activity area. Assign an equal number of students to stand by each card. When the music starts, the students begin the activity in their designated spot. When music stops, they rotate to the next card. You can complete the rotation once or twice as time allows.

Lesson Focus: Soccer Skills

Punting   Punting, which is used only by the goalkeeper, can be done either standing still or on the run. The ball is held approximately waist high with both hands out away from the body, over the kicking leg, which will be the right or left, whichever is dominant (instructions assume the right leg is dominant). Step on the left leg as the kicking leg swings back, then forward as the ball is dropped. The right leg is slightly bent with the toe

pointed. The ball should contact the foot on top of the foot (on the shoelaces). At the time of contact, straighten the kicking leg for more power. Place students in two lines (25 to 30 feet apart), facing each other. Partners are directly across from each other. With one ball per set of partners, students practice punting back and forth (using foam balls). Stress punting accurately to the partner. Begin with a standing-still punt and then progress to the running punt.

Throw-ins   Throw-ins occur during soccer play when the ball goes out of bounds. The team not kicking the ball out of bounds gets to have a throw-in at the spot where the ball went out of bounds. This is the only time the ball is touched with the hands during a game of soccer. The person throwing in must observe the following rules or the other team gets the ball.

- Both hands must be on the ball.
- The ball must be released from over the head.
- The thrower must face the field, standing outside the sideline.
- The thrower may not step on to the field until the ball has been released.
- Both of the thrower's feet must stay in contact with the playing surface until the ball is released.
- The thrower cannot touch the ball again until another player has contacted it.

Target Throw-in   Students are dribbling in a designated area. The object is for the players dribbling the soccer ball to protect the ball with their body. Several players roving the perimeter of the playing area have foam balls or soccer balls in their hand. They try to throw their ball (using the correct throw-in technique) and hit one of the balls being dribbled. If contact is made, the thrower becomes a dribbler and the person whose ball was hit becomes a thrower. As students advance in skill level, add more throwers.

Closing Activity: Technique Talk

Students sit in a circle. Students describe how to perform a successful throw-in—the technique required and the rules that must be followed.

Student Assessment

Evaluate students' punting technique and accuracy with a checklist and scoring rubric (see Appendix B for a sample rubric).

Success for All

- In Target Throw-in, if throwers do not possess the throwing accuracy to hit the soccer balls, change to a less-skilled drill. For example, scatter soccer balls in a designated area (a square area). Students stand around the square and throw balls at the stationary soccer balls. Every hit scores a point for the class.
- When practicing punting, students may have trouble dropping the ball and then kicking it. These students may begin by kicking (punting) a foam ball that is being held by the teacher.

Classroom Activity: Speeches–Throw-ins and Punting

Have two sets of partners present their speeches on punting and throw-ins (see Lesson 3.2).

Lesson 3.7 Lead-up Soccer Games: Sideline Soccer

NASPE Standards 1, 3, 4, and 5

Lesson Objectives

- Students will be able to maintain their heart rate in their training zone during the introductory and fitness activities (to develop physical fitness).
- Students will be able to score a goal while playing Sideline Soccer.
- Students will be able to involve all their team members when playing Sideline Soccer.

Equipment Needed

Four cones, one soccer ball, 12 to 15 jump ropes

Activity Descriptions

Introductory Activity: Timed Run

Mark off two lines, or set up cones approximately 22 yards apart. Students stand at one line and on the teacher's signal run to the other line (or cones). They have 15 seconds to get to the other line. At the end of 15 seconds, have them go again; gradually take a few seconds off so they have a shorter amount of time to get from one side to the other. This is an endurance activity.

Fitness Development: Jump Rope

You will need one jump rope for every two students. Have one student jump rope while a partner does crunches. Then partners switch roles. Continue switching, alternating activities like jumping jacks, sitting or standing stretches, push-ups, and the like. The teacher can call out the exercises or post them on cards throughout the area so students can work at their own pace.

Lesson Focus: Sideline Soccer

A rectangle playing area must be established by painting lines or using cones. On the short end of the playing area, mark a goal area by placing cones approximately seven or eight feet apart. Divide the class in half, with one half on one long side of the rectangle and the other half on the other side (see figure). One team should wear pinnies. Have the first four players from one end of the line come onto the field from both sides. The object is for each team to score a goal through the goal area. They may use the players on the field as well as the players on the sideline.

When a goal is scored, the players on the field go to the opposite end of the line and the next group of players comes out. Everyone must have several chances to play

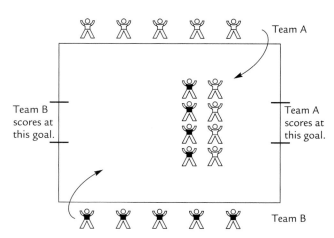

Setup and Starting Positions for Sideline Soccer

on the field, so if scoring does not occur in two minutes, call a time-out and bring in the next group of players.

Only the active players on the field can score a goal; sideline players cannot. However, sideline players play an active role in stopping the ball from going out of bounds by trapping the ball and passing it to one of their players on the field. In addition, teachers can encourage the involvement of the sideline players by establishing rules such as "the offensive team has to have two sideline players kick the ball before it can score."

Students may not push or interfere with others while playing. Rough play should be called and the opposing team awarded the ball (or awarded a point). If the ball goes out of bounds, the opposite team is allowed a throw-in at the point the ball went out of bounds.

Closing Activity: Respect Rap

Students sit in a circle. Students discuss how to include all their teammates (including sideline players) when playing Sideline Soccer. Why should all be included?

Student Assessment

- Take a ten-second heart rate during the fitness activity to ascertain whether students are working in their training zone.
- Record the number of teams who were able to score during Sideline Soccer.

Success for All

- Do not allow several players to dominate play during Sideline Soccer. Teach players how to play as a team.

If some students insist on simply dribbling down the field and scoring (without involving their teammates), instigate rules that necessitate involvement. For example, three passes have to occur before a goal can be scored.

- Consider having two games of Sideline Soccer going on so one game could be quite competitive and the other game could be more recreational.

Classroom Activity: Speeches—Blocking and Goalkeeping

Have two sets of partners present their speeches on blocking and goalkeeping (see Lesson 3.2).

Lesson 3.8 Lead-up Soccer Games: Three-on-Three

NASPE Standards 1, 3, 4, and 5

Lesson Objectives

- Students will be able to maintain an increased heart rate during the introductory and fitness activities (to develop physical fitness).
- Offensive players will be able to move the ball down the field and score at least once.
- Students will be able to include all team members in their team play.
- Players will be able to observe the rules for playing Three-on-Three.

Equipment Needed

One soccer ball for each student, cones

Activity Descriptions

Introductory Activity: Freeze Tag

One or two players are "it," and the object is to freeze as many other players as possible. Tagged players become frozen and stand in place with legs spread apart. They can be unfrozen when someone goes under their legs.

Fitness Development: Teacher-Led Exercises

Refer back to Lesson 3.1.

Lesson Focus: Lead-up Soccer Games

Dribble Mania   Refer to Lesson 3.4 for a description of Dribble Mania.

Take Away   Refer to Lesson 3.2 for a description of Take Away.

Three-on-Three   Designate teams with six members each, consisting of three offensive and three defensive players. Offensive players wear pinnies. Teams are

scattered throughout a large playing area, and each has a goal area established with two cones. Don't try to establish sidelines. Players just play in the general area in front of their goal. Play Rock, Paper, Scissors to see which team has the ball first. After that, the opposing team gets the ball whenever a goal is scored, when a shot for a goal travels beyond the end line, when a foul occurs, or when an opponent takes the ball away from the offensive team. The opposing team takes possession of the ball with a throw-in from about 30 feet in front of the goal area.

Closing Activity: Behavior Blurb

Students sit in a circle. Students discuss the extent to which their team was able to be independently responsible (without aid from the teacher) for playing the game Three-on-Three by the rules.

Student Assessment

- Using a checklist with scoring rubric, determine the level of independent responsibility that players can handle as they play Three-on-Three.
- Finish checklist evaluation of dribbling ability for all students if not already completed.

Success for All

Assist teams if they need help adapting their play to include all their team members.

Classroom Activity: Speeches—Dribbling and Tackling

Have two sets of partners present their speeches on dribbling and tackling (see Lesson 3.2).

Lesson 3.9 Lead-up Soccer Games: Sideline Soccer

NASPE Standards 1, 2, 4, and 5

Lesson Objectives

- Students will be able to maintain an increased heart rate during the introductory and fitness activities (to develop physical fitness).
- Each team will be able to score at least once while playing Sideline Soccer.
- Students will be able to include all team members while playing Sideline Soccer.
- Students will be able to discuss offensive strategies that lead to scoring opportunities.

Equipment Needed

One soccer ball

Activity Descriptions

Introductory Activity: Partner Tag
Refer to Lesson 3.1 for a description of Partner Tag.

Fitness Development: Fitness Challenges
Refer to Lesson 3.4 for a description of the Fitness Challenges.

Lesson Focus: Sideline Soccer
Refer to Lesson 3.7 for a description of Sideline Soccer.

Closing Activity: Concept Cues
Students sit in a circle. Students discuss offensive strategies they used that led to scoring opportunities.

Student Assessment

Continue assessment checklist on passing and trapping skills while students play Sideline Soccer.

Success for All

- Do not allow several players to dominate play during Sideline Soccer. Teach players how to play as a team. If some students insist on simply dribbling down the field and scoring (without involving their teammates), instigate rules that necessitate involvement. For example, three passes have to occur before a goal can be scored.
- Consider having two games of Sideline Soccer going on so one game could be quite competitive and the other game could be more recreational.

Classroom Activity: Dance Presentation

Have one group demonstrate and teach their dance to their classmates (see Lesson 3.3).

Lesson 3.10 Frisbee Skills

NASPE Standards 1, 4, and 5

Lesson Objectives

- Students will be able to jog for five minutes (to develop physical fitness).
- Students will be able to catch the Frisbee on 50 percent of the throws.
- Students will be able to throw accurately to others using all three throwing techniques.

Equipment Needed

One Frisbee for every two students

Activity Descriptions

Introductory Activity: Animal Tag

Have the entire class line up side by side at a designated starting point. Give each student one of four animal designations, for example, lions, tigers, bears, and giraffes. Choose a boy and a girl to be "it" and have them come to the center of the playing area. The girl calls off the first animal and the students with that designation run to the other end of the playing area trying not to get tagged by the "its." Tagged students go to one sideline, and those not tagged go to the other. Then the boy calls the next animal, and students with that designation run to the other end of the playing area as before. The girl and boy continue alternating animal groups. At the end of the game, select two new children to be "it." Play quickly to keep everyone active.

Fitness Development: Timed Run/Walk

Have a designated track or route mapped out with cones. The class has to jog or walk for five minutes. As students become fitter, they should jog more and walk less during the five-minute period. Students who can jog the entire time may be ready to increase the time period. Stress that students keep moving and not stop. When walking, they should walk briskly.

Lesson Focus: Frisbee Skills

Backhand Throw and Catching   Refer to Lesson 3.5 for a description of Backhand Throw and Catching.

Backhand Curve   Tilt hand one way or the other and the Frisbee will curve accordingly.

Backhand Bounce   Throw at the ground or floor and the Frisbee will bounce up for a partner to catch.

Designate partners and have children practice the above throws, emphasizing throwing accuracy.

Frisbee Keep Away   Groups of three or four students each stand in circles. Make sure the circles are large. One person in the middle tries to get the Frisbee from the others in the group. If the middle person gets the Frisbee, that person joins the circle and the player who threw the Frisbee is then in the middle.

Closing Activity: Technique Talk

Students sit in a circle. Students verbally review the techniques for all three Frisbee throws.

Student Assessment

Using a checklist and scoring rubric, evaluate basic throw and catch techniques while partners are practicing.

Success for All

- Visually impaired students may have to throw objects that beep rather than the Frisbee.
- Help students who are unsuccessful at throwing by placing your hands over their hands as they throw.
- Help students who are unsuccessful at catching by being the thrower (who throws quite accurately, thus making catching easier).

Classroom Activity: Dance Presentation

Have one group demonstrate and teach their dance to classmates (see Lesson 3.3).

Lesson 3.11 Soccer Skills: Kicking for Goal

NASPE Standards 1, 2, 4, and 5

Lesson Objectives

- Students will be able to maintain increased heart rate during the introductory and fitness activities (to develop physical fitness).
- Students will be able to kick for goal successfully at least once.
- Students (playing goalie) will be able to successfully stop a kick for goal at least once.
- Students will be able to operate independently when performing the drill Kicking for Goal.

Equipment Needed

Twenty cones, 12 to 15 soccer balls

Activity Descriptions

Introductory Activity: Partner Tag

Refer to Lesson 3.1 for a description of Partner Tag.

Fitness Development: Teacher-Led Exercises

Refer to Lesson 3.1 for a description of Teacher-Led Exercises.

Lesson Focus: Soccer Skills

Warm-up Round   Designate partners. Partners dribble and pass around the perimeter of the soccer field. Do one round at a jog, the next round at a faster speed.

Kicking for Goal   This drill provides practice for offensive players (kicking for goal) and for goalies. Have four or five goal areas designated (with cones) and have a designated line approximately 15 feet in front of the goal area. Place two players in front of the goal (to be goalies). Three or four players, each with a ball, are spread around the goal area facing the goal. They practice taking shots from a stationary position at the goal. For this drill, assume the goalies are in the penalty area of the field. Thus they may use arms and hands to stop the ball, may take four steps while in possession of the ball, and may clear the ball from the area by punting, passing, or throwing. The player who kicked for goal retrieves the ball whether it crossed the end line without scoring or is cleared by a goalie. After five minutes or so, rotate the goalies out and place two of the kickers in as goalies. Perform the same drill, but have the offensive players take their goal shots as they are dribbling toward the goal (instead of from a stationary position).

Sideline Soccer   Refer to Lesson 3.7 for a description of Sideline Soccer.

Closing Activity: Technique Talk

Students sit in a circle. Students review the technique the goalie should use to successfully stop a kick for goal.

Student Assessment

Continue recording the number of teams that were able to score during Sideline Soccer.

Success for All

Based on the student assessment data collected, make sure all students have several successful scoring experiences. Make any necessary adaptations to the drills and games to make this happen.

Classroom Activity: Speeches—Passing and Shooting for Goal

Have two sets of partners present their speeches: passing and shooting for goal.

Lesson 3.12 Modified Soccer

NASPE Standards 1, 4, and 5

Lesson Objectives

- Students will be able to maintain increased heart rate during the introductory and fitness activities (to develop physical fitness).
- Teams will be able to demonstrate sufficient independent behavior to play modified soccer successfully.
- Students will be able to include all teammates when playing modified soccer.
- Students will be able to play by the rules when playing modified soccer.

Equipment Needed

Four cones, 12 to 15 jump ropes, three soccer balls

Activity Descriptions

Introductory Activity: Leapfrog
Refer to Lesson 3.4 for a description of Leapfrog.

Fitness Activity: Circuit Activity
You will need four cones and jump ropes for half of the class. Set the cones at the corners of the movement area. Half of the class performs locomotor skills around the four cones while the other half performs jump rope. When students in the locomotor group finish a lap around the cones, they trade places with the jump ropers. The teacher designates the locomotor skill to be performed.

Lesson Focus: Modified Soccer

Verbal Explanation A regulation soccer team is made up of three forwards, three midfield players, four backline defenders, and one goalie. The forwards are the main line of attack. They should have good dribbling skills and shooting skills. This is the group that will be responsible for scoring. Midfield players tend to be the power of the team. They should have good passing and tackling skills as well as a high level of cardiorespiratory endurance. Back-line defenders should work well together and know when to take the ball from the other team. They should keep the ball clear of their own penalty area and not pass or dribble in the direction of their own goal. Goalies should be quick, have good ball-handling skills, and be able to make last-minute decisions.

Physical educators usually adapt regulation soccer for elementary school students in order to provide maximum participation for students and to recognize that students of this age are not capable of playing on a large field with lots of players and complicated rules. Modified soccer is played on a smaller playing field with fewer players and simplified rules.

The field dimensions are 20 by 40 feet. For field markings, see the following figure. Each team has seven players: three forwards, three defenders, and one goalie. Both teams should wear pinnies.

Rules for Modified Soccer

- The teacher designates which team is on offense first (or do Rock, Paper, Scissors). Play begins with a kick by the offensive team from the middle of the field. All other players must be five feet from the kicker.
- After a goal, the opposing team kicks off from the middle of the field (as when the game started). Each score counts one point.

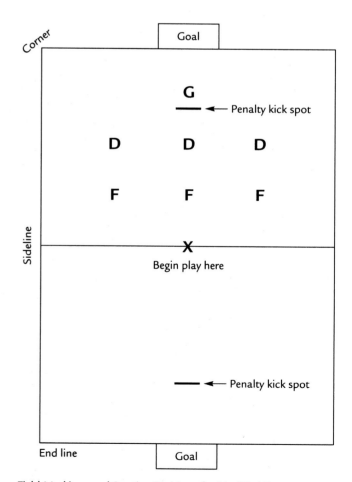

Field Markings and Starting Positions for Modified Soccer

- When the ball goes out of bounds over the sideline, the opposing team does a throw-in at the spot the ball went out.
- When the ball goes out of bounds over the end line (not scoring a goal), the opposing team does a throw-in at the corner nearest the spot the ball went out.
- When a foul is committed, a free kick is awarded to the opposing team. For serious fouls (pushing, etc.) occurring near the goal, the injured team may be awarded a penalty kick. One player from the injured team takes one kick at the goal from ten feet away. The only defensive player who can defend the goal area is the goalie. All other players are just watching.

Play Modified Soccer   Designate teams (and positions) and assign fields. Students officiate their own games with teacher assistance. Have several games going on at the same time if space allows.

Closing Activity: Concept Cues

Students sit in a circle. The teacher presents scenarios to the students to determine whether they understand the rules for playing modified soccer (e.g., What happens if a player fouls an opponent—near the goal, away from the goal? What happens if the ball travels out of bounds over the sideline?).

Student Assessment

While students play, finish completing any of the checklists being used to assess soccer skills.

Success for All

Consider assigning students to teams based on whether they want a competitive or recreational game spirit.

Classroom Activity: Speeches—Trapping and Penalty Kick

Have two sets of partners present their speeches: trapping and penalty kick.

Lessons 3.13 and 3.14 Modified Soccer

NASPE Standards 1, 2, 4, and 5

Lesson Objectives

- Students will be able to maintain increased heart rate during the introductory and fitness activities (to develop physical fitness).
- Teams will be able to demonstrate sufficient independent behavior to play modified soccer successfully.
- Students will be able to include all teammates when playing modified soccer.
- Students will be able to play by the rules when playing modified soccer.

Equipment Needed

Cones to mark playing fields, 12 to 15 soccer balls

Activity Descriptions

Introductory and Fitness Activity: Warm-up Round

Designate partners. Partners dribble and pass around the perimeter of the soccer field. Do one round at a jog, the next at a faster speed.

Lesson Focus: Modified Soccer

Skill Review Based on the observations from previous game play, select some of the drills from the unit to use as a review. Select drills that incorporate the skills the students need to practice the most in order to be successful in the game. Or select drills that include skills you still need to evaluate.

Play Modified Soccer Designate teams (and positions) and assign fields. Students officiate their own games with teacher assistance. Have several games going on at the same time if space allows.

Closing Activity: Fun Feelings

Students sit in a circle. Students discuss the fun they have when playing soccer. Ask students to express the feelings they have when playing soccer. Obviously a number of feelings occur (joy when scoring, etc.).

Student Assessment

While students play, finish completing any of the checklists being used to assess soccer skills.

Success for All

Consider assigning students to teams based on whether they want a competitive or recreational game spirit. Competitive teams could do a short round-robin tournament.

Classroom Activity: Dance Presentation

Have one group demonstrate and teach their dance to classmates (see Lesson 3.3).

Lesson 3.15 Frisbee Golf

NASPE Standards 1, 4, and 5

Lesson Objectives

- Students will be able to maintain an increased heart rate during the introductory and fitness activities (to develop physical fitness).
- Students will be able to catch the Frisbee on 50 percent of the throws.
- Students will be able to throw accurately to others using all three throwing techniques.
- Students will be able to improve their scores while playing Frisbee golf.

Equipment Needed

Exercise cards, 12 to 15 Frisbees, music and music player

Activity Descriptions

Introductory Activity: Timed Run

Mark off two lines, or set up cones approximately 20 meters apart. On the teacher's signal, all students run to the other cone or line in 15 seconds. At the end of 15 seconds, have them go again; gradually take a few seconds off so they have a shorter amount of time to get from one cone or line to the other. This is an endurance activity.

Fitness Development: Group Exercises with Instructional Cards

Divide the class into four or five groups. Have numbered instructional cards placed randomly around the activity area. Each card designates one activity, such as jumping jacks, crab-walk, crunches, push-ups, stretches, or bear walk. Have each group move to a card. When the music starts, students begin the activity on their group's card; when it stops, they jog to the next card and begin again when the music resumes. Continue rotating through the numbered cards until each group has been at all the cards.

Lesson Focus: Frisbee Skills

Review Skills Select drills to review from Lesson 3.5 and Lesson 3.10 based on students' needs. Designate partners and review necessary skills.

Catching Variations As partners play catch, have them try to catch the Frisbee behind the back, under the leg, and then on a finger.

Long Pass Throwing Have one partner run downfield for a pass (as when playing football). Throw a long, accurate pass so the partner does not have to stop or slow down to make the catch.

Hoop Throw Work on throwing accuracy by having students throw the Frisbee through a hoop held by a partner.

Frisbee Golf Lay out a course (like a golf course) with hula hoops serving as the target (like the cup on the green). Designate starting points for each target with cones. Students play the course individually and see how many throws it takes to get the Frisbee into each hoop. The number of targets you lay out depends on the space available. Unless you have a very large outdoor area, you may have to split the class in half, with half practicing their drills while the others play Frisbee golf. Then switch groups.

Closing Activity: Concept Cues

Students sit in a circle. Students identify what technique improvements they were able to implement that allowed them to better their scores for each round of Frisbee golf.

Student Assessment

Record scores from Frisbee golf and determine whether students are becoming more accurate with additional practice.

Success for All

Students can play "best throw" Frisbee golf (like "best ball" in golf). Designate partners; each player has a Frisbee. Both partners get to throw at the target. The next throw (by both partners) is taken from the spot of the best previous throw. Keep partner scores (rather than individual scores).

Classroom Activity: Dance Presentation

Have one group demonstrate and teach their dance to their classmates (see Lesson 3.3).

Movement Form: Fundamental Skills

FIFTEEN LESSONS FOR THE CLASSROOM, GRADES K–2
Rebecca Nicholas, Belle Plaine Elementary, Belle Plaine, Kansas

Lesson 4.1 Toss and Catch/Movement Levels

NASPE Standard 1

Lesson Objective

Students will be able to continuously toss to self and catch an object at various levels.

Equipment Needed

Foam ball or foam ring for each student

Activity Descriptions

Using a foam ball or foam ring, see how many ways students can toss and catch at a high, medium, and low level. If needed, discuss where a high, medium, and low level would be and have a student demonstrate. Students stand by their desk and toss and catch a foam ball to themselves at a high level, medium level, and low level ten times each.

Also, students draw themselves on a piece of paper and draw and label the ball at high, medium, and low levels.

Students stand by their desk and toss and catch a foam ball. Challenge students to practice the following skills, tossing to self and catching:

- Toss and catch the foam ball with both hands.
- Toss with the left hand and catch with both hands.
- Toss with the right hand and catch with the right hand.
- Toss with the left hand and catch with the left hand.
- Toss with the right hand and catch with the left hand.
- Toss with the left hand and catch with the right hand.

Students work by themselves on these challenges and then try the same challenges with a partner.

Student Assessment

Use a checklist and observe students. If students demonstrate high, medium, and low levels and catch the object 90 percent of the time, check off for mastery.

Success for All

For visually impaired students, use a brightly colored ball or a ball that beeps.

Lesson 4.2 Striking

NASPE Standard 1

Lesson Objective

Students will demonstrate striking objects (continuously) using hands or other objects.

Equipment Needed

Balloon (blown up) for each student, soft foam tube for each student

Activity Descriptions

- Students stand by their desk and tap a balloon to self, trying to keep it continuously in the air.
- Challenge students to see how many times they can tap it with the right hand, then the left hand, and then alternating hands.
- Tap the balloon as high as possible and then as low as possible without the balloon touching the floor.
- Tap the balloon with different body parts (head, elbow, forearm, knee, foot, and shoulder).
- Tap the balloon using a soft foam tube. Tap the balloon with one end of the golf tube and then try tapping with both ends of the tube alternately. Hold the golf tube with both hands and tap the balloon in the middle of the golf tube.
- Challenge students to keep the balloon in the air with a partner (tapping back and forth) in a stationary position and then while walking. Use the desks for a "net" if desired.
- Push desks to the center of the room. Designate groups of five members each. The group members form a circle and try to keep one balloon in the air—then two balloons, then three balloons.

Student Assessment

Using a checklist, observe students. If students can keep the balloon in the air ten or more consecutive times with hits to self, check off for mastery.

Success for All

Use foam balls if students can easily perform these tasks with balloons.

Lesson 4.3 Dribbling with Hands

NASPE Standard 1

Lesson Objective

Students will be able to dribble a ball from a seated, kneeling, and standing position.

Equipment Needed

Playground ball, beach ball, or basketball (junior-high size) for each student

Activity Descriptions

- Using playground balls or basketballs, students dribble a ball while sitting down, kneeling, and standing up.
- Students sit by their desk with legs crossed and dribble the ball continuously. They then move to a kneeling position—still dribbling continuously—and finally, standing in place.
- Students perform the above with their right hand, with their left hand, and finally, alternating hands.
- Using a playground ball or basketball, students continuously dribble while moving from a sitting position to a kneeling position to a standing position.

- Students begin dribbling by their desk in a sitting position. Keeping the ball going, they move to a kneeling position and then a standing position. Challenge students to reverse the activity by starting from a standing position, moving to a kneeling position, and then to a sitting position while keeping the ball going.

Student Assessment

Using a checklist, observe the students to see whether they can dribble at least ten consecutive times while in a seated position, ten consecutive times in a kneeling position, or ten consecutive times in a standing position. Students who demonstrate one of these challenges are checked off for mastery.

Success for All

Use balls of appropriate size (small enough so students can handle the ball with one hand)—junior-high sized basketballs, eight-inch playground balls.

Lesson 4.4 Dribbling with Feet

NASPE Standard 1

Lesson Objective

Students will demonstrate the ability to dribble a beanbag with their feet.

Equipment Needed

Beanbag or yarn ball for each student

Activity Descriptions

Move the desks to one side of the room. Each child has a beanbag or yarn ball. Students are lined up across the width of the room (no more than three deep). Place floor tape (on the floor) in a straight line from each group to the opposite wall. Challenge the students to do the following:

- Move down the floor dribbling the bag or ball (by tapping it with the inside of each foot—first with one foot, then the other). After all three students have performed, they dribble back to their original position. Repeat this a number of times.
- Do the same drill as above, but switch objects. Those with balls now have bags and vice versa.
- Do the same drill with tennis balls and eight-inch playground balls.

Emphasize short taps so the ball is controlled at all times. Emphasize moving in a straight line (along the masking tape).

Student Assessment

If the student can dribble the width of the room (with the object under control), check off for mastery.

Success for All

Allow students to practice mostly with the object they are having the most success in dribbling.

Lesson 4.5 Throwing at Targets

NASPE Standard 1

Lesson Objective

Students will be able to throw accurately, using correct technique (underhand and overhand), at a target and into a wastebasket.

Equipment Needed

Sixty beanbags and 10 to 15 bowling pins

Activity Descriptions

Using beanbags and bowling pins, students demonstrate underhand and overhand throwing skills. Students move their desks to make a large empty space in the middle of the room. Ten or more bowling pins of two different colors are placed alternately in a line to form a dividing line (for example, five yellow pins and five orange pins). Students are divided into two groups and stand side by side on opposite sides. Each student begins with two beanbags. Students are challenged to toss the beanbags underhanded at the bowling pins. A throwing line may need to be established by placing a yardstick or piece of tape on the floor. One group throws at the yellow pins and one group at the orange pins. When all five pins of one color are knocked down, a point is awarded to that team. The next game is played with overhand throws. One or two students from each team may toss the beanbags back to the players until the five pins have been knocked down.

Using the same large empty space in the middle of the room, place hula hoops or a wastebasket to throw into. Students practice throwing underhand and overhand from the throwing line.

Student Assessment

Use a checklist and observe students. If students throw with the appropriate action (underhand or overhand) when designated by the teacher, check off for mastery.

Success for All

For students with visual impairments, assign them a partner who lines them up with the target, tells them how far away the target is, what the target is (bowling pin, wastebasket), and provides feedback regarding the outcome of their toss.

Lesson 4.6 Dribbling with Hands

NASPE Standard 1

Lesson Objective

Students will be able to continuously dribble a ball, using the hands, without losing control.

Equipment Needed

Beach ball, playground ball, or junior-high sized basketball for each student

Activity Description

Using a playground ball or basketball, students dribble continuously, without losing control. Students stand by their desk and are challenged to dribble continuously in the following ways:

- Can you dribble in front of you?
- Can you dribble behind you?
- Can you dribble at knee level? Waist level?
- Can you dribble higher than your head? Lower than your knees?
- Can you dribble as fast as you can?
- Can you dribble as slow as you can?

Challenge the students to walk around the room while dribbling without interfering with others.

Using playground balls or basketballs, students begin dribbling while walking. They are challenged to jog while dribbling, if space permits. Cones may be used for obstacle dribbling, and the students weave in and out of the cones while dribbling. Try switching hands to dribble with the opposite hand, and then dribble with alternating hands.

Push the desks to one side of the room. Divide students into groups of five members each. Each group lines up behind one cone facing another cone placed across the room. When the signal is given to start, the first person in each group begins dribbling to the opposite cone, dribbles around it, and dribbles back to the group. Then the next person takes a turn. Each time a person gets back, a point is added to the team's score. Teams are challenged to see how many points they can make as a group before the signal is given to stop. The teams are challenged to improve their scores each time the game is played.

Student Assessment

Using a checklist, observe students. If they can successfully dribble around the cone (without losing control of the ball), check off for mastery.

Success for All

- Provide more room for students in wheelchairs.
- Use balls that beep for visually impaired students.
- Assign partners to help students who have motor coordination problems.

Lesson 4.7 Rhythm

NASPE Standard 1

Lesson Objective

Students will be able to complete the Pease Porridge Hot actions at least one time without mistakes (perform rhythmic movements that increase hand-eye and foot-eye coordination).

Equipment Needed

None

Activity Descriptions

Pease Porridge Hot   Without music, children sing the verses while performing the actions. Designate partners. Partners stand facing each other.

ACTION	WORDS
Slap own thighs, Clap own hands together, Slap partner's hands (both hands)	Pease porridge hot
Repeat above	Pease porridge cold

Slap own thighs,
Clap own hands together,
Slap partner's right hand
  with your right hand
Slap partner's left hand
  with your left hand
Clap own hands together
Slap partner's hands
  (both hands)
	Pease porridge in the
	  pot nine days old

Use the same actions for the second verse:	Some like it hot Some like it cold Some like it in the pot Nine days old.
Find a new partner and repeat as desired.	

Stomp, Stomp, Stomp   Without music, children say the following rhyme and perform the following actions. Designate partners. Partners stand facing each other.

ACTION	WORDS

Stamp feet three times
  (on tap, tap, tap)
	Let your feet go
	  tap, tap, tap

Clap own hands three times
  (on clap, clap, clap)
	Let your hands go
	  clap, clap, clap

Wiggle fingers	Let your fingers wiggle free
Do a right elbow swing	Come, my partner, swing with me

Student Assessment

Check off for mastery if the student can perform both verses of Pease Porridge Hot without any mistakes (and without breaking the rhythm).

Success for All

Students with motor impairments may need to perform the rhymes and actions at a slower tempo.

Lesson 4.8 Catching

NASPE Standard 1

Lesson Objective

Students will be able to catch, with properly positioned hands, a gently thrown ball.

Equipment Needed

Foam or yarn ball for each student

Activity Descriptions

Using foam or yarn balls, students play catch with a partner, demonstrating proper catching skills. Students face a partner about ten feet away. Students toss and catch the ball using the hands only. When the ball is caught at or above chest level, the catcher's fingers should be pointed upward. If the ball is caught below chest level, the catcher's fingers are pointed downward. Catches should be made with the hands only, without trapping the ball against the chest or catching the ball with the arms.

Students face a partner ten feet away and begin playing catch. When a catch is made without having to move, that student takes one step backward. Each time a catch is made, the student who caught it takes a step backward. When someone misses, a step forward is taken. Students play and see how far apart they can get.

Student Assessment

Using a checklist, observe students playing catch with a partner. Students should be able to catch the balls that are well thrown 90 percent of the time. When the ball is thrown up high, the fingers should be pointed upward, and when the ball is thrown down low, the fingers should be pointed downward. Students should catch with their hands (no trapping the ball against the chest or catching with the arms).

Success for All

The teacher (or a partner) may assist a motor-impaired student by placing his or her hands around the student's hands to help the student catch. This technique will help the student feel how to catch and will allow her or him to be successful.

Lesson 4.9 Jumping Rope

NASPE Standard 1

Lesson Objective

Students will be able to repeatedly jump a self-turned rope.

Equipment Needed

Twenty-five individual jump ropes

Activity Descriptions

Students will demonstrate the ability to jump rope continuously, turning the rope themselves. Designate groups of twos or threes. When the music starts, one person begins jumping and continues jumping until the music stops (for about 30 seconds). If music isn't available, a whistle can be used to signal students to start and stop. Students try to keep jumping the entire time when it is their turn (without any misses). When the music stops, the rope is handed to the next person. When students are not jumping rope, they do their choice of exercises until it's their turn to jump rope. Exercises could include windmills (twisting the upper body from side to side), hurdle stretches, bent-knee sit-ups, push-ups, arm circles, and side bends.

Students get into groups of three or four members each. Students in each group take turns jumping the rope. Each group member jumps and counts the number of jumps completed, but students jump only until they miss. Each completed jump counts as one point. After each team member jumps, count team points. Then count class points by adding all of the team points to see how many points the entire class made together. The emphasis shouldn't be on which team made the most points but on how many points all of the groups made together. For each contest, the class is challenged to make more points than were made before.

Student Assessment

In the first activity listed, teachers have the opportunity to watch each student jump individually in a stationary position. If students can jump ten or more times in a row, turning their own ropes, check off for mastery.

Success for All

For students who cannot jump the rope repeatedly, consult Box 9.1, which contains some lead-up activities.

Lesson 4.10 Jumping and Landing

NASPE Standard 1

Lesson Objective

Students will be able to jump and land using a combination of one-foot and two-feet takeoffs and landings.

Equipment Needed

Twenty-five individual jump ropes

Activity Descriptions

Students will demonstrate the ability to take off with one foot, landing on both feet, and take off with both feet, landing on both feet. Students stand by their desk with a book or cone on the floor in front of them. They practice by standing on one foot, jumping over the cone on that same foot, and landing on both feet at the same time.

Then students jump over the cone, taking off and landing on both feet at the same time.

Students get a partner and two short jump ropes. They spread the jump ropes a few feet apart and take turns jumping over the ropes, taking off with one foot and landing on two. Partners watch each other to make sure the movement is performed correctly. When both have done it correctly two times each, spread the ropes a little farther apart. Continue this until they can no longer make the jump without landing in the middle of the ropes. Then, by doing the same activity, the students can see how far they can go by taking off from two feet and landing on two feet.

Another good activity for teaching jumping and landing is playing hopscotch. A hopscotch court can be made with chalk on the sidewalk, by using flat plastic rings called "olympet rings" found in sports equipment catalogs, or by placing masking tape on a tile floor. In this activity, students take off with one foot, land on two, take off with one foot, land on the same foot, and take off with two feet, landing on one. For a full description of how to play hopscotch, consult Appendix C.

Student Assessment

Observe students while they're playing the partner activity with the jump ropes. When observing a pair of students, ask them to demonstrate taking off with one foot and landing on two. After observing the skill a few times, ask them to demonstrate jumping from both feet and landing on both feet at the same time (not one foot and then the other). If students can demonstrate a one-feet takeoff and a two-feet landing and a two-feet takeoff with a two-feet landing a few times each, check off for mastery.

Success for All

For students with motor impairments, allow partners to help them balance while performing the jumps and playing hopscotch. Simply allow the performer to hold the partner's hand, arm, or shoulder as the partner stands or walks beside the performer.

Lesson 4.11 Identifying Body Parts

NASPE Standard 1

Lesson Objective

Students will be able to identify a variety of body parts.

Equipment Needed

Picture of a person (25 copies) and crayons

Activity Descriptions

- Students stand by their desk or sit on the floor in a circle. The teacher holds up a picture of a person and points to one of the body parts in the picture. Students name the body part and then touch the same body part on their body.
- Students get a partner and stand 20 feet apart, facing each other. The teacher calls out a body part and the students skip toward their partners and touch the designated body part to their partner's body part. For example, if the teacher calls out "elbow," the partners touch their own elbow to their partner's elbow. Then they skip back to their places. Different ways of moving (different locomotor patterns or different animal walks) can be used as well as calling out different body parts.
- Students stand by their desk or sit on the floor in a circle. The teacher plays Simon Says with the students. The teacher says to the students, "Simon says touch your knees." The students then touch their own knees. If the teacher simply says "touch your knees," the students shouldn't do it, because "Simon" didn't say to do it. Continue with other body parts.
- Students sit at their desk and are given a picture of a person. They are asked to draw an X on each body part as the teacher names it. Have students use different colors of crayons for different body parts. For example, "using a red crayon, draw an X on the knee. Using a blue crayon, draw an X on the shoulder."

Student Assessment

Use a checklist and observe students for mastery. If students know eight body parts, check off for mastery. The eight body parts for kindergarten level could be wrist, knee, shoulder, ankle, elbow, back, ear, and eye. For first and second graders, introduce the anatomical names for the common body parts, name the body parts in another language, or learn the names of the muscles and bones of the body.

Success for All

- Use partners for the nonpartner activities, if necessary, for the success of a particular child.
- Use the bright colors of the crayons so students with color blindness can be successful (or know the particular colors your student cannot see and don't use those colors).

Lesson 4.12 Catching

NASPE Standard 1

Lesson Objective

Students will be able to catch a ball.

Equipment Needed

A variety of throwing items (15), (such as yarn balls, Koosh balls, Nerf footballs, sponge balls, foam rings, Nerf soccer balls, playground balls, plastic bowling pins), music and music player

Activity Descriptions

Students stand by their desk. Students in the first column of desks turn to face their partner, who is the person across from them in the second column of desks. Designate partners in the same way for columns three and four. The partners are going to play catch by tossing various items to each other. Place one catching item on the desks in columns one and three. Students stand as far apart as possible (with the desk with the throwing item on it in between them) and wait for the music to start. When the music starts, students begin playing catch, trying to make as many catches as possible before the music stops. Music is played for 30 seconds. When the music stops, they put the throwing item back on the desk and rotate clockwise to a new desk. Each time they rotate, they play catch with a different piece of equipment and try to make more catches than they made at the previous position. Throws should be made underhanded. The rotation can be completed several times.

Student Assessment

Catches should be made with the hands—without trapping the ball against the body, without catching with the arms instead of the hands, and without dropping the object. If the object is caught three out of five times (given tosses that can be caught), check off for mastery.

Success for All

Use throwing items that beep for students with visual impairments.

Lesson 4.13 Balancing

NASPE Standard 1

Lesson Objective

Students will be able to balance on different body parts.

Equipment Needed

Floor tape, five boards (2 inches by 4 inches by 8 feet), hula hoops

Activity Descriptions

Place pieces of tape ten feet in length on the floor around the room. The tape could be placed in separate lines, a square, or another fun shape. Students walk on the tape forward and sideways as challenged by the teacher.

Boards are fun for students to walk on, too. Eight-foot lengths by four to six inches wide are a good size to work with. Place boards in various patterns on the floor. *L* and *Z* shapes are good choices, as the students like to turn the corners. Students walk the boards, touching heel to toe with each step and sideways in both directions going left and right.

Students stand by their desks and are challenged to balance on different body parts. For example:

- Balance on one foot (do both left and right foot).
- Balance on two hands and one foot.
- Balance on one hand and one foot.
- Balance on both feet and one hand.
- Balance on one knee and both hands.
- Balance on bottom, one hand, and one foot.
- Balance on two knees and two elbows.
- Balance on bottom, one elbow, and one foot.
- Balance on both knees, both hands, and head.
- Balance on stomach and two hands.

Using a hula hoop (or jump rope formed into a circle), students balance on different body parts as challenged by the teacher. Students stand by their desk inside a hula hoop (each student has a hoop). Students are challenged to balance on different body parts inside, outside, and over their hoops. For example:

- Balance on two body parts inside your hoop and one body part outside your hoop.
- Balance on one foot inside your hoop and two hands outside your hoop.
- Balance on three body parts inside your hoop.
- Balance on both knees outside your hoop and both elbows inside your hoop.
- Balance on four body parts over your hoop.

Student Evaluation

- Use a checklist and observe the students walking forward heel to toe and sideways in both directions (left and right) the length of the tape, line, or board without stepping or falling off. Check off for mastery.
- Use a checklist and observe students. If students balance on the body parts specified by the teacher (and hold for 20 seconds), check off for mastery.

Success for All

- Provide a helper if a student needs help balancing.
- Provide an alternative experience for students in wheelchairs. Individualize this experience and have the students practice the balancing skills they need (e.g., balancing books on their lap, getting books from their backpack located on the back of the wheelchair, etc.).

Lesson 4.14 Toss to Self and Catch

NASPE Standard 1

Lesson Objective

Students will be able to toss a ball to themselves and catch it before it bounces twice.

Equipment Needed

Playground ball or beach ball for each student

Activity Descriptions

Students stand by their desks and do the following:

- Toss a playground ball (head high) and catch it before it bounces twice.
- Toss a playground ball (above the head), turn around once, and catch it before it bounces twice.

- Toss a playground ball (above the head), clap once, and catch it before it bounces twice.

Student Assessment

Using a checklist, observe the students as they toss their ball in the air above their heads and catch it before it bounces twice. If they catch it without dropping it and the toss is made above the head (five times), check off for mastery.

Success for All

For those students who consistently cannot catch the ball, allow them to toss and catch balloons, scarves, or beanbags.

Lesson 4.15 Pathways

NASPE Standard 1

Lesson Objective

Students will be able to draw and travel three different pathways (straight, curved, and zigzag).

Equipment Needed

Notebook paper and crayons, segmented jump rope for each student

Activity Descriptions

Students sit at their desks and are asked to draw a straight pathway first, a curved pathway second, and a zigzag pathway last.

Students stand by their desks and are asked to walk in a letter *S* shape and are told that the letter *S* represents a curved pathway. Students are asked to walk in a letter *Z* shape and are told that the letter *Z* is a zigzag pathway. Finally, the students are asked to walk in a letter *I* shape and are told that the letter *I* represents a straight pathway.

Push the desks to one side so students have an area in which to move freely. Students are challenged to move in different ways in the three pathways (straight, curved, and zigzag). The following are challenges that can be used: skip, gallop, hop, jump, walk forward and backward, and move as high and low as possible while moving in straight, curved, and zigzag pathways.

Using segmented jump ropes, students form the three different pathways. Students place the jump rope in a straight line representing a straight pathway, in the letter *S* or *C* for a curved pathway, and in the letter *Z* for a zigzag pathway. After forming a pathway with the jump rope, students straddle the rope and practice jumping down the pathway.

Student Assessment

While giving students different challenges, observe and use a checklist to evaluate them. Students should be challenged to travel in certain ways (such as skipping, hopping, jumping, etc.) while moving in the pathways. If students demonstrate the pathways correctly while traveling, check off for mastery.

Success for All

Students who might be unsuccessful may be paired with a partner.

APPENDIX A

Progressive Activities for Motor Skill Development

Appendix A contains activities that (1) teach gross motor activities (including locomotor, nonlocomotor, and manipulative skills) and fine motor activities, and (2) reinforce rhythmic development. Each group of activities is presented in a progressive manner beginning with simple activities and ending with more challenging activities. When using the manipulative activities, we suggest you have the students master individual activities before attempting the partner and small group activities.

Progressive Activities to Reinforce Walking

1. Walk to a count of ten; then freeze.
2. Walk, changing directions, levels, pathways, and speeds. Repeat, walking in time with a drum beat.
3. Walk forward eight steps, backward eight steps, and sideways eight steps. Repeat the pattern.
4. Walk like animals to music ("Walk Like the Animals" record by Kimbo). Kimbo records are available from Kimbo Educational (www.kimboed.com /dance).
5. Walk beside a partner and stay in rhythm with each other.
6. Follow the Leader with a partner while walking.
7. **Walk Tag:** One partner is "it." The one who is "it" counts to ten before walking to tag the partner. When tagged, the new "it" must count to ten before beginning the chase.
8. **Estimate:** Estimate the number of steps it will take to walk the width of the gym.
9. **The Marching Game:** Song on the CD titled "Physical Ed" by Learning Station, P.O. Box 1316, Melbourne, FL 32902, 1-800-789-9990.
10. **Ve'David:** Folk dance as choreographed in *Two Left Feet and a Beat* by J. Mehrhof and K. Ermler 2000, Emporia, KS: Mirror Publishing (P.O. Box 1708, Emporia KS 66801).

Formation: Single circle with partners
Action:
- All holding hands, walk clockwise (four counts).
- Walk away from the center (four counts).
- Walk toward the center (four counts).
- Walk away from the center (four counts).
- Girls walk into center of the circle (four counts) and out (four counts).
- Boys walk into center of the circle (four counts) and out (four counts).
- Partners do elbow swings (eight counts).
- Repeat the dance.

Country of origin: Israel
Alternative Music: "Let's Twist Again" by Chubby Checker from the Sun Jamming Series

Progressive Activities to Reinforce Running

1. Standing with feet still, practice moving the arms forward and backward (in opposition) in a movement similar to that of the wheels of a train.
2. Moving in personal space, jog in place while lifting knees high and slapping them with the palms of the hands.
3. Jog forward concentrating on the forward and backward movement of the arms.
4. Jog forward concentrating on high knee lift.
5. Jog forward concentrating on taking big strides.
6. Jog forward concentrating on looking straight ahead.
7. Run in general space, changing direction every eight drumbeats.
8. Jog in a figure eight to the drumbeat (forward and then backward). Jog in the pattern of other shapes: circle, square, triangle.
9. Watch a partner jog. First watch the arm movement and then the leg movement and tell what the partner is doing well.

10. Practice shuttle relays while running.
11. Practice relays around an oval; focus on the hand-offs.
12. Jog slowly for ten yards, run at a medium speed for ten yards, sprint for ten yards. Repeat, gradually increasing distances.
13. Run to a drumbeat, stop when drumbeat stops, do a front pivot turn and throw imaginary ball against the wall. Repeat the pattern with a rear pivot turn.

Progressive Activities to Reinforce Galloping and Sliding

1. **Fox and Hound:** The lead foot always stays in front. The back foot catches up but never passes the lead foot. Pretend that the lead foot is the fox and the back foot is the hound trying to catch the fox. The fox always gets away. Continue play, switching the lead foot.
2. **16-8-4-2:** Gallop with one lead foot for 16 steps, switch to the other foot leading for 16 steps, then continue for 8 steps with each lead foot, then 4 steps each, then 2. Repeat, galloping to a drumbeat.
3. **Watch the Leader:** All students focus on the teacher. If the teacher points forward, the students gallop forward; if he or she points to the right, the students slide to the right; to the left, the students slide to the left; and backward, the students gallop backward. Variation: do the same as above while the students are dribbling a ball with their hands or feet.
4. Slide to a drumbeat. Slide to the right eight counts, then to the left eight counts.
5. Face a partner, hold both hands, slide as above.
6. Gallop, holding hands (one hand) with a partner. Stay in rhythm with the partner.
7. Slide and change lead foot every eight counts, then four counts, then two counts (always moving in direction of the lead foot). Use a drumbeat.
8. **Horses in the Corral:** Rhythmic movement as choreographed in *Two Left Feet and a Beat* by Mehrhof and Ermler.
   Music: "Yes, We Can" from Muppet Music Mix
   Formation: Scattered
   Part A
   - Gallop in a controlled space (the Corral) for 32 counts.
   - Tap the right toe for eight counts; tap the left toe for eight counts (horse's feet).
   - Repeat all.
   Part B
   - Pretend to sit on the horse and ride or gallop in place for 16 counts.
   - "Horse's feet" for eight counts right and eight counts left.
   - Repeat all.

Part C
   - Lasso movement for eight counts high and right.
   - Lasso movement for eight counts low and right.
   - Lasso movement for eight counts high and left.
   - Lasso movement for eight counts low and left.
9. Repeat this pattern consecutively: Slide (to the right), slide, jump turn (½ turn), gallop (forward), gallop, run (forward), run. Repeat this sequence but begin with a slide to the left.
10. Slide to the right four times, pivot and throw imaginary ball against the wall. Repeat with slides to the left.

Progressive Activities to Reinforce Jumping

1. With the feet stationary, practice swinging the arms forward and backward (in same direction) while bouncing the knees up and down.
2. Swing arms three times, bend knees, and reach hands above head while jumping high. Say "1, 2, 3, Reach!"
3. Tie scarves onto a long jump rope. Hang the jump rope between two volleyball poles. Students each stand under a scarf and then jump to touch the scarf with both hands.
4. Jump and turn in the air (try ¼ turn, then a ½ turn, and then a full turn).
5. **Jog and Jump:** Students jog and when they hear the teacher blow the duck call or other noisemaker, they jump.
6. Partners stand on opposite sides of a volleyball net while they simultaneously jump to touch the palms of their hands to their partner's palms. Slide three steps sideways after each jump and repeat, going the length of the net.
7. **Happy Birthday:** Rhythmic movement as choreographed in *Two Left Feet and a Beat* by Mehrhof and Ermler.
   Music: "A Cat Had a Birthday" from Sesame Street: Hot! Hot! Hot! Dance Songs
   Formation: Scattered
   Introduction: March in place for 16 counts
   Part A
   - Jump to the right side (two counts). Jump to the left side (two counts). Jump to the right side (one count). Jump to the left side (one count). Jump to the right side (one count). Pause (one count).
   - Jump to the left side (two counts). Jump to the right side (two counts). Jump to the left side (one count). Jump to the right side (one count). Jump to the left side (one count). Pause (one count).
   - Repeat Part A.

Part B

- The students make the sounds of the animals whose names are stated (cat, duck, rooster, lion, cow).
- Walk in a small circle around self for eight counts.

8. ***Seven Jumps:*** "All Purpose Folk Dances," RCA, LPM 1623.
   - A Danish dance originally danced by men. Dancers should hold the balance position for the duration of the sustained note.
   - Chorus. Single circle. Younger children skip or gallop during the entire chorus. More advanced students perform seven step-hops to the right and jump on the eighth count. Repeat step-hops to the left.
   - Balance motionless on each sustained note of beeps.
   - Complete the following order of movements, adding one sustained balance each sequence.
     - Beep 1: Lift right knee.
     - Beep 2: Lift right knee, lift left knee.
     - Beep 3: Lift right knee, lift left knee, kneel and place right knee on floor.
     - Beep 4: Lift right knee, lift left knee, kneel and place right knee on floor, place left knee on floor.
     - Beep 5: Lift right knee, lift left knee, kneel and place right knee on floor, place left knee on floor, and place right elbow on floor.
     - Beep 6: Lift right knee, lift left knee, kneel and place right knee on floor, place left knee on floor, place right elbow on floor, and place left elbow on floor.
     - Beep 7: Lift right knee, lift left knee, kneel and place right knee on floor, place left knee on floor, place right elbow on floor, place left elbow on floor, and place head on floor.
     - Repeat the chorus between sustained notes.
9. Jump in and out of hoops, over long and short jump ropes.
10. Perform this pattern eight times consecutively: jump, jump, hop (right), hop (right), walk (left), walk (right), jump, jump, hop (left), hop (left), walk (right), walk (left).
11. ***Jump Band Activities:***
    - *Basic Step:* Start outside of bands, right and left in, right out two beats, left and right in, left out two beats (right, left, right, right, left, right, left, left).
    - *Straddle Jump:* In, in, out, out; both feet moving together.
    - *Side by Side:* Double jump in feet together, both feet in two beats, both feet out two beats.
    - *Straddle Run:* Start inside, right, left, out; in a running pattern.

- *High Tens:* Two jumpers face each other using basic step; counts one and two, slap own thighs; counts three and four, high tens to partner.

Progressive Activities to Reinforce Hopping

1. Stand on one foot and count to ten.
2. Stand on one foot, bend knee, and push up to hop once. Try on other leg.
3. Stand on a poly spot; hop up and down five times on one leg. Switch to other leg and repeat.
4. Hop in and out of a hoop.
5. Hop on top of several poly spots laid on the floor in a straight line.
6. Hop twice on the right foot and twice on the left foot, moving forward. Repeat this pattern to a fast or slow drumbeat.
7. Hop the length of the gym on the right foot; return to the start hopping on the left foot.
8. Estimate how many hops it will take to cross the play area. Repeat on each leg. Repeat trying to use a smaller number of hops.
9. Hop along a line, crossing back and forth over the line with the right foot. Repeat with the left foot.
10. Hop holding hands with a partner (stay in rhythm with each other).
11. Repeat this pattern moving forward across the gym floor: step (right foot), step (left foot), step (right foot), hop (right foot), step (left foot), step (right foot), step (left foot), hop (left foot). This is a Schottische step.

Progressive Activities to Reinforce Skipping

1. ***Skipping Song:*** For two- and three-year-olds: "Lift one foot and then the other, lift one foot and then the other, lift one foot and then the other, I will skip some day!" *For three- and four-year-olds:* "Hop on one foot and then the other, hop on one foot and then the other, hop on one foot and then the other, I will skip some day!" *For four- and five-year-olds:* "Walk and hop and walk and hop now, walk and hop and walk and hop now, walk and hop and walk and hop now, I will skip some day!" "Skip and skip and skip all day long, skip and skip and skip all day long, and skip and skip and skip all day long, I have learned to skip!"

2. ***Giant Skips:*** All students start on a line. Using slow skipping steps, overexaggerate the knee lifts, lifting knees high in the air as you skip across the area, and also overexaggerate the swing of the arms,

pumping the hands high as the knee lifts into the air.
3. Skip (forward, backward, in a circle, with a partner, to a drumbeat).
4. Skip to music ("Rhythms for Basic Motor Skills" record by Kimbo).
5. Repeat the pattern moving forward across the gym floor: skip, skip, run, run, run.

Progressive Activities to Reinforce Leaping

1. Stand on one poly spot on one foot. Leap onto another poly spot landing on the other foot.
2. Stand with toes touching a line. Take three giant steps backward; then run and leap over the line.
3. Leap over a poly spot, a small hoop, or an olympet (a small flat hula hoop) ring.
4. One partner lies on the floor while the other partner practices leaping over the still partner.
5. Three or four students stand in a single file. Place four or five cones in a straight line eight to ten feet apart. Students run and leap over all the cones. After leaping over the cones, they run back to the start.
6. Leap over low hurdles.
7. Perform a rhythmic pattern: leap, tap; leap, tap; leap, tap, tap (leap slightly to the right with the right foot and tap left foot beside right foot, leap slightly to the left on the left foot and tap right foot beside left foot, leap slightly to the right again on the right foot and tap left foot beside right foot twice). Repeat, beginning with slight leap to the left.

Progressive Activities to Reinforce the Roll

INDIVIDUAL ACTIVITIES

1. Roll an 8½-inch playground ball around body while sitting on the floor.
2. Roll ball on top of legs, arms, tummy, and chest and around the waist.
3. Roll ball to an elephant space (a large empty area), and run to stop the ball before it quits rolling.
4. Roll ball to hit different targets, such as bowling pins or cones, or on top of carpet squares, poly spots, or bases.

PARTNER ACTIVITIES

1. In a sitting straddle position, roll a ball back and forth to a partner.
2. While standing, roll a ball back and forth with a partner.

3. One student stands with legs in straddle position while partner tries to roll the ball between the straddled legs.
4. One student moves in general space while the partner rolls the ball to the moving student.

SMALL GROUP ACTIVITIES

1. **Bowl-a-Rama:** Divide the class into groups of four to six children each. Each child has one ball. The object is to roll the ball toward other groups, trying to keep the balls from collecting close to your group. When balls are rolled toward your group, collect them and roll them toward another group.
2. **Roll and Run:** Half of the class stands with legs in a straddle position while the other half rolls their ball between the legs of classmates. After the ball either goes between the legs of or beside the classmates, the roller runs to retrieve the ball and roll toward a different person.

Progressive Activities to Reinforce the Overhand Throw

INDIVIDUAL ACTIVITIES

1. Overhand throw toward a wall.
2. Overhand throw toward a target on the wall.
3. Overhand throw for distance to see how far the object can be thrown.
4. **Go and Throw:** While music is playing, each student jogs while carrying a ball. When music stops, overhand throw the ball against a wall. When music starts, begin jogging again. This activity may also be done with partners. Each partner has a ball, and when the music stops, overhand throw the ball to the partner.

PARTNER ACTIVITIES

1. Overhand throw to a stationary partner.
2. **One Step Back:** Throw and catch with a partner. Each time the object is caught, the person who made the catch takes one step backward. If the object is dropped, the catcher does not take a step back.
3. Overhand throw to a moving partner.
4. Overhand throw to a stationary partner while moving.
5. Jump and throw to a partner.

SMALL GROUP ACTIVITIES

1. **Flew the Coop:** Two or three students try to complete ten overhand throws to each other using a rubber chicken or object other than a ball, before the other team touches or intercepts the chicken or object (similar to a keep-away game).

2. *Lifesaver:* Persons holding the chickens or other designated objects are "it" for the entire game. Upon being tagged by "it," the caught person kneels on one knee. The teacher then tosses the "Lifesaver" ball (a foam ball) to that person, who stands up, uses an overhand pattern to throw the ball to another caught person, then returns to the game.

Progressive Activities to Reinforce the Catch

INDIVIDUAL ACTIVITIES

1. Toss a scarf to self and catch at high levels, medium levels, and low levels.
2. Toss the scarf under the leg and catch.
3. Toss and catch the scarf on different body parts.
4. Place scarf on top of a ball, underhand toss the ball into the air, catch the ball after it bounces, and then catch the scarf.
5. Toss a beanbag to self and catch at various levels.
6. Toss a beanbag to self, clap hands twice, and catch the beanbag.
7. Toss a Slo-Mo ball or a beach ball to self above head, let it bounce on ground, and then catch it using the hands.
8. Toss a Slo-Mo ball or a beach ball to self; catch with hands before ball bounces.
9. Toss and catch a six-inch foam ball.
10. Underhand toss a foam ball against the wall; catch after one bounce.
11. Underhand toss a foam ball against the wall; catch before the ball bounces.

PARTNER ACTIVITIES

1. Underhand toss a scarf to a partner; the partner catches it using the hands.
2. Both partners toss scarves straight up in the air and run forward to catch the partner's scarf.
3. Slide a beanbag on floor for the partner to stop, using hands.
4. Slide a beanbag to the right or left of the partner so the partner must track the object before stopping it with the hands.
5. Bounce a Slo-Mo ball to a partner and catch it using extended hands.
6. Clap hands before catching a ball bounced by a partner.
7. A partner underhand tosses a Slo-Mo ball to a partner, who catches it before it bounces.
8. A partner overhand throws a foam softball to a partner.
9. A partner overhand throws a foam softball to a partner at various levels.

10. A partner overhand throws a foam softball to a moving partner.
11. *Beanbag Tag:* Students work with partners; each pair has one beanbag. When the music starts (or on the teacher's signal), the students begin to toss the beanbag back and forth, making good tosses to the partner. When the music stops (or on the teacher's second signal), the person with the beanbag is "it" and will walk quickly to tag the partner with the beanbag. Begin tossing and catching either when the partner is tagged or when the music begins again.

SMALL GROUP ACTIVITIES

1. *Star Juggle:* Form groups of five students standing in a circle formation. The first person tosses a beanbag to the person straight across from him or her. Continue tossing the beanbag to someone in the group who is *not* standing by the tosser. Continue this cycle until all have caught the beanbag. The first person then adds another beanbag and then another while the group continues tossing and catching.
2. *Anything Goes:* Form groups of four or five students. All have foam or lightweight balls. Count together "1, 2, 3," and all underhand toss the ball into the air and then try to catch a different ball than the one tossed. Variation: Each person in the group has a different object to toss—for example, a ball, a beanbag, a Fox-tail, a scarf, a Whiffle ball.

Progressive Activities to Reinforce the Kick

INDIVIDUAL ACTIVITIES

1. Practice kicking a scarf, balloon, or Balzac (a balloon inside a covering made of cotton material) up in the air.
2. *Kick and Run:* Place a ball on the ground, take three giant steps back, and run forward kicking the ball as far as possible. Run after the ball and kick it again. Try to pick up the ball before it stops rolling.
3. Place a ball on a poly spot in line with a target; kick the ball to try hitting the target. Use targets such as bowling pins, cones, tennis ball cans, or Pringles cans.
4. *Kick Off:* Stand a foam football on a tee. Take three steps backward. Start with the kicking foot and run, using three steps toward the tee. Kick the ball as far as possible.

PARTNER ACTIVITIES

1. Place a ball on a poly spot; kick the ball to a partner. Switch after three kicks.

2. One partner rolls ball to the other, who kicks the ball. Switch after three kicks.

3. **Partner Kickball:** A partner rolls the ball to a kicker, and the kicker kicks the ball and runs to touch one base and return to the starting position. The partner who rolled the ball retrieves the kicked ball and attempts to touch the kicker's base before the kicker crosses home plate. Switch after three kicks.

SMALL GROUP ACTIVITIES

1. **Kick It:** Get a piece of equipment out of the hoop (balloon, Balzac, or scarf) and practice kicking that equipment. After ten kicks, put it back in the hoop and get a different piece of equipment.

2. **Move It:** Form groups of four to six children. Each person has an eight-inch ball, a soccer ball, a beach ball, or a Slo-Mo ball. All stand behind a designated line. Each player kicks his or her ball to hit the cage-ball (a large inflated ball with a circumference of 48 to 72 inches). See how far the group can move the cageball in a designated time.

3. **Defend the Pin:** The group stands in a large circle. Three players stand inside this larger circle defending three bowling pins. One ball is put into play as the outside circle tries to kick the ball and knock down one of the bowling pins. If a kicker knocks down a pin, that player becomes the defender and the defender takes the kicker's place. The kickers need to quickly pass the ball to get the defenders moving. Once the group gets good at moving the ball, add another ball. Students must keep the ball on the ground.

4. **Continuous Kickball** (J. Mehrhof and K. Ermler 2001. Physical Essentials. Emporia, KS: Mirror): Divide the class into two teams. One team is the kicking team; the other team is in the field. Place six to eight balls in a hoop beside the teacher. The teacher rolls a ball to the first kicker, who kicks the ball and runs the bases. As soon as the first ball is kicked, the next ball is rolled to the next kicker. The fielders have to get the ball and place it back in the hoop as quickly as possible. The object is for the kicking team to empty the hoop and for the fielding team to have all the balls back in the hoop before the last runner gets home!

Progressive Activities to Reinforce the Strike

INDIVIDUAL ACTIVITIES

1. **Hit and Go:** Each child has an empty two-liter bottle and a Slo-Mo ball, beach ball, or foam ball. Lay the ball on the ground and then strike the ball using the bottle. Run to the ball and strike it again. Try to strike the ball before it stops rolling.

2. **Off the Wall:** Each child has a two-liter bottle and a Slo-Mo ball, beach ball, or foam ball. Drop the ball; after it bounces, strike it against the wall. Catch the ball after it rebounds off the wall. Variation: How many times can the student continuously strike the ball against the wall?

3. **Strike and Run:** Using a paddle or an empty two-liter bottle, strike a six- to eight-inch foam ball off the batting tee. After striking the ball, lay the paddle down, run and get the ball, come back, and try again.

4. **Score:** Straddle the poly spot that is ten feet away from a target. Drop the ball and after the bounce, strike it using the hand and try to make it hit the target. Move to a different target after retrieving the ball. Targets might include a large box, a trash can, a hula hoop, or a poster or shape taped on the wall.

5. **Keep It Up:** Each person has a small paddle and a balloon. Tap the balloon up in the air using the paddle. Count by twos while tapping the balloon. Say the alphabet while striking the balloon.

PARTNER ACTIVITIES

1. **Back and Forth:** Divide the class into partners. Each individual has a bottle, and partners share a Slo-Mo ball, beach ball, or foam ball. With the ball on the ground, the partners strike the ball back and forth. Beginners should stop the ball before hitting it and then should progress to striking it as it moves toward the striker.

2. **Strike and Spell:** Think of a spelling word. Spell that word with the partner while striking the ball back and forth to each other using a hand, paddle, or racket. Say a letter each time the ball is hit.

SMALL GROUP ACTIVITIES

1. **Four-Square Tennis:** Four students, each in a square of a Four-Square box, play the game of Four-Square hitting the ball using a paddle or a racket. Begin using a Slo-Mo ball or a large ball. As skill improves, use a smaller ball, such as a tennis ball.

2. **Volleyball Tennis:** Place three or four per team on one side of a low volleyball net. Using tennis rackets, players hit a tennis ball back and forth over the net. Each team is allowed a maximum of three hits per side before returning the ball. An unlimited number of bounces may occur on each side. Variation: Limit the number of hits and bounces allowed by each team before returning the ball. Depending on skill level, use regulation tennis balls and rackets or a high-bounce foam ball and smaller rackets.

Progressive Activities to Reinforce the Volley (Set and Pass)

INDIVIDUAL ACTIVITIES

1. Use various body parts to tap a balloon up in the air.
2. Use various body parts to tap a scarf or trash bag up in the air.
3. Spell a word while tapping a balloon.
4. Hands together and volley a balloon on the forearms.
5. Volley the balloon hitting it above the head.
6. Volley and catch the ball. Volley two consecutive times and catch the ball. Continue adding a volley for each successful step completed.
7. Count the number of volleys completed in one minute.
8. Volley a trainer volleyball against a wall.
9. Volley the ball to land inside of a hoop.

PARTNER ACTIVITIES

1. Volley a balloon back and forth between partners. More experienced students may use a volleyball trainer.
2. Stand on opposite sides of a bench, a jump rope, or a hoop and volley a balloon back and forth.
3. Say the alphabet while volleying a balloon or trainer volleyball with a partner.
4. Volley the object to your partner, turn around or touch the ground, and be ready to hit the object again.
5. Alternate volleying a Balzac (a balloon inside a covering made of cotton material) into a wall with a partner.

SMALL GROUP ACTIVITIES

1. *Progressive Volleying:* Assign four or five students per circle. The group is challenged to complete ten consecutive volleys using a balloon. After that feat has been completed, they attempt to volley a Balzac consecutively. The last challenge is to volley a trainer volleyball ten consecutive times.
2. *Three on Three:* Three players stand on each side of a volleyball net. Each time players must complete a minimum of two volleys before returning the ball to the other team. A point is scored each time two hits are completed before sending the ball over the net.

Progressive Activities to Reinforce the Dribble with Hands

INDIVIDUAL ACTIVITIES

1. Dribble ball on top of a poly spot or inside of a hoop.
2. Dribble while moving around general space.
3. Dribble while moving around obstacles.
4. Dribble with right hand while spelling words; then spell words while dribbling using left hand.
5. Dribble with one hand while tossing a scarf with the other hand. Switch hands. Invent ways to dribble and toss the scarf.
6. Place a scarf on top of a ball. Underhand toss the ball up in the air, dribble the ball when it returns to the ground, and then catch the scarf. Switch hands.
7. *Rainbow Round-Up:* Each student has a ball that bounces. Scattered on the floor are several different-colored cones and poly spots. Do the following activities:
   - Dribble around as many different cones as possible.
   - Dribble to a spot, put your foot on that spot, and bounce the ball five times.
   - Dribble around a cone; then find a spot that is the same color, stop on that spot, and dribble five times.
   - Increase the difficulty by having the students dribble with the nondominant hand.
8. *Wipe Out:* Each student has a ball that bounces. During the drum solo of the song "Wipe Out" students pass the ball against a wall using various passes learned. During the verse part of the song, students are challenged to dribble using right hand, left hand, alternating hands, and fancy dribbling they invent.

PARTNER ACTIVITIES

1. *Top This:* Divide the class into partners. One person spins a top and tells the partner how to dribble the ball until the top stops. Examples: dribble with right hand only, dribble with the left hand only, alternate hands, dribble to the wall and back, dribble twice with right hand and twice with left hand. When the top stops spinning, the partners switch positions.
2. *Follow the Leader:* One partner, the follower, must dribble in the manner of the other partner, the leader. Begin with stationary dribbling and then dribble while moving around the space. Switch roles.
3. *Partner Catch:* While facing each other, partners toss one scarf back and forth while dribbling a ball. Variations: Each partner has a scarf; toss both scarves at the same time; toss scarf straight up in the air and dribble forward to catch partner's scarf.
4. *Partner ABC Dribbling:* Challenge your partner with a spelling word and listen as the partner bounces the ball and spells the word.

SMALL GROUP ACTIVITIES

1. *Balzac Keep It Up:* Assign four to six students per group; each student has a ball to dribble, and each group has one Balzac (a balloon inside a covering

made of cotton material). In circle formation, all dribble with one hand while using the free hand to volley the Balzac to teammates. Count the number of consecutive volleys.

2. ***Quick Feet:*** Half the class dribbles a ball while the other half rolls yarn balls or beanbags attempting to touch feet of the dribblers. If a dribbler's feet get touched, that person must dribble in stationary space while performing ten side straddles with legs, then return to the game. Switch roles after designated time.

3. ***Spicy Hot Chicken:*** Five or six students form a circle and dribble a ball with one hand. Count the number of catches made passing a rubber chicken to each other in one minute. Students must keep dribbling the ball continuously while the group tosses the chicken. Try dribbling with both right and left hand.

4. ***Roll 'em:*** Assign four or five students per group. A wall chart lists six ways to dribble: (1) right hand, (2) left hand, (3) alternating hands, (4) moving at a low level, (5) moving while walking backward, and (6) fancy dribbling. The group rolls a die to determine how to dribble; the number on the die indicates which number on the wall chart the group is to follow. Everyone in the group dribbles across the room using that dribble; they dribble back to the starting position, and the die is rolled again.

Progressive Activities to Reinforce the Dribble with Feet

INDIVIDUAL ACTIVITIES

1. Dribble around the area. When the music stops, see how quickly you can stop the ball on top of a poly spot.

2. Tap the ball back and forth between the feet.

3. Dribble around the area using different directions, pathways, and speeds.

4. Dribble the ball in a pathway to spell out your name.

5. ***Obstacle Course Dribbling:*** Dribble the ball around, through, over, and under different obstacles. Change the order of the obstacles and repeat.

6. Dribble around as many cones as possible in a designated time.

7. Using colored poly spots and colored cones, dribble around a cone and then dribble to a spot that is the same color as the cone and trap the ball on that spot. Repeat going around different-colored cones.

8. Choose three favorite colors. Dribble around cones that are those colors, making a pattern. Continue dribbling around those three colors.

9. Dribble the ball and listen for the leader to call out the word "stop." Then trap the ball with your foot as quickly as possible.

10. Dribble the ball and listen for the leader to call out a body part. Use that body part to stop the ball.

PARTNER ACTIVITIES

1. ***Follow the Leader:*** One person dribbles around the area while the partner follows, also dribbling a ball. Switch roles after a short time.

2. ***Partner Dribble Tag:*** All players must dribble the ball using feet. The person who is "it" counts to five before dribbling the ball in an attempt to make the ball touch the partner's ball. The partner dribbles to keep the "it" person's ball from tagging the partner's ball. When no further than an arm's length away from the partner, the player who is "it" may use a soft kick to try to tag the partner's ball. Partners switch roles after the ball has been tagged or after the teacher signals them to switch (after one minute).

SMALL GROUP ACTIVITIES

1. ***World Cup Dribbling:*** Each student has a ball. Half of the class performs sideways straddle jumps while raising and lowering the ball behind their head, pretending to perform a two-hand overhead pass but not releasing the ball. The other half of the class attempts to dribble and pass the ball between the legs of the students performing the straddle jumps. If the ball goes between the legs, the dribbler shouts "Gooooal!" and continues on to another set of legs. Switch positions after a short time.

2. ***Soccer Stuck in the Mud:*** Designate four or five students to be "it"; those who are "it" are identified by dribbling the same-colored balls. All of the players are dribbling the balls using their feet. If a colored ball hits a player's ball, that player must stand with legs straddled and may return to the game after another player passes his or her ball through the frozen player's legs.

3. ***Dribble Tag:*** All dribble a ball around half of the area. The object is to touch someone else's ball with your ball. If your ball is touched by another ball, proceed to the other half of the gym and continue playing the game on that side of the room.

Progressive Activities to Reinforce the Punt

INDIVIDUAL ACTIVITIES

1. Students underhand toss a Slo-Mo ball and try to get it to land on a poly spot located about two to three feet in front of them. Repeat in order to practice tossing the ball in the correct area.

2. Toss a Slo-Mo ball or lightweight ball; let the ball bounce once and then kick the ball using instep of the foot.

3. Facing a wall, drop the ball (Nerf ball) and kick it before it touches the ground.
4. Facing an open space, drop the ball and then kick it to see how far it can go before it touches the ground.
5. Facing an open space, drop the ball and kick it to see if it can land inside the hula hoops that have been placed out in the field area.
6. Practice punting a ball over a long jump rope that has been tied to two volleyball standards about ten feet off the ground.
7. Practice punting the ball high but a short distance.
8. Practice punting one ball a short distance, and on the next try attempt to punt the ball a longer distance.

PARTNER ACTIVITIES

1. Practice punting back and forth with a partner. Each time the partner catches the punt, take two steps backward, increasing the distance.
2. **Punt Challenge:** Count to see how many times you and your partner can punt and catch a ball in 30 seconds. One point is awarded for each catch.
3. **Three Elephants:** The partner overhand passes the ball to the punter. After the punter receives the ball, the passer counts "one elephant, two elephants, three elephants," and the punter tries to punt the ball as quickly as possible before "three elephants" is said.
4. **Punt for the Stars:** One person punts the ball. The nonpunting partner counts out loud as fast as possible after ball is kicked and stops counting when the ball is caught. The object is to kick the ball high in order to achieve a higher number.

SMALL GROUP ACTIVITIES

1. **Punt and Run:** Divide the students into two groups—one group on the punting side and one on the receiving side. All students on the punting side punt at the same time. The receiving side tries to catch one of the punts. After catching a punt or retrieving one that has bounced, they run the ball back to the punting side. Then the two groups switch positions.
2. **Hike, Punt, Catch:** Assign players in groups of three. One player is the center and hikes the ball to the punter; the punter punts the ball and the receiver tries to catch the punt. Switch roles after three punts.

Progressive Activities to Reinforce the Set Shot

INDIVIDUAL ACTIVITIES

1. **L-1:** Make an *L* shape with the dominant arm, holding an imaginary ball. Straighten the arm to make

the numeral 1. Continue practicing this to reinforce the arm movement when shooting a set shot.
2. **Squat L-1:** Bend the knees before making the L-1; extend the arms and legs concurrently while making the 1. Repeat.
3. Practice L-1 using a ball.
4. Practice Squat L-1 using a ball.
5. **Dribble and Shoot:** Each student stands on a poly spot with a ball. On the teacher's signal, students shoot one set shot to self; after catching the ball, they dribble to another poly spot and shoot. Students continue attempting to shoot to self from each of the poly spots in the room.
6. Practice the set shot, pushing the ball against a wall.
7. Practice the set shot against a wall, aiming for a large square target taped on the wall about six to nine feet high.
8. **Uno, Dos, Tres:** Mark three different lines on the wall, three feet, six feet, and nine feet from the floor. Practice set shots attempting to touch the ball to each line.
9. **Consecutive Uno, Dos, Tres:** Using the lines of the previous game, students must hit the three-foot line before attempting the six-foot line; then they must hit the six-foot line before aiming for the nine-foot line. If they hit all three in order, they yell "Uno, Dos, Tres!" and begin again.
10. Practice the set shot into a hoop hanging from a basketball rim. The lower height increases success for the students.
11. Practice the set shot into an eight-foot basketball rim.

PARTNER ACTIVITIES

1. **Shoot and Rebound:** A student performs a set shot against the wall; the partner retrieves (rebounds) the ball and then the partner shoots. Continue alternating the shooting and retrieving (rebounding) positions.
2. **Shoot the Hoop:** A student holds a hoop vertically over the head. The partner performs a set shot aiming for the ball to go through the hoop. After the shooting partner makes five shots through the hoop, partners switch positions.
3. **Partner Uno, Dos, Tres:** Play the *Uno, Dos, Tres* game described above in the individual activities section, with partners sharing one ball. Partners must alternate which line they are aiming for, switching shooters after each attempt.

SMALL GROUP ACTIVITIES

1. **Group Shoot:** Assign groups of three, each group with two balls. One student in the group uses the set shot to aim for the lines on the walls. Each time a student hits a line, the group is awarded two

points. The second person rebounds or retrieves the balls after they have been shot and passes them to the third person, who hands the balls to the shooter. After 30 seconds, all players in the group rotate positions. Add the points of all three players for a final score.

2. *Horse:* Assign groups of three, with one ball per group. Players form a single file line behind the shooter. The first person shoots to hit a line taped on the wall from any distance on the floor the shooter chooses. If the ball hits the line, the second person must attempt from that same distance. If the second person hits the line, the third person must try from that distance. A person who misses a shot directly after someone has successfully hit the line is given a letter from the word *horse*. A player who misses five shots must begin spelling *horse* again. The object of the game is to have the fewest letters. This game may also be played using a basketball hoop as the target.

Progressive Activities to Reinforce the Overhand Serve

INDIVIDUAL ACTIVITIES

1. Practice underhand tossing a ball above the head. Let the ball bounce after the toss.
2. Practice underhand tossing to lift the ball in front of the body, about two feet higher than the head, and have the ball land on a poly spot one foot in front of the dominant foot.
3. Stand two feet from a wall, facing the wall. To practice tossing the ball straight up, toss the ball parallel to the wall, reaching for a height about two feet above the head.
4. *Bend and Stretch:* Bend the arm so the hitting hand is behind head. Stretch or extend the hand above the head, aiming to hit an imaginary ball. Repeat several times.
5. *Toss and Tap:* Underhand toss a ball, bend and stretch the arm so the hand taps the ball easily. The object is to tap the ball when the arm is extended above the head.
6. Practice overhand serving the ball against a wall. Stand about 10 to 15 feet from the wall before serving.
7. Practice overhand serving the ball against a wall. Stand about 10 to 15 feet from the wall before serving, aiming the ball to hit above a six-foot line that has been taped on the wall.
8. Stand 20 feet from the wall and practice hitting the ball on the wall above a six-foot line that has been taped on the wall.
9. Practice serving a ball over a six-foot-high net.

PARTNER ACTIVITIES

1. Find a partner who is close to the same height. The nonserving partner stands on the same side as the hitting arm of the server with the arm extended above the head. The serving partner underhand tosses the ball, attempting to toss the ball about two feet higher than the partner's outstretched arm. This activity is good practice for a high-ball toss.
2. *Serve and Catch:* A student serves the ball against the wall. After the ball hits the wall, the partner tries to catch it. If the partner catches the ball before it bounces, the partner gets to serve the ball. If the partner misses the ball, the other partner serves again. After serving three consecutive serves, players switch positions.
3. *Movin' on Back:* One player is positioned on each side of the net. One player serves the ball. If the other player catches the ball, that player rolls the ball under the net to the server, who takes one step backward and serves from that position. If the catching partner misses the ball, the serving partner serves from the same position. After five serves, the players switch positions.
4. *Serving ABCs:* A student overhand serves the ball to a partner. Each time the partner catches the ball, the partners earn a letter of the alphabet. The object is to see how many letters they earn in two minutes.
5. *Moving Partner:* A partner stands on the side of the net opposite the server. The server aims to serve the ball so the partner can catch it without moving. If the ball is caught, the catching partner moves to another position on the floor. The server must now attempt to serve to that position. Partners switch after three serves.

SMALL GROUP ACTIVITIES

1. *Hit the Craters:* Assign six to eight players to a net. Half the group is positioned on each side of the net; one side is the serving side (each server needs a ball); the other side is the retrieving side. On the teacher's signal, the servers overhand serve the ball, attempting to get the balls to land inside the hoops (craters) that have been placed on the opposite side of the net. For each ball that lands inside a hoop, the team playing on that court receives one point. Retrievers return the balls to the servers by rolling them under the net. After one minute of serving, the servers and retrievers switch positions, adding points together to obtain a total.
2. *Cooperative Serving:* Assign four to six players to each side of a net. Use multiple nets to accommodate all students. One player overhand serves the ball over the net. The other players try to catch the ball after it has been served and quickly return the ball over the net using an overhand serve. The object is to see

how many consecutive overhand serves can be made over the net within two or three minutes.

Progressive Activities to Reinforce Ball Passes

INDIVIDUAL ACTIVITIES

1. Using both hands on the ball, practice throwing the ball against a wall.
2. With both hands on the ball, practice throwing the ball at different levels on the wall: high, medium, and low.
3. With both hands on the ball, throw the ball against the wall, let the ball bounce once on the floor, and then catch it. Step backward one step after each throw. See how far you can stand away from the wall to throw the ball using both hands and still have the ball hit the wall.
4. *Thirty-Second Challenge:* Count the number of times the ball can bounce off the wall in 30 seconds. Students must use two hands on the ball to pass it against the wall.
5. *Wipe Out:* Play the song "Wipe Out." During the verse, students dribble a ball around the room. During the chorus or drum part, students perform a chest, bounce, or overhead pass against the wall as identified by the teacher.
6. *Side Slide:* Practice chest passes against the wall while sliding feet sideways. Slide six steps to the right and six to the left, trying to attempt six passes in six sideways steps. Change the number of slides according to the space provided.

PARTNER ACTIVITIES

1. Share one ball with a partner. When the music begins, the partner with the ball chooses a pass. The partners continue practicing that pass until the music stops. When the music stops, the person with the ball chooses a different pass to practice. Continue as before.
2. Share one ball with a partner. When the music begins, the partner with the ball chooses a pass. The partners continue practicing that pass until the music stops. When the music stops, the person with the ball is "it" and chases the partner. If the partner is tagged, the duo begins passing again. When the music begins again, all stop running and begin passing again. The partner with the ball always chooses the pass to be used.
3. *Move the Penny* (Physical Essentials 2001): Partners place a penny on the floor between them. Practicing bounce passes to one another, they attempt to bounce the ball on the penny, moving the penny closer to their partner.

4. *Pass and Move:* Partners holding the ball stand stationary; partners without the ball are moving. After passing the ball to a partner, the person without the ball moves to an open space to receive a pass from the partner.

SMALL GROUP ACTIVITIES

1. *Keep Away:* Assign groups of six and divide the groups into two teams of three players each. Members of one team try to use the three types of passes to move the ball to their teammates. When the opposing team intercepts the ball, that team gets to control and pass the ball.
2. *Consecutive Keep Away:* This game is the same as above except the object of the game is to complete ten consecutive passes before the ball is intercepted.
3. *Ordered Keep Away:* This game is the same as above except the team in control of the ball must establish an order in which the balls are passed. Player 1 must always pass to player 2, who must always pass to player 3, and so on. Each team must attempt to complete ten consecutive passes maintaining the order that has been established.

Progressive Activities for Body Awareness

1. Transfer weight from two body parts to two different body parts.
2. Transfer weight from two body parts to three different body parts.
3. Transfer weight from two body parts to one body part.
4. Balance on three different body parts.
5. Balance on two different body parts.
6. Balance on one body part.
7. Make a wide shape.
8. Make a wide shape and then a narrow shape.
9. One partner makes a twisted shape and the other partner makes a round shape.
10. Jump off a folded mat, land and roll.
11. Jump off a folded mat, make a wide shape in the air, land and roll.
12. Jump off a folded mat, throw a ball while in the air to your partner.
13. Do beginning Yoga postures (use "Yoga for Kids" record by Kimbo).

Progressive Activities for Space Awareness

1. Clap your hands at a high, medium, and low level.
2. Toss a beanbag and catch at a high level three times. Then catch at a low level three times.

3. Stand in a personal space and stretch as far as you can to the sides and toward the sky.

4. With hands on the floor (as the base of support) move the rest of your body around in own personal space.

5. Skip around general space flapping your arms like the wings of a bird.

6. Gallop fast near a classmate, change directions quickly, and gallop away with the other foot being the lead foot.

7. Use a different locomotor skill and a different pathway each time the music stops.

8. To the drumbeat, walk fast and continue walking anywhere in gym without touching anyone or anything.

9. Practice dribbling a ball forward, backward, sideways, up, and down. First walk, then jog, then run.

10. Dribble a ball with your feet in a straight pathway, then switch to a curved pathway, and finally use a zigzag pathway.

11. Throw your foam ball over the net to a large empty space.

12. Throw your foam ball over the net and try to have your ball land inside a hoop or small space.

Progressive Activities for Qualities of Movement

1. Raise arms above your head fast, lower them down slowly.

2. Move fast in your personal space, then on the signal freeze.

3. Gallop fast, hop slow, gallop fast, hop slow.

4. Jog, run faster, sprint to the finish line, then jog again.

5. Stand across the gym from a partner. Run fast to meet your partner in the middle but stop just before you touch each other. How close can you be to each other without touching?

6. In your special area, make your arms strong, your back strong, your neck strong, your stomach strong, hands and legs strong.

7. March with strong legs, then tiptoe with quiet legs; march to music ("Traditional Marches" record by Kimbo).

8. Imagine that you are lifting a very heavy box above your head.

9. Pretend that you are sneaking up to scare your brother or sister, jump and make a loud noise when you see him or her.

10. Pretend you are tipping a basketball into the hoop; now pretend you are slam-dunking it into the hoop.

11. Pretend you are a floppy rag doll (use "Pretend" record by Kimbo).

Progressive Activities for Relationships

1. Spread your arms, fingers, and legs far apart. Put them back close together.

2. Slide your feet far apart and close together quickly.

3. Dribble the ball near your feet, in front of your body, to the side of your body, and below your knees.

4. Jump over your hoop. Land in your hoop. Skip around the outside of your hoop.

5. Jog and dribble a ball while following close behind a partner who is moving in different pathways.

6. One partner is the leader and dribbles in a high, medium, or low level; second partner must dribble in a level different from his or her partner.

7. Face your partner. One partner dribbles the ball in his or her personal space. Second partner must mirror his or her partner's dribble.

8. Face your partner. One partner dribbles the ball in her or his personal space. Second partner must match partner's dribble.

9. One partner is the leader and dribbles using different pathways, levels, and directions. Second partner tries to follow partner's movements as closely as possible (like Follow the Leader).

10. Stand beside a partner on a bench, each holding a ball. Jump off the bench together, tossing a ball to yourself, and try to land at the same time as your partner while catching the ball.

11. Teach beginning square dance patterns (use "Get Ready to Square Dance" record by Kimbo).

Progressive Activities for Nonlocomotor Skills

1. Bend, then stretch your fingers, arms, legs, tummy, and back.

2. Twist your wrist, arm, leg, waist, and foot. Try to twist two different body parts at the same time. Then try three different body parts.

3. Jump and turn to face a different direction.

4. Jump and turn to perform a 180-, then a 360-degree turn.

5. Push hard against a wall trying to knock it down.

6. One partner sits on a carpet square that is turned upside down. The sitting partner holds onto a jump rope while the standing partner pulls her or him to the other side of the room.

7. Begin by lying on the floor. Slowly rise up pretending you are a flower growing. Then a rainstorm comes with hail and causes the flower to collapse down to the ground.

8. Swing your arms below your waist trying to keep flies off your legs; then sway your arms above your head waving to people in a hot air balloon.
9. As you run across the gym, dodge the cones and hoops on the floor.
10. As you run across the gym, dodge the fellow classmates standing in the hoops attempting to grab the scarf you have tucked in your waistband.
11. Swing, shake, twist, etc. ("Walter the Waltzing Worm" and "Getting to Know Myself" records by Kimbo).

FINE MOTOR ACTIVITIES

1. Practice spinning tops with right and left hand.
2. Use clothespins to pick up cotton balls.
3. Sort buttons by color and shape.
4. Balance golf tees upside down on a flat surface.
5. Use clay to form different objects.
6. Turn Eye Poppers inside out. Obtain Eye Poppers from Oriental Trading Company, 4206 S. 108th St., Omaha, NE 68137; 402-331-5511 or www.oriental.com.
7. Spin Flying Dragonflies between the palms of the hands and then watch them fly. Older students may try to catch them. Flying Dragonflies are also available from Oriental Trading Company (see number 6 above).
8. Stack the lids of two-liter bottles.
9. Play Pick Up Sticks.
10. Play with marbles.
11. Play Jacks.
12. Spin Jammer activities:
    - Spin on fingers.
    - Change from hand to hand.
    - Sit down and stand up while spinning.
    - Spin and walk, jog, and the like to the other side of the play area.
    - Spin and then transfer the Spin Jammer onto different fingers.
    - Perform curl-ups until Spin Jammer stops spinning.

Spinning a Flying Dragonfly.

Moving Spin Jammer from one finger to another.

Turning Eye Poppers inside out.

Rubrics for Locomotor and Manipulative Skills

When creating rubrics for use in your classes, please consider the following:

1. It is best for rubrics to have an even number of levels to keep the person assessing from choosing the middle level. For instance, in a four-level rubric, level three would be the expected level for all students. Levels one and two would be below expectations and level four would identify those who performed above expectations.
2. The level titles at the top of the rubric may be represented in a variety of fashions. Some rubrics merely use numerals, such as 1, 2, 3, 4. Some use the letters A, B, C, D. Or, as can be seen in these samples,

one could use beginner, beginner plus, intermediate, and advanced (to correspond to the Stages of Performance outlined in Chapter 2). This text provided a variety of creative titles that may serve as motivators for some learners. Teachers are encouraged to use the titles most appropriate for the students in their classroom.
3. The descriptors that specifically identify differences in the levels should use student-friendly words that are identical to the cues used to teach the skills.
4. "Short and simple" best describe quality rubrics.

We have developed the following rubrics for use by classroom teachers and physical educators.

Walk Rubric

Student Name: _____

	BEGINNER	BEGINNER PLUS	INTERMEDIATE	ADVANCED
Trunk lean	Minimal to exaggerated	Slightly forward or backward	Leans slightly forward	Leans slightly forward in a relaxed fashion
Arm swing	Minimal to erratic	Hooking action across body	Rhythmical forward and backward	Purposeful, yet relaxed and rhythmic
Foot placement	Wide base of support	Slightly wider than necessary, toe in or toe out	Roll from heel to ball of foot, toe points straight ahead	Consistent roll from heel to ball in good alignment
Knee bend	Very little	Bend with effort	Bends freely	Relaxed
Head placement	Focused all around	Looks up or down	Looks forward	Looks forward

Run Rubric

Student Name: _____

	Middle School Champ	High School Champ	College Champ	Olympian
Trunk lean	No lean	Limited lean	Leans forward slightly	Relaxed forward slightly
Arm swing	No swing to exaggerated swing	Hooking action across body	Bent arm, moving forward/backward	Powerful swing, moving forward and backward
Knee and thigh lift	Limited	45 degrees to ground	Parallel to ground	Parallel to ground
Head/eye placement	Watching all around	Looks up or down	Looks forward	Looks forward
Stride	Mini steps, wide stance	Medium-sized step	Big step	Consistent, rhythmic, big steps

Gallop and Slide Rubric

Student Name: _____

	Midget	Rookie	Semipro	Pro
Trail leg	Way behind or swing in front before touching ground	Sometimes behind lead foot, sometimes beside	Stays behind lead foot	Always behind lead foot with good balance
Flight	Unpredictable, very low to very high	Medium to high	Low	Efficiently low
Rhythm	Uneven	Sometimes uneven, sometimes even	Smooth and even	Extremely rhythmic and controlled

Jump Rubric

Student Name: _____

	School Champ	League Champ	State Champ	National Champ
Arm swing	No arm swing	Limited arm swing	Backward then upward	Very powerful backward and upward
Knee bend	No knee bend or exaggerated knee bend	Slight knee bend	45 degree	45 degree
Arm extension	No arm extension	Limited arm extension	Hands reach above head	Hands, arms, trunk reach to full extension

Hop Rubric

Student Name: _____

	STILL LEARNING	IMPROVING	GOOD	SUPERB
Body lean	None	Slight	Adequate	Relaxed
Arm swing	None	Slight	Adequate	Powerful
Nonsupport leg	Frequently touches the ground	Extremely low or extremely high	Parallel to ground	Parallel and powerful lift

Skip Rubric

Student Name: _____

	JOEY	WALLABY	KANGA	BIG RED
Arm swing	None	Not in opposition to legs	In opposition to legs	Opposition to legs with power swing
Knees	Very little lift	Slight lift	Good lift	Powerful lift
Step hop	None	Not balanced	Balanced	Balanced with great rhythm

Leap Rubric

Student Name: _____

	1	2	3	4
Trunk lean	None	Slight to exaggerated	Adequate forward	Forward and relaxed
Arm extension	No extension	Extension to same leg	Extension to opposite leg	Extension with power to opposite leg
Leg extension	No extension	Slight extension	Adequate extension	Extension with power

Roll a Ball Rubric

Student Name: _____

	BUNNY	LOP-EARED BUNNY	RABBIT	HARE
Arm swing	None	Minimal and often aligned with same leg	Adequate with opposition to legs	With purpose and with opposition to legs
Legs	No involvement	Step with same leg as arm	Step forward in opposition to arm	Step forward in opposition and good knee bend
Follow through	None	Minimal	Adequate	In straight alignment in direction intended

Overhand Throw Rubric

Student Name: _____

	LITTLE LEAGUE CHAMP	COLLEGE CHAMP	DIVISION CHAMP	WORLD SERIES CHAMP
Stand sideways	Faces target directly	Stands partially toward target and partially sideways	Regularly stands sideways	Always stands sideways in a good straddle position
Eyes on target	Never watches target	Begins watching target, when throwing does not watch target	Regularly watches target	Always watches target and ready for next move
Rotate hips and shoulders	Never rotates hips and shoulders	Rotates hips and shoulders a little	Rotates hips and shoulders	Always rotates hips and shoulders and generates exceptional power
Step with opposition	Never steps at all	Steps with same foot as throwing arm	Steps with opposition to throwing hand	Always steps with powerful opposition
Follow through to opposite hip	No follow through	Follow through to same hip as throwing arm	Follow through to opposite hip	Exceptional, powerful follow-through to opposite hip

Catch Rubric

Student Name: _____

	LITTLE LEAGUE	AMERICAN LEGION	COLLEGE WORLD SERIES	WORLD SERIES
Eyes on object	Never watches object	Sometimes watches object	Always watches object	Always watches object and always looks for next play
Catch with hands	Catches using straight arms	Traps against chest	Catches using hands	Always catches with hands and is ready for the next play
Bend arms as they contact object	Straight arms bent toward chest	Arms bend sometimes	Always bends arms to absorb force	Bends arms to absorb force and gets ready to throw again if necessary

Kick Rubric

Student Name: _____

	City Champ	National Champ	Olympic Champ	World Cup Champ
Watch the ball	Never watches the ball	Watches ball prior to leg swing, does not watch ball when ball is contacted	Watches the ball when the ball is contacted	Watches ball closely and concentrates on what part of ball the foot contacts
Kick with shoelaces	Kicks with toe	Kicks with toe or with laces	Kicks with laces	Always kicks with laces and directs ball with control
Bend kicking leg	Kicking leg is straight	Leg is bent a little	Good bend of kicking leg	Exceptional bend in leg
Step-hop with kicking leg	Kick is merely a push, no step	Lands on kicking leg after the kick	Step forward with nonkicking leg and then hop onto nonkicking leg after kick	Rhythmic step-hop action with high follow through

Strike Rubric

Student Name: _____

	On the Bench	Sub	Starter	Pro
Rotate trunk/hips	No trunk or hip rotation	Limited trunk/hip rotation	Adequate trunk/hip rotation	Aggressive trunk/hip rotation
Swing level	Vertical swing	Diagonal swing	Level swing	Swing adjusts well to control placement
Sideways step toward target	No stepping motion	Step with leg furthest from pitcher	Step sideways with foot toward pitcher	Step sideways to adjust placement of ball
Watch the ball	Watches the pitcher, not the ball	Minimal focus on the ball	Adequate focus on ball	Watches bat contact ball

Volley Rubric

Student Name: _____

	BEGINNING PLAYER	HIGH SCHOOL STAR	COLLEGIATE PLAYER	OLYMPIAN
Eyes focused on ball	Eyes do not focus on ball	Does not watch ball with every contact	Regularly watches ball as it is contacted	Watches ball during contact and continues watching it after contact
Fingertips or forearms consistently contact ball	Fingertips never contact ball, sometimes ball contacts forearms between wrist and elbow	Fingertips and forearms hit ball in clumsy manner	Fingertips and forearms regularly contact ball with soft touch	Fingertips and forearms always consistently contact ball with exceptional touch
Legs bent before contact	Legs kept extended, no bend	Limited leg bend	Legs bent in adequate fashion	Player moves around the floor with legs consistently bent
Legs extend during contact	Legs always straight, therefore not able to extend	Very limited extension	Good leg extension at time of contact	Legs always extend fully during contact in correct, timely manner to impart good power

Dribble Using Hands Rubric

Student Name: _____

	MIDGET	ROOKIE	SEMIPRO	PRO
Eyes focused ahead	Eyes not focused on anything	Eyes always looking on the ball	Eyes sometimes on the ball and sometimes looking ahead	Eyes always looking around and ahead
Pushing action controlled from finger pads	Out of control slapping action	Uses both palm of hand and finger pads	Most of the time uses finger pads to control the ball	Always uses finger pads to control the ball
Ball is bounced waist high	Unpredictable ball bounce	Sometimes too high and sometimes too low	Most of the time ball is waist high	Ball is always waist high or at adjusted height as needed

Dribble Using Feet Rubric

Student Name: _____

	CITY CHAMP	NATIONAL CHAMP	OLYMPIC CHAMP	WORLD CUP CHAMP
Eyes focused ahead	Eyes rarely focused on anything	Usually focuses on ball	Eyes focus ahead	Eyes focus ahead and look for good plays
Inside and outside of foot used to control ball	Uses toes	Uses toes, and sides of foot	Uses both inside and outside of foot to control	Expert ball control using appropriate side of foot
Ball kept within two feet of body	Ball is far from body	Sometimes ball close and sometimes far from body	Ball regularly kept close to feet	Ball is always very close to feet

Punt Rubric

Student Name: _____

	ROOKIE CHAMP	DIVISION CHAMP	LEAGUE CHAMP	SUPER BOWL CHAMP
Trunk lean	None	Very little or too much backward lean	Lean back slightly at contact	Lean back slightly at contact in relaxed mode
Ball drop	Push ball downward too far or too close from foot	Toss ball too high or too close or far from foot	Toss ball to correct height most of the time with good alignment to foot	Consistently tosses ball to correct height with excellent alignment to foot
Ball contact	Rarely contacts ball with any part of foot	Contacts ball with foot on toe or area other than instep	Contacts with instep at knee level or lower	Consistently contacts with instep at knee level or lower and has good accuracy when aiming at target
Hop	No hop on nonkicking foot	Hops on kicking foot	Hops on nonkicking foot after contact with ball	Hops on nonkicking foot and maintains excellent balance

Set Shot Rubric

Student Name: _____

	NEBRASKA	OKLAHOMA	TEXAS	KANSAS
Trunk lean	No lean	Too much forward or backward lean	Slight forward lean	Slight forward lean in relaxed position
Fingers	Fingers not touching ball	Fingers close together	Fingers spread out on ball	Fingers in relaxed position on ball
Hand placement	Both hands under the ball	Each hand on side of ball	Shooting hand behind ball and other hand on side of ball	Correct hand position with relaxed follow-through after the shot
Legs	No leg flexion to extreme leg flexion	Minimal leg flexion and extension	Good leg flexion and extension	Consistently uses correct amount of leg flexion and extension

Overhand Serve Rubric

Student Name: _____

	STATE	USTA	U.S. OPEN	WIMBLEDON
Trunk lean	No lean	Little forward or backward lean	Leans forward as contacts ball	Leans forward as contacts ball in relaxed fashion
Ball toss	No control	Tosses ball too high, too low, and not in correct placement in front of body	Tosses ball slightly in front of body and at arm's length above head	Consistently tosses ball with correct height and correct distance in front of body
Ball contact	Rarely able to contact the ball	Contacts the ball at head height or lower	Contacts ball with hitting arm extended above head	Contacts ball with hitting arm extended above head, hand centered behind the ball and with heel of hand
Step	No forward step	Step forward with same foot as hitting arm	Step forward in opposition to hitting arm	Step forward powerfully in opposition to hitting arm

Ball Pass Rubric

Student Name: _____

	HUSKERS	SOONERS	LONGHORNS	JAYHAWKS
Trunk lean	No trunk lean	Minimal to exaggerated trunk lean	Slight forward lean	Powerful forward lean
Finger placement	Fingers on bottom and/or top of ball	Fingers directly behind ball	Fingers on side of ball and slightly behind the ball	Fingers in relaxed correct position on ball
Step	No step	Minimal step forward	Full-stride step forward	Step forward in direction of throw
Arms—overhead and chest	Arms have little to no extension	Arms partially extended after ball is released	Arms extended toward target after releasing ball	Arms fully extended with added wrist action
Arm—bounce	Arms have little to no extension	Arms partially extended, but ball is bounced halfway between self and target	Arms extended toward floor, aiming ball three-fourths distance between self and target	Arms fully extended with accurate ball placement and added wrist action

Recess Games and Activities

Hopscotch

SPACE Dirt or cement area

EQUIPMENT Small stone or beanbag

BENEFITS
- Controlling large body movements
- Tossing objects with accuracy

GRADE LEVEL 3–6

SAFETY CONCERNS Children should wear tennis shoes.

RULES Students need to draw on the ground the hopscotch court shown in the figure. The drawing can be done with chalk on a cement surface or with a stick on a dirt surface. Squares should be drawn big enough to accommodate the size of the player's foot, but not so big as to leave little challenge for the players. Two or three students participate per court. Each student needs something to toss into the squares (a small flat stone or a small beanbag). Children can take turns beginning games or they can play Rock, Paper, Scissors to determine who goes first (see note below). The first player tosses the stone into square one, then hops (in the single squares) and jumps (in the double, connected squares), moving from square 1 through square 8 and back again.

A player cannot hop or jump in a square that has a stone in it, and on the way back the player picks up the player's own stone and carries it back to the starting point. Squares with stones in them must be hopped over (continuing on to the next consecutively numbered square). The object of the game is to progress from square 1 to square 8 and back again without stepping on any lines and without stepping in any squares that contain a stone. If successful, the player tosses the stone into square 2 and continues as before. If not successful, the next player takes a turn. As players toss stones into the various squares, the stone must land in and stay in the square. If the stone does not stay in the square, it's the next player's turn, and the player who just tossed the stone places it in the appropriate

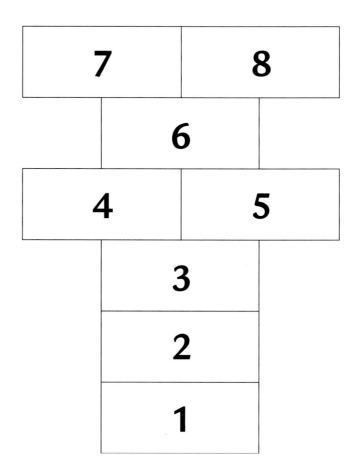

square and begins there on her or his next turn. The first player to toss into all eight squares and complete the eight up and back sequences wins the game. The number of squares can be increased (using the established pattern) to increase the difficulty of the game.

Note: Play Rock, Paper, Scissors as follows: Two players begin by saying "one, two, three." On "three," each child extends a hand in one of the following positions:
- Two fingers *V*-shaped for "scissors"
- A clenched fist for "rock"

■ An open hand for "paper"

The winner is determined by the rule that paper covers rock, rock breaks scissors, and scissors cut paper.

Tetherball

SPACE Area immediately surrounding the tetherball pole on the playground

EQUIPMENT Nothing in addition to the ball already mounted on the pole

BENEFITS Develops eye-hand coordination

GRADE LEVEL K–6

SAFETY CONCERNS Children playing the game need to watch the ball all the time so they are not struck by the ball, and children not playing the game should not be in the area of the pole.

RULES Two children play the activity at any given time. The object is to hit the ball to the other person as the ball swings around the pole. Usually no score is kept.

Jacks

SPACE Cement area that is level and smooth

EQUIPMENT Set of jacks with a jack ball

BENEFITS
■ Develops fine motor skill
■ Develops eye-hand coordination

GRADE LEVEL 3–6

SAFETY CONCERNS None

RULES For practice purposes, each player should have a set of jacks (containing at least ten jacks) and a ball. Once students master the activity, they will want to challenge each other and play in groups of two or three. The first player throws the jacks out onto the cement surface. Then the player tosses the ball into the air (with one hand), picks up one jack (with the same hand), transfers the jack to the other hand, and catches the ball after it bounces only once (with the original hand). This action occurs for each of the ten jacks and is called "ones." The player then continues with twos, threes, and so forth to tens. For example, when doing fours, the player tosses the ball, picks up four jacks (in one scoop), and catches the ball. Then the player tosses the ball again, scoops up another four jacks, and catches the ball. On the last toss, since there are only two jacks left, the player picks up only two jacks. When doing tens, the player must scoop up all ten jacks at once. When a player misses, it becomes

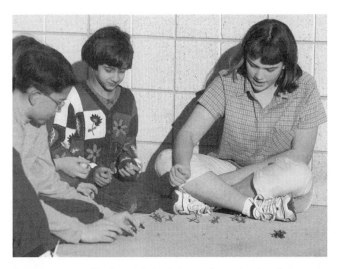

A recess game of jacks can help these students develop fine motor skills.

another player's turn. A player misses in any of the following ways:
■ Causing any other jack (meaning jacks not targeted to be picked up in that scoop) to move by touching it with the hand or fingers
■ Not being able to catch the ball
■ Allowing the ball to bounce more than once before catching it
■ Dropping any of the jacks that were scooped up

A player who misses begins his or her next turn at the throw that was missed. So a player who missed while doing twos begins the next turn by doing twos again. The first player to complete tens wins the game.

STRATEGY Learning to throw the jacks is a skill. The player wants to spread the jacks out when tossing for ones, twos, threes. But as the number of jacks to be scooped up increases, the jacks need to be thrown closer together in order to give the player time to scoop up all the jacks in one scoop.

Walking

SPACE Dirt, grass, or blacktop path around the playground

EQUIPMENT None

BENEFITS Develops cardiorespiratory fitness

GRADE LEVEL K–6

SAFETY CONCERNS
■ Children should wear tennis shoes to prevent injuries to feet and ankles.
■ Students should stay clear of debris on the path.
■ Students should wear appropriate clothing.

RULES For distance, pace, and target heart rate for various age children, consult "Walk for Fun and Fitness" by C. Milne (*Strategies* 7[6]: 5–8 [1994]). Students should be encouraged to walk at least three times a week in order to develop cardiorespiratory fitness. Students of the same age do not have to walk at the same pace. Students who want to walk faster than the set pace can be allowed to pass other students by moving slightly to the left and passing by the left side of the person who is walking more slowly. Some students like to spend recess talking to their friends. Teachers can encourage these students to walk while they visit with each other.

Hula Hoops

SPACE Cement or hard-packed dirt area

EQUIPMENT Hula hoops (one per child)

BENEFITS
- Increases flexibility
- Increases agility
- Increases coordination

GRADE LEVEL K–6

SAFETY CONCERNS Have enough space so children can avoid interfering with other children even if they mishandle the hoop.

Individual Activities
- Toss the hoop into the air and catch it.
- Spin the hoop on the ground and run around it as many times as possible before it stops spinning.
- Spin the hoop on various body parts (arm, leg, neck, waist, knees).
- Spin the hoop on one arm and, without stopping the spin, change to the other arm.
- With two hands on the hoop, toss it in the air and "ring yourself."
- Skip (jump rope) the hoop, moving forward and backward.
- Run and roll the hoop alongside of you (first with the right hand, then with the left).
- Roll the hoop slowly as you walk beside it, and try to dive through it while it is in motion (do this on a grassy area).

- Toss the hoop out in front (low to the ground) and add backspin so when it hits the ground it will return to you.
- Spin the hoop around the ankle of one foot and jump over the hoop with the other foot every time it spins by (this is an advanced skill).

Partner Activities
- Toss the hoop from partner to partner; catch it without letting it touch the ground.
- Spin the hoop to your partner and back.
- Ring your partner by tossing the hoop over her or his head and letting it drop to the floor.
- "Wring the dishrag" with your partner. (This activity is described in the Classroom Activity for Lesson Plan 2.15. This time, however, partners hold the same hula hoop instead of holding hands.)

Jumping Rope

SPACE Packed dirt or blacktop surface

EQUIPMENT One short rope per child for Individual Activities and one long rope per four to five children for Group Activities

BENEFITS Develops cardiorespiratory fitness and coordination

GRADE LEVEL K–6

SAFETY CONCERNS Space students so they do not hit each other with the ropes.

Individual Activities
- Turn the rope forward and jump the rope (*jump* means to take off and land on both feet).
- Turn the rope forward and hop the rope, first with the right foot, then with the left foot, then alternating from one foot to the other (*hop* means to land on one foot).
- Jump the rope and say the alphabet.
- Jump the rope and count by twos (fours, etc.).
- Jump the rope and see how many times you can do so without missing. Say "Teletubbies, dressed in white, went upstairs, to turn on the lights. How

Hula hoops can be used in many types of activities that develop agility and coordination.

many lights, did they use? 1, 2, 3, 4, . . ." (until the child misses).

- Turn the rope backward and do the two activities explained above.
- "Skip" the rope (turning forward and then backward).
- Turn the rope forward and cross your arms in front of your body, jumping the rope while it is crossed in front of the body. Uncross your arms as the rope comes back over your head.
- Turn the rope backward and cross the rope.
- Turn the rope forward and do a straddle jump (a *straddle jump* means jumping with your feet together then far apart, as when doing jumping jacks).
- Stand beside a line on the ground. Turn the rope forward and jump left and right across the line as you jump the rope (think of this as the "Skier").
- Have a partner stand facing you. Turn the rope forward and have the partner jump with you.
- Turn the rope forward and have a partner run in and begin jumping with you. Then have the partner run out (this is an advanced skill).
- Run the rope around the playground; just run as usual and time the rope turns to go under your running feet.

Group Activities

Generally with one long rope, two children will be turning the rope and two or three children will be in line to take their turn jumping; thus children sing songs that limit the time one person can jump. After the song is over, the jumper jumps out and the next person in line jumps in.

- Sing: "(Name) be nimble, (name) be quick, (name) jump over the candlestick. Oh jump and jump and jump so high, but you'd better jump out or (name of next person in line) will cry."
- Sing: "One, two, buckle my shoe. Three, four, shut the door. Five, six, pick up sticks. Seven, eight, lay them straight. Nine, ten, a big fat hen. Eleven, twelve, ring the bell. Thirteen, fourteen, don't be mean. Fifteen, sixteen, be squeaky clean. Seventeen, eighteen, refried beans. Nineteen, twenty, that's a-plenty."
- Play school: The players try to complete all grades of the school (K–12). For kindergarten, the player runs through the turning rope (without stopping to jump and without getting hit by the rope). For first grade, the player runs in, jumps once, and runs out. For second grade, the player runs in, jumps twice, and runs out. The player continues the same sequence for the rest of the grades. A player who misses during a certain grade must try to complete that grade again on the next turn. Misses occur when the player is struck with the

rope while running in or out and when the player misses while jumping.

Children in grades 3–6 who are skilled long rope jumpers are ready to practice the following long rope advanced skills:

- Double Dutch: Two turners (facing each other) have two long ropes (one rope in each hand). Ropes are turned in the direction of the other rope. Ropes are turned continuously but alternately, meaning the ropes will not hit the floor at the same time, but will hit the floor alternately. So the jumper will have to jump "fast time," as he or she will be jumping each time one of the ropes hits the floor. "Fast time" can be a two-foot jump done quickly, or the jumper can jump the ropes with one foot alternately (right, left, right, left, etc.). Hint for the jumper to get into ropes once they are turning—stand near the shoulder of one of the turners and enter from that angle.
- Egg Beater: Four turners stand in a square. Turners standing opposite each other have one rope, so the two ropes lie at right angles to each other (one on top of the other where they meet in the middle). The ropes are turned at exactly the same time, so they rise and fall together and hit the floor at the same time. One rope is turned clockwise and the other counterclockwise. Jumper runs into the middle, either "front door" or "back door," and jumps as many times as desired and then runs out.

Keep-It-Up

SPACE Small grassy play area

EQUIPMENT Regulation or Nerf volleyballs (one ball for every four or five players)

BENEFITS
- Develops volleyball setting skills
- Develops coordination

GRADE LEVEL 3–6

SAFETY CONCERNS Be sure players are not too near other playground activities.

RULES Four or five players form a circle. The group volleys the ball among themselves (using volleyball overhead and underhand volleying skills). The goal is to increase the number of times the group can volley without the ball going out of control and hitting the ground. To increase difficulty, have each player call out the name of the person they are hitting the ball to (thus demanding that players have more control of where their hits go).

Note: Younger children can practice volleying back and forth with a partner (not with a group). Be sure to use a Nerf ball.

A recess game of Keep-It-Up is a challenging and fun way to develop coordination and volleyball skills.

1	**2**
3	**4**

Four-Square

SPACE Hard, dirt area or blacktop surface

EQUIPMENT Four-Square court drawn, painted, or taped; one rubber ball or volleyball for each Four-Square court. The court is a large square divided into quarters with each quarter measuring five to eight feet on a side.

BENEFITS Develops ball-handling skills

GRADE LEVEL K–6

SAFETY CONCERNS None

RULES One player stands in each square with other players waiting for a turn. (Keep the number of players waiting to two or three.) The game begins with the player in square 1 dropping the ball in his or her square and hitting it underhand after the ball bounces. The player may hit the ball to any of the other three players. The player who receives the ball lets it bounce once in her or his square and then hits it to another square. Play continues in this manner until a miss occurs. Misses include hitting the ball overhand, the ball landing on lines between the squares (but the ball on an outside line is considered good), a player stepping into another player's square to hit the ball, a player catching or holding the ball before hitting it, and a player hitting the ball with a body part other than the hand. A player who misses goes to the end of the waiting line, and then all players move up (the player in square 2 moves to square 1, the player in square 3 moves to square 2, the player in square 4 moves to square 3), and the new player starts in square 4.

Toss the Ball

SPACE Small grassy play area

EQUIPMENT One ball per group of four or five children

BENEFITS Improves throwing and catching skills

GRADE LEVEL K–6

SAFETY CONCERNS With young children use Nerf balls to prevent injuries.

RULES Players stand in a circle with one player in the center. The player in the center has the ball. The center player throws the ball to each player in turn around the circle. Each player throws the ball back to the center player. Each player is given an opportunity to be the center player.

Note: Repeating the game with different types of balls (volleyballs, tennis balls, footballs, basketballs) allows children to develop a variety of throwing and catching skills. Young children can throw and catch beanbags when playing this game.

Modified Soccer

SPACE Grassy playing field with a court approximately 50 feet by 100 feet. Mark the four corners of the field with traffic cones, and mark the goal areas (on each end line) with cones 4 to 8 feet apart in the center of the of 50-foot side.

EQUIPMENT One soccer ball and eight traffic cones

BENEFITS
- Improves eye-foot coordination
- Develops ball-handling skills
- Develops cardiorespiratory fitness

Soccer can help children develop cardiorespiratory fitness, coordination, and a variety of physical skills

■ Develops soccer skills

GRADE LEVEL 3–6

SAFETY CONCERNS
■ Children should wear tennis shoes.
■ This should be played as a noncontact sport.
■ Students must keep their body in control so other players are not injured.

RULES Place five to seven players on each team spread throughout their half of the field. The object of the game is to kick the ball through the opponent's goal. The ball cannot be handled with the hands at any time. Kickoff by the center player begins the game. Which team gets to kick off is determined by a coin toss or by playing Rock, Paper, Scissors. After a point is scored, a kickoff by the team scored against restarts the game. If the ball goes outside the playing area (not between the goal markers), it is given to the team who did not last touch the ball. A player from that team kicks the ball back into the playing field from the sideline where the ball went out of bounds. If a player touches the ball with the hands or runs into other players (body is out of control), the ball is dropped to the field at that spot and the opposing team kicks the ball into play from that spot. One point is awarded for each goal.

Newcomb

SPACE Grassy area about 20 feet by 40 feet

EQUIPMENT One ball, volleyball net dividing the area in half (mounted on volleyball standards)

BENEFITS
■ Students develop throwing and catching skills.
■ Students learn to rotate positions.
■ Students learn to coordinate with teammates.

GRADE LEVEL 3–6

SAFETY CONCERNS
■ Children should wear tennis shoes.
■ Begin with a soft ball and progress to regulation balls.

RULES Place four players on each side of the net. The ball is thrown back and forth over the net. Each team attempts to keep the ball from touching the ground on its side of the court by catching the ball thrown from the opposite side of the net. A point is scored by the serving team whenever the opposing team (1) allows the ball to touch the ground (on its side of the court), (2) allows the ball to go out of bounds (on its side of the court), or (3) fails to get the ball back over the net. If the serving team does any of those things, then the other team gets to serve. Serving rotation occurs as in regulation volleyball. A serve occurs by throwing the ball (with an overhead motion) over the net.

Note: Various types of balls (volleyballs, tennis balls, beanbags, etc.) can be thrown. In addition, scoops (with their appropriate ball) can be used to change the character of the game.

Target Frisbee

SPACE Grassy area 30 feet long

EQUIPMENT Three Frisbees, one hula hoop, and one cone (for each group of three players)

BENEFITS Develops Frisbee-throwing skill

GRADE LEVEL K–6

SAFETY CONCERNS Throw in a direction that is away from other children playing on the playground.

RULES Each of the three players (in turn) stands beside the cone and throws the Frisbee toward the hula hoop, which is placed on the ground a certain distance in front of the cone. Begin with the hoop placed close to the cone (five feet away), and then gradually move the hoop further and further away. The object is to throw the Frisbee into the hoop. Players score two points for throwing the Frisbee so it lands completely inside the hoop and score one point if it lands so it's touching any part of the hoop. Once *all* the players have thrown their Frisbees, they can retrieve the Frisbees, lengthen the throwing distance (if so desired), and play again.

Frisbee Golf

SPACE Soccer field or similar size grassy area to construct "golf" holes of different lengths and shapes

EQUIPMENT One Frisbee for each child participating, one hula hoop for each "hole" to serve as the cup, one cone to mark the starting spot for each hole. If you construct dogleg holes, you'll need extra cones to mark the route to get to the cup.

BENEFITS Develops Frisbee-throwing skill

GRADE LEVEL K–6

SAFETY CONCERNS Construct the holes so children playing one hole will not interfere with other holes. Teach children to crouch down and cover their head if another player yells "fore" (meaning a Frisbee is coming their way). Teach children not to begin playing a hole until the player in front of them has finished the hole.

RULES Children can begin playing the "course" at any hole and then progress clockwise around the course. Beginning where the cone is placed at each hole, the player tries to throw the Frisbee to the hula hoop in the least number of throws possible. Keep a total throwing score for each "round" and try to do better the next time.

Half-Court Basketball

SPACE Blacktop area 20 feet by 30 feet

EQUIPMENT One basketball and a basketball goal

BENEFITS
- Develops cardiorespiratory fitness
- Develops ball-handling skills
- Develops shooting skills

GRADE LEVEL 3–6

SAFETY CONCERNS
- Players should wear tennis shoes.
- Players should always be in control of their body.
- Players should not make contact with other players.

RULES The game is played just like regulation basketball, except when a goal is scored, the ball is taken (by the team just scored against) to the edge of the blacktop area (opposite the basketball goal). From there the ball can be put into play by throwing it to a teammate or dribbling it into play. Players can play two on two, three on three, or four on four.

Spin Jammers

SPACE Blacktop area

EQUIPMENT Spin Jammers (nine-inch, not ten-inch)

BENEFITS Develops eye-hand coordination

GRADE LEVEL K–6

SAFETY CONCERNS
- Space individuals so they do not interfere with each other.
- Individuals should have their body under control.

Activities
- Spin on a finger (provide spin with the opposite hand).
- Spin; then change from hand to hand while the Spin Jammer is spinning.

Playing with Spin Jammers is a fun way to develop hand-eye coordination.

- Spin; then sit down and stand up while spinning.
- Spin; then walk, jog, or the like to the other side of the room.
- Spin; then transfer the Spin Jammer onto different fingers of the same hand.
- Spin; then do curl-ups until Spin Jammer stops spinning.
- Spin; then hand the Spin Jammer back and forth between partners (until the spinning stops).
- Spin; then toss the Spin Jammer between partners (until the spinning stops).
- Spin; then toss the Spin Jammer behind the back, over the shoulder, to catch it in front.
- Spin; then toss the Spin Jammer under a lifted leg to catch it on the other side.

Pogo Sticks

SPACE Blacktop area

EQUIPMENT Pogo sticks

BENEFITS
- Improves dynamic balance
- Improves cardiorespiratory endurance

GRADE LEVEL 3–6

SAFETY CONCERNS

- Space individuals so they do not interfere with each other.
- Individuals should have their body under control.

Activities

- Bounce once and jump off.
- Bounce twice and jump off.
- Bounce three times and jump off.
- Bounce up and down in place as many times as possible.
- Bounce while staying on the pogo stick for longer periods of time.
- Bounce while moving forward.
- Bounce while moving sideways.
- Bounce while moving in a square pattern (circle, triangle, etc.).
- Bounce holding the stick with only one hand (circle free hand above the head as if swinging a lariat).

Chinese Jump Ropes

SPACE Blacktop area

EQUIPMENT Chinese Jump Ropes (long, stretchable circle ropes)

BENEFITS

- Develops eye-foot coordination
- Develops cardiorespiratory fitness
- Improves balance

GRADE LEVEL K–6

SAFETY CONCERNS

- Jumpers should wear tennis shoes.
- Do not move the level of the rope *while* someone is jumping.

RULES The game needs three players. Two players stand facing each other, place the rope behind their ankles (feet two feet apart), and then back up until the rope is stretched taut. With the rope at ankle level, the third player then jumps a pattern in and out of the two ropes. If successful, the rope is moved up to midcalf level and then up to knee level, and so forth until the jumper misses. When the jumper misses, another player takes a turn. All three players rotate turns in that manner. The goal is to be the one who can jump the pattern at the highest level. The jumper stands in the middle of the two ropes and performs the following basic pattern:

- Jump right: Jump to the right, landing with the right rope between the feet.
- Jump left: Jump to the left, landing with the left rope between the feet
  Repeat three times.
- In: Jump, landing with both feet in the middle of the ropes.

Games using Chinese Jump Ropes can build fitness and improve balance and coordination.

- Out: Jump, landing with both feet outside the ropes.
- In: Jump, landing with both feet in the middle of the ropes.
- On: Jump, landing with each foot *on* the ropes.

The pattern is performed smoothly with no hesitation between the jumps. Here are two more fun movements:

- Jump and turn 180 degrees.
- Jump and turn 360 degrees.

Source: Videotape by Mel Aimee Productions, titled "Mel Aimee Chinese Jump Rope."

Flag Football

SPACE Grassy field approximately 35 feet by 70 feet. Mark the four corners of the field with traffic cones.

EQUIPMENT Football (junior-sized Nerf football), set of flags for each player

BENEFITS

- Improves eye-hand coordination
- Improves cardiorespiratory endurance
- Develops throwing and catching skills
- Develops running and dodging skills
- Develops ability to play as a team

GRADE LEVEL 3–6

SAFETY CONCERNS

- Children should wear tennis shoes.
- This should be played as a noncontact sport.
- Students should have their body under control.

RULES Place seven players on each team. Designate players as one of the following: line person, center, quarterback, running back. The object of the game is to run or throw the football over the opponent's end line (scores six points). Play begins with a kickoff. Which team kicks off can be determined by who wins Rock, Paper, Scissors. After a score occurs, play continues with the team who just scored kicking off to the other team. To score, the ball is moved downfield by the center hiking the ball to the quarterback, who then runs with the ball, hands the ball off to another player, or throws (passes) the ball to a teammate. The play stops when an opponent pulls off one flag from the player who has the football or the player with the football crosses the end line. The offensive team gets six plays to get the ball across the end line. If the end line is not crossed in those six plays, then the opponents take over the ball at that spot on the field

Lesson Plan Resource Materials

This appendix contains materials for several of the lesson plans included in the book.

Human Letters, pp. 500–504

LESSON 2.3 CLASSROOM ACTIVITY, P. 409
The 26 human-letter alphabet cards can be copied (adjusted to any size you choose), mounted on construction paper, and laminated for greater durability. The individual letters can then be cut around the square so that you end up with a deck of cards. Students draw a card from the deck and then use their body to make the letter the way it is shown on the card.

Animal Movement Cards, pp. 505–517

LESSON 2.4 CLASSROOM ACTIVITY, P. 411
The 26 animal movement cards can be copied (adjusted to any size you choose), mounted on construction paper, and laminated for greater durability. Students can choose a card or a teacher can show the class a card as a cue. Students are instructed to move like the animal on the card.

Loco Locomotor Hats, pp. 518–525

LESSON 2.6 INTRODUCTORY ACTIVITY, P. 414
Copy the eight Loco Locomotor hats and mount them on heavier paper or poster board. Make a heavy paper band to go around the head and hold the hat in place. Students should perform the activity indicated on the hat the teacher is wearing.

Carpet Square Activities, pp. 526–538

LESSON 2.6 CLASSROOM ACTIVITY, P. 415
The Carpet Square activity described in Lesson 2.6 integrates movement and reading. The 25 activity cards included here can be copied (adjusted to any size you choose), mounted on construction paper, and laminated for greater durability. Randomly distribute the numbered pages to each carpet square. Students can do this activity alone or in small groups. Children read the activity card and then perform the activity that is described. When finished with one activity, students find the next number and continue until they've done all 25 activities.

Math Shapes, pp. 539–541

LESSON 2.7 INTRODUCTORY ACTIVITY, P. 416
The six math shape cards can be copied (adjusted to any size you choose), mounted on construction paper, and laminated for greater durability. Each card includes a number and a locomotor skill. Begin with cards scattered on the gym floor. Students find a card and then move to touch the number of walls indicated by the number on the card, using the locomotor skill specified on the card. The activity continues until all students have completed the activity for each shape.

Physical Education Bingo, pp. 542–562

LESSON 2.8 CLASSROOM ACTIVITY, P. 418
Three types of cards are included here for Physical Education Bingo. There is one sheet of Physical Education pieces, 30 student bingo cards, and 30 cards with bingo numbers and activities for use by the teacher. The cards can be copied (adjusted to any size you choose), mounted on construction paper, and laminated for greater durability; copy enough bingo pieces for all students to have a supply. The instructor calls out the number and activity; if a student's card contains the number and the student can perform the activity, the student may place a Physical Education piece on the appropriate square on her or his card. See p. 418 for complete instructions for Physical Education Bingo.

HUMAN LETTER CARDS: Lesson 2.3 Classroom Activity

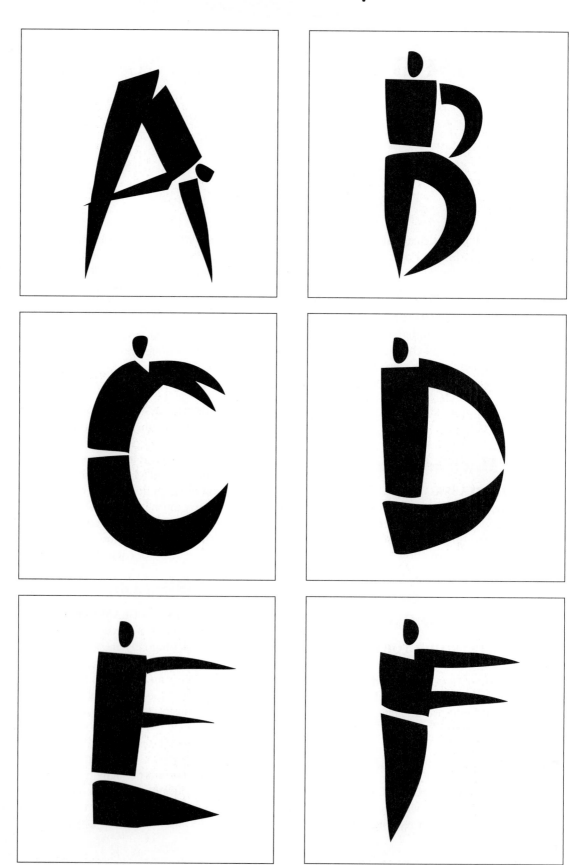

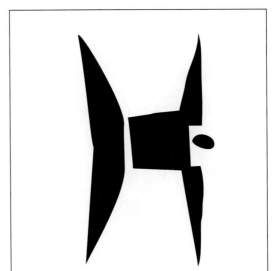

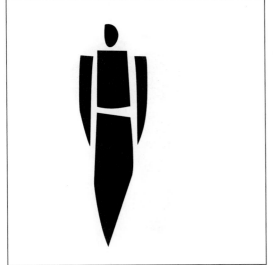

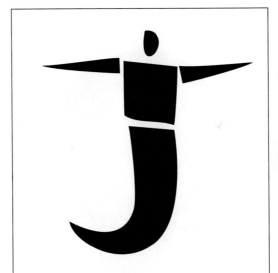

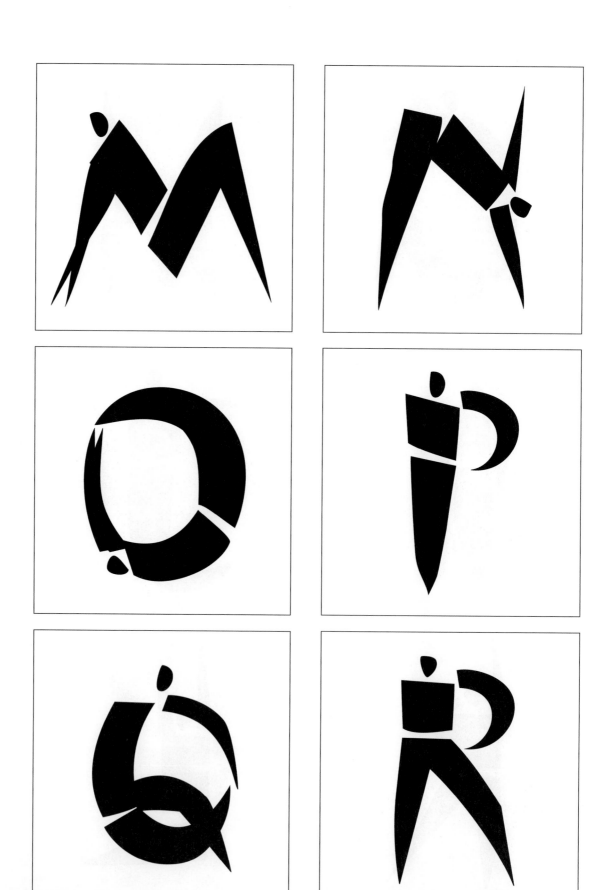

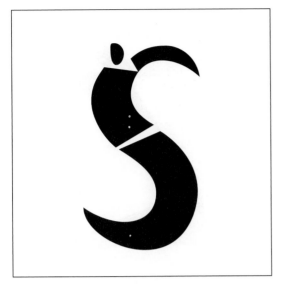

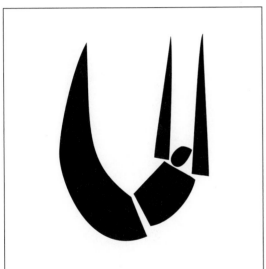

ANIMAL MOVEMENT CARDS: Lesson 2.4 Classroom Activity

ALLIGATOR

BIRD

CHICKEN

DUCK

ELEPHANT

FROG

GORILLA

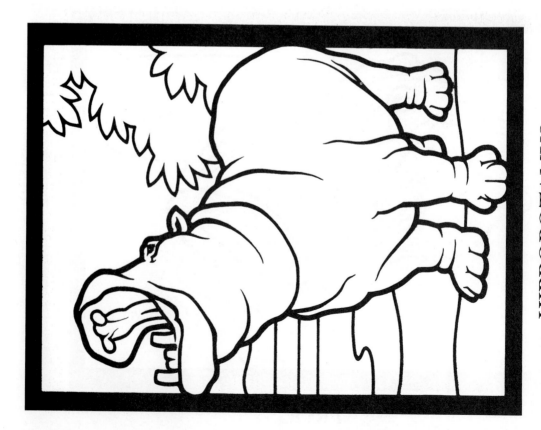

HIPPOPOTAMUS

IGUANA

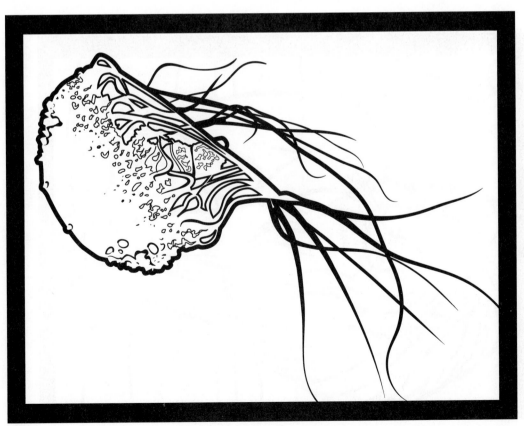

JELLYFISH

KANGAROO

LION

MOOSE

NEWT

OPOSSUM

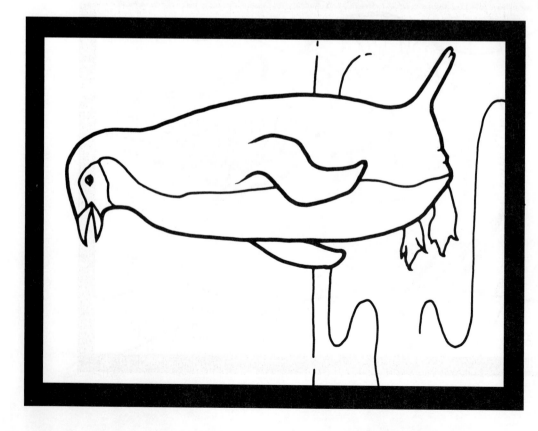

PENGUIN

QUAIL

RABBIT

SEAL

TIGER

UNICORN WHALE

VULTURE

WOLF

XENU

YAK

ZEBRA

LOCO LOCOMOTOR SKILLS HATS: Lesson 2.6 Introductory Activity

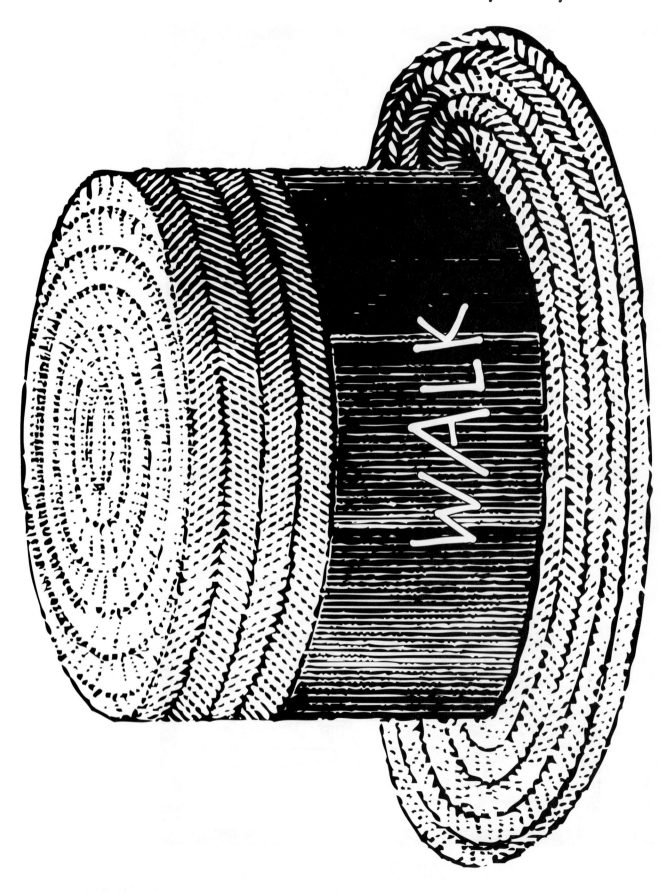

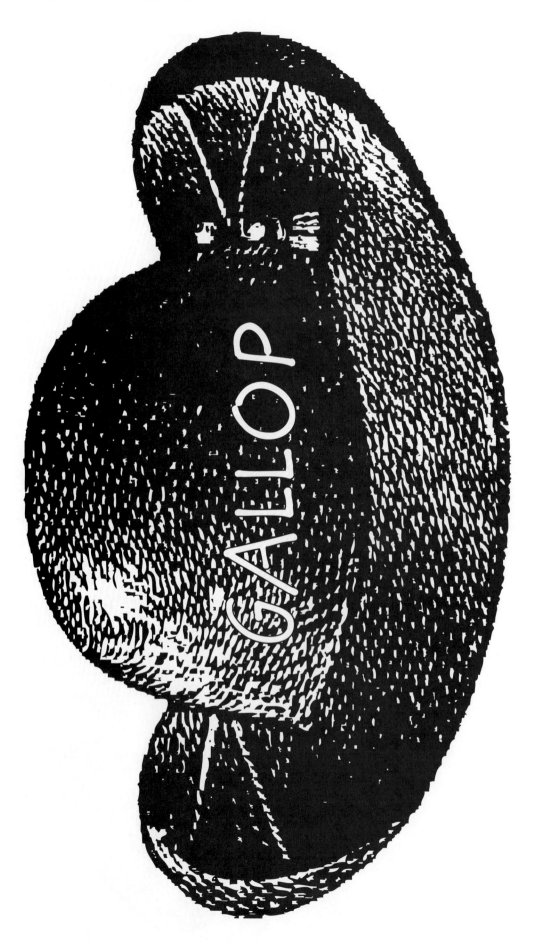

CARPET SQUARE ACTIVITY CARDS: Lesson 2.6 Classroom Activity

2

Pick up the square. Put it over your head and back to the ground 10 times.

1

Gallop around the square 10 times.

4

Jog in place 60 running steps.

3

Lie on your back with the square on your chest. Push it up and down 15 times.

6

Lie on your back and do 15 bicycles.

5

Put your head on the square and walk around the square 1 time.

Do not move the square.

Jump as
high as
you can
20 times.

Skip
around
your
square
10 times.

10

Jump up and down 1 time for each letter in your last name while yelling each letter.

9

Walk, toe to heel, around the square 5 times.

12

Close your eyes. Put your arms straight out to the side of your body. Touch your nose with your left hand, then your right hand, 10 times each.

11

Crab-walk around the square 8 times.

14

Touch your big toe to your head 5 times.

13

Hop on your right foot 4 times, then on your left foot 4 times. Right 3, left 3, right 2, left 2, right 1, left 1.

16

Put 2 body parts on the square and balance for 10 seconds.

15

Jump into the air with a quarter turn on each jump 12 times.

18T

Touch your toes 4 times.

17T

Jump into the air 5 times with arms above your head.

20

Do 5 bent-knee crunches.

19

Hop on 1 foot with 1 hand in the air 5 times.

22

Stand over the square with your hands above your head. Touch the square 10 times.

21

Touch your nose to the square 5 times while doing push-ups.

24

Touch your head to the square 5 times.

23

Make 3 funny faces while standing on the square.

25

Pat head and rub stomach 5 times while jumping up and down on both feet on the square.

MATH SHAPE CARDS: Lesson 2.7 Introductory Activity

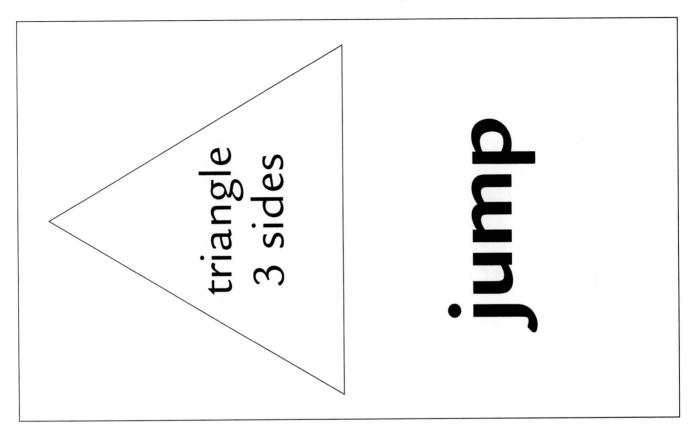

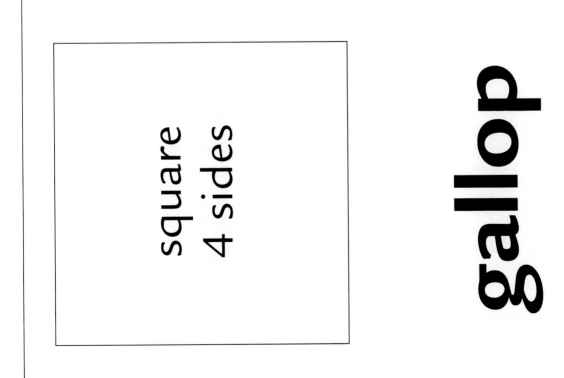

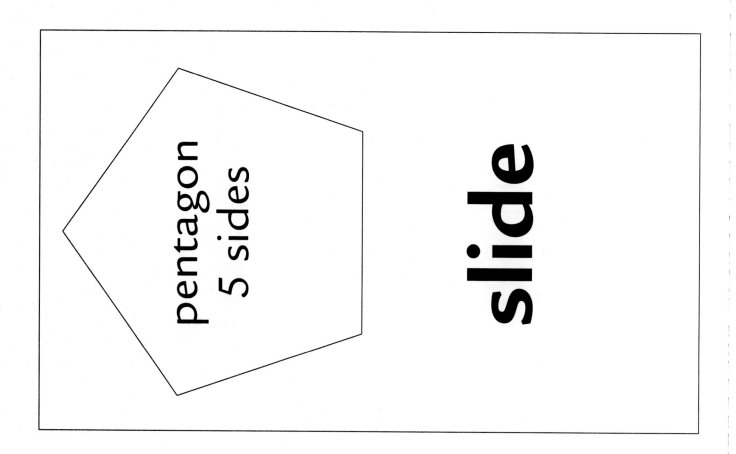

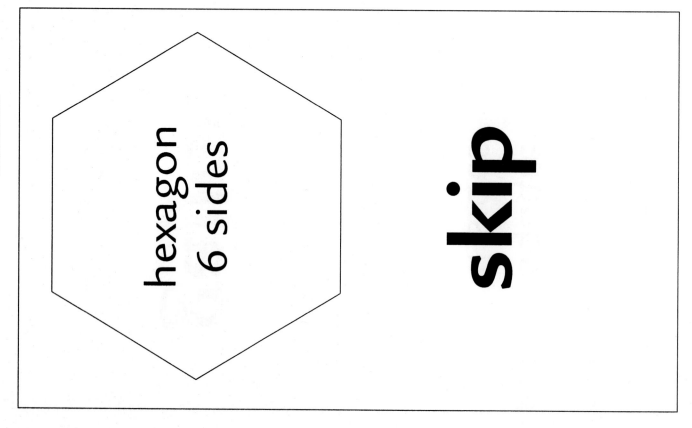

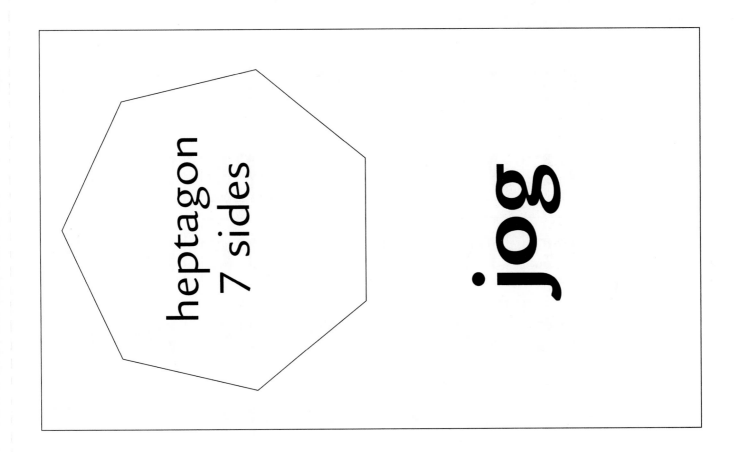

heptagon
7 sides

jog

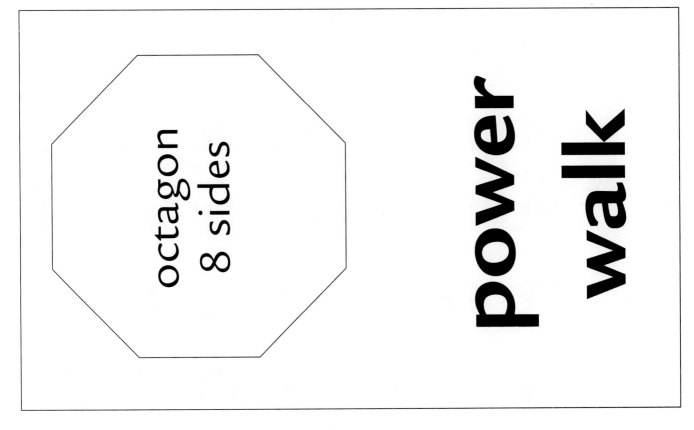

octagon
8 sides

power
walk

PHYSICAL EDUCATION BINGO (Physical Education Pieces):
Lesson 2.8 Classroom Activity

PHYSICAL EDUCATION BINGO (Student Bingo Cards):
Lesson 2.8 Classroom Activity

MOVEMENT BINGO

3	6	5
10	7	9
8	2	1

MOVEMENT BINGO

2	5	6
7	3	10
4	9	8

MOVEMENT BINGO

8	9	4
1	7	2
6	5	10

MOVEMENT BINGO

2	8	10
7	3	1
4	9	5

MOVEMENT BINGO

2	6	4
10	7	8
9	3	1

MOVEMENT BINGO

9	5	7
6	3	1
4	2	8

MOVEMENT BINGO

6	3	5
1	8	2
9	4	10

MOVEMENT BINGO

7	9	5
1	3	2
6	4	10

MOVEMENT BINGO

6	2	5
10	8	3
7	4	1

MOVEMENT BINGO

8	5	7
3	2	1
4	10	9

MOVEMENT BINGO

6	3	5
1	8	2
9	4	10

MOVEMENT BINGO

6	9	2
3	10	1
4	7	5

MOVEMENT BINGO

7	9	5
1	3	2
6	4	10

MOVEMENT BINGO

6	8	7
3	10	1
4	2	5

MOVEMENT BINGO

9	5	6
8	3	1
4	2	10

MOVEMENT BINGO

3	10	1
5	6	9
8	4	7

MOVEMENT BINGO

6	2	5
10	8	3
7	4	1

MOVEMENT BINGO

8	5	7
3	2	1
4	10	9

MOVEMENT BINGO

6	3	5
1	8	2
9	4	10

MOVEMENT BINGO

6	9	2
3	10	1
4	7	5

MOVEMENT BINGO

6	8	7
3	10	1
4	2	5

MOVEMENT BINGO

7	9	5
1	3	2
6	4	10

MOVEMENT BINGO

8	9	4
1	7	2
6	5	10

MOVEMENT BINGO

2	8	10
7	3	1
4	9	5

MOVEMENT BINGO

3	6	5
10	7	9
8	2	1

MOVEMENT BINGO

2	5	6
7	3	10
4	9	8

MOVEMENT BINGO

2	6	4
10	7	8
9	3	1

MOVEMENT BINGO

9	5	7
6	3	1
4	2	8

MOVEMENT BINGO

9	5	6
8	3	1
4	2	10

MOVEMENT BINGO

3	10	1
5	6	9
8	4	7

PHYSICAL EDUCATION BINGO (Instructor Bingo Cards):
Lesson 2.8 Classroom Activity

MOVEMENT BINGO 1

Can you run?

MOVEMENT BINGO 2

Can you skip?

MOVEMENT BINGO 3

Can you gallop?

MOVEMENT BINGO 4

Can you slide?

MOVEMENT BINGO 5

Can you jump?

MOVEMENT BINGO 6

Can you leap?

MOVEMENT BINGO 7

Can you hop?

MOVEMENT BINGO 8

Can you walk backward?

MOVEMENT BINGO 9

Can you walk at a low level?

MOVEMENT BINGO 10

Can you walk at a high level?

BEANBAG BINGO 1

Can you place the beanbag on your foot, gently swing your leg forward, and then catch the beanbag?

BEANBAG BINGO 2

Can you toss the beanbag into the air and clap before you catch it?

BEANBAG BINGO 3

Can you toss the beanbag into the air, touch your foot, and catch it?

BEANBAG BINGO 4

Can you toss the beanbag with your right hand and catch it?

BEANBAG BINGO 5

Can you toss the beanbag with your left hand and catch it?

BEANBAG BINGO 6

Can you toss the beanbag, touch your head and shoulders, and then catch it?

BEANBAG BINGO 7

Can you toss the beanbag under your leg and catch it?

BEANBAG BINGO 8

Can you toss the beanbag into the air, touch your knees, and catch it?

BEANBAG BINGO **9**

Can you toss the beanbag under your arm and catch it?

BEANBAG BINGO **10**

Can you toss the beanbag back and forth from one hand to the other?

SCARF BINGO **1**

Can you toss the scarf and catch it?

SCARF BINGO **2**

Can you move the scarf like a windshield wiper?

SCARF BINGO **3**

Can you move the scarf in a figure 8?

SCARF BINGO **4**

Can you move the scarf in a circle overhead?

SCARF BINGO   5

Can you move the
scarf like a
slithering snake?

SCARF BINGO   6

Can you move the
scarf in a circle in
front of your body?

SCARF BINGO   7

Can you toss the
scarf, clap your
hands, and catch it?

SCARF BINGO   8

Can you toss the
scarf with your right
hand and catch it?

SCARF BINGO   9

Can you toss the
scarf with your left
hand and catch it?

SCARF BINGO   10

Can you move the
scarf up and down
like you are
painting?

Content Included in Each Movement Form

Basic Movement Skills

1. Basic movement skills and concepts are explained in depth in Chapter 3 and summarized in the movement map (Figure 3.1):
   a. Body movements
   b. Body awareness
   c. Space awareness
   d. Qualities of movement
   e. Relationships
2. Progressive learning activities are listed in Appendix A (individual and partner activities).
3. Activities in this movement form that are present in the book can be found by consulting Appendix F. Go online and manipulate the Excel file to find basic movement activities for the grade level of your choice.

Basic Game Skills

1. The basic game skills are combinations of locomotor, nonlocomotor, and manipulative skills needed to play low organized games and games that lead up to regulation sports (e.g., softball/baseball, basketball, volleyball, football, soccer, tennis, badminton, and bowling). The basic game skills include the following:
   a. Throwing and catching
   b. Running and kicking
   c. Striking (with hand and instruments) and dribbling (with hand or foot)
   d. Chasing, fleeing, and dodging
   e. Rolling a ball
2. Progressive learning activities are listed in Appendix A (small group activities).
3. Activities in this movement form that are present in the book can be found by consulting Appendix F. Go online and manipulate the Excel file to find basic game skills appropriate for the grade level of your choice.

Creative and Rhythmic Movements

1. This movement form includes any activity where the purpose is to develop the body's rhythmic abilities and/or to develop the body's ability to express ideas, concepts, and emotions through movement. Generally, activities in this movement form are categorized as follows:
   a. Basic locomotor and nonlocomotor skills to music
   b. Manipulative skills to music
   c. Creative rhythms
   d. Folk dance
   e. Square dance
   Records listed below are available from Kimbo Educational (noted as Kimbo, www.kimboed.com/dance) or from Educational Record Center (noted as ERC, www.erckids.com).
2. Suggested learning activities in each category are as follows:
   a. Basic locomotor and nonlocomotor skills to music (Kimbo)
      i. Songs with actions ("Six Little Ducks," "Five Little Monkeys," and "Three Little Kittens")
      ii. Marching/fitness ("Traditional Marches")
      iii. Rhythm awareness ("Toes Up, Toes Down")
      iv. Locomotor skills ("Rhythms for Basic Motor Skills")
      v. Nonlocomotor skills ("Walter the Waltzing Worm")
   b. Manipulative skills to music (Kimbo)
      i. Jumping rope ("Jump Aerobics")
      ii. Lummi sticks ("Simplified Rhythm Stick" for grades K–3, "Lively Music for Rhythm Stick Fun" for grades 4–6)
      iii. Balls, ribbons and hula hoops ("Ball, Hoop and Ribbon Activities")

iv. Parachute ("Playtime Parachute Fun" for grades K–3, "Rhythmic Parachute Play" for grades 2–6)

v. Beanbags ("Bean Bag Activities")

vi. Scarves ("Musical Scarves and Activities")

c. Creative rhythms (Kimbo)

   i. Animal walks ("Walk Like the Animals")

   ii. Beanbags and scarfs ("Body Bingo")

   iii. Emotions ("Pretend," "Ideas, Thoughts & Feelings," and "Getting to Know Myself")

   iv. Dance a story or poem (as it is read aloud)

d. Folk dance

   i. For grades K–3

      1. "Simple Folk Dances" (Kimbo)

         a. Danish Dance of Greeting (Denmark)

         b. Shoemaker's Dance (Denmark)

         c. Bleking (Sweden)

         d. Chimes of Dunkirk (France)

         e. Swedish Clap Dance (Sweden)

      2. "Folk Dance Fundamentals" (ERC)

         a. How Do You Do, My Partner (Sweden)

         b. I See You (Sweden)

         c. Kinderpolka (Germany)

         d. The Wheat (Czechoslovakia)

      3. "Hokey Pokey" (ERC)

         a. Hokey Pokey (American)

         b. Skip to My Lou (American)

         c. Pop Goes the Weasel (American)

         d. Oh Susanna (American)

      4. "Around the World in Dance" (ERC)

         a. Bingo (American)

         b. Cherkessia (Israeli)

      5. "Songs about Native Americans" (Kimbo)

         a. A Place Called Home

         b. The Circle of Life

   ii. For grades 4–6

      1. "All Time Rhythm Favorites" (ERC)

         a. La Raspa (Mexico)

         b. Pattycake Polka (American)

         c. If You're Happy and You Know It (American)

      2. "All Time Favorite Dances" (Kimbo and ERC)

         a. Bunny Hop (American)

         b. Cotton-Eyed Joe

         c. Virginia Reel

      3. "Contemporary Tinikling" (Kimbo)

         a. Tinikling (Phillipines)

      4. "Children's Folk Dance" (Kimbo and ERC)

         a. Troika (Russia)

         b. Jump Jim Jo (American)

         c. Go Round and Round the Village (England)

         d. Schottische (Scotland)

         e. Fado (Portugal)

      5. "Authentic Indian Dances and Folklore" (Kimbo)

         a. Rain Dance

         b. Corn Dance

e. Square dance

   i. For grades K–3

      1. "Get Ready to Square Dance" (Kimbo and ERC)

         a. Cotton-Eyed Joe

         b. Turkey in the Straw

      2. "Square Dancing Made Easy" (Kimbo and ERC)

         a. Flop-Eared Mule

         b. Old Dan Tucker

         c. Yee-Ha!

         d. Basketball Square Dance

         e. Whoopin' It Up

         f. Possum Stomp

   ii. For grades 4–6

      1. "Get Ready to Square Dance" (Kimbo and ERC)

         a. Oh Belinda

         b. Shoo Fly

         c. Comin' Round the Mountain

         d. Tie a Yellow Ribbon

      2. "Basic Square Dances" (ERC)

         a. Red River Valley

         b. Take a Little Peek

         c. Divide the Ring

         d. Duck for the Oyster

         e. Girls to the Center

         f. Hinkey Dinkey Parlez-Vous

3. Activities in this movement form that are present in the book can be found in Appendix F. Go online and manipulate the Excel file to find creative and rhythmic skills appropriate for the grade level of your choice.

Body Management Skills and Gymnastics

1. For students in elementary school, this movement form concentrates on the body moving in space without equipment (e.g., forward roll) or moving in relationship to stationary equipment (e.g., balance beam). Emphasis is on body weight transfer and body control during movements. This movement form includes skills in

   a. Tumbling

   b. Stunts (individual and partner)

   c. Gymnastics

   Stunts, tumbling, and gymnastics skills should be co-taught by the classroom teacher and the physical educator. Consult with the physical educator for correct performance and safety issues relating to these skills.

2. Learning activities in this movement form may include the following:

   a. Tumbling (transferring body weight)

      i. Shoulder roll

      ii. Forward roll

GRADE LEVEL	LOCATION	CATEGORY	NAME OF ACTIVITY	NASPE STANDARD(S)	MOVEMENT FORM	SKILL(S)	KNOWLEDGE CONTENT	INTEGRATION AREA	CHAPTER	PAGE IN TEXT
3-4	Classroom	Lesson 2.9 Classroom Activity	Tinikling Workout	1, 5	Cooperative	Tinikling	Technique		LP	420
3-4	Classroom	Lesson 2.10 Classroom Activity	Jacks	1, 5	Cooperative	Jacks	Respect for others		LP	421
3-4	Classroom	Lesson 2.11 Classroom Activity	Lummi Sticks	1, 5	Cooperative	Lummi sticks	Respect for others		LP	422
3-4	Classroom	Lesson 2.12 Classroom Activity	Lummi Sticks	1, 5	Cooperative	Lummi sticks	Self-expression		LP	423
3-4	Classroom	Lesson 2.13 Classroom Activity	"La Raspa"	1, 4, 5	Cooperative	"La Raspa" dance	Respect for partner		LP	425
3-4	Classroom	Lesson 2.14 Classroom Activity	Lummi Stick Circle	1, 5	Cooperative	Lummi sticks	Cooperation		LP	427
3-4	Classroom	Lesson 2.15 Classroom Activity	Partner Stunts	1, 5	Cooperative	Partner stunts	Respect for partner		LP	429
3-4	Gymnasium	Lesson 2.1	Phrase Craze, "Bunny Hop"	5	Cooperative	Locomotor movements	Teamwork		LP	404
3-4	Gymnasium	Lesson 2.2	Coordinate Coordination, Parachute Grapevine	2, 4, 5	Cooperative	Variety	Directional movement		LP	406
3-4	Gymnasium	Lesson 2.3	Quack You Up Activities	4, 5	Cooperative	Variety	Working with partner		LP	408
3-4	Gymnasium	Lesson 2.4	Color Dribble, Goalie Kick and Punt, Partner Dribble and Pass	1, 2, 5	Cooperative	Soccer	Working with partner		LP	410
3-4	Gymnasium	Lesson 2.5	Group Ball Juggle, Scarf Juggle, Group Scarf Juggle	1, 5	Cooperative	Juggling	Cooperation		LP	412
3-4	Gymnasium	Lesson 2.6	Fun Fitness Activities: Tennis Ball Take, Team Bowling	1, 4, 5	Cooperative	Bowling and fitness	Cooperation	Math	LP	414
3-4	Gymnasium	Lesson 2.7	Dribble/Pivot/Pass, Snatch Basketball	1, 2, 4, 5	Cooperative	Basketball	Teamwork		LP	416
3-4	Gymnasium	Lesson 2.8	See and Spell	1, 5	Cooperative	Locomotor movements	Word jumble	Spelling	LP	417
3-4	Gymnasium	Lesson 2.9	Let's Go Jumping	1, 4, 5, 6	Cooperative	Jumping rope	Self-expression		LP	419
3-4	Gymnasium	Lesson 2.10	Station Rotation	1, 4, 5	Cooperative	Variety	Cooperation		LP	421
3-4	Gymnasium	Lesson 2.11	Lummi Stick Partners	1, 4, 5	Cooperative	Lummi sticks	Respect for partner		LP	422
3-4	Gymnasium	Lesson 2.12	Four-Square	1, 4, 5	Cooperative	Throwing and catching	Taking turns		LP	423
3-4	Gymnasium	Lesson 2.13	"La Raspa" (Folk Dance)	1, 4	Cooperative	Bleking steps, elbow swing	Respect for partner		LP	424
3-4	Gymnasium	Lesson 2.14	Caterpillar Walk, Skin the Snake	1, 4, 5	Cooperative	Group walking	Cooperation		LP	426
3-4	Gymnasium	Lesson 2.15	Ball Progression (One Person), Ball Progression (Two People)	1, 4, 5	Cooperative	Bouncing and catching	Respect		LP	428
3-5	Classroom	Integrated Game	Presidential Race	3	Game skills	Running, tagging, dodging	Geography	Social studies	8	243
3-5	Playground	Integrated Game	Newton's Laws	3	None	Variety	Force, motion	Science	8	244
3-6	Classroom	Classroom Learning Station 4.1	Coronary HD Risk Factors	3	Fitness	None	Health: heart disease	Art	4	127
3-6	Classroom	Classroom Learning Station 5.1	Locomotor Sign Language	5	Basic movement	Locomotor skills	Sign language	Spelling, language arts	5	164
3-6	Classroom	Classroom Learning Station 12.1	Including Others	5	Cooperative	None	Cooperation and creativity	Art, social studies	12	373
3-6	Classroom	Instant Activity 2.3	Child-Designed Physical Activity	2	Game skills	Soccer: kicking for goal	Critical thinking		2	42
3-6	Classroom	Instant Activity 4.4	Determining Heart Rates	4	Fitness	Running in place	Health: pulse		4	102
3-6	Classroom	Instant Activity 4.5	Heart Rate and Activity	4	Fitness	Marching and jogging in place	Health: heart rates		4	102
3-6	Classroom	Instant Activity 11.3	The Krinkle Slide	1, 6	Body management	Body positioning	Enjoyment		11	335
3-6	Classroom	Instant Activity 12.3	Learning Names	6	Cooperative	Body positioning	Teamwork		12	364
3-6	Classroom	Quick Lesson 1.6	Opposite Hand	5	Basic movement	Throwing	Individual differences		1	24
3-6	Classroom	Quick Lesson 4.5	Muscular Strength	3	Fitness	None	Health: strength	Writing, library skills	4	119
3-6	Classroom	Quick Lesson 12.2	Classroom Dribbling	1, 2	Basic movement	Dribbling with hand	Technique	Social studies	12	372

TABLE 1 Activity Listing by Grade Level (*continued*)

GRADE LEVEL	LOCATION	CATEGORY	NAME OF ACTIVITY	NASPE STANDARD(S)	MOVEMENT FORM	SKILL(S)	KNOWLEDGE CONTENT	INTEGRATION AREA	CHAPTER	PAGE IN TEXT
3–6	Classroom	Special Event 4.1	Are We There Yet?	3	Fitness	Walking and jogging	Health: cardiorespiratory workout	Social studies	4	132
3–6	Gymnasium	Special Event 2.1	Health & Movement Fair	5	Basic movement	Variety	Growth and development	Writing, drawing, math	2	51
3–6	Playground	Quick Lesson 1.3	Chase the Leader	4	Fitness	Jogging	Fitness: training principles	Health	1	21
3–6	Playground	Quick Lesson 1.5	Create Your Own Sport	5	Game skills	Student created	Game rules	Social studies	1	23
3–6	Playground	Quick Lesson 3.3	Partner Kickball	3	Game skills	Rolling, kicking	Fitness: endurance	Math	3	87
3–6	Playground	Special Event 11.1	Friday Afternoon Game Day	1	Game skills	Variety	Game rules	Social studies	11	343
4–5	Classroom	Integrated Game	I Have, Where Is	3	Fitness	Running	State capitals	Social studies	8	244
4–6	Classroom	Classroom Learning Station 7.1	Creating Bumper Stickers	3	Fitness	Fine motor skills	Healthy lifestyles	Science	7	228
4–6	Classroom	Instant Activity 7.1	Portraying Words and Phrases Through Movement	2, 6	Cooperative	Variety	Critical thinking		7	206
4–6	Classroom	Instant Activity 9.1	Mac the Crab	4	Fitness and Rhythm	"Macarena"	Fitness is fun	Music	9	273
4–6	Classroom	Instant Activity 9.2	Push-up Hockey	4	Fitness	Push-ups	Fitness is fun	Music	9	276
4–6	Classroom	Opening Scenario 6.1	Opening Scenario 6.1	1	Rhythmic movement	Walking and skipping	Accepting others	Social studies	6	167
4–6	Classroom	Quick Lesson 4.1	How Arteries Become Clogged	4	Fitness	Scooters	Health: blood flow	Spelling	4	115
4–6	Classroom	Quick Lesson 4.2	Measuring Blood Pressures	3	Fitness	None	Health: blood pressure	Music	4	116
4–6	Gymnasium	Opening Scenario 10.1	Opening Scenario 10.1	5, 6	Cooperative	Striking	Cooperation and problem solving		10	295
4–6	Playground	Quick Lesson 3.4	Major League Throw and Catch	4	Game skills	Throwing and catching	Fitness: strength	Geography: state capitals	3	88
5–6	Classroom	Lesson 3.2 Classroom Activity	"How To" Speeches	1	None	Soccer	Technique	Writing, speaking	LP	435
5–6	Classroom	Lesson 3.3 Classroom Activity	Line Dance Development	1, 5, 6	Rhythmic movement	Line dancing	Creativity		LP	437
5–6	Classroom	Lesson Plan Unit 3 Introduction	Journal Entries	1, 6	None	Soccer	Self-awareness	Writing	LP	432
5–6	Gymnasium	Box 6.5	Sample PE Lesson Plan	1	Rhythmic movement	Square dance	Accepting others		6	193
5–6	Gymnasium	Lesson 3.1	Dribbling the Ball, Trapping and Passing, Circle Kickball	1, 4, 5	Game skills	Ball handling: soccer	Technique and strategy		LP	433
5–6	Gymnasium	Lesson 3.2	Take Away, Stop That Ball	1, 2, 4, 5	Game skills	Defensive skills: soccer	Technique and strategy		LP	435
5–6	Gymnasium	Lesson 3.3	Circle Kick, Forward Ho!	1, 4, 5	Game skills	Offensive skills: soccer	Technique		LP	436
5–6	Gymnasium	Lesson 3.4	Dribble Mania, Soccer Keep Away	1, 3, 5	Game skills	Dribbling, passing, kicking: Soccer	Technique and responsibility		LP	438
5–6	Gymnasium	Lesson 3.5	Frisbee Backhand Throw	1, 4, 6	Game skills	Throwing and catching: Frisbee	Technique and throwing		LP	439
5–6	Gymnasium	Lesson 3.6	Punt, Throw-in, Target Throw-in	1, 3, 5	Game skills	Punting, throwing-in: soccer	Technique		LP	440
5–6	Gymnasium	Lesson 3.7	Lead-up Soccer Games: Sideline Soccer	1, 3, 5	Game skills	All soccer skills	Technique and strategy		LP	442
5–6	Gymnasium	Lesson 3.8	Lead-up Soccer Games: Three-on-Three	1, 3, 5	Game skills	All soccer skills	Technique and strategy		LP	444
5–6	Gymnasium	Lesson 3.9	Lead-up Soccer Games: Sideline Soccer	1, 2, 4, 5	Game skills	All soccer skills	Technique and strategy		LP	445
5–6	Gymnasium	Lesson 3.10	Backhand Throw and Catch, Backhand Curve, Backhand Bounce, Frisbee Keep Away	1, 4, 5	Game skills	Throwing and catching: Frisbee	Technique		LP	446
5–6	Gymnasium	Lesson 3.11	Kicking for Goal	1, 2, 4, 5	Game skills	Kicking: soccer	Technique		LP	447
5–6	Gymnasium	Lesson 3.12	Modified Soccer	1, 4, 5	Game skills	All soccer skills	Game rules		LP	448
5–6	Gymnasium	Lesson 3.15	Frisbee Golf	1, 4, 5	Game skills	Throwing	Technique		LP	451
5–6	Gymnasium	Lessons 3.13 and 3.14	Modified Soccer	1, 2, 4, 5	Game skills	All soccer skills	Rules, enjoyment		LP	450

TABLE 2 Activity Listing by Movement Form

MOVEMENT FORM	NASPE STANDARD(S)	GRADE LEVEL	CATEGORY	NAME OF ACTIVITY	LOCATION	SKILL(S)	KNOWLEDGE CONTENT	INTEGRATION AREA	CHAPTER	PAGE IN TEXT
Basic movement	1	K-2	Lesson 4.1	Toss and Catch/Movement Levels	Classroom	Tossing and catching	Technique		LP	453
Basic movement	1	K-2	Lesson 4.2	Striking	Classroom	Striking and catching	Technique		LP	454
Basic movement	1	K-2	Lesson 4.3	Dribbling with Hands	Classroom	Dribbling with hand	Technique		LP	455
Basic movement	1	K-2	Lesson 4.4	Dribbling with Feet	Classroom	Dribbling with feet	Technique		LP	456
Basic movement	1	K-2	Lesson 4.5	Throwing at Targets	Classroom	Throwing	Technique		LP	457
Basic movement	1	K-2	Lesson 4.6	Dribbling with Hands	Classroom	Dribbling with hand	Technique		LP	458
Basic movement	1	K-2	Lesson 4.7	Pease Porridge Hot; Stomp, Stomp, Stomp	Classroom	Moving to music	Rhythm recognition		LP	459
Basic movement	1	K-2	Lesson 4.8	Catching with Sponge or Yarn Balls	Classroom	Throwing and catching	Technique		LP	460
Basic movement	1	K-2	Lesson 4.9	Jumping Rope	Classroom	Jumping rope	Technique		LP	461
Basic movement	1	K-2	Lesson 4.10	Jumping and Landing	Classroom	Jumping and landing	Technique		LP	462
Basic movement	1	K-2	Lesson 4.11	Identify Body Parts	Classroom	Body awareness	Body part identification		LP	463
Basic movement	1	K-2	Lesson 4.12	Catching: Using Different Objects	Classroom	Throwing and catching	Technique		LP	464
Basic movement	1	K-2	Lesson 4.13	Balancing	Classroom	Balance	Technique		LP	465
Basic movement	1	K-2	Lesson 4.14	Toss to Self and Catch	Classroom	Tossing and catching	Technique		LP	466
Basic movement	1	K-2	Lesson 4.15	Pathways	Classroom	Locomotor skills	Pathways		LP	467
Basic movement	1	K-2	Quick Lesson 2.1	Exploration with Balloons	Classroom	Striking	Movement concepts	Math	2	49
Basic movement	1	K-3	Lesson 1.3 Classroom Activity	Beanbag Stunts	Classroom	Beanbags	Focus on the beanbag		LP	384
Basic movement	1	K-3	Lesson 1.8 Classroom Activity	Moon Throw	Classroom	Throwing	Technique and accuracy		LP	392
Basic movement	1	K-3	Lesson 1.10 Classroom Activity	Spelling Toss/Throw	Classroom	Tossing	Accuracy		LP	395
Basic movement	1	K-3	Lesson 1.11 Classroom Activity	Target Bowling	Classroom	Rolling and tossing	Technique		LP	396
Basic movement	1	K-3	Lesson 1.12 Classroom Activity	Volleying	Classroom	Volleying	Technique		LP	397
Basic movement	1	K-3	Quick Lesson 7.1	Movement Exploration with Beanbags	Classroom	Tossing a beanbag	Movement concepts	Math	7	227
Basic movement	1	K-3	Lesson 1.11	Form Bowling, Target Bowling, Pin Bowling	Gymnasium	Ball handling: bowling	Technique		LP	396
Basic movement	1	K-6	Classroom Learning Station 3.1	Fine Motor Station	Classroom	Fine motor skills	Technique: handling small objects	Math, spelling	3	89
Basic movement	1	K-6	Instant Activity 1.1	Dice Math	Classroom	Throwing	Math skills	Math	1	5
Basic movement	1	K-6	Quick Lesson 1.1	Match the Diagram	Classroom	Locomotor skills	Movement concept: pathways	Social studies	1	19
Basic movement	1, 2	K-3	Instant Activity 3.1	Collapse	Classroom	Collapsing	Movement concepts		3	56
Basic movement	1, 2	K-3	Opening Scenario 2.1	Opening Scenario 2.1	Playground	Throwing	Technique: throwing		2	31
Basic movement	1, 2	3-6	Quick Lesson 12.2	Classroom Dribbling	Classroom	Dribbling with hand	Technique	Social studies	12	372
Basic movement	1, 2, 5	K-3	Lesson 1.3	Manipulative Skills: Beanbags	Gymnasium	Beanbags	Throwing technique		LP	383
Basic movement	1, 3, 5	K-6	Instant Activity 1.2	Striking Practice	Classroom	Striking	Technique: striking		1	8
Basic movement	1, 3, 5	K-6	Special Event 1.1	Celebrating Nat. PE & Sport Week	Playground	Teacher selected	Importance of fitness	Writing	1	28
Basic movement	1, 4	K-3	Lesson 1.9	Line Dribbling, Passing Game, Shooting Game, Basket Shooting	Gymnasium	Ball handling: basketball	Technique		LP	394
Basic movement	1, 4	K-3	Lesson 1.10	Cone Dribbling, Follow the Leader	Gymnasium	Ball handling: basketball	Technique		LP	395

MOVEMENT FORM	NASPE STANDARD(S)	GRADE LEVEL	CATEGORY	NAME OF ACTIVITY	LOCATION	SKILL(S)	KNOWLEDGE CONTENT	INTEGRATION AREA	CHAPTER	PAGE IN TEXT
Cooperative	1	3–4	Lesson 2.7 Classroom Activity	Trash Can Shoot	Classroom	Throwing	Technique		LP	416
Cooperative	1, 2, 4, 5	3–4	Lesson 2.7	Dribble/Pivot/Pass, Snatch Basketball	Gymnasium	Basketball	Teamwork		LP	416
Cooperative	1, 2, 5	3–4	Lesson 2.4	Color Dribble, Goalie Kick and Punt, Partner Dribble and Pass	Gymnasium	Soccer	Working with partner		LP	410
Cooperative	1, 4	3–4	Lesson 2.13	"La Raspa" (Folk Dance)	Gymnasium	Bleking steps, elbow swing	Respect for partner		LP	424
Cooperative	1, 4, 5	3–4	Lesson 2.13 Classroom Activity	"La Raspa"	Classroom	"La Raspa" dance	Respect for partner		LP	425
Cooperative	1, 4, 5	3–4	Lesson 2.12	Four-Square	Gymnasium	Throwing and catching	Taking turns		LP	423
Cooperative	1, 4, 5	3–4	Lesson 2.6	Fun Fitness Activities: Tennis Ball Take, Team Bowling	Gymnasium	Bowling and fitness	Cooperation	Math	LP	414
Cooperative	1, 4, 5	3–4	Lesson 2.10	Station Rotation	Gymnasium	Variety	Cooperation		LP	421
Cooperative	1, 4, 5	3–4	Lesson 2.11	Lummi Stick Partners	Gymnasium	Lummi sticks	Respect for partner		LP	422
Cooperative	1, 4, 5	3–4	Lesson 2.14	Caterpillar Walk, Skin the Snake	Gymnasium	Group walking	Cooperation		LP	426
Cooperative	1, 4, 5	3–4	Lesson 2.15	Ball Progression (One Person), Ball Progression (Two People)	Gymnasium	Bouncing and catching	Respect		LP	428
Cooperative	1, 4, 5, 6	3–4	Lesson 2.9	Let's Go Jumping	Gymnasium	Jumping rope	Self-expression		LP	419
Cooperative	1, 5	3–4	Lesson 2.9 Classroom Activity	Tinikling Workout	Classroom	Tinikling	Technique		LP	420
Cooperative	1, 5	3–4	Lesson 2.10 Classroom Activity	Jacks	Classroom	Jacks	Respect for others		LP	421
Cooperative	1, 5	3–4	Lesson 2.11 Classroom Activity	Lummi Sticks	Classroom	Lummi sticks	Respect for others		LP	422
Cooperative	1, 5	3–4	Lesson 2.12 Classroom Activity	Lummi Sticks	Classroom	Lummi sticks	Self-expression		LP	423
Cooperative	1, 5	3–4	Lesson 2.14 Classroom Activity	Lummi Stick Circle	Classroom	Lummi sticks	Cooperation		LP	427
Cooperative	1, 5	3–4	Lesson 2.15 Classroom Activity	Partner Stunts	Classroom	Partner stunts	Respect for partner		LP	429
Cooperative	1, 5	3–4	Lesson 2.5	Group Ball Juggle, Scarf Juggle, Group Scarf Juggle	Gymnasium	Juggling	Cooperation		LP	412
Cooperative	1, 5	3–4	Lesson 2.8	See and Spell	Gymnasium	Locomotor movements	Word jumble	Spelling	LP	417
Cooperative	1, 5	3–4	Lesson 2.5 Classroom Activity	Juggling	Classroom	Juggling	Success		LP	413
Cooperative	2, 4, 5	3–4	Lesson 2.2 Classroom Activity	Grapevine Circle	Classroom	Grapevine step	Cooperation		LP	407
Cooperative	2, 4, 5	3–4	Lesson 2.2	Coordinate Coordination, Parachute Grapevine	Gymnasium	Variety	Directional movement		LP	406
Cooperative	2, 6	4–6	Instant Activity 7.1	Portraying Words and Phrases Through Movement	Classroom	Variety	Critical thinking		7	206
Cooperative	3	2–6	Quick Lesson 8.1	Olympic *Jeopardy*	Classroom	None	Olympic facts	Social studies, language arts	8	258
Cooperative	4, 5	3–4	Lesson 2.6 Classroom Activity	Carpet Squares	Classroom	Variety	Cooperation		LP	415
Cooperative	4, 5	3–4	Lesson 2.3	Quack You Up Activities	Gymnasium	Variety	Working with partner		LP	408
Cooperative	5	K–6	Instant Activity 6.2	Cooperative Musical Chairs	Classroom	Walking	Cooperation		6	172
Cooperative	5	K–6	Instant Activity 10.4	Stand Up, Sit Down	Classroom	Standing up	Cooperation		10	306
Cooperative	5	3–6	Classroom Learning Station 12.1	Including Others	Classroom	None	Cooperation and creativity	Art, social studies	12	373
Cooperative	5	K–6	Special Event 7.1	Challenge Play Day	Playground	Variety	Cooperation and creativity		7	229
Cooperative	5	3–4	Lesson 2.1 Classroom Activity	"Shoemaker's Dance"	Classroom	"Shoemaker's Dance"	Teamwork and success		LP	404
Cooperative	5	3–4	Lesson 2.1	Phrase Craze, "Bunny Hop"	Gymnasium	Locomotor movements	Teamwork		LP	404

TABLE 2 Activity Listing by Movement Form (*continued*)

MOVEMENT FORM	NASPE STANDARD(S)	GRADE LEVEL	CATEGORY	NAME OF ACTIVITY	LOCATION	SKILL(S)	KNOWLEDGE CONTENT	INTEGRATION AREA	CHAPTER	PAGE IN TEXT
Cooperative	5, 6	4–6	Opening Scenario 10.1	Opening Scenario 10.1	Gymnasium	Striking	Cooperation and problem solving		10	295
Cooperative	5, 6	K–4	Instant Activity 10.3	Stretches	Classroom	Shapes	Cooperation		10	302
Cooperative	5	K–6	Instant Activity 5.1	Similarities and Differences	Classroom	Locomotor skills	Accepting others		5	137
Cooperative	5	K–6	Quick Lesson 5.2	Getting to Know Your Classmates	Classroom	Variety	Accepting others	Social studies	5	163
Cooperative	5	K–6	Special Event 5.1	Simulation Activities	Classroom	Variety	Accepting others	Math, spelling	5	165
Cooperative	5	K–6	Instant Activity 7.2	New Ways to Bowl	Classroom	Variety	Critical thinking		7	207
Cooperative	5, 6	2–6	Quick Lesson 5.1	All-Star Bulletin Boards	Classroom	None	Accepting others	Math	5	162
Cooperative	6	K–1	Special Event 8.1	Read and Romp Day	Gymnasium	Variety	Cooperation and creativity	Reading, math, language arts	8	262
Cooperative	6	K–6	Instant Activity 6.3	Target Toss Math	Classroom	Tossing	Math skills		6	173
Cooperative	6	K–6	Instant Activity 12.1	Hi Five	Classroom	Locomotor skills	Accepting others		12	348
Cooperative	6	2–6	Classroom Learning Station 8.1	How Many in Our Theme?	Classroom	None	Subject integration		8	261
Cooperative	6	3–4	Lesson 2.3 Classroom Activity	Human Letters	Classroom	Letter formations	Letter recognition	Reading	LP	409
Cooperative	6	3–4	Lesson 2.4 Classroom Activity	Animal Movement Cards	Classroom	Variety	Self-expression		LP	411
Cooperative	6	3–4	Lesson 2.8 Classroom Activity	P.E. Bingo	Classroom	Variety	Number recognition		LP	418
Cooperative	6	3–6	Instant Activity 12.3	Stepping Stones	Classroom	Body positioning	Teamwork		12	364
Fitness	2	K–6	Integrated Game	Circuit Training Through the Muscular System	Classroom	Variety	Muscle identification	Science	8	246
Fitness	3	K–6	Integrated Game	Spell Around the Room	Classroom	Running	Spelling	Language arts	8	241
Fitness	3	K–6	Integrated Game	North and South Wind	Classroom	Running, tagging, dodging	Weather	Social studies	8	243
Fitness	3	K–6	Quick Lesson 6.1	The Benefits of an Active Lifestyle	Classroom	None	Fitness: benefits	Art, math	6	195
Fitness	3	K–6	Integrated Game	Junk the Junk Food	Gymnasium	Running	Junk food, pathways	Health	8	247
Fitness	3	K–6	Quick Lesson 11.1	Walking and Stretching	Playground	Walking and stretching	Technique	Math	11	339
Fitness	3	1–3	Quick Lesson 4.6	Muscular Endurance	Classroom	Abdominal curl	Health: endurance	Science	4	120
Fitness	3	1–3	Quick Lesson 4.7	Flexibility	Classroom	Stretches	Health: flexibility	Science	4	121
Fitness	3	1–3	Quick Lesson 4.8	Walking	Playground	Walking	Technique: walking	Math	4	124
Fitness	3	1–6	Classroom Learning Station 4.2	How to Determine the Heart Rate	Classroom	None	Health: taking pulse rate	Math	4	128
Fitness	3	1–6	Classroom Learning Station 4.3	Which Muscle Is Which?	Classroom	None	Health: bones and muscles	Spelling	4	130
Fitness	3	1–6	Quick Lesson 4.9	Heart Rate Games	Classroom	Locomotor skills	Fitness: continuous movement	Writing	4	125
Fitness	3	1–6	Quick Lesson 4.4	How Hard Am I Working?	Playground	Walking and jogging	Health: perceived exertion	Geography	4	118
Fitness	3	2–3	Integrated Game	Jump Rope Bingo	Classroom	Jumping rope	Math skills	Math	8	242
Fitness	3	2–5	Integrated Game	Walk Across Your State	Classroom	Walking	Geography	Social studies	8	243
Fitness	3	2–6	Integrated Game	Odds and Evens	Classroom	Running	Math skills	Math	8	242
Fitness	3	2–6	Quick Lesson 4.3	The Circulatory System	Classroom	Walking	Health: blood flow	Science	4	117
Fitness	3	3–6	Classroom Learning Station 4.1	Coronary HD Risk Factors	Classroom	None	Health: heart disease	Art	4	127
Fitness	3	3–6	Quick Lesson 4.5	Muscular Strength	Classroom	None	Health: strength	Writing, library skills	4	119
Fitness	3	3–6	Special Event 4.1	Are We There Yet?	Classroom	Walking and jogging	Health: cardiorespiratory workout	Social studies	4	132
Fitness	4	3–6	Quick Lesson 1.3	Chase the Leader	Playground	Jogging	Fitness: training principles	Health	1	21
Fitness	3	4–5	Integrated Game	I Have, Where Is	Classroom	Running	State capitals	Social studies	8	244
Fitness	3	4–6	Classroom Learning Station 7.1	Creating Bumper Stickers	Classroom	Fine motor skills	Healthy lifestyles	Science	7	228

MOVEMENT FORM	NASPE STANDARD(S)	GRADE LEVEL	CATEGORY	NAME OF ACTIVITY	LOCATION	SKILL(S)	KNOWLEDGE CONTENT	INTEGRATION AREA	CHAPTER	PAGE IN TEXT
Fitness	3	4–6	Quick Lesson 4.2	Measuring Blood Pressures	Classroom	None	Health: blood pressure	Music	4	116
Fitness	3, 4	K–6	Opening Scenario 11.1	Opening Scenario 11.1	Playground	Walking	Fitness is fun		11	323
Fitness	3, 4, 5	K–6	Special Event 6.1	Parents' Night: Fitness and Wellness	Gymnasium	Teacher selected	Fitness: concepts	Reading, writing, health	6	198
Fitness	4	K–3	Instant Activity 4.2	The Heart Beating	Classroom	None	Health: pumping heart		4	99
Fitness	4	K–3	Instant Activity 4.3	Listening to the Heart	Classroom	Running and marching	Health: stethoscope		4	101
Fitness	4	K–6	Instant Activity 4.1	Impaired Breathing	Classroom	None	Health: smoking		4	98
Fitness	4	K–6	Integrated Game	Speed It Up	Classroom	Running	Heart rate	Science	8	245
Fitness	4	K–6	Integrated Game	Relaxation Walking	Classroom	None	Relaxation	Health	8	247
Fitness	4	K–6	Lesson 1.2 Classroom Activity	Desk Aerobics	Classroom	Variety	Fitness is fun		LP	382
Fitness	4	K–6	Quick Lesson 1.4	Jump for Fitness	Classroom	Jumping	Fitness: pulse rates	Science	1	22
Fitness	4	K–6	Classroom Learning Station 6.1	Exercise Bands	Classroom	Exercises with bands	Fitness: exercise progression	Science, health	6	197
Fitness	4	K–6	Integrated Game	Muscle Tag	Playground	Running, tagging, dodging	Muscle identification	Science	8	245
Fitness	4	3–6	Instant Activity 4.4	Determining Heart Rates	Classroom	Running in place	Health: pulse		4	102
Fitness	4	3–6	Instant Activity 4.5	Heart Rate and Activity	Classroom	Marching and jogging in place	Health: heart rates		4	102
Fitness	4	4–6	Instant Activity 9.2	Push-up Hockey	Classroom	Push-ups	Fitness is fun		9	276
Fitness	4	4–6	Quick Lesson 4.1	How Arteries Become Clogged	Classroom	Scooters	Health: blood flow	Spelling	4	115
Fitness	7	K–6	Quick Lesson 1.7	My Physical Activity Journal	Classroom	Student created	Fitness: awareness		1	25
Fitness and Rhythm	4	4–6	Instant Activity 9.1	Mac the Crab	Classroom	"Macarena"	Fitness is fun	Music	9	273
Game skills	1	K–6	Classroom Learning Station 9.1	Bowling	Classroom	Rolling	Technique: rolling	Math	9	286
Game skills	1	K–6	Integrated Game	Fist Dribble	Classroom	Dribbling with hand	Math skills	Math	8	242
Game skills	1	K–6	Lesson 1.5 Classroom Activity	Blob Tag	Classroom	Soccer	Technique		LP	387
Game skills	1	K–6	Lesson 1.7 Classroom Activity	Dribbling Sequences	Classroom	Basketball	Technique		LP	391
Game skills	1	3–6	Special Event 11.1	Friday Afternoon Game Day	Playground	Variety	Game rules		11	343
Game skills	1, 2, 3	K–3	Lesson 1.4	Cone Dribbling, Pin Kickball, Kickers and Trappers	Gymnasium	Kicking and dribbling: soccer	Technique		LP	385
Game skills	1, 2, 3	K–3	Lesson 1.5	Dribble Scramble, Bull's-Eye, Soccer Keep Away	Gymnasium	Kicking and dribbling: soccer	Technique		LP	387
Game skills	1, 2, 4, 5	5–6	Lesson 3.9	Lead-up Soccer Games: Sideline Soccer	Gymnasium	All soccer skills	Technique and strategy		LP	445
Game skills	1, 2, 4, 5	5–6	Lesson 3.11	Kicking for Goal	Gymnasium	Kicking: soccer	Technique		LP	447
Game skills	1, 2, 4, 5	5–6	Lesson 3.2	Take Away, Stop That Ball	Gymnasium	Defensive skills: soccer	Technique and strategy		LP	435
Game skills	1, 2, 4, 5	5–6	Lessons 3.13 and 3.14	Modified Soccer	Gymnasium	All soccer skills	Rules, enjoyment		LP	450
Game skills	1, 3	2–6	Opening Scenario 9.1	Opening Scenario 9.1	Playground	Throwing, catching, kicking	Game rules		9	265
Game skills	1, 3, 5	5–6	Lesson 3.4	Dribble Mania, Soccer Keep Away	Gymnasium	Dribbling, passing, kicking: soccer	Technique and responsibility		LP	438
Game skills	1, 3, 5	5–6	Lesson 3.6	Punt, Throw-in, Target Throw-in	Gymnasium	Punting, throwing-in: soccer	Technique		LP	440
Game skills	1, 3, 5	5–6	Lesson 3.8	Lead-up Soccer Games: Three-on-Three	Gymnasium	All soccer skills	Technique and strategy		LP	444
Game skills	1, 3, 5	5–6	Lesson 3.7	Lead-up Soccer Games: Sideline Soccer	Gymnasium	All soccer skills	Technique and strategy		LP	442

TABLE 2 Activity Listing by Movement Form (*continued*)

MOVEMENT FORM	NASPE STANDARD(S)	GRADE LEVEL	CATEGORY	NAME OF ACTIVITY	LOCATION	SKILL(S)	KNOWLEDGE CONTENT	INTEGRATION AREA	CHAPTER	PAGE IN TEXT
Game skills	1, 4	K-3	Lesson 1.7	Dribbling and Passing	Gymnasium	Ball handling: basketball	Technique		LP	391
Game skills	1, 4, 5	5-6	Lesson 3.10	Backhand Throw and Catch, Backhand Curve, Backhand Bounce, Frisbee Keep Away	Gymnasium	Throwing and catching: Frisbee	Technique		LP	446
Game skills	1, 4, 5	5-6	Lesson 3.12	Modified Soccer	Gymnasium	All soccer skills	Game rules		LP	448
Game skills	1, 4, 5	5-6	Lesson 3.15	Frisbee Golf	Gymnasium	Throwing	Technique		LP	451
Game skills	1, 4, 5	5-6	Lesson 3.1	Dribbling the Ball, Trapping and Passing, Circle Kickball	Gymnasium	Ball handling: soccer	Technique and strategy		LP	433
Game skills	1, 4, 5	5-6	Lesson 3.3	Circle Kick, Forward Ho!	Gymnasium	Offensive skills: soccer	Technique		LP	436
Game skills	1, 4, 6	5-6	Lesson 3.5	Frisbee Backhand Throw	Gymnasium	Throwing and catching: Frisbee	Technique and throwing		LP	439
Game skills	2	K-3	Lesson 1.4 Classroom Activity	Word Recognition	Classroom	None	Word recognition		LP	385
Game skills	2	2-4	Opening Scenario 3.1	Opening Scenario 3.1	Classroom	Throwing and catching	Technique: throw and catch		3	53
Game skills	2	3-6	Instant Activity 2.3	Child-Designed Physical Activity	Classroom	Soccer: kicking for goal	Critical thinking		2	42
Game skills	3	3-5	Integrated Game	Presidential Race	Classroom	Running, tagging, dodging	Geography	Social studies	8	243
Game skills	3	3-6	Quick Lesson 3.3	Partner Kickball	Playground	Rolling, kicking	Fitness: endurance	Math	3	87
Game skills	4	4-6	Quick Lesson 3.4	Major League Throw and Catch	Playground	Throwing and catching	Fitness: strength	Geography: state capitals	3	88
Game skills	5	3-6	Quick Lesson 1.5	Create Your Own Sport	Playground	Student created	Game rules	Social studies	1	23
Game skills	5	K-6	Special Event 12.1	Traditional Games, Dances, and Activities	Classroom	Student selected	Cultural differences	Social studies	12	375
Game skills	6	K-6	Classroom Learning Station 1.1	Today's Popular Sports	Classroom	Teacher selected	Teacher selected	Reading, spelling, library skills	1	27
Rhythmic movement	1	K-2	Quick Lesson 3.1	Olympic Runner	Classroom	Running	Technique: running	Language	3	85
Rhythmic movement	1	K-6	Instant Activity 1.3	Marching	Classroom	Marching	Moving to music		1	13
Rhythmic movement	1	4-6	Opening Scenario 6.1	Opening Scenario 6.1	Classroom	Walking and skipping	Accepting others	Social studies	6	167
Rhythmic movement	1	5-6	Box 6.5	"Oh, Johnny!"	Gymnasium	Square dance	Accepting others		6	193
Rhythmic movement	1, 4, 6	K-3	Lesson 1.2	Mulberry Bush	Gymnasium	Locomotor and nonlocomotor movements	Self-expression		LP	381
Rhythmic movement	1, 4, 6	K-6	Lesson 1.13	Manipulative Skills: Rope Jumping	Gymnasium	Jumping rope	Technique		LP	398
Rhythmic movement	1, 5	K-3	Lesson 1.14	Lummi Sticks	Gymnasium	Lummi sticks	Social interaction		LP	399
Rhythmic movement	1, 5	K-3	Lesson 1.15	"Kinder-Polka"	Gymnasium	"Kinder-Polka"	Technique		LP	401
Rhythmic movement	1, 5	K-3	Lesson 1.15 Classroom Activity	"Kinder-Polka"	Classroom	"Kinder-Polka"	Technique		LP	402
Rhythmic movement	1, 5, 6	5-6	Lesson 3.3 Classroom Activity	Line Dance Development	Classroom	Line dancing	Creativity		LP	437
Rhythmic movement	4	K-3	Lesson 1.13 Classroom Activity	Jump to Music	Classroom	Jumping rope	Fitness is fun		LP	398
Rhythmic movement	5, 6	K-6	Instant Activity 9.3	Follow the Leader	Classroom	Student created	Creativity		9	280
Rhythmic movement	6	K-6	Lesson 1.14 Classroom Activity	Creative Sequences	Classroom	Lummi sticks	Self-expression		LP	400
Rhythmic movement	6	K-6	Special Event 9.1	Create and Share	Classroom	Student created	Enjoyment and self-expression	Music	9	294

TABLE 3 Activity Listing by Integration Area

INTEGRATION AREA	GRADE LEVEL	LOCATION	CATEGORY	NAME OF ACTIVITY	NASPE STANDARD(S)	MOVEMENT FORM	SKILL(S)	KNOWLEDGE CONTENT	CHAPTER	PAGE IN TEXT
Art	3–6	Classroom	Classroom Learning Station 4.1	Coronary HD Risk Factors	3	Fitness	None	Health: heart disease	4	127
Art, math	K–6	Classroom	Quick Lesson 6.1	The Benefits of an Active Lifestyle	3	Fitness	None	Fitness: benefits	6	195
Art, music	K–6	Classroom	Quick Lesson 9.1	Student Voices	6	None	None	Enjoyment and self-expression	9	284
Art, social studies	3–6	Classroom	Classroom Learning Station 12.1	Including Others	5	Cooperative	None	Cooperation and creativity	12	373
Drawing, health, writing	K–6	Classroom	Classroom Learning Station 2.1	Are We All the Same?	5	Basic movement	Jumping	Growth and development	2	50
Drawing, math, writing	3–6	Gymnasium	Special Event 2.1	Health & Movement Fair	5	Basic movement	Variety	Growth and development	2	51
Geography	1–6	Playground	Quick Lesson 4.4	How Hard Am I Working?	3	Fitness	Walking and jogging	Health: perceived exertion	4	118
Geography: state capitals	4–6	Playground	Quick Lesson 3.4	Major League Throw and Catch	4	Game skills	Throwing and catching	Fitness: strength	3	88
Health	K–6	Classroom	Integrated Game	Relaxation Walking	4	Fitness	None	Relaxation	8	247
Health	K–6	Gymnasium	Integrated Game	Junk the Junk Food	3	Fitness	Running	Junk food, pathways	8	247
Health	3–6	Playground	Quick Lesson 1.3	Chase the Leader	4	Fitness	Jogging	Fitness: training principles	1	21
Health, reading, writing	K–6	Gymnasium	Special Event 6.1	Parents' Night: Fitness and Wellness	3, 4, 5	Fitness	Teacher selected	Fitness: concepts	6	198
Health, science	K–6	Classroom	Classroom Learning Station 6.1	Exercise Bands	4	Fitness	Exercises with bands	Fitness: exercise progression	6	197
Health, writing, drawing	K–6	Classroom	Classroom Learning Station 2.1	Are We All the Same?	5	Basic movement	Jumping	Growth and development	2	50
Language arts	K–1	Classroom	Integrated Game	Letter of the Week	3	Body management	Variety	Letter recognition	8	241
Language arts	K–2	Classroom	Integrated Game	How Can I Get There?	1	Body management	Spatial awareness	Movement concepts	8	241
Language arts	K–2	Classroom	Quick Lesson 3.1	Olympic Runner	1	Rhythmic movement	Running	Technique: running	3	85
Language arts	K–6	Classroom	Integrated Game	Alphabet Balloons	1	Body management	Striking	Spelling	8	241
Language arts	K–6	Classroom	Integrated Game	Punctuation Shuffle	1	Body management	Locomotor skills	Punctuation	8	241
Language arts	K–6	Classroom	Integrated Game	Jumping Words	5	Body management	Shapes	Spelling	8	242
Language arts	K–6	Classroom	Integrated Game	Spell Around the Room	3	Fitness	Running	Spelling	8	241
Language arts, reading, math	K–1	Gymnasium	Special Event 8.1	Read and Romp Day	6	Cooperative	Variety	Cooperation and creativity	8	262
Language arts, social studies	2–6	Classroom	Quick Lesson 8.1	Olympic *Jeopardy*	3	Cooperative	None	Olympic facts	8	258
Language arts, spelling	3–6	Classroom	Classroom Learning Station 5.1	Locomotor Sign Language	5	Basic movement	Locomotor skills	Sign language	5	164
Library skills, reading, spelling	K–6	Classroom	Classroom Learning Station 1.1	Today's Popular Sports	6	Game skills	Teacher selected	Teacher selected	1	27
Library skills, writing	3–6	Classroom	Quick Lesson 4.5	Muscular Strength	3	Fitness	None	Health: strength	4	119
Math	K–2	Classroom	Quick Lesson 2.1	Exploration with Balloons	1	Basic movement	Striking	Movement concepts	2	49
Math	K–3	Classroom	Quick Lesson 7.1	Movement Exploration with Beanbags	1	Basic movement	Tossing a beanbag	Movement concepts	7	227
Math	K–6	Classroom	Instant Activity 1.1	Dice Math	1	Basic movement	Throwing	Math skills	1	5
Math	K–6	Classroom	Integrated Game	Fruit Basket Upset Math	1	Body management	Locomotor skills	Math skills	8	243
Math	K–6	Classroom	Quick Lesson 1.2	Challenge Long Jump	2	Body management	Long jump	Movement concept: force	1	20
Math	K–6	Classroom	Integrated Game	Double Dice	3	Body management	Locomotor skills	Math skills	8	242
Math	K–6	Classroom	Classroom Learning Station 9.1	Bowling	1	Game skills	Rolling	Technique: rolling	9	286
Math	K–6	Classroom	Integrated Game	Fist Dribble	1	Game skills	Dribbling with hand	Math skills	8	242
Math	K–6	Playground	Quick Lesson 11.1	Walking and Stretching	3	Fitness	Walking and stretching	Technique	11	339

TABLE 3 Activity Listing by Integration Area (*continued*)

INTEGRATION AREA	GRADE LEVEL	LOCATION	CATEGORY	NAME OF ACTIVITY	NASPE STANDARD(S)	MOVEMENT FORM	SKILL(S)	KNOWLEDGE CONTENT	CHAPTER	PAGE IN TEXT
Math	1-3	Playground	Quick Lesson 4.8	Walking	3	Fitness	Walking	Technique: walking	4	124
Math	1-6	Classroom	Classroom Learning Station 4.2	How to Determine the Heart Rate	3	Fitness	None	Health: taking pulse rate	4	128
Math	2-3	Classroom	Integrated Game	Jump Rope Bingo	3	Fitness	Jumping rope	Math skills	8	242
Math	2-6	Classroom	Quick Lesson 5.1	All-Star Bulletin Boards	5, 6	Cooperative	None	Accepting others	5	162
Math	2-6	Classroom	Integrated Game	Odds and Evens	3	Fitness	Running	Math skills	8	242
Math	3-4	Gymnasium	Lesson 2.6	Fun Fitness Activities: Tennis Ball Take, Team Bowling	1, 4, 5	Cooperative	Bowling and fitness	Cooperation	LP	414
Math	3-6	Playground	Quick Lesson 3.3	Partner Kickball	3	Game skills	Rolling, kicking	Fitness: endurance	3	87
Math, art	K-6	Classroom	Quick Lesson 6.1	The Benefits of an Active Lifestyle	3	Fitness	None	Fitness: benefits	6	195
Math, language arts, reading	K-1	Gymnasium	Special Event 8.1	Read and Romp Day	6	Cooperative	Variety	Cooperation and creativity	8	262
Math, spelling	K-2	Playground	Quick Lesson 3.2	Meet and Part	2	Basic movement	Locomotor skills	Technique	3	86
Math, spelling	K-6	Classroom	Classroom Learning Station 3.1	Fine Motor Station	1	Basic movement	Fine motor skills	Technique: handling small objects	3	89
Math, spelling	K-6	Classroom	Special Event 5.1	Simulation Activities	5	Cooperative	Variety	Accepting others	5	165
Math, writing, drawing	3-6	Gymnasium	Special Event 2.1	Health & Movement Fair	5	Basic movement	Variety	Growth and development	2	51
Music	K-6	Classroom	Special Event 9.1	Create and Share	6	Rhythmic movement	Student created	Enjoyment and self-expression	9	294
Music	4-6	Classroom	Quick Lesson 4.2	Measuring Blood Pressures	3	Fitness	None	Health: blood pressure	4	116
Music	4-6	Classroom	Instant Activity 9.1	Mac the Crab	4	Fitness and Rhythm	"Macarena"	Fitness is fun	9	273
Music, art	K-6	Classroom	Quick Lesson 9.1	Student Voices	6	None	None	Enjoyment and self-expression	9	284
Reading	3-4	Classroom	Lesson 2.3 Classroom Activity	Human Letters	6	Cooperative	Letter formations	Letter recognition	LP	409
Reading, math, language arts	K-1	Gymnasium	Special Event 8.1	Read and Romp Day	6	Cooperative	Variety	Cooperation and creativity	8	262
Reading, spelling, library skills	K-6	Classroom	Classroom Learning Station 1.1	Today's Popular Sports	6	Game skills	Teacher selected	Teacher selected	1	27
Reading, writing	K-2	Classroom	Special Event 3.1	Who Wants to Be a Millionaire?	2	Basic movement	None	Technique	3	90
Reading, writing, health	K-6	Gymnasium	Special Event 6.1	Parents' Night: Fitness and Wellness	3, 4, 5	Fitness	Teacher selected	Fitness: concepts	6	198
Science	K-3	Classroom	Classroom Learning Station 11.1	Low Balance Beam	1	Body management	Balancing	Technique	11	341
Science	K-6	Classroom	Integrated Game	Circuit Training Through the Muscular System	2	Fitness	Variety	Muscle identification	8	246
Science	K-6	Classroom	Integrated Game	Speed It Up	4	Fitness	Running	Heart rate	8	245
Science	K-6	Classroom	Quick Lesson 1.4	Jump for Fitness	4	Fitness	Jumping	Fitness: pulse rates	1	22
Science	K-6	Playground	Integrated Game	Muscle Tag	4	Fitness	Running, tagging, dodging	Muscle identification	8	246
Science	1-3	Classroom	Quick Lesson 4.6	Muscular Endurance	3	Fitness	Abdominal curl	Health: endurance	4	120
Science	1-3	Classroom	Quick Lesson 4.7	Flexibility	3	Fitness	Stretches	Health: flexibility	4	121
Science	2-5	Classroom	Integrated Game	Water Molecules	2	Basic movement	Nonlocomotor and locomotor	Water	8	245
Science	2-6	Classroom	Quick Lesson 4.3	The Circulatory System	3	Fitness	Walking	Health: blood flow	4	117
Science	3-4	Classroom	Integrated Game	Magnetic Field	2	Basic movement	Nonlocomotor/Locomotor	Magnetism	8	244
Science	3-5	Playground	Integrated Game	Newton's Laws	3	None	Variety	Force, motion	8	244
Science	4-6	Classroom	Classroom Learning Station 7.1	Creating Bumper Stickers	3	Fitness	Fine motor skills	Healthy lifestyles	7	228
Science, health	K-6	Classroom	Classroom Learning Station 6.1	Exercise Bands	4	Fitness	Exercises with bands	Fitness: exercise progression	6	197
Social studies	K-6	Classroom	Quick Lesson 1.1	Match the Diagram	1	Basic movement	Locomotor skills	Movement concept: pathways	1	19

INTEGRATION AREA	GRADE LEVEL	LOCATION	CATEGORY	NAME OF ACTIVITY	NASPE STANDARD(S)	MOVEMENT FORM	SKILL(S)	KNOWLEDGE CONTENT	CHAPTER	PAGE IN TEXT
Social studies	K–6	Classroom	Quick Lesson 5.2	Getting to Know Your Classmates	5	Cooperative	Variety	Accepting others	5	163
Social studies	K–6	Classroom	Integrated Game	North and South Wind	3	Fitness	Running, tagging, dodging	Weather	8	243
Social studies	K–6	Classroom	Special Event 12.1	Traditional Games, Dances, and Activities	5	Game skills	Student selected	Cultural differences	12	375
Social studies	K–6	Classroom	Special Event 10.1	Grandparents' Day	5	None	Variety	Individual differences	10	322
Social studies	K–6	Playground	Quick Lesson 10.1	Scooters as Wheelchairs	5	Body management	Scooters	Individual differences	10	319
Social studies	2–5	Classroom	Integrated Game	Walk Across Your State	3	Fitness	Walking	Geography	8	243
Social studies	3–5	Classroom	Integrated Game	Presidential Race	3	Game skills	Running, tagging, dodging	Geography	8	243
Social studies	3–6	Classroom	Quick Lesson 12.2	Classroom Dribbling	1, 2	Basic movement	Dribbling with hand	Technique	12	372
Social studies	3–6	Classroom	Special Event 4.1	Are We There Yet?	3	Fitness	Walking and jogging workout	Health: cardiorespiratory	4	132
Social studies	3–6	Playground	Quick Lesson 1.5	Create Your Own Sport	5	Game skills	Student created	Game rules	1	23
Social studies	4–5	Classroom	Integrated Game	I Have, Where Is	3	Fitness	Running	State capitals	8	244
Social studies	4–6	Classroom	Opening Scenario 6.1	Opening Scenario 6.1	1	Rhythmic movement	Walking and skipping	Accepting others	6	167
Social studies, art	3–6	Classroom	Classroom Learning Station 12.1	Including Others	5	Cooperative	None	Cooperation and creativity	12	373
Social studies, language arts	2–6	Classroom	Quick Lesson 8.1	Olympic *Jeopardy*	3	Cooperative	None	Olympic facts	8	258
Speaking, writing	5–6	Classroom	Lesson 3.2 Classroom Activity	"How To" Speeches	1	None	Soccer	Technique	LP	435
Spelling	1–6	Classroom	Classroom Learning Station 4.3	Which Muscle Is Which?	3	Fitness	None	Health: bones and muscles	4	130
Spelling	3–4	Gymnasium	Lesson 2.8	See and Spell	1, 5	Cooperative	Locomotor movements	Word jumble	LP	417
Spelling	4–6	Classroom	Quick Lesson 4.1	How Arteries Become Clogged	4	Fitness	Scooters	Health: blood flow	4	115
Spelling, language arts	3–6	Classroom	Classroom Learning Station 5.1	Locomotor Sign Language	5	Basic movement	Locomotor skills	Sign language	5	164
Spelling, library skills, reading	K–6	Classroom	Classroom Learning Station 1.1	Today's Popular Sports	6	Game skills	Teacher selected	Teacher selected	1	27
Spelling, math	K–2	Playground	Quick Lesson 3.2	Meet and Part	2	Basic movement	Locomotor skills	Technique	3	86
Spelling, math	K–6	Classroom	Classroom Learning Station 3.1	Fine Motor Station	1	Basic movement	Fine motor skills	Technique: handling small objects	3	89
Spelling, math	K–6	Classroom	Special Event 5.1	Simulation Activities	5	Cooperative	Variety	Accepting others	5	165
Writing	K–6	Classroom	Classroom Learning Station 10.1	Tell Me Something About You	5	None	None	Individual differences	10	320
Writing	K–6	Playground	Special Event 1.1	Celebrating Nat. PE & Sport Week	1, 3, 5	Basic movement	Teacher selected	Importance of fitness	1	28
Writing	1–6	Classroom	Quick Lesson 4.9	Heart Rate Games	3	Fitness	Locomotor skills	Fitness: continuous movement	4	125
Writing	5–6	Classroom	Lesson Plan Unit 3 Introduction	Journal Entries	1, 6	None	Soccer	Self-awareness	LP	432
Writing, drawing, health	K–6	Classroom	Classroom Learning Station 2.1	Are We All the Same?	5	Basic movement	Jumping	Growth and development	2	50
Writing, drawing, math	3–6	Gymnasium	Special Event 2.1	Health & Movement Fair	5	Basic movement	Variety	Growth and development	2	51
Writing, health, reading	K–6	Gymnasium	Special Event 6.1	Parents' Night: Fitness and Wellness	3, 4, 5	Fitness	Teacher selected	Fitness: concepts	6	198
Writing, library skills	3–6	Classroom	Quick Lesson 4.5	Muscular Strength	3	Fitness	None	Health: strength	4	119
Writing, reading	K–2	Classroom	Special Event 3.1	Who Wants to Be a Millionaire?	2	Basic movement	None	Technique	3	90
Writing, speaking	5–6	Classroom	Lesson 3.2 Classroom Activity	"How To" Speeches	1	None	Soccer	Technique	LP	435

Glossary of Key Terms and Concepts

ability: A learner's perception of how well, in general, she or he is capable of performing.

active learning time (ALT): The time students are participating successfully in lesson activities that leads to achieving the lesson objectives.

active supervision: The teacher is positioned to keep all students in view; moves around to keep students in sight; scans the class to detect problems early; watches and gives feedback to everyone all the time; and instills safety procedures into every lesson.

aerobic: With oxygen; an exercise intensity in which adequate oxygen is delivered to the muscles and the activity can be performed without stress and exhaustion.

affective objectives: Lesson objectives that indicate what the student values, believes, or feels as well as how the student is expected to interact with others.

agonistic interactions: Behaviors such as arguments or rough-and-tumble play.

anaerobic: Without oxygen; exercise that is so intense that the circulatory system cannot meet demands for oxygen, and exercise will stop unless intensity decreases.

assessment: The collection of data (measurement) and the use of the data to make informed decisions (evaluation).

athletics: Organized sports activities with skilled players and officials who monitor players and enforce the rules.

authentic assessment: Assessment that takes place in a real-life rather than artificial setting.

back-to-the-wall: An active supervision technique in which a teacher moves around the perimeter of class activity (keeping his or her back to the wall) so all students are in view at all times.

basic game skills: Skills that combine the use of the four components of movement (body, space, effort, and relationships) and the fundamental movement skills (locomotor, nonlocomotor, and manipulative) to play low organized games and games that lead up to regulation sports.

basic movement skills: Locomotor, nonlocomotor, and manipulative skills underlying the movements specific to certain games and sports.

benefits of regular physical activity: Improved movement skills and physical fitness levels; stress reduction; healthy mental state; feelings of success; improved cooperation skills; and reduced risk of coronary heart disease, diabetes, hypertension, obesity, and certain cancers.

best practices: Activities conducted using up-to-date instructional methods, appropriate skill progressions, and proper supervision techniques, and providing safety knowledge to students.

bodily-kinesthetic intelligence: The ability to control one's bodily motions and handle objects skillfully.

body awareness: What the body can do—transferring body weight; balancing or weight bearing; being in flight, such as when running, jumping, or leaping; assuming different shapes to perform a variety of skills; focusing the gaze.

body composition: The relationship of body fat to lean body weight, the weight of the nonfat components of the body, primarily muscle mass and bone.

body management skills and gymnastics: Activities concerned with the control of movement and the transference of body weight during movement.

body movements: The way the body moves within space or while stationary. The three specific components include locomotor movements, nonlocomotor movements, and manipulative movements.

body type: A general description of body shape and build based on fat and muscle distribution. Three main body types have been identified: mesomorph (muscular), ectomorph (thin, slight of build), or endomorph (rounded, possibly plump).

Brain Gym: A set of activities developed by Dennison and Dennison (1989) that stimulate the mind and body to prepare a child to learn; each activity addresses specific academic skills and behavioral or postural correlates, categorized as midline movements, lengthening activities, energy exercises, and deepening attitudes.

brain-based education: Theory that the brain changes physiologically as the result of challenging, nurturing experiences and that emotions and cognition cannot be separated.

brain-based learning: Enhancing the learning process through physical activity, which compels both sides of the brain to communicate and allows greater brain growth.

breach of duty: Unreasonable conduct, in that a teacher has failed to provide the required standard of care for students.

bullying: Overt aggression with the purpose of intimidating others.

583

calming activities: Activities such as stretching exercises, relaxation techniques, calming musical transitions, or five minutes of free time, as a bridge between vigorous recess time and return to academic work.

cardiorespiratory fitness: Related to the capacity of the cardiovascular system to deliver oxygen to the muscles and tissues.

cardiorespiratory system: The heart, lungs, and associated arteries, veins, and small blood vessels that are involved in circulation of the blood in the body.

caring community: Students and teachers are partners in the teaching and learning process; students establish caring, respectful relationships with one another; students are encouraged to interact with one another, make their own choices, and work together in positive, supportive ways.

causal relationship: The teacher's action or inaction was the immediate cause of an injury to another person.

challenge activities: A group of students solve a movement challenge while working as a team; roles include organizer, praiser or recorder, encourager, and summarizer.

cholesterol: A fatlike substance implicated in narrowing of the arteries in coronary heart disease; it can be manufactured within the body or consumed in the diet from animal fat; it is a necessary component of various steroid hormones and cell membranes. Generally cholesterol is subdivided into high density lipoprotein (HDL), the "good" cholesterol, and low density lipoprotein (LDL), the "bad" cholesterol.

closed motor skill: A skill performed in an environment where the object waits to be moved or the context does not change.

cognitive objectives: Lesson objectives that specify what a student will know intellectually.

collaboration: Relationship between physical education and classroom teachers in which they work together to fulfill the movement needs of the students and to develop successful curriculum integration activities; teachers work together to pool their resources for the benefit of students.

congruent feedback: Feedback from an external source that is directly related to the task children were asked to practice.

consequences (for misbehavior): An action, naturally occurring or imposed by the teacher, that relates to the inappropriate behavior, makes the child accountable for his or her behavior, and keeps the child's dignity.

continuous activity: Prolonged activity without rest periods, normally aerobic in nature and moderate in intensity; predominate type of activity recommended for the development of cardiorespiratory fitness in adults.

cool-down: Activities such as gradually decreasing the intensity of an exercise or walking; the heart rate slows down, breathing is less labored, and walking prevents blood from pooling in the lower extremities.

cooperative activities: The teacher develops and assigns an activity to groups that work together to complete movement tasks; groups include a facilitator, harmonizer, resource manager, and recorder.

cooperative movement skills: Tasks, games, and activities that require cooperation with partners or groups to accomplish the movement or game goal.

COPEC: Council on Physical Education for Children.

creative and rhythmic movements: Rhythmic forms such as movement to music, dance, and manipulative activities using equipment.

cultural integration: Learning games from other cultures teaches students that all cultures are valued.

curriculum: All of the experiences of the learner in an educational setting; a prescribed course of study.

curriculum guide: Specifies the particular content to be mastered at each grade level; contains the district or school's physical education philosophy, grade-level program goals and benchmarks, and program content; may also include yearly plans for various grade levels.

curriculum integration: Including movement in the classroom (academic) curriculum and academic subjects in the physical education curriculum.

developmental readiness: Having attained the age, fitness, and skill levels required to perform a particular activity.

developmentally appropriate movement activities: Movement activities designed with the students' cognitive, psychomotor, and affective ability levels in mind.

differentiation: The progression of skill development from the gross movements of infants to the more refined and useful movements of children.

direct competition: Competition in which the object is to impede the progress of others and that results in a winner and a loser or losers; inappropriate for elementary school children.

direct instruction: Teaching method where the teacher controls all aspects of the lesson and serves as the only source for learning information; used primarily to present new information quickly and provide initial practice of new motor skills.

direct teaching methods: The teacher takes total responsibility for planning, implementing, and evaluating the lesson; directs when students begin the activity, where the activity occurs, and how the activity is to be performed; and serves as the expert during the lesson. The teacher is the source of all information; students communicate directly with the teacher and little with each other; the teacher provides answers to questions.

distributed practice: The principle that individuals learn better and more quickly when their efforts on a task are distributed over time with frequent short breaks rather than concentrated in longer periods of time.

dominant culture: The values, beliefs, and behaviors expressed and expected by the majority of the people within a given geographical region.

duty: The requirement that teachers conduct their job with a certain standard of care that protects students against foreseeable harm and unreasonable risk of injury.

educate the whole child: Beliefs (and theories and practices related to those beliefs) that emphasize the learner is a whole human being who interprets educational experiences holistically. Thus teaching practices and learning experiences should be presented holistically (recognizing the child's integration of his or her physical, social, emotional, and intellectual aspects).

effort: A learner's rating of how hard she or he tried to perform well in a given situation.

emotional disturbances: Common characteristics of these conditions include inability to learn, which cannot be explained by intellectual, sensory, or health factors; inability to build or maintain satisfactory interpersonal relationships; inappropriate displays of behavior or feelings; generally unhappy or depressed mood; tendency to develop physical symptoms or fears associated with personal or social problems.

environment: The context in which the performer does a skill or in which the object is acted upon by the performer.

equilibration theory: Piaget's theory that peer interactions during play facilitate cognitive conflict and subsequent reequilibration.

exercise: Physical activity that is planned, structured, repetitive, and purposive to improve or maintain physical fitness.

extrinsic motivation: Sources of reinforcement from outside the individual.

feedback: The teacher should observe carefully; discuss both correct and incorrect technique; focus on improving the most important error; provide consistent, specific, and immediate feedback.

fetal alcohol syndrome: Birth defects resulting from prenatal alcohol use by the mother.

fine motor skills: Using small muscle groups for precise movements, typically of the hands and fingers, with eye-hand coordination.

fitness education: The part of a movement education curriculum that emphasizes the importance of physical activity and physical fitness to a healthy and productive quality of life, and the ability to sustain a reasonable intensity of exercise in order to perform daily and sport activities with a minimum of stress and effort.

fitness testing: Measuring cardiorespiratory fitness, muscular strength, muscular endurance, flexibility, and body composition.

fitness and wellness concepts and activities: The knowledge base in fitness and wellness, and any curriculum activities structured to improve children's fitness.

flexibility: The ability of a limb or body part to move through its complete range of motion; movement of a body part around a joint.

flow experiences: Activities that are exhilarating and challenging, provide enjoyment, and build internal motivation.

foreseeability: The teacher must have been able to predict the likelihood of an injury occurring given the situation in question.

formative evaluation: Occurs frequently; helps students identify areas that need improvement; aids the teacher in planning; usually not used for grading.

free to play: Playground activities chosen and structured by children, not adults.

games: Movement activities with arbitrary rules established and enforced by the participants.

general modifications: Modifications to activities or equipment to allow students to participate who have specific disabilities or delays in strength, speed, endurance, balance, coordination, or accuracy.

general space: The area within which children can move freely without touching anyone or anything.

grade-level benchmarks: Description of the specific student behavior that indicates a student has achieved a program goal.

grade-level goals: Specifically written to allow the program goals to be interpreted for the developmental needs of children of different ages and maturity.

gross motor skills: Using large muscle groups for activities such as running, jumping, skipping, throwing, kicking, or body rolling.

health: Physical, mental, and social well-being, and the absence of disease and infirmity (WHO 1947).

health promotion: The science and art of helping people change their lifestyle to move toward a state of optimal health (O'Donnell 1986).

health risk factors: Conditions and behaviors that increase the risk of developing a chronic disease.

health-related physical fitness: The aspects of fitness related to improving health and achieving an active lifestyle, which include cardiorespiratory endurance, muscular strength and endurance, body composition, and flexibility.

hearing impairment: Permanent or fluctuating hearing impairments or deafness that adversely affect a child's education performance.

heart rate: The number of times the heart beats per minute.

heredity ("nature") versus environment ("nurture") argument: The debate over whether individual and group behavior is a product of heredity and thus predetermined, or a product of experience and learning and thus could be altered.

hypertension: Medical term for high blood pressure.

inclusion: Placing children with disabilities in the regular classroom.

indirect competition: Activities that encourage children to improve individual accomplishments, achieve self-set goals or preset standards, and engage in cooperative play.

indirect teaching methods: Students are active in decision making or development of the lesson; they may discover, explore, share, or create knowledge, or decide when to begin the activity, whom to work with, and the order of various activities. Students rely less on the teacher as the source of information; they communicate more with each other than the teacher and obtain and share information from videos, books, task sheets, and wall signs.

individual or partner practice: Used for independent practice of specific motor skills, with self or partner evaluation; the teacher monitors students to provide feedback and keep them on task.

Individuals with Disabilities Education Act (IDEA): Passed by Congress in 1990, it mandates the term *disability* instead of the term *handicapped*, and defines physical education for individuals with disabilities as the development of physical and motor fitness; fundamental motor skills and patterns; skills in aquatics, dance, and individual and group games and sports; and occurring through special or adapted physical education, movement education, and motor development.

infusion-based approach: In teacher education programs, refers to including information about disabilities in program content so that each content area is covered relative to students with and without disabilities; part of the process of successfully integrating children with disabilities into the classroom, and of learning about the diverse needs of all children.

instrumental aggression: Overt aggression with the purpose of obtaining a desired object, territory, or privilege.

integration: The coordination of muscle and sensory systems, such as movements of the hands and fingers along with use of the eyes to perform refined skills.

intermittent activity: Activity in short bouts with frequent brief rest periods; can be moderate or vigorous.

interpersonal intelligence: The ability to notice and make distinctions among other individuals and in particular among their moods, temperaments, motivations, and intentions.

intrapersonal intelligence: The ability to form an accurate model of the self and to use this information to guide behavior.

intrinsic feedback: Feedback that comes from within the body through sensory modes, such as vision or hearing.

intrinsic motivation: Sources of reinforcement within the child.

learning about movement: Learning that emphasizes the development of physical fitness and skilled motor performance.

learning disability: A disorder in one or more of the basic psychological processes involved in understanding or using language to accomplish tasks; common characteristics include disorders of attention; poor motor abilities; perceptual and information-processing problems; failure to develop cognitive strategies for learning; oral, reading, or written language difficulties; inappropriate social behavior.

learning styles: Listener (prefers verbal descriptions); thinker (analyzes movement challenges); kinesthetic learner (likes to feel what the body should do); and visual learner (likes to see a visual model).

learning through movement: Learning that emphasizes how participating in movement experiences contributes to the development of the whole person, socially, emotionally, intellectually, and physically.

least restrictive environment: element within the law (PL 101-476) that requires students with disabilities to be educated with their nondisabled peers to the maximum extent possible.

lesson objectives: Written in performance or behavioral terms, they direct the student to do something that is observable and measurable.

lesson plan: Written for each class period; includes movement form, grade level, NASPE standard, program benchmark, lesson objectives, materials and equipment, approximate time, activity description, alternate activities, class organization, and student assessment.

linguistic intelligence: The ability to use language in different forms—speaking, reading, and writing.

locomotor movements: Movements that propel the mover around an area.

locomotor skills: Walking, running, galloping, sliding, jumping, hopping, skipping, and leaping.

logical-mathematical intelligence: The ability to use numbers effectively, see patterns, and see things from a logical point of view.

manipulative movements: Movements in which the hands or feet control objects such as a pen or a ball.

manipulative skills: Both fine motor skills using the hands or fingers (playing jacks, stringing beads) and gross motor skills using the large muscles of the body—rolling, throwing, catching, kicking, striking, volleying, dribbling with hands or with feet, punting, passing, making a set shot or an overhand serve.

mass media: Sources of information (especially electronic in nature) readily available to individuals (e.g., television, computer and Internet games, video games, and movies) that influence the socialization of children within our culture.

maximum participation: Movement activities that provide many skill repetitions for every child; games that require all children to be actively moving all the time.

mental disability: Significantly subaverage general intellectual functioning, along with deficits in adaptive behavior; common characteristics include having a short attention span; being slow to understand and follow directions; being loveable and wanting to please; exhibiting delayed physical, motor, and perceptual motor skills.

motor development: Changes that occur in human movement across the life span as a result of physical growth and maturation.

motor learning: Relatively permanent change in performance as a result of practice or experience.

motor skill competency: The level of achievement reached by an individual in being able to perform various movement activities.

movement: How the body moves for purposes of physical exercise, self-expression, play, competition and cooperation, or enjoyment.

movement educator: Classroom teachers who teach physical education but do not have the same professional preparation as physical educators.

movement exploration: Used for lower elementary children to explore movement possibilities; the teacher controls when, how, and with whom the activities are performed.

movement map: Categorizes the underlying components involved when the body moves.

multiple intelligences theory: Gardner's theory that individuals have eight independent intelligences—bodily-kinesthetic, linguistic, logical-mathematical, musical, spatial, naturalist, interpersonal, and intrapersonal—that combine to form each person's unique cognitive structure.

muscular endurance: The ability of a muscle to perform a contraction repeatedly.

muscular strength: The ability to create a large amount of force at one time; such as how much weight can be lifted in one repetition.

musculoskeletal system: The muscles and bones of the body.

musical intelligence: The ability to use the core set of musical elements—pitch, rhythm, and timbre.

NASPE: National Association for Sport and Physical Education.

NASPE content standards: National physical education standards that specify what students should know, value, and be able to do.

naturalist intelligence: The ability to understand, relate to, categorize, classify, and explain things encountered in the natural world.

nature vs. nurture: See **heredity versus environment.**

neglected children: Children, not welcomed by their peers, displaying behavior that is anxious, withdrawn, and hovering.

negligence: Failing to act as a reasonably prudent person would act in similar circumstances; to prove negligence, five factors must have been present: duty, breach of duty, injury occurred, causal relationship, and foreseeability.

nonlocomotor movements: Movements that are stationary or that do not propel the mover around an area.

nonlocomotor skills: Bending, stretching, twisting, turning, pushing, pulling, rising, collapsing, swinging, swaying, dodging, spinning, shaking, and balancing.

open motor skill: A skill performed in an environment where the object is in motion or the context is changing.

opportunity to respond (OTR): A measure of the number of appropriate, successful task responses made by students.

organizational routines: Minimize the time needed to complete nonacademic tasks by establishing standard routines for entering and leaving the gymnasium; getting drinks of water and using the restroom during class; responding to the teacher's signal during lessons; and obtaining and returning equipment.

orthopedic and physical impairments: Includes impairments caused by congenital anomaly; by disease; or from other causes such as cerebral palsy, amputations, fractures, or burns.

overload principle: To improve a fitness component, a person must do a little more work than normal; as the muscles, heart, and respiratory system adapt to the increased requirements, the person is able to do more work.

overt aggression: A type of aggression consisting of behaviors that hurt others, such as hitting, kicking, or threatening to do so. See **instrumental aggression** and **bullying.**

parental influence on children's activity levels: Parents can socialize their children to be physically active through encouragement, direct involvement, facilitation, and role modeling.

peer mediators: A program in which fourth and fifth graders are trained in resolving conflicts by a social worker, and use these skills during noon recess periods to help students resolve issues that arise.

perceived exertion: Understanding how much effort is being made and being able to rate it on a scale called **rating of perceived exertion.**

performance levels: Beginning (learner first attempts a skill); intermediate (learner is more advanced but has not mastered the skill; advanced (learner has mastered the skill).

personal space: Space that is used while in a stationary or moving position in a very small area; space that only one person can occupy.

philosophy of education statement: Indicates the writer's view of the purpose of education, how educational practices will be implemented to meet the stated purpose, and values and beliefs about the program.

physical activity: Any bodily movement produced by skeletal muscles that results in energy expenditure above the resting level.

physical education: A planned sequence of developmentally appropriate movement activities, games, and sports designed by the teacher or the school district to educate students about and through movement. Also, instructional time in the curriculum during which students learn about movement, practice physical skills, learn to value the importance of being active, and work with all their classmates.

physical education teacher: A person who has completed an undergraduate degree in physical education pedagogy and is certified by the state to teach physical education in K–12 schools; also called physical educator.

physical environment: The area, indoors or outdoors, where children perform physical activities, and which must be maintained for safe use.

physical fitness: The vigor and energy needed to perform moderate to vigorous levels of physical activity without undue fatigue. Also, using movement to strengthen the body systems in order to lead a healthier life.

physically educated person: A person who is physically fit; has skills to perform a variety of physical activities and participates in these activities regularly; knows the benefits of physical education; and values physical activity's contribution to a healthy lifestyle.

PL 94-142: The federal Education for All Handicapped Children Act (1975); reauthorized in 1990 as the Individuals with Disabilities Education Act, PL 101-476; states that children with disabilities have the right to a free and public education and must be educated in the least restrictive educational environment possible.

play: Movement activities that children do during their free time.

Play Fair: A program of noncompetitive games to make recess more fun, less competitive, and more inclusive (Chuoke and Eyman 1997).

Playground Leader: A program in which fourth graders are trained to direct activity stations during recess periods (Calo and Ingram 1994).

playground meetings: Meetings for first- and third-grade students and their teachers following afternoon recess to let students discuss playground concerns and explore possible solutions (Thompson, Knudson, and Wilson 1997).

positive transfer: The positive influence on learning a new skill, or using a skill differently, by past experience with another skill.

praise: Verbal statements or body actions that communicate positive messages to children about their movement performance.

principles of training: The overload principle; specificity of exercise; and progression or progressive resistance.

problem-solving activities: The teacher poses a movement problem and a group of students figure out how to organize to complete the assignment and solve the problem.

program effectiveness: Assessed by collecting data to determine how many students reached each benchmark.

progression principle: Gradually increasing the intensity of exercise so the body has time to adapt.

prosocial interactions: Relationship-enhancing interactions such as engaging in social conversations or cooperative play.

prosocial skills: Specific skills that help children learn a broad array of behaviors for resolving conflicts.

psychomotor objectives: Lesson objectives that indicate what the student will physically perform.

Public Law 108–265; Section 204: Federal mandate requiring school districts with federally funded school-meals programs to develop and implement local wellness policies for schools.

punishment (for misbehavior): An action imposed on the student by the teacher when the student behaves inappropriately. The action is not related to the misbehavior, for example, if a student hurts someone's feelings, the student is given a time-out instead of apologizing to the harmed student.

qualities of movement: How the body moves, defined by the factors of time (speed of movement), effort (strength of movement), and flow (control of movement).

rating of perceived exertion: Understanding how much effort is being made and being able to rate it on a scale.

recess: Play time provided to give students a break from academic learning. Also, the time during which children can play or talk with friends and can freely choose with whom and what they want to do, within broad limits.

recess behavior: Typical actions and interactions of students during free play time on the playground.

recreational activity skills: Activities for recreational purposes done outdoors (canoeing, hiking, biking, in-line skating, etc.).

rejected children: Children, not welcomed by their peers, who tend to display aggression toward peers (e.g., takes equipment away, issues threats, teases).

relational aggression: A type of aggression in which children ostracize their peers or withdraw their friendship from peers.

relationship (in movement): How the body relates to others, objects, equipment, rules, and boundaries.

risk management plans: Programwide or school-wide plans designed to reduce the number and severity of injuries and the likelihood of litigation arising from those injuries.

rough-and-tumble play: A physically vigorous set of behaviors characterized by positive affect and playful facial expressions.

rules of conduct: A set of behaviors that identify how students are to interact with each other and with their environment. Students and parents should be involved in establishing rules of conduct for the playground.

school-level program goals: Written by curriculum builders and based on the developed philosophy of education, the NASPE content standards, state standards (if available), and any unique local circumstances.

scope of program content: The depth and breadth of movement forms to be taught.

scoring rubric: The criteria used to judge performance and the rating scale used to judge level of achievement based on the criteria.

self-management techniques: To help students learn to identify and solve their own behavior problems, teachers build a student-teacher partnership; emphasize student behavior as a choice; find causes and solutions for behavior problems; are consistent in responding to behaviors; adapt actions to individual students and situations; create consequences for inappropriate behavior; hold class meetings; and involve parents and guardians.

sensory impairments: Visual impairments including partial sight and blindness; auditory impairments including permanent or fluctuating hearing impairments and deafness.

sequence of program content: Order in which movement forms are taught.

***Shape of the Nation* report:** Published by NASPE (2002); lists physical education requirements in the states.

shared responsibility: Teachers and students work together to establish a learning environment in which students manage their own behavior and most of the class time is spent on learning rather than management.

share control: Allowing children some choices within each lesson and/or some choices as to the units being offered in the movement program.

significant tools: Skills and perceptions possessed by successful people; perceptions of personal capabilities, significance in primary relationships, personal power; intrapersonal, interpersonal, systemic, and judgmental skills.

skill demonstrations: In direct teaching, the teacher talks about how to perform a skill while demonstrating it or while other students are demonstrating it; in indirect teaching, the demonstration may be on videotape or a task sheet or wall sign showing pictures of correct technique.

skill-related fitness: Attributes associated with performance objectives that include speed, agility, strength, explosive power, and coordination.

socialization: The process through which children acquire a sense of personal identity, learn what people in the surrounding culture believe, and discover how to behave according to cultural expectations.

socialization about movement: Society uses movement to help children develop appropriate sex-role identity and gender role; and to learn the role of physical activity in life, the appropriate activity partners and appropriate activities, and the importance of winning.

socialization agent: Any individual, group, or organization that influences a person's behavior or sense of self; for children, main socialization agents are family, peers, school, and mass media.

socialization through movement: By playing together, children learn cooperation, friendship, fairness, doing what's right, and what social and moral conduct is acceptable or not acceptable in their society.

social skills: Decision-making, interpersonal, and personal responsibility behaviors that children need to learn and use in social settings.

space awareness: Where the body moves, whether in personal or general space.

spatial intelligence: The ability to create a graphic likeness of spatial information, to have a good sense of direction, and to perceive the relationships among colors, lines, shapes and forms, and space.

special friends: A program that assigns two children without intellectual disabilities to initiate interactions with and include in play activities a child with a disability (Ronning and Nabuzoka 1993).

specificity principle: Training the particular muscles and systems needed for a particular exercise.

sports: Organized games that have established, accepted, and published rules of play.

stages of performance: Beginning level of learning a skill—learner attempts to understand the movement, is clumsy and awkward, becomes overwhelmed by the visual stimuli of the environment, tires easily from mental fatigue. Intermediate level—refinement of the movement with more consistency and fewer errors, movement is less mentally taxing, learner has developed mental idea of movement and is less distracted by environment. Advanced level—skill has become almost automatic, little conscious thought needs to be given during performance of movement, performer is consistent from one attempt to the next and can detect and correct errors in the movement.

standard of care: The level of protection of students that teachers are required to provide against foreseeable harm and unreasonable risk of injury.

student behavior as a choice: The teacher helps students choose responsible behaviors by establishing a caring classroom community; teaching social skills to shape student behavior; and implementing discipline strategies that build self-management skills.

student conduct rules: Established rules specifying how children should behave with peers, in certain activity areas, with particular equipment, and in both indoor and outdoor physical activity settings.

summative evaluation: Occurs at the end of instruction; provides a summary of accomplishments; often used to determine a grade or prepare a progress report.

surgeon general: Federal official who provides written documents as to the benefits of regular physical activity for persons of all ages and recommends that schools provide quality daily physical education taught by specialists.

task (skill) progressions: A series of lesson activities that allow students to progress from performing simple to more complex tasks.

task variation: Calls for practicing motor skills using a variety of equipment, situations, teaching styles, and movement forms in order to keep students interested in practicing.

teacher-child ratio for recess supervision: Teachers are less effective in monitoring and influencing children's behavior and children exhibit more aggressive behaviors when the teacher-child ratio is high; 1 teacher to 40 students is recommended.

teacher-student relationship: Teachers' positive relationships with all students can promote relationships between students by showing that each student, including those with disabilities, makes a valuable contribution to the class.

Title IX: Part of the federal Educational Amendments Act of 1972; requires equal educational opportunities for boys and girls; in physical education, all except some contact sports must be coeducational.

tort law: Provides the basis for awarding compensation for losses suffered as a consequence of the intentional or unintentional actions of others that result in harm or as a consequence of situations of omission.

transitioning: The process of organizing and moving students into and between designated activity formations.

understanding and accepting diversity: Respecting those who are different from oneself in race, religion, color, disability, national origin, gender, size, or age.

verbal cues: Short word sequences to prompt correct technique performance of motor skills, for example, with the skill of catching, cues could be "reach, watch, and hug."

vestibular system: The system originating in the inner ear that assists in maintaining static and dynamic balance.

visual impairment: Partial sight or blindness that adversely affects a child's education performance.

warm-up: Activities such as brisk walking, calisthenics, or other large-muscle activity that prepare the body for activity by increasing the heart rate and blood flow to the muscles.

water skills: Swimming strokes, water games, water aerobics, diving, and water safety techniques.

wellness: A holistic term that encompasses emotional, spiritual, physical, mental, and social well-being.

yearly plan: Listing of movement form and primary content of lesson for each week of physical education program.

Index